International Relations Theories

New to this edition

- Updated chapters and case studies reflect new developments in world politics.
- A new chapter on critical theory expands coverage of a key school of thought.

International Relations Theories

Discipline and Diversity

THIRD EDITION

Edited by

Tim Dunne,

Milja Kurki, and

Steve Smith

OXFORD
UNIVERSITY PRESS

OXFORD

UNIVERSITY PRESS

Great Clarendon Street, Oxford OX2 6DP,
United Kingdom

Oxford University Press is a department of the University of Oxford.
It furthers the University's objective of excellence in research, scholarship,
and education by publishing worldwide. Oxford is a registered trade mark of
Oxford University Press in the UK and in certain other countries

First edition published 2007
Second edition published 2010

Impression: 2

British Library Cataloguing in Publication Data

Data available

ISBN 978-0-19-969601-7

Printed in Italy by
L.E.G.O. S.p.A—Lavis TN

Preface

Welcome to the third edition of *International Relations Theories*. The responses to the first two editions have been overwhelmingly positive and so we have kept changes to this new edition to a minimum. We cover the same theoretical ground as in the previous edition except for one major change. In light of the fact that there has been some demand for a detailed run-through of the critical theoretical literature, we decided to devote an entire chapter to this important theoretical orientation in the discipline. The new chapter contribution on critical theory is written by Steven C. Roach.

All the chapters have been updated to reflect recently published work and the cases have been revisited to include considerations of new developments in world politics.

Rationale for the book

Underpinning the ethos of the book are a number of thematics about theory and the nature of the discipline of International Relations (IR). When using this term, we are following the important convention that distinguishes between capital IR denoting the academic study of International Relations, and lower-case international relations which is shorthand for the object of the discipline's investigations (the actors, interests, institutions, and identities on a global scale). This distinction enables us to examine the sociology of knowledge of IR as a discipline: how and when it became a distinct subject, what kinds of topics get taught, where the subject is studied, what kinds of research get funded. If we were to do away with the distinction, we would end up assuming that there is a direct read-across from the discipline to the interactions that constitute the real world of international relations.

What thematics, then, underpin this book? We highlight seven as follows:

1. Theory is the discipline's centre of gravity. Academic IR is a broad church. It includes a number of very active sub-fields, many of which are motivated by applied agendas. We would argue that the centre of gravity of the field is IR theory (a point made by Ole Wæver in the concluding chapter). It is no coincidence that histories of the discipline tend to map directly onto the major theoretical contestations or debates.

2. Theory helps us to explain the world of international relations. All contributors agree that theory is central to explaining the dynamics of world politics, whether one is interested in regionalism, identity, security, or foreign policy. To put it more graphically, there is no hiding place from theory; there is no alternative but to engage with issues concerning causation, interpretation, judgement, and critique. The introduction and the opening chapter deal at some length with what theory is, how it is interpreted differently, and what is at stake in applying theory to the world.

3. Theoretical diversity is to be valued. All books on IR theory include a variety of different theoretical positions, particularly the historically dominant traditions of realism, liberalism, and Marxism: latterly, it is commonplace, especially in US-based scholarship, to include constructivism in the mix. We go much further in terms of defending diversity. To these four we have added the English school (resurgent in the last two decades), feminism, critical theory and poststructuralism (powerful critical voices since the 1980s), and two relatively recent theories in the form of postcolonialism and green theory. The order of the chapters proceeds along a continuum, from established at the beginning of the book to the newer theories at the end. This does not mean, however, that we believe the established traditions ought to be discounted for being 'old': indeed, the fact that we allocate two chapters to realism and neorealism, and liberalism and neoliberalism, underscores the importance we attach to these two rich theoretical perspectives as well as recognizing the presence of a significant fault-line within each.

4. Theoretical diversity is contested. Related to the above, we are aware of the fact that the positive value we attach to theoretical diversity is not universally shared. Many established scholars think that the core of the discipline—the focus on inter-state dynamics of conflict and cooperation—is being undermined. We disagree. We think more is better, and that theoretical pluralism not only enables old issues to be addressed in new ways, but also opens up new agendas which speak more directly to changing threats and potentialities. As Steve Smith shows in his introduction, inside the thick walls of the academy, this debate has generated a great deal of anxiety. Those committed to a particularly narrow concept of theory as a set of propositions formulated as testable hypotheses have unnecessarily sought to *discipline* diversity.

5. The limits to theoretical diversity. The book does not have a clear answer to the question whether there are limits to theoretical diversity. On the one hand, the arguments we advance for letting new voices be heard must be extended into the future. Yet on the other, we agree with Ole Wæver that theoretical innovation *within* existing perspectives is more likely (hence the proliferation of different 'wings' within each overarching theory, discussed in the chapters themselves).

6. Choosing between theories. Those who advocate theoretical diversity need to confront the question—often posed by students—how to decide between them. The introduction goes into this issue in some detail. At this stage we remind our readers that each contributor is defending his or her particularly theory. As Milja Kurki and Colin Wight put it in the first chapter, it is important that we remember theorists are 'selling' their ideas. They may not always admit to the weaknesses in their own position, which is why it is important for 'buyers' to read the alternatives.

7. Diversity and the reinvention of the discipline. The penultimate chapter by Colin Hay differs from the previous fourteen chapters in that it is not 'selling' a particular IR theory in the same sense as the others. Instead, the reader will find an analysis of the impact globalization is having on mainstream IR theories such as realism. Rather than concluding that changes in global politics have brought the legitimacy of the entire discipline into question, both Hay in Chapter 15 and Wæver in Chapter 16 recognize that there are powerful structures at work which will ensure the ongoing resilience of International Relations.

How to use the book

We anticipate that students will read the book in different ways, and that course tutors will recommend the book for different purposes. With some certainty, we can predict that all IR theory courses will cover *some* of the ground contained in the volume. It is equally certain that only a few IR theory courses will cover *all* of the same ground.

The book has been compiled in such a way that tutors and students can read chapters as though they are free-standing. However, for those courses that follow more closely the progression established throughout, we anticipate that there will be a pay-off in terms of cumulative learning. We think this is particularly true in the case of the introduction and the two opening chapters which cover contextual issues to do with the relationship between IR theory, and the social sciences, and between IR theory and ethical inquiry. Furthermore, many similar themes are interwoven through various chapters—understanding constructivism is going to help the reader to comprehend what is meant by feminist constructivism in a later chapter.

Each chapter has followed the same format, and incorporates many of the learning aids which have proved to be highly successful in companion volumes such as Baylis, Smith, and Owens (eds.), *Globalization of World Politics,* also published by Oxford University Press and in its fifth edition.

Acknowledgements

We would like to thank Kirsty Reade our editor at Oxford University Press, and our previous editors Ruth Anderson and Nicki Sneath. Throughout the six-year lifespan of the book and its two previous editions they have been extremely positive about the book and their input has been invaluable. We would also like to thank Jodie Hobbs, an editorial assistant with the first edition, and Madeleine Fagan who helped us compile a consolidated bibliography and the glossary for the second edition.

Our final debt is to our students. It would be unthinkable to be involved in a project of this kind without the shared experience of talking about theory to excited (and sometimes frustrated) students. In a very particular sense, the three editors directly shared this experience in that Steve taught both Tim and Milja; the former at the University of East Anglia in the late 1980s and the latter at Aberystwyth in the early 2000s. This book will have succeeded if it can stimulate the minds of the next generation to engage critically with the ever-changing discipline of International Relations.

Tim Dunne, Milja Kurki, Steve Smith
May 2012

Brief Contents

Detailed Contents

About the Contributors

David Campbell is a writer and producer, specializing in photography, multimedia, and politics. He is a member of the Durham Centre for Advanced Photography Studies in the UK and Honorary Professor in the School of Political Science and International Studies at the University of Queensland, Australia, and has been the A. Lindsay O'Connor Professor in the Peace and Conflict Studies Program at Colgate University. He is the author/editor of six books and some fifty articles and essays, most notably *Writing Security: United States Foreign Policy* and *Politics of Identity and National Deconstruction: Violence, Identity and Justice in Bosnia*, both of which are published by the University of Minnesota Press, and writes a blog on photography, multimedia, and politics at www.david-campbell.org.

Tim Dunne is Professor of International Relations and Director of Research of the Asia-Pacific Centre for the Responsibility to Protect at the University of Queensland. He is an editor of the *European Journal of International Relations* and has written and edited nine books, including *Worlds in Collision: Terror and the Future of Global Order* (co-edited with Ken Booth, 2002) and *Foreign Policy: Theories, Actors, Issues* (co-edited with Steve Smith and Amelia Hadfield, 2008).

Robyn Eckersley is Professor in the School of Social and Political Sciences, University of Melbourne, Australia. She is the author of *Environmentalism and Political Theory: Toward an Ecocentric Approach* (1992) and *The Green State: Rethinking Democracy and Sovereignty* (2004), co-author of *Special Responsibilities: Global Problems and American Power* (2012) (with M. Bukovansky, I. Clark, I., R. Price, C. Reus-Smit, C., and N. Wheeler); co-author of *Globalization and the Environment* (2013) (with P. Christoff), and has edited six books, the most recent of which are *Political Theory and the Ecological Challenge* (with Andrew Dobson, 2006) and *Why Human Security Matters: Rethinking Australian Foreign Policy* (with D. Altman, J. Camilleri, and G. Hoffstaedter).

Toni Erskine is Professor of International Politics at Aberystwyth University in Wales, UK. She is also Honorary Professor of Global Ethics at RMIT University in Melbourne, Australia. She is past Chair of the International Ethics Section of the International Studies Association (2008–10), and was Lurie-Murdoch Senior Research Fellow in Global Ethics at RMIT University (2008–11) and British Academy Postdoctoral Fellow at Cambridge University (1999–2002). Her recent publications include *Embedded Cosmopolitanism: Duties to Strangers and Enemies in a World of 'Dislocated Communities'* (2008) and (edited with Richard Ned Lebow) *Tragedy and International Relations* (2012). She is currently working on a monograph entitled *Locating Responsibility: Institutional Moral Agency and International Relations*.

K. M. Fierke is Professor of International Relations at the University of St Andrews. She has previously held positions at Queen's University Belfast; Nuffield College, Oxford University; and Amsterdam School for Social Science Research, University of Amsterdam. She is the author of: *Critical Approaches to International Security* (2007); *Diplomatic Interventions: Conflict and Change in a Globalizing World* (2005); *Changing Games, Changing Strategies: Critical Investigations in Security* (1998); *Political Self-Sacrifice: Agency, Body and Emotion in International Relations* (forthcoming); as well as co-editor of *Constructing International Relations: The Next Generation* (2001).

Siba N. Grovogui is Professor of International Relations Theory and International Law at The Johns Hopkins University. He holds a PhD from the University of Wisconsin at Madison and is the author of *Sovereigns, Quasi-Sovereigns, and Africans: Race and Self-Determination in International Law* (1996) and *Beyond Eurocentrism and Anarchy: Memories of International Order and*

Institutions (2006). Grovogui is currently completing manuscripts on human rights and on the genealogy of the 'international'. He is also collaborating on an NSF-funded research project on the rule of law under a World Bank-initiated experiment in Chad around an oil and pipeline development project.

Colin Hay is Professor of Political Analysis at the University of Sheffield where he is founding co-director of the Sheffield Political Economy Research Institute (SPERI). He has held visiting posts at Harvard University, MIT, and the University of Manchester. He is the author, co-author, or editor of a number of books. These include: *The Political Economy of European Welfare Capitalism* (2012); *The Oxford Handbook of British Politics* (2009); *Why We Hate Politics* (2007, winner of the WJM Mackenzie Prize); *European Politics* (2007); *The State: Theories and Issues* (2006); *Political Analysis* (2002); *British Politics Today* (2002); *Demystifying Globalization* (2000); *The Political Economy of New Labour* (1999); and *Re-stating Social and Political Change* (1996, winner of the Philip Abrams Memorial Prize). He is co-founder and co-editor of the journals *Comparative European Politics* and *British Politics*, and lead editor of *New Political Economy*.

Milja Kurki is Professor in International Relations theory at Aberystwyth University. She is the author of *Causation in International Relations* (2008) and *Democratic Futures* (forthcoming) and the co-editor of *Conceptual Politics of Democracy Promotion* (2011). She is an associate editor of *International Relations* and currently the Principal Investigator of a European Research Council-funded project on theoretical and conceptual underpinnings of democracy promotion, entitled 'Political Economics of Democratisation'.

Richard Ned Lebow is Professor of International Political Theory at King's College London and a Bye-Fellow of Pembroke College, Cambridge. He is also James O. Freedman Presidential Professor Emeritus at Dartmouth College. His most recent books are *The Politics and Ethics of Identity: In Search of Ourselves* (2012) and, co-edited with Toni Erskine, *Tragedy and International Relations* (2012).

John J. Mearsheimer is the R. Wendell Harrison Distinguished Service Professor of Political Science at the University of Chicago, where he has taught since 1982. He has written extensively about security issues and international politics more generally. He has published five books: *Conventional Deterrence* (1983), which won the Edgar S. Furniss, Jr. Book Award; *Liddell Hart and the Weight of History* (1988); *The Tragedy of Great Power Politics* (2001), which won the Joseph Lepgold Book Prize; *The Israel Lobby and US Foreign Policy* (with Stephen M. Walt); and *Why Leaders Lie: The Truth about Lying in International Politics* (2011). He has also written many articles for academic journals such as *International Security*, and popular magazines such as *Foreign Policy* and the *London Review of Books*.

Steven C. Roach is an Associate Professor of International Politics in the Department of Government and International Affairs at the University of South Florida. Among his most recent books are: *Critical Theory of International Politics: Complementarity, Justice and Governance* (2010); *Governance, Order and the International Criminal Court: Between Realpolitik and a Cosmopolitan Court* (2009); *Critical Theory and International Relations: A Reader* (2008); and *International Relations: The Key Concepts* (with Martin Griffiths and Terry O'Callaghan, 2008).

Mark Rupert is Professor of Political Science at Syracuse University's Maxwell School of Citizenship and Public Affairs, and teaches in the areas of International Relations and political economy. Mark's research focuses on the intersection of the US political economy with global structures and processes. He is the author of *Producing Hegemony* (1995); *Ideologies of Globalization* (2000); and *Globalization and International Political Economy* (with Scott Solomon, 2005).

Bruce Russett is Dean Acheson Research Professor of International Politics at Yale University. He received his BA in political economy from Williams College in 1956, a Diploma in Economics from King's College, Cambridge in 1957, and a PhD from Yale in 1961, as well as honorary doctorates from Uppsala University in 2002 and Williams College in 2011. He has also held appointments at Columbia, Harvard, MIT, Michigan, North Carolina, the Free University of Brussels, the Richardson Institute in London, the Netherlands Institute for Advanced Study, the University of Tel Aviv, and Tokyo University Law School.

Laura Sjoberg   is Associate Professor of Political Science at the University of Florida. She is author of *Gender, Justice, and the Wars in Iraq* (2006); *Mothers, Monsters, Whores: Women's Violence in Global Politics* (with Caron Gentry, 2007); and *Gendering Global Conflict: Towards a Feminist Theory of War* (forthcoming). She is currently editor of the *International Feminist Journal of Politics*, and has edited several books and special issues, including, most recently, *The State of Feminist Security Studies: A Conversation* (in the December 2012 issue of *Politics and Gender*, with Jennifer Lobasz). Her work has been published in more than two dozen political science and International Relations journals, and she currently serves as the chair of the International Studies Association Committee on the Status of Women.

Steve Smith   is Vice-Chancellor of the University of Exeter and Professor of International Relations. He has written or edited fifteen books. His most widely read work is *Explaining and Understanding International Relations* (co-authored with the late Professor Martin Hollis). He was the editor of the prestigious Cambridge University Press/British International Studies Association series from 1986 to 2005. In 2003–4 he was President of the International Studies Association. He is an Academician of the Social Sciences (AcSS).

Jennifer Sterling-Folker   is Professor of Political Science at the University of Connecticut. Her books include *Theories of Cooperation and the Primacy of Anarchy* and the edited volume *Making Sense of International Relations Theory*. She is the author of articles and book chapters on a variety of theoretical subjects including constructivism, neoclassical realism, global governance, and identity politics in China–Taiwan relations. She is co-editor of the BISA journal, *Review of International Studies*.

J. Ann Tickner   is Professor Emerita, University of Southern California. She is the author of *Gender in International Relations: Feminist Perspectives on Achieving Global Security* (1992) and *Gendering World Politics: Issues and Approaches in the Post-Cold War Era* (2001). Her work has appeared in *International Studies Quarterly*, *International Political Science Review*, and *Millennium*. She was President of the International Studies Association in 2006–7.

Ole Wæver   is Professor of International Relations at the University of Copenhagen and director of the Centre for Advanced Security Theory. He has written or edited twenty books and published in international journals such as *Journal of Peace Research*, *International Affairs*, *Cooperation and Conflict*, *Journal of International Affairs*, *Journal of Common Market Studies*, *Review of International Studies*, *International Organization*, and *Millennium*. His most recent books are *Regions and Powers: The Structure of International Security* (with Barry Buzan, 2003), *10x10* (ed. with Rasmus Kleis Nielsen and Ole Dahl Rasmussen, 2007), and *International Relations Scholarship around the World* (edited with Arlene B. Tickner, 2009).

Colin Wight   is Professor of International Relations at the University of Sydney. Prior to this he worked at the Department of International Politics at Aberystwyth, the Department of Politics in Sheffield, and the University of Exeter. He is the author of *Agents, Structures and International Relations* (2006). He is currently Editor in Chief of the *European Journal of International Relations*. He has published articles in *International Studies Quarterly*, *European Journal of International Relations*, *Political Studies*, and the *Philosophy of the Social Sciences*.

Guided Tour of Learning Features

This text is enriched with a range of learning tools to help you navigate the text material and reinforce your knowledge of International Relations theory. This guided tour shows you how to get the most out of your textbook package and do better in your studies.

 Reader's Guide

This chapter addresses how critical international theory h
first assessing the ideas of Frankfurt School theorists, it
School's critiques of authoritarianism and repression hav
early and later critical International Relations (IR) theorists.
gence and the features of the various strands of critical in
normative and political economy theory. The former str

Reader's Guides

Reader's Guides at the beginning of every chapter set the scene for upcoming themes and issues to be discussed, and indicate the scope of coverage within each chapter.

International morality and ethics

Postcolonialism associates the development of int
political economies with specific kinds of violenc
association is not new; nor does it imply that one shou
In the first instance, postcolonial critics find inspiration
ethical, and moral thinkers worldwide who believe

Analysis

The main section of the chapter, where contributors examine the defining ideas of the theory in question, as well as the central fault-lines within each position.

Case study: from Bush to Obama—US globa twenty-first-century imperialism?

In a series of important books, realist scholar Andrew Bacev
suggested that the very nature of the US state and the ways
shaped by two inter-related historical processes: the deep e
American culture, and a corresponding drive to sustain glob
privileged access to the world's goods, energy, and credit. W

Case Studies

Students frequently point to the abstract nature of a great deal of theoretical discussion. While this text maintains that certain philosophical issues should not be sidelined, it also recognizes the value of showing the application of theory to concrete political problems. The case studies will facilitate class discussion and debate and help you to bridge theory and practice in your assessments.

 Featured book

Hans Morgenthau, *Politics among Nations: The Struggle for Power an*

Hans Morgenthau's *Politics Among Nations*, first published i
lifetime. It was the principal IR text in North American from
generations of American college students were taught the p
power and the balance of power as guarantees of security. T

Featured Book/Articles

Spotlights on key books or articles introduce you to prominent works in the field and expand your knowledge of the available literature.

Questions

1. What are the core criticisms made by the first wav
   socialist theories? Is green political theory modernis

2. What is the cause of the ecological blindness of trad

3. In what ways has the second wave of green political

4. Why are green IR theorists critical of dominant dis

Questions

A set of carefully devised questions has been provided to help you assess your comprehension of core themes, and may also be used as the basis of seminar discussion and coursework.

Further reading

Buzan, B., Held, D., and McGrew, A. (1998), 'Realism vi
   ***International Studies**, 24: 387–98.*
A fascinating exchange about the consequences of glob
a (qualified) realism and the key proponent of cosmopc

Cerny, P. G. (1997), 'Paradoxes of the Competition Stat
   ***Government and Opposition**, 32/1: 251–74.*

Further Reading

To take your learning further, reading lists have been provided as a guide to finding out more about the issues raised within each chapter topic and to help you locate the key academic literature in the field.

Important websites

Council of Women World Leaders. **www.womenworldl**
WomanSTATS Project. **www.womanstats.org**
UN Division for the Advancement of Women. **www.un.**
Women In International Security. **wiis.georgetown.edu**
MADRE, an international women's human rights organi:

Important Websites

At the end of most chapters you will find an annotated summary of useful websites to guide further research into International Relations.

article remains the most influential application of Habermas's di
it involve the formulation of the **logic of communication** to bridg
approaches, but it also develops the discursive elements of c
argumentation, and reasoning within the context of the dec
international institutions, including international law, diplomac
(see Price and Reus-Smith 1998). In this way, Risse is able to expli
of anarchy as a 'thin lifeworld' (a repository of interest and value
social context of state action) and the discursive requirements for
in the decision-making processes of international institutions.

Glossary Terms

Key terms are bold-faced in the text and defined in a glossary at the end of the book to aid exam revision.

Guided Tour of the Online Resource Centre

The Online Resource Centre that accompanies this book provides students and instructors with ready-to-use teaching and learning materials. These resources are free of charge and designed to maximize the learning experience.

www.oxfordtextbooks.co.uk/orc/dunne3e/

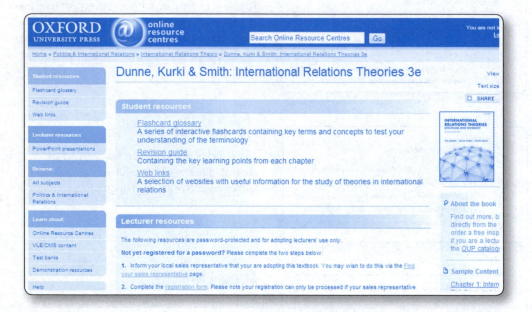

Revision Guide

Key points that summarize the most important arguments developed within each chapter topic.

Important Websites

Annotated web links, organized by issue area, have been provided to point you in the direction of different theoretical debates, important treaties, working papers, articles, and other relevant sources of information.

Flashcard Glossary

A series of interactive flashcards containing key terms and concepts has been provided to test your understanding of International Relations theory terminology.

PowerPoint Slides

These complement each chapter of the book and are a useful resource for preparing lectures and handouts. They allow lecturers to guide students through the key concepts and can be fully customized to meet the needs of the course.

Introduction: Diversity and Disciplinarity in International Relations Theory

STEVE SMITH

The study of international relations has classically focused on the analysis of the causes of war and the conditions of peace. Such an agenda seemed particularly pertinent in the twentieth century in the aftermath of two World Wars. Study of the use of force continues to motivate International Relations (IR) scholars and students even now as we move well into the second decade of the twenty-first century. For example, the question of the legitimacy and effectiveness of the 2011 Libya intervention continues to open up fissures between governments and within civil societies, just as the 2003 Iraq war did previously. Various narratives exploring the motivations for and the conditioning factors leading to such military interventions are put forward. One narrative argues that states have a right to fight preventive wars against those who could pose a mortal threat to them if they are allowed to build-up their military power unchecked—a claim forcefully made by the George W. Bush administration after the 9/11 attacks on the USA. Another narrative argues that states have a duty to fight humanitarian wars to protect civilians at risk of (or experiencing) egregious atrocity being committed.

Both kids of 'war talk' have been heard since the turn of the century. Yet, set against these contending justifications for the use of force, we should also bear in mind the objections to both pre-emption and humanitarian intervention. Indeed, objections to both kinds of warfare converge on one key point: whether justified by fear or by a sense of moral duty, interventions are 'really' about furthering the national interests of those great powers doing the intervening.

The causes of war and the justifications for intervention are not the only questions of concern, nor the only divisive questions, in the study of international relations today. Different kinds of questions have increasingly puzzled contemporary students and researchers of international relations, questions such as:

- Are cooperative relations between competing hegemonic states, such as the USA and China?
- What role can international institutions play today in altering the preferences of powerful international actors?
- How are global power relations to be identified and where, and with whom, does power lie in world politics?
- What are the limits and possibilities of progress in tackling urgent world political problems, from poverty to the threat or experience of chronic insecurity, and from terrorism to climate change?

This book is explicitly aimed at helping you think through such questions—both traditional questions concerning the causes or war and wider emerging questions in world politics. But why should we concern ourselves with theory when we deal with such questions? At first sight, you might think that surely we do not need theory to answer them: we just go and ask world political actors why they do what they do, how they intend to act, and what they think will happen in the future. Thus we can dispense with academic theories.

There are at least two main problems with this position: the first, and less important one, is that such a position requires us to believe what world leaders said in reply to our questions. Maybe, for example, state leaders lie about the reasons for going to war. Or maybe American or Chinese administrations will not be entirely forthcoming in their strategic thinking. Perhaps not all international actors reveal their hand when they claim to do their utmost to tackle climate change. Therefore, we might not get to the 'real' reason for international behaviour simply by relying on the explanations given by leaders.

The second, and more fundamental, problem in taking the views of actors at face value is that the world is rarely so simple that people can be completely aware of why they are acting in certain ways. Perhaps George W. Bush or Tony Blair, when deciding to go to war in Iraq, were looking for evidence of a clear and present danger to justify a feeling about what was 'right'. Perhaps those advocating decisive military action against Colonel Gaddafi genuinely thought their motivations were strictly humanitarian. Like all of us, they could not be entirely aware of the many reasons, personal and political, that triggered the particular course of action. The same goes for other state actors: not only may the US or China not want to expose all of their reasons for specific actions in public, but also, they may not be entirely sure why they hold particular views of their adversaries, nor why particular patterns of interactions have been resorted to. Also, many international actors may be quite unaware of the ways in which their thought and policy is already shaped by particular ideological or moral commitments, thus excluding from view other ways of coming at global interactions and problems. Thus, while global corporations tackle climate change, they may do so in good faith but yet remain unconscious of the ways in which particular assumptions about market efficiency and the imperative for economic growth limits their ability to advance the kind of changes needed to tackle the problem. It seems then that we need to locate the 'reasons' actors have for their actions in wider contexts, ones that the actors themselves may not even recognize.

Both of these objections place us immediately in the realm of theory, since we have to make assumptions about actors' behaviour and the extent to which they are either being truthful about their reasons or fully aware of the context within which they are acting.

This position could strike some readers as a bit harsh, since they might argue that surely world political actors know exactly what they are doing. My simple response is to ask each reader to think through their own behaviour: why is it that we feel what we feel, think what we think, say what we say, and do what we do? We know that in fact we are often not sure of our reasons, and sometimes catch a glimpse of ourselves acting in accordance with what is fashionable or what is consistent with a particular rationale which we hope will be publicly acceptable. In short, in the social world it is not enough simply to base our accounts of individuals solely on the reasons they give for their actions. The social world is one in which individuals exist within powerful economic, political, social, gendered, racial, linguistic, and moral structures. We might be able to *describe* action fairly easily (Prime Minister Tony Blair said that he supported the US President in going to war against Iraq), but it is far more difficult to *explain* it (why was the action undertaken?). And, when it comes to explaining action, we are, whether we like it or not, in the realm of theory.

Theories offer accounts of why things happened, and the fact that they offer a wide range of reasons for action reflects the fact that they have very different assumptions. Hence, you will get very different answers to world political puzzles and problems from the different theories represented in this book. In fact, if you were to ask each of the authors of the chapters what they think of any global confrontation whether it is the so-called global war on terror, or the challenge of China's rise, or the battle against climate change, I suspect that you would get distinctly different answers from each advocate. Some of the differences would result from the fact that the authors focused on different aspects of world politics: some might focus on political economy issues; others might look at the role of international law and institutions; others might concentrate on notions of maximizing power; while others still would see world political problems as sites where unequal identities are constructed so as to reinforce power structures. Yet other differences would be because the authors saw the world in very different ways from one another: some would see a world of power and security; others would see a world of meaning and community; while others still would see a world of economic forces capturing political actors.

These differences sometimes worry students new to the discipline of IR, since they expect some kind of 'right' answer, and are often frustrated when teachers of the subject keep referring them back to a range of theories, each of which has a different take on the question. In my view, this is an absolutely central issue, and I hope in this introduction to show why, in the case of the social world, it is indeed interpretation all the way down. To be completely clear from the outset, I do not think that we can evaluate accounts of why people act as they do in a way that leads to one definitive story; in the social world *there is always more than one story to tell*.

In this introduction I want to do three main things. First I want to explain why we (the three editors) have chosen to cover the theories that we have, and to say something about our view of international theory and its relationship to the world, an important issue which features prominently in the text through the use of case study analysis. Second, I want to look at the kind of assumptions about theory that underlie each of the approaches. Finally, I want to discuss explicitly the issue of how one might make a choice between the rival theories covered in this book.

All these theories but the bodies keep piling up[1]

The book includes eight chapters on distinct theories of International Relations (IR), with two positions being divided across classical and neo-variants: realism/structural realism, liberalism/neoliberalism, the English school, constructivism, Marxism, critical theory, feminism, poststructuralism, green theory, and postcolonialism. These eight theoretical accounts stand alongside chapters that reflect on IR theory and its relationship to social science, normative theory, globalization, and the discipline's identity. The existence of so many theories of IR does lead to one obvious query: why is there such a range of contending positions? In the history of the discipline of IR there have always been debates between competing theories. Kurki and Wight cover the history of these debates in **Chapter 1**, so I am not going to rehearse them here: suffice it to state that from the earliest days of its existence as a discipline, the main debate has been between forms of realism and liberalism. In recent years this debate has been between versions of realism and liberalism known as neorealism and neoliberalism. Although there are clear linkages between classical and 'neo' variants, we allocated them separate chapters because we think that the later versions contain distinctly different assumptions about the nature of theory. Marxism has been the other main approach to studying international relations, and by the 1980s it was commonplace to speak of the three approaches (realism, liberalism, and Marxism) as constituting an 'interparadigm debate'. This is how most of the textbooks of the 1980s and 1990s represented international theory and, as a consequence, this is how theory was taught.

From the vantage point of today, it seems that there were a number of problems with this way of thinking about IR theory. First, it exaggerated the amount of debate: what actually happened was that realism dominated the discipline given that it claimed to explain the bipolar structure of the international system, while liberalism was able to cover secondary issues to do with institutions and trade, with Marxism being invoked to explain relative economic power and structural inequality. This notion of an interparadigm debate hinted at a kind of intellectual pluralism, whereby there was a level playing field on which the theories competed. Yet, the priority accorded to explaining the military confrontation enabled realism to assume primacy. The key point to note is the power of assumptions about 'what' the world of international relations consisted of in determining the explanatory power of the rival theories. Thus, since international relations was defined as being about war, the theory that would appear to be most useful in explaining it, not surprisingly, would be the one that focused on war. I am not saying that war is not a feature of world politics, only that the dominance of realism and neorealism reflected often implicit, unstated, 'common-sense' assumptions about the content of world politics.

But it was another problem that caused most reflection among those who felt uneasy at the notion of intellectual pluralism implied by the idea of an interparadigm debate. The phrase suggested that the three approaches were all vying for attention in terms of their ability to explain *the same world*. The rather unsettling worry was that the three approaches were actually focusing on rather different features of international relations, and thus they were not in debate at all; what they disagreed about was which events should be the focus of the discipline. Thus, whereas realism might focus on the Cold War, liberalism might concentrate on international economic relations between the leading capitalist economies, and

Marxism might stress the patterns of world trade and investment that create divisions between the 'haves' and the 'have-nots'. If you accept this argument, then it follows that the dominance of one theory is the result of a prior assumption about the main things in world politics that need explaining. This leads to a rather destabilizing thought, which is that something as seemingly 'academic' and 'non-political' as deciding which theory is of most help in explaining international relations might in fact be a very political act, because which theory you see as being the most useful will depend on what you want to explain, and this, in turn, will depend on your values and beliefs about what international relations is all about. Put very simply, if you live in a wealthy part of the world, where there are no apparent military threats, you might think that the key features to be explained are those concerned with the economic relations between the main wealthy powers. If you live in a conflict zone, where the survival of your society is at issue, you might well want a theory that explains conflict. Finally, if you are in a very poor part of the world, you may see the central features of world politics as those related to the creation and support of differences between national levels of wealth.

This sense of dissatisfaction with the comforting notion of an interparadigm debate led to what many have called the fourth **great debate** in IR, between what can broadly be called **rationalist** and **reflectivist** theories. This debate was launched by Robert Keohane in his 1988 International Studies Association (ISA) presidential debate, and referred to the tensions then emerging between rationalist approaches, such as neorealism and neoliberalism, on the one hand and reflectivist approaches, such as feminism and poststructuralism, on the other. To simplify things a bit, the chapters in this book dealing with neorealism and neoliberalism would be seen by Keohane as rationalist, whereas most of the others, with two main exceptions, would be seen by him as reflectivist; the exceptions would perhaps be constructivism, normative theory, and the English school, all of which can best be understood as overlapping the rationalist/reflectivist divide (see individual chapters for details on how). The key difference between rationalist and reflectivist approaches is that, broadly speaking, rationalist accounts are **positivist**, whereas reflectivist approaches oppose positivism. Again, the Kurki and Wight chapter discusses this distinction in detail; for now it is enough to note that the central differences between rationalist and reflectivist accounts are **epistemological** and **methodological**, and only secondarily about what the world is like (**ontology**). That is to say that the fourth debate is one about how we know what we claim to know. In this important sense, the main dividing line between the significant theories of IR for the last two decades has been their attitude towards positivist accounts of knowledge.

Since the interparadigm debate of the 1980s, there has been an explosion of theories about international relations. Most of these theories have opposed the dominance of rationalist approaches (neorealism and neoliberalism), primarily on epistemological grounds. Rationalist theories accept a notion of **foundationalism**, whereby there are secure grounds for making knowledge claims about a world that is separate from the theories commenting on it. Rationalist theories sometimes claim that their accounts are more accurate than others because, due to their systematic scientific approach, they can capture the essence of the way the world is in an empirically justifiable way. By way of contrast, reflectivist approaches do not share a commitment to the form of foundational positivism found in rationalist approaches. This has caused a significant problem for reflectivist approaches, because they have been dismissed by leading rationalist scholars for not being legitimate social science.

Keohane made this point in his ISA presidential address: he claimed that reflectivism's main weakness was the lack of a research programme:

> Until the reflective scholars or others sympathetic to their arguments have delineated such a research program and shown in particular studies that it can illuminate important issues in world politics, they will remain on the margins of the field, largely invisible to the preponderance of empirical researchers, most of whom explicitly or implicitly accept one or another version of rationalistic premises.
>
> Keohane 1989: 173

What was needed, he went on to add, was for reflectivist scholars to develop 'testable theories' without which 'it will be impossible to evaluate their research programme' (1989: 173–4).

More recently, Stephen Walt, in a highly influential review of the state of IR theory, argues that although the key debate has been, and continues to be, that between realism and liberalism, there is a third approach which he sees as the main alternative to these two. But for Walt this alternative approach is not one of the main reflectivist approaches; instead it is constructivism, which concedes a great deal of philosophical ground to rationalism. But he goes further than this: Walt explicitly rejects reflectivism 'because these scholars focused initially on criticizing the mainstream paradigms but did not offer positive alternatives to them, they remained a self-consciously dissident minority for most of the 1980s' (1998: 32).

Walt sets out the main features of these three 'paradigms' (realism, liberalism, and constructivism) in a figure representing a classical Greco-Roman building with three pillars. Under the heading of constructivism he lists its 'unit of analysis' as 'individuals' and its 'main instruments' as 'ideas and discourse'. Its 'main limitation' is that it is 'better at describing the past than anticipating the future'. It is not just that this is a very thin account of constructivism but also that constructivism is portrayed as the only approach that deals with ideas, discourse, and identities, which a variety of reflectivist theorists would see as their core concerns. Not only does Stephen Walt effectively silence more radical theoretical approaches, he understates the value of constructivism. This is evident in his belief that 'the "compleat diplomat" of the future should remain cognizant of realism's emphasis on the inescapable role of power, keep liberalism's awareness of domestic forces in mind, and occasionally reflect on constructivism's vision of change' (1998: 44). By way of contrast, Walt argues that 'realism is likely to remain the single most useful instrument in our intellectual toolbox' (1998: 43).

The current situation is one where there is a wide range of theories of IR. It is very important to stress that while some of these are trying to explain the same features of world politics, others are focusing on very different aspects. The problem is that many of the mainstream (rationalist) theorists deny the legitimacy of *both* sets of alternative theories. Those that are offering competing accounts of the same phenomena are usually deemed illegitimate, as not being 'proper' social science, while those focusing on other features of world politics (such as poverty, gender, race, international law, the environment, etc.) are dismissed as not dealing with the most important features of world politics (usually defined as inter-state war). In an important respect, the dismissal of work as illegitimate (in terms of epistemology) is in many ways more insidious than a dismissal on the grounds that the features focused on (that is to say, on grounds of ontology) are not central to international relations.

None of this means that the traditionally dominant mainstream approaches are out-dated or peripheral to an explanation of international relations. Indeed, by giving each of the historically dominant traditions two chapters, we hope that we have made clear the importance that we place on these theories. In our view, they are absolutely central to explaining international relations but, equally importantly, we do not feel that they are sufficient on their own. We believe that there are other accounts that explain areas of international relations, and we feel that our job as editors is to offer as wide a range of accounts as possible in this book. We believe that the reader needs to understand both that the historically dominant approaches are vitally important for an understanding of international relations, and that these need to be complemented by other accounts that are equally legitimate.

Some established scholars in the discipline, such as Kal Holsti, regret this proliferation of theories, and the disappearance of a discrete field of inquiry. As he puts it:

> It is hard to say that there is any longer a particular core to the field. . . . Our field should be basically concerned with the relations between states, and relations between societies and non- state actors to the extent that those relations impinge upon and affect the relations between states. When we go far beyond these domains, we get into areas of sociology, anthropology, and social psychology that are best dealt with by people in those disciplines.
>
> Holsti 2002: 621

He adds:

> I am somewhat concerned that too many people may be spending time discussing great issues of epistemology and metaphysics . . . But beyond a certain point . . . concern with epistemology may lead us to lose sight of the subject matter. The greatest texts of our field were written by those who were deeply immersed in the subject, and not by epistemologists.
>
> Holsti 2002: 623

We disagree with Holsti. We believe that the field is now much healthier because of the proliferation of theories. Not only has this resulted in a significant rethink about what the field consists of, it has also led to a questioning of the main assumptions of the ontology and epistemology of the discipline. Together we see these developments as opening up space for much more debate, and, crucially, to legitimize a wider variety of theories. On the one hand, then, the range of theories allows us to think about more aspects of international relations than before, and because they are often based on epistemological positions far removed from positivism they also allow us to reflect on just how we think about the world. This widening of theories has been achieved in part by a much closer engagement with other social sciences, so that sociological or anthropological accounts of international relations are every bit as worthy as conventional political or economic accounts. We see this situation as better than that of most of the last century, when one theory (realism) dominated the discipline, and one view of knowledge construction (positivism) reigned supreme. But, of course, there is no denying that this plurality of approaches does raise some significant problems, most obviously how to choose between theories.

What do the theories share?

Despite the very significant differences between the theories dealt with in this book, it is important to note that they share three significant assumptions. First, and chief among these, is their shared commitment to the importance of theory in understanding the world. In direct contrast to those who see theory as irrelevant or optional, all the authors in this book think that theory is central to explaining international relations. We need to stress the importance of this assumption, since many continue to believe that theory merely gets in the way of understanding the world, and at worst is simply a way of making things more complicated than they really are. In our view, the option of non-theoretical accounts of the world is simply not available. All observation of international relations has to be carried out in the language of some theory or other. The choice, then, is one of whether you are aware of the assumptions you are bringing to your study of the world or not. Indeed, texts that begin by saying that they are only looking at 'the facts' are theoretically laden: this is because what counts as 'the facts' is either something that is explicitly linked to a theory, or is instead the result of powerful and unstated assumptions.

Second, all the theories have a history, though not always within the discipline of IR. These histories mean that comparing theories is not easy, since they emerge from very different intellectual traditions. Therefore many of the chapters use the word 'theory' in specific ways: we need to stress this to the reader, since the different usage results directly from the historical and intellectual heritage of each approach. Thus, the chapters on feminism, poststructuralism, green theory, and postcolonialism are developed from work that has mainly appeared in other academic disciplines, mostly in the last fifty years. By way of contrast, the chapters on classical realism, liberalism, Marxism and critical theory, and the English school are each referring to a long-standing approach that goes back much further, in most cases at least a century. The debates on social science and international political theory—discussed in the first two chapters—also have a long history, if not explicitly within the confines of IR theory but rather within the disciplines of philosophy or political theory and ethics. Finally, the chapters on neorealism, neoliberalism, constructivism, and the effects of globalization are all focused on the main theoretical developments in IR over the last twenty years.

Third, each of the chapters makes claims about the linkages between theory and practice, though, again, they do this in a variety of ways. Some of the chapters that follow treat theory as something akin to a toolkit, whereby the reader can, by understanding certain key concepts, apply them to the world and thereby understand it better. The four chapters on classical realism, classical liberalism, neorealism, and neoliberalism are good examples of this notion of theory. Other chapters present theory as something that critiques the existing dominant order and offers ways of emancipating individuals from that order: the chapters on green theory, Marxism, critical theory, and postcolonialism are good examples of this version of theory. Still other chapters, such as those on feminism, poststructuralism, international political theory, the English school, globalization, and constructivism, are more concerned with what gets presented as the core issues represented in the discipline, and how they relate to identity. Thus, the theories we cover in this book offer a variety of ways of approaching the relationship between theory and practice: the range varies from helpful toolkit all the way through to human emancipation, and this, again, raises the question: what is the role of theory?

For most of its history as a separate discipline, IR has been dominated by one specific answer to this question, which is that theory has the role of explaining the world. That is to say that the job of theories is to report on the world—this is very much the 'toolkit' model of theory. According to this view, theories are devices to explain a world that exists apart from them. Such a belief was a very strong assumption of positivism. This view of theory is known as an 'explanatory' view. It means that theories explain a world that is 'out there', and explaining it means making sense of it. But there is another view of theory which is that theories 'constitute' the world that they are explaining. By this we mean only that theories can never be separate from the world, they are an intrinsic part of it. Therefore, there can never be a 'view from nowhere', and *all* theories make assumptions about the world, both ontological ones (what features need explaining) and epistemological ones (what counts as explanation). The critically important point here is that whereas positivist theories claim that non-positivist theories are illegitimate because they are not neutral (i.e. they make explicit assumptions about ontology and epistemology, take for example the chapter on feminism) the problem is that positivist theories fail to recognize that they do exactly the same thing but this time by maintaining a separation between observer and observed, and between theory and the world. It is this claim that needs contesting. All theories are located in space, time, culture, and history, and, simply put, there is no possibility of the separation from these that positivism requires.

Therefore, this book starts with a chapter that introduces the major debates in the discipline of IR with regards to the philosophy of social sciences. It is followed by a chapter charting the role and scope of so-called normative theorizing in IR. As Erskine points out, normative theory can be considered by more of a subfield of IR than a distinct and singular theoretical position. We then have four chapters dealing with the traditional mainstream theories: classical realism, structural realism, liberalism, and neoliberalism. These are followed by three chapters dealing with approaches that share much with the mainstream, but which have been seen as developments of it, or as significantly distinct enough to constitute separate intellectual traditions: the English school, Marxism, and constructivism. Finally, we have a set of five chapters which are importantly 'critical' of the traditional mainstream: critical theory, feminism, poststructuralism, postcolonialism, and green theory. We end the book with two chapters, each of which serves as a conclusion. The chapter on globalization looks at contemporary international relations and discusses whether such a thing as globalization exists and whether the assorted phenomena of globalization render traditional state-centric theories of IR redundant. The final chapter looks at the current nature of the discipline of IR and the ways in which the theories discussed in this book relate to the emerging structure of debate in the field. As you will see, these chapters have important things to say about the linkage between how the discipline has traditionally defined the subject matter of international relations and how then one might decide which theory was of most use in explaining that world.

Diversity and disciplinarity

The picture that emerges from this book is that the discipline of IR is, we believe, far more relevant to the world of international relations than it has been at any point in its history. We made this claim in the first edition and we continue to make it, despite being challenged on this since the last edition by a leading theorist who makes a twofold challenge: first, questioning the extent to which IR is genuinely characterized by theoretical pluralism, and second, casting doubt on whether pluralism per se is something to be valued (Schmidt 2008). I have defended our claims in this regard elsewhere (Smith 2008) and will not rehearse these arguments here again. Suffice it to say that IR theory is now far more pluralist than it was just thirty years ago, particularly outside of the North American mainstream. This diversity has generated different answers to perennial questions in IR about actors, issues, causes, and consequences. In light of the fact that we do not believe that political questions about justice, power, and rights, lend themselves to singular answers, we regard pluralism as being a positive development in the discipline.

Yet, the existence of this growing body of distinctly different theories has given all students of IR two main problems. The first is whether there can be said to be a discipline of IR at all after the proliferation of theories, many of which have their intellectual basis in different social sciences. The final chapter of this book deals with this question in detail, but, similarly, the penultimate chapter on globalization implies that if we start our analysis of international relations from an economic perspective we get a much altered view of what are the core features to be explained by any theory. In an important sense the editors of this book are relaxed about what the proliferation means for the identity of the discipline, since we believe that what matters most is the ability of theories to explain the world as it is seen from a variety of different cultural, economic, gendered, political, ethnic, and social locations. One problem of an insistence that the boundaries of the discipline should be clear, precise, and fixed, is that this absolutely determines what counts as acceptable scholarship. We prefer boundaries to a discipline that can alter, as our views of the political shift according both to our identity as observers and to the agenda that we wish to explain. In this light, we note that the discipline has played a role in recreating the realist world of great power dominance, simply because that is what generations of IR academics taught as 'reality' or the 'real world' to their students. In that sense, too much concern with maintaining the boundaries of an academic discipline looks dangerously like a very conservative move to privilege the existing power distribution in the world. We feel that the current diversity in the discipline offers far more in the way of opportunity to examine a variety of policy concerns and issues than has ever been the case in the discipline's history. Taken together, the theories in this book create space for thinking about what international relations consists of and what are its most salient features. In this important sense, if the discipline is facing an identity crisis because the old certainties are no longer quite so secure, then we think that this is a positive and empowering development.

However, the second problem created by the proliferation of IR theories is much deeper. This is the question of how one chooses which theory to use. Traditionally, this has not been a problem for the discipline, since the answer was always a choice between realism and liberalism, with realism being dominant. This was largely the case because, if the subject was defined by the presence of war, then realism seemed to be the best theory to explain war. If one's focus was international cooperation, then liberalism was appropriate; and the debate between these two theoretical strands constituted the founding debate within IR. Today, not only is there a set of well developed and powerful alternative theories, but these theories dispute the core assumptions about the content of the field.

This situation raises the question of the grounds on which we make a choice between theories. For many new undergraduate students of IR this is a major worry, since they want to be guided to the 'right' answer. And, of course, this is why realism has been so powerful, because it explicitly sees itself as the best account of the persistence of inter-state war and competition. We feel that there is much more at stake in answering this question. In my view, the first criterion involved in making a choice between theories has to be the issues you wish to explain. Thus, if you are interested in the future of the environment, it is likely that green theory will be as good a place to start as any. That does not mean that only green theory can offer explanations, but it does give the reader a place to start their thinking about which is the most appropriate theory. It would be tempting to leave the issue of theory choice here, since I could imply that the theories in this book are all dealing with different, discrete, aspects of the same world of international relations, and that you could adopt a kind of 'pick and mix' attitude towards theory. Accordingly you might think it sensible to use, say, green theory when discussing the environment, feminism when discussing global gender inequalities, and structural realism when looking at great power rivalry in the Asia–Pacific. But though this might seem comforting, I do not think that this move is possible. This is because the various theories are not like parts of a jigsaw that can be neatly combined together with each explaining one part of international relations. Rather I think that the theories in this book are like different coloured lenses: if you put one of them in front of your eyes, you will see things differently. Some aspects of the world will look the same in some senses, for example shapes, but many other features, such as light and shade of colour, will look very different, so different in fact that they seem to show alternative worlds.

In thinking about this you might like to visualize Martin Hollis's excellent example of a mobile hanging over a child's bed, a metaphor he regularly used in his teaching. The view that the various theories each explain part of the world of international relations is akin to the view that someone standing looking at the child's mobile will see the same mobile as the child lying on the bed, albeit from different angles. There is nothing incommensurable about their two perspectives; simple geometric analysis can show how their different views of the mobile can be combined together—they are just different views of the same mobile. Yet Hollis always argued, persuasively in my view, that the social world is not like this. The theories we use cannot simply be combined together so as to add up to different views of the same world of international relations; instead, they actually *see* different worlds. Thus a Marxist writer, though they will focus on power, will see a different form of power (ultimately economic) to that seen by a classical realist (ultimately political). Similarly, a classical liberal will not see cooperation over environmental issues in anything like the same way as a green theorist will see them. Finally, think of, say, a feminist writing about the global power structure, and compare it to a neorealist account. It is not possible simply to add up these various accounts of international relations to get one overarching theory. Theories are *part* of the social world, they can never be separate from it, and thus they constitute the social world in which we live. Each defines the problems to be examined differently, and may well define how we know things about those problems in different ways. Thus the social location of the observer will influence which theory they see as most useful, simply because that location will predispose that observer to define some features of international relations as key and others as less relevant.

But in putting forward this view of theory we need to be clear that we are not saying that each theory is equally good at explaining everything. It is not a case of 'anything goes'. Our view is that a variety of theories will claim to offer explanations for the same kinds of features of international relations. We believe that there are grounds for choosing between them, though we want to stress that these grounds are nothing like as restrictive as positivists claim. Thus while we do not think that theory choice is simply a matter of whatever appeals to a reader on a given day, we do think that the grounds cannot be those of one dominant view of epistemology and methodology.

All of this brings us back to where we started this chapter. There are many theories that offer explanations to real world problems and dilemmas. You will find some of them persuasive, others less so. Our argument is not that each of these theories should be deemed equally appropriate, or helpful, or valid. Decisions over which theories are tenable and which are not should be determined, respectively, by the reader of this book or the proponent of the theory concerned. The judgement cannot be made by advocates of another theory that its rivals are either irrelevant or illegitimate. We also want to point out that there are epistemological difficulties with combining different theories, although both critical realism and the English school attempt to provide theories which are a synthesis of more than one position.

Many treatments of IR avoid the problem of **incommensurability** by focusing only on those theories that share an epistemological grounding (e.g. neoliberalism and neorealism). That makes 'debates' relatively easy. We have not chosen to deal with theories of IR in that way. Instead we have tried to offer you a wide choice of theories and leave you with the somewhat unsettling task of having to decide which theory you find most useful in explaining and understanding international relations, and then answering the question of why that is the case. We think that this gives you a real choice, and, although at first sight it may be a little disturbing to question whether it is possible to use theory as a toolkit to answer different issues and problems, we do think the fact of theoretical diversity in IR forces readers to confront questions about how to choose between theories. Such questions are unavoidable; previously they have been overlooked because of the tendency to present only compatible theories of IR. The diversity represented in this book promises a discipline that is of more relevance to people in a variety of locations than has hitherto been the case. The editors of this book strongly believe that it is better to open up space for analysis and debate, even though that will lead to difficult ethical and philosophical questions about theory choice, than it is to close down debate and insist that the only theories that are 'right' are those which fit into preconceived, and often hidden, assumptions about what international relations consists of. It is our strong view that this diversity is to be celebrated rather than disciplined (as some traditionalists would prefer).

Diversity may be unsettling because it leaves the reader facing some fundamental problems about how to make a choice between rival theories; but at the very least it does make it possible to confront orthodoxy, to develop theory relevant to a wider range of humanity, and, ultimately, to accept that our choice of theories to explain the world of international relations can never be a neutral act. Theory is always socially located, always has an unavoidable relationship to power, and can never be defended by resort to one foundational account of what is 'truth'. In this sense, our aim is not so much to provide the reader with one account of international relations but to offer a choice of IR theories that allow us to make sense of our multi-layered and cultural complex world, as well as to recognize the processes and difficulties involved in coming to understand them.

Note

1. This phrase could be found, at one time, on the office wall of Nicholas J. Wheeler, my former colleague in Aberystwyth.

 Visit the Online Resource Centre that accompanies this book for lots of interesting additional material. **www.oxfordtextbooks.co.uk/orc/dunne3e/**

1

International Relations and Social Science

MILJA KURKI AND COLIN WIGHT

 Reader's Guide

This chapter provides an overview of the key philosophy of social science debates within International Relations (IR) theory.[1] Often IR theorists do not address the philosophy of social science explicitly, but nevertheless philosophical issues are implicit in their claims. Since the mid-1980s, 'meta-theoretical' debates surrounding the philosophy of social science have played an important and highly visible role in the discipline. This chapter explores both the implicit and explicit roles played by meta-theoretical assumptions in IR. It begins with a brief historical overview of the philosophy of social science within IR. The contemporary disciplinary debates surrounding the philosophy of social science are then examined. The final section highlights some of the key ways in which meta-theoretical positions shape theoretical approaches to the study of world politics.

Introduction

The philosophy of social science has played an important role in the formation, development, and practice of IR as an academic discipline. Often issues concerning the philosophy of social science are described as meta-theoretical debates. **Meta-theory** does not take a specific event, phenomenon, or series of empirical real world practices as its object of analysis, but explores the underlying assumptions of all theory and attempts to understand the consequences of such assumptions on the act of theorizing and the practice of empirical research. One way to think about this is in terms of theories about theories.

The role of meta-theoretical debates is frequently misunderstood. Some see meta-theorizing as nothing more than a quick precursor to empirical research. Others see it as a distraction from the real issues that should concern the discipline. However, it is impossible for research to proceed in any subject domain in the social sciences in the absence of a set of commitments embedded within positions on the philosophy of social science. In this sense, meta-theoretical positions direct, in a fundamental way, the manner in which people theorize and, indeed, 'see' the world.

To put this in philosophical terminology, all theoretical positions are dependent upon particular assumptions about **ontology** (theory of being: what is the world made of? what objects do we study?), **epistemology** (theory of knowledge: how do we come to have knowledge of the world?), and **methodology** (theory of methods: what methods do we use to unearth data and evidence?). On the basis of these assumptions researchers may literally come to 'see' the world in different ways: ontologically in terms of seeing different object domains, epistemologically in terms of accepting or rejecting particular knowledge claims, and methodologically in terms of choosing particular methods of study. Meta-theoretical positions have deep, if often unrecognized, consequences for social analysis. Being aware of the issues at stake in meta-theoretical debate, and of their significance in terms of concrete research, serves as an important starting point for understanding IR theory and facilitates a deeper awareness of one's own meta-theoretical orientation.

Meta-theoretical debates surrounding the philosophy of social science in IR have tended to revolve around two interrelated questions. Is IR a science or an art? What does the 'scientific' study of world politics entail? A position can be taken on the question of whether IR can be a science only on the basis of some or other account of what science is, and an account of what we think IR is. Hence, the questions of what science is, and what IR is, are prior to the question of whether IR can be a science. This inevitably takes the discussion into the terrain of the philosophy of science. This seems a long way from the concerns of a discipline focused on the study of international political processes, and the frustration of some within the discipline concerning meta-theoretical debate is understandable. Yet, there is no way to avoid these issues and at a minimum all contributors to the discipline should understand the assumptions that make their own position possible; as well as being aware of alternative conceptualizations of what IR theory and research might involve.

For a large part of the history of the field a particular philosophy of science has dominated. The influence of **positivism** as a philosophy of science has shaped not only how we theorize about the subject, and what counts as a valid question, but also what can count as valid forms of evidence and knowledge. Such is the influence of positivism on the disciplinary imagination that even those concerned to reject a scientific approach to IR tend to do so on the basis of a general acceptance of the positivist model of science. There are two points worthy of note in this respect. First, despite the acceptance of the positivist model of science by both advocates and critics alike, understandings of positivism, its meaning and its consequences for the discipline, are rudimentary. Second, it is noteworthy that within the philosophy of science positivism has been discredited as a valid account of scientific practice. Had the discipline been prepared to take the philosophy of social science, and by extension the philosophy of science, more seriously, a long and potentially damaging commitment to particular forms of positivism might have been avoided. This does not mean that all research underpinned by positivist principles is invalid. Indeed, we believe that scholars who might be considered to be working in the positivist tradition have made some of the most important and lasting contributions to the discipline. Nonetheless, this view of science is highly contested and there is no reason to insist that all research should fit this model. Equally, a rejection of the positivist model of science need not lead to the rejection of science.

This chapter argues that social science debates within the discipline can be moved forward by a comprehensive re-examination of what science is. Hence, besides reviewing the historical and contemporary philosophy of social science debates in IR, the chapter also points towards new accounts of science that have been introduced to the discipline in the last decade or so; accounts that hold the promise of reformulating our understanding of the aims and methods of IR as a social science. Science, we argue, is not based on a dogmatic insistence on the certainty of its claims but, rather, rests on a commitment to constant critique.

The philosophy of social science in IR: a historical overview

The discipline of IR, in common with all the social sciences, has been deeply divided on many issues throughout its history. A common way of narrating this history is in terms of the **great debates** surrounding these key issues. In many respects debate is the wrong term to use, since in some of them a group of theorists situated their own approach as a direct counter to previous ways of thinking, without generating a substantial set of responses (Schmidt 1998). Some of the debates, however, were genuine and scholars within the discipline have often been prepared to engage with one another over substantial areas of disagreement. Although there is no consensus on the exact number of great debates, four are generally accepted to have played an important role in shaping the discipline (Wæver 1996).

The first debate refers to the exchanges between the realists and idealists before, during, and immediately after the Second World War. This was primarily waged over the role of international institutions and the likelihood that the causes of war might be ameliorated. The second debate emerged in the 1960s. It pitted the traditionalists, who were keen to defend a more humanistic methodology, against the modernizers, who aimed to introduce a greater level of methodological rigour to the discipline. The interparadigm debate of the 1970s and 1980s focused on disagreements among the realist, pluralist, and Marxist perspectives on how best to understand and explain international processes. Finally, the most recent debate, which some IR theorists call the fourth debate, has centred on deep-seated disagreements about what the discipline should study and how it should study it. While these debates have often highlighted the paradigmatic divisions between different and distinct IR theoretical schools of thought, an often-unrecognized issue has cut across and underpinned all the debates. This is the issue of whether or not IR can be, or should be, a form of inquiry based upon scientific principles.

Science and the first debate

The first great debate in the discipline is said to have taken place between the idealists and the realists. The idealists were driven by a desire to develop a set of institutions, procedures, and practices that could eradicate, or at least control, war in the international system. They were motivated by the horrors of the First World War and they sincerely believed that there must be a better way to organize international affairs. The most visible, and historically important, aspect of their programme cohered in Woodrow Wilson's Fourteen-point Plan for a new postwar order. However, the most enduring contribution of the idealists in terms of disciplinary development was the idea of an academic discipline constructed to study the world of international politics. For the idealists, ignorance and lack of understanding was a primary source of international conflict. A better understanding of international processes was required if control of the system was to be achieved. The idealists believed progress was only possible if we could develop and use reason to control the irrational desires and frailties that infect the human condition. The pinnacle of human reason in the service of effective control was science. This thinking led to the establishment of an academic department of international politics located in Aberystwyth, Wales. The aim of this new discipline was the production of a body of knowledge that could be used in the furtherance of peace. Although the idealists never clearly articulated what they meant by science, they were committed to producing knowledge that was scientific.

The absence of a clear account of science in the early years of the discipline is understandable given that the philosophy of science was itself not yet fully established as an academic field of study. Science, to the Enlightenment mind, was self-evident. Yet the realist critique of the idealists was to challenge the extent to which the knowledge produced by the idealists was scientific. In particular, realists challenged the 'unsystematic' and value-driven idealist approach to IR. Both E. H. Carr (1946, 1987) and Hans Morgenthau (1947, 1948a; discussed in more detail in **Chapter 3**) accused the idealists of focusing their attention on how the world 'ought' to be, as opposed to dealing with how it objectively was. In a scathing attack Carr famously concluded that the difference between realism and idealism was analogous to that between science and alchemy (1946: 1–11).

Neither Carr nor Morgenthau, however, can be said to have uncritically embraced a naive view of science. Carr was only too well aware of the problematic status of facts and associated truth claims. His celebrated notion of the 'relativity of thought' and his sophisticated treatment of historical method can hardly be said to constitute an uncritical commitment to science. Likewise, Morgenthau went to great lengths to distance his approach to political science from attempts to construct 'iron laws' comparable to those discovered in the natural sciences (Morgenthau 1947). Despite his belief that international politics was governed by 'objective laws' rooted in human nature, Morgenthau articulated a series of telling objections to any attempt to construct a science of international politics modelled on the natural sciences. After all, if international politics was governed by 'objective laws' rooted in human nature, then the true causes of war were to be found in biology, and any nascent science of IR could provide only suggestions for dealing with a realm of human activity that was to a great extent predetermined. Morgenthau's account of IR was not concerned to provide a series of in-depth explanations of the workings of the world but, rather, aimed at articulating a series of techniques and modes of operation for dealing with a world on the basis of a simple, but enticing, explanation. Nonetheless, despite these caveats, and the limited nature of debate surrounding understandings of science within the discipline, the status of science was clearly important in the early period of the development of the subject. In the second great debate, however, it was to take centre stage.

Science and the second debate

The second debate took the 'rhetorical' arguments about science and gave them methodological substance. Drawing on the **behaviourist** revolution in the social sciences, a new breed of 'scientific' IR scholars, such as David Singer and Morton Kaplan, sought to define and refine systematic scientific methods of inquiry for the discipline of IR. The behaviourist research instigated fierce resistance from those committed to a more historicist, or interpretive, form of IR.

For the proponents of the behavioural revolution, IR could move forward only if it consciously modelled itself on the natural sciences. By the time the second debate had emerged in IR the philosophy of science was a well developed and institutionally located academic discipline. Moreover, within the philosophy of science one view had come to dominate; although ironically just as IR was to formalize its vision of science the consensus within the philosophy of science had already begun to unravel. The model of science that had dominated was called positivism, and the behaviourists in IR embraced it enthusiastically. There are many versions of positivism and such was its promotion and reception in IR that it has come to be a synonym for science. This is a regrettable move since it effectively closes down all debate on what kind of science IR might be; if IR is to be a science, it must be modelled on positivist principles.

Positivism suggests that scientific knowledge emerges only with the collection of observable data. The collection of sufficient data, it was presumed, would lead to the identification of patterns that would in turn allow the formulation of laws. The importance of observable data for this approach cannot be over-stressed. The inscription on the Social Science Research Building façade, at the University of Chicago, reads, 'If you cannot measure it, your knowledge is meagre and unsatisfactory'. This stress on observable data and measurement led the proponents of the new scientific model to engage in a series of sharp criticisms of the account of science adhered to by many realists and other IR scholars. Many of the core concepts of 'classical' realism were deemed to be lacking in specificity and were not susceptible to measurement. Power and the national interest, for example, if they were to be studied according to the principles of the new science, needed increased levels of clarity and specification; anything that could not be rigorously measured and subject to testing was to be purged from the new ontology. New methods were developed and the mathematical modelling of international processes took pride of place. The behaviouralists hoped that through the relentless accumulation of data, knowledge would progress and control would follow.

The behaviouralist criticisms of the traditional approach did not go unchallenged. Many argued that the core concepts of the discipline were simply not susceptible to the kind of austere data collection procedures advocated by the new model of science. Chief among them was the English school theorist Hedley Bull, but the traditionalists also included some of the initial defenders of science in IR such as Morgenthau (see exchanges in Knorr and Rosenau 1969). For these theorists, systematic inquiry was one thing, the obsession with data collection and manipulation on positivist lines was another. Study of IR for Bull and Morgenthau involved significant conceptual and interpretative judgements, something that the behaviourist theorists in their focus on systematic data collection and scientific inference seemed not to adequately recognize. The dispute over science also developed a geographical aspect. Although there were some advocates of the new science in Britain and Europe it was largely a US-led development. Despite the fact that the austere version of science advocated by the behaviouralists was significantly watered down over the passage of time, the underlying principles of that approach remain deeply embedded within the account of science that continues to dominate the discipline. It was also to have a lasting effect on the methodological techniques taught in graduate schools, with hypothesis testing, statistical analysis, and data manipulation becoming indispensable requirements of all methodological training.

Science and the interparadigm debate

In the 1970s and 1980s the so-called interparadigm debate ostensibly moved IR away from the 'methodological' issues of the 1960s. The question of science was not an explicit component of this debate because to a large extent a consensus had emerged around a commitment to positivism. Indeed, it could be argued that this debate could take the form it did only as a result of a general shared commitment to the principles of science. All parties to the interparadigm debate accepted the validity of a broadly conceived positivist account of science. Certainly, the fascination with data collection, the insistence on measurement, hypothesis testing, and the statistical analysis of the early behaviouralists had been modified and toned down but, nonetheless, no one seriously attempted to argue that these were not important aspects of the study of international phenomena. Despite the consensus on science, however, issues surrounding the nature of scientific inquiry quickly resurfaced; in particular, the problem of theory choice and the alleged **incommensurability** of differing theoretical perspectives.

Much of this was indebted to Thomas Kuhn's (1962) ground-breaking study of the history of science. Kuhn had argued that science developed through two distinct phases. In its 'revolutionary' phase, science was marked by theoretical fragmentation. New modes of thought would arise and challenge traditional ways of thinking. Although the revolutionary phase ensured that theoretical innovation was always possible, Kuhn argued that such phases did not lead to a progression in terms of a body of cumulative knowledge. In a revolutionary phase, the theoretical protagonists expend their energy on attempting to gain theoretical dominance as opposed to increasing the overall stock of knowledge surrounding a subject domain. Knowledge could only progress, Kuhn argued, in periods of what he called normal science. In an era of normal science one theoretical school, or what Kuhn called a **paradigm**, would dominate. In such periods knowledge could progress because everyone was in agreement on the validity of the chosen paradigm and hence the vast majority of scholars were working in a particular subject using agreed methods and techniques and could compare their findings.

Kuhn's model of scientific development was enthusiastically embraced by the discipline. Since its inception the discipline had been attempting to develop a body of cumulative knowledge surrounding international processes. Yet, after decades of study there was still very little agreement on key issues. Despite the disagreements between them, the realists and behaviouralists had suggested that progress could be achieved only by adopting a more scientific mode of study. Kuhn's model suggested a different, more conservative, conclusion. The discipline needed the adoption of a single paradigm around which research could converge. In the mid-1970s three paradigms vied for theoretical dominance; realism, Marxism, and pluralism. The question was how to compare them. Which paradigm should the discipline adopt in order to move forward? Kuhn provided no answers. Indeed, he suggested that there was no answer; paradigms were incommensurable; they simply could not be compared. Theory choice became largely a matter of aesthetics; or what one of Kuhn's critics was to call 'mob psychology' (Lakatos 1970: 178).

It is ironic that although the interparadigm debate did not directly involve disputes over the nature of science it was the period of disciplinary development in which the philosophy of science began to play a substantial and explicit role. The conservative nature of Kuhn's model, and the fact that theory choice becomes a matter of taste, ensured that some scholars would look to alternatives. Karl Popper (1959) became an important influence, but it was the importation of Imre Lakatos's (1970) model of research programmes that was to have the greatest impact, and it is his model that is generally adopted by the more scientifically orientated 'positivist' wing of the discipline.

Science, the fourth debate and beyond

What we call the 'fourth debate' emerged in the mid-1980s. (Note that this debate is somewhat confusingly also referred to as the 'third debate' by some IR theorists.)[2] This debate has most explicitly focused on the issue of science in the disciplinary history of IR. Since the discipline is still largely in the middle of this debate we will deal with it as a contemporary issue and discuss it in terms of the cleavages and divisions around which the discipline is currently organized. There are many ways to characterize the 'fourth debate'; as a debate between explaining and understanding, between positivism and postpositivism, or between rationalism and reflectivism. This section will examine these different terms and through them the key philosophical positions in contemporary IR.

Explaining and understanding

The terms explaining and understanding come from Max Weber's distinction between Erklären and Verstehen, and were popularized in IR by Hollis and Smith in the early 1990s (see Featured Book box). Another way of describing this distinction is in terms of a scientific approach versus an interpretive or hermeneutic approach. While explanatory theorists seek to emulate the natural sciences in following scientific methods and in seeking to identify general causes, advocates of understanding focus on the analysis of the 'internal' meanings, reasons, and beliefs actors hold and act in reference to (Hollis and Smith 1990). For the advocates of understanding, social meanings, language, and beliefs are said to constitute the most important (ontological) aspects of social existence. Explanatory theorists do not generally disagree with this claim; however, they do not see how such objects can be incorporated into a scientific framework of analysis. Scientific knowledge, for the explanatory theorist, requires empirical justification; and meanings, beliefs, and ideas are not susceptible to validation by such techniques. Without such justifications, knowledge claims can be nothing more than mere speculation. Advocates of an interpretive approach, on the other hand, argue that we should be guided in our analytical procedures by the most important factors impacting on human behaviour (beliefs, ideas, meanings, reasons), not by an a priori commitment to something called science.

Clearly, a particular vision of what science is frames this debate. The explanatory theorist reduces the ontological complexity of the social world to those aspects of it that can be observed and measured. Thus the ontology adopted by this approach is shaped by epistemological and methodological concerns. This leads to a sharp split between these two approaches in terms of methodology. Explanatory theorists privilege quantitative methods, or attempt to quantify qualitative data. Supporters of understanding adopt interpretive

Featured book

Martin Hollis and Steve Smith (1990), *Explaining and Understanding International Relations* (Oxford: Clarendon Press).

Steve Smith and Martin Hollis were in many ways responsible for the rise of the meta-theoretical turn in International Relations (IR) scholarship. Their book is a classic text which explicates how assumptions about science permeate the study of international relations. Martin Hollis, a highly respected philosopher had specialized in the analysis of hermeneutics, Wittgensteinian philosophy, and philosophies of action and Steve Smith, a theorist of international relations and foreign policy, at the University of East Anglia jointly taught a course exploring philosophical underpinnings of IR. It was this course that provided the motivation for their co-authored book, and which reflected, in a highly productive manner, not only the coming together of different specialisms, but also a dialogical approach to the discussion of philosophical matters. The conclusion to this text is especially effective in demonstrating how deep philosophical debates are embedded in debates about world politics as well as famously claiming always at least 'two stories to tell' about world political events, which cannot easily be combined into one single overall 'truth'. Hollis and Smith characterized these stories as Explaining and Understanding. While the intricacies of people's motivations and reasoning (e.g. the reasons a leader might have for starting a war) could be understood through an interpretive research agenda, this approach runs the risk of leaving out what others can consider the most crucial 'explanatory' factors, such as the role external factors have in directing thoughts, actions, and options (e.g. state leader's positioning within military alliances, actors' positioning in market structures). When we consider world political issues, whether it be the causes of the Iraq war or of global poverty, debates about the role of agency and structure, internal understanding and external explanation, are key to how we approach the debates.

   Hollis and Smith also powerfully demonstrated that how we debate the causes of international political developments is highly dependent on, and reflective of, the philosophical underpinnings we adopt—whether implicitly or explicitly. This is an interesting implication to highlight for one might consider that Hollis and Smith's own argument—that there are always (at least) two mutually irreconcilable stories to tell about international relations—is an important political move in the study of IR. By arguing that not all stories could be reduced to a scientific agreement on a single truth, the text can be seen as an important 'political' defence of, first, the integrity of reflectivist IR research and, second, of political as well as theoretical pluralism. Yet this argument is not without its problems. First, why only two stories? Second, are academic accounts of global politics really little more than stories? Third, if the stories we tell about international relations are not in some sense comparable, and hence we cannot judge between them, are all stories equally valid?

methods (qualitative, discursive, historical), shunning the generalizing approach of the explainers. This debate also has epistemological consequences insofar as explanatory theory emphasizes observation as perhaps the only way of generating valid knowledge, whereas the understanding side of the debate concentrates attention on the interpretation of unobservable, and hence immeasurable, contexts of action.

Positivism and postpositivism

Underpinning the explanatory framework is a positivist vision of science. This account of science has its roots in an empiricist epistemology. Often the terms positivism and **empiricism** are confused in the discipline. Positivism is a theory of science, and generally most positivists adopt an empiricist epistemology. However, not all empiricists embrace positivism, so it is important to maintain the distinction between the two terms. Equally, it is possible to accept the validity of empirical data without adopting a positivist account of science. As an epistemology, the empiricist approach to the acquisition of knowledge is premised on the belief that the only genuine knowledge we can have of the world is based on those 'facts' that can be experienced by the human senses. The implication of this empiricist epistemology for science is that scientific knowledge is secure only when based on empirical validation. This is why positivists privilege observation, empirical data, and measurement; what cannot be an object of experience cannot be scientifically validated.

The key assumptions of the positivist view of science and social explanation can be summarized as follows. First, for positivists, science must be focused on systematic observation. The aim of the philosophy of science is to produce a set of logically rigorous guidelines concerning appropriate methodological techniques and criteria for ensuring that knowledge claims are grounded in appropriate observations. Indeed, for positivists the validity of science rests on these rigorous methodological guidelines; it is these guidelines that allow us to distinguish between scientific knowledge and mere 'belief'. Second, all positivists believe that the collection of sufficient data, generated through repeated instances of observation, will reveal regularities, which are indicative of the operation of general laws. These general laws are only the expression of relationships between patterns among observable events and there is nothing more going on behind the data. Any attempt to introduce non-observable processes, mechanisms, and events as explanations of the data are considered inadmissible. This belief in the importance of regular patterns when linked to the insistence on empirical validation becomes important in terms of how positivists conceive of causal analysis. For the positivists, causal relations are discovered through the detection of regular patterns of observable behaviour.

Third, because positivists emphasize the importance of observation, they avoid talking about 'realities' that cannot be observed. This directs them away from developing 'deep ontological' conceptual systems that aim to grapple with unobservable entities such as 'discourses' or 'social structures'. This insistence on observation means that positivists are not, as they are sometimes described, naive realists.[3] Positivists do not believe in an external world independent of humanity (Kolakowski 1969). The positivist motto was *esse est percipi* (to be is to be perceived), which makes existence logically dependent upon perception (Hollis 1996). When non-observable entities are referred to, they are treated in wholly instrumental terms. These non-observables are useful fictions that help explain the data, but positivists refrain from giving them ontological significance. It follows that positivists emphasize the instrumental function of knowledge. Knowledge has to be useful not truthful (Waltz 1979). It is partly this commitment to the instrumental validation of knowledge that makes positivists some of the most vehement critics of the role of meta-theory within IR.

The positivist approach to social explanation has been modified in significant ways since the 1960s as the positivist philosophy of science has adapted itself as a result of a range of criticisms. The so-called 'soft' postbehaviourist form of positivism is still significant in contemporary IR. It underpins, for example, the influential contribution to social analysis of King, Keohane, and Verba (1994). They aim to build a unified logic of inference for both quantitative and qualitative inquiry, and foreground the role of observation and measurement. Indeed, they aim to rescue social science from speculative and unsystematic social inquiry by showing that the 'scientific logic of inference' can be applied in qualitative studies. By demonstrating how qualitative analysis can become 'scientific', King, Keohane, and Verba hoped to force qualitative approaches to 'take scientific inference seriously', hence allowing these approaches to start making 'valid inferences about social and political life' (King, Keohane, and Verba 1994: 3, ix).

Against the positivist insistence on a 'science' of human behaviour, a diverse range of post-positivist positions has emerged. It is tempting to categorize these postpositivists as articulating a version of the interpretive understanding position detailed above. However, whilst many postpositivists draw inspiration from interpretive thinkers, the term 'postpositivist' can be used to refer to approaches that draw on a wider range of intellectual traditions; what unites them all is a commitment to reject positivism as a valid approach to the study of social processes.

Some postpositivists are influenced by developments from within the philosophy of science and attempt to use these to articulate a non-positivist version of science (see the section on scientific realism for more detail). These postpositivists reject both the positivist account of science and the hermeneutic alternatives. Importantly, for these postpositivists it is only a particular version of science that is rejected, not the idea of science itself. Many feminist theorists (discussed in more detail in **Chapter 10**), who would rightly be considered postpositivists, are also keen to develop more sophisticated versions of science. And many postpositivists are keen to repudiate the positivist account of science that has dominated the discipline and accept the importance of meanings, beliefs, and language without adopting a hermeneutic perspective. This is particularly the case in relation to postmodern, or poststructuralist, theories (discussed in more detail in **Chapter 11**). The interpretive approach rests on the conviction that meanings and beliefs are the most important factors in the study of social processes and that social inquiry could play an important role in uncovering the deep meanings that exist beneath the surface appearance of observed reality. This conviction relies on the belief that there are hidden meanings to be had. Poststructuralist theorists are sceptical of this viewpoint and have no wish to return to what they term the 'hermeneutics of suspicion'. Poststructuralists are also sceptical of the validity of all knowledge claims and reject the idea that science produces anything like true knowledge, even in terms of the natural sciences.

In many respects, the positivist/postpositivist designation represents a particular moment in the history of the discipline. It marks a particular period in time when the positivist orthodoxy had begun to crumble in the philosophy of science, and the effect of this was felt throughout the social sciences. It is an accident of history that this collapse occurred at the same time as a range of new social theories, and philosophies, was emerging. These new theories all rejected the positivist vision of science and, in particular, its application to the social sciences. Yet in many respects this rejection of positivism was all they shared in common and it is incorrect to infer that this necessarily requires them to adopt an interpretive philosophy and methodology.

Rationalism and reflectivism

The rationalist/reflectivist divide takes the explaining/understanding divide and the positivist/postpositivist debate and encapsulates them both under a single label. This terminology, utilized by Robert Keohane (1988) in his address to the International Studies Association, can be associated with the explanation/understanding and positivist/postpositivist divides, but also has particular additional connotations. Keohane takes his label of rationalism directly from rational choice theory. Rational choice theory is essentially a methodology constructed from a commitment to a positivist account of science. The rational choice theorist accepts the general complexity of the social world but ignores the majority of it in order to produce predictions based on a particular understanding of individuals. According to rational choice theorists we should treat individuals, and by extension states, as utility maximizers, and ignore every other aspect of their social being. This does not mean that rational choice theorists actually believe this is a correct description of what an individual is. However, they do believe that if we treat individuals in this manner we may be able to generate a series of well grounded predictions concerning behaviour on the basis of observed outcomes. Keohane accepts the limitations of this approach, but argues that it has been spectacularly successful in terms of knowledge production (Keohane 1988). This approach is deductive as opposed to the inductive bias of previous forms of positivism, but, nonetheless, observation, measurement, and the attempt to specify general universal laws are still at the heart of this form of analysis. The approach is deductive because it begins with a theory of the individual and then utilizes observation and hypothesis testing to substantiate, or falsify, a set of claims relating to behaviour on the basis of this view. It is an approach to explanation that is compatible with the wider positivist tradition in IR, but it is not synonymous with it. It is for this reason that the term rationalism has been associated with both the explanatory and the positivist tradition in IR.

In his now (in)famous speech, Keohane (1988) also noted the emergence of a series of theories that were sharply critical of mainstream rationalist approaches to the discipline—critical theory, constructivism, poststructuralism, and feminism. He called these approaches reflectivist, due to the fact that they rejected the classical positivist/explanatory approach to IR theory and research, emphasizing instead reflexivity and the non-neutral nature of political and social explanation. He noted the potential of these approaches to contribute to the discipline but, in a direct reference to Lakatos's account of science, suggested that they could be taken seriously only when they developed a 'research programme'. This was a direct challenge to the new theories to move beyond criticism of the mainstream and demonstrate, through substantive research, the validity of their claims. Many of the so-called reflectivists have seen this as nothing other than a demand that they adopt the model of science to which Keohane and the mainstream are committed. On the other hand, the mainstream has been reluctant to take the knowledge claims of reflectivist scholars seriously, because they challenge the very status of the ontological, epistemological, and methodological assumptions upon which the mainstream depend.

Beyond the fourth debate? Rethinking IR as a science

The debates between explaining and understanding and rationalism and reflectivism have produced a dichotomous logic that has fashioned two wings of the discipline: a 'pro-science' viewpoint versus an 'anti-science' position. Typically, this debate has been framed around positivism as the dominant account of what science is. While positivism and its debate with the anti-science faction of the discipline has been the dominant issue in IR, recent developments in the philosophy of science and the philosophy of social science suggest that this way of framing the issues is unproductive. Significant strides have been taken in the philosophy of science to move beyond positivism: positivism is no longer seen to be the only valid account of science and has been challenged by scientific realism. A comprehensive account of scientific realism is beyond the scope of this chapter; however, the important contribution it makes in terms of social science is to reject any attempt to arrive at a set of clearly defined procedures that fix the content of the scientific method. For scientific realists, each science must arrive at its own mode of operation on the basis of the object domain under study (see, for example, Roy Bhaskar 1978, 1979). Because object domains differ in fundamental ways, scientific realists claim it would be inappropriate to expect methods deployed in one science to have a universal application. Hence the social sciences should not be attempting to copy the natural sciences, not least because given the immeasurable distinctions within the various natural sciences it is impossible to identify a set of procedures and techniques that are adopted by all.

For scientific realists, what makes a body of knowledge scientific is not its mode of generation, but its content. Contra a positivist account of science, a body of knowledge is not declared scientific because it has followed a particular set of procedures based upon empirical 'facts' but, rather, because it constructs explanations of those facts in terms of entities and processes that are unknown and potentially unobservable. For scientific realists, scientific knowledge goes beyond appearances and constructs explanations that often run counter to, and even contradict, observed outcomes. Social science involves the study of the complex and interacting social objects that produce the patterns we observe. Because of their unobservable nature, most social objects have to be 'got at' through careful conceptualization. This is always a complex process that involves mutually constituted processes between agents and the objects of knowledge; yet social knowledge, however imperfect and embedded in conceptual and discursive frameworks, is knowledge of something—something called social reality.

Epistemologically, scientific realists are relativists; they argue that no epistemological position has priority in the acquisition of knowledge for there are always many ways in which to come to know the world. But this does not mean that all views are equally valid and they believe in the possibility of rationally adjudicating between competing knowledge claims. What is important to science is that any and every claim is open to challenge and, moreover, that all claims require epistemological support. This does not mean that these epistemological supports are always predicated on facts, or other such empirical data, but it does mean that those concerned to challenge particular claims make clear the evidential basis on which the challenge is made. Science, it is argued, rather than being committed to a dogmatic insistence on the certainty of its claims, rests on a commitment to constant critique.

Methodologically, it follows that scientific realists adopt a pluralist approach: contrary to the positivist emphasis on quantitative methods and the interpretive emphasis on qualitative methods, scientific realists emphasize methodological pluralism. Because the social world is ontologically highly complex, and there are many ways to come to know the world, it is better that one does not restrict methods a priori. A student of democratic peace, for example, should not study only regular patterns in history (positivist approach), nor simply interpret particular decision-makers' perceptions ('understanding' approach), but should make use of multiple ways of obtaining data. Because the social world is ontologically complex, it is better that one does not take an a priori position on either methodology or epistemology.

Scientific realism has already made major contributions to social theory and the development of research techniques in other social sciences, and it is now beginning to make an impact in IR. It has played a major role in the development of constructivism, although not all constructivists have embraced it. Alexander Wendt (1999) is perhaps the most notable theorist to embed his theory explicitly in a scientific realist framework, and it underpins his attempt to construct a *via media*, or middle ground, between rationalism and reflectivism. However, Wendt's adoption of scientific realism has been criticized by other scientific realists on the grounds that he has failed to move sufficiently beyond the parameters of the current debate and that he remains basically locked into a modified commitment to positivism. Another version of scientific realism has emerged which uses the label critical realism to differentiate itself from Wendt's account. Critical realists such as Patomäki and Wight (2000) take scientific realist ideas further in important respects. Notably, they argue that the dichotomy between rationalism and reflectivism is mirrored in the distinction between an approach that focuses on materialist issues, and one that concentrates on ideas. For critical realists, both ideas and material factors are important in producing social outcomes, and both need to be integrated into the research process. According to critical realists, the question of whether material factors or ideational issues are the most important in determining outcomes is an empirical matter that can be decided only on the basis of research that examines the relationship and interplay of both. So while critical realists agree that meanings and ideas matter they insist that ideas always emerge in a material context, and that the meanings we give to events are, in part, a consequence of how these events were materially constructed, composed, and represented.

The emergence of scientific and critical realism in IR is an important new trend in the discipline. It has opened up new potentially constructive avenues for meta-theoretical and theoretical debate in IR. By refusing to juxtapose explaining and understanding and causal and non-causal analysis, by rejecting an a priori commitment to either material or ideational factors, and by refusing to endorse either the positivist model of science, or the rejection of science advocated by some reflectivists, it has enabled the discipline to move forward from the fourth debate and allowed the non-positivist theoretical perspectives to be appreciated in a new light; as scientific contributors to the discipline. Yet, this vision of science too continues to be contested in the field. Pragmatist, positivist, and deconstructionist critics continue to debate the validity of this account of science (Monteiro and Ruby 2009; see also Forum on Critical Realism in Review of International Studies, Neumann et al. 2012). Moreover, there has been a developing trend that views these meta-theoretical debates as barriers to constructive dialogue in the field. David Lake, for example, has argued that 'isms are evil' (Lake 2011). Likewise, Rudra Sil and Peter Katzenstein, argue that the discipline should embrace a form of 'analytical eclecticism' in terms of theory choice and that we need to move 'beyond paradigms' (Sil and Katzenstein 2010). Whilst intuitively attractive, the fundamental differences that separate competing visions of what the study of IR should involve mean that paradigms are most likely here to stay. However, there are alternative ways to think about what the dividing lines are, and in particular, Patrick Jackson's *The Conduct of Inquiry in International Relations* provides a different way of thinking about these issues (Jackson 2011).

Exploring the key implications of meta-theoretical differences in IR theory

In this final section we examine how meta-theoretical assumptions influence the manner in which IR theorists formulate different understandings of certain issues: such as the nature of theory, the possibility of objectivity, the criteria to be used in theory-testing, and the relationship of theory and practice. In many respects these issues emerge out of the debates already considered in this chapter, and in some cases they are constitutive of them. In the chapters that follow many of these issues will re-emerge, even if only implicitly. In highlighting the often implicit role of meta-theory we hope to alert students to the multiple ways in which meta-theoretical assumptions influence IR theory and research.

Types of theory

It is reasonable to assume that a book dealing with IR theory would provide a clear account of what theory is. Unfortunately there is not one but many. This makes a direct comparison between theoretical claims often difficult if not impossible; being aware of the many different types of theorizing means that comparison is not always possible and alerts us to the fact that different types of theories have different aims.

One of the most common types of theory is what we will term explanatory theory. This is probably the type of theory most students initially think of when they use the term theory. Explanatory theory attempts to 'explain' events by providing an account of causes in a temporal sequence. Thus, for example, we can think of theories that attempt to explain the end of the Cold War in terms of a series of connected events occurring over time. For positivists, this type of theory must produce verifiable (or falsifiable) hypotheses which can be subject to empirical test. Another common type of explanatory theory does not attempt to link particular events in causal sequences but, rather, attempts to locate the causal role played by particular elements in the chosen object domain and, on the basis of this analysis, draw conclusions and predictions aimed at exercising control. A good example of this type of explanatory theory is neo- or structural realism (see **Chapter 4**). According to neorealists such as Waltz (1979) theory can be considered a simplifying device that abstracts from the world in order to locate and identify key factors of interest. Once these factors are identified this type of theory aims at predicting a large range of outcomes on the basis of a few important causal factors. For this type of explanatory theory it is not important that the theory provides a realistic model of the world but, rather, that the theory is 'useful' in terms of its predictive capacity.

Explanatory theories are sometimes said to be 'problem-solving theories'. This distinction comes from Robert Cox (1981) who claims that this type of theory is concerned only with taking the world as given and attempting to understand its modes of operation. As such, problem-solving theories are often said to be concerned only with making the world work better within clearly defined, and limited, parameters. In opposition to explanatory theories, Cox identified another type of theory which he called 'critical theory'. Cox's category of critical theory is confusing since the content of the term critical is dependent on a political context. What one theorist considers critical may be considered dogmatic by another. However, there is a form of theorizing that we think does merit the label 'critical'. By critical theory we mean that type of theory which begins with the avowed intent of criticizing particular social arrangements and/or outcomes (see Roach's view in **Chapter 9**). Hence a theory might be considered critical in this sense if it explicitly sets out to identify and criticize a particular set of social circumstances and demonstrate how they came to exist. We want to phrase it in this manner since it is highly probable that this type of critical theory builds its analysis on the basis of an examination of the causal factors that brought the particular unjust state of affairs about. On this account of critical theory there is no necessary conflict between the identification of an unjust state of affairs and a consideration of the causes of that state of affairs. Hence it is possible for a theory to be both explanatory and critical. Many feminist theories fit this model. They identify a particular set of social arrangements that are considered unjust and locate those social conditions in a set of particular causal circumstances. Interestingly, many feminists also take the additional step of indicating how an eradication of those causal factors might make the world better in some or other way.

Once a theorist takes the step of indicating alternative futures or social modes of operation that do not currently exist, but might be brought into being, they have entered the realm of normative theory. This will be discussed in more detail in **Chapter 2** but generally speaking it is fair to say that normative theory examines what 'ought' to be the case. Normative theory comes in strong or weak versions. In the weak version the theorist is concerned only to examine what ought to be the case in a particular domain of interest. Theories of justice, for example, can be considered normative in that they debate not only what justice is, but also what it ought to be. The strong version of normative theory is often called 'utopian' in that it sets out to provide models of how society ought to be reorganized. Marxist theory can be considered strongly utopian in this manner. This type of theorizing has been neglected for some time now, mainly because the term utopian has negative connotations associated with 'unrealistic' expectations.

Another common type of theory is known as constitutive theory. Constitutive theory does not attempt to generate, or track, causal patterns in time, but asks, 'How is this thing constituted?' This type of theory can take many forms. In one sense constitutive theory entails the study of how social objects are constituted. State theory, for example, does not always ask how the modern state came to be, but can focus solely on questions, such as, 'What is a state?', 'How is a state constituted?', 'What functions does the state play in society?'. However, the term constitutive theory is also used in the discipline in another sense: to refer to those authors who examine the ways in which rules, norms, and ideas 'constitute' social objects. For these theorists, the social world (and perhaps the natural world) is constituted through the ideas, or theories, that we hold. For this type of constitutive theory, it becomes important to theorize the act of theorizing.[4]

The last type we wish to discuss is theory considered as a lens through which we look at the world. Many positivists would be unhappy at labelling this theory. It is certainly not theory in the sense of a coherent and systematic set of logical propositions that have a well formulated and specified set of relationships. However, many social theorists do not think that the ontology of the social world permits a view of theory that allows such clearly defined sets of relationships. Instead, they are concerned to explore how social actors navigate their way through social events and processes. In order to make sense of this we need to comprehend what these social processes mean to them, and we do this by understanding the varied ways in which they make sense of the social world. All social actors view the world in particular ways, and these views of the world do not always display as much coherence, or logic, as one might expect of a systematic and well defined theory. Yet, if the theorist is to grasp how social actors understand the world, they need to be aware of the lens through which those actors view, and act in, the world.[5]

Question of objectivity

Another important issue of contention that arises in meta-theoretical debates is that of objectivity. One of the key notions of Western thought, particularly since the Enlightenment, has been the search for truth, and the ideas of truth and objectivity are closely related. It is important, however, to distinguish between truth and objectivity. There are many theories of truth, and some theories deny that there is, or can be, such a thing.[6] Philosophers have addressed the issue of truth in various ways and we cannot go into them at length here. The confusion of truth with objectivity arises due to the fact that the term objective has two closely related meanings. In the first sense, an objective claim can be said to be a statement relating to external facts as opposed to internal thoughts or feelings. Hence, it is possible to talk in this sense of something being objective independent of any belief or statement about it. It is easy to see how this can be confused with truth. Something that is said to be the way it is independent of any belief is a common-sense way of talking about truth. This is not, however, how most philosophers, or scientists, think about truth. Truth is typically understood by philosophers and scientists to express a relationship between the world (however defined) and a statement referring to that world; or to a set of beliefs or statements that can be said to be true if they have been arrived at through a given set of procedures. Truth expresses a relationship between language and the world, or a set of human conventions about what counts as 'true'. For many philosophers the idea of an external world having a 'truth' independent of any belief about it is nonsense. External objects may exist independent of theory but they could not be said to be true in any meaningful sense of the word. They have an existence, but to exist is not the same thing as to be true.

The second sense of objective is more interesting in terms of disciplinary debates. Objectivity in this sense relates to a statement, position, or set of claims that is not influenced by personal opinions or prejudices. Objectivity thus refers to the attempt by the researcher to remain detached, dispassionate, impartial, open-minded, disinterested, judicial, equitable, even-handed, fair, unprejudiced. Very few, if any, theorists in IR believe that we can ever produce a set of statements that can be said to be accurate in terms of representing the external world exactly as it is. The main lines of debate surround the extent to which we might aspire to knowledge that approximates this goal, how we might justify and provide evidential support to show how one claim fares better than another in this respect, and how objective, in the sense of impartial, we might be.

Positions on these issues deeply divide the discipline. Most positivists, for example, strive for objective knowledge by attempting to define methods and criteria for knowledge production that minimize the influence of value-biased judgements. This point of view seems persuasive in that striving for systematic and rule-governed procedures relating to knowledge production seems preferable to knowledge acquisition on the basis of an unsystematic and haphazard set of procedures. Positivists argue that, although knowledge is never perfect, through the observance of agreed-upon research criteria, we can aim to make some justifiable judgements between competing knowledge claims. Neoliberals (see **Chapter 6**), for example, might claim that while their account of the role of institutions is not the only one, nor necessarily an absolute truth, it is still empirically the most valid one in relation to a number of instances. Because this theory can be validated by empirical observations and patterns, and can be used to predict state behaviour, it can be considered more truth-approximating than many others.

For theorists informed by more interpretive approaches to knowledge, social knowledge is by definition always 'situated knowledge'; knowledge claims can never be formulated outside the influence of social and political context. It follows that we must accept that knowledge systems are always socially and politically informed and socially, politically, and ethically consequential. Poststructuralists take this view on knowledge to entail that claims about 'reality' are always constructions of particular discursive and social systems and are always implicated in power relations. They are also sceptical of truth claims due to the fact that such claims have often driven some of the most violent episodes of human interaction. When a group of people firmly believes that they alone possess the truth they can become dogmatic and attempt to implement policies on the basis of that truth, with little or no regard for alternative views. Being sceptical of truth claims then becomes not only a philosophical belief but a political position aimed at preventing totalitarian forms of politics.

Other interpretive theorists are concerned to maintain some notion of objectivity even if they reject the idea of truth. Constructivists, for example, recognize that there is no way to produce statements about the world that might be said to be true in the sense of providing complete and accurate accounts of the way the world is, but they do aspire to objectivity in the sense of attempting to remove bias and gaining support for claims by negotiation within the scientific community. In some respects this position can be said to resemble the position advocated by many positivist scholars. However, for constructivists, the overriding considerations for arriving at judgements relating to knowledge claims are intersubjective agreement as opposed to empirical evidence.

Scientific and critical realists accept large parts of the interpretivist position regarding objectivity, and argue that while we always interpret the world through our own socially positioned lenses, and while there is no easy way to prove the truth of a particular theory, not all theories are equal. Importantly for scientific realists, it is precisely because the world is the way it is independent of any theory that some theories might be better descriptions of that world, even if we do not know it. It then becomes a task of deciding which theory is the most plausible. In determining this, scientific realists rule nothing out and privilege no one factor; they are epistemological opportunists. For scientific realists there is not one set of procedures for adjudicating between knowledge claims that covers all cases. Each case must be assessed on its own merits and on the basis of the evidence it supplies. For scientific realists, scientific and explanatory activity is rendered meaningless if we are not accounting for something real in more or less objective ways.

Theory testing and theory comparison

Related to the issue of truth and objectivity is the question of how to evaluate and compare our theoretical frameworks. Positivists argue that only systematic empirical observation guided by clear methodological procedures can provide us with valid knowledge of international politics, and that we must test theories against the empirical patterns in order to compare theories. Interpretivists, and many other postpositivists, on the other hand, insist that there is no easy or conclusive way of comparing theories, and some go so far as to suggest that theories are incommensurable; in other words, theories cannot be compared because either the grounds for their knowledge claims are so different, or they see different worlds (Wight 1996). Scientific and critical realists accept that theory comparison and testing always require recognition of the complexity of judgements that are involved, and an awareness of, and reflection on, the social and political context in which such judgements are formed, as well as analysis of the potential consequences of our judgements. They accept that positivist observational criteria are often a poor guide to choosing between theories if applied in isolation and without adequate critical reflection. Scientific and critical realists argue that theory comparison must be based on holistic criteria: not merely on systematic observation but also conceptual coherence and plausibility, ontological nuance, epistemological reflection, methodological coverage, and epistemological pluralism. They also accept that all judgements concerning the validity of theories are influenced by social and political factors and hence are potentially fallible.

The consequences of how we test and evaluate the validity of knowledge claims are fundamental to any theory. Depending on our different criteria of evaluation, some approaches literally get legitimated while others are marginalized. These kinds of judgements have important theoretical and empirical consequences for the kind of world we see but, also, political consequences for the kind of world our theoretical frameworks reproduce. The important thing to note in engaging with the theoretical frameworks in the chapters of this book and in comparing their validity is that there are multiple criteria for theory testing and comparison in IR. Although some social scientists have assumed that criteria regarding the predictive and instrumental empirical value of a theory provide superior criteria for theory testing, the interpretive and scientific realist positions on theory comparison also have their strengths. Indeed, having been dominated by the rather narrow criteria for theory comparison for some time, IR theory should, in our view, start to make more use of the holistic criteria. Science, after all, need not be defined by empirical methods alone but can also be seen to be characterized by ontological, epistemological, and methodological pluralism and reflectivity.

Theory and practice

Another key aspect at stake in meta-theoretical debate within the discipline has been a discussion over the purpose of social inquiry. For some the purpose of social inquiry is to gain adequate knowledge of social reality to ground and direct policy-making (Wallace 1996). Others argue that the relationship between theory and practice is more complex than this. Booth (1997) and Smith (1997), for example, argued that the role of theory is often practical in a different sense from what is understood by those who argue for a policy-relevant IR. Wallace and others, Booth and Smith argue, make too much of a separation between theory and practice: they assume that theory is not practice and that 'practice' entails 'foreign policy-making' devoid of theoretical groundings. Booth and Smith, and alongside them many critical theorists, argue that theory can in itself be a form of practice, that is, if we accept that theory constitutes the world we live in, by advancing a theory one may either reproduce or change mindsets and, hence, social realities. Equally, all practice is predicated on the basis of some or other theory. As Booth and Smith point out, a policy-maker's view of the world is not necessarily untheoretical: it is actually deeply embedded in social and political points of view.

As the chapters in this book will reveal, theorists from different camps tend to hold different views on this issue. The traditionally dominant perspectives of realism and liberalism, along with their neo-variants, tend to lean towards Wallace's point of view, while many of the newer perspectives, especially feminism, poststructuralism, and postcolonialism, tend to put an emphasis on the role of theorizing itself as a form of world political practice. Again, the key point advanced here is that there is no agreed-upon understanding of the relationship of theory and practice: a position on theory and practice is directed by a meta-theoretical and theoretical framework; and the way one conceives of the relationship of theory and practice has important consequences for how one views the purposes of IR theorizing itself.

Conclusion

This chapter has aimed to provide the reader with an understanding of the nature and importance of meta-theoretical, or philosophy of social science, debates within IR. We have examined the manner in which discussion concerning the nature of inquiry in the discipline has shaped both the history of the discipline and the contemporary theoretical landscape. We have argued that positivist models of science have dominated, but that recent engagements with the nature of science are creating possibilities for new kinds of understandings of IR as a social science. We also examined a number of important issues that are at stake in the way in which theorists from different theoretical schools come to understand and study the world and how they propose to validate or reject knowledge claims. We would like to conclude by highlighting another aspect of debate within the discipline that students should be aware of.

All sciences are social environments with their own internal dynamics and modes of operation. As a set of social practices taking place within a structured social environment, the discipline of IR has a unique internal political structure that is both shaped by the manner in which debate occurs and which shapes the contours of that debate. In examining and evaluating the theoretical approaches outlined in the following chapters, students should be aware that all the theoretical schools of thought in IR and all meta-theoretical positions that underpin them— including ours—are attempting to get their audience to 'buy in' to the argument. In this respect IR theorists resemble salespeople, and what they are selling is their theory. Words such as 'critical', 'sophisticated', 'simplistic', 'naive', and 'dogmatic' are not neutral descriptions of theoretical positions but, rather, are deployed to either delegitimate alternative views, or prove the superiority of one approach over all others. However, much like any good customer, the student would be well advised to reflect critically on the limitations inherent in all the approaches presented to them, even the most persuasive. It is important to remember that all theoretical and underlying meta-theoretical positions are subject to criticism and dispute. Indeed, viewing IR through the philosophy of social science reminds us that all claims to knowledge are open to challenge from other perspectives. Recognizing this does not necessarily lead to relativism, but to a certain humility and degree of reflection with regard to the claims we make and reject in studying world politics.

Realizing that all theories are 'selling you' a perspective is also important in highlighting the politics of the theoretical and meta-theoretical decisions we make. Each theoretical and meta-theoretical avenue involves a number of judgements about what is an important object of inquiry and what is, or is not, a valid knowledge claim. These judgements have consequences for the kind of world we come to see, for how we account for processes within it, and for how we act in that world. Meta-theoretical and theoretical debates, then, are not abstract philosophical exercises but are also potentially politically consequential for the kind of world we live in. *Caveat emptor* (let the buyer beware).

? Questions

1. What is meta-theory? What role does meta-theoretical debate play in IR scholarship?

2. What role has the debate over science played in the discipline of IR historically?

3. Is IR a science or an art? What is at stake in this debate? What does the 'scientific' study of world politics entail?

4. What is meant by the terms positivism/postpositivism, explaining/understanding, rationalism/reflectivism?

5. Should we think of the contemporary meta-theoretical debates in IR (between positivism and postpositivism, explaining and understanding and rationalism and reflectivism) as debates between mutually incompatible positions?

6. What are the key assumptions of scientific realism? What is the significance of scientific realism in disciplinary debates?

7. How should we conceptualize the role of theory in the discipline? What do different conceptions of theory have to offer?

8. Can we have value-neutral knowledge of world politics?

9. Can we judge some theories to be better than others? If so, what is involved in making such judgements?

10. What is the purpose of IR theorizing?

11. How significant is the fourth debate in the contemporary discipline of IR? Has it, and should it be, transcended? What is the significance of meta-theoretical debates for IR theory and research?

12. Which meta-theoretical leanings do you find persuasive? Why? How would you justify the validity of your position against your critics?

Further reading

Cox, R. (1981), 'Social Forces, States and World Orders: Beyond International Relations Theory', *Millennium: Journal of International Studies*, 10/2: 126–55.
A key piece outlining a critique of 'problem-solving theory' in IR.

Hollis, M. and Smith, S. (1990), *Explaining and Understanding International Relations* (Oxford: Clarendon Press).
An influential account of the meta-theoretical debates over explaining and understanding in the context of IR.

King, G., Keohane, R. O., and Verba, S. (1994), *Designing Social Inquiry; Scientific Inference in Qualitative Research* (Princeton, NJ: Princeton University Press).
A key work outlining a positivist approach to qualitative research.

Knorr, K. E. and Rosenau, J. N. (1969) (eds), *Contending Approaches to International Politics* (Princeton, NJ: Princeton University Press).
A collection of key articles by the contenders in the second debate.

Nicholson, M. (1996), *Causes and Consequences in International Relations: A Conceptual Study* (London: Pinter).
A positivist introduction to philosophy of social science in IR.

Patomäki, H. and Wight, C. (2000), 'After Post-Positivism? The Promises of Critical Realism', *International Studies Quarterly*, 44/2: 213–37.
This article outlines the contributions of a critical realist approach to theorizing science in IR.

Smith, S., Booth, K., and Zalewski, M. (1996) (eds), *International Theory: Positivism and Beyond* (Cambridge: Cambridge University Press).
A collection of essays evaluating the contributions of the positivist/postpositivist debate in IR.

Wallace, W. (1996), 'Truth and Power, Monks and Technocrats: Theory and Practice in International Relations', *Review of International Studies*, 22/3: 301–21. See also responses by Booth and Smith in issues 23/2 and 23/4.
These articles constitute an interesting debate over the relationship of theory and practice in IR theory.

Wendt, A. (1999), *Social Theory of International Politics* (Cambridge and New York: Cambridge University Press).
An important constructivist work with a strong philosophy of social science element. Notably, this book introduces scientific realist themes to IR theory.

 ## Notes

1. We have used the terminology of International Relations (IR) only as a matter of convenience and convention. We do not mean to imply that this restricts the discipline to the study of relations between international actors. We prefer the term 'global' since we think the discipline does, and should, study the totality of global interactions among a vast range of actors.

2. Some other authors in this volume follow Lapid (1989), and refer to this as the third debate. However, we follow Wæver's (1996) distinction between the interparadigm and the fourth debate.

3. It may be that many so-called 'positivists' within the discipline are 'naive' realists, since they are often unreflective about the philosophy underpinning their research practices. However, positivism, as a philosophy of science, is clearly not realist in a 'naive' sense.

4. This type of theory can also be interpreted as causal if causal analysis is equated with analysis of causal powers carried within objects. Because many critical realists see causal analysis as analysis of causal powers, they would not necessarily see constitutive theory as a form of non-causal theorizing, as many other postpositivists do.

5. Importantly, this provides yet another point of critique through which critical theories might be constructed. For the critical theorist can take these views of the social actor and be critical of them. Hence if a group of social actors has the view that X group needs to be eradicated because of belief Y, and if the social theorist shows belief Y to be false, then the theorist must necessarily be critical of both belief Y and the view that group X needs to be eradicated.

6. The dominant theories of truth are the 'correspondence theory', the 'coherence theory', the 'conventionalist, or consensus, theory', and the 'pragmatic theory'. The correspondence theory of truth sees truth as correspondence with objective reality. Thus, a sentence is said to be true if it refers to a state of affairs that exists in the world. Most scientists and many philosophers hold some version of the correspondence theory of truth. It is the dominant theory of truth for most positivists in IR. The coherence theory sees truth as coherence with some specified set of sentences or, more often, of beliefs. For example, a belief held by an individual is true if it is coherent with all or most of their other beliefs. Usually, coherence is taken to imply something stronger than mere consistency: justification, evidence, and comprehensiveness of the belief set are common restrictions. The consensus theory holds that truth is whatever is agreed upon or, in some versions, might come to be agreed upon, by some specified group. This tends to

be the theory of truth adopted by many of the postpositivists who argue that truth is constructed by social processes, which are historically and culturally specific, and shaped through the power struggles within a community. Pragmatism sees truth as the success of the practical consequences of an idea, i.e., its utility.

 Visit the Online Resource Centre that accompanies this book for lots of interesting additional material. **www.oxfordtextbooks.co.uk/orc/dunne3e/**

Normative International Relations Theory[1]

TONI ERSKINE

 Reader's Guide

This chapter provides an introduction to normative International Relations (IR) theory. The first section sets out the distinct history, influences, and some of the categories which this field brings to the study of international relations. The second section adopts quite a different aim. Instead of continuing to explain the important ways in which normative IR theory is unique within IR, it maintains that the central concerns and contributions of this field can be understood as engagements with the hidden ethical assumptions of a range of IR approaches. The final section looks at a case of civilians being shot at a checkpoint at the start of the 2003 war in Iraq. An analysis of the circumstances in which the civilians were killed, and of the arguments surrounding such casualties in war, illustrates some of the challenging questions and moral dilemmas confronted by normative IR theorists, along with the conceptual tools that these theorists employ in responding to them.

Introduction

International politics has an unavoidable ethical dimension.[2] Wars, for example, are judged to be 'just' or 'unjust'; their conduct is deemed 'moral' or 'immoral'. Crises as diverse as genocide, famine, and climate change prompt calls that states, individual human beings, international organizations, and even transnational corporations (TNCs) have 'moral responsibilities' to engage in both preventive measures and remedial action. The same actors are 'guilty' and held to account either for not responding to such calls or for contributing to the crises in the first place. And, when confronted with problems in world politics, scholars and state leaders alike champion specific conceptions of who counts, variously giving priority to the rights and well-being of 'co-nationals', 'fellow citizens', or 'allies' – or, alternatively, extolling the equal moral worth of 'all humankind'. In the process, the **moral standing** of a range of others, whether 'foreigners', 'illegal immigrants', 'enemies', or even 'non-human animals', might be diminished or precluded – and with profound implications. In short, *moral judgements matter*. Appraisals of right and wrong conduct, blame for particular actions, omissions and outcomes, assertions of moral requirements and prohibitions, and declarations of those who do (or do not) warrant equal ethical consideration are powerful and prevalent aspects of international politics. We are told, for example, that the torture of detainees in Abu Ghraib prison in Iraq was 'disgusting and wrong' (Blair 2004), that 'the international community is guilty of sins of omission' in the context of the Rwanda genocide (Annan 2004), that 'the United States has a moral responsibility to act' to create a nuclear weapons-free world (Obama 2009a), and that everyone, globally, has an equal 'right to adequate food' (United Nations 1999). But, on what basis are such ethical assessments and prescriptions made? How can the values and moral principles that we invoke to respond to practical problems in world politics best be explained and understood? From where do they derive their authority? Can they be evaluated, criticized, and revised? If so, how? Who counts, and to what degree, when we talk about obligations to others? And, who – or what – are the agents charged with meeting these obligations?

Normative IR theory is one label for a field of study that addresses exactly these questions. This body of work draws on a rich combination of arguments, distinctions, and concerns from political theory, moral philosophy, and the relatively new discipline of IR. In doing so, it encompasses a variety of approaches and theories which, nevertheless, share the aim of exploring moral expectations, decisions, and dilemmas in world politics. Contributions to this area of scholarship take concepts such as justice, duty, and rights, which have been central to the political theorist's traditional focus on the bounded community, and extend them to the international, or global, level. In the process, normative IR theory has adopted – and adapted – conceptual categories such as communitarianism and cosmopolitanism from political theory. Moreover, it borrows from moral philosophy means of designating different types of ethical reasoning, such as deontology and consequentialism. It is important to note, however, that even while normative IR theory is deeply influenced by these philosophical sources, work within this field is characterized by an acute awareness of practical issues in international politics. This means that even when positions within normative IR theory are inspired by discourses outside the discipline of IR, they nevertheless share themes and vocabularies with other IR approaches.

Unfortunately, there has been a great deal of reticence in IR as a whole to address the ethical dimension of world politics. Work within normative IR theory thereby distinguishes itself from other theoretical approaches to international relations by directly and openly broaching questions of morality. Importantly, though, this does not mean that contributions to normative IR theory are completely removed from other theorizing in IR. Instead, this body of work engages with, explores, and extends many assumptions underlying the wide range of approaches addressed in this volume. This chapter will elaborate on both of these claims. First, it will address in more detail what is meant by normative IR theory as a discrete body of work by identifying its own particular history and influences, as well as two of its key conceptual distinctions. Second, it will suggest that contributions to this field make explicit – and often take to a logical conclusion – significant (although latent or denied) ethical assumptions from across the spectrum of different theoretical perspectives employed in IR. Finally, this chapter will turn to issues that have sparked passionate debate during recent wars, including those in Afghanistan and Iraq: civilian casualties and the price that should be paid to avoid them. There is no single normative IR theory answer to, or analysis of, practical problems in world politics. This case study will aim to provide an example of the types of questions and conundrums addressed by those who contribute to this important field of scholarship, along with an illustration of some of the concepts and categories that they employ.

Normative IR theory: defining a distinct field of scholarship

The subtitle of this volume is 'discipline and diversity'. These are extremely apt themes for an account of normative IR theory as a discrete area of scholarship. The relationship of normative IR theory to the discipline of IR, and the (often overlooked) diversity within normative IR theory itself, are complex and crucial issues in understanding this body of work. Both issues will be addressed in this section. Before beginning this overview of the field, however, it is necessary to offer a few preliminary caveats about the label being used here to describe it.

First, although a number of theorists refer to 'normative IR theory' (Frost 1986, 1996; Brown 1992; Cochran 1999; Jackson and Sørensen 2007; Erskine 2008a), there are alternative names given to the same body of work. Normative IR theory is also often referred to as 'international political theory' (IPT) (Beitz 1979/1999; Linklater 1982/1990; Hutchings 1999; Brown 2002) or simply 'international ethics' (Beitz et al. 1985; Nardin and Mapel 1992; Nardin 2008; Shapcott 2010). This array of labels does not indicate a case of multiple or confused identity on the part of the community of scholars who contribute to this field. There are good reasons for each variation – highlighting the field's debt to political theory, its focus on ethical questions, or its ties with IR, for example. While no label manages to encompass all of these characteristics, those who adopt these different labels are talking about the same general area of study. In other words, they agree on how to describe their intellectual community, even if they disagree on what to call it. A second caveat perhaps goes without saying, but is important enough to emphasize nonetheless. Normative IR theory addresses the ethical dimension of the relations between a whole range of actors in the global realm. No one writing in the field understands it to deal exhaustively with the relations between states or nations, despite the literal meaning of the term 'international'.[3] A third significant caveat about the label normative IR theory concerns what the theorists working in this area mean by 'normative'. This can be a misleading concept. 'Normative' as it is generally understood can mean prescriptive, as in standard-setting, or it can mean relating to standards of behaviour, norms, and values. As Chris Brown usefully points out, 'the danger is that two different kinds of intellectual activity will be confused: the setting of standards, and the study of how (and what and by whom) standards are set' (Brown 1992: 3). As long as we qualify that normative IR theory is concerned specifically with *moral* norms (or those that carry a sense of obligation rather than merely mapping patterns of behaviour) then the field is more accurately described by the second, broader connotation of 'normative'. This body of work does include attempts to evaluate and prescribe principles, policies, and practices, but it is also concerned with explaining and understanding the ethical dimension of international politics. Finally, designating this body of work 'normative IR theory' does not imply that other work being done in IR is somehow *not* normative in the sense of being uninformed by values or devoid of underlying ethical assumptions. Rather, it emphasizes that normative IR theory is *primarily* and *explicitly* concerned with the ethical dimension of world politics in a way that other work in IR arguably is not.

History and Influences

Normative IR theory is often presented as an exciting, new area of scholarship – one that has really only emerged over the last thirty-five years or so. It is also frequently heralded as having a distinguished history that can be traced back hundreds of years, if not millennia. So, which account is correct? The short answer is that both are. The longer and more interesting answer is that these two accounts focus on separate aspects of the field's history and key influences. Moreover, each offers a different perspective on the relationship that normative IR theory enjoys with the discipline of IR.

Terry Nardin has described the corpus of work that focuses on ethics in international relations as a 'newcomer' within IR (Nardin 2008: 595). This portrayal makes a lot of sense. A relatively recent body of normative theorizing about international relations appeared not only against a backdrop of committed behaviourialism within the discipline, but also in the wake of a long period in which moral philosophers had been more concerned with abstract analytical questions than with real-world moral dilemmas (Brown 1992: 82–106). In other words, this scholarship represented a double departure: away from a 'scientific' study of IR, and also away from what had become a rather rarefied study of ethics. A number of things happened both in academia and in world politics that were conducive to this seemingly novel focus.

First, a tangle of international problems in the 1960s and 1970s threw up extremely challenging ethical dilemmas, and these motivated a group of philosophers to concentrate on practical questions in world politics. For example, the Cold War policy of nuclear deterrence, the Arab-Israeli Six Days War of 1967, and the Vietnam War (1959–75), including incidents such as the shocking My Lai massacre of 1968, spurred philosophers to turn their attention to the ethics of war after a long period of scholarly neglect. They asked whether it is morally permissible to threaten violence (in the form of nuclear attack) that it would be unacceptable to execute; when, if ever, the resort to force is justified; and, how organized violence should be conducted (see, for example, Ramsey 1968/2002; Wasserstrom 1970; Nagel 1972; Walzer 1977/2006). In the process, a body of thought known as the just war tradition experienced a philosophical 'reawakening' (Johnson 1991: 20). Similarly, the reality of poverty and famine in many African countries, and in regions such as East Bengal (now Bangladesh), inspired moral philosophers to address the problem of blatant inequality in the global distribution of resources and wealth and to consider our moral obligations to 'distant strangers' (see, for example, Singer 1972; O'Neill 1975, 1986; Shue 1980). Is it fair that some people live in abject poverty simply because of the accident of where they were born? What duties – if any – do we have towards those starving in another continent?

Second, and also around the same time, the American political theorist John Rawls published a hugely influential work, *A Theory of Justice* (1971). In this groundbreaking book, Rawls addressed questions of distributive justice, primarily within the state, and introduced his now famous thought experiment, the 'original position'. Within Rawls' hypothetical original position, one has no knowledge of, among other things, one's own particular skills and talents, class, social status, historical position, sex, and conception of the good (Rawls 1971: 137, 1975: 537). From this starting point, Rawls maintains that individuals, free from bias and prejudice, would agree to principles of justice for society. One principle that would be arrived at under these conditions is the 'difference principle', or the stipulation that social and economic inequalities be arranged so that they are 'to the greatest benefit of the least advantaged' (Rawls 1971: 302–3). Not only was this an important impetus for further theorizing about justice within the state, but it also incited passionate responses by those who were concerned with timely questions of distributive justice *beyond* the boundaries of the state, and who were critical of Rawls' merely marginal (and conservative) treatment of justice in the international realm. These critics saw potential in applying variations on Rawls' original position to the problem of global inequality (Barry 1973; Beitz 1979/1999; Pogge 1989). Although this influence came from academia rather than the world of practice, once again ethical questions about international politics were shown to be highly relevant – and in urgent need of attention.

Finally, within IR itself there was a growing disquiet during the 1980s and 1990s with the discipline's 'positivist bias' and an acknowledgment among some that the expulsion of values and ethical questions from the realm of legitimate scholarship had resulted in both a poverty in theorizing and an inability to grapple with some of the most pressing questions arising in international relations (Frost 1986, 1996; Smith 1992). On this point, it is notable that the 'behavioural revolution' that propelled North American IR was never a leading force in the British study of international relations. The so-called 'English school', with its 'traditional' or 'classical' methodological approach (see **Chapter 7**), did not aspire to explain the world through covering laws grounded in observable facts and subject to empirical scrutiny, but, rather, drew on philosophy, history, and law to make judgements about international relations. Although the North American conception of IR dominated the discipline, the conceptual space for non-positivist scholarship left open on the other side of the Atlantic arguably contributed to the fact that many of the theorists who championed a 'normative turn' in IR were either British or had strong links with the British intellectual community.

In sum, the latter part of the twentieth century saw important work within moral philosophy focus on real-world practical problems in international politics, Rawls' influential treatise in political theory inspire attention to questions of justice beyond the borders of the state, and a frustration with the silences on ethical issues generated by an ostensibly value-free discipline of IR. This combination of influences provided fertile ground for a new variety of theorist – one who was informed by movements within moral philosophy and political theory, but firmly situated within an IR not exclusively defined by positivism. The result was pioneering work by a collection of 'normative' IR scholars throughout the 1980s and early 1990s (including Hoffmann 1981; Linklater 1982/1990; Nardin 1983; Frost 1986, 1996; Brown 1992), discussion of a new, distinct area of IR theorizing, and, in 1993, the establishment of 'International Ethics Section' of IR's largest scholarly body, the International Studies Association (ISA). A proliferation of second-generation works in normative IR theory has followed (including Cochran 1999; Hutchings 1999; Robinson 1999; Shapcott 2001; Caney 2005; Lu 2006; Erskine 2008a; Lang 2008; Heinze and Steele 2009; Pattison 2010; Beardsworth 2011). These more recent works have found it less necessary to defend the legitimacy of engaging in normative endeavours, and, instead, have sought to challenge, extend, and revise the categories and aims of this body of scholarship – as well as apply them to a host of new practical problems in world politics.

Significantly, this account of normative IR theory as a corpus of work that only began to emerge over the last thirty-five years, and that has been defined as a distinct area of IR scholarship even more recently, meshes with its portrayal as a newly conceived 'subfield' within the discipline of IR (Nardin 2008: 595). Normative IR theory, from this perspective, is a young, and perhaps still somewhat immature, sibling in a growing family of IR theories. Such a narrative provides an important part of the story outlining the history and influences of this area of scholarship – and perhaps provides the most accurate account from the perspective of those contributing to other approaches within the discipline. Yet, on its own, it threatens to neglect another aspect of the history and influences of this body of work – and, indeed, to overlook an important part of how it defines itself.

According to a different story, normative IR theory has its roots in the work of great philosophers like Plato, Aristotle, Kant, Hegel, and Marx. This account of normative IR theory is less in tune with its description as a new subfield in IR that has only recently emerged due to a fortuitous confluence of intellectual circumstances. Instead, it portrays normative IR theory as representing a rich tradition of thought, which already provided a complete and compelling theoretical framework for the study of international relations at the time that this study was 'disciplined' (Brown 1992). This comprehensive theoretical framework, grounded in moral philosophy and political theory, was temporarily abandoned when the new discipline of IR veered off in a radically different, behaviouralist direction. In other words, IR took an unfortunate 'detour' away from its normative beginnings, and the current flourishing of normative IR theory sets the discipline back on its original track (Smith 1992). From this perspective, normative IR theory is not a young sibling in a rapidly-expanding family of IR theories. Rather, it is a long-forgotten and distinguished ancestor, whose branch of the IR family tree had been temporarily obscured by the birth and ascendance of 'scientific' approaches to the study of international relations, and whose significance and distinct lineage has only recently been re-acknowledged.

So, can both accounts of the history and influences of normative IR theory really be correct? They *can* – simply because they are two aspects of the same story. This field is able to claim a long intellectual history; and, the past thirty-five years have provided the ideal context for both a rediscovery of these roots and the growth of their contemporary offshoots within a more broadly conceived discipline of IR. This history brings to the study of international relations unique theoretical tools, distinctions, and insights from political theory and moral philosophy, some of which will be focused on in a moment. Yet, this body of contemporary scholarship also situates itself within IR. Normative IR theorists do not set themselves apart from the rest of IR (even while they do co-opt into their ranks some philosophers who would not call themselves IR scholars). Instead, they re-define the boundaries of legitimate IR scholarship so that the 'facts' that we study *include* the values that variously define who we are and guide our actions. Importantly, normative IR theory does not entail a single substantive theory of international relations. Instead, contributors to the field adopt what are often very different theoretical positions. One way of organizing this diversity has been to establish a division between 'cosmopolitan' and 'communitarian' approaches.

Cosmopolitanism and communitarianism

We are all members of a variety of communities and associations, participants in different practices, and pulled (sometimes in conflicting directions) by a range of loyalties. One may be British (and Welsh), or American, for example; an active member of the Aberystwyth University Students' Union; a pianist, a political scientist, a physicist, or a farmer; a supporter of both the Labour Party and Liverpool Football Club, or of the Democratic Party and New

York Yankees; Jewish, or Christian, or Muslim; someone's brother or sister, son or daughter. As conceptual categories employed within normative IR theory to describe distinct worldviews, cosmopolitanism and communitarianism provide radically different accounts of the moral significance of these particular identities, memberships, and shared practices – and where we stand in relation to them when we confront ethical dilemmas. They also allow correspondingly divergent accounts of who matters – and how much – when we consider our duties to those outside such affiliations.

Cosmopolitanism can mean two different things and it is important to begin by distinguishing between them. *Political* cosmopolitanism advocates the elimination or radical transformation of state borders, with the aim of achieving either a world government or some system of representation that transcends political divisions. *Ethical* cosmopolitanism champions what might be called a global 'sphere of equal moral standing' (Erskine 2008a: 15–23). According to this perspective, neither friends, nor family, nor fellow citizens count for more than others. In defining their respective positions, adherents to both types of cosmopolitanism invoke the phrase 'citizen of the world'. Political cosmopolitans understand this quite literally: we will become citizens of the world upon the creation of a world state, or perhaps some sort of global democratic system. Ethical cosmopolitans use the same phrase metaphorically: we are already citizens of the world because we have duties to everyone else globally. It is this latter vein of cosmopolitanism that has been central to debates within normative IR theory.

Ethical cosmopolitanism can be considered compatible with a variety of political arrangements. It might be argued to allow a system of discrete, sovereign states, or may even be considered inextricably tied to political cosmopolitanism and require the creation of a world state. The crucial point is that ethical cosmopolitan positions adamantly deny that political borders – as well as cultural, affective, national, religious, and ideological divides – can demarcate a class of 'outsiders'. From an ethical cosmopolitan perspective, we have duties to all others *as human beings*. How this inclusive purview is achieved is important – and also controversial. Fundamental to an ethical cosmopolitan stance (as it is generally understood) is a perceived need to bracket, or abstract from, particular ties and loyalties. Proponents of this move maintain that only then can one achieve an 'impartial' point of view from which no one is excluded. (Here it might be helpful to think back to Rawls' thought experiment – the original position – which some prominent cosmopolitans, like Charles Beitz (1979/1999), have applied at the global level.) From an ethical cosmopolitan perspective thus conceived, the fact that one is British or American, Christian or Muslim, someone's son or daughter, is irrelevant for the purpose of arriving at moral judgements. Yet, for critics of ethical cosmopolitanism, this route to inclusion generates grave concern. If we shed all of the particular aspects of our identities that make us who we are, what is left? How can such shadows of ourselves engage in ethical reasoning?

Communitarianism expresses just this concern. Communitarians criticize cosmopolitan positions for suggesting that one can disregard the particularity of one's life in order to make decisions from an impartial point of view. They counter that membership in particular communities, and participation in their practices, are morally defining. As a **moral agent** (or bearer of duties), one is first and foremost British or American, Muslim or Christian, someone's son or daughter. In the words of the philosopher Alasdair MacIntyre (1981/1985: 220), these sorts of identities and roles necessarily define one's 'moral starting point'. To abstract from them would be to render oneself incapable of ethical reasoning.

Normative IR theory has taken the term 'communitarianism' from political theory. To avoid confusion, it is important to note that the meaning of the term has undergone a subtle transformation during the process of adoption. While the communitarianism of normative IR theory is placed in opposition to cosmopolitanism, within political theory, communitarianism constitutes one side of a debate with liberalism. Furthermore, the communitarian stance within normative IR theory is characterized in a way that treats the morally defining community and the state synonymously. Communitarian political theorists do not, generally, make the same equation. In other words, normative IR theory's variation on communitarianism is uniquely *state-centric*. The resulting points of contact with those classical realist positions that espouse (often overlooked) ethical stances mean that we might usefully refer to this state-centric variation as 'communitarian realism' in order to distinguish it from its political theory counterpart (Erskine 2008a: 83–6). It should be noted that it is more difficult than with cosmopolitanism to identify contemporary normative IR theorists who fall squarely within this idealized communitarian category. Nevertheless, one prominent example of a broadly communitarian position in relation to ethical questions in international relations is Mervyn Frost's 'constitutive theory' (Frost 1986, 1996).

Even as communitarian positions offer what might be compelling alternatives to the seemingly detached individual of cosmopolitan arguments, they fall foul of other alleged weaknesses. Namely, critics argue that a communitarian perspective forces one to give preference to fellow community members. For the communitarian realism of normative IR theory, the charge is, more specifically, that this stance grants priority to fellow citizens. Although state borders have only instrumental value from a cosmopolitan position, they are morally defining from this communitarian perspective. The danger, then, is that the borders of one's state demarcate those who are 'insiders' in the sense of having equal moral standing. If this is the case, then communitarians might have *some* duties towards those who are not fellow citizens, but these 'outsiders' have reduced moral standing. This has potentially far-reaching repercussions, as will be addressed below, in the case of duties of restraint in war.

The categories of cosmopolitanism and communitarianism can provide extremely useful tools for analysis. Specifically, they can help us to understand and represent the relationship between the *source* of our values (or our 'moral starting point'), and the *scope* of our obligations to others. This proposed dichotomy gained prominence after being employed in 1992 by Brown in his seminal work, *International Relations Theory: New Normative Approaches*. Brown's framework for analysis was initially offered with the clear provisos that not every theoretical stance falls easily on one or the other side of the cosmopolitan/communitarian divide, and that this classification is necessarily an imperfect means of organizing a range of complex positions. Its purpose is to highlight important features of these positions, not to represent each perfectly. The categories of cosmopolitanism and communitarianism have become central to a great deal of work done within normative IR theory – both as they are applied and discussed in the context of practical problems in world politics, and as they are challenged and re-worked by those offering alternative frameworks. Crucially, neither cosmopolitanism nor communitarianism points to a particular policy position. Indeed, the *same* substantive position – whether a justification of the division of the globe into discrete, sovereign states or of the prohibition against killing civilians in war – can be supported from *both* moral perspectives. Nevertheless, because these different worldviews appeal to distinct sources of value, and produce concomitantly disparate accounts of whether non-community members possess equal moral standing, they would necessarily offer very different defences of the same policy. This somewhat complex point will also be illustrated in the case study.

Consequentialism and deontology

Cosmopolitanism and communitarianism are competing, idealized worldviews. They help us to think about moral identity, the source of our moral values, the corresponding scope of our obligations to others, and how our actions are motivated. Consequentialism and deontology are two different types of normative theory. They provide moral frameworks to guide and evaluate our decisions regarding what we ought to do. Like cosmopolitanism and communitarianism, they are best introduced in contrast to one other.

Consequentialist theories require that we make choices according to the state of affairs that will result from our actions. Even the unintended consequences of our actions have to be taken into account. There are different variations on consequentialism, but each focuses primarily on the effects of actions, rather than on the actions themselves.[4] So, for example, one possible (albeit rather crude) consequentialist argument might be that torturing a suspected terrorist during interrogation is justified, and even required, if the information to be gained is likely to save a thousand people. In other words, moral judgement on what is right and wrong relies on weighing the projected benefits that an action will produce against the possible harms. (Utilitarianism is one prominent type of consequentialist position, according to which good and bad consequences are understood in terms of happiness and suffering.) For some, this mode of reasoning is excessively permissive and cannot provide a guide to moral action. According to these critics, the problem is that *any* action – including a harm like killing innocents or engaging in torture – can be morally justified based on its projected consequences. Even though an appeal to consequences could also be made in opposition to such actions (if the harm that would result were deemed to outweigh the good according to some calculation), many people find a mode of argument that could (even contingently) permit such acts unacceptable. However, consequentialism can also be criticized for being excessively demanding: all acts are either morally forbidden or required; and, calculating the potential consequences of each act can be an extremely difficult, if not impossible, task. Just imagine having to judge every choice as either right or wrong based on its multiple, and possibly long-term, consequences.

According to a very different class of moral decision-making, some acts are wrong in themselves, regardless of their consequences. Killing one innocent person, or engaging in torture, for example, is unconditionally wrong and cannot be justified even if the act would save a thousand others. Such a view is referred to as 'deontological', a label derived from the Greek word *deon*, meaning 'duty' (Davis 1991: 205). For the deontologist, torture and the killing of innocents, for example, are unacceptable means to pursuing *any* end (regardless of how noble). Morality requires that one's motives and the means that one deploys are good. Both Kantian ethics and the natural law tradition provide important examples of deontological reasoning. Some people find this sort of strict commitment to 'keeping one's hands clean' (even when this may result in horrible consequences) deeply problematic. There is also the issue of the practicality of insisting on absolute adherence to certain principles, such as the prohibition against killing innocents. What about the circumstances of war, when killing some civilians seems unavoidable? One deontological (and very controversial) response to this problem brings us to the 'doctrine of double effect' (DDE).

The DDE is a complex argument that is compatible with *some* deontological positions and frequently discussed by normative IR theorists in the context of the ethics of war. The DDE states that it is permissible to perform an action even if it results in *foreseeable* harm, as long as this harm is not directly intended. The notion of 'intention' does a lot of work here. The goodness or badness of the action is judged according to the intention underlying it. Yet, the concept of intention is used more narrowly than we would probably use it in daily conversation. This requires some explanation, and, again, an example might prove useful. The intentional killing of non-combatants is prohibited in war. This is an absolute prohibition. Yet, the application of the DDE allows one to distinguish between the 'direct' killing of civilians, which is prohibited, and the so-called 'collateral' killing of civilians, which is conditionally permissible.[5] So, the killing of civilians might be a foreseen consequence of an attack on a military target, for example. In other words, we know that if we hit the military target, some civilians living nearby will also be killed. According to the DDE, it is nonetheless permissible to perform this action *if the deaths of these civilians are unintended*. It is important to reiterate that 'unintended' here does not mean that we are unaware that these consequences are likely. It simply means that killing the civilians is not part of our objective. This is what many critics find difficult to accept. Does it really make sense to say that we *know* that our actions will produce some harmful result, but that this is just an unfortunate 'side-effect', which we do not really 'intend'? Some complain that DDE provides an all-too-convenient excuse for any attack on civilians. However, there are strict limits on when DDE can be invoked. For the foreseeable bad consequences to be deemed truly unintended (and therefore permissible), they cannot be a means to fulfilling one's objective. This means that killing civilians for the purpose of gaining a military advantage by undermining morale, for example, *cannot* be justified by the DDE. Moreover, the application of the DDE in war is constrained by the consequentialist principle of proportionality, according to which permissible actions must clear the additional hurdle of producing more good than harm.

An introduction to the sophisticated arguments surrounding the concepts of consequentialism and deontology is necessary in order to grasp prominent positions in normative IR theory (see Brown 1992: 41–4, 91–3) – and to understand and assess ethical judgements underlying specific policies in international politics (see Harbour 1999). Along with cosmopolitanism and communitarianism, deontology and consequentialism provide important examples of the categories and conceptual tools that normative IR theorists bring to the study of international relations. Yet, in addition to outlining the theoretical roots and vocabularies that set normative IR theory apart from the rest of the discipline, it is revealing to identify points of contact that normative IR theory has with other IR approaches. This will be the aim of the next section, which explores IR's implicit ethical assumptions.

Normative IR theory: exploring IR's implicit ethical assumptions

The following three insights are central to normative IR theory: 1) norms matter in world politics; 2) sites of value affect issues of inclusion; and 3) the global realm is one of *moral* agents, and, therefore, moral responsibilities. In addition to informing important contributions to normative IR theory, each of these assumptions is latent in a wide range of approaches to the discipline. The purpose of this section is to outline briefly each insight, and its centrality to normative IR theory, before suggesting that it connects in significant ways to other IR approaches – even those that claim to eschew ethical endeavours.

Norms matter

Norms are, perhaps unsurprisingly, central to normative IR theory. The norms upon which normative IR theorists focus carry prescriptive force: they embody established codes of what actors should do, or refrain from doing, in certain circumstances. As guides to what is required, permitted, or prohibited, they are widely understood to have moral weight. They embody moral expectations. To distinguish the prescriptive and moral character of norms as they are being referred to here from the weaker concept of norms as simply describing what is 'usual' or 'conventional', it is useful to emphasize that we are speaking of *moral* norms.

The category of *international* moral norm might elicit scepticism. It suggests near-universal agreement in a realm that is generally characterized more by division and dispute than by consensus. The sceptic might point out that there are no principles in international politics that can boast universal adherence. Indeed, it would be ludicrous to attempt to argue that what are widely claimed to be moral imperatives in world politics – such as the prohibition against targeting non-combatants or the duty to prevent and suppress genocide – are never transgressed. Civilians are intentionally targeted and responses to genocide are sidestepped or stalled until tens of thousands are massacred. Moreover, it would be an exercise in futility to maintain that there is unanimous agreement on the source of authority for such principles. Norms are variously understood to be grounded in convention, in notions such as rationality, human rights, or human nature, in the will of God (however understood), or even dismissed as the cynical constructs of those trying to engender legitimacy for their own projects. So, how can we possibly talk about shared moral norms at the international level? Here, Mervyn Frost's careful account of what he calls 'settled norms' in international politics is extremely valuable. Frost defines such principles not by whether they are universally observed, or even uniformly grounded, but, rather, by the perceived need either to keep their infringement clandestine, or to provide special justification for any attempt to override or deny them (Frost 1996: 105–6). In short, such principles are not openly transgressed without pointed justifications and excuses. They are tacitly respected, even in their abrogation. According to Frost, this provides evidence of the existence of international moral norms. Frost's definition allows us to identify a number of international moral norms, including the prohibition against targeting civilians in war, and the duty to prevent and suppress genocide. Such norms profoundly affect our actions, and the way that we justify them. They are *facts* that can be identified and studied.

Even though many IR theories view norms and values as having no place in scholarship, the strong underlying assumption that 'norms matter' can, nevertheless, be identified outside normative IR theory. A number of theoretical approaches recognize the significance of moral norms. As Richard Ned Lebow maintains (**Chapter 3**), the importance of a system of norms is appreciated by classical realism. The English school focuses on institutions, practices, and norms. Moreover, constructivism takes as its subject matter normative beliefs and arguments. Indeed, Richard Price has asserted that 'one of its main substantive contributions to the field has been to show that moral norms – and thus ethics – matter in world politics' (Price 2008: 317). Normative IR theory concurs on the importance of ethics, and, indeed, makes ethical questions the very subject of study. But, it also takes this engagement with moral norms and values a few steps further. Whereas some other theoretical approaches acknowledge the significance of norms, they do not go as far as to evaluate them – whether this means judging their internal coherence or assessing the degree to which they are consistent with broader systems of values. Normative IR theory confronts the wider contexts of meaning and interpretation within which moral norms in international politics are situated. In addition to engaging in the explanatory, empirical task of identifying and describing prominent moral norms, it also has the tools to evaluate, challenge, and revise them.

Sites of value affect moral inclusion

The question of 'who counts?' when we think about international politics is an extremely important one. Not being granted equal moral standing can mean not being shown restraint in war, not being considered a bearer of rights, or not being party to, or a beneficiary of, deliberations over distributive justice. When 'foreigners', 'barbarians', or even 'illegal enemy combatants' (to take a term from the Bush Administration) are deemed 'outsiders' in this way, the repercussions are profound. Significantly, the source of our values, or what we understand to be our moral starting point, can affect those to whom we grant equal moral standing. This is a crucial insight of work done within normative IR theory. Two positions – ethical particularism and ethical universalism – are particularly important in this context. Ethical particularism describes a position whereby one engages in moral reasoning from the perspective of his or her own particular ties and relationships, practices, and context. Within normative IR theory, communitarianism is an example of ethical particularism. Ethical universalism describes a position according to which one stands apart from all local loyalties and affiliations when engaging in moral reasoning. Moral cosmopolitanism, as it is generally understood, is an example of ethical universalism. While communitarians are often charged with favouring those with whom they stand in particular relationships; cosmopolitans claim to recognize the equal moral standing of all human beings. Normative IR theorists explore and challenge these conclusions and ask, for example, whether some accounts of cosmopolitanism exclude certain others, and how communitarian positions might be reconceived in order to be more inclusive. Some theorists endeavour to reconcile the two positions. Two powerful points surface in this body of work. First, the sites of value that we claim affect the degree to which our moral gaze can include others. Second, we can, and should, interrogate and revise these moral starting points in order to extend moral inclusion. Indeed, according to Molly Cochran, '[n]ormative IR theory . . . seeks shared principles for extended moral inclusion and social reconstruction in international practices' (Cochran 1999: 2). Diminishing the class of 'outsiders' is something that we can actively endeavour.

All IR theories make normative assumptions, even when these are not explicitly acknowledged. Moreover, these assumptions are anchored in specific conceptions of value and rely on certain moral starting points. These, in turn, affect how far our duties to others extend. For example, many classical realists implicitly adopt a variation on ethical particularism, akin to the communitarianism of normative IR theory, which treats the state as a source of value in a way that has consequences for the possibility of any robust extension of moral inclusion beyond its borders. Neoliberals pursue cooperation in a way that relies on a thin (and merely implicit) community of values. Feminism can be defined by 'its ethical attentiveness to inclusivity and relationships' (True 2008: 419), yet the move by a number of feminists of locating their moral starting points in particular, caring relationships has consequences for their ability to establish ethical concern for those outside these relationships (see, for example, Robinson 1999). And, the English school notion that international society is to some extent reliant on shared values, which are embedded in the 'diplomatic culture of elites', 'Christianity', 'Europe', or 'civilization' (Hurrell 2002: 147), begs questions of who is thereby excluded. While all of these positions demonstrate a link between the source of our values and those who we recognize as having equal moral standing, it is normative IR theory that explores, and makes explicit, this relationship – in addition to seeking ways of increasing moral inclusion.

The global realm is one of moral agents and moral responsibilities

A final key insight of normative IR theory is that purposive actors in world politics are *moral agents*. Moral agents are defined by their capacities for deliberating over possible courses of action and their consequences and acting on the basis of this deliberation. Such capacities render moral agents vulnerable to the assignment of duties and the apportioning of moral praise and blame in relation to specific actions. In other words, there is a crucial link between the concepts of moral agency and moral responsibility. We can talk about moral responsibility with respect to moral agents in two senses: in the forward-looking sense associated with claims to duty and obligation, in terms of acts that ought to be performed or forbearance that must be observed; and in the backward-looking sense of accountability and blame (or sometimes praise), for acts and omissions (Erskine 2003b). Quite simply, for the normative IR theorist, the global is an ethical realm and the various actors that inhabit it are not immune to charges of moral responsibility.

Latent assumptions regarding moral agency are held in common by a number of diverse theoretical approaches within IR. Indeed, IR does not hesitate to portray certain collective bodies as agents, or purposive actors. These agents are described as having interests, aims, and sophisticated decision-making capacities. For example, classical realist, neorealist, neoliberal institutionalist, and some constructivist positions, assume that states are agents. In fact, this assumption is fundamental to their positions. Some theorists move beyond this focus on the state and present other bodies, such as TNCs and intergovernmental organizations (IGOs) like the United Nations, as agents with sophisticated capacities. Important positions on moral agency and responsibility logically accompany such assumptions (Erskine 2008b). We need to ask what moral responsibilities these actors have, and when they can be held to account for failing to discharge their duties. Yet, most IR theorists fail to acknowledge that the capacities that they attribute to these bodies mean that these bodies qualify as moral agents. If the implicit assumptions of moral agency in IR were recognized and explored, this would open up a host of important questions about moral responsibility in international politics. The failure to take this additional, logical step from assumptions of agency to the recognition of moral agency is the result of IR's enduring methodological predisposition away from addressing ethical questions. Here, again, normative IR theory's attention to the ethical dimension of international politics raises new possibilities for understanding and evaluating the world that we live in. One arena in which attention to the moral responsibilities of a range of actors is illuminating is in analyses of war – the context of the subsequent case study.

Case study: duties to 'enemies' and civilian casualties in Iraq

On 31 March 2003, at an intersection near Karbala, Iraq, a car sped towards a checkpoint held by soldiers of the US Army's 3rd Infantry Division. The company commander, Captain Ronny Johnson, was anxious. Only two days before, an Iraqi army officer had committed suicide by bombing a similar checkpoint, killing four members of the same Infantry Division. Johnson radioed one of his forward platoons of Bradley Fighting Vehicles to inform them of the possible threat. The car kept hurtling towards the checkpoint. 'Fire a warning shot!' ordered Johnson. Becoming increasingly concerned, his next command was to shoot a machine gun round into the radiator of the approaching vehicle. When it seemed that no action had been taken, he instructed his officers to 'stop [messing] around!' He then bellowed into the company radio network: 'Stop him, Red 1, stop him!' This final order was followed by loud cannon fire.

> 'Cease fire!' Johnson yelled over the radio. Then, as he peered into his binoculars from the intersection on Highway 9, he roared at the platoon leader, 'You just [expletive] killed a family because you didn't fire a warning shot soon enough!' (Branigin 2003)

The Bradley's cannon had ripped open a car carrying women and children.

The number of civilians reported to have been in the vehicle when the high-explosive rounds hit their target varies. The Pentagon issued a statement that the vehicle was carrying thirteen women and children, seven of whom were killed at the scene (US Department of State 2003). William Branigin, a *Washington Post* journalist who was with the troops at the time of the shooting, and whose eyewitness account is relied on here, reported that fifteen Iraqi civilians had been travelling in the car that approached the checkpoint, and that ten were killed immediately. He recorded that of these ten, five were children who appeared to be under the age of five years old.

All of the reports that followed the incident agreed that the vehicle was full of civilians, that they did not, as had been feared, pose a military threat, and that the killing of these 'innocents' was a horrible and deeply regrettable act. International condemnation of the deaths of these Iraqi civilians followed. This public outcry – and the lament of the army captain when he saw that 'a family' had been targeted – were vivid manifestations of the widespread belief that, even amidst the violence and chaos of war, categories of right and wrong, moral and immoral endure. The soldiers on the ground were moral agents and expected to make difficult ethical decisions. An analysis of this snapshot of moral deliberation and judgement captures normative IR theory's concern with defining and evaluating particular moral principles and responsibilities. It also focuses on the broader contexts of

(continued)

meaning, justification, value, and (often divided) loyalty in which moral principles and responsibilities are embedded.

There are many different approaches to the ethics of war; some people adopt religious perspectives while others take one of a number of possible secular starting points (for an excellent survey, see Nardin 1996). To date, the most influential Western body of thought pertaining to the ethics of war, and one that has produced principles that have, over time, been codified in international treaties and agreements, is known as the just war tradition. The just war tradition is a valuable place to start in attempting to understand the moral categories that were invoked following the killing of Iraqi civilians at the checkpoint in March 2003.

The just war tradition and the moral norm of non-combatant immunity

Just war thinking is the result of various periods of historical development, draws on a broad range of sources, encompasses divergent views on specific concepts and principles, and, perhaps above all, is constantly evolving. It therefore makes sense to talk about a 'tradition', rather than a single 'theory', of just war thinking (Johnson 1984: 12). This tradition sets limits on the use of force, and is thereby opposed to the notion of unrestrained war. However, it also licences the use of force in certain circumstances, thereby simultaneously setting itself against pacifism, which sees war as necessarily morally wrong. The just war tradition has developed around two categories of principles of restraint, which are usually labelled with the Latin terms *jus ad bellum* (governing the justice of resorting to war) and *jus in bello* (pertaining to just conduct in war). It is the *jus in bello* principle of 'non-combatant immunity', or 'discrimination', that is of primary importance in understanding the difficult ethical deliberations – and impassioned responses – to this particular case.

 Featured book

Michael Walzer (1977/2006) *Just and Unjust Wars: A Moral Argument with Historical Illustrations*. 4th edn. (New York: Basic Books).

Michael Walzer's *Just and Unjust Wars* is the single most influential contemporary contribution to just war thinking. Walzer was motivated to write this book by his staunch opposition to American conduct in Vietnam. He also wanted to demonstrate that one can make moral arguments about war, and challenge the justice of particular policies and practices, in a way that cannot be dismissed as merely subjective, or as the articulation of personal feelings and preferences. It is possible to describe, interrogate, analyse, and re-articulate our shared judgements and justifications about war in a way that reveals the reality of our deepest moral commitments.

This is exactly what Walzer does in this re-working of the just war tradition. In the process, he coins his own terms for its two main categories. Walzer calls his variation on *jus ad bellum* (pertaining to the resort to war) the 'legalist paradigm' and his articulation of *jus in bello* (pertaining to the conduct of hostilities) the 'war convention'. In addition to the way that Walzer carefully uncovers moral principles in each category by exploring specific historical cases, one of the most interesting features of this book is its underlying tension between cosmopolitan and communitarian perspectives.

Walzer's cosmopolitanism is most apparent in his detailed account of the principle of non-combatant immunity, his main focus within the war convention. Walzer defends the immunity of non-combatants in terms of their underlying humanity. (Although there is not enough space to recount them here, his stories of 'naked soldiers' (1977/2006: 138–43) provide illuminating examples of this position.) Writing in the context of an example from the First World War, and maintaining that soldiers should fire 'warning shots' to protect enemy civilians, even when this puts the soldiers themselves at greater risk, Walzer asserts that 'the structure of rights stands independently of political allegiance; it establishes obligations that are owed, so to speak, to humanity itself and to particular human beings and not merely to one's fellow citizens.' (1977/2006: 158)

Even given these clear cosmopolitan commitments, at times Walzer seems to adopt a communitarian realist perspective. This is particularly apparent in Walzer's treatment of 'supreme emergency', or a situation in which, he maintains, extreme measures might legitimately be taken to defend the political community (1977/2006: 251–68). 'Can soldiers and statesmen override the rights of innocent people for the sake of their own political community?', he asks. Despite his erstwhile adamant defence of non-combatant immunity, grounded in a theory of human rights, he concedes that, 'I am inclined to answer this question affirmatively, though not without hesitation and worry.' His 'hesitation and worry' tell us that he is aware of this tension in his work – and that he is unsure how to resolve it. Walzer's honesty in confronting such tensions makes *Just and Unjust Wars* a particularly rewarding – and challenging – book.

According to the principle of non-combatant immunity, only combatants are morally acceptable intended objects of organized violence. This principle is an excellent example of deontological reasoning. It states forcefully that non-combatants must never be targeted, regardless of the perceived merits in any particular case of the resort to indiscriminate warfare. The resulting distinction between permissible and prohibited targets of attack is understood to be a cardinal feature of the ethics of war. It is 'the basis of the rules of war' (Walzer 1977/2006: 136).

Yet, the principle of non-combatant immunity is not simply a central feature of just war thinking. Encoded in international law, it is outlined in the Hague Conventions of 1907, the Geneva Conventions of 1949, and, most explicitly, in the 1977 Protocols to the Geneva Conventions (see Roberts and Guelff 1989). And, it is a prominent and powerful moral norm in international politics. As well as the violation of this principle being greeted with near universal condemnation, there is a perception that an explicit commitment to it is necessary if one's conduct in war is to be deemed legitimate. President Bush stated at the start of the Iraq war that '[p]rotecting innocent civilians is a central commitment of our war plan' (Bush 2003). When non-combatants *are* killed, painstaking accounts are offered to explain or deny these apparent transgressions: exonerating claims of 'collateral damage' and statements of 'error' are put forth; assertions that those targeted actually warranted the status of combatant are sometimes rehearsed;[6] or reasons are given for temporarily overriding the norm. To refer back to Frost's definition of a 'settled norm' in international politics, it is significant that any derogation from the principle of non-combatant immunity is, indeed, understood to require special justification.

The Checkpoint Incident and 'Collateral Damage'

The killing of Iraqi women and children at the checkpoint in March 2003 is a challenging case for the idea that we have duties to our 'enemies' (or those members of a community against which one's own community is at war), which require us to grant them equal moral standing with our compatriots. It also forces us to question, in light of our broader moral commitments, the way that the principle of non-combatant immunity is conventionally applied – and to consider revisions.

The civilian deaths at the checkpoint were clearly not deliberate. Of course, the soldiers must have recognized the possibility of accidentally killing civilians when they opened fire on the vehicle; they could

(continued)

only guess at who was inside. Yet, we can assume that they did not want to kill civilians. Such an act would not have contributed to any military objective. Indeed, given that avoiding civilian casualties was thought to be fundamental to maintaining the legitimacy of the war effort, civilian deaths would have been perceived as markedly counterproductive. Moreover, if we leave the question of the legitimacy of the war as a whole aside (which most just war theorists would implore us to do when considering particular cases of conduct), the 3rd Infantry Division was engaged in a legitimate military activity: securing an intersection near Karbala and screening vehicles for Iraqi guerrillas, who posed a real threat to the American forces.

People might disagree on how to apply just war principles to this incident (just as they disagree on the fine points of the principles themselves). Yet, there is a strong argument to be made that the absolute prohibition against intentionally killing non-combatants was *not* violated; nor was the principle of proportionality. Even without the 'warning shots', upon which Johnson placed so much emphasis, the civilian deaths can be seen as 'collateral damage', and thereby permissible. The idea that collateral civilian deaths are morally permissible is generally considered to be an inherent feature of the norm of non-combatant immunity – despite the controversial nature of the DDE upon which this permissibility relies. Indeed, the notion of collateral damage is frequently invoked by practitioners and policy-makers, as well as by scholars. Nevertheless, in this case, there was a notable concern among the 3rd Infantry Division that something had gone wrong. This apprehension was evident in debates over whether, and how soon, warning shots had been fired. Combined with sharp condemnations from outside observers, this unease gestures towards moral expectations that go beyond simply requiring that civilian casualties be proportionate side-effects of intended targets.

According to Michael Walzer, writing long before the 2003 war in Iraq,

> soldiers are supposed to accept (some) risks in order to save civilian lives. . . . They are the ones who endanger civilian lives in the first place, and even if they do this in the course of legitimate military operations, they must still make some effort to restrict the range of the damage they do. . . . It is not kindness that is involved here, but duty . . .

(Walzer 1977/2006: 151)

Walzer argues that not intending to kill civilians is insufficient; we must actively endeavour not to kill them. In other words, it is necessary to take steps to avoid killing non-combatants, even when this means that soldiers have to accept risks to themselves in the process. Walzer's proposed revision to the DDE forces us to ask what risks soldiers should take to protect 'enemy' civilians. This brings us back to another question, touched upon earlier in this chapter: Do we have duties first and foremost to our fellow citizens, or do we have duties to fellow human beings as such?

Sources of Value and Scope of Obligations

The idea of restraint in the conduct of war, and, specifically, defences of the norm of non-combatant immunity, are generally defended from a cosmopolitan perspective. This should not be surprising. For the cosmopolitan, everyone has equal moral standing, whether compatriot or foreigner, ally or enemy. From this perspective, one's opponent in war is, above all, a fellow human being. Although the just war tradition possesses a particularly Christian heritage, the idea of an inclusive community of humankind is central to its contemporary, often secular, interpretations. A cosmopolitan lens would portray the Iraqis who approached the American checkpoint in the spring of 2003 as human beings to whom the principle of discrimination necessarily applied. Moreover, when it was clear that they were, potentially, civilians, this cosmopolitan lens would generate a moral expectation that the soldiers take risks to themselves in endeavouring to protect the immunity of these others. Enemy civilians, the cosmopolitan would maintain, should be protected no less arduously than the civilians that these soldiers had left at home.

Of course, a cosmopolitan moral outlook is not the only one available to the normative IR theorist. Communitarianism provides a markedly different account of both our source of values and the force of any duties that we might owe to the enemy. Communitarian realism locates value in the particular political community, thereby granting a degree of moral concern to fellow citizens that neither extends to, nor can be compromised by, consideration of those beyond the borders of the state. The practical implications of such a position can be far-reaching when the state is engaged in war. Seen through a communitarian realist lens, the moral standing of non-citizens is qualified, and both concern and obligation towards them is attenuated. This might mean that moral norms of restraint are abandoned. Importantly, though, moral arguments for restraint *can* be made from a communitarian realist perspective. They are, however, different than cosmopolitan defences. Even if the moral standing of one's enemies is qualified, or not recognized at all, one's compatriots are granted full moral standing from a communitarian realist perspective. It is therefore *possible* for a communitarian realist to argue that civilian populations must be spared attack in time of war. The desired protection of *one's own* non-combatant population, combined with the quest for reciprocal treatment, could motivate the exercise of restraint towards the enemy. It is crucial to note, though, that this is a weak motivation for adherence to moral norms of restraint compared to the cosmopolitan's commitment to the enemy's underlying humanity.

With respect to the war in Iraq and the checkpoint incident, both moral worldviews are revealing. And, arguably, both came into play as the soldiers at the checkpoint were faced with the problem of what to do. A cosmopolitan perspective explains the importance placed on warning shots – even though such a strategy exposes one's fellow soldiers to greater risk. Adopting a communitarian realist moral worldview highlights the loyalties that the soldiers on either side of the war have towards their compatriots, and, in doing so, uncovers a deep tension between these loyalties and norms of restraint that are justified in terms of our common humanity. Communitarian realism provides an account of why one might place the well-being of one's own community and fellow citizens above obligations to protect enemy civilians by failing, for example, to issue a warning shot in extreme circumstances.

Who is Responsible?

Finally, with its focus on *moral* agency, normative IR theory creates conceptual space to ask 'who – or what – is responsible?' (Erskine 2003a, 2008b). One might question, for example, who had a duty to ensure that civilians were not killed at the intersection near Karbala, and who can be blamed if warning shots were not fired, or other precautions to avoid civilian deaths were not taken. There is no single – or easy – answer to these questions. To conclude this case study, it might be useful to suggest some of the possibilities open to normative IR theorists to explore.

Individual soldiers, as moral agents, have obligations to safeguard civilians. Arguably, one must begin by asking whether the soldiers who fired the shots that killed the women and children at the checkpoint took the necessary precautions to avoid civilian deaths. Or, were Iraqi suicide bombers responsible for placing their civilian compatriots at risk when they masqueraded as innocent motorists in the days before this incident? What about the officer giving the orders? Could Johnson's impassioned calls to 'stop him!' have been interpreted as a command to dispense with warning shots and eliminate the threat? Of course, the decision to engage in war comes from higher up still. What about governments and state leaders? Finally, to what extent are the citizens of democracies, who are so comfortably far removed from such shootings, morally responsible for civilian deaths that result from the wars in which their states engage? And, can some citizens (university students and lecturers who study these issues, for example) be held to even greater account for not doing more to influence their respective governments to adopt different courses of action?

Conclusion

What can the above snapshot of a few tense, and ultimately tragic, moments at the start of the war in Iraq tell us about normative IR theory – and about the world we live in? To start quite specifically, the case highlights the weight granted to the moral norm of non-combatant immunity. More generally, it demonstrates that moral norms have great effect in international politics. They set out principles and practices to which we have perceived obligations to adhere, thus propelling and constraining actors at all levels. They not only exert formidable force in the world of practice, but also represent *facts* for the normative IR theorist to study. It makes eminent sense, therefore, to talk about the normative IR theorist's task of providing an account of international moral norms as, at least in part, an empirical endeavour. These norms are things that can be observed and studied – even if, for the normative IR theorist, they are *also* things that can be evaluated and revised.

The incident at the checkpoint also highlights the specific idea that soldiers have duties to exercise restraint in war. These duties can require soldiers to accept risks to themselves and to their compatriots in order to safeguard their enemies. More broadly, it demonstrates the tension between our loyalties to fellow community members and our commitments to fellow human beings. It forces us to think about how the influence of certain moral norms can best be explained and justified, how adherence to them is motivated, and how different worldviews include and exclude others. Normative IR theorists take these to be fundamental questions. But, they do not stop their inquiry here. By paying attention to the systems of values and multiple loyalties that frame principles and practices, normative IR theorists also question and assess, and often seek to revise and transform, our understanding of moral guidelines in international politics.

Moreover, the killing of the Iraqi civilians raises questions of moral responsibility – questions of who, for example, might be blamed for these deaths. Such questions reverberate loudly and clearly in the real world of international politics, but are all-too-often evaded within the discipline of IR. We regularly ask who has an obligation to do something, or who should be held to account for some harm. These are critical and complex issues. Normative IR theory follows the practical world of international politics by paying attention to questions of *moral* agency and responsibility. Importantly, normative IR theory also prompts us to ask a host of additional questions about the case study that have not been touched on here. For example, was the war in Iraq just? Could it be justified on the grounds of self-defence – or perhaps as a so-called 'humanitarian' war? Do we have to alter our moral expectations of conduct in war in light of realities such as suicide bombers? And, how do our responses to these questions affect our analysis of the shooting of the civilians at the checkpoint?

Normative IR theory as a distinct area of study within IR was initially propelled by problems surrounding both war and global inequality, but the field has since tackled a multitude of other problems. These include themes such as global warming and humanitarian intervention. Moreover, the so-called 'War on Terror' reinvigorated interest in the ethics of war, and brought with it new topics for study, including the ethics of torture, the status of non-state actors in armed conflict, the justice of pre-emptive force, and our duties to others *after* wars end. Each is still hotly debated, the final two with renewed passion in light of the nuclear threat associated with Iran (and considerations of the moral permissibility of a 'pre-emptive strike') and the ongoing instability in Libya following the 2011 intervention (and claims to 'a moral responsibility to Libya' to 'rebuild the peace' (Murphy 2011)). Significantly, none of the issues, insights, or questions listed here would appear on our radar screens as IR scholars if we did not acknowledge the importance of the *ethical dimension* of international politics. Although normative IR theory has often been treated as lying at the periphery of the discipline of IR, the issues addressed by this body of scholarship are situated resolutely at the very heart of international politics. Indeed, normative IR theory embraces theoretical perspectives and priorities that the discipline cannot ignore if it is to be both meaningful to those who study it and relevant to practice.

Questions

1. What unique features does normative IR theory bring to the study of international relations?

2. Are norms things that we can identify and explore in international relations, or are they just a matter of speculation?

3. Why has IR been particularly unreceptive to addressing ethical questions? Is this changing?

4. What are some prominent examples of international moral norms? Are they 'settled norms' according to Frost's criteria?

5. Should 'foreigners' and one's fellow citizens be given equal moral consideration? If so, why? If not, why not?

6. Even though a cosmopolitan perspective assumes that all human beings have equal moral standing, can it nevertheless be criticized for excluding some others? If so, in what ways? If not, why not?

7. Some critics claim that new wars, new weapons, and new types of enemy have rendered the just war tradition obsolete. Are just war principles of restraint still relevant and applicable? (You might want to think specifically about the principle of 'non-combatant immunity', or 'discrimination', and modern realities such as 'humanitarian' wars, 'suicide bombers', and child soldiers.)

8. Do you think that torture is ever morally permissible? Are you employing deontological or consequentialist reasoning in arriving at your answer?

9. Why is the doctrine of double effect so controversial?

10. Which moral perspective provides a more compelling account of policies conducted during the 'War on Terror', cosmopolitanism or communitarianism? (Think of policies such as the classification of 'illegal enemy combatants', the torture of detainees, and the policy of pre-emptive war.) Explain your answer.

11. Should citizens in a democracy be considered morally responsible for the unjust conduct of a war in which their state engages? If so, why? If not, why not?

12. Which actors in international politics have obligations to respond to environmental degradation and climate change? What is the most compelling way of defending such obligations?

Further reading

Beitz, C. R. (1979/1999), *Political Theory and International Relations*, 2nd edn. (Princeton: Princeton University Press).
An important example of ethical cosmopolitanism and one of the catalysts for the emergence of normative IR theory in the 1980s and 1990s. Beitz draws on John Rawls' *A Theory of Justice* and proposes a *global* 'original position' in order to tackle questions of international distributive justice.

Brown, C. (1992), *International Relations Theory: New Normative Approaches* (London: Harvester Wheatsheaf).
A seminal work in the field of normative IR theory and the best introduction available to the categories of communitarianism and cosmopolitanism. The debates on critical theory and postmodernism addressed in Part III have moved on since the work was published, but the book remains essential reading.

Cochran, M. (1999), *Normative Theory in International Relations: A Pragmatic Approach* (Cambridge: Cambridge University Press).
An excellent example of 'second generation' normative IR theory, this book responds directly to the work of theorists like Brown, Frost, and Linklater. Cochran aims to 'reconcile the poles' of the communitarianism/cosmopolitanism divide by adopting an antifoundationalist stance inspired by American pragmatism.

Erskine, T. (2003) (ed.), *Can Institutions Have Responsibilities? Collective Moral Agency and International Relations* (New York and Basingstoke: Palgrave Macmillan).
A collection of high-quality essays that introduces a new agenda to normative IR theory. The contributions to this book ask 'who – or what – has moral responsibilities in international relations?' and explore whether formal organizations can be considered moral agents in a way comparable to individual human actors.

Frost, M. (1996), *Ethics in International Relations* (Cambridge: Cambridge University Press).
An influential example of a contemporary communitarian position in normative IR theory. Frost champions a neo-Hegelian position, which he labels 'constitutive theory', and aims to reconcile the 'settled norms' of state sovereignty and human rights.

Harbour, F. V. (1999), *Thinking About International Ethics: Moral Theory and Cases from American Foreign Policy* (Boulder, CO: Westview Press).
A valuable introduction to the categories of deontology and consequentialism as applied to international relations. Harbour presents these moral perspectives as tools for analysing cases in American foreign policy.

Nussbaum, M. and J. Cohen (1996/2002) (eds.), *For Love of Country?* (Boston: Beacon Press).
With short and thought-provoking essays that contemplate and criticize ethical cosmopolitanism, this volume is excellent for sparking discussion. The debate here is couched in terms of 'cosmopolitanism' vs. 'patriotism', but many of the themes in normative IR theory's communitarian/cosmopolitan divide are colourfully covered.

O'Neill, O. (1986), *Faces of Hunger: An Essay on Poverty, Justice and Development* (London: Allen & Unwin).
A robust example of a deontological approach to famine and poverty in international politics, which O'Neill describes as a '(maverick) Kantian theory of obligation'. This provides a useful contrast to Singer's consequentialist approach (listed here).

Orend, B. (2006), *The Morality of War* **(Peterborough, Ont.: Broadview Press).**
Clear and accessible, this is an excellent complement to Michael Walzer's outstanding *Just and Unjust Wars*. Published almost thirty years after Walzer's book first appeared, *Morality of War* provides an up-to-date analysis of the issues addressed by Walzer, while also making an original contribution to just war thinking.

Singer, P. (1972), 'Famine, Affluence, and Morality', *Philosophy & Public Affairs*, **1/2: 229–43.**
A demanding, controversial, and frequently-cited example of a consequentialist approach to the problem of famine and poverty in international politics, which adopts a specifically utilitarian perspective. Like O'Neill, Singer is a philosopher whose applied ethics helped to influence work done in normative IR theory.

Important websites

The Stanford Encyclopedia of Philosophy is an outstanding on-line source of refereed articles, which offers accessible and comprehensive accounts of a range of concepts relevant to normative IR theory. See, for example, the entries on 'war', 'international justice', and 'deontological ethics'. **http://plato.stanford.edu/**

The website of the Carnegie Council on Ethics and International Affairs includes a valuable library of transcripts, audio and video material, interviews, and articles, as well as a section for 'educators and students' – all on the theme of ethical decisions in international affairs. **http://www.cceia.org/index.html**

The website of the International Ethics Section of the International Studies Association (ISA), the largest scholarly association for the study of international relations, provides information on the activities of scholars working in normative IR theory/international political theory/international ethics. This site includes summaries of recently published books that engage with international ethics. **http://www.isanet.org/ethics/**

Notes

1. I would like to thank Chris Brown, Frances Harbour, Susanna Karlsson, Anthony Lang, Jr., and Cian O'Driscoll for providing incisive written comments on a previous draft of this chapter. I am also grateful to Richard Ned Lebow, Nicholas Wheeler, and Howard Williams for their valuable engagements with specific sections.

2. In this chapter, I will use the terms 'ethical' and 'moral' interchangeably.

3. Nevertheless, Simon Caney's discomfort with the limits of the term 'international' has prompted him to coin the phrase 'global political theory' as yet another alternative to normative IR theory (Caney 2005).

4. The more common category of consequentialist theories, known as 'act-consequentialism', analyses the effects of each act. 'Rule-consequentialism', by contrast, weighs the costs and benefits of general adherence to a set of rules.

5. Note that 'civilians' are not the only 'non-combatants'. Surrendered and injured soldiers, for example, are also categories of non-combatants, and therefore prohibited targets of attack. However, the specific example of civilian deaths will be explored in relation to the principle of non-combatant immunity in this chapter.

6. Debates over where to draw the line between combatants and non-combatants, and why the principle of discrimination rests on a morally relevant distinction, are multifaceted and important. Non-combatants are frequently described as deriving their immunity from their 'innocence'. For most contemporary theorists, the term innocence refers to what is often called 'material' rather than 'moral' innocence – signifying (with semantic reference to its Latin root) those who are 'not harming'. There is no question that those killed at the checkpoint shooting were both non-combatants and innocents.

 Visit the Online Resource Centre that accompanies this book for lots of interesting additional material. **www.oxfordtextbooks.co.uk/orc/dunne3e/**

Classical Realism

RICHARD NED LEBOW

 Reader's Guide

Classical realism represents an approach to international relations that harks back to fifth century Greek historian Thucydides and his account of the Peloponnesian War. It recognizes the central role of power in politics of all kinds, but also the limitations of power and the ways in which it can readily be made self-defeating. It stresses sensitivity to ethical dilemmas and their practical implications and the need to base influence, whenever possible, on shared interests and persuasion. In this chapter, I examine the core assumptions of classical realism through the texts of ancient and modern writers, contrast their ideas with neo-realism and other variants of modern realism, and analyse the Anglo-American intervention in Iraq in terms of the tenets of classical realism.

Introduction

There is widespread recognition that the realist tradition reached its nadir in neorealism. In his unsuccessful effort to transform realism into a scientific theory, Kenneth Waltz, father of neorealism, denuded the realism of its complexity and subtlety, appreciation of agency and understanding that power is most readily transformed into influence when it is both masked and embedded in a generally accepted system of norms. Neorealism is a parody of science. Its key terms like power and polarity are loosely and haphazardly formulated and its scope conditions are left undefined. It relies on a process akin to natural selection to shape the behaviour of units in a world where successful strategies are not necessarily passed on to successive leaders and where the culling of less successful units rarely occurs. It more closely resembles an ideology than it does a scientific theory.

Like most ideologies, neorealism is unfalsifiable, and its rise and fall has had little to do with conceptual and empirical advances. Its appeal lies in its apparent simplicity and certainty; something that says more about its adherents that it does about the theory. Its decline was hastened by the end of the Cold War, which many scholars understood as critical test case for a theory that sought to explain the stability of the bipolar world. The end of the Cold War and subsequent collapse of the Soviet Union also turned scholarly and public attention to a new range of political problems to which neorealism was irrelevant.

The decline of neorealism encouraged many realists to return to their roots. They read great nineteenth and twentieth century realists like Max Weber, E. H. Carr and Hans Morgenthau in search of conceptions and insights relevant to contemporary international relations. Weber and Morgenthau in turn were deeply indebted to the Greeks – to the tragic playwrights and Thucydides, where the tradition of classical realism originates.

Classical realism has displayed a fundamental unity of thought across nearly 2500 years. The principal thinkers in this tradition – Thucydides, Niccolò Machiavelli, Carl von Clausewitz and Hans J. Morgenthau – are concerned with questions of order, justice and change, at the domestic, regional and international levels. Classical realists stress the similarities, not the differences, between domestic and international politics, and emphasize the importance of ethics and community in promoting stability in both domains. In keeping with their tragic understanding of life, they recognize that communal bonds are fragile and easily undermined by the unrestrained pursuit of unilateral advantage by individuals, factions and states. When this happens, time-honoured mechanisms of conflict management like alliances and the balance of power may not only fail to preserve the peace but may make domestic and international violence more likely. Like Greek playwrights, classical realists tend to regard history as cyclical, in the sense that efforts to build order and escape from fear-driven worlds, while they may succeed for a considerable period of time, ultimately succumb to the destabilizing effects of actors who believe they are too powerful to be constrained by law and custom.

This chapter explores the thought of two of the most important classical realists writers on international affairs: Thucydides (460- c. 390 BCE.), a fifth century Athenian general and writer who authored an account of the Peloponnesian War between Athens and Sparta, and their respective allies; and Hans J. Morgenthau (1904–79), a German born lawyer who came to the United States as a refugee during the Second World War, taught for many years at the University of Chicago, and was arguably the most influential postwar theorist of international relations.[1] There are the many similarities in their outlooks, some of which derive from the tragic view of life and politics they shared.

The first section explores the Classical Realist reflections on community. Thucydides and Morgenthau believe that the tensions between individuals and communities could be reconciled in part at a deeper level of understanding. This is because a well-functioning community is essential to the intelligent formation and pursuit of individual interests. The principles of justice on which all viable communities are based, also allow the efficient translation of power into influence. Membership in a community imposes limits on the ends and means of power. Failure to subordinate individual or state goals to the requirements of justice leads to self-defeating policies of overexpansion. Classical realists understand great powers to be their own worst enemies when success and the hubris it engenders encourage them to see themselves outside of and above their community. Such a self-understanding blinds them to the need for self-restraint and prompts aggressive and self-defeating foreign policies.

The second section of the chapter explores change and transformation. Classical realists categorize political systems in terms of their principles of order, and the ways in which these principles shape the identities of actors and the discourses in terms of which they frame their interests. For Thucydides and Morgenthau, changes in identities and discourses are often the result of major economic, social and political changes. They understand hegemonic wars – conflicts that involve most or all of the great powers—as more the consequence than a cause of domestic and international transformations. This is a very different understanding of cause and effect from neo- and other modern realists, and has important implications for the kinds of strategies classical realists think useful in maintaining or restoring order. In this regard, they put at least as much emphasis on values and ideas as they do on power.

The third section of the chapter examines the understanding classical realists have of the nature and purpose of theory. Thucydides constructed no theories in the modern sense of the term, but he is widely regarded as the first theorist of international relations. Morgenthau is explicitly theoretical. They are nevertheless united in their belief that theoretical knowledge is not an end in itself, but a starting point for actors to work their way through contemporary problems and, in the process, come to deeper forms of understanding.

The fourth section of the chapter offers a case study of Anglo-American intervention in Iraq to overthrow Saddam Hussein. I argue that it is characterized by three pathologies that are well-described by classical realism but to which modern realists are largely oblivious. The first is the inability of actors to formulate interests intelligently and coherently outside of a language of justice. The second is hubris, and how it often leads to tragic outcomes that are the very opposite of those intended. The third is the inappropriate choice of means, and the generally negative consequences of choosing means at odds with the values of the wider community.

I conclude with a brief discussion of tragedy. Thucydides should be considered the fourth great tragedian of fifth century Athens. His account of the Peloponnesian War (431–404 BCE) is constructed in the form and style of a tragedy. Morgenthau wrote no tragedies, but his thinking, like many educated Germans of the nineteenth and twentieth century, was deeply steeped in a tragic understanding of life and politics. It lies at the core of his theory and his thoughts about the appropriate means of reconstituting political order.

Classical realism on order and stability

Community, order, and stability

Most realists have a straightforward answer to the problem of order: effective central authority. Governments that defend borders, enforce laws and protect citizens make domestic politics more peaceful and qualitatively different from international politics. The international arena remains a self-help system, a 'brutal arena where states look for opportunities to take advantage of each other' (Mearsheimer, 1994–5). Survival depends on a state's material capabilities and its alliances with other states (Waltz, 1979: 103–104). Thucydides and Morgenthau are not insensitive to the consequences of anarchy, but do not distinguish international from domestic politics. For classical realists, *all* politics is an expression of human drives and subject to the same pathologies. They see more variation in order and stability *within* domestic and international systems than they do between them, and explain it with reference to the cohesiveness of society, domestic or international, and the channels into which it channels human drives and passions.

Thucydides devotes equal attention to internal developments in Athens and external developments in the several theatres of war. He describes parallel developments in Athens and Greece and encourages us to understand them as the outcomes of similar and reinforcing processes. His city states run the gamut from highly ordered and consensual to those who succumb to civil war. These differences have nothing to do with the presence or absence of rulers, but with the cohesiveness of the community (*homonoia*). When communal bonds are strong, as in Periclean Athens, and in Greece more generally before the Peloponnesian War, conventions (*nomoi*) restrained individuals and cities. When community breaks down, as in Corcyra in the 420s, so does order. Thucydides would have agreed with Aristotle's observation that law 'has no power to compel obedience beside the force of habit' (*Politics*: 1269a20).

Morgenthau's understanding of the relationship between domestic and international politics mirrors that of Thucydides. At the outset of his famous text, *Politics Among Nations*, he makes a sharp distinction between international and domestic politics which he then systematically undermines. *All* politics, he insists, is a struggle for power that is 'inseparable from social life itself' (1948a: 17–18). In many countries, laws, institutions and norms direct the struggle for power into ritualized and socially acceptable channels. In the international arena, the struggle cannot so readily be tamed. The character of international relations nevertheless displays remarkable variation across historical epochs. In the eighteenth century, Europe was 'one great republic' with common standards of 'politeness and cultivation' and a common 'system of arts, and laws, and manners' (1948a: 159–66). Morgenthau often spoke of the parallel between international relations in the eighteenth century and pre-Peloponnesian War Greece. In both epochs, 'fear and shame' and 'some common sense of honor and justice' induced leaders to moderate their ambitions (1948a: 270–84). The sense of community was ruptured by the French Revolution, and only superficially restored in its aftermath. It broke down altogether in the twentieth century when the principal powers became divided by ideology as well as by interests. In the 1930s, four major powers—Germany, the Soviet Union, Japan and Italy – rejected the very premises of the international order. The Soviet Union continued to do this in the postwar era, leading to a conflict with the United States and reducing international politics 'to the primitive spectacle of two giants eyeing each other with watchful suspicion' (1948a: 285).

Morgenthau recognized the same variation in domestic politics. In strong societies like Britain and the United States, norms and institutions muted the struggle for power, but in weak societies like Nazi Germany and Stalin's Soviet Union, they broke down. Politics in these latter countries was every bit as violent and unconstrained as in any epoch of international relations. For Morgenthau, as for Thucydides, communities and the identities and norms they help to create and sustain are the most critical determinants of order, at home and abroad.

Balance of power

Contemporary realists consider military capability and alliances the foundation of security. The Greeks were not insensitive to the value of alliances. Aristotle observed that 'When people are friends, they have no need for justice, but when they are just they need friends as well' (*Nicomachean Ethics*: 1155a: 24–6). Thucydides, and classical realists more generally, recognize that military power and alliances are double-edged swords; they are as likely to provoke as to prevent conflict.

Book One of Thucydides leaves no doubt that Athenian efforts to construct a favourable balance of power were an instrumental cause of war. Its alliance with Corcyra (present day

Featured book

Hans Morgenthau, *Politics among Nations: The Struggle for Power and Peace* (New York: Alfred A. Knopf)

Hans Morgenthau's *Politics Among Nations*, first published in 1948, went through six editions in his lifetime. It was the principal IR text in North American from the early 1950s until the late 1970s. Two generations of American college students were taught the principles of realism, the importance of power and the balance of power as guarantees of security. The principles of political realism Morgenthau set out in *Politics Among Nations* were: 1) that politics is governed by objective laws with their roots in unchanging human nature; 2) that realism perceives the world through the concept of 'interest understood in terms of power'; 3) that, while interest is to be universally defined as power, the meaning and content of interests may shift and change; 4) that realism was a perspective aware of the moral significance of political action; 5) that moral aspirations of a single community or a state may not be universally valid or shared; 6) and that realism as a tradition of thought was distinct in its focus on the autonomy of the political realm and decisions made within it.

To Morgenthau's regret, many who used his text in their courses paid less attention to the ethical dimensions of foreign policy, which he considered equally important. Initially written to wean Americans from law-based, idealistic foreign policies, Morgenthau was convinced by the mid-1960s that the lesson of realism had been overlearned. He complained that *Realpolitik*, divorced from any ethical considerations, was the mindset responsible for intervention in Indochina and the disastrous war that followed.

In the post-Cold War world, there has been renewed interest in Morgenthau by scholars motivated by related theoretical and political agendas (see for example Williams, 2007). Those interested in recapturing IR theory from the narrow positivism of Kenneth Waltz and his followers have turned to Morgenthau and other founding texts of classical realism for inspiration. They have drawn from them different conceptions of theory, the importance of actors vs. so-called structures, and the lesson that the most successful foreign policies are those that serve the international community at large. These lessons provide starting points for the development theories intended to challenge the continuing pursuit of hegemony by American leaders and its national security establishment.

Corfu) led to a violent encounter with the Corinthian fleet and raised the prospect of a wider war with Sparta. Athens then took peremptory action against Megara and Potidaea, and made war difficult to prevent. Sparta's alliance with Corinth dragged it in turn into a war with Athens that many Spartiates would have preferred to avoid. Nowhere in his text does Thucydides offer an example of an alliance that deterred war, and by the logic of the balance of power some should have. His Mytilenean Debate and Melian Dialogue suggest several reasons for this unrelieved pattern of deterrence failure. Chief among them is the pursuit of unrealistic goals, motivated by the appetite and spirit, which encourage wishful thinking in the form of downplaying risks and exaggerating the likelihood of success. In Sparta, this led the war party to ignore the strategic advantages of Athenian sea power, which made it all but invulnerable to even a successful invasion (Thucydides 1954: 1.86–8).

Deterrence was also defeated by the breakdown of community and the conventions it sustained. Athenians increasingly succumbed to the impulses of self-aggrandizement (*pleonexia*). In the Sicilian debate, the sensible and cautious Nicias tries to educate Athenians about the size and population of Sicily, the military readiness of its largest city, Syracuse, and warms of the dangers of sailing against an island so far away when there are undefeated enemies close to home. Alcibiades dismisses these risks out of hand and appeals to the greed of his audience. Recognizing that arguments against the expedition will not succeed, Nicias now tries to dissuade the assembly by insisting on a much larger force and more extensive provisions than were originally planned. To his surprise, the more he demands, the more eager the assembly becomes to support the expedition, convinced that a force of such magnitude will be invincible. Carried away by the prospect of gain, Athenians became immune to the voice of reason, and committed the second fateful misjudgement – the alliance with Corcyra being the first – that led to Athens' defeat (Thucydides 1954: 6.10–26).

For Morgenthau, the universality of the power drive means that the balance of power was 'a general social phenomenon to be found on all levels of social interaction' (1958: 49, 81). Individuals, groups and states inevitably combine to protect themselves from predators. At the international level, the balance of power has contradictory implications for peace. It might deter war if status quo powers outgun imperialist challengers and successfully demonstrate their resolve to go to war in defence of the status quo. Balancing can also intensify tensions and make war more likely because of the impossibility of accurately assessing the motives, capability and resolve of other states. Leaders understandably aim to achieve a margin of safety, and when multiple states or alliances act this way, they ratchet up international tensions. Even when the balance of power fails to prevent war, Morgenthau reasons, it might still limit its consequences and preserve the existence of states, small and large. He credits the balance with having done this for much of the eighteenth and nineteenth centuries (1948a: 155–9, 162–6, 172; 1958: 80).

For Morgenthau, the success of the balance of power for the better part of two centuries was less a function of the distribution of capabilities than of the existence and strength of international society that bound together the most important actors in the system. When that society broke down, as it did from the first partition of Poland in 1772 through the Napoleonic Wars, the balance of power no longer functioned to preserve the peace or existence of the members of the system (1948a: 160–6). International society was even weaker in the twentieth century, and its decline was an underlying cause of both world wars. Morgenthau worried that the continuing absence of a robust international society in the immediate postwar period had removed all constraints on superpower competition. By the 1970s, he had become more optimistic about the prospects for peace. Détente, explicit recognition of the territorial status quo in Europe, a corresponding decline in ideological confrontation, the emergence of Japan, China, West Germany as possible third forces, and the effects of Vietnam on American power had made both superpowers more cautious and tolerant of the status quo (1972: preface). Perhaps most importantly, daily Soviet-American contacts, negotiations and occasional agreements had gone some way toward normalizing relations and creating the basis for a renewed sense of community.

Thucydides and Morgenthau understand politics as a struggle for power and unilateral advantage. The differences between domestic politics and international relations are of degree, not of kind. Military capability and alliances are necessary safeguards in the rough-and-tumble world of international relations, but cannot be counted on to preserve the peace or the independence of actors. Order, domestic and international, ultimately rest on the strength of community. When states and their rulers are bound by a common culture, conventions and personal ties, competition for power is restrained in its ends and means. In this context, a balance of power might prevent some wars and limit the severity of others. In the absence of community, military capability and alliances are no guarantee of security, and can provoke wars they were intended to prevent. States like Athens, and leaders like Napoleon and Hitler cannot be deterred. Morgenthau understands the seeming paradox that the balance of power works best when needed least.

Interest and justice

Contemporary realists define interest in terms of power. For the most part, they equate power with material capabilities. According to Kenneth Waltz (1979:153) 'the political clout of nations correlates closely with their economic power and their military might.' Many contemporary realists also believe in the primacy of self-interest over moral principle, and regard considerations of justice as inappropriate, even dangerous foundations on which to base foreign policies. At best, appeals to justice can serve to justify or mask policies motivated by more concrete material interests. Classical realists consider capabilities only one source of power and do not equate power with influence. Influence for them is a *psychological* relationship, and like all relationships, based on ties that transcend momentary interests. Justice enters the picture because it is the foundation for relationships and of the sense of community on which influence and security ultimately depend.

The first level of Thucydides' history depicts the tension between interest and justice and how it becomes more acute in response to the exigencies of war. It reveals how interest and justice are inseparable and mutually constitutive at a deeper level. In his funeral oration, Pericles describes Athens as a democracy, but Thucydides (1954: 2.37.1) considers the constitutional reforms of 462–1 to have created a mixed form of government (*xunkrasis*). Behind the facade of democracy, he tells us, lay the rule of one man — Pericles (1954: 2.37.1, 2.65.9–10). The democratic ideology, with which he publicly associated himself, moderated class tensions and reconciled the *dēmos* to the economic and political advantages of the elite. When the gap between ideology and practice was exposed by the behaviour of post-Periclean demagogues, class conflict became more acute and politics more vicious, leading to the violent overthrow of democracy by the regime of the Thirty in 404 and its equally violent restoration a year later. Justice, or at least a belief in justice, was the foundation for community.

Athenian imperialism underwent a similar evolution. The empire was successful when power was exercised in accord with the social conventions governing Greek speech and behaviour. Post-Periclean Athens consistently chose power over principle, lost its *hegemonia*, alienated allies and weakened its power base. In 425, during the Mytilenean debate, Cleon tells the assembly to recognize that their empire is a despotism (*turannis*) based on military power and the fear it inspires (Thucydides 1954: 3.37.2). In 416, the Athenian commissioners in the Melian Dialogue divide people into those who rule and those who are subjects (1954: 5.95) To intimidate allies and adversaries alike, they acknowledge their city's need to expand Runaway imperialism of this kind stretched their resources to their breaking point. Interest defined outside of the language of justice is irrational and self-defeating.

Thucydides' parallel accounts of Athenian domestic politics and foreign policy indicate his belief that coercion is a grossly inefficient and ultimately self-defeating basis of influence. The sophist Gorgias (circa 430) personified *logos* (words) as a 'great potentate, who with the tiniest and least visible body achieves the most divine works' (Diels and Kranz 1956: frg. 82, B11). Employed in tandem with persuasion, it 'shapes the soul as it wishes.' Thucydides leads us to the same conclusion. Persuasion can maintain the position of the 'first citizen' (*stratēgos*) of Athens vis a vis the masses and that of the hegemon vis a vis its empire and effectively mask the exercise of power. To persuade, leaders and hegemons must live up to the expectations of their own ideology. For Athens, this meant providing benefits to citizens and allies, and upholding the principles of order on which the polis and its empire were based.

Perhaps the most frequently quoted line from *Politics Among Nations* is Morgenthau's assertion at the outset that 'the concept of interest defined in terms of power' sets politics apart 'as an autonomous sphere of action' and makes a theory of politics possible (1960: 5). Morgenthau then subverts this statement to develop a more nuanced understanding of the relationship between interest and power. These contradictions can be reconciled if we recognize that Morgenthau distinguishes between theory and in practice. The former aspires to create an abstract, rational ideal based on the underlying and unchanging dynamics of international politics. It represents the crudest of templates. Policy is always concrete, rarely rational, and has to take into account many considerations outside of politics.

The contrast between theory and practice is equally apparent in Morgenthau's conceptualization of power. He thinks of power as an intangible quality with many diverse components, which he catalogues at some length. But in the real world, the strategies and tactics leaders use to transform the raw attributes of power into political influence are just as important as the attributes themselves. Because influence is a psychological relationship, leaders need to know not only what buttons are at their disposal but which ones to push in diverse circumstances. There are no absolute measures of power, because it was always relative and situation-specific. Levers of influence that A could use against B might be totally ineffectual against C. The successful exercise of power required a sophisticated understanding of the goals, strengths and weaknesses of allies, adversaries and third parties. But above all, it demands psychological sensitivity to the others' needs for self-esteem.

People seek domination but most often end up subordinate to others (Morgenthau 1947: 145). They try to repress this unpleasant truth, and those who exercise power effectively employ justifications and ideologies to help them do this. Whenever possible, they attempt to convince those who must submit that they are acting in their interests or those of the wider community (Morgenthau 1958: 59). 'What is required for mastery of international politics,' Morgenthau insisted, 'is not the rationality of the engineer but the wisdom and moral strength of the statesman' (1948a: 172).

Like Thucydides, Morgenthau understands that adherence to ethical norms is just as much in the interest of those who wielded power as it is for those over whom it is exercised. He makes this point in his critique of American intervention in Indochina, where he argues that intervention will fail and erode America's influence in the world because the ends and means of American policy violate the morality of the age. There is a certain irony to Morgenthau's opposition. Two decades earlier, he had written *Politics Among Nations*, in large part to disabuse an influential segment of the American elite of the naive belief that ethics was an appropriate guide for foreign policy and that international conflicts could be resolved through the application of law. Intervention in Indochina indicated to him that American policymakers had 'over learned' the lesson; they had embraced *Realpolitik* and moved to the other end of the continuum. Morgenthau is adamant that morality, defined in terms of the conventions of the epoch, imposes limits on the ends that power seeks and the means employed to achieve them (1947: 151–68).

For classical realists – including Machiavelli—justice is important for two different but related reasons. It is the key to influence because it determines how others understand and respond to you. Policy that is constrained by accepted ethical principles and generally supportive of them provides a powerful aura of legitimacy that helps to reconcile less powerful actors to their subordinate status. Influence can also be bought through bribes or compelled by force, but influence obtained this way is expensive to maintain, tenuous in effect and usually short-lived. By contrast, a demonstrable commitment to justice, can create and maintain the kind of community that allows actors to translate power into influence in efficient ways.

Justice is important in a second instrumental way. It provides the conceptual scaffolding on which actors can intelligently construct interests. In this respect, a commitment to justice is a powerful source of self-restraint, and restraint is necessary in direct proportion to one's power. Weak states must generally behave cautiously because of external constraints. Powerful states are not similarly restricted, and the past successes that made them powerful breed hubris, encourage their leaders to make inflated estimates of their ability to control events and seduce them into investing their assets and reputation in risky ventures. As in Greek tragedies, these miscalculations often lead to catastrophe, as they did for Athens, Napoleon and Hitler. Internal restraint and external influence are thus closely related. Self-restraint that prompts behaviour in accord with the acknowledged principles of justice both earns and sustains the *hegemonia* that makes efficient influence possible.

Classical realism and change

Change and modernization

Modern realists classify international systems on the basis of their polarity (uni-, bi- and multipolar). System change occurs when the number of poles changes. This is thought to be the result of shifts in the balance of material capabilities. Rising powers may go to war to remake the system in their interests, and status quo powers to forestall such change. For some realists, this cycle is timeless and independent of technology and learning. Others believe that nuclear weapons have revolutionized international relations by making war too destructive to be rational. In their view, this accounts for the otherwise anomalous peaceful transformation from bi- to multipolarity at the end of the Cold War (Mearsheimer 1990; Waltz 1993; Wohlforth 1994–5).

For classical realists, transformation has a different meaning and is associated with processes we have come to describe as modernization. It brings about shifts in identities and discourses, and with them, changing conceptions of security.

Thucydides' language (1954: 1.15) encourages readers to draw an analogy between individual pursuit of wealth and Athenian pursuit of power. The empire is based on the power of money (*chrēmatōn dunamis*). It generates revenue (*chrēmatōn prosodōi*) to build and maintain the largest navy in Greece. Athens is so powerful relative to other city states that it can dominate them by force. For Greeks, tyrants were rulers without any constitutional basis who dispensed with reciprocity and took what they wanted. Gyges of Lydia was the first known tyrant, and not coincidentally, Lydia was thought to be the first city to have introduced money. Like a tyrant, Athens no longer needed to legitimize its rule or provide the kind of benefits that normally held alliances or city states together. Wealth encouraged the 'orientalization' of Athens, a perspective common to Herodotus and Thucydides. It led to a deep shift in Athenian values, superficially manifested in an increasing reliance on force. This pattern of behaviour was a reflection of changing goals; that of honour (*timē*) increasingly gave way to that of acquisition. And *hegemonia* – rule based on the consent of others—was replaced by control (*archē*) exercised through threats and bribes.

Thucydides' account of the Peloponnesian War is rich in irony. Athens, the tyrant, jettisons the traditional bonds of friendship and reciprocity in expectation of greater rewards only to become trapped by a new set of more onerous obligations. As Pericles recognizes in his funeral oration, Athens maintained its *hēgemonia* by demonstrating generosity to its allies. 'In generosity,' he tells the assembly, 'we are equally singular, acquiring our friends by conferring not by receiving favors' (Thucydides 1954: 2.40.4). The post-Periclean empire must maintain its *archē* by constantly demonstrating its power and will to use it. It must keep expanding, a requirement beyond the capabilities of any state. Athenians discover this bitter truth with their crushing defeat in Sicily.

Morgenthau's understanding of modernization is similar. It led to a misplaced faith in reason undermined the values and norms that had restrained individual and state behaviour. Morgenthau draws on Hegel and Freud. In his *Phenomenology of the Spirit* (1807) and *Philosophy of Right* (1821), Hegel warned of the dangers of homogenization of society arising from equality and universal participation in society. It would sunder traditional communities and individual ties to them without providing an alternative source of identity. Hegel wrote on the eve of the industrial revolution and did not envisage the modern industrial state with its large bureaucracies and modern means of communication. These developments, Morgenthau argues, allow the power of the state to feed on itself through a process of psychological transference that makes it the most exalted object of loyalty. Libidinal impulses, repressed by the society, are mobilized by the state for its own ends. By transferring these impulses to the nation, citizens achieve vicarious satisfaction of their aspirations, including those that society would otherwise make them repress. Stalin's elimination of the Kulaks (wealthy peasants), forced collectivization, and purges, and Hitler's foreign conquests to exterminate the Jews were all expressions of the transference of private impulses onto the state and the absence of any limits on the state's exercise of power. Writing in the aftermath of the great upheavals of the first half of the twentieth century, Morgenthau came to understand communal identity as far from an unalloyed blessing: it allows people to fulfil their potential as human beings, but also risks turning them into 'social men' like Eichmann who lose their humanity in the course of implementing the directives of the state.[2]

The intellectual transformation Morgenthau attributes to the Enlightenment bears striking similarities to the proto-Enlightenment of fifth century Greece. In both epochs, the assertion of the individual, widespread belief in the power of reason and the triumph of secular over religious values had far-reaching political implications. The biggest difference between the two periods was in technology; the modern Enlightenment made possible the industrial revolution and machine age warfare. Nuclear weapons are an outgrowth of this process, and for Morgenthau, 'the only real revolution which has occurred in the structure of international relations since the beginning of history.' War between nuclear powers would no longer an extension of politics by other means but mutual suicide (1958: 76; 1960: 326)

Restoring order

Thucydides and Morgenthau wrote in the aftermath of destructive wars that undermined the communities and conventions that had sustained order at home and abroad. Neither thought it feasible to restore the old way of life, aspects of which had become highly problematic even before the onset of war. They searched instead for some combination of the old and the new that could accommodate the benefits of modernity while limiting its destructive potential.

Thucydides wanted his readers to recognize the need for a synthetic order that would combine the best of the old and the new, and avoid, as far as possible, their respective pitfalls. The best of the new was its spirit of equality (*isonomia*), and the opportunity it offered to all citizens to serve their polis. The best of the old was its emphasis on excellence and virtue (*aretē*), which encouraged members of the elite to suppress their appetite for wealth and power, and even their instinct for survival, in pursuit of valour, good judgement and public service. The Athenians displayed *aretē* at Marathon and Salamis where they risked their lives for the freedom of Greece (Thucydides 1954: 2.20, 25, 41,43, 4.81.2). By the end of the fifth century, *aretē* had progressed through three stages of meaning: from its original Homeric sense of fighting skill, to skill at anything to moral goodness. Thucydides uses all three meanings, and has Pericles (1954: 2.34.5) introduce a fourth in his funeral oration where *aretē* now describes the reputation a state can develop by generous behaviour toward its allies. Thucydides offers an idealized view of Periclean Athens as an example of the kind of synthesis he envisages. It is the very model of a mixed government (*xunkrasis*) that allowed the capable to rule and the masses to participate in government in meaningful ways. It successfully muted tensions between the rich and the poor and the well-born and men of talent, and stood in sharp contrast to the acute class tensions and near stasis of Athens when ruled by demagogues.

Thucydides may have hoped that inter-city relations could be reconstituted on similar foundations. The same kinds of inequalities prevailed between cities as within them. If the power of tyrants could give way to aristocracy and mixed democracy, and the drive for power and wealth be constrained by the restoration of community, the same might be done for inter-polis relations. Powerful cities might once again see it in their interest to wield influence on the basis of *hegemonia*. Power imbalances could be 'equalized' through the principle of proportionality; the more powerful cities receiving honour in degree to the advantages they provided for less powerful cities. Thucydides wrote his history, I believe, to advance this project.

Thucydides is a stern sceptic and rationalist, but one who supports religion because he considered it to be a principal pillar or morality and conventions. In his view, the radical sophists had done a disservice to Athens by arguing that laws and conventions were arbitrary justifications for economic and political inequality. Thucydides wrote for a small, intellectually sophisticated elite, who, like himself, were unlikely to accept conventions as god given. He appeals to them with a more sophisticated defence of convention that does not require rooting it in man's nature. By demonstrating the destructive consequences of the breakdown of conventions, he makes the case for their necessity and the wisdom of those in authority to act *as if* they believed they derived from nature. For Thucydides, language and conventions are arbitrary but essential. His history, like a tragedy, provides an 'outside perspective' for elites to generate a commitment to work 'inside' to restore what is useful, if not essential, to justice and order.

For Morgenthau, the absence of external constraints on state power is *the* defining characteristic of international politics at mid-century. The old normative order was in ruins and too feeble to restrain great powers (1958:60; 1947: 168). Against this background, the Soviet

Union and the United States were locked into an escalating conflict, made more ominous by the unrivalled destructive potential of nuclear weapons. The principal threat to peace was nevertheless political: Moscow and Washington were 'Imbued with the crusading spirit of the new moral force of nationalistic universalism,' and confronted each other with 'inflexible opposition' (1948a: 430). The balance of power was a feeble instrument in these circumstances, and deterrence was more likely to exacerbate tensions then to alleviate them. Bipolarity could be help to preserve the peace by reducing uncertainty—or push the superpowers toward war because of the putative advantage of launching a first strike. Restraint was needed more than anything else, and Morgenthau worried that neither superpower had leaders with the requisite moral courage to resist mounting pressures to engage in risky and confrontational foreign policies.

Realism in the context of the Cold War was a plea for statesmen, and above all, American and Soviet leaders, to recognize the need to coexist in a world of opposing interests and conflict. Their security could never be guaranteed, only approximated through a fragile balance of power and mutual compromises that might resolve, or at least defuse, the arms race and the escalatory potential of the various regional conflicts in which they had become entangled. Morgenthau insists that restraint and partial accommodation are the most practical *short-term* strategies for preserving the peace (1948a: 169; 1958: 80). A more enduring solution to the problem of war would require a fundamental transformation of the international system that made it more like well-ordered domestic societies. By 1958, the man who twenty years earlier had heaped scorn on the aspirations of internationalists, insisted that the well-being of the human race now required 'a principle of political organization transcending the nation-state' (1958: 75–6).

Morgenthau's commitment to some form of supranational authority deepened in the 1970s. Beyond the threat of nuclear holocaust, humanity was threatened by the population explosion, world hunger and environmental degradation. He had no faith in the ability of nation states to ameliorate any of these problems. But if leaders and peoples were so zealous about safeguarding their sovereignty, what hope was there of moving them toward acceptance of a new order? Progress would only occur when enough national leaders became convinced that is was in their respective national interests. The series of steps Europeans had taken toward integration illustrated the apparent paradox that 'what is historically conditioned in the idea of the national interest can be overcome only through the promotion in concert of the national interest of a number of nations' (1958: 73).

Thucydides and Morgenthau grappled with successive phases of modernization and their social, political and military consequences. They understood these consequences, and modernization itself, as an expression of evolving identities and discourses. Human beings were never entrapped by their culture, institutions or language, but constantly reproducing, changing and reinventing them. The central problem for Thucydides and Morgenthau was that old procedures were being abandoned or not working, and being replaced by new and dangerous practices that had entered without much warning. They recognized that stable domestic orders, and the security that they might enable, could only be restored by some synthesis that blended the old with the new. This synthesis had to harness the power of reason, but make allowance for the disruptive passions that often motivated individuals, classes and political units. It had to build community, but could not ignore powerful centrifugal forces, especially self-interest at the individual, group and national levels, that modernization had encouraged and legitimated. The biggest challenge of all was to construct the new order through the willing agency of representatives of the old order in cooperation with the newly empowered agents of modernity.

Given the nature of the challenge, it is not surprising that classical realists are better at diagnosis than treatment, to use Thucydides' medical metaphor. Thucydides is the most sophisticated of classical realists. Perhaps by design, he offered no explicit synthesis, but contented himself with identifying an earlier synthesis—Periclean Athens—that might serve as a model, or at least a starting point, for thinking about the future. Morgenthau addresses the problem of order at two levels: he seeks stop-gap political measures to buy time for states-men to grasp the need to transcend the state system. Their works remain possessions for all time, if only because of their insights into human nature, war and political order. But also because of their recognition of the great difficulty of reconciling tradition and modernity by conscious, rational designs.

Classical realism on the nature of theory

Aristotle (*Nicomachean Ethics*: 141a–b) thought it unlikely that human investigations could ever produce *epistēmē*, which he defined as knowledge of essential natures reached through deduction from first principles. Thucydides does not directly engage questions of epistemology, but one can readily infer that he shared this understanding of the limits of social inquiry. One of his recurrent themes is the extent to which human behaviour is context dependent; similar external challenges provoke a range of responses from different political cultures. As those cultures evolve, so do their foreign policies, a progression I documented in the case of Athens. There is also variation within culture. Thucydides' accounts of the Spartan decision to go to war, the plague in Athens, the Mytilenian Debate and civil war in Corcyra all reveal that individuals respond differently to the same or similar situation in very different ways.

Morgenthau explicitly denies the possibility of general laws and of predictions based on more limited kinds of generalizations. Morgenthau conceives of the social world as 'a chaos of contingencies,' but 'not devoid of a measure of rationality.' The social world could not be reduced to a limited set of social choices because of the irrationality of actors and the inherent complexity of the social world. The best a theory can do 'is to state the likely consequences of choosing one alternative as over against another and the conditions under which one alternative is more likely to occur or to be successful than the other' (Morgenthau 1966: 77).

Theōrie, *theōrein* and *theōrōs*, are all post-Homeric words having to do with seeing and visiting. The noun (*theōrōs*) meant 'witness' or 'spectator.' A *theōrōs* was dispatched to Delphi by his polis to bring back a full account of the words of the oracle. He might also be sent to religious and athletic festivals, and it is here that the word picked up its connotation of spec-tator. Over time, the role of the *theōrōs* s became more active; a *theōrōs* was expected not only to describe what he had seen but to explain its meaning.

Thucydides comes closest to the model of the *theōrōs*; he provides readers with a descrip-tion of events that has interpretations of their meaning embedded in it. Morgenthau con-ducts independent theoretical inquiries in which brief historical accounts, more properly described as examples, are used for purposes of illustration. But in the best tradition of the Greeks, he aspires to develop a framework that actors can use to work their way through contemporary problems. Morgenthau insists that 'All lasting contributions to political science, from Plato, Aristotle, and Augustine to the *Federalist*, Marx and Calhoun, have been responses to such challenges arising from political reality (1966: 77). Great political thinkers confronted with problems that could not be solved with the tools at hand, and developed new ways of thinking, and often use past experience to illuminate the present. Beyond this, Thucydides and Morgenthau seek to stimulate the kind of reflection that leads to wisdom and with it, appreciation of the need for self-restraint. For all three classical realists, history is the vehicle for tragedy and the teacher of wisdom.

Case study: classical realist analysis of Iraq

Anglo-American intervention in Iraq is not a subject that can easily be addressed in a short case study. Its origins, implementation and consequences warrant lengthy analysis, and are likely to be the subject of considerable controversy for decades to come. My goal here is different: I want to use classical realism as a framework for analysing the case. I describe intervention as a tragedy in the Greek sense of the term, and concentrate on the United States because the key decisions were made in Washington.

One of the principal themes of tragedy and classical realism is that people who act outside of a community, and hence, outside of a language of justice, are incapable of formulating interests in an intelligent and coherent manner. They are moved by passions and hope, not be reason and careful calculation. Thucydides, as we have seen, portrays the Athenian invasion of Sicily in this light. His paired speeches of Alcibiades and Nicias reveal the emotional nature of the decision and how poorly connected it was to any strategic logic or estimation of the likely costs. Policymaking in the Bush administration was similar. There was no public debate, and leaders seemed to be moved as much by emotion as rational calculation (Hersh 2004; Mann 2004; Woodward 2004; Daalder and Lindsay 2005).

Our tragedy begins with the end of the Cold War and the collapse of the Soviet Union. American neoconservatives hailed what they called the 'unipolar moment,' and revelled in the unrivalled power of the United States. Mistaking power for influence, they felt no reason why their country should be bound by treaties, agreements and norms that constrained its pursuit of its interests. The move toward unilateralism began with the Clinton administration but accelerated under Bush (Lebow 2003: 310–23). One of the most striking features of American unilateralism is how often it was manifest in pursuit of goals that could not reasonably be said to be in the American interest. Good examples are opposition to the International Criminal Court, European negotiations with Iran, and efforts to limit global warming through treaty arrangements, from all which, in the judgement of most American analysts, the US had much to gain.

In Greek tragedies, success and power are the principal causes of hubris. American intoxication with power and disregard—even contempt—for America's traditional allies and the wider international community, led the Bush administration to embrace risks foreign policy initiatives. This is most evidence in Iraq. Sanctions against Saddam Hussein gave evidence of working, albeit at considerable humanitarian cost, but the administration was not satisfied with mere containment. Vice President Cheney, Secretary of Defense Donald Rumsfeld, Undersecretary of Defense Paul Wolfowitz and National Security Advisor Condoleezza Rice sought Saddam's removal, and made no attempt to hide their objective. Their conversations with lesser officials and the media indicate that they were offended by the survival of the Saddam regime, and expected that his overthrow would allow Washington to remake the map of the Middle East and dramatically increase its influence world-wide. They assumed that Iraqis would welcome American 'liberators' with open arms, accept their émigré puppet Ahmed Chalabi as their new ruler, and at one fell swoop gain significant leverage over Saudi Arabia, Iran and the Palestinians. They further expected that a successful high-tech military campaign that removed Saddam by 'shock and awe' with few American casualties would intimidate North Korea and encourage widespread 'bandwagoning,' making other countries more intent on currying favour with Washington.

The available evidence indicates that these officials rarely, if ever, consulted with acknowledged Middle East experts in State or the Central Intelligence Agency (CIA), ignored reports and estimates that ran counter to their expectations and put great pressure on the CIA and other organizations within the American intelligence community to confirm their views. This has been well-documented with regard to 'evidence' that Saddam had, or was developing, weapons of mass destruction (WMDs).

Trust in hope rather than reason also characterized military planning. Donald Rumsfeld insisted on invading on the cheap, and ordered the Joint Chiefs of Staff to jettison their war plan calling for 400,000 troops and to produce one requiring no more than 125,000. Contrary to wishes of field commander General Tommy Franks, he also insisted that army begin withdrawing forces thirty days after the fall of Baghdad. The CIA contributed to rosy picture the administration had former. It advised that principal opposition would come not from Saddam's Red Guard, but from paramilitary forces with money and ample diverse weapons caches. The National Intelligence Council's (NIC) 38 page assessment of postwar Iraq mentioned internal opposition only once, in conclusion and in an off-hand way. It did warn, however, that there would be trouble if the Americans were perceived as occupiers. The CIA's regional officers worried about insurrection, but George Tenet, Director of Central Intelligence, and keen to please the President, made sure that their fears not reported in the NIC's estimate.

Giving in to pressure from Rumsfeld, the CIA exaggerated the effectiveness of Iraq's infrastructure. The air force and navy were accordingly instructed not to target the electrical grid, but the system collapsed anyway. Getting the lights back on and rebuilding hospitals, schools and sewage facilities became a major struggle for which the occupying forces were initially unprepared. Rumsfeld and his planners thought the bureaucracy would remain intact and could merely be reformed, as was the true in the occupations of Germany and Japan! The White House, Secretary of Defense and military were working with inadequate intelligence because Iraq had long been treated as a 'Tier 2' threat, in contrast to Iran and North Korea. The US had no more than a handful of agents on the ground, and relied on refugees, foreign intelligence and excellent photo intelligence. Intelligence supplied by Chalabi and refugees associated with him was given credence by Rumsfeld and Rice despite repeated warnings from the CIA and State Department's Bureau of Intelligence and Research that it was exaggerated or entirely fabricated (Phillips 2005: 68–73). State Department planning for the occupation, a task force that drew in 75 experts on all aspects of the Arab world, was terminated by Rumsfeld on the ground that they were not fully committed to transforming Iraq (Woodward 2004: 282–4). The Pentagon's occupation plans, based on Rumsfeld's most optimistic scenario, were only designed to secure the oil ministry and oil fields, and secondarily to search for weapons of mass destruction. None of the latter were ever found.

Inadequate plans and occupation forces alienated many Iraqis and allowed those who were disgruntled to loot arsenals and seize weapons, ammunition and explosive that they would later use against American occupation forces and American-trained police. In the resulting chaos, looting substituted for shopping. American proconsul Jake Garner, relying on advice provided by Chalabi and other refugees, was totally detached from the local scene. His replacement, Paul Bremer, disbanded the 400,000 man Iraqi army, unwisely let them keep their guns, and many promptly joined the insurgency. (Diamond 2004: 32–9; Phillips 2005: 198–9). There was no effective dialogue with local forces until well after the insurrection was underway, and house-to-house searches, and other measures designed to nip the insurgency in the bud, only intensified it. American generals would repeatedly claim over the next two years that the insurgents were losing, and would even cite increases in the number of their attacks as evidence. Within a year, the Bush administration was in a quagmire, not unlike Vietnam. None of the options open to it were promising, the American public had increasingly turned against the war and the president's popularity had reached an all-time low in the polls.

(continued)

The Bush administration's experience in Iraq drives home one of the most important insights of classical realism: that great powers are their own worst enemies. President Obama campaigned against the war but when he entered office American opinion remained deeply divided over the right course of action. Obama committed his administration to a gradual build-down of forces in Iraq. Following the recommendations of conservative foreign policy and military advisors, he decided to focus American military and developmental efforts in Afghanistan, now increasingly threatened by a resurgent Taliban because for some years American forces and attention had been diverted to Iraq. The American buildup in Afghanistan, with the participation of forces from other NATO countries has been expensive and costly in lives. Despite the 'surge' intervention of 30,000 more US troops, the Taliban has continued to expand its influence, transforming Afghanistan into another Iraq. American forces have been in Afghanistan for more than ten years as this edition goes to press. The Obama administration feels pressure to withdraw its forces but also to keep a significant number in the country to keep the Karzai regime from collapsing and the Taliban from returning to power.

The military opposition to the US in Afghanistan has received funding and training from Pakistani, drawing the US into a confrontation with that country. Relations deteriorated dramatically when US military team staged a raid in May 2011 on a house in Abbotabad in northwest Pakistan to kill Osama bin Laden. In response, Pakistan's military intelligence stepped up their support of insurgents in Afghanistan, leading to higher casualty rates among American forces. The so-called 'War on Terror' has spread into Yemen and parts of Africa, where the US has begun more actively hunting down al-Qaeda forces, often using rockets fired from unmanned drones to eliminate them. These efforts have met with some success but have also killed innocent civilians, arousing opposition locally and internationally. What started as a local operation in Afghanistan to hunt down Osama bin-Laden has escalated into an extremely costly multi-country and multi-region struggle that gives no evidence of making the US and the West any safer from terrorism. It has also led to a precipitous decline in US influence and prestige. In retrospect, this vast and arguably counterproductive effort is tragic in that it has produced the very opposite outcome envisaged by the Bush administration when it initially sent forces to Afghanistan.

Conclusion: the tragic vision

The chorus in *Antigone* praises human beings as the most inventive of all creatures who reshape the goddess earth with their ploughs, yoke horses and bulls, snare birds and fish in the twisted mesh of their nets and make paths through the turbulent seas with their ships. But they destroy what they create, kill what they love most and seem incapable of living in harmony with themselves and their surroundings. The juxtaposition of man's achievements and transgressions is a central theme of Greek tragedy and classical realism. Like the chorus in Antigone, Thucydides and Morgenthau recognized the extraordinary ability of human beings to harness nature for their own ends, and their propensity to destroy through war and civil violence what took them generations to build. Their writings explore the requirements of stable orders, but they remained pessimistic about the ability of the powerful to exercise self-restraint. Like Aeschylus, they saw a close connection between progress and conflict. They understood that violent challenges to the domestic and international orders are most likely in periods of political, economic social and intellectual ferment.

Thucydides was a friend of Sophocles and Euripides, and the only one of our three authors who wrote what might be called a tragedy. In the late eighteenth century, German intellectuals turned to tragedy as a model for reconstituting ethics and philosophy. Morgenthau was deeply influenced by this latter development. He was intimately familiar with the corpus of ancient and modern literature and philosophy. His intellectual circle included his colleague and fellow émigré Hannah Arendt, who had studied with philosopher Martin Heidegger, wrote about tragedy and applied its lessons to contemporary politics, as did American-born theologian Reinhold Niebuhr.

Morgenthau came to understand tragedy, he wrote to his British colleague, Michael Oakeshott, as 'a quality of existence, not a creation of art' (1948b). His postwar writings, beginning with *Scientific Man vs. Power Politics*, repeatedly invoke tragedy and its understanding of human beings as the framework for understanding contemporary international relations. The principal theme at which he hammers away is the misplaced faith in the powers of reason that have been encouraged by the Enlightenment. But he is equally wary of emotion freed from the restraints of reason and community. 'The *hybris* of Greek and Shakespearean tragedy, the want of moderation in Alexander, Napoleon, and Hitler are instances of such an extreme and exceptional situation' (1947: 135). Although he never used the Greek word, *sophrosunē* (prudence and self-restraint) his German and English writings and correspondence making frequent use of its equivalents: *Urteilskraft* [sound judgement] and prudence. He offers them, as did the Greeks, as the antidotes to hubris. Tragedy, and its emphasis on the limits of human understanding, also shape his approach to theory. Political leaders and theorists alike would do well to dwell on this lesson of history.

 Questions

1. In what ways does Thucydides' account of the Peloponnesian War bridge realism and constructivism?

2. To what extent do Thucydides and Morgenthau attribute the decline and downfall of great powers to their own policy choices versus foreign threats?

3. What other writers on political and international affairs might be considered classical realists? What about Sun Tzu, Machiavelli, Carl von Clausewitz, John Herz and E. H. Carr?

4. When Thucydides and Morgenthau write about ethics, do they have in mind a particular ethical code?

5. What are the principal ways in which classical realists differ from neorealists?

6. To what extent can George Bush or Barrack Obama be considered tragic figures?

7. To what extent can ethical precepts guide foreign policy in a world where there are fundamental disagreements about what is ethical?

8. Describe the respective understandings Thucydides and Morgenthau have of theory. In what ways were they similar and different? How do they differ from the neopositivist understanding of theory that underlies most so-called 'mainstream' theory building in the social sciences?

9. Analyse the respective understanding Thucydides and Morgenthau have of the ability of the balance of power and deterrence to preserve the peace.

10. How would classical realists characterize the similarities and differences between American intervention in Vietnam and Iraq, and between both of those and Soviet intervention in Afghanistan?

11. How do classical realists conceive of influence? What is its relation to power?

12. Has our understanding of international politics progressed at all beyond that of Thucydides?

Further reading

Mervyn Frost, James Mayall, Nicholas Rengger and Richard Ned Lebow (2003, 2005) Two Symposia on 'Tragedy, Ethics and International Relations,' *International Relations* 17/4: 480–503 and 19/4: 324–36.
A useful debate on the relevance of tragedy to contemporary international relations.

Herz, John (1950) 'Idealist Internationalism and the Security Dilemma,' *World Politics* 2/12: 157–80.
A recent discussion of the prospects of international transformation by one of the great classical realists and originator of the concept of the security dilemma.

Lebow, Richard Ned (2003) *The Tragic Vision of Politics: Ethics, Interests and Orders* **(Cambridge: Cambridge University Press).**
Develops the concept of classical realism and uses it to critique modern realism and its belief that foreign policies should not be based on ethical considerations.

Morgenthau, Hans J. (1947) *Scientific Man vs. Power Politics* **(London: Latimer House).**
A classical realist critique of behavioral of behaviouralism.

Morgenthau, Hans (1960) *Politics Among Nations*, **3rd ed. (New York: Knopf).**
A foundational work of modern classical realism.

Reus-Smit, Christian (1999) *The Moral Purpose of the State: Culture, Social Identity, and Institutional Rationality in International Relations* **(Princeton: Princeton University Press).**
Explores the links between ethics, politics and identity.

Thucydides, *History of the Peloponnesian War* **(1954), trans. Rex Warner (London: Penguin Books).**
The original text of classical realism.

Important website

Columbia International Affairs Online (CIAO): access through subscriber university URLs. The best up-to-date website for articles and documents on foreign affairs and international relations. **http://classics.mit.edu/Thucydides/pelopwar.html** for the text of Thucydides' History of the Peloponnesian War.

Notes

1. See Lebow (2003: 68–70, 217–20) for brief biographies.
2. Morgenthau and Hannah Arendt were friends and colleagues, and their extensive correspondence suggests that they drew on each other's insights in their work. Morgenthau was favourably impressed by Arendt's *Eichmann in Jerusalem: A Report on the Banality of Evil* (1964).

Visit the Online Resource Centre that accompanies this book for lots of interesting additional material. **www.oxfordtextbooks.co.uk/orc/dunne3e/**

4 Structural Realism

JOHN J. MEARSHEIMER

 Reader's Guide

This chapter examines a body of realist theories that argue that states care deeply about the balance of power and compete among themselves either to gain power at the expense of others or at least to make sure they do not lose power. They do so because the structure of the international system leaves them little choice if they want to survive. This competition for power makes for a dangerous world where states sometimes fight each other. There are, however, important differences among structural realists. In particular, defensive realists argue that structural factors limit how much power states can gain, which works to ameliorate security competition. Offensive realists, on the other hand, maintain that the system's structure encourages states to maximize their share of world power, to include pursuing hegemony, which tends to intensify security competition. The subsequent analysis revolves around four questions. Why do states want power? How much power do they want? What causes war? Can China rise peacefully (the thematic of the case study)?

Introduction

Realists believe that power is the currency of international politics. Great powers, the main actors in the realists' account, pay careful attention to how much economic and military power they have relative to each other. It is important not only to have a substantial amount of power, but also to make sure that no other state sharply shifts the balance of power in its favour. For realists, international politics is synonymous with power politics.

There are, however, substantial differences among realists. The most basic divide is reflected in the answer to the simple but important question: why do states want power? For classical realists like Hans Morgenthau (1948a), the answer is human nature. Virtually everyone is born with a will to power hardwired into them, which effectively means that great powers are led by individuals who are bent on having their state dominate its rivals. Nothing can be done to alter that drive to be all-powerful. A more detailed treatment of classical realism can be found in **Chapter 3**.

For structural realists, sometimes called neorealists, human nature has little to do with why states want power. Instead, it is the structure or architecture of the international system that forces states to pursue power. In a system where there is no higher authority that sits above the great powers, and where there is no guarantee that one will not attack another, it makes eminently good sense for each state to be powerful enough to protect itself in the event it is attacked. In essence, great powers are trapped in an iron cage where they have little choice but to compete with each other for power if they hope to survive.

Structural realist theories ignore cultural differences among states as well as differences in regime type, mainly because the international system creates the same basic incentives for all great powers. Whether a state is democratic or autocratic matters relatively little for how it acts towards other states. Nor does it matter much who is in charge of conducting a state's foreign policy. Structural realists treat states as if they were black boxes: they are assumed to be alike, save for the fact that some states are more or less powerful than others.

There is a significant divide between structural realists, which is reflected in the answer to a second question that concerns realists: how much power is enough? **Defensive realists** like Kenneth Waltz (1979), whose book is discussed as a featured text, maintain that it is unwise for states to try to maximize their share of world power, because the system will punish them if they attempt to gain too much power. The pursuit of hegemony, they argue, is especially foolhardy. **Offensive realists** like John Mearsheimer (2001) take the opposite view; they maintain that it makes good strategic sense for states to gain as much power as possible and, if the circumstances are right, to pursue hegemony. The argument is not that conquest or domination is good in itself, but instead that having overwhelming power is the best way to ensure one's own survival. For classical realists, power is an end in itself; for structural realists, power is a means to an end and the ultimate end is survival.

Power is based on the material capabilities that a state controls. The balance of power is mainly a function of the tangible military assets that states possess, such as armoured divisions and nuclear weapons. However, states have a second kind of power, latent power, which refers to the socio-economic ingredients that go into building military power. Latent power is based on a state's wealth and the size of its overall population. Great powers need money, technology, and personnel to build military forces and to fight wars, and a state's latent power refers to the raw potential it can draw on when competing with rival states. It should be clear from this discussion that war is not the only way that states can gain power. They can also do so by increasing the size of their population and their share of global wealth, as China has done over the past few decades.

Let us now consider in greater detail the structural realists' explanation for why states pursue power, and then explore why defensive and offensive realists differ about how much power states want. The focus will then shift to examining different structural realist explanations about the causes of great power war. Finally, I will illuminate these theoretical issues with a case study that assesses whether China can rise peacefully.

Why do states want power?

There is a simple structural realist explanation for why states compete among themselves for power. It is based on five straightforward assumptions about the international system. None of these assumptions alone says that states should attempt to gain power at each other's expense. But when they are married together, they depict a world of ceaseless security competition.

The first assumption is that great powers are the main actors in world politics and they operate in an anarchic system. This is not to say that the system is characterized by chaos or disorder. Anarchy is an ordering principle; it simply means that there is no centralized authority or ultimate arbiter that stands above states. The opposite of anarchy is hierarchy, which is the ordering principle of domestic politics.

The second assumption is that all states possess some offensive military capability. Each state, in other words, has the power to inflict some harm on its neighbour. Of course, that capability varies among states and for any state it can change over time.

The third assumption is that states can never be certain about the intentions of other states. States ultimately want to know whether other states are determined to use force to alter the balance of power (**revisionist states**), or whether they are satisfied enough with it that they have no interest in using force to change it (**status quo states**). The problem, however, is that it is almost impossible to discern another state's intentions with a high degree of certainty. Unlike military capabilities, intentions cannot be empirically verified. Intentions are in the minds of decision-makers and they are especially difficult to discern.

One might respond that policy-makers disclose their intentions in speeches and policy documents, which can be assessed. The problem with that argument is policy-makers sometimes lie about or conceal their true intentions. But even if one could determine another state's intentions today, there is no way to determine its future intentions. It is impossible to know who will be running foreign policy in any state five or ten years from now, much less whether they will have aggressive intentions. This is not to say that states can be certain that their neighbours have or will have revisionist goals. Instead, the argument is that policy-makers can never be certain whether they are dealing with a revisionist or status quo state.

The fourth assumption is that the main goal of states is survival. States seek to maintain their territorial integrity and the autonomy of their domestic political order. They can pursue other goals like prosperity and protecting human rights, but those aims must always take a back seat to survival, because if a state does not survive, it cannot pursue those other goals.

The fifth assumption is that states are rational actors, which is to say they are capable of coming up with sound strategies that maximize their prospects for survival. This is not to deny that they miscalculate from time to time. Because states operate with imperfect information in a complicated world, they sometimes make serious mistakes.

Again, none of these assumptions by themselves says that states will or should compete with each other for power. For sure, the third assumption leaves open the possibility that there is a revisionist state in the system. By itself, however, it says nothing about why all states pursue power. It is only when all the assumptions are combined together that circumstances arise where states not only become preoccupied with the balance of power, but acquire powerful incentives to gain power at each other's expense.

To begin with, great powers fear each other. There is little trust among them. They worry about the intentions of other states, in large part because they are so hard to divine. Their greatest fear is that another state might have the capability as well as the motive to attack them. This danger is compounded by the fact that states operate in an anarchic system, which means that there is no nightwatchman who can rescue them if they are threatened by another country. When a state dials the emergency services for help, there is nobody in the international system to answer the call.

The level of fear between states varies from case to case, but it can never be reduced to an inconsequential level. The stakes are simply too great to allow that to happen. International politics is a potentially deadly business where there is the ever-present possibility of war, which often means mass killing on and off the battlefield, and which might even lead to a state's destruction.

Great powers also understand that they operate in a self-help world. They have to rely on themselves to ensure their survival, because other states are potential threats and because there is no higher authority they can turn to if they are attacked. This is not to deny that states can form alliances, which are often useful for dealing with dangerous adversaries. In the final analysis, however, states have no choice but to put their own interests ahead of the interests of other states as well as the so-called international community.

Fearful of other states, and knowing that they operate in a self-help world, states quickly realize that the best way to survive is to be especially powerful. The reasoning here is straightforward: the more powerful a state is relative to its competitors, the less likely it is that it will be attacked. No country in the western hemisphere, for example, would dare strike the USA, because it is so powerful relative to its neighbours.

This simple logic drives great powers to look for opportunities to shift the balance of power in their favour. At the very least, states want to make sure that no other state gains power at their expense. Of course, each state in the system understands this logic, which leads to an unremitting competition for power. In essence, the structure of the system forces every great power—even those that would otherwise be satisfied with the status quo—to think and act when appropriate like a revisionist state.

One might think that peace must be possible if all of the major powers are content with the status quo. The problem, however, is that it is impossible for states to be sure about each other's intentions, especially future intentions. A neighbour might look and sound like a status quo power, but in reality is a revisionist state. Or it might be a status quo state today, but change its stripes tomorrow. In an anarchic system, where there is no ultimate arbiter, states that want to survive have little choice but to assume the worst about the intentions of other states and to compete for power with them. This is the tragedy of great power politics.

The structural imperatives described above are reflected in the famous concept of the **security dilemma** (Herz 1950; see also Glaser 1997). The essence of that dilemma is that most steps a great power takes to enhance its own security decrease the security of other states. For example, any country that improves its position in the global balance of power does so at the expense of other states, which lose relative power. In this zero-sum world, it is difficult for a state to improve its prospects for survival without threatening the survival of other states. Of course, the threatened states then do whatever is necessary to ensure their survival, which, in turn, threatens other states, all of which leads to perpetual security competition.

How much power is enough?

There is disagreement among structural realists about how much power states should aim to control. Offensive realists argue that states should always be looking for opportunities to gain more power and should do so whenever it seems feasible. States should maximize power, and their ultimate goal should be hegemony, because that is the best way to guarantee survival.

While defensive realists recognize that the international system creates strong incentives to gain additional increments of power, they maintain that it is strategically foolish to pursue hegemony. That would amount to overexpansion of the worst kind. States, by their account, should not maximize power, but should instead strive for what Kenneth Waltz calls an 'appropriate amount of power' (1979: 40). This restraint is largely the result of three factors.

Defensive realists emphasize that if any state becomes too powerful, **balancing** will occur. Specifically, the other great powers will build up their militaries and form a balancing coalition that will leave the aspiring hegemon at least less secure, and maybe even destroy it. This is what happened to Napoleonic France (1792–1815), Imperial Germany (1900–18), and Nazi Germany (1933–45) when they made an attempt to dominate Europe. Each aspiring hegemon was decisively defeated by an alliance that included all, or almost all, of the other great powers. Otto von Bismarck's genius, according to the defensive realists, was that he understood that too much power was bad for Germany, because it would cause its neighbours to balance against it. So, he wisely put the brakes on German expansion after winning stunning victories in the Austro–Prussian (1866) and Franco–Prussian (1870–1) Wars.

Some defensive realists argue that there is an **offence–defence balance**, which indicates how easy or difficult it is to conquer territory or defeat a defender in battle. In other words, it tells you whether or not offence pays. Defensive realists maintain that the offence–defence balance is usually heavily weighted in the defender's favour, and thus any state that attempts to gain large amounts of additional power is likely to end up fighting a series of losing wars. Accordingly, states will recognize the futility of offence and concentrate instead on maintaining their position in the balance of power. If they do go on the offensive, their aims will be limited.

Defensive realists further argue that, even when conquest is feasible, it does not pay: the costs outweigh the benefits. Because of nationalism, it is especially difficult, sometimes impossible, for the conqueror to subdue the conquered. The ideology of nationalism, which is pervasive and potent, is all about self-determination, which virtually guarantees that occupied populations will rise up against the occupier. Moreover, it is difficult for foreigners to exploit modern industrial economies, mainly because information technologies require openness and freedom, which are rarely found in occupations.

In sum, not only is conquest difficult but, even in those rare instances where great powers conquer another state, they get few benefits and lots of trouble. According to defensive realism, these basic facts about life in the international system should be apparent to all states and should limit their appetite for more power. Otherwise, they run the risk of threatening their own survival. If all states recognize this logic—and they should if they are rational actors— security competition should not be particularly intense, and there should be few great power wars and certainly no **central wars** (conflicts involving all or almost all the great powers).

Offensive realists do not buy these arguments. They understand that threatened states usually balance against dangerous foes, but they maintain that balancing is often inefficient, especially when it comes to forming balancing coalitions, and that this inefficiency provides opportunities for a clever aggressor to take advantage of its adversaries. Furthermore, threatened states sometimes opt for **buck-passing** rather than joining a balancing coalition. In other words, they attempt to get other states to assume the burden of checking a powerful opponent while they remain on the sidelines. This kind of behaviour, which is commonplace among great powers, also creates opportunities for aggression.

Featured book

Kenneth Waltz (1979), *Theory of International Politics* (Reading, MA: Addison-Wesley).

Kenneth Waltz's *Theory of International Politics* (1979) is structural realism's foundational text, and probably the most influential book written in international relations over the past fifty years. Its core thesis is that the absence of a higher authority that states can turn to in a crisis, coupled with their interest in survival, leaves states little choice but to compete with each other for power. It makes sense to have more power than your rivals if you have to depend on yourself when trouble comes knocking. After all, stronger states are less likely to be attacked than weaker states.

Waltz maintains, however, that states should not attempt to maximize their power, because efforts to acquire more power can easily backfire. They should definitely not seek hegemony. Indeed, their main goal should be to ensure that other states do not gain power at their expense. 'The first concern of states', he emphasizes, 'is not to maximize power, but to maintain their positions in the system'. Furthermore, Waltz does not suggest that going to war to gain power makes good strategic sense. In essence, there are real limits on the severity of security competition in Waltz's world, which is why he is sometimes labelled a 'defensive' realist.

States should temper their appetite for power, Waltz argues, because of the prevalence of balancing behaviour. States almost always check rival states that seek to become especially powerful. Threatened states can build up their own capabilities—'internal balancing'—or join together and form a balancing coalition—'external balancing'. Because 'balances of power recurrently form,' says Waltz, aggressive states should expect to be stopped by their potential victims.

Theory of International Politics contains several other important ideas. Waltz argues that bipolar systems are more peaceful than multipolar systems and that economic interdependence makes conflict more likely. He also introduces the important distinction between balancing and **bandwagoning**, the latter referring to states joining forces with a rising state that is winning wars and gaining power. He maintains that, 'Balancing, not bandwagoning, is the behavior induced by the system', because states do not want to be vulnerable to a powerful partner. Finally, Waltz makes the controversial argument that cooperation among states is difficult because of concerns about 'relative gains'. Making deals is difficult, he suggests, because states worry that the other side will gain a bigger share of the pie and shift the balance of power in its favour.

Offensive realists also take issue with the claim that the defender has a significant advantage over the attacker, and thus offence hardly ever pays. Indeed, the historical record shows that the side that initiates war wins more often than not. And while it may be difficult to gain hegemony, the USA did accomplish this feat in the western hemisphere during the nineteenth century. Also, Imperial Germany came close to achieving hegemony in Europe during the First World War.

Both defensive and offensive realists agree, however, that nuclear weapons have little utility for offensive purposes, except where only one side in a conflict has them. The reason is simple: if both sides have a survivable retaliatory capability, neither gains an advantage from striking first. Moreover, both camps agree that conventional war between nuclear-armed states is possible but not likely, because of the danger of escalation to the nuclear level.

Finally, while offensive realists acknowledge that sometimes conquest does not pay, they also point out that sometimes it does. Conquerors can exploit a vanquished state's economy for gain, even in the information age. Indeed, Peter Liberman argues that information technologies have an 'Orwellian' dimension, which facilitates repression in important ways (1996:

126). While nationalism surely has the potential to make occupation a nasty undertaking, occupied states are sometimes relatively easy to govern, as was the case in France under the Nazis (1940–4). Moreover, a victorious state need not occupy a defeated state to gain an advantage over it. The victor might annex a slice of the defeated state's territory, break it into two or more smaller states, or simply disarm it and prevent it from rearming.

For all of these reasons, offensive realists expect great powers to be constantly looking for opportunities to gain advantage over each other, with the ultimate prize being hegemony. The security competition in this world will tend to be intense and there are likely to be great power wars. Moreover, the grave danger of central war will arise whenever there is a potential hegemon on the scene.

The past behaviour of the great powers has been more in accordance with the predictions of offensive rather than defensive realism. During the first half of the twentieth century, there were two world wars in which three great powers attempted and failed to gain regional hegemony: Imperial Germany, Imperial Japan, and Nazi Germany. The second half of that century was dominated by the Cold War, in which the USA and the Soviet Union engaged in an intense security competition that came close to blows in the Cuban Missile Crisis (1962).

Many defensive realists acknowledge that the great powers often behave in ways that contradict their theory. They maintain, however, that those states were not behaving rationally, and thus it is not surprising that Imperial Germany, Imperial Japan, and Nazi Germany were destroyed in those wars they foolishly started. States that maximize power, they argue, do not enhance their prospects for survival; they undermine it.

This is certainly a legitimate line of argument but, once defensive realists acknowledge that states often act in strategically foolish ways, they need to explain when states act according to the dictates of their structural realist theory and when they do not. Thus, Waltz famously argues that his theory of international politics needs to be supplemented by a separate theory of foreign policy that can explain misguided state behaviour. However, that additional theory, which invariably emphasizes domestic political considerations, is not a structural realist theory.

The theories of defensive realists such as Barry Posen, Jack Snyder, and Stephen Van Evera conform closely to this simple Waltzian template. Each argues that structural logic can explain a reasonable amount of state behaviour, but a substantial amount of it cannot be explained by structural realism. Therefore, an alternative theory is needed to explain those instances where great powers act in non-strategic ways. To that end, Posen (1984) relies on organizational theory, Snyder (1991) on domestic regime type, and Van Evera (1999) on militarism. Each is proposing a theory of foreign policy, to use Waltz's language. In essence, defensive realists have to go beyond structural realism to explain how states act in the international system. They must combine domestic-level and system-level theories to explain how the world works.

Offensive realists, on the other hand, tend to rely exclusively on structural arguments to explain international politics. They do not need a distinct theory of foreign policy, mainly because the world looks a lot like the offensive realists say it should. This means, however, that they must make the case that it made strategic sense for Germany to pursue hegemony in Europe between 1900 and 1945, and for Japan to do the same in Asia between 1931 and 1945. Of course, offensive realists recognize that states occasionally act in strategically foolish ways, and that those cases contradict their theory. Defensive realists, as emphasized, have a fall-back position that is not available to offensive realists: they can explain cases of non-strategic behaviour with a separate theory of foreign policy.

What causes great power war?

Structural realists recognize that states can go to war for any number of reasons, which makes it impossible to come up with a simple theory that points to a single factor as the main cause of war. There is no question that states sometimes start wars to gain power over a rival state and enhance their security. But security is not always the principal driving force behind a state's decision for war. Ideology or economic considerations are sometimes paramount. For example, nationalism was the main reason Bismarck launched wars against Denmark (1864), Austria (1866), and France (1870–1). The Prussian leader wanted to create a unified Germany.

Wars motivated largely by non-security considerations are consistent with structural realism as long as the aggressor does not purposely act in ways that would harm its position in the balance of power. Actually, victory in war almost always improves a state's relative power position, regardless of the reason for initiating the conflict. The German state that emerged after 1870 was much more powerful than the Prussian state Bismarck took control of in 1862.

Although isolating a particular cause of all wars is not a fruitful enterprise, structural realists maintain that the likelihood of war is affected by the architecture of the international system. Some realists argue that the key variable is the number of great powers or poles in the system, while others focus on the distribution of power among the major states. A third approach looks at how changes in the distribution of power affect the likelihood of war. Finally, some realists claim that variations in the offence–defence balance have the greatest influence on the prospects for war.

The polarity of the system

A longstanding debate among realists is whether **bipolarity** (two great powers) is more or less war-prone than **multipolarity** (three or more great powers). It is generally agreed that the state system was multipolar from its inception in 1648 until the Second World War ended in 1945. It was only bipolar during the Cold War, which began right after the Second World War and ran until 1989.

It is tempting to argue that it is clear from twentieth-century European history that bipolarity is more peaceful than multipolarity. After all, there were two world wars in the first half of that century, when Europe was multipolar, while there was no shooting war between the USA and the Soviet Union during the latter half of that century, when the system was bipolar.

This line of argument looks much less persuasive, however, when the timeline includes the nineteenth century. There was no war between any European great powers from 1815 to 1853, and again from 1871 to 1914. Those lengthy periods of relative stability, which occurred in multipolar Europe, compare favourably with the 'long peace' of the Cold War. Thus, it is difficult to determine whether bipolarity or multipolarity is more prone to great power war by looking at modern European history.

Proponents of these rival perspectives, however, do not rely on history alone to make their case; they also employ theoretical arguments. Realists who think bipolarity is less war-prone offer three supporting arguments. First, they maintain that there is more opportunity for great powers to fight each other in multipolarity. There are only two great powers in bipolarity, which means there is only one great power versus great power dyad. In multipolarity, by contrast, there are three potential conflict dyads when there are three great powers, and even more as the number of great powers increases.

Second, there tends to be greater equality between the great powers in bipolarity because, the more great powers there are in the system, the more likely it is that wealth and population, the principal building blocks of military power, will be distributed unevenly among the great powers. And, when there are power imbalances, the stronger often have opportunities to take advantage of the weaker. Furthermore, it is possible in a multipolar system for two or more great powers to gang up on a third great power. Such behaviour is impossible, by definition, in bipolarity.

Third, there is greater potential for miscalculation in multipolarity, and miscalculation often contributes to the outbreak of war. Specifically, there is more clarity about potential threats in bipolarity, because there is only one other great power. Those two states invariably focus on each other, reducing the likelihood that they will misgauge each other's capabilities or intentions. In contrast, there are a handful of great powers in multipolarity and they usually operate in a fluid environment, where identifying friends from foes as well as their relative strength is more difficult.

Balancing is also said to be more efficient in bipolar systems, because each great power has no choice but to directly confront the other. After all, there are no other great powers that can do the balancing or can be part of a balancing coalition and although lesser powers can be useful allies they cannot decide the overall balance of power. In multipolarity, however, threatened states will often be tempted to pass the buck to other threatened states. Although buck-passing is an attractive strategy, it can lead to circumstances where aggressors think they can isolate and defeat an adversary. Of course, threatened states can choose not to pass the buck and instead form a balancing coalition again the threatening state. But putting together alliances is often an uncertain process. An aggressor might conclude that it can gain its objectives before the opposing coalition is fully formed. These dynamics are absent from the simple world of bipolarity, where the two rivals have only each other to think about.

Not all realists, however, accept the claim that bipolarity facilitates peace. Some argue that multipolarity is less war-prone. In this view, the more great powers there are in the system, the better the prospects for peace. This optimism is based on two considerations. First, deterrence is much easier in multipolarity, because there are more states that can join together to confront an especially aggressive state with overwhelming force. In bipolarity, there are no other balancing partners. Balancing in multipolarity might be inefficient sometimes, but eventually the coalition forms and the aggressor is defeated, as Napoleonic France, Imperial Germany, Imperial Japan, and Nazi Germany all learned the hard way.

Second, there is much less hostility among the great powers in multipolarity, because the amount of attention they pay to each other is less than in bipolarity. In a world with only two great powers, each concentrates its attention on the other. But, in multipolarity, states cannot afford to be overly concerned with any one of their neighbours. They have to spread around their attention to all the great powers. Plus, the many interactions among the various states in a multipolar system create numerous cross-cutting cleavages that mitigate conflict. Complexity, in short, dampens the prospects for great power war.

With the end of the Cold War and the collapse of the Soviet Union many realists argue that **unipolarity** has arrived (Wohlforth 1999). The USA, in other words, is the sole great power. It has achieved global hegemony, a feat no other country has ever accomplished. Other realists, however, argue that the post-Cold War system is multipolar, not unipolar. The USA, they maintain, is by far the most powerful state on earth, but there are other great powers, such as China and Russia.

What are the consequences for international stability if the international system is unipolar? Such a world is likely to be more peaceful than either a bipolar or multipolar world. Most importantly, there can be neither security competition nor war between great powers in unipolarity, because it includes just one great power. Furthermore, the minor powers are likely to go out of their way to avoid fighting the sole pole. Think about the western hemisphere, where the USA clearly enjoys hegemony. No state in that region would willingly start a war with the USA for fear of being easily and decisively defeated. This same logic would apply to all regions of the world if the USA was a global hegemon.

There are two caveats to this line of argument. If the hegemon feels secure in the absence of other great powers and pulls most of its military forces back to its own region, security competition and maybe even war is likely to break out in the regions it abandons. After all, the sole pole will no longer be present in those places to maintain order. On the other hand, the hegemon might think that its superior position creates a window of opportunity for it to use its awesome military power to reorder the politics of distant regions. A global hegemon engaged in large-scale social engineering at the end of a rifle barrel will not facilitate world peace. Still, there cannot be war between great powers in unipolarity.

Balanced or imbalanced power

Rather than look to the number of great powers to explain the outbreak of war, some realists argue that the key explanatory variable is how much power each of them controls. Power can be distributed more or less evenly among the great powers. Although the power ratios among all the great powers affect the prospects for peace, the key ratio is that between the two most powerful countries in the system. If there is a lopsided gap, the number one state is a preponderant power, simply because it is so much more powerful than all the others.[1] However, if the gap between numbers one and two is small, there is said to be a rough balance of power, even though power might not be distributed equally among all the great powers. The key point is that there is no marked difference in power between the two leading states.

Some realists maintain that the presence of an especially powerful state facilitates peace. A preponderant power, so the argument goes, is likely to feel secure because it is so powerful relative to its competitors; therefore, it will have little need to use force to improve its position in the balance of power. Moreover, none of the other great powers is likely to pick a fight with the leading power, because they would almost certainly lose. However, war among the lesser great powers is still possible, because the balance of power between any two of them will at least sometimes be roughly equal, thus allowing for the possibility that one might defeat the other. But, even then, if the preponderant power believes that such wars might upset a favourable international order, it should have the wherewithal to stop them, or at least make them unusual events.

The historical case that proponents of this perspective emphasize is the period between Napoleon's defeat in 1815 and the outbreak of the First World War in 1914. There were only five wars between the great powers during these hundred years (1853–6, 1859, 1866, 1870–1, 1904–5), and none was a central war like the two conflicts that bracket the period. This lengthy period of relative peace—sometimes called the *Pax Britannica*—is said to be the consequence of Britain's commanding position in the international system. Conversely, the reason there were central wars before and after this period is that Napoleonic France and Imperial Germany, respectively, were roughly equal in power to Britain.

Other realists take the opposite view and argue that preponderance increases the chance of war. Indeed, central wars are likely when there is an especially powerful country in the system. A preponderant power, according to this perspective, is a potential hegemon. It has the wherewithal to make a run at dominating the system, which is the best guarantee of survival in international anarchy. Therefore, it will not be satisfied with the status quo, but instead will look for opportunities to gain hegemony. When there is rough equality among the great powers, no state can make a serious run at hegemony, ruling out deadly central wars. Great power wars are still possible, but the fact that power tends to be rather evenly distributed reduces the incentives for picking fights with other great powers.

Proponents of this viewpoint argue that the Napoleonic Wars were largely due to the fact that France was a potential hegemon by the late eighteenth century. The two world wars happened because Germany was twice in a position during the first half of the twentieth century to make a run at European hegemony. The long period of relative peace from 1815 to 1914 was not due to the *Pax Britannica*, because Britain was not a preponderant power. After all, no balancing coalition ever formed against Britain, which was hardly feared by Europe's continental powers. The reason there were lengthy periods of peace in Europe during these hundred years is that there was a rough balance of power in multipolar Europe. Unbalanced multipolarity, not balanced multipolarity, increases the risks of great power war.

Power shifts and war

Other realists maintain that focusing on static indicators like the number of great powers or how much power each controls is wrongheaded. They claim that instead the focus should be on the dynamics of the balance of power, especially on significant changes that take place in the distribution of power (Copeland 2000). Probably the best known argument in this school of thought is that a preponderant power confronted with a rising challenger creates an especially dangerous situation, because a central war usually results. The dominant state, knowing its days at the pinnacle of power are numbered, has strong incentives to launch a preventive war against the challenger to halt its rise. Of course, the declining state has to act while it still enjoys a decided power advantage over its growing rival. Some scholars argue that the rising power is likely to initiate the war in this scenario. But that makes little sense, because time is on the side of the ascending power, which does not need a war to catch up with and overtake the leading state.

The origins of the two world wars are said to illustrate this line of argument. Germany was the dominant power in Europe before both conflicts, but each time it faced a rising challenger to its east: Russia before 1914 and the Soviet Union before 1939. To forestall decline and maintain its commanding position in the European balance of power, Germany launched preventive wars in 1914 and 1939, both of which turned into devastating central wars.

The offence–defence balance

As noted, some defensive realists argue that there is an offence–defence balance which almost always favours the defence, and thus works to dampen security competition. As such, that balance is a force for peace. Some defensive realists, however, allow for significant variation in the balance between defence and offence, and argue that offensive advantage is likely to result in war, while defence dominance facilitates peace. For example, the Second World War occurred because the tank and the dive bomber, when incorporated into a blitzkrieg doctrine, markedly shifted the offence–defence balance in the offence's favour. On the other hand, there was no shooting war between the USA and the Soviet Union during the Cold War, because the coming of nuclear weapons sharply shifted the balance in the defence's favour.

In sum, a variety of structural arguments attempt to explain when great power war is more or less likely. Each has a different underlying causal logic and each looks at the historical record in a different way.

Case study: can China rise peacefully?

The Chinese economy has been growing at an impressive pace since the early 1980s, and many experts expect it to continue expanding at a similar rate over the next few decades. If so, China, with its huge population, will eventually have the wherewithal to build an especially formidable military. China is almost certain to become a military powerhouse, but what China will do with its military muscle, and how the USA and China's Asian neighbours will react to its rise, remain open questions.

There is no single structural realist answer to these questions. Some realist theories predict that China's ascent will lead to serious instability, while others provide reasons to think that a powerful China can have relatively peaceful relations with its neighbours as well as the USA. Let us consider some of these different perspectives, starting with offensive realism, which predicts that a rising China and the USA will engage in an intense security competition with considerable potential for war.

The rise of China according to offensive realism

The ultimate goal of the great powers, according to offensive realism, is to gain hegemony, because that is the best guarantor of survival. In practice, it is almost impossible for any country to achieve global hegemony, because it is too hard to project and sustain power around the planet and onto the territory of distant great powers. The best outcome that a state can hope for is to be a regional hegemon, which means dominating one's own geographical area. The USA's 'Founding Fathers' and their successors understood this basic logic and they worked assiduously to make the USA the dominant power in the western hemisphere. It finally achieved regional hegemony in 1898. While the USA has grown even more powerful since then, and is today the most powerful state in the system, it is not a global hegemon.

States that gain regional hegemony have a further aim: they seek to prevent great powers in other geographical regions from duplicating their feat. Regional hegemons do not want peer competitors.

Instead, they want to keep other regions divided among several major states, who will then compete with each other and not be in a position to focus on them. Thus, after achieving regional dominance, the USA has gone to great lengths to prevent other great powers from controlling Asia and Europe. There were four great powers in the twentieth century that had the capability to make a run at regional hegemony: Imperial Germany (1900–18), Imperial Japan (1931–45), Nazi Germany (1933–45), and the Soviet Union (1945–89). In each case, the USA played a key role in defeating and dismantling those aspiring hegemons. In short, the ideal situation for any great power is to be the only regional hegemon in the world.

If offensive realism is correct, we should expect a rising China to imitate the USA and attempt to become a regional hegemon in Asia. China will seek to maximize the power gap between itself and its neighbours, especially Japan and Russia. China will want to make sure that it is so powerful that no state in Asia has the wherewithal to threaten it. An increasingly powerful China is also likely to try to push US military forces out of Asia, in much the same way as the USA pushed the European great powers out of the western hemisphere in the nineteenth century. China can be expected to come up with its own version of the Monroe Doctrine.

From China's perspective, these policy goals make good strategic sense. Beijing should want a militarily weak Japan and Russia as its neighbours, just as the USA prefers a militarily weak Canada and Mexico on its borders. All Chinese remember what happened in the last century when Japan was powerful and China was weak. Furthermore, why would a powerful China accept US military forces operating in its backyard? US policy-makers, after all, become incensed when other great powers send their military forces into the western hemisphere. They are invariably seen as a potential threat to US security. The same logic should apply to China.

It is clear from the historical record how US policy-makers will react if China attempts to dominate Asia. The USA does not tolerate peer competitors, as it demonstrated in the twentieth century; it is determined to remain the only regional hegemon. Therefore, the USA will work hard to contain China and ultimately to weaken it to the point where it is no longer a threat to control the commanding heights in Asia. In essence, the USA is likely to behave towards China in much the same way as it behaved towards the Soviet Union during the Cold War.

China's neighbours are also sure to fear its rise, and they too will do whatever they can to prevent it from achieving regional hegemony. In fact, there is already evidence that countries like India, Japan, and Russia, as well as smaller powers like Singapore, South Korea, and Vietnam, are worried about China's ascendancy and are looking for ways to contain it. In the end, they will join a US-led balancing coalition to check China's rise, in much the same way as Britain, France, Germany, Italy, Japan, and even China, joined forces with the USA to contain the Soviet Union during the Cold War.

The rise of China according to defensive realism

In contrast to offensive realism, defensive realism offers a more optimistic story about China's rise. For sure, defensive realists recognize that the international system creates strong incentives for states to want additional increments of power to ensure their survival. A mighty China will be no exception; it will look for opportunities to shift the balance of power in its favour. Moreover, both the USA and China's neighbours will have to balance against China to keep it in check. Security competition will not disappear altogether from Asia as China grows more powerful. Defensive realists are not starry-eyed idealists.

Nevertheless, defensive realism provides reason to think that the security competition surrounding China's rise will not be intense, and that China should be able to coexist peacefully with both its neighbours and the USA. For starters, it does not make strategic sense for great powers to pursue hegemony, because their rivals will form a balancing coalition and thwart—maybe even crush—them. It is much smarter for China's leaders to act like Bismarck, who never tried to dominate Europe, but still made Germany great, rather than like Kaiser Wilhelm or Adolf Hitler, who both made a run at hegemony and led Germany to ruin. This is not to deny that China will attempt to gain power in Asia. But structure dictates that it will have limited aims; it will not be so foolish as to try to maximize its share of world power. A powerful China with a limited appetite should be reasonably easy to contain and to engage in cooperative endeavours.

(continued)

The presence of nuclear weapons is another cause for optimism. It is difficult for any great power to expand when confronted by other powers with nuclear weapons. India, Russia, and the USA all have nuclear arsenals, and Japan could quickly go nuclear if it felt threatened by China. These countries, which are likely to form the core of an anti-China balancing coalition, will not be easy for China to push around as long as they have nuclear weapons. In fact, China is likely to act cautiously towards them for fear of triggering a conflict that might escalate to the nuclear level. In short, nuclear weapons will be a force for peace if China continues its rise.

Finally, it is hard to see what China gains by conquering other Asian countries. China's economy has been growing at an impressive pace without foreign adventures, proving that conquest is unnecessary for accumulating great wealth. Moreover, if China starts conquering and occupying countries, it is likely to run into fierce resistance from the populations which fall under its control. The US experience in Iraq should be a warning to China that the benefits of expansion in the age of nationalism are outweighed by the costs.

Although these considerations indicate that China's rise should be relatively peaceful, defensive realists allow for the possibility that domestic political considerations might cause Beijing to act in strategically foolish ways. After all, they recognize that Imperial Germany, Imperial Japan, and Nazi Germany made ill-advised runs at hegemony. But they maintain that the behaviour of those great powers was motivated by domestic political pathologies, not sound strategic logic. While that may be true, it leaves open the possibility that China might follow a similar path, in which case its rise will not be peaceful.

There are other structural realist perspectives for assessing whether or not China's rise will be peaceful. If the world is unipolar, as some structural realists argue, then the growth of Chinese power will eventually put an end to unipolarity. When it does, the world will be a more dangerous place, since there cannot be war between great powers in unipolarity, while there certainly can be if both China and the USA are great powers. Furthermore, if Japan acquires nuclear weapons, Russia gets its house in order, and India continues its rise, there would be a handful of great powers in the system, which would further increase the potential for great power conflict.

Of course, one might argue that China's ascendancy will lead to bipolarity, which is a relatively peaceful architecture, even if it is not as pacific as unipolarity. After all, there was no shooting war between the superpowers during the Cold War. Indeed, the security competition between them was not especially intense after the Cuban Missile Crisis. It was more dangerous before then, mainly because the USA and the Soviet Union had to come to grips with the nuclear revolution and also learn the rules of the road for dealing with each other under bipolarity, which was then a new and unfamiliar structure. China and the USA, however, would have the benefit of all that learning that took place during the Cold War, and could deal with each other from the start much the way that Moscow and Washington dealt with each other after 1962.

Not all structural realists accept the argument that bipolarity is more prone to peace than multipolarity. For them, a return to bipolarity would be a cause for pessimism. However, if the rise of China were accompanied by the emergence of other great powers, the ensuing multipolarity would give these realists more cause for optimism.

Finally, for structural realists who believe that preponderance produces peace, the rise of China is ominous news. They argue that US power has had a pacifying effect on international politics. No other great power, and certainly no minor power, would dare pick a fight with the USA as long as it sits at the pinnacle of world power. But that situation would obviously change if China reached the point where it was almost as powerful as the USA. Preponderance would disappear, and without it the world would be a much more dangerous place. Indeed, these realists would argue that the USA would have strong incentives to launch a preventive war against China to forestall decline.

In sum, there is no consensus among structural realists about whether China can rise peacefully. This diversity of views is not surprising since these same realists disagree among themselves about how much power states should want as well as what causes war. The only important point of agreement among them is that the structure of the international system forces great powers to compete among themselves for power.

Conclusion

It was commonplace during the 1990s for pundits and scholars to proclaim that the world was rapidly becoming more peaceful and that realism was dead. International politics was said to have been transformed with the end of the Cold War. Globalization of the economic sort was supposedly tying the state in knots; some even predicted its imminent demise. Others argued that Western elites were for the first time thinking and talking about international politics in more cooperative and hopeful terms, and that the globalization of knowledge was facilitating the spread of that new approach.

Many argued that democracy was spreading across the globe and, because democracies do not fight each other, we had reached 'the end of history' (classical liberalism is discussed in **Chapter 5**). Still others claimed that international institutions were finally developing the capacity to cause the major powers to act according to the rule of law, not the dictates of realism.

In the wake of September 11, that optimism has faded, if not disappeared altogether, and realism has made a stunning comeback. Its resurrection is due in part to the fact that almost every realist opposed the Iraq War, which has turned into a strategic disaster for the USA and the UK. But, more importantly, there is little reason to think that globalization or international institutions have crippled the state. Indeed, the state appears to have a bright future, mainly because nationalism, which glorifies the state, remains a powerful political ideology. Even in Western Europe, where there has been unprecedented economic integration, the state is alive and well.

Furthermore, military power is still a critical element in world politics. The USA and the UK, the world's two great liberal democracies, have fought five wars together since the Cold War ended in 1989. Both Iran and North Korea remind us that nuclear proliferation remains a major problem, and it is not difficult to posit plausible scenarios where India and Pakistan end up in a shooting war that involves nuclear weapons. It is also possible, although not likely, that China and the USA could get dragged into a war over Taiwan, or even North Korea. Regarding China's rise, even the optimists acknowledge that there is potential for serious trouble if the politics surrounding that profound shift in global power are handled badly.

In essence, the world remains a dangerous place, although the level of threat varies from place to place and time to time. States still worry about their survival, which means that they have little choice but to pay attention to the balance of power. International politics is still synonymous with power politics, as it has been for all of recorded history. Therefore, it behoves students of IR to think long and hard about the concept of power, and to develop their own views on why states pursue power, how much power is enough, and when security competition is likely to lead to war. Thinking smartly about these matters is essential for developing clever strategies, which is the only way states can mitigate the dangers of international anarchy.

 Questions

1. Why do states in international anarchy fear each other?
2. Is there a reliable way to determine the intentions of states?
3. Is China's rise likely to look like Germany's rise between 1900 and 1945?
4. Does it make sense for states to pursue hegemony?
5. Why was the Cold War not a hot war?

6. Does it make sense to assume that states are rational?

7. Is balancing a reliable deterrent against aggressive states?

8. What is the security dilemma and is there a solution to it?

9. Is the USA a global hegemon?

10. Is unipolarity more peaceful than bipolarity or multipolarity?

11. Is realism relevant in contemporary Europe?

12. What is the tragedy of great power politics?

 ## Further reading

Brown, M. E., Coté Jr, O. R., Lynn-Jones, S. M., and Miller, S. E. (2004) (eds), *Offense, Defense, and War* **(Cambridge, MA: MIT Press).**
Contains key articles by structural realists, including Robert Jervis's seminal article, 'Cooperation under the Security Dilemma', *World Politics*, 1978.

Copeland, D. C. (2000), *The Origins of Major War* **(Ithaca, NY: Cornell University Press).**
Sophisticated brief for the claim that major wars are caused by sharp changes in the balance of power.

Dickinson, G. L. (1916), *The European Anarchy* **(New York: Macmillan Company).**
Short, but brilliant book which introduced the concept of international anarchy.

Dunne, T. and Schmidt, B. (2004), 'Realism', in J. Baylis and S. Smith (eds), *The Globalization of World Politics*, **3rd edn (Oxford: Oxford University Press).**
An accessible chapter which charts the major debates within and about realism.

Glaser, C.L. (2010), *Rational Theory of International Politics: The Logic of Competition and Cooperation* **(Princeton, NJ: Princeton University Press).**
A thorough explication of defensive realism that treats it largely as a normative theory.

Mearsheimer, J. J. (2001), *The Tragedy of Great Power Politics* **(New York: Norton).**
The most comprehensive statement of offensive realism.

Posen, B. R. (1984), *The Sources of Military Doctrine* **(Ithaca, NY: Cornell University Press).**
A smart book that sets out the limits of structural realism for explaining military doctrine.

Schmidt, B. C. (1988), *The Political Discourse of Anarchy* **(Albany: State University of New York Press).**
A history of the early years of the discipline of International Relations which shows the dominance of realism.

Snyder, J. (1991), *Myths of Empire: Domestic Politics and the International Ambition* **(Ithaca, NY: Cornell University Press).**
Excellent case studies on how the great powers behaved in the twentieth century from a defensive realist perspective.

Van Evera, S. (1999), *Causes of War: Power and the Roots of Conflict* **(Ithaca, NY: Cornell University Press).**
An important study which argues that the offence–defence balance explains much of international history.

Walt, S. M. (1987), *The Origins of Alliances* **(Ithaca, NY: Cornell University Press).**
Influential work on the prevalence of balancing behaviour in international politics.

Waltz, K. N. (1979), *Theory of International Politics* **(Reading MA: Addison-Wesley).**
Seminal book that lays out the fundamentals of structural realism but with a defensive realist bent.

 ## Important websites

Interviews with Robert Jervis, John Mearsheimer, Stephen Walt, and Kenneth Waltz
http://globetrotter.berkeley.edu/conversations/alpha.html

Introduction to realism www.geocities.com/virtualwarcollege/ir_realism.htm

Coalition for a Realistic Foreign Policy attempts to push US foreign policy in a realist direction
www.realisticforeignpolicy.org/

 ## Note

1. The presence of a preponderant power is not the same as unipolarity, because a preponderant power is not the only great power in the system. In unipolarity, there is a single great power.

 Visit the Online Resource Centre that accompanies this book for lots of interesting additional material. www.oxfordtextbooks.co.uk/orc/dunne3e/

5 Liberalism

BRUCE RUSSETT

Reader's Guide

The most important transformation in world politics over the past sixty years derives from the concurrent and interlinked expansion of three key phenomena associated with liberalism and its emphasis on the potentially peace-promoting effects of domestic and transnational institutions. One is the spread of democracy throughout most of the world. A second is the multiple networks of communications, trade, and finance often summarized as globalization. The third is the multiplication of inter-governmental organizations, especially those composed primarily of democratic governments. Each of these supports and extends the other in a powerful feedback system envisioned by Immanuel Kant. Moreover, each creates a set of norms and interests which dramatically reduce the risk of violent conflict among the countries so linked. Contemporary Europe constitutes the prime example of these processes at work, but they are not limited to Europe or to developed economies.

Introduction

The world is full of testimony to tragedy. Governments oppress their own people and commit aggression against their neighbours. World politics is conducted in a condition of anarchy as that term was used by the Greeks: not chaos, but 'without a ruler', having no overarching authority to enforce order. There is some order, but on a globe far from ready for world government, most order is not something imposed from above.

Realists say that every country is potentially an enemy of every other—intentionally or not, a threat to their security and very existence. In the absence of a world state they are caught forever in this precarious condition of freedom and risk. This tradition, like the anarchy that underlies it, has a history from Thucydides, Niccolo Machiavelli, and Thomas

Hobbes, and shapes the perspective of many policy-makers. Yet there are restraints on the use of force. States do not fight all others even when purely realist principles dominate; they are constrained by geography, the coincidence of national interests expressed in alliances, and the balance of power. Deterrence forms the heart of survival, but deterrence—and especially nuclear deterrence—is an uncertain and dangerous way of avoiding war. Treating all international politics as unending struggle, and everyone as a potential enemy, risks becoming a self-fulfilling prophecy.

A competing perspective deserves equal attention. This perspective, sometimes labelled liberal-institutionalist, is associated with classical analysts like John Locke, Hugo Grotius, and Immanuel Kant. Kant proposed that 'republican constitutions', commercial exchange embodied in 'cosmopolitan law', and a system of international law among republics governed domestically by the rule of law would provide the basis for sustained peace. The alternative would be the peace of 'a vast grave where all the horrors of violence and those responsible for them would be buried' (Kant [1795] 1970). Peace was not simply an ideal to Kant. He believed that natural processes of self-interest could impel rational individuals to act as agents to bring a just peace. He was also realistic in acknowledging that nations must act prudently until a 'federation' of interdependent republics is established.

Key 'liberal' assumptions in Kant's framework include the belief in the rational qualities of individuals, faith in the feasibility of progress in social life, and the conviction that humans, despite their self-interest, are able to cooperate and construct a more peaceful and harmonious society. Liberal internationalism arising from Kant has transposed these beliefs to the international sphere by emphasizing the fact that war and conflict can be overcome, or mitigated, through concerted changes in both the domestic and international structures of governance.

The Kantian perspective has frequently been characterized as antithetical to realism. That is an error. Kant accepted Hobbes's description of conflict among many of the nations, but went far beyond it. The pacific federation he envisioned is more accurately a confederation, and not a world state. Its members remain sovereign, linked only by partially federal institutions as in Europe today, or by collective security alliances. The difference between the two traditions is that Kant sees democratic government, economic interdependence, and international law and organizations as means to overcome the security dilemma of the international system.

Kant contended that the three elements of his pacific federation would strengthen over time to produce a more peaceful world. Individuals desire to be free and prosperous, so democracy and trade will expand, which leads naturally to the growth of international law and organization to facilitate these processes. He held that peace among republican states does not depend upon a moral transformation of humanity if even devils understand how to promote their own interests in cooperation. Kant was an empiricist who taught anthropology and geography; he drew on the history of his native Königsberg—once a member of the Hanseatic League of trading states in northern Europe. He knew that the achievement of durable peace is not mechanical, nor is the outcome determined. Human agents must learn from their own and others' experience, including the experience of war.

Featured book

Michael Doyle (1997), *Ways of War and Peace* (New York: N.N. Norton).

In *Ways of War and Peace* Michael Doyle traces the development of IR theory starting with Thucydides on the Peloponnesian War nearly 2,500 years ago. Doyle was one of the first IR theorists in the modern era to advance the Kantian idea of a liberal peace. In this illustrative text, Doyle not only provides a detailed account of classical liberal thought, he shows how it developed alongside two historical alternatives—that of realism and Marxism.

Classical realists such as Thucydides were aware of the primacy of power politics. As he argued in The History of the Peloponnesian Wars, it was the growth of Athenian power, and the fear this aroused in the Spartans, that led to war between the two most powerful Greek city states. This classic realist statement focuses on the inherent vulnerability of independent states in any anarchic system. Yet it is not just a statement about shifting power balances, it is also about agency: how individual leaders interpret the shifts and choose the actions they take to protect their security. Personality and domestic politics are part of his story. Statesmanship requires good judgement, and morality resides in a commitment to the safety of one's own people. Hobbes, writing in seventeenth-century England after a vicious civil war, emphasized the need for a powerful leader to enforce order so as to protect his rule at home and his ability to defend his state in the anarchic international system. Nearly all states then had such powerful leaders, or if not suffered from their absence.

Subsequent realist theorists, such as Jean-Jacques Rousseau in 1756, experienced more variation in how states were governed, and thought carefully about how democracy, revolution, and cultural differences might affect the ability of states to survive internationally. Kant in part built on this view, developing it much more fully in his concern with republican government and commercial relations. Kant's difference was in his strong rationalist view that leaders could perceive and even create a different system of rules and incentives for cooperation by which, in their own self-interest, they might be able to tame the threats inherent in international anarchy. By the twentieth century, Marxist thinkers like Lenin developed a sharply different view. They held that economic imperatives would create states controlled by monopolistic commercial interests, whose states would inevitably fight bitterly as they sought ever-expanding markets abroad. Joseph Schumpeter, by contrast, believed that industrialization would produce more democratic leaders and that rising international commerce would tame militaristic imperialism.

Doyle makes us aware of how classical accounts of realism, liberalism, and Marxism developed in the minds of important theorists and activists in the context of very different political and economic conditions. The legacy of these competing schools of thought, along with changing global economic and political realities, continues to shape contemporary theory and policy concerned with our own and others' interests.

Four big changes in the world

As background for the following discussion three graphics show key changes in the world over the past century and especially over recent decades. The first illustrates the long-run decline in battle deaths from violent conflicts in which one or more states were participants. It includes battle deaths from interstate wars, intrastate (civil) wars, internationalized interstate wars (like Afghanistan and Iraq in this century), and wars of colonial liberation. There was a peak of violence immediately after the Second World War, and then three progressively lower mountains. (Battle deaths during the Second World War years were on average ten times greater than in the 1951 postwar peak.) The trend since late in the Cold War (ending roughly 1989) has been lower in all types of wars. It is essential to keep a longer perspective to understand that the most recent decline is not just a temporary downward spike. In fact, deadly violence has been declining sharply over many centuries.[1]

The big drop in world conflict was not easily recognized. Conflict always draws media attention. While the graph in Figure 5.1 does not include incidents in which terrorists go abroad to strike targets associated with a foreign state, only about 4,000 people died from such acts in all of 200–8—less than 2 per cent of the battle deaths from wars in same period (www.systemic peace.org/conflict.htm Figure 5, accessed 21 December, 2011). Even a big terrorist attack with weapons of mass destruction could not approach the level of death and destruction had there been a Cold War nuclear exchange.

No single cause can account for the decline in global conflict deaths. However, this chapter makes a case that major contributions to that decline in destruction have been three great advances associated with liberalism in the post-Second World War era, and especially since the end of the Cold War. Two more graphs illustrate these trends.

Figure 5.2 shows the drastic decline in the number of autocracies (dictatorships) in the world, and the even greater increase in the number of democracies as defined by the degree of free political competition permitted by their institutions. (The dotted line is for 'anocracies', a category between the extremes.) By 2006, and for the first time in history, half the countries in the world were governed democratically.

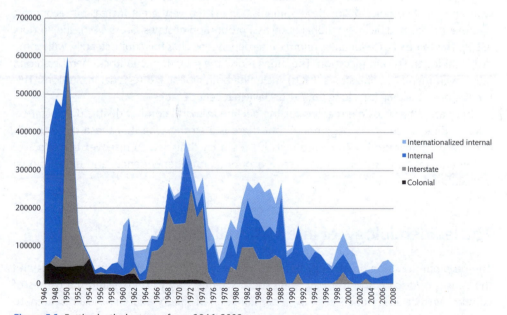

Figure 5.1 Battle-deaths by type of war, 1946–2008

Source: B. Lacina and N. P. Gleditsch dataset, UCDP/Human Security Report Project dataset.

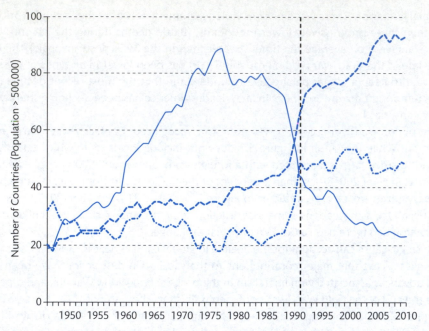

Figure 5.2 Global changes in political system types, 1950–2010

Source: M. Marshall and B. Cole, Global Report 2011: Conflict, Governance, and State Fragility, p. 10, http://www.systemicpeace.org/GlobalReport2011.pdf

Figure 5.3 plots the percentage increase in the number of democracies since 1950, along with lines for two other major developments. One is the very great increase in economic openness, measured by international trade as a proportion of states' Gross Domestic Product (GDP). This trend of widespread economic interdependence has built quite steadily, with some drops during the recent recession. The other shows the growth in countries' membership in intergovernmental organizations (IGOs), including both global and regional institutions. This too has been building for a long time, especially in recent decades.

There are other possible reasons for the decline in world combat deaths (for instance, nuclear deterrence or US hegemony), but there is a strong case that these three trends deserve particular credit. That case rests on research designed to discover the effect of key liberal Kantian variables—democracy, economic interdependence, and international institutions—on peace.

The 'epidemiology' of international conflict

The research draws on an analogy between the way medical scientists try to understand the causes of disease and the way some social scientists try to understand the causes of conflict. Medical researchers seek, by a combination of theory and empirical research, to identify conditions that promote or prevent fatal diseases. Much of their research is *epidemiological* in character. They look at the distribution of particular diseases in large

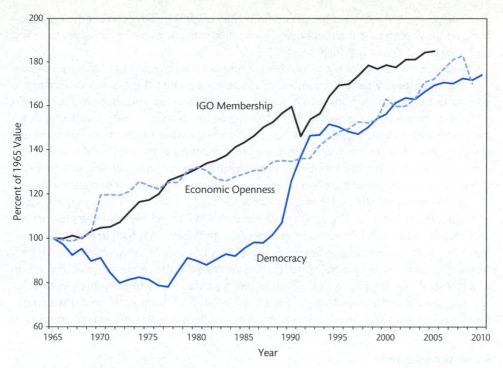

Figure 5.3 Growth of liberal influences since 1950

Sources: Government type: M. Marshall and B. Cole, Global Report 2011: Conflict, Governance, and State Fragility, Figure 12. http://www.systemicpeace.org/GlobalReport2011.pdf Trade: http://pwt.econ.upenn.edu/php_site/pwt_index.php IGOs: http://www.correlatesofwar.org/COW2%20Data/IGOs/IGOv2.3.htm

populations to discover why some individuals contract a disease while many others do not. Huge databases—about who dies where and when of various diseases, and about the life experience of those individuals—help researchers to uncover the causes, and to advise on prevention or treatment.

An epidemiological study of the causes of heart disease might show that smokers run a much higher risk of heart attack than non-smokers. So too do those who consume a diet high in saturated fats, or who engage in little physical exercise. No single risk factor is a perfect predictor. Many people who do not smoke have heart attacks. Many smokers live a long time without a heart attack. The predictions are probabilistic, about greater and lesser risks. Each influence operates somewhat independently of the others. That is, smoking increases the risk of a heart attack regardless of diet. So a doctor might say, 'Based on your age, sex, family history, and lifestyle, statistically you run a 4 per cent risk of having a heart attack in the next year. You can't totally eliminate that risk, but if you quit smoking (or go on a diet, or get off the couch) you can cut it in half. And if you quit smoking, go on a diet, *and* get off the couch—you can cut the risk by three-quarters.' Similar conclusions can be derived by analysing countries' behaviour in war and peace.

The following analysis uses an information base on international relations, analogous to the life histories of individuals. It consists of data on relations between virtually all countries in the world in each year over the period from 1885 to 2001. It can consider the expansion of democracy, economic interdependence, and international organizations over time and their effects in different historical periods.[2]

Countries can in principle fight any other country, but they typically fight only a few, so the data are organized by pairs of countries, or *dyads*. For example, it looks not at Germany in general, but rather its relations with Austria, Italy, Japan, Sweden, and so forth. It asks which kinds of dyads are prone to conflict and which are apt to remain at peace. Looking at dyads over more than a century gives nearly half a million cases, where a case is the experience of one *pair of countries in one year*. From them one can compute the likelihood that a pair of countries sharing a certain constraint on conflict (such as a common alliance, or both being democracies) experienced the onset of a serious militarized dispute in a particular year.

The analysis uses information compiled independently by many scholars and organizations, from standardized sources. The conflict data include all militarized interstate disputes, not just wars. Wars are (fortunately) rare events and, as with rare diseases, it is hard to find general patterns for where and why they erupt. Including all uses of violence between countries gives a better chance of finding general patterns. Here we consider the results for *fatal* disputes, in which at least one combatant died. These incidents are far more common than wars. Other analyses show that the constraints on war do not differ much from those on militarized disputes. The influences, and their measures, include the following realist and Kantian constraints.

Realist constraints

Power ratio

One way to reduce the likelihood of going to war is to deter it by military strength. Most deterrence theorists argue that conflict is best prevented by a great predominance of power for one side. When power is unbalanced the outcome of conflict is usually predictable, and the weaker side generally will not fight because it knows it will lose. In Thucydides' words, 'the strong do as they will and the weak do as they must'. To assess the effect of power on the likelihood of conflict, we use information about states' material capabilities—economic, demographic, and military. Together they tap a combination of elements that can be used immediately for military purposes (soldiers and expenditures) and longer-term military potential that matters in a protracted conflict. It is a reasonable measure of power over a century-long period. The power ratio is the stronger state's capability index divided by that of the weaker member.

Allies

Allies share important strategic and security interests. If they have military disputes among themselves, they risk weakening their common front against a country each perceives as an enemy. During the Cold War, NATO allies (save for Greece and Turkey) did not fight each other.

Distance and size

Two other realist influences are distance and size. Distance makes it harder and more costly to exert military power. Neighbours can readily fight, and are more likely to have competing interests for territory, control of natural resources, or common ethnic groups that may provoke conflict. Great powers typically have strong military forces able to exercise force at a distance, and wide-ranging—even global—interests to fight for.

Kantian constraints

Liberal institutionalists, however, insist that the realist perspective does not exhaust the list of constraints on war over which states can and do exercise some control. States do not fight all others at all times and places where the realist constraints are weak. To the realist influences we add the three Kantian influences: that democracies will refrain from using force against other democracies; that economically important trade creates incentives to maintain peaceful relations; and that international organizations can constrain decision-makers by positively promoting peace.

Democracy

The first Kantian influence suggests that democracies will rarely fight or even threaten each other. Democracies may also be more peaceful with all kinds of states. Many studies support the first proposition. But the claim that democracies are more peaceful in general is much more controversial. Two plausible explanations for why democracies at least do not fight each other are as follows:

One explanation is about norms. Democracies operate internally on the principle that conflicts are to be resolved peacefully by negotiation and compromise, without resort to the threat or use of organized violence. Democratic peoples and their leaders recognize other democracies as operating under the same principles in their internal relations, and so extend to them the principle of peaceful conflict resolution. Negotiation and compromise between democratic states are expected, and the threat of violence is both unnecessary and illegitimate. Dictatorships, by contrast, are expected to operate more on Hobbesian principles, making threats, taking advantage of weak resolve, and using force. Thus dictatorships in their relations with other dictatorships, or with democracies, will not be subject to the same restraints.

The other explanation is about institutions. Democratic leaders who fight a war are held responsible, through democratic institutions, for the costs and benefits of the war. The costs often outweigh the benefits, and many of the costs are borne by the general public. Democratic leaders who start wars risk being voted out of office—especially if they lose, or the war is long or costly. In anticipating this political judgement, democratic leaders will be reluctant to fight wars, especially wars they are likely to lose. When facing another democracy, both sets of leaders will be restrained. Dictators, however, are better able to repress opposition and to stay in power after a war. By repression they can keep more of the benefits and impose more of the costs on their peoples than can democratic leaders. So they may be less hesitant to fight anyone, either a democracy or another dictatorship.

It is likely that both explanations operate, depending on the circumstances. In our database, the measure of democracy incorporates several restraints on government, notably institutions and procedures through which citizens can express their preferences in truly competitive elections, and institutional constraints on the exercise of executive power. No democracy is perfect, nor are even the most totalitarian governments totally without restraints on arbitrary rule. Many states combine some mixture of authoritarian and democratic features. So we use information from the source cited in Figure 5.2, which ranks each country on a full scale of −10 to +10. An international conflict can result from the actions of either state. Nonetheless, the likelihood of conflict depends primarily on how undemocratic the less democratic state is. The greatest risk is between a dictatorship and a democracy, and the least between two highly democratic states.

International trade

Commercial interaction has a solid place among parents of the liberal tradition, as well as in Kant. Sustained commercial interaction becomes a medium of communication whereby information about needs and preferences are exchanged, across a broad range of matters ranging well beyond the specific commercial exchange. This may result in greater mutual understanding, empathy, and mutual identity across boundaries. A complementary view stresses the self-interests of rational actors. Trade depends on expectations of peace with the trading partner. Violent conflict endangers access to markets, imports, and capital. It may not make trade between disputing states impossible, but it certainly raises the risks and costs.

The larger the contribution of trade between two countries to their national economies, the stronger the political base that has an interest in preserving peaceful relations between them. We measure the importance of trade for each state in a dyad as the sum of its imports from and exports to the other state, divided by its GDP. A given volume of trade will exert greater economic and political impact on a small country than on a big one. Similar effects can be expected from international investments.

International organizations

IGOs include both almost-universal organizations like the United Nations (UN) or the International Monetary Fund (IMF), and those focused on particular types of countries or regions. They may be multi-purpose, or 'functional' agencies directed to specific goals like military security, promoting international commerce and investment, health, environmental concerns, or human rights. The means by which they may promote peace also vary greatly, on a range that may include separating or coercing norm-breakers (UN peacekeeping is an example), mediating among conflicting parties, reducing uncertainty by providing information, expanding members' material interest to be more inclusive and longer-term, shaping norms, and generating narratives of mutual identification. IGOs vary widely in effectiveness.

The network of international organizations is spread very unevenly across the globe. Some dyads in Europe share membership in over a hundred IGOs; other dyads share few or even none (e.g. the USA and China during much of the Cold War). Our measure is the number of IGOs to which both states in the dyad belong. This crude index equates all types and strengths of IGOs in a simple count. Using such a crude measure is likely to underestimate the conflict-reducing effect of IGOs. Later we consider a more refined measure, taking into account the kind of countries which constitute IGOs' membership. Other refinements could consider the degree to which IGOs built strong institutions, or their different purposes.

Almost all of these influences are measured on scales. They propose, for example, that the more trade or democracy between countries the less chance they will fight each other. So these are probabilistic statements, not absolute or deterministic laws; for example, that democratic countries will never fight each other. International relations are not so simple.

Analysing the global experience of a century

To uncover the relative importance of these various influences on the risk of interstate conflict we use a statistical technique like that employed by epidemiologists. It estimates the independent effect of a change in any one variable while holding the effect of all other variables constant. Analyses must minimize the danger of wrongly imputing causation. For example, trade may promote peace, but also peace may enhance trade. So one must get the sequencing right. Statistical methods cannot *prove* causation, but theory helps strengthen causal inference. After more than a decade of vigorous debate, many social scientists of international relations generally accept the results given here.

Table 5.1 shows how much lower the risk of a fatal militarized dispute would be if the two countries were allied, or if both were both democratic, and so forth. It gives the percentage change in the risk associated with a change in each variable that might be affected by political action. (It controls for the effects of the 'background' influences—geographical proximity and size—but does not show them because they are not readily affected by policy.) The percentages show the effect of changing the value of each separate influence, from what it would be if the dyad were at the average level for all states to the ninetieth percentile for that influence. This shows the relative impact of each one individually. Finally we see the effect if all the Kantian influences were together at the ninetieth percentile. The changes shown here should not be taken as precise, but they do approximate those of other research. The average annual risk of a fatal dispute is about 6 in 1,000, meaning that most dyads avoid fatal disputes most of the time. But the risk varies substantially depending upon both realist and Kantian factors.

Unequal power generally does deter weak states from challenging strong ones. If the power of the stronger state is increased from a near-even balance to the ninetieth percentile

Table 5.1 Percentage change in risk that a pair of countries will experience the onset of a fatal militarized dispute in any one year, 1886–2001

Keep all influences at mean or median values except	Percentage change
Make the countries Allied	−09
Increase Power Ratio to the 90th percentile	−61
Increase both Democracy scores to the 90th percentile	−43
Increase higher Democracy score to 90th percentile, and decrease lower Democracy score to 10th percentile	+197
Increase Trade/GDP to the 90th percentile	−56
Increase number of IGO memberships to the 90th percentile	−31
Increase Democracy, Trade, and IGOs together	−83

of imbalance, the chance of a militarized dispute emerging is cut by 61 per cent. But that demands a forty-fold growth in relative power. Since our measures include such basic determinants of power as population and industrial capacity, that big an increase is really unattainable for any nation. Alliance, the other realist influence, has little effect (9 per cent) in reducing the risk of a fatal dispute.[3]

Although a Kantian perspective does not contest the influence of power, it predicts relationships that realist theory does not predict, and these predictions are confirmed. If both states are in the ninetieth percentile on the democracy scale rather at the average level, the risk of fatal violence conflict is much lower, by 43 per cent. Disputes between very authoritarian states (both in the tenth percentile) are much more common: an increase of 39 per cent from the average level. Conflicts are, by far, most likely if one state is in the ninetieth percentile and the other in the tenth one: a risk increase of almost 200 per cent.[4] Economic interdependence also has a very strong effect. If both states are in the 90th percentile of trade dependence rather than in the middle, the chance of violent conflict goes down by more than half. In this analysis the effect of IGOs appears somewhat weaker, but still reduces risk by nearly a third when both states are in the ninetieth percentile. When all three influences operate together, they reduce the risk of a fatal dispute by 83 per cent. This is strong support for Kant's liberal propositions.

We also tested whether Huntington's (1996) famous 'clash of civilizations' thesis made a difference. Using his categorization of eight civilizations, we asked if dyads of countries from different civilizations were more likely to get into disputes than were those from the same civilization. The answer was no if the realist and Kantian influences were included—they did all the explanatory work; and differences in civilizations added nothing more. The same answer emerged when we asked whether disputes were especially likely between Islamic and Christian countries. The answer was no, both during the Cold War years and the following years up through 2001. The clash of civilizations could become a self-fulfilling prophecy, but it has not yet done so.

The benefits of the Kantian variables are not just phenomena of the bipolar nuclear era of democratic capitalist states against their communist rivals. Similar relationships existed in the pre-Cold War era, both before the First World War and in the interwar years. Furthermore, they continued to operate in the post-Cold War era after 1989.

Are democracies peaceful in general?

A dyadic perspective, however, does not tell us whether democracies, or even fully Kantian states, maintain more peaceful relations with all other states. In a world of countries with very different political and economic systems, they may still come into conflict with some of them. In fact, any statement that democracies are especially peaceful monadically (more peaceful in general) must be carefully qualified. A sweeping claim that democracies are peaceful in general ignores the dangers democracies face in the realm of power politics in an incompletely Kantian world. The dyadic claim by definition includes both the dynamics of domestic political interactions between leader and potential opposition, and the interactions between two independent states. The monadic claim completely ignores the latter.

One important refinement of the simple relationship arises as follows. Suppose that democratic states comprise only a small minority of states in the entire system. That was true of the nineteenth and twentieth centuries until after the end of the Cold War. Add to that some evidence that the most peaceful dyads are democracies with each other, with autocratic dyads being more conflict prone, and mixed dyads (democracies–autocracies) even more so. The combination of many mixed dyads in such a system and greatest hostility being between mixed dyads means that the average difference in total conflict involvement by democracies and autocracies may appear slight. Perhaps we might see a stronger monadic effect in a system where democracies are a strong majority. We do know that geographical neighbourhoods in which democracy is the predominant form of government are especially peaceful (Gleditsch 2002).

Another big qualification concerns which side starts or escalates the fight, raising a largely peaceful diplomatic dispute up to a militarized one, or a low-level militarized dispute to full-scale war. Here the evidence is stronger: even when democracies are involved in diplomatic disputes with dictatorships they are less likely than the dictators to initiate the use of violence and less likely to escalate any violence to a high level (Huth and Allee 2002). Thus the dictator's action tends to produce the fight. Sometimes, however, great powers—even democratic ones—may take 'preventive' military action to defeat potential challengers before they become big threats.

All great powers are war-prone. Their power and interests may draw them into fights far from home. They must rely on their own power to protect themselves. Small or weak states, however, can contribute little to the chance that a strong state will win a war. Thus small states have a great incentive to free-ride on a big ally's military efforts. A big state, by contrast, can make all the difference for the survival of a weak one.

Moreover, great powers are less constrained by trade and IGOs. Mutual trade in a dyad constrains the political system of the bigger state less than that of the smaller one, since that trade represents a lower percentage of its GDP. For example, US–Guatemalan trade is a 500 times larger share of Guatemala's GDP than it is of the US economy. Also, great powers depend less on regional or functional IGOs for their security than do many mid-sized and smaller states. So the difference in total conflict involvement between democratic and autocratic great powers may be small. Just five countries—the USA, the UK, France, plus regional powers India and Israel—account for nearly 80 per cent of the violent conflicts by democracies. A similar pattern emerges for dictatorships, with the Soviet Union and China at the high end.

Finally, democratic political systems vary greatly in how, and how effectively, they can restrain their leaders. Nor should one forget the influence of particular leaders' personalities and perspectives, such as a 'we-versus-them' attitude or a belief that peace is served by forcibly transforming other states' regimes. Untangling this complex interplay of influences is necessary to comprehend why a monadic **democratic peace** may be hard to identify in a world that still contains many autocracies.

A self-perpetuating system?

This is only part of the Kantian perspective on world politics, which is about an interdependent system of influences, which are seen to exist in a series of 'feedback loops' with each of the major forces strengthening the other. This understanding is expressed in Figure 5.4. The

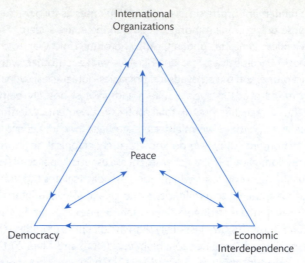

Figure 5.4 The Kantian Triangle

relationships discussed so far are represented by the arrows running from each of the apexes of the triangle toward the centre, directly promoting peace. Reverse arrows run back from the centre. Each represents a relationship that is supported by theory and some evidence. Democracy is easier to sustain in a peaceful environment. States in conflict with other states restrict information about government activities and limit public criticism, but states at peace need fewer restraints on democracy. Trade and peace are reciprocally related. Traders are reluctant to trade with, or invest in, countries with which political relations may be disrupted at any time. While many IGOs are created to reduce or manage tensions between adversaries, most IGOs depend on peaceful relations among their members to be effective, and are most often formed when peace seems probable.

   The arrows around the sides are also important. Along the base of the triangle, democracies trade more with each other, knowing that trade agreements are more likely to be kept, and foreign property rights respected, under a stable rule of law. In turn, trade typically promotes mutual prosperity, which contributes to the development and stability of democracy. Along the right side of the triangle, open trading systems require institutions and rules to make government and commercial actions predictable. In turn, the institutions encourage commerce by helping to lower barriers and resolving conflicts of interest.

   The two arrows on the left indicate not only that democracies join and utilize international organizations, but that IGOs are increasingly involved in promoting democracy. Some of this activity is carried out by global organizations, notably the UN. Much more is done by regional organizations like the European Union, the Organization for Security and Cooperation in Europe, and the Organization of American States. These regional organizations are especially important because they are composed mostly of democracies. They possess a range of powerful carrots and sticks to attract new member states who want to become democratic, and to support member democratic governments against overthrow from within. IGOs composed mostly of democracies are also especially effective in maintaining peace among their members—even with whatever non-democratic governments may be within the organization. They help to mediate conflicts, help governments make credible commitments to peace and democracy (by being able to apply sanctions against governments that would break their commitments), and socialize elites to norms of democratic practice and peace. At least half of the peace-promoting influence of all IGOs identified earlier can be attributed to the regional IGOs composed mostly of democracies. And they have an indirect impact on peace by promoting democracy—first down the left side of the triangle, and then from the democratic corner into the centre (Pevehouse 2005; Pevehouse and Russett 2006).

Over the past sixty years this full set of influences has become an increasingly broad, deep, and stable set of relationships among many countries. It is most evident among the members of the European Union (EU). The case study gives more detail. Yet it is not limited to the EU, encompassing also nearly all economically advanced democracies and many poorer democracies (most institutionalized in Latin America). Democracy cannot be created as rapidly in the Middle East as it was in Europe, Latin America, and parts of Asia with some democratic experience. Governing elites vigorously resisted the Arab Spring of 2011. Given the depth and endurance of Middle East conflicts, it is too much to expect new democracies there to be inherently peaceful, especially with Israel. But in the long run the peace and prosperity of the Kantian community can peaceably attract new governments and peoples.

That does not mean it will inevitably include all states in the system, or that the process cannot be reversed. A severe economic shock, like a global depression, could reverse its momentum. The immediate effect would be felt in trade and finance, which, magnified by a rise in protectionist policies, would sharply weaken economic restraints on international conflict. International organizations would find it harder to defend free trade, and democratic governments could fall—as they did during the depression of the 1930s. All this could lead to greater international conflict and war, continued deterioration in economic conditions and **international institutions**, and a feedback reversal of the world's hard-won gains. An economic downturn could also be started by a major war or really massive terrorist attacks. Nonetheless, the system now has a great deal of institutional and normative resistance built into it.

The continuity and stability in this system suggests another way to think about how these restraints work—by changes in the international system as a whole. Global increases in the average level of democracy, interdependence, and IGO involvement represent not just what is happening to pairs of states that share those characteristics, but to the dominant norms and institutions of the whole system. States at the low end on these characteristics may be peacefully induced, by threats or rewards, to observe international norms. Even dictatorships can find it in their interest to do so. (Libya's renunciation of nuclear weapons in 2003 was achieved by negotiation rather than by military action.)

The world is not as Hobbesian as in previous eras. It was once common for aggressors simply to eliminate states. Twenty-two internationally recognized states were forcibly occupied or absorbed during the first half of the twentieth century, but no state has permanently lost its sovereignty through external conquest since the Second World War. Democracies with democratic neighbours feel less threatened. When democracies fight dictatorships they usually fight well—winning nearly 80 per cent of all their wars, and more than 90 per cent of those they choose to start (Reiter and Stam 2002).[5] So as the proportion of democracies in the international system grows, autocracies must be more concerned about weakening themselves in war. If most great powers become democratic, peace among them would reduce the incentive for wars with non-democratic states across great power spheres of influence. If international norms and institutions for resolving disputes grow, even non-liberal states may be impelled to use regional or international organizations to help settle their disputes rather than accept the political and economic costs the liberal community could impose on them for using force.

Case study: the European Union

Sometimes a vicious circle of conflict and violence can be broken by deliberate policy. The most prominent reversal occurred in Western Europe after the Second World War. With tens of millions dead, their economies in shambles, and cities in ashes, the new European leaders, including Konrad Adenauer, Alcide de Gasperi, Jean Monnet, and Robert Schuman, decided to break the old pattern. Informed by a set of classical liberal insights, they set up an intricate system of mutually reinforcing political, economic, and social elements, creating a set of virtuous circles to promote peace.

Democracy

They believed that the breakdown of democracy had played a key role in destroying peace. The Second World War could readily be blamed on authoritarian or totalitarian states, especially Germany, Japan, and Italy. So the initial task was to establish stable democratic institutions and to root out old nationalist and authoritarian ideologies. In this they were aided by the total defeat and discrediting of the old leaders (some of whom were executed for war crimes) and by institutional changes put in place by the allied occupation of Western Germany.

Economic integration

Dictatorships had arisen largely because of the breakdown of the world economy in the 1930s and the Great Depression. Governments tried to protect their citizens' income by the competitive imposition of tariffs and other trade barriers. They preferred to preserve jobs at home rather than to import goods produced by foreign workers. This kind of economic policy has a basis in eighteenth-century practices of mercantilism to strengthen a state's security by promoting exports, discouraging imports, and bringing an inflow of gold and foreign currency that the state could tap to build its power. In Germany, the Weimar Republic, established in 1918 after the forced abdication of Kaiser Wilhelm, was distrusted by supporters of the old autocratic system. Millions of Germans who were impoverished by unemployment and inflation in the 1930s turned away from democracy and toward Hitler, who promised prosperity and glory.

After the Second World War, Europe's new leaders understood that real prosperity would require the efficiencies of a market bigger than that of any one European country. A complex network of economic interdependence would underpin democracy, and also strengthen peace directly. War would be economically irrational: businessmen, companies, and workers would suffer, and would use their political power to oppose it.

Economic integration began with industries important to an economy's war potential. In 1951 the leaders formed the European Coal and Steel Community to ensure that Germany could not again turn its heavy industries into a war machine. A similar plan for the nuclear industry (Euratom) followed. American policy-makers supported integration. They insisted that Marshall Plan aid for European recovery from the Second World War be coordinated by a new institution, the Organization for European Economic Cooperation. That ultimately became global, as the Organization for Economic Cooperation and Development (OECD) with members around the world, including several newly industrialized countries.

International institutions

Economic interchange required organizations empowered to make rules that encouraged and protected it. All the benefits of free trade could not be achieved if member states had radically different labour or social policies. That meant dismantling regulatory barriers to free movement not just of goods, but of services, capital, and people. Then the legal gaps had to be filled by new regulations. Common environmental policies and health standards were needed so producers in countries with lax standards would not have a market advantage over those in countries with strict controls. Economic policies had to be coordinated, and fluctuations in the relative value of national currencies brought under control. One form of economic liberalization led to others. The European Common Market became the European Community and ultimately the European Union. At each stage the institutions assumed broader functions. The process was so successful that other countries wanted to join, in time bringing the EU to its current total of twenty-seven members.

The EU has some supranational powers. It collects taxes (called fees) from all its member states. The European Commission enforces a wide range of common regulations. The Council is an executive body where important decisions are made by a weighted-voting scheme, so that a small minority of Europe's population or countries cannot block action. The European Parliament is directly elected by the citizens of member states (though its powers are limited). The European Court of Justice settles conflicts between different institutions of the EU and takes referrals from states for the interpretation of EU regulations, and EU laws prevail over national ones. A non-EU institution, the European Court of Human Rights, elaborated a bill of rights to which citizens may appeal against their national govern- ments. Court rulings required Britain to permit homosexual men and women to serve in its military and to restrict the use of corporal punishment in its schools. In 1999 a European Central Bank took over the vital area of monetary policy, with the Euro becoming the common currency for seventeen member states. Decisions on taxing and spending, however, remained under national control, leading many of the Eurozone states to take on excessive public debt and balance of payments deficits that could not be sustained. This became a full-blown crisis in 2011, and remains a serious threat to economic growth and perhaps even political stability.

Thus in many ways the EU acts as an intergovernmental body, with its member states retaining important elements of their traditional sovereignty in critical areas. For example, they do not have a common foreign policy, nor, in significant form, common defence institutions. The Common Security and Defence Policy institution has a command structure and small military force for peacekeeping operations. But it was incapable of conducting, or even agreeing on, action in Libya in 2011. Instead the task fell to NATO, with the USA an essential actor.

All this began in the Cold War, when the USA urged its allies to be more integrated and thus stronger. However, integration outlasted the Cold War, expanded far beyond the initial Cold War allies, and became far deeper. Growth rates for democracy and IGOs in Europe were similar to those for the world in Figure 5.3, from starting points about twice as high. Intra-European trade started lower than for the world, but its growth rate was very much higher. Whether Europe will become even more integrated, or less, is an open question. Yet its experience so far shows how virtuous circles can solidify peaceful relations while states retain many of their traditional characteristics. The system has produced stable peace among its members—an extraordinary achievement compared with centuries of catastrophic warfare.

Promoting order in anarchy

This analysis has implications for a particularly dangerous and important pair of countries: the USA and China. First, we can calculate the mid-1960s, risk factors for a fatal dispute from all the influences at that time. The two countries were not geographically close or contiguous, reducing the risk. But since both were big powers, with wide interests and power projection capability, the risk increased. America was predominant in power over China, but not hugely so, implying a moderate risk. None of the Kantian influences helped reduce the risk. Mao's China was very totalitarian on the political scale (–9). US–China trade was nil; as were shared IGO memberships (China was not even in the UN).

By comparison, some influences at the beginning of the twenty-first century were still unchanged: same geographical location, both great powers. But with the very rapid growth of China's economy relative to that of the USA, the power ratio had moved substantially closer to equality: a dangerous development by our analysis. However, all the liberal Kantian influences had come into play. China had liberalized somewhat, moving up to –7 on the political scale. Chinese–American trade flourished. Their trade is a smaller part of US GDP than of China's GDP—but even the USA's trade/GDP ratio is in the ninetieth percentile. Finally, they now share membership of many IGOs. China is in virtually all of the universal organizations, and in many smaller functional and North Pacific regional organizations, to which the USA also belongs. On this basis we can revise the risk factors. Even controlling for the more dangerous power balance, we find more than a 50 per cent reduction in risk under current conditions from the position in the 1960s.

Engagement is working. Yet its success cannot be assumed, and some elements of deterrence remain. China's political liberalization lags appreciably. Demands for democratization may be brutally suppressed once again or, alternatively, get explosively out of hand. Major environmental degradation may create extensive political and economic problems. Finally, the status of Taiwan remains a major threat to peace, requiring careful statesmanship by China, Taiwan, and the USA. A big war between the world's two biggest powers would be a tragedy, but it is not impossible.

Some countries, though not all, do learn to live peaceably with each other despite a centuries-long history of violent competition. There is order to be discerned and nurtured within the anarchy. The assumption that everyone is a potential enemy, not anarchy itself, is what drives the Hobbesian security dilemma. Many countries can and do get along with numerous others, rarely threatening to use military force. They operate substantially by principles of negotiation and compromise, in an order of cooperation and reciprocation broadly consistent with basic precepts of moral behaviour. This kind of order does not demand a moral transformation of humanity so much as it requires a careful structuring of relationships to channel self-interest in directions of mutual benefit.

Of course, not all states are at present part of this order. Those not bound by mutual ties of democracy, economic interdependence, and international institutions have a much weaker basis for cooperation. Where Kantian linkages are still weak, the Hobbesian dilemma may remain (perhaps with Iran and North Korea). Yet even with such states more stable relationships may be created, perhaps stumblingly, as in the early days of USA–China relations.

Conclusion: power, hegemony, and liberalism

The USA is sometimes described as hegemonic, with the burdens, benefits, and temptations dominance implies. It does not always behave as a Kantian state. With military spending nearly as great as that of all the rest of the world, it is tempted to rely on the armed force that money and high technology create. But hegemony cannot last forever. A Kantian liberal perspective on world politics can provide means for sustaining a stable peace when military advantage fades. Promoting democracy (but rarely imposing it by force, and then only in response to aggression), deepening linkages of international trade, and extending the multilateral network of IGOs offers the possibility of strengthening existing peaceful relations and expanding their scope to most of the world. Doing so depends less on the material elements of power than on soft power, on perceptions that the USA is acting on legitimate principles and following agreed rules. Doing so can serve both American interests and those of many other states and peoples.

Being the strongest power in the world does not mean being able to dictate all the important political, military, or economic outcomes. Moreover, predominant power can stimulate a 'balancing' reaction against itself. Fear of domination is an obvious motivation, but for other members of the Kantian community it is probably less important than distrust of American judgement and behaviour. Many Europeans do not fully trust Americans to act according to Kantian principles of negotiation and compromise. Nevertheless, a power-balancing alliance cannot easily be formed. Europe is not yet ready to act as a single foreign policy actor. Because of the great gap in power between the USA and even the biggest second-tier states, any such alliance would require many members. That raises the problem of collective action among members of an alliance without a strong leader, and consequently the temptation for each member to pursue its separate interests.

This 'free-riding' problem existed even in the great Cold War alliance epitomized by NATO. Indeed, NATO's success in deterring the outbreak of conflict in Europe was a direct cause of its collective goods problem. So long as the US nuclear deterrent seemed reliable, other NATO members had little incentive to contribute large forces of their own. Consequently the US spent twice as large a percentage of its GDP on defence than the average of all other NATO members. This suggests the difficulty of achieving common action when collaboration might be in the common interest.

Incentives to free-ride on international security continue. The more US policy in the 'war' against terrorism seems unwise, or in the narrow interest of the USA and a very few of its allies, the more other states will resist it. Some may not want to be protected as the Americans intend. Others, especially European states, have conflicting interests. One is the demographic and economic pressures that limit their willingness to spend on defence rather than care for ageing populations. Another is the presence of tens of millions of poorly assimilated Islamic workers and their families. The incentives to avoid doing anything that might inflame Islamic sentiments are very real. All this implies the possibility of an inadequate response to global terrorism. Yet a broad defeat could bring down the whole global economy and Kantian system.

This chapter is not about predictions, but about possibilities. Democratic liberties can be debased, the inequalities of capitalism may run wild, a global authority could become a leviathan, peace does not always mean justice. Nor can we take for granted the continued growth of liberal influences. Real people—leaders, elites, voters—make choices. They can discover constructive patterns of behaviour and act accordingly. We are not condemned to choose between being passive victims and being caught in endless cycles of violence. Openings exist for actions that can be other-regarding while still self-interested. In the daylight we can see Hobbes's realist vision as the nightmare it is, and Kant's liberal one as the partial reality it has become.

Questions

1. Which realist explanations of IR does liberalism accept, and which does it reject?

2. Was Kant just an idealist philosopher, or did he have a solid understanding of international relations?

3. What changes in the world, other than the three liberal influences, might help explain the decline in battle deaths, and why?

4. How do liberals try to explain why democracies rarely fight each other, and which do you find most or least plausible?

5. Why might one think democracies may not be peaceful in their relationships with dictatorships?

6. Does trade reduce conflict, or conflict reduce trade, or both, and why?

7. What kinds of IGOs might be most useful in promoting democracy, trade, and peace?

8. What are the strengths and limitations of applying epidemiological analysis to the analysis of violent international conflict?

9. How would you account for the beginnings of European integration?

10. What European institutions do you think are most important to ensuring peace in Europe?

11. What policies might democratic states follow to prevent a possible war between the USA and China?

12. What conditions might produce a reversal of the 'virtuous circles' that have brought increasing peace to much of the world?

 Further reading

Bueno de Mesquita, B., and A. Smith (2011), *The Dictator's Handbook* **(New York: Public Affairs).**
Elections and why democratic leaders avoid war better than dictators.

Chiozza, G., and H. Goemans (2011), *Leaders and International Conflict* **(Cambridge, UK: Cambridge University Press).**
Dictators may start international conflicts to discourage violent coups at home.

Geiss, A, Brock, L., and Muller, H. (2006) (eds), *Democratic Wars: The Dark Side of the Democratic Peace* **(London: Palgrave).**
Some democracies are less peaceful than others.

Howorth, J. (2001), *Security and Defence Policy in the European Union.* **(London: Palgrave), 2nd edn.**

Lipson, C. (2003), *Reliable Partners: How Democracies Have Made a Separate Peace* **(Princeton, NJ: Princeton University Press).**
Open political debate makes democracies' international commitments credible.

MacMillan, J. (1998), *On Liberal Peace: Democracy, War and International Order* **(London: Tauris).**
Liberal pacifism as an evolving political tradition.

Russett, B. (1993), *Grasping the Democratic Peace: Principles for a Post-Cold War World* **(Princeton, NJ: Princeton University Press).**
Democratic peace in the contemporary world, ancient Greece, and anthropology.

Rousseau, D. (2005), *Democracy and War: Institutions, Norms, and the Evolution of International Conflict* **(Stanford, CA: Stanford University Press).**
A broad-gauged discussion of institutions as more important than norms.

Important websites

Human Security Report Project, http://www.hsrgroup.org/human-security-reports/20092010/text.aspx

Polity IV Project: Political regime characteristics, global conflict, etc. http://www.systemicpeace.org/

Trade and GPD Data, http://pwt.econ.upenn.edu/php_site/pwt_index.php

Correlates of War project. Conflict, national power, alliances, etc. http://www.correlatesofwar.org/

Bibliography by Dan Reiter, Democratic Peace Theory. http://oxfordbibliographiesonline.com/

 Notes

1. Pinker (2011) emphasizes the long-term decline; Goldstein (2011) particularly credits UN peacekeeping in recent decades.

2. The sources, definitions, and decisions needed to turn concepts and hypotheses into measures for statistical analysis are discussed in a comprehensive report by Russett and Oneal (2001), and more recent results in Pevehouse and Russett (2006).

3. The effect of alliances is not statistically significant, but all the other percentages are highly significant, meaning that the odds that the sign should be the opposite from what we find are less than one in a thousand.

4. Mansfield and Snyder (2005) claim that states in incomplete transition from autocracy toward democracy are war-prone, especially if their central governments are weak. But wars under those conditions are extremely rare, almost non-existent in the twentieth century (Narang and Nelson 2009).

5. This statement has been contested. See Brown et al. (2011).

 Visit the Online Resource Centre that accompanies this book for lots of interesting additional material. www.oxfordtextbooks.co.uk/orc/dunne3e/

6

Neoliberalism

JENNIFER STERLING-FOLKER

 Reader's Guide

Neoliberalism argues that international institutions facilitate international cooperation. It acknowledges that cooperation can be difficult to achieve in anarchic conditions, but it argues that institutions allow states to overcome a variety of collective action impediments. How institutions do so, and how they might be redesigned to more efficiently obtain cooperative outcomes, is the primary focus of neoliberal analysis. This chapter revolves around a series of questions that are relevant for understanding neoliberal contributions. How did neoliberalism emerge? What are the barriers to international cooperation? How does neoliberalism study international institutions? The World Trade Organization (WTO) is used as a case study to illustrate the importance of institutional design for international free trade cooperation.

Introduction

The central concern of neoliberalism involves how to achieve cooperation among states and other actors in the international system. International cooperation occurs when states 'adjust their behaviour to the actual or anticipated preferences of others' so that 'the policies actually followed by one government are regarded by its partners as facilitating realization of their own objectives, (Keohane 1984: 51). To most observers, the desirability of achieving beneficial collective outcomes in IR would seem obvious. Yet the ability to do so in an anarchic international system has been relatively difficult historically. In fact, neoliberalism concurs with structural (or neo-) realism that international cooperation can be difficult to obtain in an anarchic international environment that fosters fear and uncertainty (see **Chapter 4**).

Yet in stark contrast to structural realism, neoliberalism argues that particular historical developments in the twentieth century have made international cooperation relatively easier to achieve now than was the case historically. These developments ensured the growth of international institutions, in both a formal and informal sense, which play a fundamental role in the daily activity of contemporary global politics. Formal institutions are multilateral organizations with physical locations, buildings, staffs, budgets, and other resources at their disposal (see also **Chapter 5**). States voluntarily create intergovernmental institutions such as the United Nations (UN) or the International Monetary Fund (IMF) in order to obtain particular collective interests. States have also created informal institutional arrangements, or **international regimes**, which consist of 'sets of implicit or explicit principles, norms, rules, and decision-making procedures around which actors' expectations converge in a given area of international relations' (Krasner 1983: 2). The concept of international regimes was developed to capture, describe, and analyse the totality of cooperative efforts, assumptions, and behaviours in a given international issue area.

Neoliberalism is a variant of liberal IR theory that focuses on the role international institutions play in obtaining international collective outcomes, and for this reason it is often called 'neoliberal *institutionalism*'. In order to examine international cooperation, neoliberalism subscribes to a state-centric perspective which, like structural realism, considers states to be unitary, rational, utility-maximizing actors who dominate global affairs. That is, states are treated as unified entities with particular, specifiable goals, rather than composites of many different domestic actors and competing interests. States are also assumed to make decisions based on a set of self-interested priorities and according to a strategic cost-to-benefit analysis of possible choices, reactions, and outcomes. In making these assumptions, neoliberalism not only mirrors structural realism but is also heavily indebted to the study of **rationality** and utility-maximization in economics.

However, unlike realism, neoliberalism is a variant of IR liberalism, and it is premised on basic liberal assumptions about the possibility of cumulative progress in human affairs. Liberalism assumes that collective benefits may be obtained through the greater application of human reasoning. Increased interaction and informational exchange among self-interested individuals and actors are also important. And all variants of liberal theory assume, to some degree, that benefits may be obtained from devising more effective institutional arrangements. Thus, in comparison to realism, neoliberalism has relatively greater faith in the ability of human beings to obtain progressively better collective outcomes that promote freedom, peace, prosperity, and justice on a global scale.

This does not mean that neoliberal scholars are idealists (see **Chapter 1**) in the traditional IR theoretical sense of the word. Neoliberalism acknowledges that impediments to collective action can be difficult to overcome in an anarchic environment. But neoliberalism argues that the structure or design of international institutions plays an important role in determining the extent to which collective goals can be realized. Policy-makers and other relevant actors can create and reshape institutional structures in order to more effectively obtain collective interests. In other words, it is possible for human beings to design international institutions that substantially mitigate the negative impact of anarchy on international collective actions. Whether or not they have done so, and how those institutions might be improved upon to do even better, is the primary subject of neoliberal institutional analysis.

How did neoliberalism emerge?

One of the early influences on neoliberalism was the pluralism literature in the 1960s and early 1970s. Pluralism challenged realist assumptions that states could be analytically treated as unitary, rational actors. Pluralists argued instead that a variety of non-state actors and processes were breaking down barriers between domestic and international affairs. Because, as Richard Little (1996: 66) explains, 'state boundaries were becoming increasingly permeable', pluralists argued that it 'was no longer possible to understand international relations simply by studying the interactions among governments'. According to the early work of Robert Keohane and Joseph Nye (1971), the term 'transnational relations' better characterized the increasingly extensive cross-national interaction occurring between states. This interaction was seen as a challenge to the authority and autonomy of national governments, which were no longer able to control outcomes or obtain interests by pursuing unilateral policies.

While this pluralist foundation informed many aspects of neoliberalism, what differed was the latter's adoption of state-centric, unitary actor assumptions. The early neoliberal litera-ture of the 1980s constituted a renewed analytical confrontation with the structural realist arguments of Kenneth Waltz (1979) in particular. In a series of neoliberal foundational texts, beginning with Robert Keohane and Joseph Nye's *Power and Interdependence* (1977), liberal scholars sought to challenge realist pessimism on its own terms by utilizing realist assump-tions. In a relatively bold analytical move, neoliberalism argued that an anarchic environ-ment of self-interested, egocentric actors did not necessarily impose debilitating realist constraints on cooperation.

These arguments were further developed in the edited volume by Stephen Krasner, *Inter-national Regimes* (1983), which outlined the concept of regimes and applied it to a variety of issue areas. The tenets of neoliberalism were given fullest expression in Robert Keohane's *After Hegemony* (1984), in which the author characterized his arguments as a variant of real-ism. This characterization spurred considerable debate within the scholarly literature of the 1980s and early 1990s between Robert Keohane (as a neoliberal) and Joseph Grieco (as a neorealist) over whether realist assumptions had been correctly adopted and applied (Grieco 1990, 1993; Keohane 1993). This so-called neo–neo debate (discussed more extensively in Ole Wæver's **Chapter 16**) explains why neorealism and neoliberalism are sometimes catego-rized together as rationalist approaches.

The analytical convergence between structural realism and neoliberalism did not please everyone. A number of critics argued that adopting the same state-centric assumptions meant that important dynamics in world politics would continue to be missed by both theo-ries (Rochester 1986; Little 1996). The unitary actor assumption remained problematic for both approaches, which faced challenges over the role that domestic politics plays in deter-mining interests and foreign policies (Rose 1998; Sterling-Folker 2002). Critics also noted that the rational actor assumption made it impossible to separate the independent causal effects of regimes from what states did or wanted (Haggard and Simmons 1987; Strange 1983). Friedrich Kratochwil and John Ruggie (1986) argued that this problem was due to an analyti-cal inconsistency between neoliberalism's chosen epistemology and its ontology. Such criti-cisms served as an important theoretical foundation for the development of constructivism, with its emphasis on process, identity, and social interaction (see **Chapter 10**).

Yet despite these challenges, and the analytical convergence to which they were responding, there were still important substantive differences between structural realism and neoliberalism that have kept them on parallel but clearly separate theoretical tracks. One of the central differences involves how they define and analyse the concept of anar-chy (Grieco 1990). Structural realists see anarchy as an all-encompassing, unchanging con-dition or environment to which humans beings are subject. The inability to control outcomes and ensure survival generates the paranoia, fear, and drive for power that are basic to a realist analysis. Alternatively neoliberals see anarchy as a vacuum that is gradually being filled with human-created processes and institutions (Sterling-Folker 2001). These have begun to counteract the inability to control outcomes and ensure survival, which means that the paranoia, fear, and drive for power induced by anarchy have been mitigated overtime as well.

The result is that the two perspectives read the Westphalian historical record very differently. Structural realists point to the ongoing warfare and military/trade competition between states as confirmation for the unchanging quality of anarchy. Neoliberal scholars concede that much of IR prior to the twentieth century seems to conform to realist expectations. But they highlight two historical developments in the twentieth century that have made realism an increasingly inaccurate description of contemporary global politics.

The first historical development was increasing **interdependence** in a variety of global issue areas due to modern technological and industrial advances. Interdependence involves a relationship of mutual dependence in which actions and interests are entwined. This relationship may produce unintended, undesirable, and reciprocal consequences, but participating actors also obtain important interests and benefits through their interconnection. It is therefore costly to one's own interests to threaten or end the relationship. The concept of interdependence as a potentially pacifying process in an anarchic environment has a long pedigree in liberal IR thought. In neoliberal analysis, it sets the stage for the historical development of common interests which can only be obtained if states successfully cooperate with one another.

For example, states have a common interest in preventing the depletion of environmental resources, which is occurring at a rapid rate due to the pace and scope of global industrialization. The problem is not confined within particular national borders, nor can it be resolved with traditional power politics, violence, or unilateral action. All states have a common interest in finding a solution to the problem, which their collective but overlapping activity has created. It is also a problem which can only be resolved through cooperative efforts among them. The same dynamics can be found in other issue areas sometimes disparagingly referred to as 'low' politics (vs. the 'high' politics of national security), such as global economics, health, refugees, or immigration. These issue areas have become increasingly important to states and, because they are characterized by interdependence, are also the areas in which there is the greatest potential for international cooperation.

The second historical development that has made realism an inaccurate description of contemporary IR is the period of **hegemonic stability** which the United States (USA) provided after the Second World War. American and British foreign policy-makers began to plan for the post-Second World War era before the outcome of the conflict had even been determined. Influenced by the Great Depression, the rise of fascism in Europe, and the global war in which they were then engaged, the Americans and British mapped out a postwar vision meant to stabilize world affairs according to their own preferences. This vision included the UN system, which was to serve as an umbrella for cooperative relations across many different issue areas.

Particular attention was paid to the capitalist economic and free trade system, which was supported by a series of formal institutions, such as the IMF and IBRD, which came to be known as the Bretton Woods system. These institutions were backed by American economic resources, and in so doing the USA was behaving as a **hegemon**, or a very powerful state which provides self-interested global or regional stability. Many international political economy (IPE) scholars argue that a hegemon is necessary for states to have confidence in and engage with free trade in an anarchic environment. By supporting the economic system in this way, the USA provided a period of hegemonic stability in the latter half of the twentieth century during which an extensive international regime evolved for capitalist economics.

While the underlying motivation for this period of hegemonic stability was economic self-interest (along with ability), the period also served as an important foundation for the growth of interdependence in economics and other issue areas. More significantly, neoliberalism posits that even if US relative power has declined, interdependence provides a rational, strategic incentive for states to continue cooperating with one another (Keohane 1984). This is because high degrees of their own economic wealth now depend on access to one another's markets and consumers. In addition, the institutions established by the hegemon serve as the physical and normative platforms for maintaining and even expanding cooperative efforts among self-interested actors. Hence cooperation, and particularly economic cooperation, could theoretically be obtained in anarchy in the absence or decline of a hegemon.

Taken together these historical developments—interdependence and hegemonic stability—have created the necessary window of opportunity for the development of common collective interests that can only be obtained through international cooperation. Not surprisingly, neoliberal claims about these developments have been subjected to intense scrutiny. Important questions have been raised about how to measure interdependence, whether interdependence is just as likely to produce violence, and how to isolate the effects of interdependence from other potential causes (Jones and Willetts 1984; Mansfield and Pollins 2003). Similarly, critics have questioned the normative bias of hegemonic stability theory, whether the USA has actually declined as a hegemon, and whether a hegemon is even necessary in the first place (Snidal 1985; Strange 1987; Lake 1993). These criticisms suggest that the assumed relationship between historical processes, international institutions, and international cooperation, which serves as the foundation for neoliberalism, is not unproblematic.

What are the barriers to international cooperation?

It would be wrong, however, to characterize neoliberalism as arguing that cooperation will be easy to achieve just because interdependence has increased. States may now share a common interest in controlling the spread of deadly viruses, nuclear weapons, trade protectionism, and environmental pollution. But simply having common interests in an effective resolution does not lead easily or automatically to that resolution. States may fail to cooperate because they lack information about one another's true preferences. They may fear that others will take advantage of a cooperative arrangement by cheating. They may be concerned that others will free-ride on the back of their cooperative efforts. They may believe, in short, that the transaction costs, or the unknown consequences and penalties, of even a potentially beneficial agreement are simply too great to risk the effort. Thus even when all actors share a common interest and would gain from a cooperative effort, there are still significant barriers to the ability of self-interested actors to cooperate.

According to structural realists, these barriers are intractable because, even when both parties have common interests and would gain from cooperation, they fear that any relatively greater gains will be employed for competitive purposes. Since they cannot trust the future intentions of their cooperative partners, actors will avoid potential agreements if they involve different pay-off levels. Alternatively, neoliberal scholars argue that the fear of these relatively greater gains do not necessarily inhibit cooperation. States can be motivated to cooperate in order to achieve absolute gains (or the total gains made regardless of the relatively greater gains of others) if their concerns over future intentions can be mitigated. It is true that in anarchy any agreement must be self-enforcing, but this does not make states incapable of recognizing when it is in their interest to curtail cheating or to trust in the future actions of others. The barriers to cooperation are inhibiting and worthy of examination, but they are not as insurmountable as structural realists would have us believe.

Neoliberal scholars have often employed game theory to analyse these cooperative difficulties.[1] The most famous illustrative game is the **Prisoner's Dilemma**, in which two

 Featured book

Kenneth Oye (1986), *Cooperation Under Anarchy* (Princeton, NJ: Princeton University Press).

Although game theory is not used by all neoliberal scholars, the concepts and language of game theory permeate neoliberal analysis. Game theory utilizes a combination of mathematics and logic to analyse strategic interaction among decision-makers. One early text that encouraged the use of game theory in neoliberalism was the collection of essays, *Cooperation Under Anarchy*, edited by Kenneth Oye (1986).

Games were categorized according to whether they were non-cooperative or cooperative. Non-cooperative games were constant-sum or zero-sum, in which a gain by one opponent automatically meant the equivalent loss by the other. Chess is a typical example, and military-security issues were characterized as zero-sum. Cooperative games were called variable-sum, positive-sum, or increasing-sum games. In these games, both opponents gain or lose unequally from their interaction. Such games also tended to be 'mixed-motive', because player preferences (or utilities) were not clearly ranked and contained both cooperative and non-cooperative motivations. The Prisoner's Dilemma is a typical example, and trade issues were characterized as variable-sum. There was disagreement among the volume's authors over whether military-security issues were actually zero-sum. Yet ultimately Robert Axelrod and Robert Keohane argued in the concluding chapter that 'economic issues usually seem to exhibit less conflictual pay-off structures than do those of military security' (Oye 1986: 231).

In issue areas characterized as mixed motive and variable sum, player pay-offs are determined by strategic bargaining. Thus game theory allowed neoliberal scholars to highlight the difficulties of negotiating a mutually satisfactory solution. Such solutions are referred to as 'pareto-optimal', because they are outcomes in which no one could gain additional benefits without making someone comparatively worse off. If there are no player defections, these solutions could also develop into 'equilibrium outcomes', in that players were prevented from unilaterally improving the outcome for their own benefit.

The condition of interdependence was argued to be important because, while it could not change interests associated with zero-sum games, it could encourage a shift in mixed-motive games to increasing-sum games. Interdependence encouraged iteration (or repeated plays), thereby allowing players to employ strategies such as 'Tit-For-Tat' and issue-linkage to reward cooperation and punish defection. Once increasing-sum games became established, none of the players could obtain their interests in the absence of agreement from the others. As the authors argued, bargaining difficulties over the pareto-optimal solution remained, but the preference for cooperation over unilateralism became embedded.

prisoners are held incommunicado by police and told that if they provide evidence against the other they will receive a reduced sentence. Both would be better off if they remained silent and thereby cooperated, yet the pay-off structure encourages each to turn against the other or defect, which means they will both receive longer sentences. One of the obvious barriers to effective cooperation in this instance is the lack of information or transparency about the potential pay-offs and hence the real value of cooperation or defection. Another barrier is the incentive to 'cheat' on one's partner or, alternatively, the fear of being cheated which involves a basic mistrust about the actual intentions of others.

The examination of the Prisoner's Dilemma and other games have allowed neoliberal scholars to more effectively isolate and analyse these sorts of barriers to international collective action in interdependent conditions (Axelrod 1981; Oye 1986). For example, neoliberal scholars discovered that iteration, or the expectation of future interaction, makes actors less likely to defect from cooperative arrangements than actors engaged in one-shot relationships. The recurrent ability to exchange information, as well as monitor one another's behaviour, reduces concerns over actual intentions and the consequences of being cheated.

At their most basic level, international institutions foster iteration by ensuring that constant and regular meetings occur between national leaders and policy-makers. This allows states to learn one other's preferences, discover they have common interests and constraints, and consider a variety of solutions to collective problems. International institutions also foster the exchange of information about one another's intentions, and they can reveal common concerns over cheating, free-riding, and other transaction costs which can then be addressed directly by negotiators and decision-makers. Transparency is enhanced, thereby reducing the apprehension that can inhibit a mutually beneficial agreement.

Because institutions play such a fundamental role in reducing these sorts of barriers to international cooperation, how they are designed and who uses them for what purpose is central to neoliberal research agendas. After all, a failure to cooperate can be due, at least in part, to the inefficient design of cooperative institutions. Since 'there are many mutually beneficial arrangements that states forgo because of the fear that others will cheat or take advantage of them', Robert Jervis has correctly observed that neoliberal scholars 'see important gains to be made through the more artful arrangement of policies' (1999: 48). This interest, in what has been called the 'rational design of institutions' (Koremenos et al. 2003), serves as the foundational context for neoliberal analysis and shapes its research agendas.

How does neoliberalism study international institutions?

Neoliberalism begins its analysis by identifying the shared self-interests that a particular cooperative effort is meant to obtain in an international institutional setting. That is, for what common purpose or goal was the institution designed? Neoliberal analysis next turns to the question of how, or whether, that particular institutional design ensures those interests are sufficiently obtained. In doing so, neoliberalism derives generalizable lessons about what aspects of the institution are more or less successful in obtaining a cooperative result. In studying cooperation and institutions in this manner, neoliberal scholars have identified three broad difficulties in international institutional design. These difficulties affect the extent to which international cooperation can be achieved.

Bargaining

The first broad theme involves the extent to which institutional design plays a role in international negotiations and **bargaining**. In order to reach a collectively-agreed decision, states need a degree of regularity in the rules and procedures for their collective decision-making. By normalizing rules and procedures, institutions reflect mutually accepted boundaries for behaviour and for the achievement of collective goals. Yet any cooperative international effort will still involve a great deal of negotiations, often among a large number of state actors with comparatively different resources and interests. The specificity and regularity of bargaining procedures also varies according to particular issue areas and its institutions, so there is variation in how well particular institutions achieve their specified goals.

Clearly great powers can have more influence over international negotiations and their outcome, as neoliberalism's critics have charged (Mearsheimer 1994–5). It may also be the case, as Gulio Gallarotti (1991) has argued, that although international institutions do serve as important forums for negotiations, they have not been particularly good managers of some collective problems because they cannot resolve serious conflict between countries. These criticisms suggest that institutional redesign will miss its mark because it does not address problems inherent to the negotiations process itself. The difficulties inhibiting cooperation lie elsewhere, with the issue area or the states involved.

In light of these criticisms, we must be careful to appropriately differentiate causal variables and take the role of power into account when examining bargaining outcomes. Yet dismissing the role of institutions, and the entire analytical enterprise of neoliberalism, on these grounds misses the extent to which sovereign states (both powerful and weak) rely on institutions as essential forums for bargaining in the first place. Nor does it negate the role that different institutional designs might play in achieving more efficacious negotiations in particular situations. Dysfunctions may certainly result from relative power, yet these do not account for every instance in which cooperation could have been more effectively achieved. In other words, there are times when the bargaining dysfunctions are within the grasp of institutional designers.

Barbara Koremenos, Charles Lipson, and Duncan Snidal (2003) have found that a number of key design features have an impact on bargaining outcomes. These features include the scope of an issue covered by the negotiations, the extent to which issues are linked, and the rules for controlling how decisions are made (including rules on voting). Issue linkage, for example, has been particularly prevalent in bargaining among European countries, where a high degree of international institutionalization developed after the Second World War. Thomas Oatley (2003) points out that the hundreds of European bilateral trade agreements following the Second World War initially constrained the significant gains that could be realized through intra-European trade. Yet these agreements also served as important stepping stones for the eventual multilateralization of European trade via regional institutions. By developing institutions such as the European Union (EU), multilateral negotiations obtained greater collective gains and made it possible to link negotiations across common issue areas. Thus issue linkage became particularly important in the European context, where the nesting of regional and global institutions lead to complex cross-cutting institutional bargaining games (Aggarwal

1998; Pahre 2003). This nesting or clustering of negotiations could not have occurred in the absence of international institutionalization.

There is debate among neoliberal scholars over whether regional or global institutional arrangements are relatively more efficacious at facilitating negotiations (Acharya and Johnston 2007; Mansfield and Reinhardt 2003). The trend toward regionalism since the 1990s has also been accompanied by a growing legalization of negotiations that has become an important subject of neoliberal analysis in its own right (Smith 2001; Goldstein et al. 2000). The legalization of international negotiations has meant that decision-making rules and dispute-resolution mechanisms are clearly defined and proceed along highly specified lines. And although the legalization of an issue area does not ensure state compliance, the process and degree of legalization in an issue area appears to influence bargaining outcomes in important ways.

For example, states now increasingly rely on international legal processes to resolve trade disputes by filing complaints over treaty violations with neutral third parties which then issue legally binding rulings. This is puzzling because, given an anarchic system of sovereign states, it is not immediately clear why states would seek to avoid an unfavourable ruling in the first place. After all, why not simply ignore a ruling one doesn't like? While there are a number of potential causes for this avoidance behaviour, as least some part of the explanation might lie with the normative value that sovereign states, as legally institutionalized entities themselves, place on any legal process (Schwartz and Sykes 2001). This suggests that the greater the extent to which an international institution can legalize a process (thereby making it transparent and clear), the greater the chances that negotiations will be successfully concluded.

Such legal clarity may also assist national decision-makers when faced with domestic pressures to enact trade barriers (Martin and Simmons 1998). Alternatively, Thomas Oatley and Robert Nabors (1998) have noted that decision-makers sometimes propose redistributive international institutions in order to defuse domestic political pressures. In doing so, decision-makers simultaneously obtain their domestic interests while contributing to the institutionalization and regulation of an international issue area. Decision-maker leadership may, in fact, be an essential element in the ability to remove bargaining obstacles at both the domestic and international levels (Young 1991). In all of these instances, neoliberal scholars have discovered that institutional design plays a role in promoting or discouraging some aspect of international bargaining, thus underscoring the relevance of its study to the achievement of collective ends.

Defection

The second broad category of institutional design problems of interest to neoliberal scholars involves the issue of **defection**. Because states fear that their cooperative partners may fail to live up to mutual agreements, states may be discouraged from engaging in cooperative projects in the first place. They may also be concerned with the ability of other states to free-ride or indirectly (and without incurring costs) benefit from their cooperative efforts. These concerns lead to an obvious question: how can international institutions be designed to alleviate concerns over defection?

The existence of international institutions already indicates that, to some extent, the problem of defection is not as inhibiting as it might first appear. After all, states create these institutions under the assumption that it is possible to lock one another into the institutional arrangements and the agreements that have been signed. In so doing, states acquire increased information about the actions and preferences of others, combined with greater knowledge about the consequences of cheating and being cheated, which reduces the temptation to cheat generally. The same has been true for concerns over free-riding, since institutions have been the forums through which states have expanded multilateral participation in the provision of collective goods. This has led some scholars to argue that since states generally follow through on their international agreements, the subject of defection is not particularly important (Chayes and Chayes, 1993).

Yet it is still the case that in an anarchic environment, in which cooperative agreement is necessarily decentralized and self-enforcing, states do not always uphold, follow through with, or fully implement the agreements they have initially reached. As George Downs, David Rocke, and Peter Barsoom have observed, 'cooperation . . . may begin with agreements that require little enforcement, but continued progress seems likely to depend on coping with an environment where defection presents significant benefits' (2001: 297). Thus the issue is not so much whether defection will occur, since obviously it can and will, but rather how to deal with it when it does. As with bargaining, relative power between states can play an important role in who defects and free-rides, as well as who has both an interest in and the capacity to challenge and pressure defectors. While international institutions generally do not have the ability or resources to punish defectors directly, neoliberal analyses demonstrate that different institutional arrangements make defection more or less likely.

Institutions can play a role in alleviating two important aspects of defection—**compliance** and enforcement. Compliance involves the extent to which states can be induced or encouraged to abide by the international agreements to which they are parties. Enforcement involves the extent to which states can be forced into compliance and possibly punished for their failure to do so. Institutional mechanisms for monitoring state behaviour are particularly important for compliance, because such monitoring makes all states aware of one another's behaviour. By providing for the systematic review of each member's practices, institutions highlight areas of potential defection and, because states are aware that their behaviour is being regularly monitored, it encourages compliance. This has been the case in issue areas such as trade, human rights, and the environment, in which countries face domestic and international pressure or institutional censure for a failure to comply with agreements. Thus a basic element in the design of international institutions has been responsibility for collecting and disseminating information about member state behaviour.

Transparency by itself, however, is usually not enough to ensure compliance. In a comparative study of institutional compliance systems, Ronald Mitchell (1994) found that increased transparency needed to be combined with reduced implementation costs, the threat of sanctions, and an emphasis on actively preventing violations rather than merely deterring them. Such integrated compliance systems made defection less likely, thus indicating that a combination of mechanisms (some of which are specific to the issue area in question) is likely to be most effective at eliciting compliance. Other mechanisms include the ability of international institutions to provide financial incentives, act as moral persuaders, serve as neutral third parties, and actively manage member state disagreements. Such management might include either the arbitration of a dispute directly or the provision of legal guidance for its resolution (Mitchell and Hensel 2007; Simmons 2002; Roben 2008).

As with bargaining, issue-linkage can become an important aspect of compliance. Institutions may serve as the forums through which issues become linked, as either a reward or punishment for behaviour, although this also varies according to the problem at hand, the relative impact of defection, and the relative power of the states involved (Mitchell and Keilbach 2003). This is particularly clear in the case of economic sanctions, or the threat of them, which may be used as an institutional means of enforcement and punishment of defectors. Yet, as Lisa Martin (1992) points out, sanctions can only be successful when all relevant parties comply with the decision to sanction. The process of getting states to go along with proposed sanctions involves what she calls 'coercive cooperation'. It depends on the relative power of interested states to persuade or threaten other states to comply with the sanctions. In order to do this effectively, interested states rely on international institutions to obtain cooperation as well as implement and monitor imposed sanctions against the defecting parties.

Another important aspect of institutional design for compliance and enforcement is the inclusion of dispute resolution mechanisms. Neoliberal analysts have discovered that flexibility in institutional compliance mechanisms is an essential design element if defection is going to be effectively discouraged. Barbara Koremenos (2001) has observed that renegotiation provisions alleviate concerns about the distributional effects of an agreement. This encourages states to both cooperate and comply, since they know that renegotiations will address subsequent distributional effects and concerns. Similarly, Peter Rosendorff and Helen Milner (2003) argue that the inclusion of escape clauses and loopholes encourages compliance, because states may refuse to sign onto an agreement if it is too rigid in the first place. In the face of increasing domestic pressures, decision-makers may feel they have no other choice but to abandon an agreement. Escape clauses, on the other hand, allow states to temporarily back out of agreements, although they must be carefully designed so that a state's reliance on them is neither too frequent nor too unusual.

Autonomy

The third, broad area of institutional design of interest to neoliberal scholars involves the issue of autonomy. While neoliberalism assumes that international institutions facilitate self-interested cooperation, it is not always clear that outcomes are due to the presence of institutions specifically. The problem lies with the neoliberal assumption that international institutions are created by states to serve their self-interests. How is it then possible to disentangle the effects of state interests from the attributes of international institutions? If institutions are implementing what states want, then why not just study the states involved? Do international institutions even have an autonomous status that can be analysed separately from the analysis of state interests?

Scholars have responded to this analytical problem in a number of ways. One approach has been to examine how international institutions act as norm entrepreneurs and agenda setters in global politics (Finnemore and Sikkink 1998). Because international institutions are generally viewed as neutral parties who represent commonly-shared values, they are accorded a certain degree of legitimacy in world affairs. This allows them to promote particular values and goals on a global scale. They derive additional authority from their control and coordination of technical expertise and information. How effectively a given institution can shape the global agenda will depend on a variety of aspects. Yet as Martha Finnemore (1996) has argued, a major element in the process involves the institution's ability to socialize states, and particular domestic constituents within those states, into global norms. In this way, the domestic political agendas and hence foreign policies of even relatively powerful states can be affected by international institutions.

Another response to the analytical problem of autonomy has been to examine how international institutions implement the tasks assigned to them by states (Joachim et al. 2008). It is important to underscore here just how numerous these tasks are in global politics. While controversies and the institutions associated with them are more likely to appear in newspaper headlines (such as WTO protests, the IMF structural adjustment programmes, or International Criminal Court indictments), the activities of daily global life are inevitably overseen by an international institution. People, goods, services, and ideas are being exchanged across national borders and around the globe every moment of the day. International institutions have been assigned the task of overseeing and implementing this daily activity and the legal agreements that accompany them.

Yet institutions 'do not simply pursue the mandates handed to them', as Michael Barnett and Martha Finnemore (2004: 5) point out, and instead institutional 'staff must transform these broad mandates into workable doctrines, procedures, and ways of acting in the world'. International institutions have an independent causal impact precisely because they oversee daily global tasks that states do not. How they do so may not always be very effective; yet this is also one of the ways in which scholars have been able to identify the independent causal impact of international institutions. That is, international institutions exhibit a variety of standard bureaucratic pathologies when implementing their missions and these cannot be traced to state intentions or interests. Such pathologies may be avoided, Barnett and Finnemore (2004) suggest, by making organizational decision-making processes more transparent and inclusive.

Finally, the question of autonomous action and implementation has led to the development of a neoliberal research programme known as **principal–agent theory**. This research examines how states (as the principals) delegate tasks and authority to international institutions which serve as their independent representatives (as agents) within particular issue areas (Hawkins et al. 2006). Delegation serves the interests of most countries, yet it also allows international institutions to independently pursue and shape multilateral agendas. Because differences arise between what states want as principals and what institutions do as agents, states simultaneously develop mechanisms for controlling organizational influence and autonomy (Pollack 1997; Nielson and Tierney 2003). Such mechanisms serve as an important source of institutional redesign. Thus the process of delegation, and the rules governing it, has evolved over time in order to more effectively promote the interests of states, even as the process paradoxically promotes institutional autonomy.

Case study: the World Trade Organization

The purpose of the World Trade Organization (WTO) is to serve as a forum for states to negotiate free trade agreements and settle trade disputes. It came into formal existence in 1995 and is part of a well-established international regime in the area of global capitalist free trade. This regime consists of numerous free trade organizations and agreements, and it depends on a variety of ideational and legal foundations. These rest, in turn, on the presumption that it is normatively valuable and beneficial to participate in the global activity of capitalist free trade (in contrast, for example, to the Marxist perspective explained in **Chapter 8**). An exclusive focus on the formal procedures and structure of the WTO would miss these important foundational elements, which is one of the reasons why the broader concept of international regimes was developed by neoliberal scholars.

Yet the institutional evolution of the WTO serves as an excellent case study for illustrating the importance of institutional design to collective goals in an anarchic environment. States developed the WTO from a prior and less formal institutional arrangement, known as the General Agreement on Tariffs and Trade (GATT), in order to better obtain their collective economic interests. The WTO's institutional design developed out of the collective experience with GATT. Some of the WTO's key institutional aspects have already been modified in response to new situations and institutional shortcomings. And the WTO has been the subject of considerable neoliberal analysis.

Origins of the WTO

Given the nature of international trade, the impetus for developing a formal institution such as the WTO had existed since the Second World War. Despite the collective benefits that can be obtained by removing trade barriers, coordinating trade liberalization can be relatively difficult to achieve and maintain. Domestic producers often pressure governments for protectionism, particularly in times of economic crisis, and these pressures are difficult for decision-makers to ignore. A particularly appropriate game for illustrating the difficulties involved is Stag Hunt (Gates and Humes 1997: 85–90). In the game, hunters must cooperate to bring down a stag which will provide all of them with considerable gain. However, any individual hunter may be tempted to defect by unilaterally pursuing a rabbit, which will cause the stag hunt to fail. The defection will provide the hunter with more immediate and unilateral but ultimately short-lived and comparatively smaller gains.

Trade liberalization operates according to a similar logic, because comparatively greater aggregate wealth can be obtained by all participants if they reduce barriers to trade. Yet in the face of immediate domestic pressures, a state will be tempted to resort to protectionism, causing other states inevitably to follow suit. The end result is that by pursuing their individual short-term interests, all states end up being economically worse off in the long run as the effects of protectionism multiply through the economic system. This pattern of behaviour could be seen during the Great Depression, in policies such as the 1930 Smoot–Hawley Tariff which effectively closed US markets to imported goods and caused other states to follow suit. The hegemonic vision of a new global economic order proposed by the Americans and British during the Second World War included a forum that would facilitate trade liberalization bargaining.

Unlike the IMF and IBRD, however, specific aspects of the proposed International Trade Organization (ITO) proved to be controversial, and the organization failed to materialize after the US withdrew its support.[2] The need for a trade negotiations framework and forum remained, however, and in the ITO's place, the US and other trading states turned to the GATT which, in anticipation of the ITO's creation, had gone into effect in 1948. GATT represented the first round of trade negotiations and tariff reductions after the Second World War. Although it was not in itself a formal IGO, GATT established a set of provisional trade rules and it created mechanisms for resolving trade-related disputes.

This trade agreement subsequently served as the institutional backbone for successive rounds of trade negotiations, which dealt with new trade difficulties as technology, economic practices, and political events evolved during the Cold War period (Spero and Hart 2003; Cohn 2005). Each round would last several years, as delegates hammered out the details of reducing particular trade barriers (often product by product particular to each member state) and address new types of barriers and practices. The Kennedy Round in the mid-1960s focused on anti-dumping practices, when states subsidize domestic industries which then export their products at below production cost. The Tokyo Round in the 1970s focused on non-tariff trade barriers, such as government subsidies for infant industries and import quotas. The Uruguay Round in the late 1980s was one of the most comprehensive, as it included negotiations on everything from agriculture to intellectual property rights.

In this way, GATT was the institutional and legal basis for the maintenance and expansion of free trade. Its membership grew steadily from roughly twenty in the late 1940s to over a hundred by the early 1980s. The goals of GATT were supported by a variety of other international and regional institutions, such as the IMF, which oversaw the fixed exchange rate system, or the EU, which promoted regional economic integration. Informal institutions, such as the Group of 7, also developed so that leaders from the major industrialized democracies could meet on an annual basis to discuss areas of mutual concern. In all of these endeavours, international institutions served as the forums for iterated interaction, thereby confirming collective intentions and behaviours. They allowed states to exchange information, to address new problems as they arose, and to reduce transaction costs that would have been associated with bilateral trade arrangements. Not surprisingly, the markets of GATT members became increasingly interdependent as the Cold War progressed.

At same time, the relative ability of the US to unilaterally control economic outcomes had begun to wane. The US announced in 1971 that it would no longer support the fixed exchange rate system. During the economic difficulties of the 1970s, including a series of oil crises, the USA found it increasingly difficult to offer and maintain an open market for its partner's products. Although this relative decline should not be overstated, since by most estimates the American economy remained one of the most influential and wealthiest, the perception of hegemonic decline relative to its trading partners impacted policy. The USA began to put pressure on its trading partners to shoulder more of the burden for maintaining a free trade system, and it became increasingly dissatisfied with GATT and the absence of stronger compliance mechanisms.

The institutional structure of GATT was becoming a problem in other ways as well. As long as GATT's membership had been limited to advanced industrial economies and a handful of other states, the informal setting was conducive to negotiations. The flexibility of GATT's institutional design and mandate allowed member states to address new trade issues as they arose. And many newly-independent states did not join GATT because they pursued isolationist development policies. This began to change by the early 1980s as the growing economies of Asia and South America became GATT members. The trend toward ever larger membership numbers, which expanded again after the Cold War, put considerable strain on the GATT's institutional structure and its negotiating procedures. With more members and a diverse set of problems at the table, each round of negotiations, and the membership committees which oversaw them, became increasingly more complex. Thus while GATT had served as an appropriate institutional framework for free trade negotiations during much of the Cold War period, its institutional design became unwieldy by the 1980s. These problems, combined with growing dissatisfaction with GATT compliance and enforcement, led to institutional reform and the development of the WTO as GATT's replacement.

WTO: its structure and its operation

The WTO differed from GATT in its legal foundations, structural parameters, and substantive mandates. It was a formal inter-governmental organization with a full Secretariat and an extensive institutional structure designed to cover all aspects of trade (not simply traded goods). Negotiating procedures and schedules (of substantive committees, working groups or parties, and Ministerial Conferences) were delineated. Organizational requirements and procedures for the accession of new members and

(continued)

observers were established. And the WTO contained one of the most highly developed dispute resolution mechanisms to be found in an international institution.

Since its creation, the WTO has served as the primary international institution through which the normative and behavioural expectations of global capitalist free trade have been extended and affirmed. Yet despite the collective will to create the WTO, the new institutional design was not without its problems. A series of initial WTO trade dispute decisions labelled nationally-legislated measures to protect the environment and labour standards as unfair trade practices. An unlikely coalition of environmental activists and labour unions protested the Seattle Ministerial Conference in 1999, charging that the WTO was an undemocratic institution which represented corporate interests. As a decentralized compliance and enforcement mechanism, the WTO's procedures for dispute resolution came under increasing scrutiny and criticism as being too effective (in the case of labour or environment) or not effective enough (because initially states could veto an undesirable decision). North–South divisions also began to emerge among members over ongoing agricultural subsidies, which stalled progress on the Doha round of negotiations that had begun in 2001.

Many of these problems, and the way in which the WTO's structure influences outcomes in general, have been the subject of neoliberal analysis. In a comprehensive neoliberal treatment of GATT to WTO institutional design and reforms, Kyle Bagwell and Robert Staiger (2004) argue that institutional modifications have not always been the most efficient from an economic perspective. Yet many of the institutional revisions which have occurred make sense, they argue, within the context of particular bargaining and defection issues which were confronting GATT and WTO negotiators at the time. Similarly Robert Pahre (2003) has argued that simply by clustering or centralizing trade negotiations within its structure, important distributional advantages have been created for WTO members.

Issue linkage has been particularly important to agricultural trade negotiations. Christina Davis (2003) has found that multilateral bargaining in the GATT/WTO led to greater liberalization because it allowed for issue linkage and because the rules and procedures for trade negotiations were highly specified. These aspects provided decision-makers with leverage against recalcitrant domestic groups. It also allowed them to demonstrate that larger economic collective interests are at stake in the negotiations. The greater application of legal procedures in the WTO's institutional design has also been significant. Eric Reinhardt (2000) has discovered, for example, that trade disputes tend to be settled earlier, and with greater concessions, if there is the potential for future legal proceedings involving trade treaty violations. That is, when trade bargaining has involved the option of adjudication, members attempt to settle the dispute via negotiations prior to such rulings.

In the area of defection, the WTO Secretariat provides for the systematic review of each member's practices. This is particularly important for an issue area such as world trade, where there is an incentive among exporters to examine data on trade treaty compliance since defection directly affects anticipated profits (McCubbins and Schwartz 1984; Pahre 2003). Yet there is considerable debate within the neoliberal literature over the efficacy of the WTO's dispute resolution mechanism and exactly how it works, both in obtaining early compliance and in how states respond to its rulings. Marc Busch (2000) has argued that an important intervening variable in whether trade cases are adjudicated is whether or not the states involved are democracies. And Keisuke Iida (2004) has argued that whether or not WTO dispute settlements are effective may have as much to do with domestic political and legislative processes as does the institutional and legal parameters of the WTO itself.

There is, finally, the issue of institutional access, delegation, and transparency within the WTO itself. The WTO's greater dispute settlement capacity was supported by developing and smaller countries, which have increasingly availed themselves of this mechanism. Yet neoliberal scholars have found that the capacity to even litigate WTO cases, and to involve expert testimony and legal experts in one's defence, may be directly correlated with relative power and resources (Busch and Reinhardt 2006). On the other hand, Bown and Hoekman (2008) argue that WTO rules are rarely enforced on smaller, poorer members and that greater institutional transparency would resolve this problem. Institutional access is also important in Manfred Elsig's (2011) application of principal–agent theory to the WTO. According to Elsig, there is a link between emerging pathologies in the WTO's negotiations process and the WTO Secretariat's declining role in that process. This suggests that increasing the Secretariat's role would produce more efficacious trade negotiations outcomes. In addition, the conflict between trade and environmental standards has already led to institutional redesign and accommodation (Schoenbaum 1997). In this way, the WTO amply demonstrates how institutional design is continually adjusted by states as they seek to better obtain their collective interests.

Conclusion

As we have seen throughout this chapter, neoliberalism is the umbrella term for liberal research programmes that focus on the role played by international institutions in achieving collective outcomes in an anarchic environment. Neoliberalism argues that international cooperation is possible, and most readily achievable, with the creation and maintenance of international institutions. In contrast to structural realism's pessimistic understanding of global politics, neoliberalism argues that states now have more interests in common and a greater ability to recognize that commonality. Far from representing a 'false promise', as structural realists such as John Mearsheimer (1994–5) have claimed, states have developed international institutions in order to overcome barriers to international collective action. International cooperation is now an embedded, enduring feature of global politics. Neoliberalism's goal is to understand how international institutions foster, maintain, and deepen this cooperation.

Yet it is also important not to overstate the case for international institutions within the context of neoliberal analysis. Neoliberal scholars are aware that institutions do not always matter. They understand that institutions can breakdown or fail to achieve a desired collective outcome. They know that institutions cannot guarantee an effective solution. They understand that institutions serve the interests of states and that these interests do not always accord with the greater good. Yet even in these contexts, there may be an important role for institutional redesign in achieving a more desirable outcome. We must be careful not to assume *a priori* that the absence or failure of a cooperative solution is due to interest conflicts among powerful states. Doing so imposes an explanation on outcome before analysis has even begun. Upon closer inspection, even powerful states often want cooperation; the problem is more typically how to obtain equilibrium solutions that are also pareto-optimal. Institutional redesign may or may not more effectively obtain such solutions, but we cannot know this before analysis has even begun.

It is, on the other hand, also important to draw attention to neoliberalism's normative assumptions about institutions and global politics. Implicit in neoliberal analysis is a faith that the growth of international institutions has been, on balance, a positive development, particularly in global capitalist affairs. This faith has been challenged on a number of grounds, most notably by Marxist and Critical Theorists (**Chapters 8 and 9**), who argue that international institutions perpetuate economic inequities. In addressing this concern, Robert Keohane (1984: 257) argued that 'improvements (as judged by cosmopolitan moral standards) are more likely to be incremental than sudden, building on the knowledge of one another created by successful cooperation.' In other words, ethical improvements are more likely if existing institutional arrangements are modified rather than simply abandoned and replaced with entirely new arrangements.

Whether this effectively addresses the concerns raised by neoliberalism's critics is an open question. By starting with realist assumptions about anarchy and state interests, both realism and neoliberalism treat the Westphalian system as a given. In so doing, both tend to reify the social structures, identities, and interests of that system (as constructivism argues, see **Chapter 10**), and reaffirm that the main criteria for evaluating Westphalia's ethical dimensions are consistent with the aggregate interests of states. International institutions are then evaluated according to whether they obtain state interests, without actually addressing the ethical dimensions of the interests in the first place. In this, neoliberalism shares some of the same dilemmas as English school pluralists (**Chapter 7**) in that it limits its ethical and analytical horizons by presuming that the current international system can best be studied as if it were a tolerable co-existence among like-minded sovereign states.

Unfortunately few neoliberal scholars directly address the ethical criticisms which have been levelled against their approach. Nor have they sought to engage other analytical perspectives in larger discussions about the trajectory of global affairs. Doing so would seem important, if only to avoid being relegated to a disciplinary niche in which only one type of phenomenon—intergovernmental organizations—is being studied. Ultimately, however, neoliberalism's strength lies in its ability to highlight the sheer ubiquity of institutions and cooperative efforts in the current system. In doing so it underscores how the ability to achieve collective action solutions has significantly increased in global affairs. The extent to which this has produced a more equitable international system can certainly be debated. But it is undoubtedly the case that contemporary global affairs exhibit more cooperative dynamics than at any other time in the Westphalian system. For this reason, international institutions, and the disciplinary perspective that puts them front and centre in analysis, are essential to the study of international relations.

 Questions

1. How does anarchy inhibit cooperation?

2. What stands in the way of achieving beneficial collective outcomes?

3. How can the barriers to international cooperation be overcome?

4. How does neoliberalism challenge structural realism?

5. Is a hegemon necessary to a capitalist free trade system?

6. What occurred historically to encourage the growth of common interests?

7. What role does information exchange and iteration play in achieving cooperative outcomes?

8. How is power relevant to a neoliberal analysis?

9. What are the pros and cons of assuming that states are unitary actors with specifiable goals?

10. What are the pros and cons of assuming that interdependence encourages cooperation?

11. How does neoliberalism study the subject of institutional design?

12. What are some of the ethical dilemmas confronting neoliberalism analysis?

13. How would neoliberalism analyse cooperation in an issue area such as environment or human rights?

Further reading

Hawkins, D. G., Lake, D. A., Nielson, D. L., and Tierney, M. J. (2006), *Delegation and Agency in International Organizations* (Cambridge: Cambridge University Press).
This edited volume maps out the principal–agent approach in a variety of applied examples.

Keohane, R. (1984), *After Hegemony: Cooperation and Discord in the World Political Autonomy* (Princeton, NJ: Princeton University Press).
One of the foundational texts in neoliberal analysis that establishes the link between interdependence, regimes, and hegemonic stability theory.

Keohane, R. O. and Nye, J. S. (1977), *Power and Interdependence* (New York, NY: Longman).
One of the foundational texts in neoliberal analysis, which explores 'complex' interdependence and its ramifications for global politics.

Koremenos, B., Lipson, C., and Snidal, D. (2003) (eds), *The Rational Design of International Institutions* (Cambridge: Cambridge University Press).
An edited volume that maps out core components in the study of international institutional design.

Krasner, S. (1983) (ed.), *International Regimes* (Ithaca, NY: Cornell University Press).
The influential edited volume on international regimes, with chapters written on a variety of regimes in particular issue areas.

Martin, L. and Simmons, B. (2001) (eds), *International Institutions: An International Organization Reader* (Boston, MA: MIT Press).
An edited volume which reprints seminal neoliberal articles as well as critiques.

Oye, K. (1986) (ed.), *Cooperation Under Anarchy* (Princeton, NJ: Princeton University Press).
This edited collection explores how game theory can be employed to examine barriers to self-interested cooperation.

 ## Important websites

World Trade Organization website. http://www.wto.org/

International documents on IGO collection, with links to organization websites, maintained by Northwestern University Library. http://www.library.northwestern.edu/govinfo/resource/internat/igo.html

 ## Notes

1. Alternatively, realist scholars have used non-cooperative game theory to illustrate military-security dynamics involving deterrence, crises, and arms races. For examples, see Steven J. Brams and D. Marc Kilgour (1991), Frank C. Zagare and D. Marc Kilgour (2000), and Barry O'Neill (1994).
2. While the ITO's charter was successfully negotiated by 1948, the US Congress refused to ratify it over concerns that it would interfere in domestic economic affairs. By 1950, and after repeated attempts to obtain ratification, President Truman withdrew his support for the ITO as well.

 Visit the Online Resource Centre that accompanies this book for lots of interesting additional material. www.oxfordtextbooks.co.uk/orc/dunne3e/

The English School

TIM DUNNE

 Reader's Guide

The principal alternative to mainstream North American theorizations of International Relations (IR) is the English school. I begin with an account of what it is and how it emerged. Thereafter, the chapter provides a reconstruction of its methodology before embarking on a substantive discussion of its master-concept of international society. I argue that the social order established by states and embodied in the activities of practitioners must be understood alongside the dynamics of the system and world society. The interplay of these three concepts is the primary theoretical contribution of the English school. In the case study section, I look at the issue of human rights as it has become central to the occupation of many contemporary English school theorists. Human rights represent a significant transformation in our understandings of justice in international relations: at the same time, they pose a challenge for international order as Hedley Bull predicted over two decades ago.

Introduction

Writing in the mid-1990s, I began a book on the history of the English school[1] with the claim that the discipline of IR had either ignored or misunderstood the writings of its leading figures (Dunne 1998). Stanley Hoffmann's widely cited historiography of the field up until the 1970s illustrated how the English school had been ignored. Hoffmann claimed there was no systematic study of the discipline outside the USA, 'only the occasional brilliant contribution such as that by Hedley Bull', but his work had been 'unconnected and unsupported' (Hoffmann 1977: 37). In making this claim, Hoffmann overlooked the systematic research programmes undertaken by the British Committee on the Theory of International Politics. While being ignored in the USA, the work of the English school was misunderstood by leading IR thinkers outside the school who viewed it as a straightforward variant of realism (Banks 1984).

Fifteen years after *Inventing International Society* was published (Dunne 1998), the English school is no longer ignored: the inclusion of the English school in influential textbooks is one indicator, as is the number of discussions about it that have appeared in leading journals (including *Review of International Studies* 2001; *Millennium* 2005). Without overstating the impact of the English school on IR today, it is probably reasonable to claim that in Britain at least it has once more become the dominant theoretical voice. Beyond its heartland, there is significant interest in its work in continental Europe as well as the USA, Canada, Australia, China, and India. Contrary to what is implied by the name, the English school was never very English and is even less so today. Despite the resurgence of interest in English school theory, there remain many detractors who view the enterprise as being conceptually underdeveloped; still others who regard it as being overly complacent about the political and social conditions which afflict the vast majority of peoples in the world. Even if the English school is regarded as flawed, it is at least being taken seriously as a distinctive approach to IR—this was not the case during the successive great debates between the three dominant paradigms in the 1970s (realism, pluralism, and structuralism) followed by the debate between neorealism and its critics in the 1980s.

Those who identify with the English school today see it as occupying the middle ground in IR alongside constructivism: this location is preferable to the dominant mainstream theories of neorealism and neoliberalism and the more radical alternatives (such as critical theory and post-structuralism). They are drawn to an English school perspective because it offers a synthesis of different theories and concepts. In so doing, it avoids the either/or framing of realism vs. idealism, as set out in the writings of many great figures during the 1930s and 1940s. It also avoids the explanatory (*versus*) interpretive dichotomy which generated so much heat during the 'fourth debate' in the 1990s. In place of these dichotomies, the English school purports to offer an account of IR which combines theory *and* history, morality *and* power, agency *and* structure.

One obvious consequence of this level of theoretical ambition is that the boundaries of the English school often appear to be unclear, which in part explains the ongoing debate about who belongs in the school and how it differs from other theoretical accounts of world politics. To shed light on these questions, it is helpful to consider some contextual issues about what exactly defines the English school and who its principal contributors are. To begin with, it is useful to reflect on why it makes sense to speak of the school as a distinct tradition of inquiry. First, there are the personal ties that grow when colleagues share institutional affiliations and belong to the same academic field—this is particularly relevant to the 1950s and 1960s when IR as a subject was in its infancy. Second, the main protagonists believed themselves to be part of a collective enterprise, and consciously sought to carry its debates forward. The emergence of a self-conscious research programme, with an open yet distinct agenda, can be seen in the writings of early post-1945 writers working in leading UK universities. Charles Manning developed a curriculum at the London School of Economics and Political Science (LSE) in which the idea of **international society** played a prominent role. In the 1950s, his colleague Martin Wight developed an approach to the subject that drew on 'three traditions' (Wight 1991)—one that was resigned to international relations being a state of war (realism), one that sought to reform its basic structure (the Grotian tradition), and one that strove to dismantle it (what Wight called 'revolutionism').

Beyond realism versus idealism

Many leading figures of the next generation attended Wight's lectures on international theory (they were not published until two decades after his death). Wight's most famous protégé was Hedley Bull who was invited by Manning to join the staff in the IR Department at the LSE in 1955. These lectures, Bull later wrote, exerted 'a profound impression on me' (Dunne 1998: 138). Like many other writers in the late 1950s, Bull was increasingly dissatisfied with the either/or choice between realism and idealism. He singled out E. H. Carr for severe criticism. His *Twenty Years' Crisis 1919–1939* (Carr 1946) was effective at undermining spurious claims to universality, such as free trade and national self-determination, yet at the same time it was flawed because Carr 'jettisons the idea of international society itself' (Dunne 1998: 143). Bull went on to conclude that this had to be the main idea out of which 'a new analysis of international relations should now begin'. In truth, it was already well under way.

The search for a new analysis of international relations was what drove Herbert Butterfield to set up the British Committee on the Theory of International Politics. The inaugural meeting was in January 1959 and the Committee persisted until the early 1980s—long after the parallel committee in the USA had broken up due to divisions between theorists and practitioners. Early discussions of the British Committee revolved around founding issues to do with the nature of IR theory, and the possibilities of establishing order given the condition of international anarchy. The best essays from this period were published in *Diplomatic Investigations*, including classic contributions from Butterfield and Wight on the balance of power, Bull on international law, and Bull and Wight on international society (Butterfield and Wight 1966). In the second phase of their research programme, the Committee looked at comparative states systems, leading eventually to Martin Wight's book *Systems of States* (1977) and Adam Watson's *Evolution of International Society* (1992). The third and final project of the Committee developed organically out of the second in that it focused on the emergence of European international society and the impact colonization and decolonization had on the rules and institutions of the newly globalized international society (Bull and Watson 1984).

By the time of Bull's death in 1984, the work inaugurated by the British Committee and those sympathetic to it was increasingly seen as being out of step with the emergence of new theories and sub-disciplines (such as foreign-policy analysis and international political economy). This is no doubt why the English school is missing in a number of reviews of the 'state of the discipline' in the 1980s (Banks 1984; Smith 1987); nor did it figure in early representations of the debate between neorealism and its critics. Yet by the mid-end of the 1990s, interest in the English school had begun to rekindle. Many influential textbooks began to include it as an alternative approach to the subject, placing it alongside realism, liberalism, and various critical approaches (Burchill et al. 1997; Brown 1997; Der Derian 1994; Jackson and Sørensen 1999). Added to these, original contributions to the history and theory of international society have proliferated, all taking the English school as their point of departure (*inter alia*, de Almeida 2003; Armstrong 1993; Buzan and Little 2000; Clark 2005, 2007; Gonzalez-Palaez 2005; Hurrell 2007; Jackson 2000; Keene 2002; Korman 1996; Navari 2009; Neumann 1996; Osiander 1994; Welsh 1995; Wheeler 2000).

This sense of a resurgent paradigm was prompted in part by the recognition that it represented a distinct position that was inhospitable to the rationalist assumptions underpinning both neorealism and neoliberalism. Moreover, in terms of substantive research questions, the English school had long focused on the kind of cultural questions and normative contestations that were rising to the top of the international agenda in the 1990s. Such momentum prompted Barry Buzan—along with Richard Little—to seek to invigorate theoretical understanding by pulling previously diverse strands together and forging them into a coherent research programme. This new phase was marked by the publication of

Buzan's agenda-setting paper 'The English School: An Under-exploited Resource in IR' in 2001 (Buzan 2001: 471–88) and culminated in two major theoretical works (Buzan 2004; Linklater and Suganami 2006).

The beginning of this chapter has provided some historical and sociological context for the emergence of the English school. What follows will be a focused analysis of their key claims. A good place to begin the remainder of the chapter is to reflect on Kenneth Waltz's dismissal of the contribution made by writers such as Martin Wight and Hedley Bull. Waltz intimated that their work was valuable but it was not really theory, at least not in a sense that would be recognized by philosophers of science (Waltz 1998). Underlying Waltz's argument is his particularly positivist view of what counts as theory, an issue dealt with comprehensively in **Chapter 1** of this volume. Nevertheless, if the English school is to appeal more widely it needs a rigorous account of exactly what it means by 'theory' and how knowledge is generated. What follows is an initial discussion on methodology, followed by an analysis of the school's conception of how the world political system ought to be understood in terms of the dynamic interplay of system, society, and community (or world society).

The interpretive mode of inquiry

The most infamous intervention into 'methodology' was Hedley Bull's 1996 paper in *World Politics* called 'The case for a classical approach'. As has often been remarked, it was more a case *against* the rigid application of scientific methods which he felt would not generate knowledge of any significance. By contrast, a **classical approach** was defined as 'that approach to theorizing that derives from philosophy, history and law, and that is characterized by explicit reliance upon the exercise of judgement' (Bull 2000: 255). One irony with regard to Bull's position in the article is that he had previously spent a good deal of time berating his colleagues in the British Committee for their disinterest in the new wave of scientific writing being developed in the USA in the early 1960s.

Bull's case for a classical approach was obscured by the polemical style he chose to adopt. Some years later, he wrote a much more considered account of what an interpretive methodology ought to involve (2000). His claims in this piece (written in 1972) serve as a good guide to the English school view of the field of IR and how to study it:

1. **The subject matter of IR.** Bull argued that the appropriate frame for IR was not 'interstate relations' or the interactions of any other 'units'. Rather, IR was about establishing a body of general propositions about 'the global political system' by which he meant states and also regions, institutions, NGOs, transnational and subnational groups, individuals, and the wider community of human kind. In tracing the connections between these actors, and the patterns generated by their interactions, Bull placed a high premium on the role of IR theory to define concepts and theorize relations between them. This emphasis upon concepts constitutes a particular kind of theorizing, one which is designed to illuminate complex changes in world order. Such an interpretive understanding of theory is at odds with the positivist pursuit of the formulation of 'testable hypotheses' (King et al. 1994).

2. **The importance of historical understanding.** Academic knowledge needs to have historical depth. Bull gives a pertinent example: it is insufficient simply to know the facts about the strategic superiority of the USA over its competitors; what is preferable is to understand how and why the USA regards itself as an exceptional power. Institutions of international society, such as law and the balance of power, must also be understood in historical context. It matters, for example, whether human rights are as seen by a child of the Enlightenment, or whether they are believed to be a twentieth-century interpretation of the natural rights tradition. These different historical understandings are vital to the diplomacy of human rights and the rationale for promoting rights beyond borders.

3. **There is no escape from values.** It is important to be aware of one's values and for these to be subjected to critical scrutiny. Values will inform the selection of topics to be studied, and the writings and statements of academics will in turn have an impact on the political process. Despite denying the possibility of separating facts about the world and our values, academicians ought to aim at a position of detachment. By this, Bull was targeting those who were obsessed with policy relevance: he believed that the pursuit of political influence was likely to significantly diminish the prospects of generating research that would be of interest to practitioners. In the other camp, the pursuit of political causes is likely to undermine the integrity of the subject and the wider academic enterprise.

4. **IR is fundamentally a normative enterprise.** Values matter not just in terms of the relationship between the researcher and their subject but are central to the subject of IR, properly studied. The central problem in world politics was, according to Bull, how to construct a form of international society that was both orderly and just. His answer to the Weberian question 'What shall we do, and how shall we live?' was not to enter the realm of 'ideal theory' with fictional assumptions and make-believe states (Rawls 2005). Unlike moral philosophers, Bull believed that the IR theorist doing normative inquiry needed to stay close to state practice. What mattered were not normative ideas per se but the ideas that practitioners believed in and sought to implement (Wight 1991). This involves elaborating the context within which actors take decisions as well as understanding that in politics values are often irreconcilable and that terrible choices have to be made.

Throughout the 1970s and early 1980s, the English school's commitment to an interpretive mode of inquiry rendered it marginal to developments inside the North American heartland of IR. Such a position of marginality was further underscored by the fact that the English school was silent during the normative and interpretive assault on positivism that began in the mid-1980s (despite having opposed positivism for over three decades). At the vanguard of this movement were Gramscian critical theorists, feminists, poststructuralists, and constructivists. Of these, constructivism emerged as a mainstream alternative to neorealism and neoliberalism. Constructivism enabled IR to cling onto its claim to have a distinctive subject matter—broadly around the interaction of sovereign actors and institutions—without buying in to neorealism's obsession with material power and immovable international structures. As noted already, constructivists began to appreciate the overlaps between their approach to IR and that of the older English school (Finnemore 1996: 17; Wendt 1999: 31). For a much more extensive discussion of constructivism, see **Chapter 9**.

Were writers such as Manning, Wight, and Bull constructivists before their time? Read Manning's *Nature of International Society* (Manning 1962), or indeed Bull's *The Anarchical Society* (1977/1995), and it is apparent that there is a degree of convergence with conventional constructivists such as John Ruggie and Alexander Wendt (Dunne 1998). Both regard the inter-state order as a fundamentally social sphere which constitutes states as agents and socializes them into following its rules and conventions. And both view norms and institutions as expressions of shared knowledge and shared values. Despite these overlaps, one could argue that as the two research programmes have evolved, significant differences have emerged. Take the example of the basic 'unit' of analysis. Wendt believes that states are the key actors and they are 'like people too' (1999: 215–24). While English school scholars sometimes attribute agency to states as a form of shorthand, they believe that the real agents in international society are the diplomats and leaders who think and act on behalf of the state and its institutions.

Knowledge of how diplomats and leaders understand 'their' world can be enhanced by being attentive to the language they use and the justifications they employ. Two important inferences can be drawn from this relationship between language and social action. First, an action will be constrained 'to the degree that it cannot be legitimated' (Skinner 2002: 156). Second, the range of possible forms of innovative action is limited by the prevailing morality of international society. Actors 'cannot hope to stretch' the application of existing rules and meanings 'indefinitely' (2002: 156).[2] International law provides a testing ground for these interpretive insights. What ostensibly appears to be an act of aggression is invariably justified as an act of self-defence. Whether this is condoned or not depends on how much 'stretch' is being demanded of the normative vocabulary. When Israel described its attack on Iraq's nuclear reactor in terms of self-defence, this was not accepted by the majority of states in international society. Yet the UN accepted the US government's argument that the use of force against the Taliban government in 2001–2 was acceptable given the attacks on New York and Washington on 11 September 2001. The key difference was a change in the normative context of international relations such that the stretch to self-defence was thought to be that much smaller after 9/11. As has already been demonstrated by new thinking in the English school, identifying and tracking the constraining power of rules and norms is a fruitful direction for an interpretive methodology (Wheeler 2000).

Reading exchanges between Waltz and his critics in the 1980s, one could be forgiven for thinking that the scientific revolution in IR is a relatively recent occurrence. Yet, as early as the late 1950s, the British Committee on the Theory of International Politics was deeply sceptical that such methods could ever generate knowledge about world politics. Almost five decades later, the English school continues to offer an alternative way of studying IR which is rooted in the history of current and past states systems, and guided by moral questions about the adequacy of the current inter-state order. The more recent challenge posed by constructivism has brought a greater conceptual clarity to many implicit assumptions in English school theorizing. For instance, the work of Wendt provides a sophisticated account of how actors are constituted by normative structures while at the same time allowing for a certain degree of material determination of the system. Such a combination of ideas and material forces is also evident in Bull's thinking, albeit that in his case it is more a matter of common sense than meta-theoretical application. Such overlaps offer mutual gains. The collective works of the English school have a great deal to say about the intersection of history, morality, and agency. What actors say, how they learn or adapt, under what conditions they act rationally, whether (and how do we know) they are speaking truthfully, and what possibilities they had to act differently. These questions can be answered using an interpretive methodology that borrows from constructivism, although is not entirely reducible to it.

International society

Having reflected on the issue of the English school's approach, the main body of the chapter will delve deeper into the idea that states form an international society, a claim that has been said to distinguish it from other theories of IR. Following Barry Buzan's path breaking book *From International to World Society?* (2004), many now hold the view that the school must not only provide a powerful account of how and why states form a society, it must also show how this domain relates to world society.

What is the status of the categories system, society, and world society? As Bull reminded us, these are 'elements' that exist 'out there' in world politics but can be known to us only through interpretive designs. The sociologist Max Weber referred to these schemas as ideal-types. In order to show the relationship between capitalism and Christianity, Weber argued, it was first necessary to distil them into a conceptual form that made it possible to speak about certain values and institutions being shared by different peoples or successive generations. So it is with system, society, and world society. All are bundles of properties that highlight certain important features while minimizing that which is thought to be less relevant. By seeking to clarify the concepts which reveal patterns in world history, the English school is working with a very different notion of 'theory' to that which is found in the dominant American approaches. Rather than 'operationalizing' concepts and formulating 'testable' hypotheses, the emphasis upon contending concepts is driven by a search for defining properties which mark the boundaries of different historical and normative orders.

Before proceeding, it is important to consider one objection to representing English school theory as a conversation between three overlapping domains: while classical English school theorists alluded to 'three traditions' (Wight) or 'three elements' (Bull), they nevertheless privileged the domain of international society in their account. Therefore, to treat the three as being of equal significance is to misunderstand the distinctive character of English school thought. I do not doubt that one of the intellectual drivers propelling the English school into existence was a rejection of realism and idealism in favour of a middle way that recognizes that institutions can moderate the dreaded dangers that are associated with life in the international anarchy. I also recognize that many publications by English school advocates in the 1990s continued to privilege the societal domain, in part due to the desire to show that the English school was not just a polite form of realism as many in the 1980s had assumed. Neither of these points undermines the claim set out in this chapter that the most persuasive case in defence of the English school is that it is potentially more illuminating than mainstream alternatives because it seeks to provide a synthetic account of global politics that avoids the series of false dichotomies thrown up by the alternatives such as power vs. norms, materialism vs. idealism, anarchy vs. hierarchy, reasons vs. causes. To do so, we need not only to think about international society as the defining marker of the English school, but also to include the other two ideal types to illustrate its boundaries and constraints. After discussing the properties and types of international society, the chapter will discuss how this domain is subjected to downward pressure generated by the system and upward pressure generated by transnational forces in world society.

International society: definition, properties, variations

According to Bull's classical definition, international society comes into being when 'a group of states, conscious of certain common interests and common values, forms a society in the sense that they conceive themselves to be bound by a common set of rules in their relations with one another, and share in the working of common institutions' (1977: 13).[3] The discussion here scrutinizes each component of this definition.

The first key element of international society is the unique character of the membership which is confined to sovereign states. What is significant here is that actors both claim sovereignty and recognize one another's right to the same prerogatives (Wight 1977). Clearly the act of mutual **recognition** indicates the presence of a social practice: recognition is fundamental to an identity relationship. Recognition is the first step in the construction of an international society. If we were to doubt for a moment the social nature of the process of recognition, then this would quickly be dispelled by those peoples in history who at some time have been or continue to be denied membership of the society of states. The history of the expansion of international society (Bull and Watson 1984) is a story of a shifting boundary of inclusion and exclusion. China was denied sovereign statehood until January 1942 when Western states finally renounced the unequal treaties. How did this happen? Membership was defined in the nineteenth century by a 'standard of civilization' which set conditions for internal governance that corresponded with European values and beliefs. Note how important cultural differentiation was to the European experience of international society: China was not recognized as a legitimate member and was denied equal sovereign prerogatives as a result. If the West and China did not recognize each other as equal members, then how should we characterize their relations? Here we see how the system–society dynamic can usefully capture historical boundaries of inclusion and exclusion. There was a great deal of 'interaction' between China and the West during the nineteenth and early twentieth centuries but this was driven by strategic and economic logics. Crucially, neither side believed themselves to be part of the same shared values and institutions: China, for example, long resisted the presence of European diplomats on its soil along with their claim to extraterritorial jurisdiction which has been a longstanding rule among European powers. In the absence of accepting the rules and institutions of European international society, it makes sense to argue that from the Treaty of Nanking in 1843 to 1942 China was part of the states system but was not a member of international society (Gong 1984).

Once it has been established who is entitled to claim the identity of a rightful member of international society, the next consideration involves thinking about what it means for a state to 'act'. Here the English school encounters criticism from empiricists who argue that collective constructs cannot have agency. What does it mean to attribute agency to collectivities like states? One straightforward answer is that states act through the medium of their representatives or office-holders. Every state employs officials who act externally on its behalf, from the lowly consulate dealing with 'nationals' who have lost their passports to the 'head of state'. In a narrowly empirical sense, therefore, this diplomatic and foreign-policy elite are the real agents of international society. This is the original sense in which the term 'international society' came into existence in the eighteenth century: in 1736, Antoine Pecquet argued that the corps of ministers formed an 'independent society' bound by a 'community of privileges'. If we are looking for the real agents of international society, then it is to the diplomatic culture that we should turn; that realm of 'ideas and beliefs held in common by official representatives of states' (Der Derian 2003; Neumann, 2012).

While sovereign states are the primary members of international society, it is important to note that they are not strictly the only members. Historical anomalies have always existed, including the diplomatic network belonging to the Catholic Church and the qualified sovereign powers that were granted to non-state actors such as the rights to make war and annex territory which were transferred to the great trading companies of the imperial era. One might also argue that influential international non-governmental organizations (INGOs) are members in so far as they give advice to institutions such as the UN and on occasions participate in the drafting of significant multilateral treaties. The other important anomaly with the membership of international society is the fact that sovereign rights are often constrained for economic or security reasons. Robert Jackson, a leading writer in the English school, pointed to the fact that post-colonial states are 'quasi' sovereigns in that they are recognized by international society but are unable to maintain an effective government internally (Jackson 1990). A related development is the temporary suspension of sovereign prerogatives by an international institution or occupying authority, a practice that follows from a period of civil conflict or external military intervention. In the colonial period this was often described as trusteeship (Bain 2003); in contemporary international society it goes under the less politically sensitive label of a 'transitional authority'.

While the element of mutual recognition is highly significant for English school understandings of international society, it is not a sufficient condition for its existence. The actors must have some minimal common interests such as trade, freedom of travel, or simply the need for stability. Here we see how aspects of the system impinge on the possibilities for a society to develop. The higher the levels of economic interdependence, the more likely it is that states will develop institutions for realizing coming interests and purposes. The independence of sovereign states, however, remains an important limiting factor in the realization of common goals. For this reason, the purposes states agreed upon for most of the Westphalian era have had a fairly minimal character centred upon the survival of the system and the endurance of the dominant units within it. The condition of general war is an example of the breakdown of order, but Bull was quick to point out that even during the Second World War certain laws of war were respected and, perhaps more significantly, the period of total war triggered an attempt to construct a new order based largely on the same rules and institutions that had operated in the pre-war era. It was this that led him to claim that 'the element of society had always existed' in the modern states system. Such a claim prompts disquiet among IR scholars trained in sophisticated social science methods. If 'society' explains the existence of order, how can it be a permanent presence in the world political system? One answer, which the English school needs to develop more fully, is to provide clearer benchmarks which enable an evaluation of how much 'society' is present in the inter-state order.

Types of international society

This criticism of the tendency in English school writings to treat international society as an unchanging entity is rebutted in part by the attempt to set out different kinds of international society. At the more minimal end of the spectrum of international societies, we find an institutional arrangement that is restricted solely to the maintenance of order. In a culturally diverse world, where member states have different traditions and political systems, the only collective venture they could all agree on was the maintenance of international order. Without order, the stability of the system would be thrown into doubt and with it the survival of the units. Yet, the extent to which states formed an international society was limited and constrained by the fact of anarchy. For this reason, international society was not to be equated with a harmonious order but, rather, a tolerable order that was better than a realist would expect but much worse than a cosmopolitan desires (Linklater 2005: 95).

In a pluralist international society, the institutional framework is geared towards the liberty of states and the maintenance of order among them. The rules are complied with because, like rules of the road, fidelity to them is relatively cost free but the collective benefits are enormous. A good example is the elaborate rules to do with ambassadorial and diplomatic privileges. Acceptance that representatives of states are not subject to the laws of their host country is a principle that has received widespread compliance for many centuries. This is one instance among many where the rules of coexistence have come to dominate state practice. Pluralist rules and norms 'provide a structure of coexistence, built on the mutual recognition of states as independent and legally equal members of society, on the unavoidable reliance on self-preservation and self-help, and on freedom to promote their own ends subject to minimal constraints' (Alderson and Hurrell 2000: 7). To fully comprehend the pluralist order, one needs only to be reminded that great powers, limited war, and the balance of power, were thought by the English school to be 'institutions'. By this term, Bull and his colleagues were pointing to the practices which helped to sustain order, practices which evolved over many centuries. For example, if the balance of power was essential to preserve the liberty of states (an argument the English school shared with classical realists, see **Chapter 3**), then status quo powers must be prepared to intervene forcefully to check the growing power of a state that threatened the general balance.

To what extent are pluralist rules and institutions adequate for our contemporary world? This is a question that has provoked widely differing responses within the English school. On one side, traditionalists like Robert Jackson believe that a pluralist international society is a practical institutional adaptation to human diversity: the great advantage of a society based on the norms of sovereignty and non-intervention is that such an arrangement is most likely to achieve the moral value of freedom (Jackson 2000). Pluralism asserts that states are entitled to equal rights regardless of their capabilities or internal arrangements. Principles of sovereign equality underpin the UN Charter and many form part of customary international law, which is as old as the inter-state order itself. Pluralists regard interventionism as a practice that threatens to undermine the liberal code of toleration and mutual respect in international society (Welsh 2012: 1201).

Critics of pluralism charge that it is failing to deliver on its promise. The persistence of inter-state wars throughout the twentieth century suggests that sovereignty norms were not sufficient to deter predatory states. Moreover, the rule of non-intervention that was central to pluralism was enabling statist elites to violently abuse their own citizens with impunity. For these reasons, both Bull and Vincent were drawn to a different account of international society in which universal values such as human rights set limits on the exercise of state sovereignty. The guiding thought here, and one that is captured by the term solidarism, is that the ties that bind individuals to the great society of humankind are deeper than the pluralist rules and institutions which separate them.

What does a **solidarist international society** entail? Bull originally defined it as the collective enforcement of international rules *and* the guardianship of human rights. It differs from cosmopolitanism in that the latter is agnostic as to the institutional arrangement for delivering universal values: some cosmopolitans believe a world government is best and others would want to abandon formal political hierarchies altogether. By contrast, solidarism is an *extension* of an international society not its transformation. Like pluralism, it is defined by shared values and institutions and is held together by binding legal rules. Where it differs is in the content of the values and the character of the rules and institutions. In terms of values, in a solidarist international society individuals are entitled to basic rights. This in turn demands that sovereignty norms are modified such that there is a duty on the members of international society to intervene forcibly to protect those rights. At this point, Bull was hesitant about what was implied by solidarism. He believed that there was a danger that the enforcement of human rights principles risked undermining international order. Until there was a greater consensus on the meaning and priority to be accorded to rights claims, attempts to enforce them—what he described as 'premature global solidarism'—would do more harm than good.

For much of the post-Cold War period, the normative debate within the English school fractured along a pluralist–solidarist divide. On one side of the divide, Jackson (2000) made a forceful case for upholding pluralist norms, while Wheeler (2000) set out a persuasive argument in defence of a solidarist account of rights and duties. From the vantage point of today this dispute looks rather narrow. In our globalized world, the dynamics of governance outstrip these traditional English school categories. Pluralism seems predicated on an inter-state model of international society that does not connect with transnational flows of goods and services let alone shared identities. Solidarism too often focuses on the enforcement of transnational liberal values by inter-governmental institutions, thereby omitting the dense networks of actors and institutions which have penetrated international society. This third understanding of international society is neatly captured by the label 'complex governance' discussed by Hurrell in the featured book.

 Featured book

Andrew Hurrell (2007), *On Global Order: Power, Values and the Constitution of International Society* (Oxford: Oxford University Press).

Many English school theorists take Hedley Bull's *The Anarchical Society* to be the classical statement of their perspective. They are right to do so. Bull's book is finely crafted. He provides the reader with a picture of international society while at the same time posing fundamental questions about how the world political system is ordered and whether this arrangement is morally defensible.

    Andrew Hurrell, a former pupil of Bull's, has written an 'anarchical society' for our times.
He reproduces what is best about classical English school writings while at the same time updating

it for the early twenty-first century. After all, *The Anarchical Society* was written before the second Cold War let alone the 9/11 attacks on the United States and the subsequent global War on Terror.

The opening part of Hurrell's book re-interprets what we understand by global order. Drawing on Bull's ideas, he argues that order is identified through goal-oriented activity. The following passage neatly captures this argument:

> Bull's classic study of order in world politics concentrated on the common framework of rules and institutions that had developed within the anarchical society of states. It was anarchical in that there was no common power to enforce law or to underwrite cooperation; but it was a society in so far as states were conscious of common rules and values, cooperated in the working of common institutions, and perceived common interests in observing these rules and working through these institutions. It was, however, a necessarily thin and fragile society in which the three fundamental goals of international social life were limited to the preservation of the society of states itself, the maintenance of the independence of individual states, and the regulation—but not elimination—of war and violence amongst states and societies.
>
> Hurrell 2007: 3

Hurrell then sets out three rival analytical frameworks for understanding what order is and how it is achieved. To the traditional categories of pluralism and solidarism, Hurrell considers the framework of complex governance. This way of thinking about order challenges the inter-state model on several fronts. With respect to international law, we see non-state actors involved in law creation and in modes of its implementation. We see private power—or network power—being wielded in ways that advantage some states and social classes while marginalizing others. Alongside these novel features, important questions remain about the enduring power of statehood and the attachment of peoples around the world to cultural difference and the legitimacy of public institutions on which it depends.

The middle part of the book looks at several contemporary issues and challenges, including nationalism, human rights, security, political economy, and the environment. Each one is considered in relation to the three analytics of pluralism, solidarism, and global order. For example, the chapter on political economy examines the complex interaction of markets in an inter-state order (pluralism); the extent to which a liberal value consensus underpins the global economic order and whether this is under challenge from emerging powers (solidarism); and the complex interplay of public and private actors, state and non-state, in the management of global markets (complex governance paradigm).

In common with *The Anarchical Society*, Hurrell ends the book by considering alternative paths to global order. One scenario is where regions become the dominant actors. Advocates of this view claim that regions provide the kind of scale that is necessary for capitalism to thrive; they are also strong enough to regulate markets to ensure a degree of stability and fairness.

If regionalism is unpersuasive, what about the fashionable idea of 'empire reborn?' (262). In a fascinating passage, Hurrell quotes the French intellectual and public official Alexander Kojeve who argued in 1945 that 'nation-states, still powerful in the nineteenth century, are ceasing to be *political* realities'. Instead, the state can only 'truly' be a state 'if it is an Empire' (265). Although such a view found considerable favour among neo-cons during the two George W. Bush administrations, it is questionable how far even the USA can be regarded as being an empire in the traditional sense. For writers such as Hurrell, remaining open to alternative pathways to global order is critical to the on-going relevance of the English school. That said, for now, international society is here to stay: the key challenge is to ensure that order-building in international society deepens its legitimacy and extends its capability to respond to new governance challenges.

International society: between system and world society

Bull and Wight recognized that a sophisticated analysis of world politics required a systemic component. Yet their discussion of Hobbesian dynamics in the 'system' is inconsistent and unpersuasive. In my view, this vital element of the English school's theorization of world politics ought to be refined rather than discarded as some have claimed (see Buzan 2004). Bull defined the system as being an arena where there was interaction between communities but no shared rules or institutions. In order for a system to come into being, there has to be sufficient intensity of interactions to make 'the behaviour of each a necessary element in the calculations of the other' (Bull 1977: 10).

The concept of a system plays three important roles in the English school's theory of world politics. First, as discussed already, the system–society distinction provides a normative benchmark for addressing the question of how far international society extends (Wight 1991: 6). Second, by looking at the formation of the system it is possible to discern mechanisms which shape and shove international and world societies. Third, the category of the system can usefully be used to capture the basic material forces in world politics—flows of information and trade, levels of destructive capability, capacities of actors to affect their environment. Let me examine each of these briefly in turn.

This view of an **international system**—or more accurately an inter-state system—shares a great deal with the use of systems theory in realist thought, both classical (**Chapter 3**) and structural (**Chapter 4**). What sets them apart is that the English school was interested in the system primarily for what it tells us about the history of international society. If one takes Bull's developmental insight into the relationship between system and society, then it is clear that the existence of a society presupposes the existence of a system. This can open up into an intriguing series of discussions as to when a system becomes a society. What level and type of interactions are required in order for the units to treat each other as ends in themselves? And under what circumstances might a society lapse back into a systemic order in which actions impact upon one another but there is no mutual recognition or acceptance of a common framework of rules and institutions? In the British Committee's writings on decolonization, the emphasis is placed on the gradual inclusion of the non-Western world into a globalized society of sovereign states. It is also important to realize that systemic interactions remain a possible future arrangement if the dominant actors in international society cease to comply with the rules and act in ways which undermine the international security. The hypothetical case of a major nuclear confrontation could become a reality only if the great powers acted in ways that were catastrophic for international society. As a result, the society collapses back into the system.

The idea of a states system is also useful to identify the current boundaries between members and those states who find themselves shunned by international society. It is in the dark recesses of the states system that pariah states and failed states find themselves. This does not mean pariahs are outside the framework of the rules and institutions entirely, only that their actions are subjected to far greater scrutiny. Actors in the states system can have structured interactions with members of international society—they may even comply with treaties and other rules—but these interactions remain systemic unless the parties grant each other mutual respect and inclusion into international society.

Thinking about the systemic domain also alerts us to the downward pressure exerted by the distribution of material power. In Bull's work we can find two important instances where the system impinges upon the society. First, he notes how general war is 'a basic determinant of the shape the system assumes at any one time' (1977: 187). Even in the Cold War, where the massive nuclear arsenals of the NATO and Warsaw Pact countries were not unleashed, the presence of these weapons was a crucial constraint on the two superpowers' room for manoeuvre. If the Soviet Union had had only conventional weapons, would the USA and its allies have tolerated the 'fall' of central European countries into the Soviet sphere of influence? Closely related to the phenomena of general war and destructive capacities as basic determinants of the system, one can find in the English school the view that there is a logic of balancing in the states system. Under conditions of anarchy, where there is no over-arching power to disarm the units and police the rules, it is in the interests of all states to prevent the emergence of a dominant or hegemonic power (Watson 1992). Those who take the balance of power seriously point to repeated instances in modern history where states with hegemonic ambition have been repelled by an alliance of powers seeking to prevent a change in the ordering principle of the system. Even if this tendency requires states to 'act' in order to uphold the balance of power, it can still be persuasively argued that the survival of the states system *demands* balancing behaviour from states such that it becomes an inbuilt feature of the system. This is contrasted with the institution of the balance of power in international society which is not mechanical but is rather the outcome of a deliberate policy of pursuing a strategy of self-preservation in the absence of world government (Wight 1978: 184).

Looking through the systemic lens shows not only the ordering of the units; it also directs our attention to the levels of technology, the distribution of material power, and the interaction capacity of the units. Together, these factors tell us a great deal about the ability of units to act and particularly their 'reach'. (Are actors local, regional, or global?) Levels of technology can be thought of as attributes of the units; an obvious case in point is whether a state has nuclear weapons technology or not. However, it is also useful to think about technology in systemic terms, particularly in areas such as communication, transportation, and levels of destructive capacity. Compare, for example, a states system in which the dominant mode of transportation is a horse-drawn wagon, as opposed to a system in which individuals and goods can be transported by supersonic jets, high-speed rail, and ships the size of several football fields placed end-to-end. As these technologies spread, 'they change the quality and character of what might be called the *interaction capacity* of the system as a whole' (Buzan et al. 1993).

What make these attributes 'systemic'? They are systemic in that for the most part they fall outside the institutional arrangement developed by states to regulate order and promote justice. By way of illustration, take the example of the place of Britain in the world from the early 1940s to the beginning of the Cold War. Throughout the war, Britain was one of the 'big three' great powers who were the architects of the postwar order. At war's end, the country was increasingly a policy-taker on the world stage and not a policy-maker despite the fact that its diplomatic network remained global, its language remained dominant, and its values ascendant. None of these soft power advantages were enough to configure the system in multipolar terms. Without wanting to imply over-determination, it is nevertheless useful to invoke the system to characterize those factors that appear immovable from the perspective of the actors, such as their geographic location, population base, and technological/economic capacity. Of course they are not immovable over the long term—even geographical 'distance' can change over time, as globalization has demonstrated in recent decades.

The third element in the English school triad is **world society**. This concept runs in parallel to international society albeit with one key difference—it refers to the shared interests and values 'linking all parts of the human community' (Bull 1977: 279). Vincent's definition of world society is something of a menu of all those entities whose moral concerns traditionally lay outside international society: the claim of individuals to human rights; the claim of indigenous peoples to autonomy; the needs of transnational corporations to penetrate the shell of the sovereign states; and the claim to retrospective justice by those who speak on behalf of the former colonial powers. It is undeniable that human rights are at the centre of the classical English school's conception of world society. An account of the development of human rights is presented in the case study below. For now, it is important to give a brief account of how cosmopolitan ideas have helped to re-configure world society.

One indicator of an evolving world society is the emergence of international humanitarian law. The UN Charter represented an important stage in this evolution, thus indicating the dynamic interplay between the inter-state and the world society domains. Justice, rights, and fundamental freedoms, were all given prominence in the Charter; subsequently, universal norms of racial equality, the prohibition on torture, and the right to development have been added (among others). Various changes in international criminal law have significantly restricted the circumstances in which state leaders can claim immunity from humanitarian crimes committed while they were in office. Similarly, the Rome Statute of the International Criminal Court adds another layer of international jurisdiction in which agents of states can be held accountable for alleged war crimes. Taken as a whole, one authority on the English school argued that they 'may be interpreted as involving a clear shift from an international society to a world society' (Armstrong 1999: 549). Such a claim, however, understates the extent to which the development of world society institutions is dependent on the ideational and material support of core states in international society.

World society is not just about the growing importance of transnational values grounded in liberal notions of rights and justice. Transnational identities can be based upon ideas of hatred and intolerance. Among a significant body of world public opinion, the strongest identification is to the faith and not to the state. This generates countervailing ideologies of liberation on the part of fundamentalist Christians and holy war on the part of Muslim extremists. In English school thinking, such dynamics can usefully be considered in the context of earlier 'revolts' against Western dominance that were apparent during the struggle for decolonization.

Case study: human rights

The extension of international law from the exclusive rights of sovereign states towards recognizing the rights of all individuals by virtue of their common humanity marks a significant normative shift in the character of world politics.[4] To put it into the conceptual vocabulary used earlier, human rights are the most obvious indicator of a move beyond a pluralist international society and its exclusive interest in the pursuit of order and the limitation of an understanding of justice that is limited to demands by sovereign states to be treated equally. Yet, as this case study suggests, for much of the post-1945 period human rights have been as much a source of division as a marker of the emergence of a solidarist international society. During the springtime of liberalism in the 1990s, human rights established an institutional presence that matched its rhetorical power: the winter of the post-9/11 era has illustrated that systemic and societal forces have reversed many previous gains as governments alter the priority accorded to national security over individual liberty (Booth and Dunne 2012). Before unpacking this argument further, let us remind ourselves of the journey human rights have taken in the modern era.

On 10 December 1948, the UN General Assembly adopted the Universal Declaration of Human Rights (UDHR). Eleanor Roosevelt, one of the main advocates, said that it had 'set up a common standard of achievement for all people and all nations' (Risse et al. 1999: 1). Human rights advocates had to wait a further three decades before such principles began to significantly constrain the behaviour of states. In the intervening period, the siren call for states to live up to respecting universal rights was muted by two factors: first, the priority accorded to national security by the leading protagonists (and their allies) during the Cold War; and, second, the fact that states did no multilateral monitoring of their human rights practices. In other words, right at the outset, human rights were overshadowed by systemic factors to do with great power rivalry and the preference by members of international society to view human rights as standards and not as enforceable commitments.

Several factors converged in the mid-1970s which together signalled a step-change in the power of the human rights regime. These can be grouped into the following themes (examined in turn: the growing legalization of human rights norms; the emergence of human rights international non-governmental organizations (INGOs); and the increased priority accorded to human rights in the foreign policies of key Western states. In terms of legalization, in 1976 the two international human rights covenants came into force. With no little historical irony, the Czechoslovak parliament ratified the two covenants in the knowledge that this would mean the treaty had enough support for the International Covenant for Civil and Political Rights (ICCPR) to come into effect. Over and above the internationalization of what Jack Donnelly calls 'an international bill of rights', other institutional changes had an important impact. The UN Human Rights Commission (UNHRC) became more active, in part helped by its expanded membership and the inclusion of states committed to make a difference. While the work of the Commission is largely that of information gathering and sharing, its role raises the status of human rights in the UN system. The appointment of a UN High Commissioner for Human Rights in 1993 took the profile to an even higher level.

Liberal states and INGOs as change agents

The 1970s also saw the emergence of international non-governmental organizations (INGOs) committed to deepening state compliance with human rights law. Dismissed by Soviet diplomats in 1969 as 'weeds in the field' (Foot 2000: 38), INGO activity was beginning to have a significant impact on state–society relations in all corners of the globe. Amnesty International is a good example. Its mission is to cajole governments into complying with human rights standards, such as freedom from torture and the preservation of human dignity. Originally set up around a clutch of activists in 1961, it had over 150,000 members in more than 100 countries by 1977 (it now has 1.8 million members). INGOs such as Amnesty perform two vital functions. They act as information networks with a capacity to communicate evidence of human rights violations to their membership and the global media. If INGOs are believed to be authoritative and independent, as Amnesty is, then this information is taken seriously both by UN bodies entrusted with monitoring human rights and by other actors in global civil society. In 1977 Amnesty won the Nobel Peace Prize and, seven years later, it was highly influential in the drafting of the 1984 Convention Against Torture. The second key role of human rights INGOs in world politics is one of criticizing governments for failing to uphold the standards they sign up to. INGOs make up the most important institution in world society.

Of the three dynamics for change, probably the most significant was the intrusion of human rights into the diplomacy of Western states. In the USA, Congress was increasingly minded to pass legislation linking aid and trade to human rights. And when Jimmy Carter became President, the cause of human

(continued)

rights found a passionate advocate, in sharp contrast to the Nixon–Kissinger era when they were thought to complicate the achievement of more important goals in the economic and security domains. In Western Europe, Norway and the Netherlands were becoming more activist in promoting human rights in their own foreign policy. Within the European Community (EC) and, after 1993, the European Union (EU), respect for human rights had always been a condition for membership. Individuals in EC states could also bring cases against their governments, indicating a much higher level of institutionalization than is the case in the UN system.

The signing of the Helsinki Final Act of 1975 illustrates each type of agency at work. This treaty was the culmination of three years of negotiation among thirty-five states involved in the Conference on Security and Cooperation in Europe (CSCE). The Eastern Bloc countries were desperate to normalize relations with the rest of Europe and have the postwar division of Europe recognized in an international treaty. The West Europeans were pushing hard for shared commitments to fundamental human rights: while this was resisted by communist states, they eventually yielded in order to realize their gains in other issue areas. The Final Act set out ten 'guiding principles for relations among European states', including 'respect for human rights and other fundamental freedom of thought, conscience, religion or belief'.[5] While the communist elites chose to emphasize other articles in the final declaration which underscored the principle of non-intervention in their internal affairs, activists inside their societies began a period of intense mobilization which did untold damage to the stability of communist rule. Within a year of the Helsinki Final Act, the normative context had become inhospitable to the status quo in Eastern Europe—the opposite of what the communist governments had hoped for when they called for a security conference (Thomas 1999: 214). Human rights had exposed, in the words of R. J. Vincent, 'the internal regimes of all the members of international society to the legitimate appraisal of their peers' (1986: 152).

Countervailing forces in the human rights regime

By the mid- to late 1990s, there was a process of 'norm cascade' under way as the influence of international human rights norm diffused rapidly (Risse et al. 1999: 21). The cascade is complete when the norms acquire a common-sense quality such that they become unchallenged (even if they are not unbroken). The 1993 World Conference on Human Rights was an important signifier of the unchallenged status of the standard, as was the signing of the ICCPR by China in 1998. These tipping points illustrate the progressive socialization of states into a framework where their internal behaviour is subject to the scrutiny of other states as well as international public opinion. As the example of the Helsinki process illustrates, the effect of the diplomacy of human rights reinforced by civil society actors and transnational networks was to delegitimize the communist system. Such a process provides a powerful counter to hard-headed realists who believe that human rights are 'just talk'.

The embedding of human rights principles and the development of institutions in world society such as Amnesty, CARE, Oxfam, the International Committee of the Red Cross, and countless others, represents a significant change in our moral sensibilities. This, however, must be checked by the realization that the diplomacy of human rights in the inter-state order presents defenders of solidarism with a number of awkward challenges. First, states may pay lip service to human rights but is this just 'cheap talk' that is likely to fall silent when the eyes of the world are not watching? Second, and perhaps more worryingly, the conduct of the US during the global War on Terror suggests that a retreat from core human rights values is not unthinkable in the world's liberal heartland. The general relegation of human rights down the agenda of core liberal states in recent years reminds us that compliance to human rights norms is contingent and reversible: human wrongs—such as torture in the name of anti-terrorism—can 'cascade' throughout global politics just as quickly as human rights-enhancing norms can be diffused. As Ken Booth has powerfully argued, there is a disjuncture between our growing cosmopolitan awareness on the one hand, and the blinding indifference of statist elites to protect and extend human rights values (Booth 1995).

Conclusion

The case study has illustrated a dimension of international relations that has been of growing importance during the late modern period. By way of an overall conclusion to the chapter, we will situate human rights more directly in the frames of system, society, and world society. The claim here is that the three ideal types provide clarity with respect to the sources of agency pushing for change and the impact this has on the rule structure. As intimated in the opening section of the chapter, a revived classical approach enables the discussion of normative questions without abandoning the quest to explain 'how it all hangs together' (Searle 1995: xi).

In relation to human rights, an English school analysis reminds us that even during the high-water mark of colonialism, the rights of individuals were never entirely distinguished. Hence the attraction of historical figures such as Hugo Grotius who believed that the law of nations was a subset of the law of nature in which the right to liberty and self-defence were universal. In the post-Enlightenment period, changes inside core states, such as the abolitionist movement in Britain in the early nineteenth century, affected change internationally in so far as the hegemonic power used its naval supremacy to end the trade in slaves. Arguably what prevented the evolution of an effective human rights regime prior to the mid-1970s were systemic factors: the condition of general war from 1914 to 1945; great power rivalry until the period of détente; and the absence of institutions in world society with the capacity to lobby and cajole states into rule-compliance.

The retreat of human rights after 9/11 also has a systemic quality that makes the challenge more than simply the product of neo-conservative ideology. Here we are driven back to the thought that there is a centripetal momentum to power such that it concentrates around a single source. Once the centralization reaches a tipping point, the conditions exist to challenge the pluralist rules and institutions upon which the post-Westphalian order has been built. This line of thought goes to the heart of debates about the role of America (and its allies in the West) in building a world order in its own image. Arguably this is a greater threat to international society than the destabilizing potential posed by on-going insecurity associated with decolonization, a concern that consistently reappeared in the later work of the British Committee. Aside from the emergence of an unbalanced power with global economic and military reach, the other significant systemic logic is that of jihadist terrorism. The willingness of coordinated networks of extremist Islamists to use violence against both civilians and government forces undermines international society's claim that is members have a monopoly on violence and have the power to regulate its use.

The appearance at the start of the twenty-first century of an imperial power seeking to wage pre-emptive war and a non-state actor wielding violence outside the framework of the laws of war could lead one to conclude that Bull was right to be concerned that the element of international society was in drastic decline. Set against this, just as the bell has tolled for the state many times before, it is possible that the element of society is resilient enough to resist the unilateralist impulses of great powers as well as the challenge of transnational networks. Whichever pathways history proceeds down, the categories of system, society, and world society will retain their relevance as explanatory tools and normative benchmarks.

Questions

1. What are the core elements of the English school's approach to IR? How, if at all, does it differ from realism?

2. Are English school writers correct in pointing to the gradual diffusion of human rights norms throughout the system? Answer the question with reference to dominant actors in both international society and world society.

3. What is the relationship between order in international society and justice claims advanced by actors in world society?

4. Do you agree with Hedley Bull's comment that 'international society has always been present' in the world political system?

5. Does the English school have an implicit theory of progress in human history?

6. When journalists report on gross human rights violations, they often claim that the international community ought to 'do something'. How would an English school theorist respond to this plea?

7. Is there any analytical purchase in categorizing the administrations of George W. Bush as being part of the system but not being part of international society? Do these categories help or hinder an account of the USA's role between 2001 and 2008?

8. Was R. J. Vincent right to argue that how governments treat their population has become the subject of legitimate scrutiny? Answer with reference to the 'Responsibility to Protect' document (listed under Important Websites).

9. Analyse Prime Minister Blair's speech 'Doctrine of International Community'. Does this suggest that international rules matter for state leaders?

10. Use the concepts of system, society, and world society (or community) to illustrate the evolution of human rights. What explanatory power do these concepts have?

11. Do you agree with Bull that international order will be undermined by solidarism?

12. Evaluate Andrew Hurrell's model of 'complex governance beyond the state'. How is it vulnerable to critique from pluralists and solidarists?

 Further reading

Bull, H. (1977/1995), *The Anarchical Society: A Study of Order in World Politics* **(London: Macmillan).**
Probably the best single work by a member of the English school. It is a defence of international society while at the same time recognizing that other historical orders have existed, and future orders are not only perceptible they may also be normatively more desirable.

Bull, H. and Watson, A. (1984) (eds), *The Expansion of International Society* **(Oxford: Oxford University Press).**
A collection of essays representing the last phase of the British Committee's work. Contributors trace the system/society boundary through various case studies: underpinning the work is a question about whether the rules and institutions of European international society can be sustained in a deeply divided world.

Butterfield, H. and Wight, M. (1966) (eds), *Diplomatic Investigations: Essays in the Theory of International Relations* **(London: Allen & Unwin).**
A collection of British Committee essays, including classics by Martin Wight on 'Western Values' and Hedley Bull on 'Society and Anarchy'.

Buzan, B. (2004), *From International to World Society* **(Cambridge: Cambridge University Press).**
Starts out as a bold reworking of the 'world society' category; in the process, reworks international society too.

Clark, I. (2011), *Hegemony in International Society* **(Oxford: Oxford University Press).**
A book of historical and sociological depth which makes the case for hegemony to be considered an institution of international society.

Hurrell, A. (2007), *On Global Order: Power, Values and the Constitution of International Society* **(Oxford: Oxford University Press).**
See the Featured Book box on p. 146.

Linklater, A. (2005), 'The English School', in S. Burchill, A. Linklater, et al. *Theories of International Relations* **3rd edn. (London: Macmillan), 93–118.**
The best chapter on the English school written for upper-level undergraduates and postgraduate students.

Ralph, J. (2007), *Defending the Society of States* **(Oxford: Oxford University Press).**
This book addresses the issues raised by the International Criminal Court from an English school perspective – offering innovative conceptual design and detailed empirical analysis of American opposition to the ICC.

Vincent, R. J. (1986), *Human Rights in International Relations* **(Cambridge: Cambridge University Press).**
Vincent shows how the post-1945 world has given us a different vocabulary for thinking about the relationship between the rights of states and the rights of individuals. He makes a persuasive argument in defence of the inviolability of basic rights.

Wheeler, N. J. (2000), *Saving Strangers: Humanitarian Intervention in International Society* **(Oxford: Oxford University Press).**
Looking at a series of Cold War and post-Cold War case studies, Wheeler shows how a new norm of humanitarian intervention emerged after 1989. In this and other work, the author sets out criteria for evaluating when interventions are legitimate.

Important websites

The English school website. This website was pioneered by Barry Buzan and has subsequently been taken on by Jason Ralph. The site is a documentation centre, including an excellent bibliography and a collection of reading lists written by leading figures in the English school. It also has information on English school papers presented at national and international conferences. **www.leeds.ac.uk/polis/englishschool/default.htm**

Responsibility to Protect. The principle that informs diplomatic debates about prevention and response to an actual, or potential, atrocity crime being committed. All the key documents, and many briefings, appear on the Asia-Pacific Centre for R2P website: **http://www.r2pasiapacific.org/**

Amnesty International (AI). A worldwide movement of people who campaign for internationally recognized human rights. It claims to be independent of ideology, religion, government, or economic interest. **http://web.amnesty.org/pages/aboutai-index-eng**

'Doctrine of International Community', Prime Minister Tony Blair's speech to the Economic Club of Chicago on 28 April 1999. Readers will find this speech engaging as it sets up a tension between Westphalian conceptions of rules and institutions with late-twentieth-century ideas about the primacy of inalienable human rights. For all its flaws, the speech illustrates the clear connections between how leaders and practitioners view the world. **www.number10.gov.uk**

Notes

1. It is important, at an early stage in the chapter, to discuss the difficulties attached to the label 'English school'. If the label is taken literally, then it is highly misleading: many of the founding members and leading lights were not English (Charles Manning was a South African and Hedley Bull was an Australian). However, it is fairly routine to sever the connection between scholarly identity and territoriality. As one Canadian defender of the English school put it, those who are in the English school 'are as likely to reside outside of England: in Wales, Australia, Canada, Norway, Germany, even the US' (Epp 1999: 48). It is worth noting that this distinction between people and place is relatively uncontroversial in the case of those critical theorists in IR who associate with the 'Frankfurt School', even though the closest they are likely to come to the famous Institute for Social Research is Frankfurt airport.

2. In his work on humanitarian intervention, Nicholas Wheeler has developed and applied both of these insights (2000).

3. Despite the centrality of the concept, one can find in the English school literature several usages. It exists either 'as a set of ideas to be found in the minds of statesmen' (Manning being an exponent), or 'as a set of ideas to be found in the minds of political theorists' (which he likens to a Wightean approach), or 'as a set of externally imposed concepts that define the material and social structures of the international system'. These contending usages of international society are mapped out by Buzan (2004: 12–15) and subjected to scrutiny in Dunne (2005).

4. This section draws heavily on the following sources: Dunne and Wheeler (1999), Foot (2000), and Risse et al. (1999).

5. The entire Helsinki Final Act document can be read at the HR Net website. See http://www.hri.org/docs/ Helsinki75.html.

 Visit the Online Resource Centre that accompanies this book for lots of interesting additional material. **www.oxfordtextbooks.co.uk/orc/dunne3e/**

Marxism

MARK RUPERT

 Reader's Guide

In discussions of world politics, it is not uncommon for Marxism to be dismissed out of hand as being preoccupied with economics rather than politics, and concerning itself with domestic rather than international social relations. In this chapter I will suggest to the contrary that Marxist theory aims at a critical understanding of capitalism as an historically particular way of organizing social life, and that this form of social organization entails political, cultural, and economic aspects which need to be understood as a dynamic ensemble of social relations not necessarily contained within the territorial boundaries of nation states. Viewed in this way, Marxism can yield insights into the complex social relationships—on scales from the workplace and the household to the global—through which human beings produce and reproduce their social relations, the natural world, and themselves. The case study section delves deeper into the insights that can be gained from Marxism in understanding the social relations underlying US global militarism.

Introduction

Marxism may be fundamentally distinguished from both the liberal and the realist traditions. Liberalism generally constructs its view of social reality in terms of individuals pursuing their private self-interest. These individuals may be led by self-interest into a social contract to create a government which will protect their lives, liberty, and property (John Locke), or to specialize and exchange with one another so as to create the germ of a market-mediated social division of labour (Adam Smith). With such contractual theories, liberalism purports to have resolved the problem of social order and cooperation among self-interested individuals. But the question of relations *among* these contractually constituted political communities remains problematic. Accordingly, the modern structural realist theory of International Relations (IR) has defined its field of inquiry in terms of a fundamental distinction between 'international' and 'domestic' politics (evident in **Chapter 4**). While the latter is held to be governed by a sovereign authority and hence allows for the authoritative resolution of disputes, the former is distinguished by the absence of these. In such an insecure 'anarchic' environment, sovereign states encounter one another with diffidence, suspicion, and, potentially, hostility. On this view, the 'high politics' of national security and power struggle necessarily dominate the horizon. Neoliberalism has sought to reintegrate into this state-centric world the liberal concern with contractual relations of cooperation, suggesting that international interdependence can create a demand for more cooperative forms of interaction which are facilitated by regimes and international organizations (as set out by Jennifer Sterling-Folker in **Chapter 6**). Thus can the 'low politics' of interdependence and routinized cooperation tame the 'high politics' of power struggle.

Viewed from the perspective of Marxist theory, both liberalism and realism (and their neo variants) are profoundly limited, and limiting, for each takes as its premise a world of precon-stituted social actors (whether self-interested individuals or security-seeking states) and is therefore unable to understand the social processes through which these kinds of actors have been historically constructed, and implicitly denies the possibilities for alternative pos-sible worlds which may be latent within those processes of social self-production. In addition to the analytical blinders which this entails, the presuppositions of liberalism and realism are exposed as embodying political commitments which are profoundly conservative in effect. In order to recover the analytical and political possibilities denied by liberalism and realism, Marxist theories have sought to illuminate processes of social self-production and the pos-sibilities they may entail.

Marxism constitutes a huge and varied tradition of scholarship and practical political activity which is probably impossible to catalogue adequately. Therefore, rather than attempting to map this extensive and varied terrain, I will instead sketch out a particular interpretation which I believe builds upon the strengths of the dialectical social philosophy developed by Karl Marx, and shows how those strengths can yield insights into the politics of global production as well as the production of global politics. I will relate this tradition of dialectical theory to strains of thought sometimes characterized as 'Western Marxism' (to distinguish them from the official state Marxisms of the twentieth-century 'East')—including the political theory of Antonio Gramsci. The Western Marxist encounter serves to highlight the many ways in which humans are socially self-productive, and suggests important critical insights which include the cultural and political, as well as the economic, aspects of that process. These conceptual tools, then, enable a much richer and politically nuanced inter-pretation of the politics of globalizing capitalism, and the role of imperial power within that process.

Historical materialism and the meaning of dialectical theory

While it may not be possible to provide a simple or straightforward definition of Marxism which would comfortably encompass all its different variants and divergent strains, one fundamental commonality is the desire to provide a critical interpretation of capitalism, understood as an historically produced—and therefore mutable—form of social life, rather than as the ineluctable expression of some essential human nature. To the extent that the ways in which we live our lives, the kinds of persons that we are, and our social relations, are all seen as historical social products, the critical question arises as to whether, and how, we might organize ourselves differently. Given the historically specific social context in which we find ourselves, are there tensions or possibilities for change which might enable us to produce a different, conceivably more equitable and democratic, future possible world? Before any such questions can be posed, however, it is necessary to exert some critical leverage on the prevailing view that social life in commodity-based society is a necessary outgrowth of the natural characteristics of individual human beings.

Contrary to Adam Smith's, and many liberals' (see **Chapters 5** and **6**), world of self-interested individuals, naturally predisposed to do a deal, Marx posited a *relational* and *process-oriented* view of human beings. On this view, humans are what they are not because it is hard-wired into them to be self-interested individuals, but by virtue of the relations through which they live their lives. In particular, he suggested that humans live their lives at the intersection of a three-sided relation encompassing the natural world, social relations and institutions, and human persons. These relations are understood as *organic*: each element of the relation is what it is by virtue of its place in the relation, and none can be understood in abstraction from that context. Insofar as humans are material beings, we must engage in some kind of productive interchange with the natural world in order to secure our survival. Insofar as we are social beings, this productive activity will be socially organized, necessarily involving thinking, talking, and planning together. And in the process of this socially productive activity, Marx believed, humans continuously remake their world (both its natural and social aspects) and themselves. If contemporary humans appear to act as self-interested individuals, then, it is a result not of our essential nature but of the particular ways we have produced our social lives and ourselves. On this view, humans may be collectively capable of recreating their world, their work, and themselves in new and better ways, but only if we think critically about, and act practically to change, those historically peculiar social relations which encourage us to think and act as socially disempowered, narrowly self-interested individuals.

The meaning of dialectic: social relations in process

This view of human social life as *relations in process* forms the core of Marx's famous **dialectical understanding of history**: humans are historical beings, simultaneously the producers and the products of historical processes. In one of his more justly famous aphorisms, Marx summarized his view of history in the following terms: 'Men [*sic*] make their own history, but they do not make it just as they please; they do not make it under circumstances chosen by themselves, but under circumstances directly encountered, given, and transmitted from the past' (2000: 329).[1]

This process is sometimes described as a dialectic of agents and structures. **Agents** are social actors, situated in the context of relatively enduring social relations or structures, often embodied in institutions. Structures generate the possibility of certain kinds of social identity and corresponding forms of action (i.e. roles which actors may play in the context of those structures), but the structures are not themselves determinative or automatic. They require human agents continuously to re-enact their structural roles. Actors or agents may enact structural roles in ways which reproduce, alter, or potentially even transform social structures in which they are embedded. 'This interplay between individual actions and the institutions that form the framework for individual action is what Marx means by dialectic' (Schmitt 1997: 50).

This dialectical, or process-oriented, approach has important implications for the way in which we study social life. As Marx himself put it, 'as soon as this active life-process is described, history ceases to be a collection of dead facts as it is with the empiricists' (2000: 181). On this view, causal explanations which posit objective 'laws' of social life may be misleading insofar as they distract us from the ways in which our world has been produced by historically situated human social agents. For if we understand history as an open-ended process of social self-production under historically specific circumstances, then we are led to inquire about the historical context of social relations in which actors are situated, to ask about the historical processes which generated that kind of social context, and to look for structured tensions in those historically specific forms of life, tensions which could open up possibilities for historically situated actors to produce social change. Further, we are encouraged to ask how our own social situation in the present relates to that of those whom we are studying. Might our own inquiries have implications for the ways in which contemporary people know and (re)produce our own social world? Is theory of politics itself political?

Marx's dialectical framework of relations in process also has important implications for the ways in which we think about politics, freedom, and unfreedom. Traditionally understood in terms of authoritative processes of rule (based upon an official monopoly of the means of coercion), or the authoritative allocation of values (who gets what, etc.), from a Marxian perspective these understandings of politics seem remarkably limited, and *limiting*. In the context of a dialectical view of history, politics appears as struggle over processes of social self-production, the ability to steer those processes in one direction or another and thus to shape the kind of world in which we will live and the kinds of persons we will become in that world. Politics, in short, concerns future possible worlds. And freedom may correspondingly be understood in terms of social self-determination—our collective ability to shape ourselves and our world. This is an expansive understanding of freedom, much broader and potentially more empowering than the traditional liberal understanding of freedom as individual choice (often expressed in a market context where the object of choice is the maximal satisfaction of the individual's private wants and needs). Based on the dialectical approach to understanding history, with its expansive conceptions of politics and of freedom, Marx developed a powerful and enduringly relevant critique of capitalist social life.

Marx and the critique of capitalism

Marx was one of the most incisive critics of a peculiarly modern form of social life—capitalism. For Marx, capitalism was not to be confused with markets or exchange, which long predated capitalism. Rather, capitalism represented a form of social life in which commodification had proceeded to such a degree that human labour itself was bought and sold on the market. One of Marx's central insights was that this situation presupposed the development of historically specific class-based relations and powers: the concomitant development of capital—socially necessary means of production reconstituted as the exclusive private property of a few—and wage labour as the compulsory activity of the many. Under the class relations of capitalism, direct producers are not personally tied to their exploiter, as were slaves in bondage to their master or feudal serfs bound to the lord's estate. In a real historical sense, then, capitalism frees workers to treat their labour as their own property. However, this freedom is complemented by a peculiarly capitalist kind of unfreedom. Insofar as means of production are under the ownership and control of a class of private owners, workers are *compelled* to sell their labour to members of this owning class in order to gain access to those means of production, engage in socially productive activity, and secure through their wages the material necessities of survival.

Marx's critique of capitalism hinged upon the claim, intelligible within the context of his dialectical theory of social self-production, that capitalism simultaneously involves historically unique forms of human freedom and unfreedom, empowerment and disempowerment. Relentless competition among private capitalists results in extension and elaboration of the social division of labour and continuous innovation is the organization of production processes. Marx believed that although capitalism develops the productive powers of human societies to historically unprecedented heights, it does so in ways which are also disabling, exploitative, and undemocratic. In these fundamental ways, capitalism is a contradictory social system, with endemic tensions, political struggles, and potential for change.

Capitalism is *disabling* insofar as this way of organizing social life distorts and obscures real historical possibilities for social self-determination. Socially empowered as never before to remake their world and themselves, people under capitalism are simultaneously prevented from realizing the full implications of their socially productive powers and the fuller forms of freedom these powers might make possible. Within the context of capitalist commodification and the ideology it supports, historically specific forms of social organization and activity take on the appearance of objective, necessary, natural, universal conditions. Marx referred to this kind of disabling mystification as 'alienation' or 'fetishism'. Insofar as these appearances involve abstracting particular elements out of the constitutive relations through which they are produced, and representing them as if they were self-subsistent, preconstituted entities, this ideological mystification may be understood as a sort of reification—the practice of conflating abstractions with reality. For example, social practices which might be seen as specific to a particular historical or social context (and hence to be potentially changeable along with that context) are instead presumed to be hard-wired into individuals as such. Thus the self-interested behaviour which Adam Smith observed among private producers in the context of a commodity society is represented as a universal human attribute, a natural 'propensity to truck, barter, and exchange' (Smith 1993: 21). Similarly, this is the significance of Mrs Thatcher's famous claim that there is no alternative to 'free market' capitalism. To the extent that we understand ourselves as isolated individuals, we confront our social environment not as our collective social product, but as an objective constraint on our individual choices. Social life becomes something which happens to us, rather than a collective way of being in the world. This is an instance of a powerful critical insight derived from Marxian theory: to the extent that people understand existing social relations as natural, necessary, and universal, they are prevented from looking for transformative possibilities, precluded from imagining the social production of alternative possible worlds. In short, they may abdicate their collective powers of social self-production. Ironically, then, the unprecedented development of productive capacity under capitalism has as its historical correlate the disempowerment of collective human producers.

A second strand of Marxian critique holds that capitalism is *exploitative*. Often couched in the arcane language of the labour theory of value which Marx adopted for the purposes of his critical engagement with classical political economy, the theory of exploitation is a complex and controversial topic (Brewer 1990: 26–36; Schmitt 1997: 100–13), but it may be more readily understandable when expressed as an instance of the disabling unfreedom discussed above. On Marx's view, capital is the *result* of socially productive activity, the creation of value by labour. Viewed as a 'thing', capital itself has no productive powers. But viewed as a social relation, capital is productive only as an accumulation of previously expended labour power, set in motion by newly expended labour power. Yet, because capitalism is characterized by private ownership of the means of production, as owner the capitalist controls the production process and expropriates its product—the *surplus value* created by labour (i.e. the product of labour above and beyond that required to sustain the workers themselves). In Marx's understanding of capitalist exploitation, the process and product of socially organized labour are subordinated to private property and incorporated into the accumulation of capital.

Of course, the capitalists' ability to control the production process and expropriate its product depends upon the successful reproduction of their class-based powers, and the insulation of these powers from more democratic, collective forms of decision-making. The third strand of Marxian critique thus highlights the degree to which capitalism creates *private social powers* located in a separate 'economic' sphere of social life, effectively off limits from explicitly 'political' public deliberation and norms of democratic accountability. This is perhaps best understood in terms of an historical contrast. Pre-capitalist modes of production such as feudalism involved the direct coercive expropriation of surplus labour by the dominant class, a landed nobility whose social powers were simultaneously economic and political. Should serfs fail to yield surplus labour to their lord, the social significance of this was not simply a private deal gone bad but rather a direct challenge to the political–economic order upon which the lord's social position rested. That the lord would respond by deploying the coercive force at his disposal would not have seemed extraordinary in a social context where economic and political aspects of social life were fused in this way.

In a modern capitalist context, however, it is relatively unusual (although certainly not unheard of) for employers to use direct coercive force as an integral part of their extraction of surplus labour. Rather, workers are compelled to work, and to submit to capitalist control of the workplace, by what Marxists often refer to as the 'dull compulsion of economic life', the relentless daily requirement to earn enough to pay the rent and put food on the table. The direct intervention of explicitly political authority and directly coercive force within the capitalist workplace is the exception rather than the rule. The social powers of capitalist investors and employers are ensconced in this depoliticized and privatized economic sphere, understood not as intrinsically political powers but as individual prerogatives attendant upon the ownership of private property. By virtue of being understood as attributes of 'private property', these powers are made democratically unaccountable (it is, after all, nobody else's business what each of us does with our own private property). Further, because of the state's structural dependence on private investment, government is effectively compelled to serve the long-term interest of the capitalist class (not necessarily congruent with that of individual capitalists). Failure to create the political conditions perceived by capitalists as a business-friendly climate would result in capitalist investors sending their capital after higher profits elsewhere and leaving the government to preside over an economic crisis which could well be politically catastrophic for incumbent office holders. Insofar as politicians of all major parties are acutely aware of this structural dependence upon the maintenance of a business-friendly climate, a range of possible policy orientations (which might be perceived as threatening to the profitability of private investment) are effectively precluded. This implicit veto power over public policy is yet another sense in which Marxists have argued that capitalism is undemocratic.

Capitalism as a system of social organization, as a way of life, presupposes as part of its structure both a privatized and depoliticized economic sphere and, correspondingly, a public, political state (see Table 8.1). Further, this separation is embodied in a variety of cultural practices and representations in which we appear to ourselves as private individuals, workers, consumers, rights-bearing citizens, confronting a pre-given world in which we must choose the most efficient means for the realization of our private purposes. In these ways, then, capitalism effectively privatizes the social powers of investors and employers, lodging these in a privatized economic sphere, understood to be separate from the sphere of politics, public affairs, or the state. Even as capitalism creates these unequal powers based on class, it masks those powers behind the apparent equality of citizens in relation to politics, the state and law, and behind the appearance of the economy (where inequality may be more obvious) as if it was an apolitical arena where questions of power can hold no meaning. To identify capitalism narrowly with the economy—and therefore Marxism with economic analysis—is to miss the crucial point that particular forms of political and cultural organization and practice are bound up with capitalist social reality, and are implicated in political struggles over the reproduction—or transformation—of that entire way of life.

None of this is incontestable in principle or uncontested in fact. A system of social organization premised upon *privatized social powers* is a system fraught with contradictions and tensions. Historical materialism highlights these powers, along with their structural and ideological defences, in order to subject them to critical scrutiny and to identify historically real possibilities for progressive social change.

Globalizing capitalism and imperial power

Among the most influential contributions of the Marxist tradition to the study of world politics have been those aimed at theorizing global hierarchies of power and wealth, including theories of **imperialism**. According to Anthony Brewer's authoritative text (1990: 25), Marx himself never actually used the term 'imperialism'. Further, Brewer's interpretation of Marx's relatively few discussions of the topic suggests that colonialism is not essential to capitalism: 'capitalism does not need a subordinated hinterland or periphery, though it will

Table 8.1 Contradictory structure of capitalism divides social life into two seemingly separate spheres

Political Sphere	Economic Sphere
Institutional locus: state	Institutional locus: market
Governing norm: Pursuit of public interests, overtly political	Governing norm: Pursuit of private wants and needs, seemingly apolitical
Social identity: citizen, member of political community	Social identity: private individual, owner of property (or not)
Political rights of citizen	Right to own property (or not)
Equality before the law	Inequality of property

use and profit from one if it exists' (Brewer 1990: 57). Although he had relatively little to say about imperialism as such, regarding the expansionary dynamics of capitalism which we would nowadays associate with globalization Marx was prescient:

> The bourgeoisie, by the rapid improvement of all instruments of production, by the immensely facilitated means of communication, draws all, even the most barbarian, nations into civilization. The cheap prices of commodities are the heavy artillery with which it batters down all Chinese walls, with which it forces the barbarians' intensely obstinate hatred of foreigners to capitulate. It compels all nations, on pain of extinction, to adopt the bourgeois mode of production; it compels them to introduce what it calls civilization into their midst, i.e., to become bourgeois themselves. In one word, it creates a world after its own image.
>
> Marx 2000: 248–9[2]

Capitalism for Marx was clearly not a purely 'domestic' phenomenon, hermetically contained within the territorial vessels of modern nation states. Its expansionist dynamics (rooted in the imperatives of competitive accumulation) overflowed those boundaries and outdistanced the geographical scope of state-based political authority. For Marx, the privatized social powers of capital have long had global horizons. Marx thought that the international activities of industrial capital (as distinct from the trading of merchant capital) were potentially transformative for the social organization of production on a world scale, spreading and intensifying the capitalist organization of production and greatly expanding socially productive powers. Consistent with his dialectical analysis of capitalism, Marx believed this process would entail both progressive and retrogressive aspects, generate massive suffering as well as the potential for qualitative and, he hoped, progressive social change.

In the early twentieth century, as the First World War loomed, a generation of Marxist writers emerged who are most appropriately associated with the theory of imperialism. Including Rosa Lumemburg, Rudolf Hilferding, Nicolai Bukharin, and most famously Vladimir Lenin, these writers argued that advanced processes of capitalist accumulation were driving the major capitalist countries into colonial expansionism. Although the precise mechanisms driving capitalism toward imperialism varied (e.g. the quest for raw materials, overproduction requiring a search for new markets, or over-accumulation compelling the export of capital), their thinking converged on the notion that advanced capitalist countries would be driven by the imperatives of capital accumulation to support the international expansion of their great monopolistic blocs of industrial–financial capital. In a finite world where much of the globe had already been colonized by one or another of the great imperialist powers, 'inter-imperialist rivalry' was seen as an overwhelmingly likely source of conflict, and the First World War would have appeared as confirmation of this. Classical theories of imperialism have been subjected to sharp criticism insofar as they represent species of economic determinism—the idea that processes intrinsic to the economy are the primary determinants of social and political life.

Western Marxism and Gramsci's theory of hegemony

The Bolshevik revolution and the rise of Official Soviet Marxism in the 'East' provided the backdrop for the development of 'Western Marxism'—a family of innovative theories which both built upon and reacted against aspects of the classical Marxist tradition (see also **Chapter 9**, for evolution of critical theory). The Marxist expectation that proletarian revolution, once ignited, would sweep the advanced capitalist world was bitterly disappointed in the early twentieth century. The Russian revolution gave birth to socialism in one nation and Marxists in the West were left to ponder the reasons why working-class revolution had failed to materialize in their own countries and, subsequently, why fascism had triumphed in some Western countries. Official Soviet Marxism soon solidified into a rigid Stalinist dogma in the service of a one-party state, stifling rather than enabling critical discourse and social self-determination. It is in this historic context that we may understand Western Marxism not just in terms of a critique of capitalism but also a corresponding critique of positivism and economic determinism as ways of understanding social life. In the apt summary of critical theorist Douglas Kellner, 'those individuals who became known as "Western Marxists" saw the need to concern themselves with consciousness, subjectivity, culture, ideology and the concept of socialism precisely in order to make possible radical political change' (1989: 12).

The Italian Marxist Antonio Gramsci, incarcerated in Mussolini's fascist prisons for the last decade of his life, was sharply critical of economistic and positivistic forms of knowledge, including forms of Marxism based on economic determinism. Gramsci insisted on situating the process of human knowledge construction in particular historical social contexts and, in a devastating critique of the economistic and scientistic Marxism of Bukharin, he derided as 'metaphysical materialism any systematic formulation that is put forward as an extra-historical truth, as an abstract universal outside of time and space' (Gramsci 1971: 437). For Gramsci, Marxism was not the objective truth of history, but was rather a way of telling the story of history from *within* a capitalist historical context, a story which could lead people to consider possible post-capitalist futures and ask themselves how, together, they might get there from here.

Accordingly, Gramsci developed a theory of **hegemony** as a subtle form of political power which relied more strongly upon consent than coercion. In a hegemonic social situation, dominant groups (classes, class fractions, and their various allies) articulate a social vision which claims to serve the interests of all, and they use selective incentives to recruit junior partners into their coalition and to divide and disable opposition. Gramsci believed that in advanced capitalist societies, in which civil society was highly developed, hegemonic power might be promoted and contested in forums of popular culture, education, journalism, literature, and art, as well as in political parties and unions. Under conditions of hegemony, subordinate social groups might be led to consent to the power of dominant groups, making the widespread use of direct (and obviously oppressive) coercive power unnecessary. However, Gramsci argued, hegemony was not seamless, a dominant ideology which simply foreclosed any possibility of critique. On the contrary, hegemony could be and should be continuously challenged throughout civil society in ongoing ideological struggles. In this way, Gramsci hoped, an atomized and depoliticized capitalist culture might be challenged by a counter-hegemonic political culture, people might be led to think of their economic lives as having political significance, and they might begin to question capitalism's structured separation of the economic from the political aspects of social life. This latter he saw as the necessary precondition for the concurrent democratization of economic, cultural, and political life, a gateway to a variety of possible postcapitalist futures (see Rupert 2009).

Global power and hegemony

The stream of explicitly critical theorizing associated with dialectical theory, Western Marxism and Antonio Gramsci, might lead us to regard with some scepticism claims of scientific objectivity associated with positivistic forms of IR theory, and the economic determinism underlying classical theories of imperialism. And, indeed, contemporary theorists have drawn upon these and related intellectual resources to begin to construct dialectical theories of world politics. Robert Cox (1986) was a pioneer in using Gramscian conceptual vocabulary to make sense of historical structures of global power.

Cox explicitly called into question prevailing modes of theorizing world politics: as a species of positivist or 'problem-solving' theory, 'Neorealism implicitly takes the production process and the power relations inherent in it as a given element of national interest, and therefore as a part of its parameters' (1986: 216–17). Assuming what needs to be explained, neorealism describes patterns in the operation of power among states without inquiring as to the social relations through which that power is produced. Moreover, those relations themselves have a history, a process of production, and they need not remain forever as we see them now. Accordingly, Cox adopts what he calls a method of 'historical structures' in which 'state power ceases to be the sole explanatory factor and becomes part of what is to be explained' (1986: 223):

> 'The world can be represented as a pattern of interacting social forces in which states play an intermediate though autonomous role between the global structure of social forces and local configurations of social forces within particular countries . . . Power is seen as emerging from social processes rather than taken as given in the form of accumulated material capabilities, that is as the result of these processes. (Paraphrasing Marx, one could describe the latter, neo-realist view as the 'fetishism of power'.)'

> Cox 1986: 225

A Gramscian critical approach to global politics would then take a relational, process-oriented perspective, and seek to show how social forces (classes, social movements, etc.), states, and world orders are bound up together in particular constellations of historical structures. It would inquire as to the ways in which those historical structures—entailing political, cultural, and economic aspects—had been socially produced, the ways in which they differentially empower various kinds of social agents, and the kinds of resistances which those power relations engender. It would seek to highlight tensions and possibilities within the historical structures of the present in order to open up political horizons and enable social agents situated within those structures to imagine, and potentially begin to realize, alternative possible worlds. The view of theory defended by Cox—and his characterization of 'problem-solving theory'—is discussed in **Chapters 1** and **9**.

More recently there has been something of a renaissance of Marxian international theory, beginning during the 1990s and gaining momentum with the US turn toward military supremacy and preventive war after 2001. A landmark contribution was Justin Rosenberg's Marxist critique of realist approaches to IR theory which, he charges, 'can perceive that the modern state seeks to mobilize the economy, but not that the economy is part of a transnational whole which produces important political effects independently of the agency of the state' (1994: 13). Instead of reifying states as everywhere and always the primary actors of world politics, Rosenberg seeks to recontextualize geopolitics within 'wider structures of the production and reproduction of social life' (1994: 6). Under social conditions of capitalist modernity, in which a structural separation of economic life and political life is effected, this 'means that the exercise of imperial power, like domestic social power, will have two linked aspects: a public political aspect which concerns the management of the states-system, and a private political aspect which effects the [transnational] extraction and relaying of surpluses.' In both spheres, actors will confront the compulsions of anarchic competition which characterize the historical structure as a whole. Rosenberg refers to this modern, capitalist geopolitics as 'a new kind of empire: the empire of civil society' (1994: 131). In the wake of Rosenberg's pioneering work, innovative Marxist theorizations of the emergence of capitalist geopolitics among a system of multiple territorial states have been constructed by Benno Techke and Hannes Lacher (see the featured book box). And with the overtly militaristic turn in US foreign policy, a veritable flowering of Marxist theorizing on world politics has ensued (see, for example, the various essays in Colas and Saull 2006; Anievas 2010).

 Featured book

Hannes Lacher (2006), *Beyond Globalization: Capitalism, Territoriality and the International Relations of Modernity* (London: Routledge).

While acknowledging Justin Rosenberg's insight that capitalist geopolitics are qualitatively different from absolutist or feudal geopolitics, Hannes Lacher offers a powerful theoretical and historical argument against the thesis that the modern state—and, by extension, the system of states—was born out of the very historical processes that gave rise to capitalism. Lacher argues instead that the emergence of a system of rivalrous territorial states—a process driven by the historically distinct politico-economic imperatives of absolutist rule in early modern Europe—*preceded* the emergence of capitalist production relations and cannot adequately be understood as their product. However, following the emergence of capitalist production relations in seventeenth-century England, the dynamics of absolutist geopolitics were transformed and the system of territorial states was *internalized* within, and became integral to, a distinctly capitalist system of transnational social relations. The nature of sovereignty itself was transformed as absolutist rule and 'politically constituted property' (characteristic of absolutism) gave way to capitalist social formations based on the formal separations of politics and the economy, domination and appropriation. In this way, Lacher argues that capitalism's 'political space has been fractured by sovereign territoriality', and this historical–structural disjuncture has put states in a position of rivalry: 'Whereas the state domestically stands apart from the competition between individual capitals, and seeks to regulate the economy through universal forms of governance like the rule of law and money, in the international sphere it is or can itself be a competitor seeking to promote the interests of its capital with political and economic means' (Lacher, in Rupert and Smith 2002: 160–1). Further, Lacher argues that capitalism's globalizing tendencies were shaped and channelled through inter-relation with rivalrous territorial states and their socio-political and geopolitical strategies. It is this dialectic of territorialization and globalization that Lacher identifies as the central dynamic through which contemporary geopolitics has been produced. In contrast to scholars who argue that the system of territorially exclusive states is likely to remain into the indefinite future as the problematic political infrastructure of economically universalizing capitalism (e.g. Wood 2003), and those who posit the more or less inevitable subsumption of nation states by global relations and processes of capitalism (e.g. Robinson 2004), Lacher views the persistence of territorially based rule as very much an open—and quintessentially political—question in the era of capitalist globalization.

Case study: from Bush to Obama—US global power as twenty-first-century imperialism?

In a series of important books, realist scholar Andrew Bacevich (2005a, 2008, 2010) has perceptively suggested that the very nature of the US state and the ways it exercises global power have been shaped by two inter-related historical processes: the deep embedding of a mass consumerist ethos in American culture, and a corresponding drive to sustain global military supremacy in order to ensure privileged access to the world's goods, energy, and credit. While Bacevich's insights are surely of the greatest significance, it is also remarkable that in order to generate those insights he has had to peer into areas of social reality systematically neglected by realism. A realist conceptual vocabulary is ill-suited to understanding of the historical development of such a global power complex and the economic, cultural, and political relations that together constitute its core. I argue that such an understanding requires an analysis of historical structures, their inter-relations and dynamics, and that historical materialism is better suited to this task than other available theories.

From this perspective, a satisfactory account would need to incorporate not just the historical structures of global capitalism (with their economic, political, and cultural aspects) but also the ideologies and actions of human agents situated within these structures. The resulting multi-layered explanatory account would resemble a sort of dialectical layer cake seeking to explain: (1) how the structures of capitalist modernity create the possibility of particular kinds of world politics; (2) how those possibilities were realized in the particular forms of the twentieth-century capitalist world order; (3) within those historical structures, the key relationship between capitalism, Fordism, and the geopolitics of petroleum; and (4) the ideologies of 'economic security' which have animated US policy-makers from the Cold War to the Bush and Obama administrations. I will be able to do no more in this context than to sketch out the broad outlines of what such an explanation might look like. That should be enough, however, to show how this kind of analysis differs from other approaches to the study of world politics.

Recall that at the heart of capitalism is a class relation between those who own the means of production and those who must sell their labour-power in order to gain access to those means of production. One of Marx's most important insights was that this class relationship presupposes a broader set of social relationships, a set of social structures which make this kind of relation possible. One of these enabling structures involved the constitution of social means of production as private property, and hence presupposed the privatization and depoliticization of economic life (recall, by way of contrast, how economic and political life had been fused under feudalism). The creation of a privatized and depoliticized economy involved the exclusion of public, political concerns from the economy, and their assignment to a separate sphere of society, one which we have come to associate with the modern state. The political states which have become integral to capitalist modernity are understood to be sovereign within their territory, and thus are enabled to legislate and regulate 'domestic' affairs. Yet, the activities of private economic actors continuously overflow those bounda-ries—in no small measure because of the dynamics of capitalism as a system of accumulation without limits, driven by the compulsions of relentless market competition. The structural contours of capitalist modernity, then, involve a system of territorially limited political authority and flows of economic activity which are not similarly limited. This structure represents a condition of possibility for imperial-ism—the exercise by states of coercive power in the service of capital accumulation—as well as systems of global hegemonic power in which coercive force is less evident and the ideological politics of consent come to the fore.

Hegemony and Fordist capitalism

These structures of capitalist modernity are not automatically self-perpetuating, but rather are continuously (re)produced, challenged, or changed by human agents under particular historical circumstances. Thus, these structures may assume distinct forms during identifiable historical periods.

During the twentieth century, Fordist industrial capitalism in the USA was setting global standards of dynamism and productivity (this itself was not simply an historical datum but the result of long and complex political struggles—see Rupert 1995). After the Second World War a transnational coalition, centred on Fordist industrial capital, emerged and promoted a hegemonic world-order project which envisioned a global economy of free trade, but one in which state managers would be able to use macroeconomic policy to sustain economic activity and levels of consumption, and in which labour unions might be tolerated or even encouraged as brokers of industrial consent, securing the cooperation of workers within the framework of Fordist mass-production industry in exchange for real wages which would grow along with productivity. In the USA and across much of the industrial capitalist world, organized labour was integrated into a hegemonic coalition which sought to rebuild the world economy along the lines of this 'corporate–liberal' model (van der Pijl 1984; Rupert 1995). Securing a measure of political stability and institutionalizing a rough correspondence between mass production and consumption, this set of historical structures enabled a period of unprecedented economic growth and capital accumulation, and institutionalized a culture of mass consumerism, especially in the wealthy global 'North'. The political economy of Fordist capitalism played a central role in the great global order struggles of the twentieth century: arguably, it was the unparalleled productive power of Fordist capitalism which enabled the geopolitical triumph of the allies over the autarkic and authoritarian capitalism of the axis powers, and subsequently of the reunified West over the Soviet bloc in the Cold War.

Fordist capitalism depended not only on politically quiescent industrial labour and predictable levels of consumer demand for the products of mass production industry; it also required fuel and lubricants for its machines, raw material for its pervasive petrochemical industry, and inputs for its increasingly mechanized and chemical-intensive agriculture. Oil, in short, was indispensable to the energy-intensive form of Fordist capitalism at the heart of the twentieth-century world order. Although the US oil industry was able to provide from domestic production the great bulk of the oil consumed by the allies during the Second World War, by the end of the war it was clear that US reserves were not sufficient to fuel the reconstruction of the capitalist world economy or its growth in subsequent decades.

Geopolitics and Fordism

Framed in terms of 'economic security', US global strategy after the Second World War aimed not just at 'containing' the power of the Soviet Union, but also at creating a world which would be hospitable to the growth of US-centred capitalism (Pollard 1985). US strategists explicitly envisioned a symbiotic relationship between the vitality and robustness of the capitalist 'free world' and globally projected US military power. The foundational vision of world order embodied in the strategy document known as NSC-68 (1950, reprinted in May 1993) led the USA into a grand strategy of globalized military containment justified by anticommunism and social self-understandings of Americans as defenders of the 'free world'. That document explicitly envisioned a political economy of military Keynesianism in which strong economic growth would be consistent with massive rearmament as well as unprecedented levels of popular consumption at home (May 1993: 75). Over postwar decades, the legitimacy of incumbent officials came to be linked to popular perceptions of their defence of and support for the 'American way of life.' As Bacevich (2005b) has perceptively argued, this involved transformations in American political culture in which freedom was increasingly conflated with consumerism in ways which have been deeply consequential for America's role in the world: 'what Americans demanded from their government was freedom, defined as more choice, more opportunity, and, above all, greater abundance, measured in material terms. . . . The aim was to guarantee the ever-increasing affluence that underwrites the modern American conception of liberty.' In these ways, the military–industrial complex and mass consumerism became embedded together in the historical structures of the US state–society complex, and Americans came to understand themselves and their place in the world in terms of social identities as 'defenders of freedom' and as 'consumers'. Viewed through the lenses of this strategic vision, protecting the

(*continued*)

free world was closely identified with promoting a vigorous US-centred capitalist world economy, and it was this worldview which appeared to justify US interventions in order to counter political forces which might inhibit the growth of US-dominated global capitalism and support those forces favourably inclined toward such a geopolitical project. In this context we can understand numerous interventions which undermined democracy or led to large-scale human rights abuses in countries around the world (Kinzer 2006)—actions that might seem profoundly puzzling from the perspective of liberal or realist theories.

Insofar as the Fordist world order depended upon ample and cheap supplies of oil which the USA could not itself provide, US strategists sought to establish predominance in the oil-rich Persian Gulf region. Pivotal to postwar US strategic dominance in the Gulf were its relations with Iran and Saudi Arabia. Franklin Roosevelt had established a strategic partnership with the Saudi ruling family in 1945: 'Roosevelt forged an agreement with Abdul-Aziz ibn Saud, the founder of the modern Saudi dynasty, to protect the royal family against its internal and external enemies in return for privileged access to Saudi oil' (Klare 2004: 3). In Iran, US influence was secured for a quarter-century by the 1953 CIA-sponsored coup in which democratically elected Prime Minister Mohammad Mossadegh, who had committed the cardinal sin of nationalizing the Anglo-Iranian Oil Company, was overthrown by forces who re-established the autocratic power of the Iranian monarch, the reliably pro-Western Shah. In light of this history, it is little wonder that the Iranian Revolution which finally ended the Shah's rule in 1979 fused a Shiite Islamic theocracy with bitter anti-Americanism (Kinzer 2003). Nor should it be surprising that the USA–Saudi relationship is deeply ambivalent, with widespread resentment of US influence (and, for the last decade, military presence) in the Kingdom finding expression through the fundamentalist Wahhabi brand of Sunni Islam which predominates there. Announced in 1980, the 'Carter Doctrine' made explicit the US commitment to prevent a hostile power from gaining a foothold in the Middle East, and US ability to project military power into the region was augmented substantially. In subsequent years, the US entered into partnership with the Saudis and Pakistanis in support of Islamist mujahedeen resisting Soviet military intervention in Afghanistan, thereby laying the groundwork for the emergence of militantly anti-Western jihadist groups such as al-Qaeda once the Soviets had been driven out (Coll, 2004). Militant Islamism did not, then, arise suddenly out of an abstract hatred of American 'freedoms' but is in some substantial part understandable as an idiom of resistance to the longstanding geopolitical project of US dominance in the region.

It is against this backdrop of global geopolitics and the ideology of economic security that we may interpret the invasion of Iraq under the guise of the War on Terror. The most hawkish elements in the administration of George W. Bush exploited the atmosphere of jingoism and fear in the USA following the terrorist attacks of 11 September 2001 to put into effect their long-cherished vision of US global military supremacy, unilateral action, and the pre-emptive use of military force deployed to create a world in which the US model of capitalist democracy is unquestioned—a strategic vision now known as the Bush Doctrine. Building on 'a position of unparalleled military strength and great economic and political influence'—a unipolar condition to which Bush referred as 'a balance of power that favors freedom'—'[t]he United States will use this moment of opportunity to extend the benefits of freedom across the globe. We will actively work to bring the hope of democracy, development, free markets, and free trade to every corner of the globe' (White House 2002: 1–2). Iraqi leader Saddam Hussein's continuing defiance of US power in a region of such enormous strategic signifi-cance effectively mocked the Bush administration's pretensions to unquestioned global supremacy. That removing Saddam was a high priority for those who formulated the Bush Doctrine should not then be surprising. The administration also hoped that a postwar client regime in Iraq would provide the USA with a base of operations in the heart of the Gulf region more reliably open to US forces than Saudi bases. Further, among the so-called neoconservatives in the administration and their intellectual guides, it was believed that a forcefully 'democratized' Iraq would lead to the spread of liberal democracy throughout the Middle East, 'drain the swamp' of authoritarianism and poverty which was believed to be the breeding ground of terrorism, and lessen the perceived threats posed to Israel. But the Iraq War cannot be properly understood in abstraction from questions of world order following in the wake of Fordist capitalism. The US remains among the most petroleum-dependent of major economies, and its mechanized military machine consumes enormous quantities in order to fuel its global power projection. Since petroleum prices are set on a global market, this makes the US susceptible to global supply disruptions and price fluctuations, even if it succeeds in reducing its own dependence on imported oil. As global demand for oil continues to grow and put pressure on available supplies, no other petroleum reserves are as significant for the future of global strategic power in a post-Fordist world as those of the Gulf region. The Bush administration's National Energy Policy task force, chaired by Vice-President Cheney, estimated that the Gulf region will be supplying around two-thirds of the world's oil needs by the year 2020 (Dreyfuss 2003: 44). In their quest for global supremacy and a capitalist world order favourable to US interests, Bush administration officials may well have believed that militarily-based strategic dominance in the Middle East, and an American hand on the world's oil tap, would represent a bargaining chip of incalculable value when dealing with potentially incompliant allies and emergent rivals (especially China) (Everest 2004).[3] On this view, the War on Terror is inextricably bound up with US attempts to achieve strategic dominance in the oil-rich Persian Gulf region, and this latter is deeply entangled with the historical structures of US-centred global Fordist capitalism.

While embracing a more multilateral style of diplomacy and backing slowly out of the major ground wars initiated by the Bush administration, President Obama has continued vigorous use of US military power to attack those perceived to be most hostile to American presence in the Middle East, south Asia, and east Africa. Obama has embraced covert operations and so-called 'targeted killings' of suspected militants and their associates, massively expanding the more secretive elements of the national security state to gather intelligence, target, and execute these attacks (Priest and Arkin 2011). This has included expanded use of so-called kill/capture teams operated by the US military's Joint Special Operations Command (JSOC) as well as drone strikes executed by the military and the CIA. As of February 2012, 'the Obama administration has carried out at least 239 covert drone strikes, more than five times the 44 approved under George W. Bush. And after promising to make counter-terrorism operations more transparent and rein in executive power, Obama has arguably done the opposite, maintaining secrecy and expanding presidential authority' (Rhode 2012).

While it may not be possible to deductively derive US global militarism from an essential underlying logic of capital, it is possible—and arguably necessary—to contextualize these ongoing military commitments in terms the historical structures of Fordist capitalism, and the US geopolitical project of economic security and military supremacy which has been its historical correlate.

Conclusion

Marxism is neither solely preoccupied with the economy, nor with domestic relations. Rather it aims at a critical understanding of capitalism as an historically particular way of organizing social life, one which entails political and cultural as well as economic relations and practices, which has never been containable within the boundaries of territorial states, and which has crucial implications for processes of social self-production on scales from the workplace and household to global order. Conceived by Marx as a dialectical theory of relations in process, the enabling implications of Marxist theory were substantially vitiated by interpretations which cast it as a form of economic determinism. Seeking to recover its ability to illuminate dialectical tensions and possibilities, Western Marxism formulated sharp critiques of economic determinism and positivistic forms of knowledge more generally. These currents led toward a re-emphasis of politics, culture, and ideology within a broadly materialist understanding of social life, pointing towards an approach which Cox (1986) described as a 'method of historical structures'. Employing an analytic approach similar to the one Cox suggests, we may understand America's global military activity as the product of a confluence of social relations and processes which traverse and interrelate social forces, states, and world orders. The structures of capitalist modernity, the historical forms they assumed in the epoch of Fordism and the hegemonic world order which emerged out of that context, strategic ideologies of economic security, and the culture of Fordist consumerism are all implicated in this story.

 ## Questions

1. What do Marxists mean when they talk about a *dialectical* understanding of history?

2. How does such a view shed critical light on liberal individualist theories, such as that of Adam Smith?

3. What are the implications of a dialectical understanding of history for the way in which we think about *politics* and *freedom*? When we see the world in terms of dialectical theory, how do we need to redefine these terms?

4. Why do Marxists believe that capitalism cannot be adequately understood as a 'domestic' phenomenon? How has this belief been reflected in the theories of imperialism?

5. What do Marxists mean when they talk about capitalism as more than just an economy? In what ways are politics and culture integral to capitalism as a way of life?

6. How does the apparent separation of economic from political spheres of social life under capitalism both create and mask privatized forms of social power? How might those powers undermine the supposedly democratic aspects of political life?

7. How do the insights of Western Marxism shed critical light on more 'economistic' forms of Marxism?

8. How does a critical understanding of capitalism as a way of life encompassing economic, political, and cultural or ideological aspects help us to make sense of US global strategy since the Second World War?

9. How does such an understanding enable us to reframe the Bush Doctrine and Obama's national security strategy as forms of twenty-first-century imperialism?

 ## Further reading

Anievas, A. (2010) Marxism and World Politics (London: Routledge).
A set of essays by prominent Marxist theorists debating materialist theorizations of geopolitics and the significance of imperialism.

Bacevich, A. (2008), *The Limits of Power* (New York: Metropolitan Books).
A highly regarded realist scholar pushes beyond the analytical bounds of realism to raise questions about the cultural, economic, and political relations underlying US global power.

Brewer, A. (1990), *Marxist Theories of Imperialism: A Critical Survey*, 2nd edn. (London: Routledge).

A comprehensive explication and critique of the various theories of imperialism to which the Marxian tradition has given rise.

Colas, A. and Saull, R. (2006) (eds), *The War on Terrorism and the American 'Empire' after the Cold War* (London: Routledge).

Essays from a variety of critical perspectives, including a number of leading Marxist theorists, reflecting on the apparent imperial turn in contemporary world politics.

Cox, R. and Sinclair, T. (1996), *Approaches to World Order* (Cambridge: Cambridge University Press).

Collected in this book are some of the most seminal essays by a leader in the neo-Gramscian tradition of international studies.

Kinzer, S. (2006) *Overthrow: America's Century of Regime Change from Hawaii to Iraq* (New York: Times Books).

An historical introduction to some of the major episodes of US imperial intervention.

Lacher, H. (2006), *Beyond Globalization: Capitalism, Territoriality and the International Relations of Modernity* (London: Routledge).

Draws on a theory of social property relations to offer a bold and powerful reinterpretation of the relationship between modern geopolitics and capitalism.

Robinson, W. I. (2004), *A Theory of Global Capitalism* (Baltimore, MD: Johns Hopkins University Press).

Robinson posits the emergence of a globalized process of capital accumulation, a transnational capitalist class, and a nascent transnational state.

Rosenberg, J. (1994), *Empire of Civil Society* (London: Verso).

Rosenberg critically situates the theory and practice of *Realpolitik* within the relations and processes of capitalist modernity.

Rupert, M. and Smith, H. (2002) (eds), *Historical Materialism and Globalisation* (London: Routledge).

Essays from a variety of scholars broadly sympathetic to historical materialism but understanding in very different ways its significance in a world of globalizing capitalism.

Rupert, M. (2009) 'Antonio Gramsci' in J. Edkins and N. Vaughan-Williams, editors, *Critical Theorists and International Relations* (London: Routledge), pp. 176–86.

A brief and accessible introduction to the life and political thought of Antonio Gramsci.

Wood, E. M. (2003), *Empire of Capital* (London: Verso).

A contemporary reinterpretation of imperialism theory from an influential Marxian political theorist.

Important websites

Marxists.org Internet Archive. A massive electronic resource including extensive selections of texts (in a variety of languages) from many major Marxist theorists, articles on the history of Marxism, and an encyclopaedia of Marxism. www.Marxists.org

The Socialist Register. Web page of a leading socialist annual containing Marxian analyses of globalizing capitalism, US imperialism, and a variety of other topics. http://socialistregister.com

Dialectical Marxism. The writings of political philosopher Bertell Ollman, one of the world's leading scholars of dialectical theory. Check out 'Class Struggle', Ollman's Marxist board game. www.nyu.edu/projects/ollman/index.php

Notes

1. Marx's language here betrays an historical context prior to the women's movement and feminist theorizations of the political economy of the household and culture of gendered privilege (see Sayer 1991: 31–2). This should not be misunderstood as implying that Marxist or socialist feminisms are inconceivable: for a striking example of this kind of work, see Barrett (1980).

2. Again, we may note in Marx's language the historically prevailing Eurocentric cultural norms of which he was himself not innocent (see Sayer 1991: 14–20). Whether Eurocentrism is intrinsic to Marxism as such is a matter of controversy. My own view, in a nutshell, is that this is not necessarily the case, especially as regards those versions of Marxism which eschew economic determinism and teleological understandings of history (Rupert 2005).

3. For a more fully developed version of these arguments, see Rupert and Solomon (2006: ch. 5).

 Visit the Online Resource Centre that accompanies this book for lots of interesting additional material. **www.oxfordtextbooks.co.uk/orc/dunne3e/**

9

Critical Theory

STEVEN C. ROACH

Reader's Guide

This chapter addresses how critical international theory has evolved over the years. By first assessing the ideas of Frankfurt School theorists, it critically examines how the School's critiques of authoritarianism and repression have influenced the thinking of early and later critical International Relations (IR) theorists. In doing so, it maps the emergence and the features of the various strands of critical international theory, including normative and political economy theory. The former strand encompasses the many implications of developing and applying Habermas's communicative action theory to IR. More importantly, it underscores an important distinction between critical international theory—which integrates and extends Frankfurt School critical theory concepts and ideas to the international level—and a critical theory of international relations that adopts a core set of themes and concepts derived from international institutional processes such as law, economy, and politics, to produce empirical knowledge of these processes. I shall argue that critical IR theorists have made important strides towards realizing and formulating the requirements for a critical theory of international relations.

Introduction

The early critical theory interventions by Robert Cox and Richard Ashley provided crucial starting points for critiquing realism and its metaphor of states as billiard balls (see **Chapters 3** and **4**). Such attempts to treat states as subjective agents and international structures as social, mutable processes would mark the growing disenchantment with realism's rigid statism/paradigmatic dominance and its failure to examine the significant transformations occurring in this system, including the fall of the Soviet Union, the spread of international human rights, and the adoption of global democratic practices to meet the demands of a growing number of marginalized individuals and peoples. But, by the mid-1990s critical international theory would encompass a wide array of different theoretical strands, including cosmopolitanism, postmodernism, postcolonialism, and critical security studies, reflecting what some would regard as a pluralistic project of emancipation in international relations (Rengger and Thirkell-White 2007) (see

Chapters 12 and 13). Thus, while the postmodern strand critiqued the repressive effects of fixed sovereign borders (Ashley and Walker 1991), pragmatic-minded critical theories, namely those inspired by Jürgen Habermas's writings on communicative action, focused on the role of discursive ethics, dialogue, and community to map the emerging modes of legitimacy and world citizenship (Linklater 1998). As we shall see, these different strands underscore an important, emerging distinction between critical international theory and a critical theory of international relations. The former adapts and extends Frankfurt School critical theory (and other critical theorists') concepts and ideas to the international level in order to interpret and/or understand the global phenomena driving the emancipatory struggle. The latter, by contrast, analyses the functional relevance of these concepts of the emancipatory project by investigating the normative and shifting empirical dynamics of global institutional processes (law, economy, and diplomacy). As such, it aspires to produce knowledge by analysing the distinctive, concrete, and universal parameters of international and global institutions, as well as the increasing interaction of agents, principles, and institutional norms at the global level (Diez and Steans 2005).

Still, this is not to say that critical IR theory lacks a core set of concepts, themes, and/or ideas to direct the emancipatory struggle beyond the repressive traits of militant ideology and dogmatism at the international level. Rather, it is to stress the ongoing struggle to develop a relevant critical theory of international relations that can accomplish two aims: (1) explain the shifting empirical dynamics of governance, and (2) allow us to understand the social genesis of norms and events/crises (Kurki 2011; Roach 2010; Linklater 2008). I shall argue that critical IR theorists have made important strides towards realizing and formulating the normative and social requirements of a critical theory of international relations.

Nonetheless, the difficulty of formulating a critical theory of international relations raises an important issue: whether the need to become more policy relevant will unduly challenge the radical orientation of critical theory or the open-ended, holistic parameters of the emancipatory project in international relations. This is an issue, as we shall see, that reflects the complex, albeit influential, legacy of the Frankfurt Institute of Social Research, or Frankfurt School, founded in 1923. A key feature of the first-generation Frankfurt School theorists' legacy, for instance, was its negative critique of the metaphysical, ideological, and social origins of authoritarianism. Jürgen Habermas, however, would redirect this negative dialectical critique towards the progressive aspects of communicative reason and social action, allowing Frankfurt School theory to evolve into a more expansive and reflexive critique of world citizenship and global governance.

The first part of this chapter introduces the reader to the legacy of the Frankfurt School. The second part then moves on to survey the prevailing normative and historical material-ist approaches derived principally from Frankfurt School theory. The normative strand, as we shall see, has produced lively debates on the practical and empirical relevance of criti-cal international theory, leading to discussion of the practical possibilities of realizing a critical theory of international relations. The third section assesses the important features and issues of these debates, including critical security studies.

The Frankfurt School

The origins of critical theory can be traced back to the modern theories of consciousness and dialectics of the Enlightenment period (Hegel 1977; Kant 1989). Kant, Hegel, and Marx are the most notable and seminal influences in this regard. But, between Hegel and Marx and the Frankfurt School stood the Western Marxists, in particular Georg Lukàcs (**Chapter 8**). In *History and Class Consciousness*, Lukàcs theorized that revolutionary movements should never be assumed to be permanent unless the derivative facts of the movement could be revised in terms of the changing social and historical circumstances. As such, if one did not examine the changing content of his or her social ideas and facts, one also risked isolating this content within the larger, holistic struggle for equality and justice (**social totality**). It was precisely this isolation that suppressed the political consciousness of individuals, allowing the hypostasized understanding of social and societal relations (as Horkheimer and Adorno called it) to register the regressive and/or authoritarian tendencies of a political regime (i.e. the Nazis' use of blood and soil to signify greater German nationalism as a closed totality).

The first-generation theorists of the Frankfurt School, then, not only sought to revise orthodox (scientific) Marxism, but also to draw on aesthetics and culture to understand the pervasive tendencies and/or influence of authoritarianism and conformism.[1] Their unorthodox critique of society was based on an intriguing contradiction: that rather than liberating man from oppression, technology, market forces (consumerism), and liberal political forces had conspired to suppress the political consciousness of man. Walter Benjamin, one of the first-generation members of the Frankfurt School, referred to this phenomenon in terms of the jargon of authenticity: the capacity of the owners of the economic and social means of production to reproduce and streamline the essence of art objects for the sake of consumption (Benjamin 1968). As Benjamin (ibid.: 221) put it:

> The authenticity of a thing is the essence of all that is transmissible from its beginning, ranging from its substantive duration to its testimony to the history which it has experienced. Since the historical testimony rests on the authenticity, the former, too, is jeopardized by reproduction when substantive duration ceases to matter. And what is really jeopardized when the historical testimony is affected is the authority of the object.

Horkheimer expressed this idea in terms of instrumental reason or the eclipse of the critical, substantive content (humanistic) of reason by formal, scientific methods/reasoning. His essay, 'Traditional and Critical Theory' analysed the political and social implications of employing reason to measure and test societal phenomena, such as mass production (Horkheimer 1992). Here he argued that traditional (scientific) theory's methodological separation between fact and value was based on a (pre-)given, unexamined conception of social reality. Such a conception ignored the social genesis of facts, leading the social scientist to champion a neutrality and objectivity that ignored the social content of facts, including the researcher's self-awareness of his beliefs and values and societal oppression. Scientific theory had not, as many social scientific theorists assumed, liberated man from oppression and deprivation. Rather, it had led to a rigid rationality *qua* Weber that limited and suppressed a meaningful engagement with the open-ended possibilities of social and political change (holistic social totality).

Horkheimer's critique of scientific reason, then, reflected a deep disenchantment with the Enlightenment principle of rationality. In *Dialectic of Enlightenment*, for example, he and Theodor Adorno claimed that the new culture industry, or network of advertisers and entertainment figures, marked the emergence of a totalizing capitalist force capable of manipulating one's desire via consumerism (Horkheimer and Adorno 1994). Herbert Marcuse (1964), another first-generation theorist, would build on this idea by arguing that technology had absorbed the radical energies of desire and eliminated the opposition between labour and capital. His and Horkheimer and Adorno's negative critiques of consumerist society helped reveal a growing complacency and conformism of capitalist societies. Unfortunately though, they failed to provide a systematic and cohesive theory of progressive social action and societal emancipation (Bronner 2002).

If anything, Horkheimer and Adorno's deep scepticism accomplished the opposite goal of revolutionary thinking: the abandonment of the cognitive possibilities for re-steering the Enlightenment project. Yet it was precisely this abandonment that became the starting point of Habermas's attempts to resituate reason in uncoerced dialogue or communicative action (Habermas 1984). And, in time, Habermas would develop the legal and democratic context of the emancipatory project, arguing that the neutrality of democratic procedures constituted an important source of mediation between the facts and norms of law (Habermas 1996). In Habermas's view, the progressive elements of reason could be realized in the struggle to reach mutual understanding, or in deliberations and discussions that required voluntary or uncoerced dialogue among citizens (Habermas 1983). This critical turn in critical theory helps to underscore the important legacy of Habermas's theory for not only the third-generation critical theorists, such as Axel Honneth, but also the development of normative critical IR theory.

Critical international relations theory

The early phase

During the Cold War era, as already mentioned, realism and its variant neorealism, dominated the field of inquiry in IR. Neorealism holds the view that the international system of states is an anarchical realm comprised of competitive states, or 'self-help' units (Waltz 1979). As the leading proponent of neorealism, Kenneth Waltz designed a reductive scientific framework that sought not only elegance but scientific rigor (see **Chapter 4**). The purpose of theory, in his view, was to describe reality. However, for early critical IR theorists, the purpose of theory was not simply to describe the reality of the international system, but to interpret reality as an open-ended totality of the changing and unfolding social relations and identities in international relations. The early critical theory interventions in IR that adopted this version of what we might call self-aware theory included the seminal works and articles by Robert Cox, Richard Ashley, and Mark Hoffman. Together these works were predicated on the idea that realism's ontological, scientific approach—which stressed objectivity through the observation of recurrent events—had impoverished our understanding of the complex, evolving social and political relations among states and other international actors (Ashley 1981: 205–6).

The central concern for these early critical theorists was an epistemological one: How did the ontological or deep (material) structure of the international system emerge in the first place? And how could we know or explain the evolving and differentiated structures of international relations (see Ruggie 1986)? Because realists had treated the anarchical structure as given or naturalized, they also ignored the origins and social content of these structures, that is, the social determinants of states' interests and motives for interaction (Cox 1981). States, in other words, were not merely units or objective entities: they were also subjective agents whose political and social interests were shaped by their interaction with other agents and changing social and historical circumstances.

But the focus on states' political interests presented its own limitation: it ignored arguably the most important agent of the emancipatory project, namely, the individual citizen whose shared values and beliefs had begun to assume more importance within a participatory network of global organizations and non-state actors. Was it not this emerging fact and its social or sociological genesis that needed to be explained to advance the emancipatory project? Here Mark Hoffman (1987) argued that Ashley had failed to advance our understanding of the non-statist features of the emancipatory project in IR. 'Realism', as he put it, 'performs an ideological function in legitimising an order in which only certain interests are realised—the technical and practical interests of states and the state system. This leaves it void of emancipatory interests, of the humanist element that is central to critical theory' (ibid.: 238). In drawing on Horkheimer's work, Hoffman claimed that the need for a critical theory of international relations lay precisely in the articulation of this humanistic element: the open-ended totality or global realm of human values and freedom—where countering the oppressive effects of state power, such as exclusion and marginalization, drove the struggle for justice and equality.

To go beyond the inter-paradigm debate, then, was to recognize the growing pluralism in the field. For Yosef Lapid, this meant recognizing the methodological value of pluralism in the IR field or, rather, achieving rigorous pluralism under what he championed as the Third Debate (Lapid 1989).[2] But here Lapid failed to explicate what he meant by a so-called pluralist rigor. Did it amount to postpositivist paradigm that would offer an alternative to the rigorous scientific approaches it critiqued? Or would it provide a constellation of critical theory approaches, a plurality of critical theory approaches clustered around principles of justice, identity, difference, and (bio-)politics? Suffice it to say, the Third Debate reflected the growing conceptual space in IR for accommodating the different critical interventions that addressed the growing complexity of international relations. By articulating the expanding scope of IR's theoretical focus to the political and social margins, the Third Debate suggested that IR's future intellectual trajectory lay principally in the development of postpositivist and/ or epistemological approaches to international relations (see Smith et al. 1996).

Note that postpositivism is a broad term that refers to an interpretive approach or critique of scientific approaches that treat facts and assumptions as independent features of theory or permanent conceptual tools for measuring and objectifying phenomena. As perhaps the most well-known radical, postpositivist approach, poststructuralism in IR is an anti-foundationalist approach that seeks to deconstruct status quo concepts and to expose the repressive features of existing practices (see **Chapter 12**). During the late 1980s and early 1990s, Ashley and R.B.J Walker attempted to steer critical theory in a poststructuralist direction by analysing the inherently unstable and arbitrary textual meanings of sovereignty (Ashley 1987; Ashley and Walker 1991).[3]

Later phase: universal morality and political economy

However, for more pragmatic-minded critical theorists, post-structuralism's anti-foundationalism also displaced the discursive elements of reason in humane governance. It obscured, in other words, the goal of explicating the requirements for recognizing individual citizens' capacity to transcend the oppressive modes of state and international governance through dialogue and the struggle for justice (Linklater 1992; Devetak 1995; Shapcott 2001). Andrew Linklater's objective in this respect was to position critical theory within IR, by explicating what he called 'modes of exclusion and inclusion' and the evolution of norms and justice into the global realm (world citizenship). In *The Transformation of Political Community*, Linklater (1998) drew on a diverse array of normative ideas, including Kant's cosmopolitan right, Habermas's communicative action theory and discursive ethics, as well as Charles Taylor and Michael Walzer's communitarianism. Here he formulated three evolving domains of critical IR theory: normative, praxeological, and sociological. The normative domain focused on the dialogical ethics of world citizenship or the individual's, state's, and group's shared moral understanding of and commitments to international justice. The sociological domain, by comparison, encompassed the social determinants of international structures of the international state system, while the praxeological domain involved the actions and tasks of implementing and enforcing the principles of justice, freedom, and equality (Roach 2008: 227). Humane governance in this sense reflected the immanent possibilities of increased representation, accountability, and participation, and the concrete opportunities for realizing these possibilities through a growing global network of political and judicial bodies. Linklater's emphasis on dialogue, then, was intended to situate Habermas's discursive ethics within this normative strand of critical IR theory and to probe the social origins and evolution of proscriptive norms and laws against serious harm in international relations (Linklater 2008).

But his emphasis on dialogical ethics also reproduced the conflict between Habermas's ideas and the early critical theorists' embrace of Hegel's theory of self-consciousness (the radical dialectics of identity). Habermas, to recall, rooted his ideas in cognition and linguistic theory in order to move beyond the metaphysical (traps) theories of consciousness, whose negativity his predecessors had embraced. His communicative action theory, therefore, displaced important elements of consciousness in Hegel's theory of recognition or identity formation: namely, the struggle for the unity of the self-consciousness, or the internal recognition of outside events as constituting our own finite ideas of our place in society and the world. Recognition theory, in other words, refers to how the struggle for respect, honour, and dignity can affect our interaction with others. It reflects how moral conflicts between individual and their institutions arise from the lack of recognition or non-recognition. In this respect, the Habermasian-inspired basis of Linklater's normative critical IR theory steered one away from the sources and dynamics of this moral dimension rooted in the struggle for recognition. This, in turn, raised an important question for critical IR scholars: How does the discourse of recognition help to explain the moral and cultural sources of conflicts in international relations? And can these sources of moral conflict help to explain the difficulties of achieving mutual understanding through uncoerced dialogue? Indeed, even if the condition for uncoerced dialogue exists at negotiations or high-level meetings, the lack of respect accompanying non-recognition or misrecognition can constitute a moral injury that undermines the willingness to listen and/or be morally persuaded by reason.

This is a problem that lies at the centre of Axel Honneth's (a third-generation Frankfurt School theorist) theory of the struggle for recognition. His theory/model stresses how societal conflicts between groups arise from moral injuries triggered by the withholding of respect and honour (Honneth 1995). Reaching mutual understanding and consensus, then, is not simply about building empathy through dialogue or the deprivation of social needs, but about (dialogical) how the withholding of recognition of a person's or group's values and dignity can lead to the distrust that erodes such empathy (the laws designed to promote fairness and curb abuse).[4] The critical IR theorist Jürgen Haacke (2005) argues that Honneth's theory provides a causal and empirical map for understanding and explaining the development and effectiveness of global institutions. Whether or not Honneth's ideas can be effectively integrated in this international context, critics of Honneth's theory of the struggle for recognition continue to argue that it downplays the overlapping or imbricated types of social oppression that limit the desired effect of recognition (Fraser 1997).

This is not to say that the normative strand of critical IR theory ignores or downplays the historical materialist strand of critical theory. Rather, it suggests that the normative and historical materialist strands may be diverging. This has led some to speculate that the division between these strands in critical IR theory may further widen (Wyn Jones 2001: 8). If this is true, then the underlying challenge for promoting an integrated project of emancipation in IR theory is to integrate the political economy and ethical strands. This challenge would at least suggest why neo-Gramscians have grappled with, and applied in novel ways, the ethics of Gramsci's ideas of hegemony to understand the changing forces and dynamics of production and global resistance movements (**Chapter 8**).

Robert Cox (1981, 1983) was the first IR scholar to tackle the international implications of Gramsci's concepts of hegemony, civil society, historical bloc, passive revolution, and organic intellectuals (see also Leysens 2008). Here his aim was to explicate the structural contradictions of international institutions/order and hegemonic state power that structural realists had dismissed (i.e. the relationship between global elites and intellectuals of social movements). Social and environmental movements had evolved out of these contradictions and the dialectical struggle to overcome the social inequalities of the international system. The goal of neo-Gramscianism was to situate these struggles within the evolution of large-scale capitalist structures and the novel trends of domination and legitimizing tactics in international relations, including the Trilateral Commission and American hegemony (Gill 1995; Rupert 1995).

But critics of this global application argue that it overextended the meaning of Gramsci's concepts. Randall Germain and Michael Kenny (1998), for instance, offered an important forum of (re)appraisal of neo-Gramscianism in a special issue of the *Review of International Studies*, which featured Mark Rupert's forward-looking approach and Germain and Kenny's sober assessment of the limits of and challenges of adapting Gramsci's concepts to global politics. As one of the sceptics of this extension of Gramsci's ideas, Ann Showstack-Sassoon (2005) argued that global forms of hegemony and civil society remained too loosely developed and incoherent to substantiate the extension of Gramsci's nation state framework (Italian state and society) to a global network of non-state actors (global civil society). Whether or not this is true, the international political economy strand of critical theory calls attention to another challenge: devising a critical theory of international relations that can provide a useful, derivative framework for understanding the ethical and empirical dimensions and dynamics of global governance. As we shall see, this underscores the important distinction already mentioned, between critical international theory and a critical theory of international politics. The latter seeks to formulate or work towards a more systematic, contextual analysis of the discursive dimensions of institutional norms and global governance, as well as the shifting institutional dynamics of decision-making processes.

Empirical challenges and institutional norms

Habermas's discursive ethics and logic, as already mentioned, seem to hold many important implications for articulating the preconditions of uncoerced dialogue and moral argumentation/persuasion for international institutions.[5] Thomas Risse's (2000) path-breaking article remains the most influential application of Habermas's discursive ethics. Not only does it involve the formulation of the **logic of communication** to bridge rationalist and constructivist approaches, but it also develops the discursive elements of communicative action, moral argumentation, and reasoning within the context of the decision-making frameworks of international institutions, including international law, diplomacy, and the balance of power (see Price and Reus-Smith 1998). In this way, Risse is able to explicate the constitutive function of anarchy as a 'thin lifeworld' (a repository of interest and values and strategies that offer the social context of state action) and the discursive requirements for arriving at rational consensus in the decision-making processes of international institutions.

Still, Risse's application is not without its problems. Perhaps the most significant is that the lack of enforcement and effective democracy at the global level requires considerable sacrifices and good faith to promote strong global spheres, or sites of the struggle for rights, democracy, and justice (Brunkhorst 2002). In addition, Risse also underestimates the considerable constraints and volatility imposed by the anarchical system on the efficacy of norms and argumentation. Jennifer Mitzen (2005), for instance, argues that the face-to-face interaction at international forums and meetings cannot prevent the quick devolution of negotiations to violence. Consensus-making in global public spheres, in this respect, also reveals the volatility of norm compliance. Here Nicole Deitelhoff and Harald Müller (2005) draw on Habermas's communicative action theory and Risse's logic of communication to analyse the causal obstacles to dialogue and norm abidance, including realpolitik factors such as state noncompliance. In their view, norm density at the international level reflects the existent yet shifting disparity between strong discursive legal international institutions and state power politics (reliable enforcement).

Deitelhoff (2009) investigates this challenge in greater detail in the context of the International Criminal Court (ICC) to address the link between legitimacy and enforcement. The ICC—which cannot actively enforce its arrest warrants, but must rely on state cooperation to bring indicted perpetrators to The Hague—must depend on its impartiality and/or legitimacy as an independent court to convince state officials to surrender perpetrators to the Court. This of course places the ICC chief prosecutor in the rather difficult position of persuading and reasoning with states to comply with the ICC under its complementarity principle, which provides for state's primary responsibility for trying war criminals. State leaders, in other words, may not comply with or learn to reason with ICC officials in a genuine manner. By the same token, the ICC chief prosecutor may elect to maintain a morally inflexible position on justice and peace by continuing to indict heads of state—even though in the case of the Sudan the chief prosecutor could have opted to pursue lesser authorities in the Sudanese government to mitigate the tensions between justice and peace (see David Kaye 2011).

Nonetheless, these applications of Habermas's discursive theory reflect important efforts to build the very incipient basis of what I have been calling a critical theory of international relations. It is also worthwhile to note Habermas's (2006) concurrent attempts to formulate a cosmopolitan theory of international law based on a revisionist idea of Kant's statist conception of cosmopolitan right. Here Habermas maps the normative requirements for a world organization consisting of three mutual complementary levels of institutional governance. But in doing so, he also recognizes the problematic implications of Hauke Brunkhorst's weak global public spheres: the structural deficit of democracy at the global level and the challenges this poses for reaching rational consensus through democratic procedure. Realpolitik, as Habermas and

Featured book

Scheuerman, W. E. (2008), *Frankfurt School Perspectives on Globalization, Democracy, and the Law* (London: Routledge).

This book's primary aim is to assess the normative and political relevance of Frankfurt School theory for understanding the challenges posed by globalization. Understanding and rethinking the global vision of cosmopolitan law and democracy remains a central normative priority for many critical theorists. More than anything, though, it requires greater appreciation of the rule of law and its expanding application through various institutions such as the International Criminal Court (ICC), the United Nations (UN), and the European Union (EU).

In Scheuerman's view, the writings of Jürgen Habermas and Franz Neumann on the law help us to frame the possibilities for developing this vision of a global rule of law. Scheuerman's central argument in the book is that critical theorists have failed to articulate the conditions of the global rule of law. While he is careful to offer his own caveat—his shortage of in-depth empirical analysis of the central implications of Frankfurt School theory—he does provide the reader with arguably the most detailed and insightful analysis of the theoretical and empirical value of the rule of law for promoting cosmopolitan democracy.

The first part of the book focuses on the first-generation Frankfurt School theorists, in particular, Franz Neumann, whose ideas on democracy and authoritarian politics, as Scheuerman points out, remains overlooked. Yet Neumann's idea of the entrepreneurial class—of being 'replaced by a bureau-cratic functionary in particular his ideas regarding monopoly capital'—suggests that private interests or capital can work against the articulation of a clear and flexible institutional basis of the global rule of law (p. 77). As such, Neumann may well have anticipated the growth of neoliberalism and how the powerful states of global institutions can undermine the democratic procedures for fair governance (i.e. the World Trade Organization (WTO)). This perspective on globalization—which stresses how monopoly capital restricts democratic consensus formations—might explain the unwillingness of WTO officials to expand the scope of the WTO's mandate into the areas of human rights, the environment, and labour.

In the second part, Scheuerman moves on to address Habermas's contribution to globalization, notably his recent body of writings on global democracy and the cosmopolitanization of the law. Here he probes the reformulation of ideas developed in Habermas's first book, *The Structural Transformation of the Public Sphere*, and their contribution to the ongoing debates on deliberative democracy and cosmopolitan democracy. He wrestles with, among other things, Habermas's sobering admission of the limits of the global public sphere, by critically examining how his institutional analysis tends to fall short in formulating the preconditions of the global rule of law for democracy. As he points out, this means not simply paying 'homage to (nonstate) governance' insofar as 'it obscures the indispensable functions existing state and new state institutions will need to perform in achieving novel forms of self-legislation and the rule of law' (p. 133).

In his view, though, Habermas avoids this trap, but fails to explicate the institutional criteria for achieving these novel forms of governance. Hauke Brunkhorst's weak democratic global spheres proves especially instructive for Scheuerman, since it raises the important question of how, amidst democratic deficits that divide at the global level (Security Council veto), we can achieve solidarity and political unity. In effect, globalization challenges this solidarity in a number of ways, including building consensus around issues such as global warming.

But if the EU is any indication, globalization can also be understood as a progressive example of globalization. Critical theorists, in his view, will need to shed further light on this progressive development. This will mean formulating the concrete institutional requirements for expanding and maintaining a more flexible global rule of law. Nonetheless, while Scheuerman's analysis may not offer the concrete institutional analysis needed to do justice to this objective, it does provide one of the most lucid and insightful reappraisals of the unmet normative tasks of critical theory in the age of rapid globalization.

many critical IR theorists concede, remains an inescapable limitation to developing a critical theory of international relations. This is one main reason why critical IR theorists need to continue developing an immanent critique of power and security.

Case study: the Arab Spring

The Arab nation stretches from Iraq to the Maghreb region of North Africa to central Africa. It arose from the rapid and sustained spread of Islam in the seventh and eighth centuries, solidifying its control and influence under the Ottoman Empire and the Kalif's institutionalization of Islam (Hourani 1991). For several centuries the rise of Islam mirrored that of the Catholic religion. Yet its trajectory in modern times diverged markedly from the Catholic religion in the West, where Protestantism and secular nationalist movements helped spur the rise of individual human rights and democracy. The Arab world's collective identity remained anchored in a strict, orthodox devotion to Islamic principles or the inseparability of political rule and religion. By the latter part of the twentieth century, some Arab states would experiment unsuccessfully with multi-party democratic elections (i.e. Algeria, Sudan), giving rise to a passionate debate on the compatibility of democracy/human rights and Islam. But this would hold little sway over the Arab dictators who continued to suppress dissent and to maintain a tight grip over state affairs; that is, until the winter of 2011 when the Arab people began to rise up against their rulers.

Sparked by a Tunisian street vendor's decision to light himself on fire to protest the government's decision to raise food prices (the vendor spent several days in the hospital before finally succumbing to his wounds a few weeks later)—which would lead to the downfall of Tunisia's dictator—the protests would soon spread to other Arab states, including Libya, Egypt, Bahrain, and Syria. Egypt would be the next authoritarian regime to fall in February 2011, followed by Libya in June 2011 (and the eventual brutal killing of Moammar Qaddafi in October of that same year). What proved most remarkable in both cases was the sheer brutality of the Arab dictators' attempts to crack down on the peaceful protests. Indeed, the Arab people's embrace of Western democracy seemed to signal the determination to fight a far more intractable common enemy, namely, the Arab rulers. As Gregory Gause (2011: 89) points out, 'The common enemy of the 2011 Arab revolts is not colonialism, U.S. power or Israel, but the Arabs' own rulers'. And yet while some regimes fell, others did not. Saudi Arabia, for instance, immediately pledged nearly $100 billion in new spending plans in March 2011. In so doing, King Abdullah, Saudi Arabia's leader, could do what the other dictators were unable, much less unwilling, to do: to invest in the social welfare of the people.

Nonetheless, the uprisings defied most if not all expectations of the stability of authoritarian governments. Many powerful states, including the USA, had embraced these dictators, believing that their support, which in the case of the US, included nearly $1 billion of military aid to the Mubarak regime, amounted to the trade-off needed to suppress Arab discontent regarding the plight of the Palestinian people and to bring stability to the region. However, this strategy of containment proved short-lived, which for our purposes raises the following question: How can critical IR theory help us to understand some of these problematic and contradictory factors? Here we need to consider four political and social dynamics of the Arab Spring: the political identity and consciousness of the Arab peoples, the failure of neoliberal policies, the political will to instantiate the rule of law, and the social media.

Many Western states believed that the dictator offered the best opportunity to liberalize the Arab regimes. Indeed, unconfirmed reports had surfaced that Saif el-Islam, Muammar Qadaffi's second oldest son and heir apparent, had planned to reform Libya's economic and political system. Meanwhile Bashar al-Assad, the President of Syria, appeared willing to follow the model of neighbouring Turkey, which under the leadership of the Prime Minister, Tajyp Erdoğan, had initiated sweeping economic and legal reforms. But the failure of these and other Arab states to liberalize their political systems testified to the rampant corruption of these regimes, as well as the unwillingness of the growing number of superwealthy elites to support the authoritarian regime (Gause 2001: 86). Nonetheless, the idea of forging a stronger economic alliance between the new wealthy elite and the state never materialized. For neo-Gramscian thinkers, it would be wrong to label this as an isolated or insignificant event. Rather, something much larger was at work, requiring a dialectical, holistic perspective on the changing social forces, or in this case, the failed attempts to enhance and legitimize elite (economic) control and the rising historical bloc of unemployed and marginalized workers and students who united together to counteract elite control.

Still, few expected the resurgence of the Arab shared identity. Abdul Nasser's Arab nationalism of the 1970s had not in this case dissipated; it had simply manifested itself in a far more passionate desire for political reform, namely, in the Arab people's demands for unity and control over their particular political fates. In this way, the collective identity of the Arab people provided a common framework for the solidarity that the dictators had sought to suppress. It had, in other words, been turned against these dictators by the people's demands for new democratic political leaders and the rule of law. In this way, the demand for the rule of law returns us to an important theme of normative critical IR theory or Habermas's and Linklater's writings: the discursive power of democratic norms and their role in promoting a global rule of law. For both, dialogue and deliberation remain crucial for the people's participation in the legal and political institutions that uphold the rule of law.

But it remains unclear how the Arab people's demand for the rule of law will play out—whether through an enlightened executive or multi-party elections that can give voice to and accommodate the Islamist demands (Islamic Law). The Salafists in Egypt, for instance, have suggested the need for strict Islamic codes to prevent political corruption. Yet any such implementation would also challenge efforts to implement civil rights and democratic reforms, such as a checks-and-balances system or the separation of church and state. Indeed, the recent crackdowns in several countries have either exposed the lawlessness of the political leaders, or the close ties between the political leaders and judiciary. The Egyptian Army (which assumed political control of the country in January 2011) and police, for instance, have not only failed in their promise to hold elections, but continue to hold themselves above the law. The soccer riots on 1 February 1 2012—which left seventy-six people dead—is but one example of the rising tensions between the people and the army. At the same time, Assad's defiance of international law, of the basic rights of civilians, has led as of March 2012, to an estimated 8,000 civilian deaths. In short, building an effective basis for participation or democratic pluralism and deliberation in these Arab states remains crucial to supporting a strong rule of law (Scheuerman 2008: 133).

Nonetheless, Wael Ghonim, the Egyptian Google Executive and one of the leaders of the political movement inside Egypt, was one of many young elites who shifted his loyalties from the state to people, primarily through the Internet. In this context, the social media was the critical tool that helped call attention to the plight of Arabs under the authoritarian regimes. It helped, among other things, to expose the Arab people's plight to the outside world and allowed for the instantaneous exchange of ideas and feelings that could organize the people. Marcuse (1964), as we saw, argued that technology repressed the desire to revolt. But in this case, Facebook and Twitter had provided an open-ended venue for countless empowered individuals to voice their dissent. The authoritarian governments, aware of the power of the social media, sought to shut down public access to the Internet. This move, however, had a counter-productive effect: it compelled the people to take to the streets to continue their exchanges and to build solidarity, in person. More important, the killings of their fellow protesters would also encourage the people to finally overcome their fear of the authoritarian regime, the product of years of repression.

In short, the social media showed how technology could play a novel, revolutionary role, rather than simply repressing the desire for change and revolt, as many of the first-generation Frankfurt School critical theorists had come to believe (see Der Derian 2001). Whether the social media will continue to assert its influence is an issue that will depend on the long-term commitments to political change. At this point, it appears that the social media will continue to play a largely transitory role: that is, it will help to inspire protestors to rise up against their governments, while failing to produce the vibrant political leadership needed to sustain and promote these revolutionary tools.

Critical security studies

The central aim of critical security studies, which emerged in the mid-1990s, is to develop an immanent critique of security policy and strategy; more concretely, to show how traditional mainstream approaches suppress cultural, social, historical, and humanistic elements in international security. Conventional, status quo security studies assume that threats arise from perceived imbalances of military capabilities and the competition between and among states. These are assumptions based on fixed, rationalist assessments of security threats, which critical security theorists argue fail to demonstrate how such threats are constructed or how these threats derive from cultural, social and political understandings (Krause 1998). Security, in other words, is a discourse or sphere of knowledge consisting of symbols, representations, and practices; and not simply strategic interests. Whether we are referring to health crises, terrorism, or nuclear proliferations, then, a security threat remains the amalgamation of many social forces, requiring critical analysis of the health, environmental, and social contexts of such threats (Fierke 2007; Booth 2005).

From this critical perspective, fear may determine how one responds to threats; but it can also fix the meaning of the symbols one uses to define such threats. In other words, if state A designates state B as an enemy whose weapons pose a threat to it, then assuming that B poses a threat to state A's intentions presupposes some given perception of state B's capacity and inclinations. But a given perception is also naturalized insofar as it exists independently of our desires and social customs. It is this independence that presupposes the basis for objectivity and neutral thinking, for prioritizing military strategy.

But this begs an important question of whether state A's lack of knowledge induces the fear of state B's, or if it represses one's capacity to adapt to his or her changing social environment. Realists, to recall, argue that knowledge of the other (state) is imperfect in international relations; that one can never fully know the intentions of the other, and therefore must prepare for the worst. This is why theory can only describe reality and why positivist approaches presume that the facts we use to test this reality remain divorced from the values that constitute this reality. But the first-generation Frankfurt School theorists, as we saw, treated this as a false dichotomy of facts and values. In their view, objectivity and neutrality reflect a pronounced disengagement from the social reality of the production of knowledge, in particular the social genesis of the facts that scientists employ to objectify (close) the truth. Here some critical security theorists have drawn more directly on the Frankfurt School to theorize about the limitations and problems of traditional security theory.

Richard Wyn Jones (1999), for instance, argues that traditional security studies remains an applied research tool rooted in instrumental reason. Scientific rationality, in this sense, assumes a neutrality that defies or ignores a holistic, humanistic understanding of security. In an insightful new study of the context of missile defence, Columba Peoples (2009) claims that justifying missile defence reflects a long-standing effort to staticize or naturalize the symbols, means, and representations of security. His point of course is that humanizing security strategies is a collective holistic effort, one that reflects a nuanced understanding of the cultural symbols that construct and change the meaning of these strategies. It is this idea of critical security studies that calls attention to the concrete possibilities of situating the meaning of security within the larger, open-ended project of emancipation.

Conclusion

Critical theory remains relevant in a number of ways. Not only does it provide us with the insights to critique the limitations of positivist approaches, but it also offers potentially practical ways of working from critical international theory to a critical theory of international relations. Perhaps more than any other theorist, Habermas continues to inspire critical international theorists to develop the causal and constitutive pathways for understanding the shifting dynamics of international institutions, including international law, diplomacy, and war. But overextending critical theory in a policy and practical direction, as we saw, can also pose the challenge of sustaining critical theory's power of critique. If, for instance, we address its role in the environmental movement, we might say that scientific rationality also contains a darker side or contradiction that environmentalists are unwilling to address: that scientific rationality might actually repress the political consciousness needed to promote political unity and solidarity in an age of globalization.

Indeed, globalization, in this sense, cuts in two ways. It can allow us to extend the emancipatory struggle beyond the nation state; but it can also challenge the development of solidarity and political unity that is necessary for promoting deliberation and/or deliberative democracy (Pensky 2005). This contradiction need not be undermining, but rather seen as the reason for inquiring further into the repressive effects of state rule. In this respect, there will remain open-ended issues with which critical international theorists will continue to grapple, including whether we are working towards an open and responsive global civil society, and whether global institutions and technological advances are helping to address the needs of marginalized and oppressed peoples. Indeed, the rapidly growing influence of the social media suggests that while more individuals are equipped with an unprecedented means empowerment, it may also be these means of empowerment that prevents a long-term sustainable and cohesive political discourse (as the social media encourages its users to move rapidly from one issue to another).

Nonetheless, as long as dogmatism and orthodoxy continue to exist, so too will the need for critical theory to expose the traits of these oppressive discourses in international relations. This should always give pause, on the one hand, for fixing our assumptions about social and political reality. On the other hand, it should give further reason to return to the first-generation Frankfurt School theorists, in particular their emphasis on the dialectical imagination. After all, it is the imagination that allows one to connect the social purpose of ideas and creative faculties with the radical desire for social change. It is also this imaginative dimension that reflects how the emancipatory project in IR remains an open-ended struggle for equality and justice: an emerging project of a critical theory of international relations that can help us to further understand and address institutional novelties and crises.

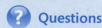 **Questions**

1. According to Max Horkheimer, how does 'traditional theory' limit one's understanding of social reality?

2. How does Habermas succeed in redirecting the negative critique of the first-generation theorists of the Frankfurt School?

3. What are two central assumptions and/or features of Habermas's theory of communicative action?

4. What are two central claims made against realism by the early critical international theorists?

5. Does the Third Debate help to explain the value of critical theory? And why?

6. How does Linklater adapt Habermas's discursive ethics to international theory?

7. What is the meaning and significance of the three domains that Linklater devises to understand the evolving modes of world citizenship?

8. What are two central features of the political economy strand of critical international theory, notably neo-Gramscianism?

9. How does Honneth's theory of the struggle for recognition complement or work against Habermas's ideas in international relations?

10. How does Thomas Risse adapt Habermas's logic of communicative action to demonstrate the explanatory role of argumentative reasoning and moral persuasion in international relations?

11. How have Habermasian-based theorists succeeded in linking discursive power with the effectiveness of global institutions?

12. In what way do critical security studies adapt Frankfurt School theory to critique the traditional concept of military or state security?

13. Given the distinction made between critical international theory and a critical theory of international relations, how would you make a strong or weak case for the emancipatory project in the context of evolving global institutions?

 Further reading

Diez, M. and Steans, J. (eds) (2005), 'A useful dialogue? Habermas and International Relations', *Review of International Studies*, **31/1.**
This 'forum' debates the empirical relevance of Habermas's communicative action theory and the prospects for formulating a Habermasian-based critical theory of international relations.

Edkins, J. and Vaughan-Williams, N. (eds) (2009), *Critical Theorists and International Relations* **(London: Routledge).**
This book consists of several concise essays that address the ideas, methods, and personal histories of 32 key thinkers that critical IR theorists draw from to study issues of identity and subjectivity in international politics.

Fierke, K. M. (2007), *Critical Approaches to International Security* **(London: Polity Press).**
A comprehensive examination of the evolution of various approaches to international security. It argues that critical approaches are now needed to address the growing complexity of these issues in the areas of military, health, and natural disaster relief.

Gill, S. (ed.) (1995), *Gramsci, Historical Materialism, and International Relations* **(Cambridge: Cambridge University Press).**
A state-of-the-art collection of essays by leading Marxists and Gramscian-inspired scholars on the methodological, theoretical and empirical relevance of Gramsci's concepts for international relations.

Linklater, A. (1998), *The Transformation of Political Community* **(London: Polity Press).**
A path-breaking book that offers an authoritative and exhaustive examination of the different immanent modes of inclusion and exclusion in international society.

Rengger, N. and Thirkell-White, B. (2007), *Critical International Theory after 25 years*, *Review of International Studies*, **33 (Special Issue) (2007).**
This special issue (re-)appraises the progress and evolution of critical international theory, offering high-quality essays that map past and new directions of this theoretical approach.

Roach, S. C. (2010), *Critical theory of International Politics: Complementarity, Justice and Governance* **(London: Routledge).**
This book investigates the intellectual currents of critical theory, from Kant to Habermas, and the recent works of Robert Cox and Andrew Linklater. It formulates a theory of complementarity that brings together critical theory and critical international theory.

Wyn Jones, R. (2001), *Critical Theory and World Politics* **(Boulder, CO: Lynne Rienner Publishers).**
A fine collection of insightful essays from leading critical theorists in IR. This advanced text, aimed primarily at graduate students, addresses key issues that very nicely size up the important role and influence of critical theory in IR.

 ## Important websites

Institute for Critical Theory at the University of California at Irvine **http://www.humanities.ucl.edu/critical/**
Features several latest books on critical theory and offers several fellowships.

Center for the Study of Developing Societies **http://csdccu.tripod.com/csdc.html/**
The center seeks to offer alternative critical viewpoints. It provides several links to important works regarding critical global studies as well as audios and videos.

John Felice Rome Center of Loyola University of Chicago **http://csdccu.tripod.com/csdc.html**
Hosts an annual conference on critical theory, which stresses the varied applications of critical theory to society and global trends.

 ## Notes

1. For an excellent historical analysis of the Frankfurt School's first-generation of theorists, see Martin Jay, *The Dialectical Imagination: The History of the Frankfurt School and the Institute of Social Research, 1923–1950* (Berkeley: University of California Press, 1973). It should be noted here that there are officially three generations of theorists belonging to the Frankfurt School.

2. This Third Debate, in this context, replaced the third debate referring to the inter-paradigm debate. However, most IR scholars, it is fair to say, prefer to call the post-positivist debate as the emerging Fourth Debate in IR.

3. This would lead to a more concerted engagement with Michel Foucault's genealogical analysis and biopolitics in IR (see Bartelson 1995; Edkins 1999).

4. It is worthwhile to note the overlap between Honneth's and Charles Taylor's the politics of recognition. The latter claims that the significant extent of a group's moral injury should entitle it to special recognition as a distinct group.

5. See Neta Crawford (2001), who offers an excellent dissection of the properties of argumentation, before deploying this analysis to explain the role of discursive reasoning in various issue areas of IR.

 Visit the Online Resource Centre that accompanies this book for lots of interesting additional material. **www.oxfordtextbooks.co.uk/orc/dunne3e/**

10

Constructivism

K. M. FIERKE

 Reader's Guide

This chapter will examine the key debates that have shaped the development of constructivism in International Relations (IR). The introduction and first section will explore the general notion that international relations is a social construction, as it emerged from the critique of more traditional theories of IR. The second and third sections will examine the demarcations that have come to distinguish various constructivisms, focusing in particular on the contrast between those who seek a 'better' social science, and therefore better theory, as opposed to those who argue that constructivism is an approach that rests on assumptions at odds with those of positivist method. The fourth section will analyse the significance of this difference for undertaking research, including questions about the role of language and causality. The final section will bring these insights to bear in relation to the War on Terror.

Introduction

In the 1980s, when the Cold War was raging with renewed force, social movements concerned about the prospect of nuclear war emerged on both sides of the Atlantic. They shared roughly the same objective, that is to bring an end to the nuclear arms race, but approached the challenge in different ways. One movement, the US Nuclear Weapons Freeze Campaign, came to the conclusion, given lessons from the Vietnam War protests, that achieving its objectives required moderation in behaviour and message. Rather than dressing like hippies, they would dress in suits, appeal to Middle America, and mobilize citizens to pressure their congressmen (sic). Their proposals were formulated in a measured way that would minimize alienating people and appeal to the wider spectrum. In another political context, across the water, the critique was somewhat more hard hitting and diverse. Rather than calling on the USA and Soviet Union to simply stop the development, testing, and deployment of nuclear weapons, protesters demanded actual disarmament and in some cases unilateral disarmament. While loose cooperation existed at the European level, in the form of European Nuclear Disarmament, movements in the Netherlands, Germany, or Italy, had a distinctive character.

These critical movements shared the aim of changing the nuclear status quo, and each was shaped by the politics of its respective location, as well as the larger context of the Cold War. I start with this example from the political world for two reasons. First, against this background, that is the mid- to late 1980s, questions began to be raised about the theories and scientific methods of IR and the extent to which they were implicated in the production of international power (see Cox 1981; Ashley 1981, 1984; Walker 1987). Challenges to the assumptions underpinning the study of IR emerged against the backdrop of a historical context where political actors were challenging the assumptions of the Cold War. As the end of the Cold War was ushered in, further questions about these changes and the social construction of IR were formulated. The failure of IR scholars to predict or initially explain the end of the Cold War, on the basis of the dominant theories of IR, reinforced the importance of these questions.

Second, the two social movements are a useful metaphor for thinking about the construction of constructivism within IR. Constructivists, broadly defined, have shared a critique of the static material assumptions of traditional IR theory. They have emphasized the social dimensions of international relations and the possibility of change. They, however, differed in their approach. Some have been more conscious of their broader audience and have shaped their critique in a language that would open a space for dialogue with mainstream scholars. Others have been more hard hitting in stating the problem and more far reaching in their critique. The two together have shaped the place of constructivism in IR. The main point—and, I might add, a very constructivist point—is that academic debate, no less than political, emerges in historically and culturally specific circumstances.

This is evident in other debates that have shaped IR theory. The debate between realism and idealism was a reflection on the weaknesses of idealism after the First World War against the background of Hitler's expansion across Europe (see Carr 1946). Attempts to solidify the scientific status of realist IR were led by European émigrés to the USA, following the Second World War. The debate between behaviouralists and traditionalists pitted scholars in the USA, who wanted to make IR into a science, against the international society theorists of the English school (see Knorr and Rosenau 1969). The postpositivist debate in the late 1980s was a reaction against the dominant place of scientific method in the American context (see Lapid 1989). The 'dialogue' over constructivism was a reaction to the third debate, or, as some prefer to call it, the fourth debate (see **Chapter 1**), and an attempt to speak across the barricades it had constructed, while addressing problems raised by the end of the Cold War.

This chapter develops various dimensions of the 'constructivist turn' (Checkel 1998) in IR. It begins with a general discussion of what it means to say that reality is socially constructed and then proceeds to a more in-depth discussion of related debates.

The social construction of reality

The idea that international relations is a social construction can be thought about in quite simple terms. To construct something is an act which brings into being a subject or object that otherwise would not exist. For instance, a material substance, such as wood, exists in nature, but it can be formed into any number of objects, for instance the beam in a house, a rifle, a musical instrument, or a totem pole. Although these represent material objects in and of themselves, they do not exist in nature but have come about through acts of human creation. Once constructed, each of these objects has a particular meaning and use within a context. They are social constructs in so far as their shape and form is imbued with social values, norms, and assumptions rather than being the product of purely individual thought or meaning. Similarly, explicitly social phenomena, such as states or alliances or international institutions, that is, the collective subjects of international relations, may build on the basic material of human nature, but they take specific historical, cultural, and political forms that are a product of human interaction in a social world.

Constructivists have highlighted several themes. First, the idea of social construction suggests difference across context rather than a single objective reality. Constructivists have sought to explain or understand *change* at the international level. Traditional theories of IR, which have often assumed the sameness of states, for instance, across time and space, have prioritized the identification of regularities for the purpose of generalization and theory construction. The dramatic changes with the end of the Cold War and in its aftermath revealed the importance of historical context and raised questions about the transition from conflict to cooperation or from peace to war.

Second, constructivists have emphasized the *social* dimensions of international relations, and have demonstrated the importance of norms, rules, and language at this level. The importance of Gorbachev's 'New Thinking' in bringing an end to the Cold War, the increasing importance of norms of humanitarian intervention, and the spread of liberal democratic values raised critical questions about the exclusive emphasis of realist theory on material interest and power. Constructivists emphasized that the latter were unable to account for some of the key issues of post-Cold War international politics and sought to provide a more complete or 'better' explanation, based on an analysis of how material and ideational factors combine in the construction of different possibilities and outcomes.

Third, constructivists have argued that, far from an objective reality, international politics is 'a world of our making' (Onuf 1989). In response to the over-determination of 'structure' in neorealist and neoliberal theory, constructivists introduced the possibility of agency and have emphasized *processes of interaction*. It is not that actors are totally free to choose their circumstances, but rather that they make choices in the process of interacting with others and, as a result, bring historically, culturally, and politically distinct 'realities' into being. In this respect, international relations is a social construction rather than existing independently of human meaning and action. States and other actors do not merely react as rational individuals but interact in a meaningful world.

The central themes of change, sociality, and processes of interaction point to the added value of constructivism within a field that has emphasized generalization across time, materiality, and rational choice. However, as already suggested, constructivists have not sung from a single hymn sheet and the meaning of constructivism in IR has been transformed over time. Here I will deepen discussion of the themes above by examining how the meaning of constructivism has been shaped by specific debates within IR.

Constructivism and rationalism

Most constructivists have presented some kind of critique of rationalism. However, unlike poststructuralism (see **Chapter 12**), this critique has not involved a wholesale rejection of scientific method. I will examine how the meaning of constructivism has been shaped out of the dialogue with rationalists. Four central points will be discussed, including the nature of being, the relationship between structures and agents, the constitution of the material world, and the role of cognition.

Social being

Ontology is a word originating with metaphysics, which refers to the nature of being and focuses on the types of objects the world is composed of. Rationalist theories of IR have an individualist ontology insofar as the basic unit of analysis is the individual (whether human or state). Neorealist theory, for instance, treats states as if they were individuals who try to maximize their ultimate aim of survival. Neorealists, such as Kenneth Waltz (1979), present individual states as the prior condition for a structure of anarchy, which then constrains their character and behaviour. In a competitive environment, generated by multiple states acting in their self-interest, to follow a different logic of action, it is argued, would be suicide. While emphasizing the individual state and the distribution of power, Waltz does bring in an element of 'socialization', insofar as the effects of structure are produced 'through socialization of the actors and through competition among them' (Keohane 1986: 63).

Arguments by neoliberals, such as Goldstein and Keohane (1993), who focus on the role of ideas, contain a similar tension between the individual and the social. Ideas are treated as causal factors that are exchanged by fully formed individuals. As Ruggie comments:

> The individuals featured in [Goldstein and Keohane's] story are not born into any system of social relationships that helps shape who they become. When we first encounter them, they are already fully constituted and poised in a problem-solving mode.
>
> Ruggie 1998: 866

Constructivists have questioned the individualist ontology of rationalism and emphasize instead a social ontology. As fundamentally social beings, individuals or states cannot be separated from a context of normative meaning which shapes who they are and the possibilities available to them. Indeed, the concept of sovereignty is first and foremost a social and constitutive category insofar as the prior condition for *recognizing* the sovereignty of individual states is a *shared understanding* and acceptance of the concept.

The relationship between the individual and the social structure is important for both rationalism and constructivism, but is conceived in different ways by each. For rationalists, structure is a function of competition and the distribution of material capabilities. Structures first and foremost constrain the actions of states. The subjects of rationalism are guided by a **logic of consequences**, that is, a rational act is one that will produce an outcome that maximizes the interests of the individual unit.

Constructivists focus more on the norms and shared understandings of legitimate behaviour, although material factors also play a role. In their view, structures not only constrain; they also constitute the identity of actors. The subjects of constructivism are guided by a **logic of appropriateness** (March and Olson 1989). What is rational is a function of legitimacy, defined by shared values and norms within institutions or other social structures rather than purely individual interests. As Ole Jacob Sending (2002: 449) states, the self, in this logic, becomes social through acquiring and fulfilling an institutional identity. In this respect, norms not only constrain behaviour; they also constitute the identities of actors. Human rights norms, for instance, constrain less because of power considerations than because human rights are a constitutive feature of liberal democratic states, in particular, and increasingly, at the international level, the identity of legitimate states. The emphasis on norms and rule following can be distinguished from instrumentally rational behaviour in that actors try to 'do the right thing' rather than maximizing or optimizing their given preferences (Risse 2000: 4)

Mutual constitution

A social structure leaves more space for **agency**, that is, for the individual or state to influence their environment, as well as to be influenced by it. The title of Alexander Wendt's famous article (1992), 'Anarchy Is What States Make of It', captures this idea. It is not that states in anarchy can, on a whim, change their circumstances. Rather, relationships evolve over time. They are not characterized, across the board, by enmity and egoism. The USA and Britain have evolved as friends, while other states are enemies. Many states within the European Union (EU) are former enemies who have learned to cooperate. Relationships are a product of a historical process and interactions over time. Wendt (1992: 404–5) illustrates this in his example of Alter and Ego, two space aliens who meet for the first time, and who, through a series of gestures, determine whether the other is hostile or friendly. Each exercises an element of choice, and thus agency, in how this relationship develops. Choice is not, however, unlimited. Alter and Ego coexist in a social relationship, and their choices are partially dependent on the response of the other. The space for choice can thus be said to be **mutually constituted**.

Rather than emphasizing how structures constrain, as rationalists do, constructivists focus on the constitutive role of norms and shared understandings, as well as the relationship between agency and structure (Wendt 1987). The subjects of international politics are not uniformly and universally rational egoists but have distinct identities shaped by the cultural, social, and political—as well as material—circumstances in which they are embedded. They are not static but ever evolving as they interact with each other and their environment.

Social facts

Rationalists assume a static world of asocial egoists who are primarily concerned with material interests. While constructivists would not deny the importance of interests, they would tie them more directly to the identity of the subject. Neither identity nor interests can be detached from a world of social meaning. As suggested in the section on mutual constitution, identity as a liberal democracy cannot be detached from an interest in complying with human rights norms. Identity as a capitalist cannot be separated from an interest in generating profit. Likewise, identities may be formed in conflict, for example, as enemies who have an interest in self-protection. Far from being detached from the material world, identity, and subsequent interest, may constitute a world populated by particular kinds of object. Missiles, for instance, are not created in a vacuum. The mass production of nuclear weapons by the USA, after the Second World War and during the Cold War, was a response to the emerging conflict with the Soviet Union. These weapons were bound up in the constitution of the Soviet Union as an enemy, defined by a distinction between capitalist and communist, among others, and related to an interest in containing that enemy.

Most objects of international relations, unlike trees, rocks, or glaciers, exist only by virtue of human acts of creation which happen in a cultural, historical, and political context of meaning. They are social facts, rather than purely material ones, that exist because of the meaning and value attributed to them. John Searle (1995: 2) argues that social facts depend on human agreement and typically require human institutions for their existence. Without the attribution of value, and the existence of financial institutions, a dollar bill or euro note would be nothing more than a piece of paper. As already suggested, sovereignty or the borders dividing states exist only by virtue of human agreement. Likewise, a nuclear weapon does not exist in nature, although objects in nature, such as sticks, can be used as weapons. It is human design and intent that shapes the material object into one with a specific meaning and use within a context, where specific identities and interests are at stake.

Social cognition

The question of intent in designing material objects or institutions raises a further issue about the role of human reasoning. Many constructivists have built on a Weberian concept of *Verstehen* or understanding which refers to the hermeneutic theme that 'action must always be understood from within', and, thus, that social meaning is a function of 'what is in people's heads' (Adler 1997: 326). The constructivist emphasis on Verstehen is interesting in so far as Weber was also one early source of the rational actor model. While rationalists highlight the rationality of decisions in terms of self-interest, thereby minimizing the role of context, constructivists have brought the social dimension back in. Inter-subjective meanings are not merely the aggregation of individual beliefs but have some independent status as collective knowledge, based on the notion that although 'each of us thinks his own thoughts, our concepts we share with our fellow men' (Toulmin 1972: 35). Verstehen is the 'collective interpretations, practices and institutions of the actors themselves' (Adler 1997: 326).

The emphasis on Verstehen highlights a similarity and difference between rationalists and constructivists. The difference is that the former emphasize the individual while the latter emphasize the social. However, looking more closely at the role of individual cognition and rationality in constructivism, the difference appears to be less stark. The logic of appropriateness emphasizes the individual (Sending 2002). The rational thought processes of Wendt's (1992) Alter and Ego are prior to social interaction. Verstehen emphasizes cognition and what is 'in the head' (Adler 1997: 326).

Constructivism, as outlined above, clearly adds a social dimension that is missing from rationalist approaches. However, it also contains some inconsistencies, which will be explored in the constructivism as middle ground section. These inconsistencies arise from the combination of a social ontology with an epistemology that rests on a separation between an external world and the internal thought processes of individuals. Constructivism, in this depiction, is cast in the positivist language of causality and hypothesis testing, complemented by a focus on the rationality of individuals, although more deeply embedded in a social context. The emphasis on the individual unit, whether human or state, fails to sufficiently problematize how the individual unit is constituted. Given the emphasis on ontology, the autonomy of the social and the role of language is obscured, both in their relation to the material world and individual cognition.

Constructivism as middle ground

Constructivism, as already discussed, has occupied a 'middle ground' between rationalist and poststructuralist approaches to IR (a ground it shares with the English school, as argued in **Chapter 7**). Initially, when the word was introduced to IR by Nicholas Onuf (1989), it referred broadly to a range of postpositivist perspectives, which shared a critique of the static assumptions of mainstream IR theory. Constructivism later became a subject of contestation, with scholars making a distinction between 'conventional' constructivism, which was said to occupy the middle ground, and more critical variations (Adler 1997; Hopf 1998; Campbell 1998a), including poststructuralism. Conventional constructivists have not rejected the scientific assumptions of positivist science to the extent that more explicitly postpositivist approaches have. As Jeff Checkel (1998: 327) argues, the quarrel with rationalists is not epistemological but ontological (see also Katzenstein et al. 1998: 675).

Epistemology is a branch of philosophy that deals with the origin and nature of knowledge and begins with a question about how we come to have knowledge of the world. Constructivists embrace an intersubjective ontology, emphasizing norms, social agents, and structures, and the mutual constitution of identity, but accept an epistemology indebted to positivism,[1] which includes hypothesis testing, causality, and explanation. Ted Hopf (1998: 171) argues that emphasis on the ontological is part of an effort to overcome some of the scepticism about constructivism—arising from a conflation with postmodern approaches—and a scepticism because constructivists are assumed to be ambivalent towards mainstream social science methods. Hopf distinguishes 'conventional' constructivism by its distance from critical theory. He refers to conventional constructivism as a 'collection of principles, distilled from social theory but without the latter's more consistent theoretical and epistemological follow through' (Hopf 1998: 181). Both rationalists and constructivists claim that no great epistemological or methodological differences divide them (Wendt 1998: 116; Katzenstein et al. 1998: 675).

By accepting a positivist epistemology, constructivists gained considerable legitimacy, such that the debate with rationalists has come to occupy an important place in the discipline (Katzenstein et al. 1998: 683). At issue in these debates is the nature of social science itself and therefore the discipline of IR, that is, the claim to a 'naturalist' conception of science (associated with the positivists) or a social one (Adler 1997: 320). The primary concern of the conventional constructivists is one of bringing the social back into a discipline that has been undersocialized (Wiener 2003: 256). The constructivist emphasis on causality, hypothesis testing, and objective (intersubjective) truths, is distinguished from poststructuralists who are 'not especially interested in the meticulous examination of particular cases or sites for purposes of understanding them in their own distinctive terms' (Ashley 1989: 278). As Adler (1997: 334) states, constructivists are interested in providing a better explanation, rather than emancipation per se.[2]

Shifting the middle ground

As Kurki and Wight argue in **Chapter 1** the discipline of IR has failed to take philosophy of social science questions seriously and has far too often embraced an otherwise discredited 'positivism'. The key issue here is whether combining an emphasis on social being (constructivist ontology) with an empiricist approach to the generation of objective knowledge (positivist epistemology) is consistent. This question is implicit in Hopf's (1998) claim that critical constructivists have a 'more consistent theoretical and epistemological follow through'. Several scholars (Kratochwil 2000: 74; Onuf 1989; Fierke and Jorgensen 2001) have examined constructivism as part of a longer lineage outside IR and with a genealogy that intersects with, but is distinct from, poststructuralism. Constructivism is, from this perspective, also an epistemological position, heavily indebted to the so-called 'linguistic turn'.[3] If, following on the linguistic turn, constructivism raises fundamental questions about the natural connection between word and thing or between symbol and the symbolized (Palan 2000: 4), is it consistent to marry a social ontology to a positivist epistemology?

Positivist epistemology rests on a correspondence theory of language. Objects are assumed to exist independently of meaning and words act as labels for objects in this reality. Hypothesis testing represents one expression of this assumption about language. It is a method of comparing scientific statements about the world with the world to see whether they correspond. By contrast, a constructivist epistemology, as a product of the linguistic turn, builds on the notion that we cannot get behind our language to compare it with that which it describes (Wittgenstein 1958). Language is bound up in the world rather than a mirror of it. The language of a knight in chess cannot be separated from the material object; it is by this language that we distinguish the knight, and the rules applying to it, from a piece of wood. To refer to the knight as a piece of wood would be to detach it from the context in which it has meaning and a use.

The distinction between conventional and critical constructivists often rests on an assumption that the former accept the existence of an objective world, while the latter emphasize 'merely' language. However, as Kratochwil (2000: 91) notes, 'hardly anyone doubts that the "world" exists "independent" from our minds. The question is rather whether we can recognize it in a pure and direct fashion or whether what we recognize is always already organized and formed by certain categorical and theoretical elements'. The either/or designation of objective world versus interpretive relativism is too stark. A more nuanced position understands language as rule-based. This issue will be discussed in more detail in the section on approach or theory.

Approach or theory

The ontology/epistemology issue is related to a further concern regarding constructivism's status as an approach or a theory. Onuf (1998: 1) argues that constructivism is not a theory but a way of studying social relations. Alexander Wendt's book, *Social Theory of International Politics* (1999), builds a constructivist *theory*. Wendt accepts certain tenets of mainstream methodology, although his is a modified commitment to positivism within a scientific realist framework (see **Chapter 1**). The problem with his approach is two-fold. On the one hand, if constructivism and positivism rely on differing assumptions about the nature of 'reality', then building a constructivist theory on a positivist epistemology is inconsistent. On the other hand, to treat constructivism as a theory in the same sense as realism is misleading; it is like comparing apples and oranges. Realism, as a substantive theory, makes assumptions about actors in the world and how they operate, that is, they are power seekers who exist in a competitive environment. This has often (in structural realist accounts specifically) been married in IR theory to positivist assumptions about the existence of an objective world and, more specific to IR, a timeless competitive anarchy where material power is supreme. The theoretical assumptions of realism could, arguably, be rethought from a constructivist angle, shifting to an analysis of how a competitive relationship is generated and reproduced out of processes of historical interaction. To this end, IR scholars have recently attempted to construct a dialogue between classical realism and constructivism (Sterling-Folker 2002; Barkin 2003; Jackson 2004).

 Featured article

Alexander Wendt (1992), 'Anarchy is What States Make of It: The Social Construction of Power Politics,' *International Organization*, 46/2: 391–425.

While constructivism was first introduced to international relations by Nicholas Onuf (1989), it is most frequently identified with Alexander Wendt's 1992 article 'Anarchy is What States Make of It'. Following closely on the end of the Cold War, the piece spoke to the processes of change that were under way at the time. Its core argument represented a departure from more structural accounts of international relations, which assume that states are constrained by a condition of anarchy. The article introduced the potential for agency in a condition of anarchy.

While starting with the neo–neo debates, Wendt's critique most directly addressed the neorealist claim that in the absence of a global authority states were left with little choice but to compete with one another in order to maximize their interests and to survive. From this perspective, both the identity and interests of states are given, as they are defined by an environment of anarchy. Wendt provides a framework for thinking about identity and interests as constructed and thus subject potentially to processes of transformation. He sets out to build a bridge between two traditions, which at the time were referred to as rationalist and reflectivist (or positivist and postpositivist) by developing a constructivist argument, drawn from structurationist and symbolic interactionist sociology.

Wendt defines identities as the basis for interests, which means that actors 'define their interests in the process of defining situations'. Institutions are relatively static sets or 'structures' of identities and interests, which are often codified as rules or norms, but only have motivational force by virtue of an actor's socialization to and participation in collective knowledge. 'Self-help' in itself is an institution within anarchy but it is not the only possible institution, since we can point to examples of more cooperative security systems. Thus power and institutions are not two opposing explanations, as is often assumed. In order to go from structure to action it is necessary to take account of the 'intersubjectively constituted structure of identities and interests in the system'. These meanings, by which action is organized, arise out of a process of interaction.

Wendt illustrates the point through the example of two mythical space aliens, Alter and Ego, who meet for the first time and, through a process of signalling, interpreting, and responding to the other, begin a process of creating shared intersubjective meanings, which may develop as either cooperative or competitive (see main text for a more lengthy discussion). Given Alter and Ego begin their relationship with a blank slate, the analysis of Mikhail Gorbachev's policy of 'New Thinking' raises a question about the extent to which an alteration of the 'game' is possible once two parties have become stuck in a negative spiral such as existed during the Cold War. He argues that actors have a capacity for critical self-reflection and choice 'designed to bring about changes in their lives'. This may happen when there is a reason to think about oneself in novel terms, for instance, due to the presence of new social circumstances, which cannot be mapped onto pre-existing self-conceptions. When these conditions are present actors can engage in 'self-reflection and practice specifically designed to transform their identities and interests' and thus to 'change the games' in which they are embedded.

The constructivist label became attached to scholars, particularly in the US, who identified with a middle ground between rationalist and poststructuralist approaches. This middle ground has emphasized a social ontology, a common epistemology with the mainstream, and a focus on the development of constructivist theory. Another constructivism shifts this middle ground, highlighting the inseparability of a social ontology *and* social epistemology. Both accept the 'possibility of a reality to be constructed', which distinguishes them from poststructuralists who problematize this possibility (Zehfuss 2002).

In the section on consistent constructivism, I argue that the second constructivism is more consistent than 'conventional' constructivism. I use the label 'consistent constructivism' to highlight that its assumptions correct the inconsistency at the core of conventional constructivism. This contrasts with the more common distinction between conventional and critical constructivism. The latter term often includes poststructuralism, while the idea of consistent constructivism presented here does not.

Consistent constructivism

Constructivists and rationalists have engaged in dialogue but method has not been on the agenda. There is a tension between a school of constructivism that sees no fundamental differences with mainstream methods and another which understands constructivism as an approach with roots in the linguistic turn. The inconsistency is most evident in relation to the role of language and rules, on the one hand, and the question of causality, on the other.

Language and rules

The role of language has been largely ignored in the debate between rationalists and constructivists. The avoidance of language is in part a reflection of the effort to create distance from poststructuralists, who are associated with interpretive relativism. It is also a reflection of the middle ground's focus on ontology. An approach to language that is consistent with the social ontology of constructivism should also occupy an epistemological middle ground. In between a view of language as either a mirror of the world or pure interpretation, is an understanding of language and action as rule-based. It is a small step from a focus on the role of norms and rules in international relations, to an acknowledgement that these only find expression and are constituted only in a language and action that is rule-based and itself infused with norms.

This conception of language rests on a distinction between rules (the concern of constructivists) and interpretation (the emphasis of poststructuralists). Following a **rule** is different from an interpretation. As Wittgenstein states,

> there is a way of grasping a rule which is *not* an *interpretation*, but which is exhibited in what we call 'obeying a rule' and 'going against it' in actual cases. Hence there is an inclination to say: every action according to the rule is an interpretation. But we ought to restrict the term interpretation to the substitution of one expression of the rule for another.
>
> Wittgenstein 1958: para. 201

The unitary view of science rests on a dichotomy between the objective and the subjective. In this view language operates as a set of labels for the objective reality or for the mental processes of individuals. A consistent constructivist approach to language challenges this dichotomy. In this view, language use is fundamentally social. We are socialized into it and in the process we do not simply learn words but how to act in the world—what it means to promise, threaten, and lie, the types of context in which these **speech acts** are appropriate or meaningful, or even what it means to formulate a hypothesis, vote, or deploy a missile. Language use is part of acting in the world. Without language we could not begin to communicate with one another, attribute meaning to objects or acts in the world, think individual thoughts, or express feelings.

Hypothesis testing in positivist science rests on an assumption that labels will be either true or false. An approach to language as rule-based requires that we 'look and see' how language is put to use by social actors as they construct their world. In a situation of change, categories of identity or action are not likely to be static. For instance, the dominant categories defining identity in communist Yugoslavia were different from those that emerged along with the conflict between Serbs, Croats, and Muslims. The category Yugoslavia subsumes all of the latter under a common identity as 'southern slavs'. By contrast, the ethnic categories construct clear historical, religious, and political distinctions between the different groups. These categories may have begun as interpretations, in that they substituted one rule of identity for another, but they became rule-like in their designation of identity and the actions that followed from this. In the transition from Yugoslavia to violent conflict, neighbours, who had lived together in peace, became the objects of ethnic cleansing.

A consistent constructivist approach to language shifts emphasis to the generation of meaning, norms, and rules, as expressed in language, by the subjects of analysis. It is also concerned less with the intentions of individuals, as suggested by conventional constructivists (March and Olson 1989; Sending 2002; Adler 1997), than the intention expressed in social action. As Wittgenstein (1958: para. 337) said, 'An intention is embedded in its situation, in human customs and institutions.'

In the example here, the 'intention' of individuals engaged in ethnic cleansing could not be separated from a social world in which neighbours had become 'dangerous others', defined as Chetnik, Ustasa, or Ottoman—terms with deep historical resonance—who had to be eliminated because of the threat they posed. Intention and action were defined in a public language by socially constituted actors. Questions of intention relate to a second category of inconsistency.

Reasons and causes

The other seeming inconsistency in the construction of constructivism vis-à-vis rationalism is the frequent emphasis on causality (Checkel 1997, 1998; Finnemore 1996: 28; Adler 1997: 329). On the surface, this appears to be merely a matter of word use. But the conflation of reason and cause raises a more serious issue, which is illustrated by the following example. Take a question about US President Bush's reasons for invading Iraq or the cause of the US invasion. Multiple possible reasons/causes have been identified: from oil, to the desire to complete unfinished business from the Gulf War, to concerns about Saddam's weapons of mass destruction, to human rights.

A hypothesis focusing on Bush's individual reasons or the cause of the invasion seeks an explanation that corresponds with the world. But truth and falsity are ultimately slippery insofar as we cannot get inside individual minds, and the competition to identify the 'true' cause or intention usually devolves into a battle of interpretations. The question can be asked in a different way, however, focusing less on the ultimate truth of why Bush or the USA undertook the invasion, and more on the social fact that the invasion happened and how it became possible. We might pose this **'how possible' question**, as Howard (2004) has, in terms of the puzzle that Iraq actually posed less of a threat to the USA than North Korea yet became the object of invasion, while the latter was the subject of negotiations. He traces how the historical pattern of interaction with the USA laid the groundwork for different policies towards these two 'Axis of Evil' states.

The 'how possible' question reveals the importance of public language and the intentionality embedded in it. It is now known that intelligence communities on both sides of the Atlantic got it wrong in (falsely) believing that Iraq had weapons of mass destruction. An explanation that the invasion was caused by Iraq's weapons of mass destruction is more accurately stated in the following terms. The reason for the invasion of Iraq, given by foreign-policy elites, was the threat posed by Saddam Hussein's weapons of mass destruction. Whether these actors believed the intelligence or manufactured it, this 'reason' made the invasion possible. The reason was the means for persuading the US public, and US soldiers, that this was a legitimate act by their government. The reason was strengthened by the link made in political discourse between Saddam and the attackers on 9/11. The premise that Saddam had weapons of mass destruction, although based on false data, established the context for justification of, that is, giving a reason for, the invasion. This reason was publicly accessible in political language. It constituted an action and a 'reality', that is, the invasion. The intention to invade was embedded in these language games and in the act of invasion itself. The recent 'practice turn' in international relations, which is a further development in these debates, would approach invasion as an international 'practice' or a socially meaningful pattern of action that is more or less competently performed (see, for instance, Adler and Pouliot 2011). The practice turn builds not only on the thought of Wittgenstein, but Bourdieu, Goffman, Foucault, and others.

To refer to a reason as a cause is an interpretation; it takes the rule by which 'giving a reason' has meaning and gives it a different meaning. However, a **reason** has a different logic than a cause. X may give a reason for her action to Y. In doing so, X explains her action. This may have an influence on Y, but, if so, it is less as a cause, in the sense that the impact of one stone on another may propel the latter in forward motion. It rather is part of a conversation where X is trying to persuade Y, and thereby legitimate her own actions in terms that can be understood and accepted by the other.

To give a reason, or to engage in many other speech acts, from promising to threatening, opens a space for the other to be engaged and respond. As a two-way relationship, this interaction is not merely a question of who has the greater material power; it is dependent on some degree of common language (the other must be able to understand what is being said and what constitutes a reason, promise, or threat), which incorporates standards of legitimacy (that is, what will suffice as a good reason, as well as conditions, relating to past words and actions, which make a promise or threat credible), the normative basis of these claims and the possibility of contestation (Wiener 2008). The latter suggests the importance of a logic of arguing and bargaining as well as one of appropriateness (see, for instance, Risse 2000; Muller 2004). Power is a factor, since, particularly in the case of threats, material capability is one, although not the only, condition of credibility. Power may also be a factor insofar as the legitimacy of a reason may be tied to social role or position (see, for instance, Barnett and Duvall 2005; Guzzini 2005). For example, Western states may give reasons for maintaining a large nuclear arsenal, which are accepted as legitimate, while the desire for even one nuclear weapon by a Middle Eastern nation, such as Iran, may be widely viewed as illegitimate and dangerous.

To call a reason a cause is to transform the meaning of the former. Obviously, the meaning of words can change over time. However, in this case, the two words are in conflict. We can replace the rule by which 'a reason' is given meaning with an interpretation that it is a 'cause', but this is like changing the direction of a signpost, which has constituted a regular use or custom (Wittgenstein 1958: para. 158).

Case study: the War on Terror

The introduction of this chapter began with the politicization of Cold War security practices in the late 1980s. The 'timeless' realist assumptions underpinning security studies were further called into question by the sudden end of the Cold War, which no one predicted; by largely non-violent revolutions in Central Europe; by the failure of the Soviet Union to step in to save its crumbling empire; and by its eventual decision to disband. For some, the attacks on the World Trade Center and Pentagon on 11 September 2001, and the War on Terror that followed, signalled a return to a world of realist security relations, given the renewed emphasis on the use of force. Contemporary structural realists, such as John Mearsheimer, have acknowledged that realism, given its focus on states, has little to say about non- state actors, such as 'terrorists' (Kriesler 2002). Realism can explain the actions of the main state protagonist, that is, the USA, and its response to the attacks, but is limited first and foremost by its assumption that states are the primary actors at the international level. 'Terrorism studies' more generally has articulated the problem as one of how states should respond to actors who use illegitimate force, and do not problematize either the identities of the actors or the objectivity of threats.

A constructivist approach to the War on Terror would move away from this emphasis on states or objective threats. It would instead explore how identities, actions, and human suffering are constructed through a process of interaction. The problem is thus one of how actors engage with one another, how they define themselves and others and how this shapes the boundaries of the world within which they act. While realists would highlight the competitive nature of states in a condition of anarchy, a constructivist might shift the emphasis to how in a particular context actors came to define their relationship in antagonistic terms. They would also see more potential for transforming this relationship. Here I examine the War on Terror as a social interaction, in which conflict has been mutually constituted, which highlights the social ontology of the conflict. I also highlight the role of language and context, as well as the role of giving reasons—as distinct from identifying cause—all of which relate to a social epistemology.

9/11 and War on Terror

The attacks on 11 September 2001 seemed to come from nowhere. Images of the attacks, shown repeatedly in the public media, contributed to a widespread experience of shock and trauma among the US population, as well as the consolidation of American identity and patriotism (Silberstein 2002). Questions of identity regard how the relationship between self and other is given meaning and how this shapes interactions between them. While identity is always relational (Wendt 1992: 397) and established in relation to a series of differences that are socially recognized (Connolly 1991: 64), the degree of difference can vary. In this case, identity was mutually constituted around a stark difference

(continued)

between good and evil. Following the attacks and the naming of the War Terror, George Bush (2001a) drew a clear line in the sand, stating 'you are either with us or you are with the terrorists.' He further stated that:

> We value life; the terrorists ruthlessly destroy it. We value education; the terrorists do not believe women should be educated, should have health care or should leave their homes. We value the right to speak our minds; for terrorists, free expression can be grounds for execution. We respect people of all faiths and the free practice of religion; our enemy wants to dictate how to think and how to worship even to Muslims.

Bush 2001b

Bin Laden, in declaring jihad on all Americans, also constructed identity in negative oppositional terms, articulating a distinction between 'infidel Crusaders' in the West and those who are a part of the Muslim *Ummah* (community).

Not only identities but the meaning of their actions grew out of this interaction. Constructivists have raised a question about how, given the existence of numerous possible threats and threatening others, some come to be elevated above others to become the focus of security efforts (Weldes et al. 1999). The Copenhagen School (Wæver 1995; Buzan et al. 1998) have theorized a process of securitization by which naming a threat as a security threat elevates it above all others. In this elevation the identification of an existential threat, that is, a threat to the survival of a community, justifies a suspension of the normal rules of politics, allowing elites to take extraordinary measures.

War is not normal politics and sometimes requires extraordinary measures. The attacks on the World Trade Center and Pentagon were a dreadful tragedy arising out of an abominable act. The question, from a constructivist perspective, is whether there were alternative frameworks for giving meaning to and responding to this attack. The framework of 'war' and securitization arguably increased the threat and contributed to the construction and deepening of conflict. In attacking the USA, Al-Qaeda communicated with violence. As George Soros argued, the Bush administration walked into a trap by responding in a way that accepted the terms of the relationship set down by Bin Laden (Cook 2004).

The coining of the 'War on Terror' in the aftermath of 9/11 confused two fields of practice that have traditionally been distinct. War has been a rule bound practice of states, which usually begins with a declaration and has a clear end. Terrorism has most often, at least in recent times, been associated with non-state actors and treated as an area of crime. In naming a war of indefinite duration involving an obscure enemy who is outside the rules of war, Bush brought the War on Terror into being, and out of the tensions contained in this double-sided term, gave reasons for a range of acts that would not otherwise have been considered acceptable.

On the one hand, war presents an existential threat which justifies extraordinary measures and limitations on democratic freedoms. The War on Terror led to the speedy passage of the Patriot Act and other measures which changed the rules of detention and allowed unprecedented government surveillance. The US government also rewrote the rules on torture, allowing acts, such as waterboarding and hooding, which would otherwise be forbidden (Sands 2008). On the other hand, the non-state protagonists were placed outside the normal rules of war, and not least the Geneva Conventions, because they were not viewed as conventional soldiers. They were placed in Guantanamo Bay which, it was argued, was outside US jurisdiction and therefore constituted a legal black hole. They were held without charge for years on end, and submitted to what has since been viewed as treatment that violated international law.

Articulating a threat or declaring a war are speech acts that bring a particular state of affairs into being. The speech act involves not only a speaker but an audience who must accept its legitimacy to be successful. Against the backdrop of 9/11 the moves of the Bush administration received unprecedented support. In the aftermath of the Iraq invasion, following the discovery that Saddam had no weapons of mass destruction, the threat became increasingly hollow. Over time the Bush administration was delegitimized which was followed by a gradual return to normal politics. This was most dramatically illustrated by the unprecedented turn out for the 2008 elections and the high level of support for Barack Obama, the candidate who was most consistently against the Iraq War. In his inaugural (2009b) and Cairo (2009c) speeches Obama presented a different American face to the world, and the Arab and Muslim world in particular, in a situation where its status had been severely damaged.

Conflict may be perpetuated by mutual negative othering. The naming of an existential threat can result in the suspension of normal politics and justify not only acts of war but other extraordinary acts, which would not normally be tolerated, such as extraordinary rendition, where primarily Muslim captives were secretly packed off to countries that practice torture, or subjected to humiliating acts in Abu Ghraib or Guantanamo Bay. In this respect, it is not only threats and violence that are constructed, but human suffering or trauma as well. Human suffering is a social construction in so far as it grows out of a particular kind of human interaction, rather than existing purely in the mind of the traumatized (Fierke 2007). Trauma that arises from an act of human intention, as distinct from natural disaster, is more difficult to come to terms with (Zinner and Williams 1999). Torture is a form of human interaction entered into with the intention of causing pain in order to elicit a mock consent to the torturer's demands (Scarry 1985). In this respect, it also represents a relation of power. If the torturer turns out to be someone who it was expected would provide protection, such as a family member or one's own state authorities, the feelings of betrayal add to the humiliation of this powerless position (Edkins 2003).

Torture has played a role in the War on Terror, damaging the lives, in particular, of those innocent individuals who were wrongly imprisoned. But trauma has had a more public expression in the War on Terror as well. As already noted, the attacks on the World Trade Center and Pentagon were experienced as a trauma by Americans, which was reinforced by repeated televised images of the planes crashing into the buildings. The shattered feelings of safety were quickly followed by a mobilization of military might first in Afghanistan and then in Iraq. Bin Laden (2001) justified the attacks in terms of the humiliation experienced by Arabs and Muslims at the hands of the West over the past eighty years. From this perspective, 9/11 was one act that formed part of a longer history of interaction, rather than the opening volley in a war. Images of violence or humiliation from Fallujah, Abu Ghraib, Guantanamo, and Palestine, flashed across the Arab and Muslim world by *Al Jazeera*, added to the widespread sense of humiliation within these communities and provided a powerful tool for recruiting Islamic 'martyrs' or 'suicide bombers' (Fattah and Fierke 2009). For both sides an experience of human suffering was the background against which identity was consolidated and acts of violence were justified vis-à-vis their respective communities.

Conclusion

The interactions of the War on Terror produced a reality, but this reality was constituted out of meanings that the two main actors brought to their interactions. The reality was therefore far more multidimensional and social than posited by epistemological approaches that assume an objective reality 'out there'. The social meaning given to identity, threats, or human suffering is expressed in language. Actors also give reasons for their actions. While the language and practices constitute an interaction and a type of relationship, and thus a reality, they also contain contradictions which have contributed to a transformation of this context.

These contradictions were evident in relation to several aspects of Bush administration policy. First, the architects of the War on Terror articulated the end of remaking the countries of the Middle East into liberal democracies; the practice of the War involved the violation of human rights, disregard for international law, and a failure to listen to the voices, even of traditional allies, who challenged, in particular, the invasion of Iraq. Second, events that exposed the failure of intelligence, such as the 9/11 attacks and the invasion of Iraq, contributed to the legitimation of more far-reaching intelligence. These surveillance measures and the suspension of many established civil liberties, in the context of a war of infinite duration, were in conflict with the end for which the war was fought, that is, the preservation of a way of life defined by openness and freedom.

The contradictions became too glaring to ignore and contributed to the increasing politicization of what had been a largely militarized response to terrorism. While the USA initially received widespread support and sympathy from the international community, this support waned over time as the practices of the Bush administration appeared increasingly to violate the rules and norms of international law. While the invasion of Afghanistan was widely seen as a justified act of self-defence in response to 9/11, the questionable legality of the Iraq invasion in 2003, practices of extraordinary rendition, the suspension of due process and Habeas Corpus in Guantanamo Bay, and the exposure of the photos of Arab prisoners being humiliated at the Abu Ghraib prison in Iraq, led to a serious loss of legitimacy and questions about whether the USA had deviated from its own basic principles in attempting to address this security threat. While these practices appeared to violate international norms and rules, this violation also revealed and reinforced the importance of these norms and rules for defining appropriate behaviour. The new US administration, elected in 2008, has emphasized the importance of respect for human rights and the law, which included rejecting the use of torture. Following his election, President Obama spoke of encouraging dialogue and diplomacy across the divisions of international society and a shift of emphasis to the politics of terrorism rather than an exclusively military response, although in practice he has not made as much progress in dismantling the War on Terror as was initially hoped. The other issue raised by the massive civilian and military casualties in Iraq and Afghanistan is the humanitarian consequences of fighting terrorism with force. As this constructivist analysis has suggested, human suffering is often drawn on to consolidate identity and mobilize military power. In this respect, a constructivist analysis opens a space for greater reflexivity on both sides of a conflict, making it possible for actors to step back and ask questions about how their own actions may contribute to the construction of the very problems they seek to address.

 Questions

1. Constructivism was a response to changes in the world of international relations. Discuss.
2. Is it more important to generalize about international relations across time or to account for processes of change?
3. Discuss the idea that international relations is a social construction.
4. How have the central themes of constructivism contributed to the discipline of IR?
5. What are the central differences between rationalists and constructivists?

6. What does it mean to say that identities and interests are mutually constituted?

7. What was at stake in the distancing of 'conventional' constructivists from poststructuralists?

8. What is the significance of thinking about constructivism as an approach or a theory?

9. Is language important in a constructivist analysis? Why or why not?

10. Critically analyse the difference between a realist and a constructivist approach to the War on Terror.

11. What is the added value of a constructivist analysis of the War on Terror?

 ## Further reading

Guzzini, S. and A. Leander, eds. (2005b) *Constructivism and International Relations: Alexander Wendt and his Critics* **(London Routledge).**
This book includes the most prominent critiques of Alexander Wendt's constructivism as well as a reply to his critics.

Fierke, K. M. and Jorgensen, K. E. (2001), *Constructing International Relations: The Next Generation* **(Armonk, NY: M. E. Sharpe).**
A transatlantic dialogue over the meaning of constructivism.

Finnemore, M. (1996), *National Interests and International Society* **(Ithaca, NY: Cornell University Press).**
An exploration of the role of norms in international relations.

Katzenstein, P. (1996), *The Culture of National Security: Norms and Identity in World Politics* **(New York: Columbia University Press).**
An edited collection of a range of empirical studies that apply a constructivist analysis.

Kratochwil, F. (1989), *Rules, Norms and Decisions: On the Conditions of Practical and Legal Reasoning in International Relations and Domestic Affairs* **(Cambridge: Cambridge University Press).**
A seminal work on the role of rules in international relations.

Onuf, N. (1989), *World of Our Making: Rules and Rule in Social Theory and International Relations* **(Columbia, SC: University of South Carolina Press).**
The work that introduced constructivism to IR.

Wendt, A. (1999), *Social Theory of International Politics* **(Cambridge: Cambridge University Press).**
The most comprehensive effort to build a constructivist theory of international relations.

Zehfuss, M. (2002) *Constructivism in International Relations: The Politics of Reality* **(Cambridge: Cambridge University Press.**
Drawing on Derrida, the book provides a comprehensive critique of constructivism and its representation of reality.

 ## Important websites

A Second Image: A Constructivism Resource. http://home.pi.be/%7Elazone/

War on Terror—Global Issues. http://www.globalissues.org/issue/235/ war- on-terror

Notes

1. A note is in order about my use of the term positivism, which is as 'essentially contested' as constructivism and is also associated with a range of philosophical traditions, many of which have been discredited in the larger scientific world. For a more detailed discussion of the meaning of positivism within IR, see Chapter 1.

2. It should be noted that 'emancipation' is a concept associated with the Frankfurt School of critical theory (see **Chapter 9**) which is distinct from poststructuralism. Poststructuralists do not generally embrace this concept. The two schools of thought tend, however, to be conflated in the contrast with conventional constructivism.

3. The linguistic turn in philosophy introduced language to the relationship between logic and world. The phrase 'linguistic turn' is often associated with Wittgenstein's later work, and particularly his *Philosophical Investigations* (1958), but it actually originated with his earlier *Tractatus Logico-philosophicus* (1922). This work influenced the logical positivism of the Vienna Circle and its conception of verification. By contrast, *Philosophical Investigations* influenced a number of different philosophers, from the constructivism of Anthony Giddens and John Searle, to the critical theory of Jurgen Habermas, as well as the poststructuralism of Richard Rorty and Jean François Lyotard.

 Visit the Online Resource Centre that accompanies this book for lots of interesting additional material. **www.oxfordtextbooks.co.uk/orc/dunne3e/**

Feminism

J. ANN TICKNER AND LAURA SJOBERG

Reader's Guide

This chapter introduces feminist perspectives on international relations. It provides a typology of feminist International Relations (IR) theories, outlining their major tenets with illustrations from specific authors. Feminist theories of IR use gender as a socially constructed category of analysis when they analyse foreign policy, international political economy, and international security. This chapter focuses on feminist perspectives on international security. Feminist security research takes two major forms: theoretical reformulation and empirical evaluation. This chapter chronicles developments in feminist reanalyses and reformulations of security theory. It illustrates feminist security theory by analysing the case of United Nations Security Council sanctions on Iraq following the First Gulf War. It concludes by discussing the contributions that feminist IR can make to the discipline of IR, specifically, and to the practice of international politics, more generally.

Introduction

Feminist theories entered the discipline of IR in the late 1980s and early 1990s. The beginnings of IR feminism are associated with a more general ferment in the field—often referred to as the 'third debate' (or sometimes as the 'fourth debate', see **Chapter 1**). Early IR feminists challenged the discipline to think about how its theories might be reformulated and how its understandings of global politics might be improved if attention were paid to women's experiences. Feminists claimed that only by introducing **gender** analysis could the differential impact of the state system and the global economy on the lives of women and men be fully understood. IR feminists critically re-examined some of the key concepts in the field—concepts such as sovereignty, the state, and security.

IR feminists have also sought to draw attention to women's invisibility and gender subordination in international politics and the global economy. Less than 10 per cent of the world's heads of state are women. IR feminists ask why this is the case and how this might affect the structure and practice of global politics. More recently, 'second generation' IR feminist empirical case studies have focused on hitherto understudied issues such as military prostitution, domestic service, diplomatic households, and home-based work, much of which is performed by women.[1] Through these studies, feminists have sought to demonstrate how vital women are to states' foreign policies and to the functioning of the global economy. Since most women speak from the margins of international politics, their lives offer us a perspective outside the state-centric focus of conventional Western international theories and broaden the empirical base upon which we build theories. Feminist scholars suggest that if we put on **gendered lenses** we get quite a different view of international politics (Peterson and Runyan 1999: 21).

Feminists define gender as a set of socially constructed characteristics describing what men and women ought to be. Characteristics such as strength, rationality, independence, protector, and public are associated with masculinity while characteristics such as, weakness, emotionality, relational, protected, and private are associated with femininity. It is important to note that individual men and women may not embody all these characteristics—it is possible for women to display masculine ones and vice versa. Rather, they are ideal types; the ideal masculine type (in the West—white and heterosexual) is sometimes referred to as 'hegemonic masculinity'. These characteristics may vary over time and place but, importantly, they are relational, meaning they depend on each other for their meaning. They are also unequal. Men, women, and the states they live in generally assign more positive value to masculine characteristics than to feminine ones—at least in the public sphere. The foreign policies of states are often legitimated in terms of hegemonic masculine characteristics; a desirable foreign policy is generally one which strives for power and autonomy and which protects its citizens from outside dangers. Appeals to these gender dualisms also organize social activity and divide necessary social activities between groups of humans; for example, since women are associated with the private sphere, it is seen as 'natural' for women to be caregivers while men's association with the public space makes them 'natural breadwinners' (Harding 1986: 17–18). While feminists rightly question the naturalness of these dichotomized distinctions, they have consequences—for women, for men, and for global politics.

In this we trace the history of the development of feminist IR. We outline a typology of IR feminist theories which build on, but go beyond, a variety of IR approaches, such as liberalism (**Chapters 5** and **6**), constructivism (**Chapter 10**), critical theory (**Chapter 9**), poststructuralism (**Chapter 12**), and postcolonialism (**Chapter 13**). We offer some reinterpretations of security as an illustration of how feminists are reformulating some of the key concepts in IR. We will illustrate our feminist analysis of security through an examination of United Nations **economic sanctions** against Iraq in the 1990s. We propose that feminist IR offers some insights into this case that other sanctions theories do not. We conclude by suggesting the contributions of feminist IR to the discipline specifically and to global politics more generally.

Gender in IR

The 'third debate' of the late 1980s was a time when many scholars in the discipline began to debate its ways of knowing (Lapid 1989). Certain scholars began to question both the epistemological and ontological foundations of a field which, in the USA especially, had been dominated by positivist, rationalist, and materialist theories. Postpositivist scholarship, which includes critical theory, some forms of constructivism, poststructuralism, and postmodernism, questions positivists' beliefs about the possibility of creating universal, objective knowledge.

Featured book

Cynthia Enloe (2010), *Nimo's War, Emma's War: Making Feminist Sense of the War in Iraq* (Berkeley: University of California Press).

Cynthia Enloe's *Nimo's War, Emma's War* provides an account of the war in Iraq through the life stories of eight women, four American and four Iraqi, as a creative and complicated way to see the war through gendered lenses. Enloe provides a window into the ways that war functions to militarize women's lives, as well as the ways that the militarization of women's lives is essential to the making and fighting of wars. Enloe traces the impacts of the war from Iraqi jails to American kitchens, and from American hospitals to Iraqi beauty parlours, showing that, despite narratives of 'progress' on women's rights in Iraq and 'success' in gender-integrating the US military, gender oppression remains.

Enloe argues that militaries and their civilian supporters rely on the existence and support of women, not only as people, but specifically *as women*, as well as on ideas about masculinity and femininity, and that the war in Iraq is no exception. In fact, she notes *masculinization—the decrease* of women's presence and women's influence—in key spheres of the war (including but not limited to the Iraqi economy, the Iraqi police forces, and the US military). She outlines a number of the roles that women are expected to fill in order to make war possible, roles that are as diverse as free care provision for wounded soldiers and prostitution as a means of supporting families. Enloe claims that these roles are linked by gender-based behavioural expectations essential for the inspiration for, and operation of, militarism in global politics.

Through rich empirical analyses, Enloe argues that militarization is pervasive, and that it is important to see the war(s) in Iraq as fought through, on, and in the lives of ordinary people, who experience the fighting very differently depending on the biological sex category to which they belong. Whether it is in Nimo's beauty parlour as politics is discussed or at Emma's dining room table as her sons talk about joining the US military, Enloe 'makes feminist sense of' the Iraq War by showing how it is fought constantly in everyday life.

In so demonstrating, Enloe does not just 'make feminist sense' of the Iraq War, she makes sense of it. She demonstrates that the war cannot be accounted for without understanding not only the war's place in history, but the war's place in the history of gender relations, and the gender relations of history and war. Looking through the experiences of the women who lived the war, Enloe compellingly demonstrates war as commonplace, embodied, felt, and gendered.

Rejecting rationalist methodologies and causal explanations, postpositivists advocate more interpretive, ideational, and sociological methods for understanding global politics. They ask in whose interests and for what purpose knowledge is constructed. For a more detailed account of the different kinds of theorizing in IR, see **Chapter 1**.

Many feminists share this postpositivist commitment to examining the relationship between **knowledge and power**. They point out that most knowledge has been created by men and is about men.[2] Although IR postpositivists have been as slow as positivists to introduce gender into their research, their epistemological critiques created space for feminist analyses in a way that other IR scholarship had not. Conventional IR relies on generalized rationalist explanations of asocial states' behaviour in an anarchic international system. IR feminist theories focus on social relations, particularly gender relations; rather than anarchy, they see an international system constituted by socially constructed gender hierarchies which contribute to gender subordination. In order to reveal these gender hierarchies, feminists often begin their examinations of international relations at the micro-level—attempting to understand how the lives of individuals (especially marginalized individuals) affect and are affected by global politics.

IR feminist research can be divided into two complementary but distinct generations: first generation, which largely focused on theory formulation, and second generation, which approached empirical situations with 'gendered lenses'. First-generation IR feminist theory was primarily concerned with bringing to light and critiquing the gendered foundations of IR theories and of the practices of international politics. Second-generation IR feminists have begun to develop their own research programmes—extending the boundaries of the discipline, investigating different issues, and listening to unfamiliar voices. These feminists use gender as a category of analysis in their studies of real-world events in global politics, incorporating feminist conceptual critiques into their analyses of specific situations. They have studied the gendered nature of the global economy, foreign policy, and security by examining specific political and economic situations in concrete historical and geographic contexts.

Typology of IR feminist theories

As in IR more generally there are a wide variety of feminist theoretical perspectives. Many of them build on, but go beyond, some of the IR perspectives discussed in other chapters, such as liberalism, constructivism, critical theory, poststructuralism, and postcolonialism. While they may disagree about the reasons, all of them are trying to understand women's subordination. IR feminists share an interest in gender equality or what they prefer to call gender emancipation. But what feminists mean by gender emancipation varies greatly, as does their understanding of the appropriate paths to reach it. We will now briefly outline the assumptions and methodological preferences of some of these approaches and refer to some exemplary writings in each. We note that there is significant overlap between these perspectives and that our typology is somewhat of a simplification, but useful for analysis.

Liberal feminism

Liberal feminism calls attention to the subordinate position of women in global politics but remains committed to investigating the causes of this subordination within a positivist framework. Liberal feminism challenges the content but not the epistemological assumptions of conventional IR. Liberal feminists document various aspects of women's subordination. For example, they have investigated the particular problems of refugee women, income inequalities between women and men, and human rights violations incurred disproportionately by women such as trafficking and rape in war. They look for women in the institutions and practices of global politics and observe how their presence (or lack thereof) affects and is affected by international policy-making. They ask what a world with more women in positions of power might look like. Liberal feminists believe that women's equality can be achieved by removing legal and other obstacles that have denied them the same rights and opportunities as men.

Liberal feminists also use gender as an explanatory variable in foreign- policy analysis. Using social scientific methods, Mary Caprioli and Mark Boyer (2001) employ quantitative social science data and statistical measures to investigate a variant of the democratic peace hypothesis—namely, whether there is a relationship between domestic gender equality and states' use of violence internationally. According to their measures of gender inequality, their results show that the severity of violence used by states in international crises decreases as domestic gender equality increases. Caprioli and Boyer are using gender as a variable to explain certain policies and policy results.

Many postpositivist IR feminists are critical of liberal feminism. They see problems with measuring gender inequality using statistical indicators. Caprioli and Boyer (2001) use national indicators, such as numbers of women in parliament and years since women gained the vote, to measure gender equality. Postpositivist feminists claim that such measures are inadequate for understanding gender inequality, which is associated with gender role expectations that keep women out of positions of power; as we mentioned earlier, gender-laden divisions between public and private spheres consign women to certain socially accepted roles. Postpositivist feminists point out that gender inequalities continue to exist in societies that have long since achieved formal equality, so we must go deeper into our investigations of gender hierarchies if we are to explain these inequalities. All these feminists use gender (as we defined it earlier) as a category of analysis to help them understand these inequalities and their implications for global politics.

Critical feminism

Critical feminism goes beyond liberal feminism's use of gender as a variable. It explores the ideational and material manifestations of gendered identities and gendered power in global politics. Many critical feminists build upon, but go beyond the work of IR scholar Robert Cox. Cox (1986) portrays the world in terms of historical structures made up of three categories of reciprocal interacting forces: material conditions, ideas, and institutions. These forces interact at three different levels: production relations, the state–society complex, and historically defined world orders. While ideas are important in legitimating certain institutions, ideas are the product of human agents—therefore, there is always the possibility of change. Critical theory is committed to understanding the world in order to try to change it.

Sandra Whitworth is a feminist critical theorist who builds on Cox's framework. In her book, *Feminism and International Relations* (1994), she claims that understandings about gender depend only in part on real material conditions of women and men in particular circumstances. She suggests that gender is also constituted by the meaning given to that reality—*ideas* that men and women have about their relationships to one another. Her research examines the different ways gender was understood over time in the International Planned Parenthood Federation (IPPF) and the International Labor Organization (ILO), and the effects that these changing understandings had on both institutions' population policies at various times in their history.

Christine Chin's *In Service and Servitude* (1998) also uses a critical feminist approach to study female domestic workers. Chin examines the increasing prevalence of underpaid and often exploited foreign female domestic workers in Malaysia during the 1970s—a time when the state was modernizing the economy. She rejects a traditional economic explanation of wage differentials to explain the importation of Filipina and Indonesian female domestic labour because, in this case, economic theory does not account for state involvement or the social dynamics around the employment of foreign domestic workers. Adopting a critical approach, Chin argues that the Malaysian state supported the importation and employment of foreign female domestic workers, who were often working in conditions not much better than slavery, as a part of a strategy to co-opt and win the support of middle-class families and decrease ethnic tensions. Her study shows that the Malaysian state, like other states, is not neutral, but an expression of class, race, and gender-based power which has won support by co-opting certain citizens while repressing others. Consistent with critical theory more generally, Chin sees her study as emancipatory—to identify existing power relations with the intention of changing them.

Feminist constructivism

IR social constructivists called for rethinking the ways we see and understand international politics by adding a social layer to IR's analyses. They emphasize the ideational rather than the material elements of global politics. Constructivist approaches range broadly—from positivist versions that treat ideas as causes to a postpositivist focus on language. All agree that international life is social and that agents and structures are co-constituted. They challenge realist assumptions about states as unitary actors; instead, they see states as the dynamic results of the social processes that constitute their existence. States and other international actors' perceptions of their own and others' identities shape their behaviour in global politics.

Constructivist feminism focuses on the way that ideas about gender shape and are shaped by global politics. Elisabeth Prügl's book, *The Global Construction of Gender* (1999), uses a linguistically based feminist constructivist perspective to analyse the treatment of home-based work in international negotiations and international law. Since most home-based workers are women, the debate about regulating this type of employment is an important one from a feminist perspective. Low wages and poor working conditions have often been justified on the grounds that home-based work is not 'real work' since it takes place in the private reproductive sphere of the household rather than the more valued public sphere of waged-based production. Prügl shows how ideas about womanhood and femininity contributed to the international community's debates about institutionalizing these workers' rights, a debate which finally culminated in the passage of the ILO's Homework Convention in 1996 due, in large part, to the lobbying of a variety of women's non-governmental organizations (NGOs). She sees gender as an institution that codifies power at every level of global politics, from the home to the state to the international system. She argues that gender politics pervade world politics, creating a set of linguistically based rules about how states interact with each other and with their own citizens. Prügl and other constructivist feminists study the processes whereby ideas about gender influence global politics as well as the ways that global politics shape ideas about gender.

Feminist poststructuralism

Poststructuralists focus on meaning as it is codified in language. They claim that our understanding of reality is mediated through our use of language. They are particularly concerned with the relationship between knowledge and power; those who construct meaning and create knowledge thereby gain a great deal of power. Feminists point out that men have generally been seen as the knowers—what has counted as legitimate knowledge in the social sciences has generally been based on knowledge about men's lives in the public sphere; women have been marginalized both as knowers and as the subjects of knowledge.

Poststructuralist feminism is particularly concerned with the way dichotomized linguistic constructions, such as strong/weak, rational/emotional, and public/private, serve to empower the masculine over the feminine. In international relations constructions, such as civilized/uncivilized, order/anarchy, and developed/underdeveloped, have been important in how we divide the world linguistically. Poststructuralists believe that these distinctions have real-world consequences. Dichotomous constructions such as these denote inferiority and even danger with respect to those on the outside—they are also gendered and have racial implications. Feminist poststructuralists seek to expose and deconstruct these hierarchies—often through the analysis of texts and their meaning. They see gender as a complex social construction and they emphasize that the spoken meaning of gender is constantly evolving and changing with context. Deconstructing these hierarchies is necessary in order for us to see them and construct a less hierarchical vision of reality.

Charlotte Hooper's book *Manly States* (2001) is an example of poststructural textual analysis. One of her central questions is what role does international relations theory and practice play in shaping, defining, and legitimating masculinities. She claims that we cannot understand international relations unless we understand the implications of the fact that it is conducted mostly by men. She asks how international relations might discipline men as much as men shape international relations. Hooper sets about answering this question through an analysis of theories of masculinity together with a textual analysis of *The Economist*, a prestigious British weekly newspaper that covers business and politics. She follows the practice of intertextuality—'the process by which meanings are circulated between texts through the use of various visual and literary codes and conventions' (Hooper 2001: 122). Through an examination of texts, graphs, photos, and advertising material, she concludes that *The Economist* is saturated with signifiers of hegemonic masculinities and that gendered messages are encoded in the newspaper regardless of the intentions of its publishers or authors. She aims to show that gender politics pervades world politics and that gender is a social construction that results from practices that connect arguments at all levels of politics and society including the international.

More recently, Laura Shepherd's *Gender, Violence, and Security: Discourse as Practice* (2008) investigates United Nations Security Council Resolution 1325, passed in 2000 to address gender issues in conflict areas, from a feminist poststructuralist point of view. Shepherd argues that the language of the resolution not only reflects reality, but is constitutive of it. She details the ways in which the Resolution's discursive construction has influenced its implementation and, ultimately, determined its failure. For example, Shepherd points to the reification of gender-based expectations that women are peaceful/passive in the Resolution's justifications for including women in peace processes, arguing that this still-gendered interpretation even in apparently gender-emancipatory international law can explain the United Nations' continued inability to adequately include women in their peace processes and/or transform these processes to be gender-aware. Shepherd's discourse-theoretical analysis of Resolution 1325 concludes that a reconceptualization of gendered violence in conjunction with security is necessary to avoid replication of the partial and highly problematic understandings of their relationship in Resolution 1325 and (therefore) in its implementation.

Postcolonial feminism

Many postcolonial writers are poststructuralists. Their particular concern is colonial relations of domination and subordination established under imperialism. They claim that these dominance relationships have persisted beyond the granting of independence to formerly colonized states and that they are built into the way the colonized are represented in Western knowledge. Arguing that the colonized must represent themselves, postcolonial scholars aim to 'speak back', a task made harder by the erasure of their history and culture. Like poststructuralist scholars more generally, postcolonial scholars argue that, in international relations, constructions of 'self' and 'other' foster racial and cultural stereotypes that denote the other—in their case ex-colonial subjects—as inferior.

Postcolonial feminism makes similar claims about the way Western feminists have constructed knowledge about non-Western women. Just as feminists have criticized Western knowledge for its false assumptions about universality when, in reality, it is knowledge constructed mainly from men's lives, postcolonial feminists see false claims of universalism arising from knowledge which is based largely on the experiences of relatively privileged Western women. Chandra Mohanty (1988) critiques some Western feminists for treating women as a homogeneous category which does not acknowledge their differences depending on their culture, social class, race, and geographical location. This ethnocentric universalism robs women of their historical and political agency. Postcolonial feminists, such as Mohanty, are concerned that Western feminists assume that all women have similar needs with respect to emancipation when, in fact, their realities are very different. Postcolonial feminists challenge Western portrayals of Third World women as poor, undereducated, victimized, and lacking in agency. Recent work in postcolonial feminist IR, including that of Lily Ling and Anna Agathangelou,[3] has analysed gender subordination as sitting at the intersection of gender, race, and culture, and blurring the boundaries between politics, political economy, and other relations of domination/subordination. Recognizing this, they seek to redress these subordinations within their own cultural context, rather than through some universal understanding of women's needs.

Gender, security, and global politics

In this section we focus on how the theoretical perspectives we have outlined and how the scholarship we have discussed contribute to our understanding of security and insecurity. Feminist definitions of security, explanations of insecurity, and suggestions as to how to improve security are very different from those of conventional IR. We begin this section by offering some feminist redefinitions of security and insecurity. Then we suggest some feminist reanalyses of security and outline some empirical evidence that feminists are using to formulate their reanalyses.

Redefining security and its subjects

Conventional IR scholars, notably realists, define security primarily in terms of the security of the state. A secure state is one that can protect its physical and moral boundaries against an 'anarchic' international system. Neorealists focus on the anarchic structure of the international system where there is no sovereign to regulate state behaviour. They portray states as unitary actors whose internal structures and policies are less important than this anarchic condition for explaining their security and insecurity. The power-seeking behaviour and military capabilities of states are seen as ways to increase their security; many security specialists believe that power-seeking in order to promote security explains much of the international behaviour of states.

In the 1980s, certain IR scholars began to challenge these explanations and to articulate broader definitions of security. Noting that most wars since 1945 have been fuelled by ethnic and nationalist rivalries and have not been fought across international boundaries, they began to examine the interrelation of military threats with economic and environmental ones. Most of the world's poorest states have active military conflicts within their boundaries. These conflicts contribute to high numbers of civilian casualties, to **structural violence**—the violence done to people when their basic needs are not met—and to environmental destruction. Critical security scholars, as they are called, began to define security in terms of threats to human well-being and survival—security of the individual and their environment, as well as that of the state.

Like critical security scholars, many IR feminists define security broadly in multidimensional and multilevel terms—as the diminution of all forms of violence, including physical, structural, and ecological. According to IR feminists, security threats include domestic violence, rape, poverty, gender subordination, and ecological destruction as well as war. Feminists not only broaden *what security means* but also *who is guaranteed security*. Most of their analyses of security start at the bottom, with the individual or the community, rather than with the state or the international system. IR feminists have demonstrated how the security of individuals is related to national and international politics and how international politics impacts the security of individuals even at the local level.

Feminist research is demonstrating how those at the margins of states may actually be rendered more insecure by their state's security policies. The Malaysian case, discussed earlier, demonstrates that the exploitation of foreign domestic servants, often thought of as a 'private' issue, was permitted by the Malaysian state in order to win support of its middle class thereby diminishing ethnic tensions—tensions that were causing threats to the security of the state. In *Sex Among Allies* (1997), a study of prostitution around US military bases in South Korea in the 1970s, Katharine Moon shows how prostitution became a matter of top-level US–Korean security politics. The cleaning up of prostitution camps, effected by imposing health standards and monitoring sex workers, was directly related to establishing a more hospitable environment for US troops at a time when the USA was pulling troops out of South Korea. Both these cases show how considerations of national security translated into insecurity for marginalized vulnerable women. Redefinitions of security and rethinking about the subjects of security prompt feminists to ask different questions, particularly about whose lives are being secured and whose are not.

Challenging the myth of protection

Our earlier definition of masculinity and femininity defined men as 'protectors' and women as 'protected'.[4] It is a widespread myth that men fight wars to protect 'vulnerable people' usually defined as women and children. Yet, women and children constitute a majority of casualties in recent wars as civilian casualties have risen from about 10 per cent at the beginning of the twentieth century to almost 90 per cent by its close. In 1999 about 75 per cent of refugees were women and children, many of them fleeing from wars. Wars make it harder for women to fulfil their care-giving responsibilities; as mothers and family providers, women are particularly hurt by the economic consequences of wars.

In *Gender, Justice and the Wars in Iraq* (2006), Laura Sjoberg demonstrates that women's presumed status as innocent civilians makes wars harder, not easier, for them, by defining them as protected without regard for their actual safety. Since women's immunity from war has been presumed, belligerents have often disregarded the degree to which war causes women to suffer disproportionately. Feminists have also drawn our attention to wartime rape; often rape is not just an 'accident' of war but, as in the case of the war in the former Yugoslavia in the 1990s, a deliberate military strategy. Instead of seeing military power as part of a state's arsenal to defend against security threats from other states, feminists see that militaries are often threats to individuals' (particularly women's) security and competitors for scarce resources on which women may depend more than men.

Looking at the effects of war through gendered lenses, we find that war is a cultural construction that depends on myths of protection. Such myths have been important in upholding the legitimacy of war. They also contribute to the delegitimation of peace which is often associated with feminine characteristics, such as weakness, concession, and idealism. Looking at these gendered constructions may deepen our understanding of the causes of war and allow us to see how certain ways of thinking about security have been legitimated while others have been silenced.

Understanding economic insecurity

Feminist analyses of military security have looked at the gendered impacts of war, particularly as they relate to the security of individuals. Feminist research on economic security highlights women's particular economic vulnerabilities. While there are obviously enormous global differences in women's socio-economic status, depending on race, class, and geographic location, women are disproportionately located at the bottom of the socio-economic scale in all societies. In order to explain this, feminists have drawn our attention to a gendered division of labour that had its origins in seventeenth-century Europe, where definitions of male and female were becoming polarized in ways that were suited to a growing division between work and home required by early capitalism. The notion of 'housewife' began to place women's work in the private domestic sphere as opposed to the public world of production inhabited by men. Even though most women do work outside the home, the association of women with gendered roles, such as housewife, caregiver, and mother, came to be seen as 'natural'. Consequently when women do enter the workforce, they are disproportionately represented in the caring professions or 'light' manufacturing industries, occupations that are chosen because of values that are often emphasized in female socialization. Women provide an optimal labour force for contemporary global capitalism because, since they are defined as housewives rather than workers, they can be paid lower wages on the assumption that their wages are supplemental to family income. Elisabeth Prügl's (1999) study of home-based labour, discussed earlier, talks about the low remuneration of home-based work which is grounded in this assumption. Nevertheless, in actual fact, about one-third of all households are headed by women.

Even when women do benefit from entry into the workforce, they continue to suffer from a double or even triple burden since women carry most of the responsibility for household labour and unpaid community work. Unremunerated labour plays a crucial role in the reproduction of labour necessary for waged work, yet it has rarely been of concern to economic analysis. A narrow definition of work as work in the waged economy, one that is used in economic accounting, tends to render invisible many of the contributions that women make to the global economy. The disproportionate poverty of women cannot be explained by market conditions alone; gendered role expectations about the economic worth of women's work and the kinds of tasks that women are expected to do contribute to their economic insecurity.

Like critical security scholars, feminists have broadened their definitions and analyses of security. But they go further by showing how important gender as a category of analysis is to our understanding of security and insecurity. Using our gendered lenses we will now examine in more detail the UN sanctions policy on Iraq during the 1990s, a case which supports this proposition.

Case study: UN sanctions on Iraq

In 1991, Iraq invaded and conquered Kuwait, claiming a right to Kuwaiti territory. The United Nations (UN) declared Iraq's invasion illegal and ultimately used military force to eject Iraq from Kuwait. This conflict is known as the First Gulf War. At the end of the First Gulf War, UN Security Council Resolution 687 left Iraq under a strict import and export embargo. According to the Resolution, the embargo would remain in place until Iraq met a list of demands imposed by the Security Council. These demands related to Kuwaiti independence, Iraqi weapons, terrorism, and liability for the Gulf War.[5] This sanctions regime, originally intended to last about a year, stretched over thirteen. It was marked by confusion, fits and starts, partial compliance, and ulterior motives. Iraq's cooperation was inconsistent at best and Saddam Hussein, the president of Iraq, often openly defied the sanctions. Throughout the 1990s, Iraq remained under one of history's longest and most strict economic sanctions regimes.

In the mid-1990s, international popular opinion turned against the sanctions because of the tragic humanitarian consequences. Many states that favoured the overthrow of the Saddam Hussein regime became critical of the sanctions. A number of UN Security Council member states, including France and Russia, turned against the sanctions. Still, a Security Council vote to lift the sanctions was never taken because such a vote would have faced certain veto from the USA. The USA, but not the UN, insisted on regime change in Iraq as a condition for lifting sanctions. Meanwhile, pictures of malnourished children were publicized by activist organizations fighting the sanctions. The USA and the UN Security Council blamed Saddam Hussein for Iraq's non-compliance, while the Iraqi government blamed the UN.

The sanctions regime was a humanitarian disaster. The impacts of a thirteen-year near-total embargo on the Iraqi economy were extensive. Before the First Gulf War, Iraq had an

(continued)

export-based economy, exporting oil. Iraq imported almost all of its food and other basic necessities. The Iraqi gross national product (GNP) fell by 50 per cent during the first year of sanctions, and declined to less than $500 in the following years. By 2000, Iraq was the third poorest country in the world. Economic decline caused a sharp decline in real wages and widespread unemployment.

These adverse economic impacts caused most Iraqis serious material problems. Often, women had less secure jobs than men because their job tenure had been shorter and they were not seen as the primary income-earners for their families. Iraq had neither the money to buy, nor the means to produce, essential supplies; before the sanctions it had imported most of its food. With no income, a crippled infrastructure, and an international law against both imports and exports, Iraq had a difficult time acquiring food. The result was catastrophic malnutrition. Households rarely had enough food and women were often the last to eat. Iraqis also lacked clean water, baby milk, vitamins, healthcare supplies, and adequate electricity. The oil-for-food programme, which was implemented by the UN Security Council, allowed some needed supplies to enter Iraq by permitting limited oil exports. While the programme did result in some food entering Iraq, its provisions failed to provide for the restoration of Iraq's oil infrastructure which had been badly damaged in the First Gulf War and had been dormant for most of the 1990s. As a result, the oil-for-food programme did not meet the basic needs of Iraqi citizens. It was not until certain members of the international community began to trade with Iraq in the late 1990s despite the sanctions that the worst humanitarian impacts dissipated.

These deprivations had severe medical impacts. Finding adequate prenatal care was next to impossible for Iraqi women; even if their children were born healthy, the lack of vitamins and baby milk meant that child mortality skyrocketed. The cancer rate rose by 400 per cent. It is estimated that the sanctions lead to the deaths of about 1 million Iraqis, half of them children and another 30 per cent women (Mueller and Mueller 1999). In a country that had previously possessed a world-class medical system, curable diseases and starvation were the leading causes of death. The educational systems also plummeted. Crime rates and prostitution rose while culture, the arts, and religious activity decreased. Joy Gordon (1999) claimed that sanctions sent Iraq back to the stone age.

Some IR analyses of sanctions

Following the success of limited sanctions on South Africa in the 1980s which contributed to the ending of Apartheid, economic sanctions were seen as a powerful but humane tool. IR analyses of the effectiveness of sanctions are informed by a variety of theoretical perspectives. Realists view sanctions as a way of raising the cost of non-compliance for the country on which sanctions are imposed until it becomes unacceptable (Baldwin 1985). Liberals explain sanctions as a way of depriving the target country of the means to commit a violation of international norms (Martin 1992). In other words, sanctions take away the resources an errant state would use to defy international will. Constructivists argue that sanctions are a socializing phenomenon, communicating a message of disapproval through the combination of negative consequences and international shame (Crawford and Klotz 1999). Scholars who focus on language see sanctions as discourse—as tools of argumentation which allow actors to demonstrate the importance of their point to other actors reticent to agree (Morgan and Schwebach 1997). Within each of these schools of thought, there are disagreements about which (if any) sanctions have worked, and how frequently they should be used. A feminist theory of sanctions draws from all these perspectives but goes beyond them, using gender as a category of analysis.

Feminists interpret sanctions on Iraq

Economic sanctions do not appear to be a security issue in the narrow sense: they are not fought with guns on a battlefield, or with bombs on airplanes. The UN Security Council did not declare war on Iraq and the sanctions on Iraq did not *look like* a conventional war. However, as we mentioned earlier, IR feminists who study war pay attention to all forms of violence, physical and structural, and to what is happening on the ground—to individuals and communities. From this perspective, economic sanctions on Iraq not only looked like a war; they looked like a war on Iraq's most vulnerable citizens.

As we have shown, the UN Security Council's sanctions regime deprived most Iraqi citizens of their basic everyday needs. The aim of the sanctions was to stir up popular discontent against the Iraqi government and its policies. In other words, sanctions tried to *hurt civilians* so they would change their government. The civilians who were hurt the most were not the rich and powerful or the decision-makers, since they had the ability to buy food and supplies on the black market. Instead, it was Iraq's most vulnerable population that suffered most— low-income people, women, children, and the elderly. Economic sanctions against Iraq constituted both physical and structural violence. *Physical* violence was incurred though frequent bombings intended to communicate UN member states' unhappiness with Iraq's non-compliance. *Structural* violence was incurred through the destruction of the economic infrastructure and the lack of nutrition and medical care that had supported Iraq's poorest citizens. By these measures feminists would conclude that economic sanctions constitute war. This being the case, we will now suggest some research questions that feminists might ask and what we might learn from their analyses.

A liberal feminist study of sanctions might ask how many women participated in the sanctions decision-making process; they might also measure the varying effects of sanctions on individuals, focusing on gender differences. From this they might conclude that, while few women were involved in constructing and implementing the sanctions policy, women suffered more than their male counterparts, both through direct deprivation and through the effects of sanctions on their homes, families, and jobs.

Feminists from all postpositivist theoretical perspectives would introduce gender as a category of analysis and investigate the role that gender played in the politics of the sanctions regime. They might investigate how both the Iraqi government and the advocates of the sanctions regime used gender as a public relations argument against their opponents. The United States characterized Iraq as a state that failed to fulfil its protector role on account of its willingness to starve its women and children in order to develop weapons. Iraq characterized its sanctioners as cruel for killing women and children to punish the government.

Feminists might investigate the political appropriation of gender categories by both sides of the conflict. IR feminists emphasize the gendered social hierarchy in global politics that fosters an atmosphere of coercive competition by valuing traits associated with masculinity (bravery, strength, and dominance) over traits associated with femininity (compromise, compassion, and weakness). Feminists might investigate the gendered discourses of competitive masculinity that each side of the sanctions war used to legitimize their actions and delegitimate the enemy's; such discourses are often manifested in times of inter-state conflict. Specifically, they might point to instances where US CIA Director George Tenet talked about penetrating Saddam Hussein's 'inner sanctum', where US President George H. W. Bush talked about protecting Iraqi women as a justification for sanctions and war, and where Saddam Hussein countered with the threat of showing the US what a 'real man' he was. It is often the case, particularly in times of conflict, that we personify enemy states in gendered

(continued)

ways, referring to them by their leaders' names. This hides the negative impacts of war on the lives of individuals—individuals who may not be responsible for the conflict in the first place. Feminists might also explore the punitive relationship between the UN Security Council and Iraq as an example of a hegemonic masculinity feminizing a weaker enemy.

Towards a feminist theory of sanctions

We suggest three major insights that feminists contribute to the study of sanctions. First, feminists look for where the women are in sanctions regimes. They see that women are disproportionately affected by comprehensive sanctions. Women and children are the most likely to be malnourished. When women are malnourished, every stage of the child-bearing process becomes more difficult. Pre-natal and infant health care is often the first facet of the healthcare system to suffer when a sanctioned economy begins to decline. Women lose their jobs and are charged with running households deprived of basic goods. An international policy of economic deprivation is felt most heavily at the level of individual households. While women suffer disproportionately from sanctions regimes, very few women are present in the decision-making process. When the sanctions on Iraq were enacted, there were no female heads of UN Security Council member states. Feminists see the sanctions regime on Iraq as an example of the systematic exclusion of women's voices from decisions about international policies that disproportionately affect them. State and inter-state security policy can cause women's (and other individuals') insecurity.

The second insight feminists have is a criticism of the gendered logic of the policy choice. Sanctions are put in place by the stronger actors in an attempt to force the weaker actor to submit to their will. They are coercive in nature—comply, or you starve. Feminists criticize the adversarial nature of international politics because it valorizes masculine values, such as pride, victory, and force, over feminine ones, such as compromise, compassion, and coexistence—values that are often seen as signs of weakness by most states and many of their citizens, women and men alike. This results in confrontational policies; policies that often hurt those at the margins of international political life the most. Postcolonial feminists would add a criticism of the assumption that the UN Security Council members somehow knew *better than Iraq* what was good for Iraqis. It is often the case that powerful people, many of whom are men, claim to know what is best for subordinate people (and often for women). IR feminists critique the gendered logic and gendered impacts of sanctions.

The third insight that IR feminists have to offer a theory of sanctions is a critical re-examination of the question of responsibility. Feminists not only look for the problems with hierarchical gender relationships in global politics, they also look for solutions. Feminists explore sanctions as both an empirical phenomenon and a gendered phenomenon. Having seen the tragic humanitarian consequences of the sanctions regime, they might ask why no one was fixing them. The Iraqi government used people's suffering to advance its political position at the expense of its most vulnerable citizens. Saddam Hussein showed no flexibility which could have saved lives. Whether or not the international community truly believed that the goal of sanctions was worth the catastrophic loss of life in Iraq or whether anyone weighed the consequences directly, many governments in the international arena were willing to let people die. Feminists draw our attention to the construction of state borders as a way to separate 'self' from 'other' and distance ourselves from the suffering of others. Feminists encourage states and their citizens to reflect on the false perception of separateness and the global hierarchies that are thereby created. Deconstructing these hierarchies might lead people to care for, rather than compete with, those others outside state boundaries.

Feminists would conclude that economic sanctions are not isolated areas of conflict within an otherwise peaceful system. Acts of coercion, physical or economic, put in place by both sides to win international competitions are not only violent, but part of a system that is condoning violence, both physical and structural. The sanctions regime on Iraq contributed to the perpetuation of a violent international system in which the most vulnerable people are rarely secure. The feminist insights from the study of economic sanctions *as war* in international relations are not only valuable for their contribution to IR's theories of sanctions, but also for their generalizability to IR's crucial questions, such as what constitutes foreign policy, what counts as war, and how war affects people.

Conclusion

We believe that feminist IR has contributed substantially to our understanding of global politics over the last twenty years. Feminists have restored women's visibility, investigated gendered constructions of international concepts and policies, and questioned the naturalness of the gendered categories that shape and are shaped by global politics. First-generation feminist IR scholars have offered theoretical reformulations while second-generation scholars have applied these theoretical reformulations to concrete situations in global politics.

We have provided a brief overview of a number of different IR feminist theories, including liberal, critical, constructivist, poststructuralist, and postcolonial. While we realize it may be an over-simplification, we created this typology to illustrate one of the major goals of feminist IR—to demonstrate that gender relationships inhere in all IR scholarship. Gender relationships are everywhere in global politics; whenever they are not recognized, the silence is loud. IR feminists suggest that all scholars and practitioners of international politics should ask gender questions and be more aware of the gendered implications of global politics. Scholars should ask to what extent their theories are constructed mainly by men and from the lives of men. Practitioners should ask how their policies impact women and whether a lack of women's voices influences their policy choices. Recognizing gender and other hierarchies of power and their implications for the lives of both women and men, allows us to begin to de-gender global politics—from inside the United Nations to inside the home.

In this chapter, we focused on feminist interpretations of security. Security is so important to states that sometimes they pursue sanctions and wars and cause structural violence in the name of preserving or enhancing security. However, in preserving state security members of the international community may violate the security of their own and others' most marginal citizens, notably, women, children, the elderly, the poor, and the sick. IR feminists study security at the individual and the community level; they notice the differential impacts of security policies on women and marginalized people more generally and interrogate the gendered nature of concepts such as war, security, and the state. The insights they produce reveal some new causes of insecurity at the global level, including gender subordination.

Gender subordination is visible at every level in the Iraq sanctions case. Individual women were disproportionately impacted by the sanctions; gendered states exploited that disparate impact by engaging in gendered discourses of masculine competition. From the policy logic to the effects, sanctions on Iraq were an example of a gendered international security policy. We have laid out a few paths feminists have used in reformulating IR's understandings of sanctions in order to make women and gender relationships visible and thereby suggest some new ways to enhance security. We hope that these suggestions offer IR scholars of all perspectives some new insights into the feminist claim that gender is not just about women but also about the way that international policies are framed, studied, and implemented.

Questions

1. More than half the world's labour comes in the form of the unpaid, home-based labour of women. If this type of labour were remunerated, labour costs in the global economy would triple. How does women's free labour affect the global economy?

2. Does it make any difference to states' foreign policies that a vast majority of policy-makers are men? Does it matter to the content of IR scholarship that most of its leading scholars are men?

3. Cynthia Enloe, a prominent IR feminist, has claimed that 'the personal is international and the international is personal' (1990: 195). What does she mean by this?

4. Sanctions against Iraq were a case of extreme humanitarian suffering and political intransigence, but other sanctions have been more successful. Do gendered lenses have anything to say about economic coercion more generally? If so, what?

5. What about the men? How does gender affect men's experiences in everyday life? In global politics?

6. Once we realize that gender plays a pervasive role in global social and political interactions, we begin to ask what we can do about it. Could global politics be de-gendered?

7. One of the major claims that feminists in IR make is that individual lives *are* global politics. How might your trip to the grocery store, choice of television programming, or choice of internet sites be global politics?

8. The debate about whether or not women should get the vote was a contentious one in most countries. Do women have something different from men to say about global politics? If so, what?

9. Many scholars who work on the humanitarian consequences of war talk about the effect of war on innocent women and children. How might women experience war differently from men?

10. Since feminist insights stretch across different perspectives on IR, this chapter raises the issue as to whether feminism belongs in one chapter of a book about IR theories. How might gendered lenses see the cases in other chapters?

11. Following the war in the former Yugoslavia in the 1990s, a number of scholars and activists argued that the international laws of war should include a prohibition against genocidal rape. What might a feminist perspective on IR contribute to the discussion of the problem of wartime rape?

12. In his 2002 State of the Union Address to the US Congress, President George W. Bush claimed that 'brutality against women is always and everywhere wrong', implying that brutality against women might justify war. Would a feminist perspective on IR agree?

 ## Further reading

Introductions to feminist IR

Peterson, V. S. and Runyan, A. S. (2009), *Global Gender Issues.* **3rd edn (Boulder, CO: Westview).**
Peterson and Runyan introduce and apply 'gendered lenses' to global politics.

Tickner, J. A. (2001), *Gendering World Politics* **(New York: Columbia University Press).**
The author of the first singly-authored book in feminist IR lays out a foundation for feminist IR in the twenty- first century.

Feminist security theory

Enloe, C. (2000), *Maneuvers: The International Politics of Militarizing Women's Lives* (Berkeley: University of California Press).
Enloe finds the relationship between gender and security in political phenomena as different as a military base and a Chiquita banana, and weaves a framework for feminist security theories from these observations.

Feminist political economy

Marchand, M. H. and Runyan, A. S. (2010) (eds.), *Gender and Global Restructuring: Sightings, Sites, and Resistances.* 2nd edn. (London and New York: Routledge).
This book addresses genderings in the global economy, going beyond the narrow limits of conventional approaches to globalization to reveal the complexities of global restructuring based on economic and social disparities.

Second generation feminist IR empirical studies

Chin, C. (1998), *In Service and Servitude: Foreign Female Domestic Workers and the Malaysian 'Modernity' Project* (New York: Columbia University Press).
Chin uses gendered lenses to show that the very private phenomena of home-based labour interacts with international relations in important, gendered ways.

Moon, K. H. S. (1997), *Sex Among Allies: Military Prostitution in U.S.–Korea Relations* (New York: Columbia University Press).
Moon demonstrates that international security policy takes place at the level of regulating individual women's lives in Korean prostitution camps.

Prügl, E. (1999), *The Global Construction of Gender: Home-Based Work in the Political Economy of the 20th Century* (New York: Columbia University Press).
Prügl examines the social, political, and economic dynamics of home-based work in the twentieth century from a feminist constructivist perspective.

Robinson, F. (1999), *Globalising Care: Ethics, Feminist Theory and International Relations* (Oxford: Westview).
Robinson derives an ethic of care from feminist theories and applies her theoretical insights to the empirical study of care for health and welfare around the world.

True, J. (2003), *Gender, Globalization, and Post- socialism: The Czech Republic after Communism* (New York: Columbia University Press).
True applies the insights of feminist theories of international political economy and international security to post- socialist Eastern Europe.

 ## Important websites

Council of Women World Leaders. **www.womenworldleaders.org**

WomanSTATS Project. **www.womanstats.org**

UN Division for the Advancement of Women. **www.un.org/womenwatch/daw**

Women in International Security. **wiis.georgetown.edu**

MADRE, an international women's human rights organization. **www.madre.org**

Global Fund for Women. **www.globalfundforwomen.org**

Notes

1. Jacqui True (2003) made the distinction that first-generation feminist work in IR was theory-building, whereas second-generation work does empirical research investigating the implications of those theories for global politics (see Moon 1997; Prügl 1999). Second-generation feminist research challenges early criticisms of feminist IR's inability to deal with empirical political situations.

2. Harding (1986) points out that the problem with purported 'objective' knowledge is that only a small percentage of voices are represented in the production of that knowledge. Specifically, most knowledge is produced by white, Western men, while the voices most often excluded from the knowledge production process are those of women and minorities.

3. See, for example, *Empire and Insecurity in World Politics: Seductions of Neoliberalism* (2009).

4. Jean Elshtain explains that the just war tradition produces a narrative of heroic, masculine soldiers (just warriors) protecting innocent, female civilians (beautiful souls), justifying violence *for* women while neglecting violence *against* women (1992).

5. See United Nations Security Council Resolution 687; S/RES/687, 1991. Resolution 687 included demands that Iraq recognize and respect Kuwait's independence; allow a demilitarized zone between Iraq and Kuwait; surrender all nuclear, biological, chemical, and long-range weapons, weapons research, and weapons-related material; accept liability for the First Gulf War in its entirety; return all Kuwaiti possessions stolen during occupation; repatriate all Kuwaiti prisoners of war; and renounce terrorist activities as legitimate politics.

 Visit the Online Resource Centre that accompanies this book for lots of interesting additional material. **www.oxfordtextbooks.co.uk/orc/dunne3e/**

12 Poststructuralism

DAVID CAMPBELL[1]

 ## Reader's Guide

The way the discipline of International Relations (IR) 'maps' the world shows the importance of representation, the relationship of power and knowledge, and the politics of identity to the production and understanding of global politics. Post-structuralism directly engages these issues even though it is not a new paradigm or theory of IR. It is, rather, a critical attitude or ethos that explores the assumptions that make certain ways of being, acting, and knowing possible. This chapter details how and why poststructuralism engaged IR from the 1980s onwards. It explores the interdisciplinary context of social and political theory from which poststructuralism emerged, and examines the misconceptions evident in the reception this approach received from mainstream theorists. The chapter details what the critical attitude of poststructuralism means for social and political inquiry. Focusing on the work of Michel Foucault, it shows the importance of discourse, identity, subjectivity, and power to this approach, and discusses the methodological features employed by poststructuralists in their readings of, and interventions in, international politics. The chapter concludes with a case study of images of humanitarian crises that illustrates the poststructural approach.

Introduction

Interpretation, mapping, and meta-theory

Every way of understanding international politics depends upon abstraction, representation, and interpretation. That is because 'the world' does not present itself to us in the form of ready-made categories or theories. Whenever we write or speak of 'the realm of anarchy', the 'end of the Cold War', 'gendered relations of power', 'globalization', 'humanitarian intervention', or 'finance capital', we are engaging in representation. Even the most 'objective' theory that claims to offer a perfect resemblance of things does not escape the need for interpretation (Bleiker 2001).

Political leaders, social activists, scholars, and students are all involved in the interpretation of 'the world' whether they engage in the practice, theory, or study of international relations. This does not mean, however, that anyone can simply make things up and have their personal opinions count as legitimate knowledge. That is because the dominant understandings of world politics are both arbitrary in the sense that they are but one possibility among a range of possibilities, and non-arbitrary in the sense that certain social and historical practices have given rise to dominant ways of making 'the world' that have very real effects upon our lives.

The dominant interpretations of 'the world' have been established by the discipline of IR, which traditionally talks of states and their policy-makers pursuing interests and providing security, of economic relations and their material effects, and of the rights of those who are being badly treated. The 'we' who talk in this way do so from a particular vantage point—often white, Western, affluent, and comfortable. These representations, then, are related to our identities, and they establish a discourse of identity politics as the frame of reference for world politics.

This highlights the relationship between **knowledge and power**. While many say 'knowledge is power', this assumes they are synonymous rather than related. The production of maps illustrates the significance of this relationship between knowledge and power. Maps are not simply passive reflections of the world of objects. They favour, promote, and influence social relations (Harley 1988).

Consider the commonly used Mercator projection (Figure 12.1). Drafted in 1569 in order to provide the direct lines necessary for navigation, it placed Europe at the centre and put two-thirds of the world's landmass in the Northern Hemisphere. This representation supported the British Empire, and later reinforced Cold War perceptions of the Soviet threat (Monmonier 1996). Contrast this to the Peters projection, developed in the 1970s (Figure 12.2). This was based on equal-area projection which emphasized the South. This

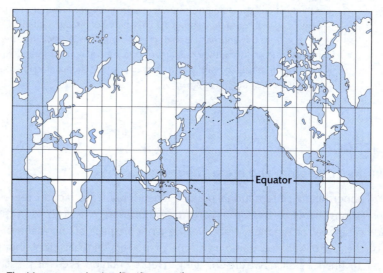

Figure 12.1 The Mercator projection (Pacific central)

Source: Oxford University Press.

projection was significant because it emerged with Third World political assertiveness in the United Nations (UN), and was promoted by UN agencies keen to secure more resources for development. The Peters projection is, therefore, a manifestation of the power relations that challenged the two superpowers in the 1970s and a form of knowledge that promoted the global South.

IR as a discipline 'maps' the world. However, it is only the critical perspectives—and poststructuralism in particular—which make the issues of interpretation and representation, power and knowledge, and the politics of identity central. Because of this poststructuralism is not a model or theory of international relations. Rather than setting out a paradigm through which everything is understood, poststructuralism is a critical attitude, approach, or ethos that calls attention to the importance of representation, the relationship of power and knowledge, and the politics of identity in an understanding of global affairs.

This means poststructuralism does not fit easily with the conventional view that IR is a discipline characterized by different paradigms competing in 'great debates' (discussed in **Chapter 1**). Instead of being another school with its own actors and issues to highlight, poststructuralism promotes a new set of questions and concerns. As a critical attitude rather than theory, poststructuralism, instead of seeing a distinction *between* theory and practice, sees theory *as* practice. This comes about because poststructuralism poses a series of meta-theoretical questions—questions about the theory of theory—in order to understand how particular ways of knowing, what counts as knowing, and who can know, have been established over time. Poststructuralism is thus an approach which comes from prior and extensive debates in the humanities and social science, in a manner akin to critical theory (**Chapter 9**), feminism (**Chapter 11**), and postcolonialism (**Chapter 13**).

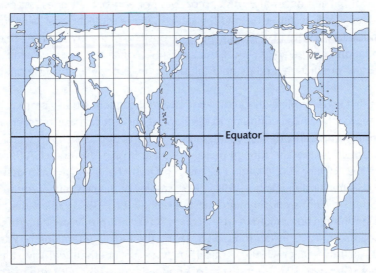

Figure 12.2 The Peters projection (Pacific central)
Source: Oxford University Press.

Poststructuralism and IR

Poststructuralism's entrance into IR came in the 1980s through the work of Richard Ashley (1981, 1984), James Der Derian (1987), Michael Shapiro (1988), and R. B. J. Walker (1987, 1993). Two important collections (Der Derian and Shapiro 1989; Ashley and Walker 1990) brought together the early studies. These focused mostly on articulating the meta-theoretical critique of realist and neorealist theories to demonstrate how the theoretical assumptions of the traditional perspectives shaped what could be said about international politics. What drove many of these contributions was an awareness of how other branches of the social sciences and humanities had witnessed significant debates about how knowledge of the world was constructed. Recognizing that the dominant approaches to IR were unaware, uninterested, or hostile to such questions, the above authors sought to connect IR to its interdisciplinary context by introducing new sources of theory. The motivation for the turn to poststructuralism was not purely theoretical, however. Critical scholars were dissatisfied with the way realism—and its revivification at that time through neorealism—remained powerful in the face of new global transformations. These scholars felt that realism marginalized the importance of new transnational actors, issues, and relationships and failed to hear (let alone appreciate) the voices of excluded peoples and perspectives. As such, poststructuralism began with an ethical concern to include those who had been overlooked or excluded by the mainstream of IR.

In focusing on the conceptual and political practices that included some and excluded others, poststructural approaches were concerned with how the relations of inside and outside were mutually constructed. For realism, the state marked the border between inside/outside, sovereign/anarchic, us/them. Accordingly, poststructuralism began by questioning how the state came to be regarded as the most important actor in world politics, and how the state came to be understood as a unitary, rational actor. Poststructuralism was thus concerned at the outset with the *practices of statecraft* that made the state and its importance seem both natural and necessary. This approach is not anti-state, it does not overlook the state, nor does it seek to move beyond the state. In many respects, poststructuralism pays more attention to the state than realism, because—instead of merely asserting that the state is the foundation of its paradigm—poststructuralism is concerned with the state's historical and conceptual production, and its political formation, economic constitution, and social exclusions.

After the first wave of meta-theoretical critiques, subsequent studies employing a poststructural approach—while continuing to develop the theoretical basis for their alternative interpretations—engaged political events and questions directly. This research includes analyses of state identity and foreign policy in Korea, Bosnia, and the USA (Bleiker 2005; Campbell 1992, 1998b, 2005); studies of the gendered character of state identity in the context of US intervention (Weber 1994, 1999); studies of the centrality of representation in North–South relations and immigration policies (Doty 1993, 1996); a deconstructive account of famine and humanitarian crises (Edkins 2000); interpretive readings of diplomacy and European security (Constantinou 1995, 1996); the radical rethinking of international order and security (Dillon 1996); critical analyses of international law and African sovereignties (Grovogui 1996); a recasting of ecopolitics (Kuehls 1996); the re-articulation of the refugee regime and sovereignty (Soguk 1999); a problematization of the UN and peacekeeping (Debrix 1999); a semiotic reading of militarism in Hawaii (Ferguson and Turnbull 1998); investigations of contemporary warfare, strategic identities, security landscapes, and representations of sovereignty (Coward 2002; Der Derian 1992, 2001; Dillon 2003; Dillon and Reid 2001; Klein 1994; Lisle and Pepper 2005); a reinterpretation of area studies (Philpott 2001); and a rethinking of finance and the field of international political economy (de Goede 2005, 2006).

This list is not exhaustive, nor is it the case that all the authors cited would willingly accept the label 'poststructural' for their work. Nonetheless, their work intersects with, and would not have been possible without, an interdisciplinary debate that called into question the authority of the positivist meta-theoretical assumptions which secured realist and other traditional perspectives in IR. Before detailing what a poststructuralist perspective involves, it is necessary, therefore, to outline the key elements of this interdisciplinary debate.

The interdisciplinary context of poststructuralism

Positivism and science in question

IR has been shaped by the influence of science and technology in the development of the modern world. The potential for control and predictive capacity that the natural sciences seemed to offer provided a model that social scientists sought to emulate. This model, **positivism**, was founded on the empiricist theory of knowledge, which argued that sensory experience provides the only legitimate source of knowledge (for more detail on positivism, see **Chapter 1**). 'Experience' refers to direct sensory access to an external reality comprising material things. As an epistemology (a meta-theory concerning how we know), the empiricist conception of knowledge understands knowledge as deriving from a relationship between a given subject (the person that knows) and a given object (that which is known).

These theoretical developments were central to a major historical transformation—the intellectual clash in the Renaissance period between the church and science which challenged the dominance of theology for social order. These intellectual developments, named as the Enlightenment, included making 'man' and 'reason', rather than 'god' and 'belief', the centre of philosophical discourse, and the construction and legitimation of the state, rather than the church, as the basis for political order. It was a moment in which knowledge intersected with power to lasting effect. Although the Enlightenment conception of knowledge was intended to free humanity from religious dogma, it was eventually transformed into a dogma itself. By the end of the nineteenth century, its dominance meant that knowledge was equated with science and reason limited to scientific reason. This dogmatization of science meant that social life is centred on technical control over nature and administrative control over humans, so that political issues became questions of order and efficiency.

The positivist account of science at the base of Enlightenment thought is founded upon three empiricist assumptions. First, **epistemic realism**: the view that there is an external world, the existence and meaning of which is independent of anything the observer does. Second, the assumption of a *universal scientific language*: the belief that this external world can be described in a language that does not presuppose anything, thereby allowing the observer to remain detached and dispassionate. Third, the **correspondence theory of truth**: that the observer can capture the facts of the world in statements that are true if they correspond to the facts and false if they do not. We can see these assumptions in Hans Morgenthau's classic text when he writes that a theory must 'approach political reality with a kind of rational outline' and distinguish 'between what is true objectively and rationally, supported by evidence and illuminated by reason, and what is only a subjective judgement, divorced from the facts as they are and informed by prejudice and wishful thinking' (Morgenthau 1978: 3–4).

Post-empiricism in science

A number of intellectual developments have demonstrated that the positivist understanding of scientific procedure that the social sciences have tried to model does not actually represent the conduct of scientific inquiry. The 'linguistic turn' in Anglo-American philosophy was a move away from the idea that language is a transparent medium through which the world can be comprehended—a view that suggested it was possible to get 'behind' language and 'ground' knowledge in the world itself—towards an account of language that understood it as embedded in social practice and inseparable from the world (Rorty 1967). Allied with the development of hermeneutic thought in continental philosophy—a tradition originally concerned with the reading of biblical, classical, and legal texts which developed into an account of the importance of interpretation to being human—these shifts contributed to a new understanding of the relationship between language and reality (see George 1994). Developments in the philosophy of science itself—especially what are called the postpositivist and post-empiricist debates (see Hesse 1980)—have also challenged the validity of the positivist account. These developments have also contributed to a reappraisal of science through social studies that question the value of 'facts' and the meaning of 'objectivity' for social inquiry (Megill 1994; Poovey 1998). Finally, the development of complexity science (including chaos theory and other new approaches to regularity) extends even further the challenge to 'common sense' assumptions of what counts as science and how it is conducted, and links contemporary understandings of science with poststructuralism (Dillon 2000). Given this, poststructuralism is in no sense anti-science.

In the philosophy of science, the post-empiricist debates focused on the core of the contention between positivists and anti-positivists: the Enlightenment conception of knowledge. For the Enlightenment the search for truth meant the search for foundations, facts that could 'ground' knowledge. The post-empiricist perspective is thus concerned with the rejection of such *foundational* thought (such as the claim that the state is the organizing principle of international relations, or that ethical theory requires established rules of justice as grounds for judging right from wrong), which it achieves through a new understanding of the subject/object relationship in theories of knowledge. Post-empiricists conceive of this relationship as one in which the two terms construct each other rather than the fundamental opposition of two pre-given entities. This undermining of the separation of subjects and objects means any claim to knowledge that relies on dichotomies analogous to the subject/object dualism (e.g. facts against values, objective knowledge versus subjective prejudice, or empirical observation in contrast to normative concerns) 'is . . . epistemologically unwarranted' (Bernstein 1979: 230, 1983).

The end result is that in place of the basic assumptions of epistemic realism, a universal scientific language and the correspondence theory of truth that lay behind positivist understandings of science and the Enlightenment conception of knowledge, all inquiry—in *both* the human sciences and the natural sciences—has to be concerned with the social constitution of meaning, the linguistic construction of reality, and the historicity of knowledge. This reaffirms the indispensability of interpretation, and suggests that all knowledge involves a relationship with power in its mapping of the world.

The reaction of IR to poststructuralism

Critical anxiety

As we shall see, these dimensions are present in and help make possible the poststructuralist accounts of politics and international relations introduced above, even as those accounts go beyond the priority given to language in the constitution of reality that marks constructivist approaches to international politics. We need to be clear, then, about the similarities and differences in the critical approaches to IR. An awareness of these distinctions, however, is something that has been absent from the responses the critical approaches have provoked in the field.

Those who have objected to the meta-theoretical critiques of realism, neorealism, and the like, particularly the way those critiques have called into question the reliance on external reality, foundations, objectivity, and the transparency of language, have often called those critiques 'postmodern', even though there are few if any scholars who use that label, and many who explicitly reject it (see Campbell 1992: 246–7).

In one of the first assessments of the meta-theoretical critiques, Robert Keohane (1988) dichotomized the field into 'rationalists' vs. 'reflectivists' and castigated the critical approaches of the latter position for lacking social scientific rigour. Keohane faulted the critical approaches for failing to embrace the empiricist standards concerning research agendas, hypothesis construction, and testing that would (in his eyes) lend them credibility. However, in making his claims, Keohane failed to demonstrate an awareness or understanding of the challenge posed by post-empiricist developments in the philosophy of science for his supposedly objective criteria (see Bleiker 1997). Subsequently accused of 'self-righteousness' (Wallace 1996), lambasted as 'evil' and 'dangerous' (Krasner 1996), castigated for 'bad IR' and 'meta-babble' (Halliday 1996), misread as 'philosophical idealism' (Mearsheimer 1994–5), and considered congenitally irrational (Østerud 1996), those named as 'postmodernists' have been anything but welcomed by the mainstream of IR (see Devetak 2001 for the best review using this term). Aside from their unwillingness to engage ways of thinking they regarded as 'foreign', these critics reacted as if the questioning of critical approaches meant that the traditional containers of politics (especially the state) and the capacity to judge right from wrong were being rejected. In so doing, they mistook arguments about the historical production of foundations for the claim that all foundations had to be rejected.

When theoretical contests provoke such vehemence, it indicates that there is something larger at stake than different epistemologies. As Connolly (2004) has argued, different methodologies express in one way or another deep attachments—understood as metaphysical commitments or existential faith—on behalf of those who advocate them. For those who take such intense objection to the critical perspectives they herd together and brand as 'postmodern', their faith is a particular understanding of science. Their attachment to that faith in science—despite the debates in the philosophy of science that demonstrate how their understanding of science cannot be supported through reason—in turn derives from an anxiety about what the absence of secure foundations means for ethics and politics. Bernstein (1983) has named this the 'Cartesian Anxiety', because in the philosophy of Descartes the quest was to find a secure ground for knowledge. The Cartesian Anxiety is the fear that, given the demise of objectivity, we are unable to make judgements that have been central to the understanding of modern life, namely distinguishing between true and false, good and bad. The challenge, though, is to escape from the straightjacket in which intellectual understanding and political life has to be organized by recourse to either one option or the other. The post-empiricist debates in the philosophy of science have demonstrated that dualistic or dichotomous frameworks are unstable. We need, in Bernstein's (1983) words, to move beyond objectivism and relativism. We need to develop modes of interpretation that allow judgements about social and political issues at home and abroad while accepting, first, that such judgements cannot be secured by claims about a pre-existing, external reality and, second, such arguments cannot be limited by invoking dichotomies such as fact/value or objective/subjective.

Poststructuralism misunderstood as postmodernism

By labelling the critical perspectives that deal with interpretation and representation in international politics as 'postmodern', the critics are suggesting that it is modernity that they believe to be under threat. If we are to understand what is meant by 'postmodernism', we also have to be concerned with modernism. What is meant by this term?

'Modernism' refers to the predominant cultural style of the period from the 1890s to the outbreak of the Second World War, encompassing the ideas and values in the painting, sculpture, music, architecture, design, and literature of that period. Modernism was part of the great upheavals in political, sociological, scientific, sexual, and familial orders in Europe and the USA. It was also part of colonialism and imperialism, in which these aesthetic and technological transformations radically affected the political, sociological, scientific, sexual, and familial orders of non-Western societies. Modernism had much to do with large technological and scientific transformations which made the early twentieth century a time of both infectious optimism and unsettled fear. It was an era which saw the industrial revolution produce mass railways, the first aircraft, automobiles, light bulbs, photography, films, and a host of other mechanical inventions. These machines offered the hope of improved social conditions, increased wealth, and the possibility of overcoming human limitations. But their impact on pre-mechanized ways of life made people fear for the existing social order, at the same time as they compressed time and space in the global order. Modernism was the cultural response to this change, evident in the abstract art of the Cubists (like Picasso and Braque) whose work distorted perspectives and favoured manufactured objects over natural environments (see Hughes 1991; Kern 1983). Its aim was to represent, interpret, and provide critical commentary on modern life.

The faith in technology of the early modernists was soon extinguished in the First World War. The great machines of promise turned into technologies of mass slaughter. The future lost its allure, and art became full of irony, disgust, and protest. In the imperial domain of Europe the questioning of modernism fuelled anti-colonial nationalism. In this context, 'modernism' was a political intervention in a specific cultural context that had global affects. But, after fascism in Europe, another world war, the Holocaust, and the process of decolonization, the critical edge of modernism was spent. Modernist cultural forms lost any sense of newness and possibility.

It is against this background that 'postmodernism' emerged during the period after the Second World War, representing and interpreting the indeterminate, pluralistic, and ever more globalized culture of the Cold War world. In literature, art, architecture, and music the term 'postmodern' designated a particular, often eclectic, approach to this cultural context. (Examples here include the painting of Andy Warhol, the intermingling of styles in the architecture of Charles Jencks, and the music of Madonna.) In this context, 'postmodernism' refers to cultural forms inspired by the conditions of accelerated time and space and hyper-consumerism that we experience in the globalized era some call 'postmodernity'.

Many of the problems associated with the concept of 'postmodernism' come from the misleading periodization associated with the prefix 'post'. Many critics of postmodernism attack it by arguing that it assumes a temporal break with modernity. They argue that the term 'postmodernity' assumes that we live in an historical epoch that is quite distinct from, and in some way replaces, 'modernity'. However, as Jameson (1991) has argued, the structure of postmodernity that critical, interpretive approaches seek to engage historically is not a new order that has displaced modernity. It is, rather, a cultural, economic, social, and political problematic marked by the re-articulation of time and space in the modern world (see also Harvey 1989). It is evident in developments such as financial speculation and flexible accumulation that depart from the modern, industrial forms of capitalism rooted in the exploitation of labour in the production process.

Much of the confusion and hostility surrounding the concept of 'postmodernism' in IR stems from the mistaken idea that those deploying an interpretative analytic to critically understand the transformations in modernity are celebrating the apparently shallow and accelerated cultural context that has challenged many of modernity's certainties. While 'postmodernity' is the cultural, economic, social, and political formation *within* modernity that results from changes in time–space relations, poststructuralism is one of the interpretative analytics that critically engages with the production and implication of these transformations.

The critical attitude of poststructuralism

Political context

In philosophical terms a number of the scholars who resist the mistaken label of 'postmodernism' are more comfortable with the term 'poststructuralism'. 'Poststructuralism' is a distinct philosophical domain which has a critical relation to structuralism, modernity, and postmodernity. The 'structuralist' philosophical movement is associated with 'modernist' cultural forces. Structuralism was a largely French philosophical perspective associated with linguist Ferdinand de Saussure and cultural critic Roland Barthes.[2] Structuralists aimed to study the social and cultural construction of the various structures that give meaning to our everyday lives. Poststructuralism is equally concerned to analyse such meaning-producing structures, but in a manner consistent with transformations in the social order of the late twentieth century.

The events that influenced poststructuralism were associated with the resistance struggles against established and imperial power blocs, such as the Algerian and Vietnam wars, the Prague Spring of 1968, the May 1968 movement in France, cultural expression in Yugoslavia, demands for Third World economic justice, and the civil rights, environmental, and women's movements in the USA and elsewhere. According to the French philosopher Giles Deleuze (1988: 150) these events were part of an international movement which 'linked the emergence of new forms of struggle to the production of a new subjectivity'. In other words, these struggles, unlike the revolutionary movements of the early twentieth century, were not concerned with freeing a universal 'mankind' from the chains imposed upon it by society, but with reworking political subjectivity given the globalizing forms of late capitalism. This context means poststructuralism has important things to say about the concept of identity in political life.

Michel Foucault: limits, ethos, and critique

The critical attitude of poststructuralism can be found in the writing of numerous thinkers.[3] For the purposes of simplicity, this chapter will focus on the work of Michel Foucault. Thinking the present historically involves an ethos of what Foucault has called 'the limit attitude'. It involves considering the limits that give meaning to our thought and practice—for example, reason and rationality is given meaning by the establishing of limits at which unreason and irrationality are said to begin. Moreover, a 'limit attitude' involves interrogating those limits, not by getting rid of, escaping, or transcending them, but by contesting and negotiating them through argumentation.

This critical attitude is consistent with the Enlightenment project to critically interrogate the conditions of human existence and is animated by an emancipatory ideal. The critical attitude is emancipatory insofar as it draws out the limits that shape existence and in so doing gives the conditions under which such limits—and the exclusions they entail—can be challenged. Although those dismissive of 'postmodernism' claim that it is an anti-modern and anti-Enlightenment position, to talk in those terms (anti- vs. pro-Enlightenment) is to replicate the either/or exclusionary logic that Foucault terms the 'blackmail of the Enlightenment'. Rather than succumbing to such gestures of rejection, Foucault argues that the attitude of modernity has had from its beginnings an ongoing relationship with attitudes of 'counter-modernity'. This agonism is itself characteristic of and inherent in the Enlightenment, for, in Foucault's terms, what connects us with the Enlightenment 'is not faithfulness to doctrinal elements but rather the permanent reactivation of an attitude—that is, of a philosophical ethos that could be described as a permanent critique of our era' (Foucault 1984: 42). Poststructuralism, then, is first and foremost an approach rather than a theory. As Foucault argues:

> The critical ontology of ourselves has to be considered not, certainly, as a theory, a doctrine, nor even as a permanent body of knowledge that is accumulating; it has to be conceived as an attitude, an ethos, a philosophical life in which the critique of what we are is at one and the same time the historical analysis of the limits that are imposed on us and an experiment with the possibility of going beyond them.
>
> Foucault 1984: 50

As an approach, attitude, or ethos, poststructuralism is inherently critical. Critique, though, is a positive rather than negative attitude. It is about disclosing the assumptions and limits that have made things as they are, so that what appears natural and without alternative can be rethought and reworked. Critique is thus also inescapably ethical, because it is concerned with change. As Foucault writes:

> A critique is not a matter of saying that things are not right as they are. It is a matter of pointing out on what kinds of assumptions, what kinds of familiar, unchallenged, unconsidered modes of thought the practices that we accept rest. We must free ourselves from the sacralization of the social as the only reality and stop regarding as superfluous something so essential in human life and in human relations as thought . . . It is something that is often hidden, but which always animates everyday behavior. There is always a little thought even in the most stupid institutions; there is always thought even in silent habits. Criticism is a matter of flushing out that thought and trying to change it: to show that things are not as self-evident as one believed, to see what is accepted as self-evident will no longer be accepted as such. Practicing criticism is a matter of making facile gestures difficult.
>
> Foucault 1988: 154–5. See Campbell 1992: ch. 9

Taking these arguments into account, we can see that poststructuralism has a lot in common with the attitude of Frankfurt School critical theory (see **Chapter 9**). Indeed poststructuralism also has much in common with the post-empiricist debates outlined earlier. It has a similar disdain for foundationalism (ideas of grounding thought on universal rules that exist independently of the observer), shares the view that language is central to the constitution of social life, and agrees that the historicity of knowledge (the historical production of knowledge in socio-cultural structures and, hence, the refutation of the idea of universal/timeless knowledge) is a major concern.

Subjectivity, identity, and power

However, poststructuralism differs from Frankfurt School thought in ways that are important to the analysis of international relations. Most importantly, poststructuralism takes a different conception of the human subject. Whereas much of Frankfurt School critical theory takes critique to involve the uncovering or emancipation of a 'humanity' whose autonomy and freedom is bound by ideology, Foucault's work involves creating 'a history of the different modes by which, in our culture, human beings are made subjects' (Foucault 1982: 208). For Foucault, the modern individual is an historical achievement. This is to say that there is no 'universal person'—a human-being that has been the unchanging basis for all history—on whom power has operated throughout all time. Rather, the individual human is an effect of the operations of power. Similarly, there is no 'human nature' shared by all members of the species—the nature of individuals, their humanity, is produced by certain power structures. Foucault's poststructuralism is thus offering the most thoroughgoing questioning of foundations around. That is because it is a questioning of foundations that includes the category of 'man' as well as the bases upon which social and political order is constructed. Foucault is thus concerned with forms of subjectivity. What are the subjects of politics? If they are 'humans', in what way is the 'human' subject constituted historically? How have the identities of women/men, Western/Eastern, North/South, civilized/uncivilized, developed/under-developed, mad/sane, domestic/foreign, rational/irrational, and so on, been constituted over time and in different places? All of which means that *identity*, *subjectivism*, and *power* are key concepts for poststructuralism.

Foucault's focus on the constitution of the subject is in accord with poststructuralism's concern with the dualisms which structure human experience. In particular, it is concerned with the interior/exterior (inside/outside) binary according to which that which is inside is deemed to be the self, good, primary, and original while the outside is the other, dangerous, secondary, and derivative. French philosopher Jacques Derrida has approached this issue through his strategy of deconstruction—reversing the original order of the binary pair of terms to demonstrate how the exclusion of the second term is central to the first (Culler 1982). In this argument, the outside is always central to the constitution of the inside; the insane is central to the constitution of what it is to be sane or rational; the criminal is central to the constitution of the law-abiding citizen; and the foreign is pivotal in understanding the domestic. In *Discipline and Punish*, Foucault (1979) demonstrates how what the prison confines is as much the identity of society outside the walls as it is the prisoners on the inside. The good, civilized society is constituted by the bad, barbaric prisoners it confines. When drug abuse and prostitution are made pathological by being criminalized, the effect is to normalize a moral order in which certain behaviours are excluded.

The critique of inside/outside dualisms leads poststructuralist thinkers to emphasize the importance of studying cultural practices. Instead of claiming that reality is understood by isolating the internal nature of the object studied (e.g. states and their desire to maximize power) poststructuralism studies the cultural practices through which the inclusions and exclusions that give meaning to binary pairs are established. This shift to cultural practices means that poststructuralist thinkers refuse to take any identity—individual or collective—as given and unproblematic. Rather, they see identity as culturally constructed through a series of exclusions. The particular events, problems, and actors that are recognized in history are thereby understood as constituted by an order always dependent upon the marginalization and exclusion of other identities and histories. This means there are considerable affinities between poststructuralism and postcolonialism.

The emphasis on practices of exclusion in poststructural accounts involves a different understanding of power. For Foucault power is not simply *repressive* (i.e. imposing limits and constraints on the infinite possibilities of the world) but is *productive* because of the imposition of limits and constraints. Relations of power establish the limitations of self/other, inside/relation to outside, but without those limitations those notions of self/inside, other/outside would not exist. The limitations are, therefore, productive: we know what that thing *is* by knowing what it is *not*. Foucault calls this productive power 'disciplinary power', power that disciplines in order to produce a certain political subject. The aim of poststructural analysis is, therefore, not to eliminate exclusion (since that is what makes meaning possible) but to understand the various forms of exclusion that constitute the world as we find it, understand how they come to be and how they continue to operate, and make possible interventions that can articulate alternatives.

Understanding discourse

Language, reality, and performance

The operations of disciplinary power, and the conceptions of subjectivity and identity to which it gives rise, take place within **discourse**. Discourse refers to a specific series of representations and practices through which meanings are produced, identities constituted, social relations established, and political and ethical outcomes made more or less possible. Those employing the concept are often said to be claiming that 'everything is language', that 'there is no reality', and, because of their linguistic idealism, they are unable to take a political position and defend an ethical stance.

These objections demonstrate how understandings of discourse are bedevilled by the view that interpretation involves only language in contrast to the external, the real, and the material. These dichotomies of idealism/materialism and realism/idealism remain powerful conceptions of understanding the world. In practice, however, a concern with discourse does not involve a denial of the world's existence or the significance of materiality. This is well articulated by Laclau and Mouffe (1985: 108): 'the fact that every object is constituted as an object of discourse has *nothing to do* with whether there is a world external to thought, or with the realism/idealism opposition. . . . What is denied is not that . . . objects exist externally to thought, but the rather different assertion that they could constitute themselves as objects outside of any discursive condition of emergence.' This means that while nothing exists outside of discourse, there are important distinctions between linguistic and non-linguistic phenomena. There are also modes of representation which are ideational though strictly non-linguistic, such as the aesthetic and pictorial. It is just that there is no way of comprehending non-linguistic and extra-discursive phenomena except through discursive practices.

Understanding discourse as involving the ideal and the material, the linguistic and the non-linguistic, means that discourses are performative. Performative means that discourses constitute the objects of which they speak. For example, states are made possible by a wide range of discursive practices that include immigration policies, military deployments and strategies, cultural debates about normal social behaviour, political speeches, and economic investments. The meanings, identities, social relations, and political assemblages that are enacted in these performances combine the ideal and the material. As a consequence, appreciating that discourses are performative moves us away from a reliance on the idea of (social) *construction* towards *materialization*, whereby discourse 'stabilizes over time to produce the effect of boundary, fixity and surface' (Butler 1993: 9, 12). Discourse is thus not something that subjects use in order to describe objects; it is that which constitutes both subjects and objects.

Discourse, materialism, and meaning

Within IR, there has been much misunderstanding of discourse in these terms. Even some constructivists (Wendt 1999) maintain a strict sense of the material world external to language as a determinant of social and political truth. When faced with poststructural arguments, they will maintain that no discursive understanding can help you when faced with something as material as a bullet in the head (Wendt 1999: 113; Krasner 1999: 51; cf. Zehfuss 2002). At first glance, this appears irrefutable. So how would a poststructuralist respond? First, they would say that the issue is not one of the materiality of the bullet or the reality of death for the individual when struck by the bullet in a particular way. The undeniable existence of that world external to thought is not the issue. Second, they would say that such a world—the body lying on the ground, the bullet in the head, and the shell casing lying not far away—tells us nothing itself about the meaning and significance of those elements. They would say that the constitution of the event and its elements is a product of its discursive condition of emergence, something that occurs via the contestation of competing narratives. Did the body and the bullet get to be as they are because of suicide, manslaughter, murder, ethnic cleansing, tribal war, genocide, a war of inter-state rivalry, or . . .? Each of those terms signifies a larger discursive formation through which a whole set of identities, social relations, political possibilities, and ethical outcomes are made more or less possible. Whichever figuration emerges as the accepted or dominant one has little to do with the materiality of specific elements and much to do with power of particular discourses materializing elements into comprehensible forms with political effects. Therefore, focusing specifically on the bullets that riddled their bodies tells us very little about those circumstances beyond the fact people died; something that occurs in many other dissimilar circumstances. Not least it fails to tell us how people, knowing full well the likely futility of their actions in the face of overwhelming force, nonetheless sacrifice themselves. That is an explanation which is going to require, among other things, that attention be paid to discourses of loyalty, pride, and the nation. If in IR we limit ourselves to the immediate cause and context of material events we will be unable to understand the larger ethical and political issues.

Discourses of world politics

Theory as the object of analysis

Understanding discourse as performative materialization, rather than linguistic construction, takes us beyond the idea that it is just a practice employed by the subjects of international relations (be they states, institutions, or trans-national actors). We need to consider not only the international relations discourse various actors are involved in but also the discourse of IR—the modes of representation that give rise to the subjects of international relations and constitute the domain to which IR theory is purportedly only responding.

This means poststructural accounts—in addition to the concern with the representations invoked by the actors of world politics—investigate the practices that constitute entities called 'actors' capable of representation. This includes the cultural, economic, social, and political practices that produce particular actors (e.g. states, non-government organizations, and the like). It also includes investigating the role of theorists and theory in representing some actors as more significant than others. In this latter sense, this means that instead of theory being understood as simply a *tool for analysis* poststructuralism treats theory as an *object of analysis*. This reorientation, which derives from poststructuralism's status as an approach to criticism rather than a critical theory per se, is no less practical in its implications. It asks, for both theorists and practitioners of international relations, how do analytic approaches privilege certain understandings of global politics and marginalize or exclude others?

This approach is evident in arguments that offer historical, theoretical, and political re-readings of the traditional concerns of IR. For example, Walker (1993) has investigated the way that many realist questions and answers have been produced via a particular reading of Machiavelli. His conclusion is that the dominant tradition in IR has endorsed a narrow ahistorical reading of the paradigmatic realist which has given us the slogans of power over ethics, ends justifying means, and the necessity of violence. Similarly, in identifying anarchy as integral to realist thought, Ashley (1984, 1988) demonstrated that its status as a 'given' is a matter not of factual observation but part of a particular discursive strategy which disciplines our understanding of the multiple and ambiguous events of world politics through hierarchies such as sovereign/anarchic, domestic/international, objective/subjective, real/ideal, is/ought, and masculine/feminine. This means that the problematization of 'reality' offers two possible solutions of which only one can be chosen: for example sovereignty or anarchy. The operation of this 'anarchy problematique' results in the mapping of world politics into zones of sovereignty and zones of anarchy, with sovereignty being normatively superior to anarchy.

 ### Featured article

Richard K. Ashley (1984), 'The Poverty of Neo-Realism', *International Organization* 38/2 Spring: 225–86.

This box gives an account of another key text by Ashley. This is one of the most important articles in the development of a critical approach to international relations. Ashley did not write of the day-to-day events of international politics. Instead, he drew upon European social theory to question how North American international relations theory was beginning to understand global affairs.

Ashley's concern was with the rise of neorealism, as manifested in the work of Robert Keohane, Stephen Krasner, and Robert Gilpin. However, it was the assumptions of a theory, rather than the personalities of people, that were Ashley's target. 'My arguments here, intentionally phrased in provocative terms, are like warning shots, meant to provoke a discussion, not destroy an alleged enemy' (p. 229).

Ashley drew inspiration from the historian E. P. Thompson's polemic against the structuralism of Louis Althusser, entitled *The Poverty of Theory* (1978). This book condemned Althusser's scientific Marxism for its reliance on positivism. Ashley thereby noted that, just as social theory was calling structuralism into question, prominent scholars in international relations were developing a new approach reliant on structuralism.

Neorealism had emerged as a response to perceived failings in classical realism, Ashley argued. In place of the subjectivism of realism, neorealists wanted to emphasize a 'scientific' approach that would identify the 'objective' structures of world politics. At the heart of neorealism was a commitment to the state-as-actor. As a result, and especially odd given the neorealist's concern with power politics, there was no concept of social power behind or constitutive of states and their interests.

The effect of these assumptions, Ashley argued, was for neorealists to treat the given international order (with the USA in a position of hegemony) as the natural order. Neorealism, Ashley said, did not to expose the limits of the given order and thereby denied history as process, the significance of practice and the place of politics. Controversially, Ashley called this a 'totalitarian project of global proportions (p. 228),' although he emphasized this referred to the logic of the theoretical assumptions rather the politics of individuals (p. 257).

Ashley's 1984 article was not just a critique; it also proposed that a 'silenced realism' (p. 264) be recovered and a theory of international political practice be developed, drawing on the work of Pierre Bourdieu, Jurgen Habermas, and Michel Foucault. Although critics like Robert Gilpin were scathing in their responses to Ashley's article, it helped shape the future of critical theory in IR.

From subjects to subjectivity

One of the most important functions of these historical and theoretical critiques has been to demonstrate that what we take to be real, timeless, and universal in both the domain of international relations and field of IR is produced through the imposition of a form of order. A poststructural approach seeks, therefore, to make strange and denaturalize taken-for-granted perspectives. Important here are the discourses of danger we consume as citizens of a modern state. In an argument examining US foreign policy towards Central America, Shapiro (1988: ch. 3) shows that foreign policy can be understood as the process of making 'strange' the object under consideration in order to differentiate it from 'us'. In the case of the construction of the 'Central American Other', the moral and geopolitical codes of US foreign policy discourse make US intervention in the region seem necessary, both in terms of US interests and the subject state's own good. Campbell (1992) developed this account to show that US foreign policy generally should be seen as a series of political practices which locate danger in the external realm—threats to 'individuality', 'freedom', and 'civilization'—thereby constructing the boundary between the domestic and the international, which brings the identity of the USA into existence. Together these arguments examine the practices of statecraft that produce 'the state' as an actor in international relations and the practices of statecraft that produce the identity of particular states. As such, these arguments are directly concerned with the state so they cannot be understood as being against the state or its importance. They focus on the production and meaning of the state rather than simply assuming or asserting that states exist naturally as particular identities.

These examples build upon poststructuralism's concern with subjectivity, identity, and power. In general, they shift analysis from assumptions about pre-given subjects to the problematic of subjectivity and its political enactment. This is achieved through three methodological precepts, which can be understood by contrasting them to the basic assumptions of the traditional approaches to IR.

Methodological precepts: interpretation, representation, politics

The most common meta-theoretical discourse among mainstream theories is committed to an epistemic realism, whereby the world comprises objects the existence of which is independent of ideas or beliefs about them. This commitment sanctions two other analytic forms common to the field: a narrativizing historiography in which things have a self-evident quality that allows them to speak for themselves; and a logic of explanation in which the purpose of analysis is to identify those self-evident things and material causes so that actors can accommodate themselves to the realm of necessity they create.

Contrary to the claims of epistemic realism, a poststructural approach maintains that because understanding involves rendering the unfamiliar in the terms of the familiar, interpretation is unavoidable and such that there is nothing outside discourse, even though there is a material world external to thought. Contrary to a narrativizing historiography, a poststructural approach employs a mode of historical representation which self-consciously adopts a perspective, a perspective grounded in the view that identity is always constituted in relationship to difference. Because of this, poststructural approaches need to be understood as interventions in conventional understandings or established practices. And, contrary to

Case study: images of humanitarian crises

As an approach that adopts a critical stance in relation to its objects of concern, poststructuralism differs from other theoretical perspectives in international relations. Because it does not seek to formulate a theory of international relations, it does not outline a detailed scheme of international politics in which some actors, issues and relations are privileged at the expense of others. As such, poststructuralism can, therefore, concern itself with an almost boundless array of actors, issues, and events. The choice of actor, issue, or event is up to the analyst undertaking a poststructural analysis. Because of this, there is no one set of actors, issues, or events that would illustrate poststructuralism better than others.

The case study chosen to illustrate poststructuralism here concerns visual images of humanitarian disaster, especially famine. Visual imagery can be approached from a range of theoretical positions, but in the way it calls attention to questions of interpretation, perspective, and their political effects it is well suited to demonstrate aspects of a poststructural account. It also reminds us that discourse should not be confined to the linguistic (Rose 2001: chs. 6, 7).

Visual imagery is of particular importance for international politics because it is one of the principal ways in which news from distant places is brought home. Indeed, ever since early explorers made a habit of taking cameras on their travels, photographs have provided much basic information about the people and places encountered on those travels. Much like cartography, these images contributed to the development of an 'imagined geography' in which the dichotomies of West/East, civilized/barbaric, North/South, and developed/underdeveloped have been prominent (Said 1979; Gregory 1995). Since the advent of technology for moving images (i.e. film, television, and video), much of the news from abroad centred on disaster, with stories about disease, famine, war, and death prominent (Moeller 1999). In the post-Cold War era, news about humanitarian emergencies has become increasingly prominent.

Humanitarian emergencies are matters of life and death. But they do not exist for the majority of the people in the world unless they are constructed as an event. This construction, which materializes these issues of life and death in particular ways, is achieved in large part through media coverage. These media materializations create a range of identities—us/them, victim/saviour—and are necessary for a response to be organized. This argument is consistent with poststructuralism's reorientation of analysis from the assumption of pre-given subjects to the problematic of subjectivity because it maintains that the event (the emergency or disaster) and the identities of those involved are the effects of discursive practices through which they are brought into being. As the development consultant Jonathan Benthall argues:

> the coverage of disasters by the press and the media is so selective and arbitrary that . . . they 'create' a disaster when they decide to recognise it. To be more precise, they give institutional endorsement or attestation to bad events which otherwise have a reality restricted to a local circle of victims. Such endorsement is a prerequisite for the marshalling of external relief and reconstructive effort.
>
> Benthall 1993:11

Pictures, especially those imprinted as photographs or frames of film, are especially apt for a poststructural analysis because they foreground questions of representation. Such pictures have been culturally produced as authoritative documents that witness atrocity and injustice, in large part because they are accepted as transparent windows on an already existing world. Through the photograph we are said to be able to view things as they are. However, technologically generated images are anything but objective records of an external reality. They are necessarily constructions in which the location of the photographer, the choice of the subject, the framing of the content, the exclusion of context, and limitations on publication and circulation unavoidably create a particular sense of place populated by a particular kind of people.

Famine images remain powerful and salient in modernity because they recall a precarious pre-modern existence industrialized society has allegedly overcome. Understood as a natural disaster in which there is a crisis of food supply, famine is seen as a symptom of the lack of progress that results in the death of the innocent (Edkins 2000). It is for this reason that famine images are more often than not

(continued)

Figure 12.3 Famine victims with aid workers, Idaga Hamus, Northern Ethiopia,1984
Source: Camerapix.

of women and children, barely clothed, staring passively into the lens, flies flitting across their faces (Figure 12.3). Content analyses of newspaper photos during the Ethiopian famine of 1984 (which gave rise to the Live Aid phenomenon) found that mothers and children featured more than any other subject (Figure 12.4). As one study noted:

> All these pictures overwhelmingly showed people as needing our pity—as passive victims. This was through a de-contextualised concentration on mid- and close-up shots emphasising body language and facial expressions. The photos seemed mainly to be taken from a high angle with no eye-contact, thus reinforcing the viewer's sense of power compared with their apathy and hopelessness. The 'Madonna and Child' image was particularly emotively used, echoing the biblical imagery. Women were at the same time patronised and exalted.
>
> van der Gaag and Nash 1987: 41

Content analyses of news images through time reveals that regardless of the context, time, or place in which famine has been observed, the same images recur (Moeller 1999: ch. 3). They recur because they are the icons of a disaster narrative, in which complex political circumstances are interpreted through an established journalistic frame of reference. In this discursive formation, outsiders come from afar to dispense charity to victims of a natural disaster who are too weak to help themselves (Benthall 1993: ch. 5). Instead of this discursive formation having to be explained in full each time, the recurrence of the iconic image of the starving child triggers this general and established understanding of famine, thereby disciplining any ambiguity about what is occurring in famine zones.

This discursive formation has effects on 'us' at the same time as it gives meaning to 'them'. Indeed, it establishes a series of identity relations that reproduce and confirm notions of self/other, developed/ underdeveloped, North/South, masculine/feminine, sovereignty/anarchy, and the like. Given that most contemporary famine imagery comes from one continent, it reproduces the imagined geography of

Figure 12.4 Mohamed Amin and Michael Buerk filming in Ethiopia,1984
Source: Camerapix.

'Africa', so that a continent of 900 million people in fifty-seven countries is homogenized into a single entity represented by a starving child (Figure 12.5). In doing this, a stereotypical famine image is not creating something from nothing. It is drawing upon established modes of representation, bringing into the present something that has been historically significant for European identity—that since the first colonial encounters 'Africa' has been understood as a site of cultural, moral, and spatial difference populated by 'barbarians', 'heathens', 'primitives', and 'savages'. This attention to the historical emergence of particular modes of representation is a feature of poststructural analysis. Understood as genealogy, this concern with history dispenses with the search for origins and deals with how dominant understandings have come to work in the present (see Foucault 1977; Ashley 1987).

As has been detailed here, the logic of interpretation that marks a poststructural analysis is concerned with the manifest political consequences of adopting one mode of representation over another. In terms of this case study, this focus would note two impacts. First, that the discursive production of 'Africa' means the majority of outsiders (more than 80 per cent of UK respondents in one survey) view the continent in wholly negative terms as a place of disease, distress, and instability.[4] Second, such representations establish the conditions of possibility for state and non-state action with regard to humanitarian crises, especially as they depoliticize the issues and render them best dealt with by humanitarian aid. Significantly, this logic of interpretation encompasses a notion of causality. But, rather than claiming a direct cause–effect relationship between pictures and policy (as in some arguments about the 'CNN effect' in international politics), this focus on the conditions of possibility posits an 'emergent causality' in which elements infuse and resonate across cultural and social domains, creating real effects without being able to specify a direct, causal link (see Connolly 2004).

The overall purpose of a poststructural analysis is ethical and political. Its emphasis on how things have been produced over time seeks to denaturalize conventional representations so as to argue that they could have been different. By repoliticizing dominant representations, poststructural analyses call

(continued)

Figure 12.5 *Daily Mirror* cover image, 21 May 2002, 'Africa's Dying Again'

Source: Mirrorpix.

attention to the inclusions and exclusions involved in producing that which appears to be natural, fixed, and timeless, and argue that the political action which follows from naturalized understandings could be pursued differently. In the context of humanitarian crises, especially famines, this would establish the following: the modern understanding of famine as starvation has been secured by visual representations of women and children as innocent victims, marginalizing in the process indigenous notions of famine as social catastrophe (Edkins 2000). Understanding famine as starvation leads to international action as humanitarian aid, directed towards the condition of individuals, whereas understanding famine as social catastrophe could lead to international action as conflict resolution, directed towards the state of the community. If followed, the consequence of this would be a complete overhaul of humanitarian action in the post-Cold War world.

the logic of causal explanation, a poststructural approach works with a logic of interpretation that acknowledges the improbability of cataloguing, calculating, and specifying the 'real causes', and concerns itself instead with considering the manifest political consequences of adopting one mode of representation over another. As such, poststructural approaches identify and explain how actors, events, or issues have been problematized. This means poststructuralism examines the 'problematizations' which make it possible to think of contemporary problems, and then examines how that discourse has emerged historically to frame an understanding of problems and solutions (Campbell 1998a: Preface).

Conclusion

From a poststructural perspective, interpretation and representation are indispensable and unavoidable when it comes to engaging both the domain of international politics and the field of IR. This claim is supported by the developments in philosophy and science which have undermined empiricist and positivist accounts of knowledge and theory. With its emphasis on the importance of language, culture, and history, the interdisciplinary context that has made critical perspectives like poststructuralism possible has challenged the 'common sense' and 'taken for granted' assumptions about reality which many traditional theories of IR have relied upon.

In assessing poststructuralism, it is important to be clear about the purpose of this body of thought. Poststructuralism is different from most other approaches to international politics because it does not see itself as a theory, school, or paradigm which produces a single account of its subject matter. Instead, poststructuralism is an approach, attitude, or ethos that pursues critique in particular ways. Because it understands critique as an operation that flushes out the assumptions through which conventional and dominant understandings have come to be (suppressing or marginalizing alternative accounts in the process), poststructuralism sees critique as an inherently positive exercise that establishes the conditions of possibility for pursuing alternatives. It is in this context that poststructuralism makes other theories of IR one of its objects of analysis, and approaches those paradigms with meta-theoretical questions designed to expose how they are structured.

Although it does not outline a specific theory of international relations, poststructuralism nonetheless offers a number of general and constructive arguments that can be used to approach the study of international politics in a different manner. Poststructuralism reorients analysis away from the prior assumption of pre-given subjects to the problematic of subjectivity. This involves rethinking the question of power and identity, such that all identities are understood as effects of the operation of power and materialized through discourse. While poststructuralism rejects empiricist understandings of knowledge, its critical approach is often empirical, using archives, images, survey data, content analysis, and the like as evidence in understanding the relationship between power and knowledge. The result of a poststructuralist analysis is itself an interpretation of international politics, and as such can (and should) be subject to the same ethos of critique that gave rise to it.

Poststructuralism has often found itself marginalized within IR. That is largely because those critical of it have misunderstood many of its central claims (especially with regard to the relationship between language and reality) and have been anxious about the effect of following its meta-theoretical questioning to its logical conclusion. Others have sought to confront poststructuralism with criticisms founded on positions that poststructuralism has questioned—arguing, for example, that poststructuralism fails to accept the existence of material reality when it has questioned the idealism/materialism dualism on which that objection depends (Laffey 2000; cf. de Goede 2003). Poststructuralism is, like all perspectives, certainly open to question. But, to be effective, critiques need to engage poststructuralism on its own terms. The starting point for an effective critique of poststructuralism involves recognizing that, instead of seeking to establish a social science, it embodies an ethical and political attitude driven by the desire to make all facile gestures difficult.

 Questions

1. What does it mean to say that abstraction, interpretation, and representation are indispensable and unavoidable?

2. How does the discipline of IR 'map' the world?

3. How are power and knowledge related? What does it mean to say they are related rather than synonymous with each other?

4. What are the key features of the positivist meta-theoretical discourse which have underpinned traditional approaches to international politics, and how have developments in the philosophy of science challenged these features?

5. What are some examples of foundational thought in IR, and what critiques have been directed at foundational thought generally?

6. What is the relationship between modernity and postmodernity, modernism and postmodernism, and why do many scholars express an anxiety about what they (mistakenly) call 'postmodernism' in IR?

7. What is the critical attitude of poststructuralism as expressed in the work of Michel Foucault, and how does it differ from traditional conceptions of social scientific theory?

8. What is meant by the claim that poststructuralism reorients analysis from pre-given subjects to the problematic of subjectivity?

9. What are the main features of Foucault's conception of power and how does it differ from traditional perspectives in IR?

10. If there is 'nothing outside discourse', does this mean that language is all there is and reality is only a product of the imagination?

11. How can poststructuralism's concern with subjectivity, identity, power, and discourse be connected to the categories and concerns of IR?

12. Should poststructuralism be viewed as a paradigm in IR? How can we assess its impact on the discipline?

Further reading

Bleiker, R. (2000), *Popular Dissent, Human Agency and Global Politics* **(Cambridge: Cambridge University Press).**
Theoretically and empirically sophisticated demonstration of how exploring questions of identity, agency, and subjectivity widens the understanding of politics and permits a conception of resistance.

Campbell, D. (1998a), *Writing Security: United States Foreign Policy and the Politics of Identity,* **revised edn. (Minneapolis: University of Minnesota Press).**
One of the first book-length studies that works with a poststructural attitude to rethink international politics, with an epilogue in the revised edition reviewing the discipline's debates around identity.

Der Derian, J. and Shapiro, M. J. (1989) (eds.), *International/Intertextual Relations: Postmodern Readings of World Politics* **(Lexington, KY: Lexington Books).**
The first collection of poststructural work, for which the publisher insisted on having 'postmodern' in the title.

Der Derian, J. (2009), *Critical Practices in International Theory: Selected Essays* **(New York: Routledge).**
This collection of essays fuses critical and poststructuralist theories in order to analyse issues as diverse as diplomacy, terrorism, intelligence, national security, new forms of warfare and the role of information technology in international relations.

Edkins, J. (1999), *Poststructuralism and International Relations: Bringing the Political Back In* **(Boulder, CO: Lynne Reinner).**
Provides a good introduction to the work of Derrida and Foucault, amongst others, emphasizing questions of subjectivity and politics.

Edkins, J. (2011), *Missing: Persons and Politics* **(Cornell: Cornell University Press).**
Informed by poststructuralist epistemology, this recent work seeks to situate individuals at the heart of international relations analysis by exploring the concept of "the missing".

Hansen, L. (2006), *Security as Practice: Discourse Analysis and the Bosnian War* **(New York: Routledge).**
Informative introductory discussion on poststructuralism, as well as how poststructuralist accounts and methodology help to understand the constitution of identity and security in the context of foreign policy.

Shapiro, M. J. and Alker, H. R. (1996) (eds.), *Challenging Boundaries: Global Flows, Territorial Identities* **(Minneapolis: University of Minnesota Press).**
A collection that demonstrates the wide range of events, issues, and topics involving the concept of identity that can be examined with a critical ethos.

Walker, R. B. J. (1993), *Inside/Outside: International Relations as Political Theory* **(Cambridge: Cambridge University Press).**
Seminal discussion that critically examines International Relations as political theory, thereby establishing the possibility for poststructural analyses.

Walker, R.B.J. (2009), *After the Globe: Before the World* **(New York: Routledge).**
Investigates the exclusionary basis of international relations as a discipline and practice and offers a reconceptualization of global political relations

Important websites

Although neither of these sites is self-consciously poststructuralist, the critical approaches to their objects of concern embodies the ethos of critique described: The Imaging Famine project. Examines media coverage of famine from the nineteenth century to the present day. Focusing on photographic images, it contains background documents, reports as well as historic and contemporary photo essays. **www.imaging-famine.org**

The Information Technology, War and Peace project. At Brown University's Watson Institute, it covers the impact of information technology on statecraft and new forms of networked global politics. **www.watsoninstitute.org/infopeace/index2.cfm**

 ## Notes

1. In addition to the editors, I am grateful to Martin Coward, Marieke de Goede, Debbie Lisle, and Simon Philpott for critical commentaries on drafts of this chapter. For revisions to the Further Reading in the 3rd edition, I would like to thank Dr Emma Hutchison. All responsibility for the final version nonetheless remains mine.

2. See the entry on de Saussure and semiotics on the Communication, Cultural and Media Studies website (www.ccms-infobase.com) for a good discussion with examples of this approach.

3. The list could include Jean Baudrillard, Helene Cixous, Gilles Deleuze, Jacques Derrida, Luce Irigaray, Jacques Lacan, Emmanuel Levinas, Jean-François Lyotard, Paul Virilio, and many, many others. It would be wrong to argue their philosophies are identical, and it would be a mistake to ignore the many differences between them. For good introductions to the range of poststructuralist philosophy, see Descombes (1981), Culler (1982), White (1991), Edkins (1999), and Hoy (2004).

4. A number of media studies demonstrate the pervasiveness of this negative imagery and its effects on understandings of the global South. For downloadable copies of studies by the UK Department for International Development, the International Broadcasting Trust, 3WE, and the VSO, see http://www. imaging-famine.org/gov_ngo.htm. The figure of 80 per cent of UK respondents comes from the 2001 VSO report, *The Live Aid Legacy*.

 Visit the Online Resource Centre that accompanies this book for lots of interesting additional material. **www.oxfordtextbooks.co.uk/orc/dunne3e/**

Postcolonialism

SIBA N. GROVOGUI

 Reader's Guide

Without impugning the eloquence and character of our precursors, any student of international relations may legitimately ask whether the likes of Thucydides, Machiavelli, Hobbes, and Kant give proper accounts of the complex, varied, and unpredictable events that characterized their times. One may also ask whether their maxims of war-making and peace-making hold lessons for the present; whether their representations of human nature, power, and interest correspond to the views and experiences of societies conquered by Europe. Postcolonialism highlights that they do not. In this light, postcolonialism offers new ways of knowing and thinking about the complex and fluid events that have shaped relations around them by stressing the varying contexts of power, identity, and value across time and space. This chapter will first explore the morality and ethics in postcolonialism before moving on to discuss Edward Said's work on 'Orientalism'. The following section discusses power and international legitimacy, focusing on the themes of the Arab Spring, particularly the discord between the Western powers of the United Nations Security Council (UNSC) and the African Union over the crisis in Libya. Finally, I will use the Suez Crisis as a case study of the manner in which postcolonial sentiments have shaped international relations after the Second World War.

Introduction

In his introduction to Frantz Fanon's *The Wretched of the Earth* (Fanon 1968), Jean-Paul Sartre, co-founder of French existentialism, stressed the impetus of postcolonialism. Having once conquered and colonized other regions, a self-identified 'Europe'[1] (later, the 'West') stipulated that the world was divided into 'five hundred million men' and 'one thousand five hundred million natives'. Upon conquest and colonization, Europe had aspired to direct world affairs by first writing the history of 'Man' in its own self-image (Trouillot 1995). It then degraded the markers of culture, arts, and science for others to the status of folklore, myths, and shamanism. Academic subjects such as Literature, Philosophy, History, and Anthropology—and now International Relations (IR)—contribute to this endeavour. Upon decolonization, Sartre reckoned, the new citizens challenged the position claimed by Europe as legislator and executor of the will of the world as well as the ultimate judge of values, desires, and interests. Not only did formerly native writers, artists, and scientists recognize themselves as 'Men' of distinct will, conscience, and agency (Pillay 2004), they imagined themselves as equal citizens of the world, equally unbound by place and time, to reflect on global politics.

I use the term postcolonialism to introduce a multiplicity of perspectives, traditions, and approaches to questions of identity, culture, and power. Postcolonialism has multiple points of origination in Africa, Asia, Australia, Latin America, and the New World (see, Gilroy 1993; Memmi 1965; Guha 1985; Spivak 1987). These regions underwent different forms of control and economies at the time of conquest. Colonial histories also explain the diversity of post-colonial accounts of society, science, and knowledge as well as their embrace of modern ideologies, of say liberalism, Marxism, postmodernism, and feminism (Mignolo 1995). This diversity has led to confusions compounded by the academic confinement of postcolonial studies to ethnic, cultural, and regional studies programmes or departments. Yet, postcolo-nialism figures in all former colonial expanses as an enterprise to offer new ways for thinking about techniques of power that constrain self-determination (Bhabha 1994; Said, 1978; Mignolo, 1995; Appadurai, 1990).

Thus, postcolonialism aspires to participate in the creation of 'truths', based on dis-tinct modes of signification and forms of knowledge (or the manners of representations) that advance justice, peace, and political pluralism. To this end, it contests rationalist, humanist, and other universalist views and their modes of signification (or ways of mak-ing sense of the world), especially where they claim that Europe possessed the finer forms of reason, morals, and law. Further, postcolonialism applies local memories, arts, and sciences to the subjects of History, Literature, and Philosophy among others. Third, postcolonialism rejects 'native essentialism', or the idea that the natives bore essential and timeless features. This idea has been abused by Western powers and postcolonial elites for the purpose of acquisition and retention of power. Finally, postcolonialism highlights the relationship between freedom and politics particularly in the settings of production of knowledge and policy-making. In the event, postcolonialism entertains the possibility of alternatives.

This chapter has two aims. The first is to highlight the insufficiencies of current interna-tional norms as means to international justice. The second is to illustrate the postcolonial ambition to undo the legacies of European imperialism (when Europe unilaterally projected power abroad) and colonialism (or settlement and rule over others) in order to transform the international order and associated notions of community, society, and morality. The chapter is divided into four sections. First, it explores the prospect of international morality and eth-ics in postcolonialism (Fanon 1968; Césaire, 2000; Said 1978; Ashcroft et al. 1989; Chatterjee 1986). This section touches upon Kantian notions of international morality and pacific union under republicanism. Second, it discusses Edward Said's *Orientalism* as one stream of postco-lonial discussions of political subjectivity and identity (Bhabha 1994; Anzaldúa 1987; Moreiras 2001), followed by a discussion of power and international legitimacy. The case study section focuses on Gamal Abdel Nasser's nationalization of the Suez Canal, in so doing seeking to demonstrate how a postcolonial perspective might orient understandings of international relations.

International morality and ethics

Postcolonialism associates the development of international order and society and its political economies with specific kinds of violence (Hulme 1992; Cheyfitz 1997). This association is not new; nor does it imply that one should give up on the idea of global orders. In the first instance, postcolonial critics find inspirations from a vast community of ecclesiastic, ethical, and moral thinkers worldwide who believed in the idea of common society of 'brotherhood' but expressed misgivings about the methods chosen by Europe to bring it about. Beginning with the conquest of the Americas, upon Christopher Columbus's 'discovery', Friars Antonio de Montesinos and Bartolomé de las Casas initiated the first protests against the treatment of native populations (Galeano 1985: 57, 84). The protests of Montesinos and Las Casas were aimed at Spain but they reverberated later in other contexts where Christian powers conquered non-European lands. The methods of European conquest and expansion varied across time and space. While conquest led to European settlement or colonization in the New World, Europe's means of control elsewhere involved political control through multiple forms of colonial administration. They varied from protectorates (based on treaties of protection) to indirect rule (dual control by a colonial administration and native rulers) to direct rule (total administrative control). In any case, protests were heard everywhere whenever European imperial powers subjected new political entities to their own will through warfare and unfavourable political compacts—some of which were aptly named treaties of concession and capitulation while others were disingenuously categorized as protection and trusteeship.

In another instance, postcolonialism is cognizant that protests by the likes of Las Casas, although significant, did not prevent modern European imperialism, colonization, and colonialism. It also acknowledges that the institutions of modern European empires, settlements, and colonies laid the foundations for what our discipline calls alternatively international order, community, and/or society. In short, the coming together of the world as a single unit is one of the hallmarks of the modernity instigated by Europe. Postcolonialism perceives an irony in this event where others might not. In any case, postcolonialism does not take it for granted that the received world is pre-ordained and given by force of nature: the world cannot be unmade but its base institutions and systems of value and interest can be refashioned to reflect today's communities. In this regard too, postcolonialism has antecedents in revolts and revolutions by slave and colonial populations that sought justice in their particular locales by rejecting the moral, legal, and cultural foundations of their enslavement.

Postcolonialism and knowledge

Brought to the level of academic practice, postcolonialism today holds the motives and intentions of advocates of global institutions and systems of values separate from discussions of the systems of truths, values, and institutions that must shape the international or global order. Beginning with 'truths', postcolonialism notes that knowledge, or what is said to be, is never a full account of events. Gaps between what is said to have happened and what actually happened can be understood frequently by examining how imperial and colonial structures shaped such institutions as academic research. For instance, we can ascertain that colonial structures of power delivered the whole world to European and Western scholars as object of study. Among them, rationalists, humanists, and other cosmopolitans had access to the whole world to which they applied the available scientific instruments, or methods of analysis, which allowed them to reach certain conclusions, or universal 'truths' about themselves and native peoples everywhere. However, as observed by Talal Asad (1983) and Said (1978), this enterprise was not a collaborative undertaking that involved 'natives' in the conceptions and implementation of its objectives. The knowledge resulting from 'observations' of and about 'natives' was neither constitutively native knowledge nor based on native concerns. Finally, imperial knowledge was not universally accessible to natives. Not even the most dedicated metropolitan observers could make up for the political and economic processes that left vast majorities of colonial populations in abject poverty and illiteracy.

Postcolonialism disputes the validity of ideas and commonplaces that figure authoritatively in academic and public discourses as 'expert knowledges' about the former colonial expanses. These ideas and commonplaces include notions of the inherence of labour, property, enterprise and capacity in race, culture, and the environment—which once served as justifications of imperialism and its distribution of value (Cohn 1996). Postcolonialism also disputes propositions by rationalists and critical theorists that Western methods, particularly rationalism and humanism, suffice as context for critiques of imperialism and colonialism and, by this token, offer the way to comfort and salvation for others (Césaire 2000; James 1989; DuBois 1989). This conceit is combined with obstinacy in the belief that the West has sole responsibility for charting the course of human history (Prakhash 1999). In addition, postcolonialism is sceptical of the prevailing rationalities and historical justifications of empire (Chakrabarty 2000). More often than not, related representations of the ends of imperialism and colonialism are self-serving (Prakhash 1999). Finally, postcolonialism is suspicious of colonial ethnography and its accounts of cultures, rituals, and their significations. More often than not, the social structures and rituals 'discovered' by colonial ethnographers reflected their own 'castes of mind' which were frequently at odds with what existed (Dirks 2001). Colonial understandings were deeply steeped in alternate forms of natural history and/or scientific racism which divided humanity into races, ethnic groups, heathens, and barbarians (Bensmaïa 2003).

A postcolonial critique of the Western tradition

Postcolonial examinations of reason, history, and culture are necessary steps to re-envisioning the future (Scott 1999). To this end, postcolonialism forwards omitted or devalued *ways of knowing* and their base-practices, or institutions, as possible expressions of valid moral concerns and, therefore, as the basis for valid formulations of value and interest. The postcolonial approach to knowledge upholds the principle of coexistence while rejecting erroneous ideas. In the first instance, postcolonialism recognizes the intrinsic merits of Western attempts and the intellectual prowess of the iconic figures that stand behind them—from Herodotus to Machiavelli, Kant, and beyond. Nor does postcolonialism impugn on the credentials of Europe and the West as purveyors of civilization. In the second instance, most postcolonial readers take Western iconic texts with degrees of irony—and depressing bemusement. Take Immanuel Kant, for instance. Kant has been recently lauded by an assortment of institutionalists who praise his republican ideas as foundation for a plausible democratic peace in a pacific union under cosmopolitan law (Doyle 1997; Russett 1993; see also **Chapter 5**). Postcolonialism does not scorn such praises, but asks questions about the logic of an international order founded upon Kant's ideas. Specifically, they always return to gaps in Kant's representations of the eighteenth century and the implications of such gaps for the validity of his theory. This 'return' to the source then serves as metaphor and a point of criticism for today's institutionalists who would change the present world without due attention to its complexity and the diverse stakes involved in change.

Irrespective of whether they hold that Kant was racist like many of his contemporaries, postcolonial scholars generally take issue with today's readings of Kant.

There are complex arguments here that cannot be exposed fully in an introductory text. But imagine, if you will, writing about moral commands, ethics, and pacific union. Imagine that you live in an era when slavery was both the reality and the most potent metaphor for the absence of liberty (Trouillot 1995). Imagine also living in an era marked by three revolutions (in the US, France, and Haiti), one of which arose from demand by actual slaves for freedom. Would you omit actual slavery and the aspiration of slaves for freedom from three major treatises on 'love' for humanity and the related moral sentiments of solidarity and hospitality? Would you expect the slave or former slave to take resulting speculations about peaceful coexistence at face value? You might, but it will not be easy to dismiss Kant's gaps as mere historical perspectives.

We can now begin to understand postcolonial suspicions about Kant's moral imperatives. From one perspective, Kant's account of the picturesque denigrates prior enactments of 'pacific union' in places beyond Europe well before the birth of European enlightenment. When imperialism transformed colonial landscapes, the picturesque was more like an assemblage of scenes of intended (unintended) crimes. The picturesque quickly lost its lustre and reveals itself as an imperial cartography in which the cosmopolitan sentiment of empathy (or colonial trusteeship) is inserted into a politics of repression, and expropriation through broken treaties and violence. This conclusion raises question about Kant's ethical and aesthetic concepts.

I do not here seek an indictment of Kant's view of slavery. I merely wish to ask whether the omission of such an important institution as slavery and enslavement from moral thought does not diminish the moral reach of resulting theories of republicanism and **cosmopolitanism**. I am therefore asking for a pause before proposing Kant as the prophet of ethics and pacific union. Although I personally favour the idea of global norms, questions remain as to their origins; how they are attained; and for what purpose. In these connections, postcolonialism draws three conclusions. The first is that it is not sufficient for theorists to simply embrace categories such as international order, international society, and international ethics. Because these concepts recall the era of European expansion and colonialism, they are not devoid of political effects. In fact, they exude a colonial anthropology in which a mythical righteous West poses as teacher for others, regardless of the context and purpose of engagement and the nature of behaviour.

Second, there is a double movement in Western moral thought involving presence (when European authorship matters to the legitimacy and purpose of discourse) and erasure (when European identity is necessarily concealed). For instance, the proposition that human rights are a universal value depends on a de-emphasis of their Western origins and the invocation of human rights by victims' groups throughout the world. On the other hand, when Western intellectuals and politicians need to underscore European superiority and 'duty' or 'right to lead', they stress that 'human rights' are civilizational markers of the West. The accentuation of Western origination of 'universal values' then bolsters the position that the West may legitimately pose as 'moral teacher' for others. Postcolonialism notes that discussions of Western universalism and moral rectitude obscure Western origination of modern forms of political violence, including Nazism, Fascism, Stalinism, total war, and other practices developed in the long march to emancipate Man. In short, the celebration of Western modernity and liberalism suppresses Western violence as a matter of political expedience.

Third, postcolonialism nonetheless embraces reason, universalism, and pragmatism. However, postcolonialism expands the meaning of these categories and remains sceptical of institutional narratives maintaining their objectivity or neutrality. These disciplinary narratives exude the sort of colonial hubris that mistakes one's 'desire' for 'reality' and one's own aspiration for universalism. Indeed, the related disciplinary perspectives are unable to speak to the world as a whole. They are the product of the kind of intellectual and moral presumptuousness that continues to lead to unpredictable (and at times dangerous) adventures disguised as liberation (like the Anglo-American invasion of Iraq) or humanitarian interventions (for instance in Somalia).

These comments are part of the suspicion that postcolonialism harbours toward today's institutional approaches to international relations (see e.g. **Chapters 5** and **6**). These approaches produce international regimes and international morality as sublime settings for the enactment of value, without prior identification of value or deliberations on the nature or origin of the proposed institutions. Specifically, liberal and neoliberal institutionalist discourses often appear as rationalizations of hegemony disguised as universal humanism. For its part, cosmopolitanism risks becoming a tangle of self-serving misrepresentations of reason, solidarity, and the common good. Finally, constructivist notions of 'mutuality' and 'co-constitution' of norms (see **Chapter 10**) appear to the postcolonial ear as an ironic attempt to embellish, as signs of 'moral suasion' and/or 'preference', the resigned entry of constitutionally-weakened and politically-defeated postcolonies into existing international regimes.

Orientalism and identities

In the English-speaking world, postcolonialism has been associated with the study of identities and cultures. This is because the concept brings to mind such works as Edward Said's *Orientalism* (1978); Gayatri Spivak's *In Other Worlds* (1987); Ngugi wa Thiong'o's *Decolonizing the Mind* (1986); Homi Bhaba's *The Location of Culture* (1994); Bill Ashcroft et al.'s *The Empire Writes Back* (1989); and Gloria Anzaldúa's *Borderlands/La Frontiera* (1987). These authors and their texts have equivalencies in the French, Spanish, and Chinese-speaking worlds. Collectively, they have generated and supported scholarly genres and journals, including *Subaltern Studies*, *Presence Africaine*, and more recently *Nepantla*. Yet, contrary to what has been charged (Hopkins 1997; Todorov 1997), the postcolonial attention to identity and culture is neither chauvinism nor an endorsement of essentialism—the idea that identities and culture have their own essential features which are impermeable to those of others. Rather than proclaim 'fixity' for identity and/or 'authenticity' for culture, postcolonialism appropriates their historical representations for their legitimate uses in more fluid postcolonial contexts.

In most of Africa, for instance, few postcolonial theorists would use the idea of nation without a degree of dread. This is because the colonial populations that now form African 'nations' cannot be said to be linguistically or culturally coherent entities outside of a European frame of reference. Frequently, African states brought together under the umbrella of the nation are groups that speak different languages and that a mere century ago lived in separate political spaces under their own rules. The processes of self-invention and self-determination produced real effects in these contexts, for instance, they allowed formerly colonial populations, such as tribes in Africa, to divest themselves of colonial subjectivity in favour of new institutions, including nations. It follows that, in these contexts, notions of authenticity, indigeneity, and the like are embraced anew but not for their prior implications which suggested inherent and fixed qualities. They are embraced because they give historical credibility or legitimacy to political or ethical projects on account of authorship (Warrior 1997; Memmi 1965).

Postcolonialism acknowledges the possibilities, that is, dangers and opportunities, contained in these rapid transformations in identity and culture particularly with respect to historical Western views of 'natives' as the modern 'barbarians'. To illustrate these points, let's return to Said's most celebrated and controversial book, *Orientalism*. The title describes its object as a phenomenon born of Europe's dominance of the world, including the Middle East. According to Said, Orientalism is not simply the space called the Orient because it is situated east of Europe. Rather, Orientalism is a technique of power based in language and processes of translation of the identities, cultures, and religion of the Middle East. Through these techniques, European (and Western) intellectuals and public officers created a mythical space that only partially bore resemblance to the place it described. Through readings of English texts, Said illustrates how colonial representations of the (formerly) colonized are institutionalized as instruments and/or features of cultural dominance. Accordingly, Orientalist texts have material existence that can be detected in the context of actual strategies of textual production.

Said helped to develop propositions about the cultural and political impact of European conquest of other regions; and thus colonization and colonialism. Said claims that the histories revealed in texts are not unearthed from fixed 'burial grounds' in the past. Orientalist histories highlight the terms and stereotypes that produced European beliefs, which inform contemporary policy-making. In this light, *Orientalism*, first, illustrates cultural and political struggles between imperial societies and colonial ones over struggles over **knowledge and power** and their respective ends. Second, Said provides useful methods for analysing imperialism and post-imperial cultural engagements. In this context, Said challenges the Western boundaries of self and other producing alternatives for rethinking these constitutive categories. He also provides empirical and methodological frames for queries about identity and culture: for instance, how humanism countenanced colonial violence (which may be found in Fanon); how liberal constitutional orders in the USA and elsewhere underwrote racism (DuBois); who 'Man' was and who spoke on 'his' behalf and about what subjects (Morrison 1993).

It is an understatement to say that Said provides useful tips for understanding Western political discourses about others. From Said's perspectives, the present terms and

Western 'public understanding' of Arab regimes as despotic, traditional, and irredeemable reiterate today yesterdays images of 'Oriental despotism' (Mill 1806–73) and of the every-day of Bedouins and others as cave-dwelling (Montesquieu 1689–1755). One can also detect echoes of Orientalism in the declared 'long war' on terrorism. The War on Terror began with the identification of the terrorist and not any denunciation or call for the renunciation of the use of violence. The war on terrorism is in actuality a war on pre-assigned terrorists who hold 'identified' beliefs and inclinations. In Western policy circles, the terrorists practice a sordid brand of Islamic fundamentalism; exude 'moral intolerance' and hatred for the West and Western way of life; and are the product of social and political decay in the Muslim world. The war on terrorism dispenses therefore with the political rationality of the terrorists in that it has been determined in advance that the terrorists have no just cause that warrants the use of force or violence. Because terrorists do not have legitimate or just cause, civilized societies (the 'victims') have the right to violently combat terrorism and, yes, kill the terrorists with all available means—now, we understand, irrespective of international conventions and norms.

Regardless of one's views of current events, one detects ideological slippages in the Orientalist continuum from actual reactions to actual events to invocations of a dubious cartography of region, religion, and culture.

These slippages have caused many critics (and not just postcolonialists) to ask themselves about the interchangeability of Pakistan, Afghanistan, and Iraq; or wonder what it means that Bin Laden and Saddam Hussein are indistinguishable in political standing; or question how it became legitimate to advocate the overthrow of the Afghan Talibans and Iraqi Ba'athist for the real sins of Al-Qaeda; and finally, to puzzle over how a majority in the USA and a minority in Britain could still hold the belief in a collusion between Saddam Hussein and Bin Laden—two men who belong to antagonist political movements.

One explanation might be that discourses on terrorism have found an easy entry point into three tenets of Orientalism: (1) the existence of separate, unequal, and hierarchical spheres of civilizations; (2) the need to maintain the boundaries between them by defending Western civilizational goods or values against corrupt ones without; and, for the Orient, (3) the necessity for 'moderate Arabs' or secular Arab groups to join the West in introducing progressive values in their region. Again, these ideas are not new. They go as far back as the end of the Crusades. Still, it is untrue that Europe has an original civilization, formed over an unbroken time span within a homogenous space. Nor is it possible to draw a boundary on a straight line between 'civilized Europe' and the violent cultures without, including a place called the Orient. One would have to negate historical co-dependencies between Europe (and the West) and other regions: for instance, Byzantium and vast expanses beyond it. One would also have to argue that Russians and Bosnian Muslims do not share ethnographic traits with say the Franks. Finally, one would have to expunge Moorish Spain from memory as the cultural antecedent of contemporary Spain.

It is somewhat mystifying, therefore, that international theorists, from Hugo Grotius, in seventeenth-century Netherlands, to James Lorimer, in nineteenth-century England, would erect metaphysical boundaries between Europe and others (Grovogui 1996). They were not alone. The Berlin Africa Conference (1884–5), which finalized colonial boundaries in Africa, was also derivative of Europe's civilizational discourse that masked actually violent processes with humanitarian overtones (Fetter 1979). Today, pretentious civilizational discourses provide sustenance to the belief that Muslim émigrés within the gates of Europe would work in tandem with Muslim barbarians beyond in order to destroy Europe (Huntington 1998). These views are mistaken about the pervasiveness of political corruption and violence in modern life. Indeed, it is near fictitious to maintain an opposition between 'total European virtue' and 'total Oriental barbarism'. For this opposition to hold, one would have to negate that Nazism and fascism were manifestations of modern European ideologies and practices. The photographs taken of Abu Ghraib provide sufficient evidence that techniques of torture and 'barbarism' are not the sole province of Middle East states.

It is beside the point that the facts of Orientalism are wrong. Its function is to sow the seeds of antipathy to the Orient and its religion and culture in the West. One view is that the European anxiety of being overtaken by Muslims has persisted because Islam does not easily lend itself to translation by the state, at least not by a democratic state. Further, individual European Muslims have remained on the margins of European societies and it is not yet certain how they and the collectives in which they exist will convey their 'gratitude' for the privileges of European citizenship. As the relatively recent French 'Affaire du Foulard' (or Head Scarf Affair) showed, multitudes of European Muslims are not ready to divest themselves of their prior Islamic traditions as condition of their entry into European political processes. On this and other scores, Orientalism has succeeded in digging deep wells of antipathy toward Islam and Muslims. Would be defenders of secular Western norms may plead innocent as they help to proliferate mistaken views on the nature of European society and Islam as a religion and practice (Asad 1993). They may also point to the antipathies toward the West among Muslims and in the Middle East, with their equal share of unfounded beliefs. But in a context of power, Orientalism has greater political effects.

It is not exaggerated to suggest that Western anxieties and antipathies toward Muslims are exerting considerable influence on debates about terrorism. For instance, outraged denunciations of Palestinian terrorism might rightly point out the cowardliness of would-be liberators and the devastating psychological toll of suicide bombing on non-combatant Israelis. They are cast as 'innocent victims' who are violated in their legitimate expectation of security. All these concerns are real in that they are pertinent to the ability of people to function in society. But, in the West, few express equally emphatic outrage about the toll of daily violence on Palestinians due to military occupation by Israel. Fewer still ask themselves whether Palestinian children may be psychological scarred by bombs that slam into any Palestinian building, any time of day, without notice, on the sole Israeli suspicion of an adverse activity in the abode. It would seem that the ethical reflex that demands that bus riders feel safe on their way home to their families, relatives, and friends would demand that fathers and mothers be able to ensure the safety of their children at home—away from the streets and the riots. Due partly to Orientalism, the Western war on terrorism depends upon moral injunctions (the equivalent of fatwa) against total violence upon civil populations on one side of the civilizational-cum-political divide. By contrast, certain protagonists incite Western foreign policy establishments to countenance total violence against Palestinian civilians (Muslims and Christians alike) caught on the other side of the civilizational divide.

Power and legitimacy in the international order

Postcolonialism begins with the truism that it is both aberrant and dysfunctional for a singular group of Eurocentric perspectives, wills, desires, values, and interests to remain hegemonic in global politics as well as in the development of such concepts as 'international order', 'international morality', and 'international law'. The inoperativeness of this state of affairs is emerging increasingly in the discipline as problematic as methodologists and empiricists revisit disciplinary archives. For postcolonialism, questions about the international order and international law and morality are even more practical than purely theoretical contestations over the veracity of disciplinary verities and their received notions of epistemology and ontology. Postcolonial questions revolved around power and legitimacy. Again, the key to postcolonial difference rests in the fact that the experiences of the conquered and colonized contrast with those of the conquerors and colonizers.

An illustration of this difference is the decision of the African Union to not endorse military action during the recent uprising that led to the downfall of Gaddafi. Reflecting both Orientalism and racism, uninformed observers opined that the decision had to do with Gaddafi's role as a power in Africa. This view is both misinformed and offensive. It is misinformed because Africa has depended on European and Western aid in proportions far surpassing Libya's assistance to small and largely insignificant projects in Africa. But the real offense— and it is of the racist and Orientalist sort—is that Africans do not hold coherent views of the world, complete with political objectives and strategies, that may collide with those of the West. To Western political strategists and ideologues, this view of Africa-as-unthinking was useful at the time of intervention because it ensured the erasure from discussions of difficult questions of legitimacy and ethics as well as complex historical relationships between, on the one hand, the West and Libya and, on the other, Gaddafi and individual Western leaders. Finally, this view also obscured African concerns about constitutional and social questions that lurked behind both the uprising and intervention.

In relating this conflict, I do not wish to speak for a uniformly-defined 'Africa' and/or for all African entities. Nor do I wish to conflate the official West and authoritative decisions made by Western leaders with the sentiments and traditions of all constituencies of what might be called the West. I only reflect on a widely held sentiment currently expressed in Africa that specific actions by Western powers about and in Libya paradoxically undermine the spirit and practice of participatory global governance. They also subvert what should have been a moment of transformation of politics at the local, national, and global levels. In short, this is a story of how the global democratic gap or what I call the global democratic deficit has widened precisely at the moment when the national democratic deficit has erupted into violent conflict. The paradox is that humanitarian concerns come once again to serve as pretext for widening the global democratic deficit and, in the case of the Middle East, re-inscribing the term of past imperial relations under new guises.

Specifically, the disagreement underlying African hostility to the Libya intervention concerned the future of global governance and international morality, both of which are held as guarantors of domestic social peace and a just constitutional order. It echoed those of generations of African anti-colonialists who opposed Western interventions in Vietnam, Madagascar, Kenya, Algeria, and Rhodesia. But the mood this time was not reflexive anti-imperialism. After all, African states largely endorsed the principle of the responsibility to protect and the establishment of the international criminal court (or ICC). Today one is quickly reminded that vast majorities of Africans variously subscribe to the notion of protection of populations and punishment of war criminals. This is to say that something else was in operation in Libya that dictated what many in the Western media called reversal on humanitarian intervention. One explanation, which I share, is that Western actions around Libya reminded equally large majorities of Africans that today's practices of humanitarianism intervention have become too inextricably entangled with hegemonic power to deserve support.

The first act of the West in Libya was to proclaim itself the bearer of the universal will. This positioning had consequences. One of them was to predicate intervention on nearly unimpeachable pretences. One recalls that NATO's intervention began with admirable pretences that, from any perspectives, were reflected in otherwise unimpeachable resolutions. The last of these resolutions, UNSC Resolution 1973, could be summarized thus: (1) 'immediate establishment of a cease-fire and a complete end to violence and all attacks against, and abuses of, civilians'; (2) 'the need to intensify efforts to find a solution to the crisis which responds to the legitimate demands of the Libyan people', aided by a Special Envoy to Libya and the Peace and Security Council of the African Union; (3) compliance by 'Libyan authorities with their obligations under international law, including international humanitarian law, human rights and refugee law'; (4) 'to protect civilians and civilian populated areas under threat of attack in the Libyan Arab Jamahiriya, including Benghazi, while excluding a foreign occupation force of any form on any part of Libyan territory'; and (5) to designate the League of Arab States as primary address 'in matters relating to the maintenance of international peace and security in the region'. These measures were to be complemented with the enforcement of a no-fly zone and an arms embargo.

These resolutions had several important features from the standpoint of the African Union. The most important part is that its intervention in favour of peaceful resolution so infuriated Western powers that they excluded it altogether from the subsequent processes of the resolution of the conflict. To be sure, the resolution recognizes that the actions of the government of Libya had been condemned by the League of Arab States, the African Union, and the Secretary General of the Organization of the Islamic Conference. But its authors trampled upon international conventions by determining that all concerns be directed to the Secretary-General of the United Nations (UN) and the Secretary-General of the League of Arab States in recognition of 'the important role of the League of Arab States in matters relating to the maintenance of international peace and security in the region'. In other words, the Western alliance not only had its power to decree the law, but also to prescribe its interpretation and to punish those who actually dared to think that the first three mandates of the resolution truly mattered.

From the perspective of the Western alliance, the sin of African states was one of gullibility: to have actually believed that the first three mandates of the resolution mattered. Africans, in other words, were naïve enough to not understand that the task at hand was the removal of Gaddafi and that resolutions merely make references to mediation in some instances to appease equally gullible domestic constituencies and the media. What is even more telling is that the Western alliance, all former colonial powers, decided unilaterally and as a matter of sovereign right that Libya was an Arab state and not African and that, for the purpose of their own intervention, the African Union had no authority over North Africa. One wonders how this dramatic change occurs so easily from one moment to the next.

These actions were not merely contemptuous of Africa and Africans. From an institutional perspective, the scale and speed with which the West dispensed with decades-old UN procedures of associating regional organization to dispute resolutions is frightening and points to the series of violations/violences that can be committed any time by the 'civilized' powers.

Having sidelined Africans and imputed all hindrances in the resolution of the conflict to Gaddafi, France, Britain, and the US could proceed as they intended toward installing the Transitional National Council, or TNC. They could count on sympathies for the Arab Spring to absolve themselves of all sins. Thus, since the UN Resolutions, the strikes have exceeded the mandate of forestalling Gaddafi's aggression to destroying the nation's infrastructure; the Western alliance has embraced assassination as a policy; and France had delivered weapons to the so-called resistance, despite the putative ban on weapons. And the new World Order lives on with or without Africa, or so the story goes.

The events leading to the intervention bore strong resemblance to those taking place in the Republic of Congo Leopoldville in the 1960s. Then, as now, a number of UNSC resolutions (143; 145; 146; and 157) had authorized peacekeeping activities in the former Belgian colony. The initial resolution spoke initially of stabilizing a chaotic political situation on behalf of the people of Congo. It soon appeared to the governments of Egypt, Ghana, and Guinea that the bland and neutral language of UN resolutions masked other motivations: to protect client elites and to institute a particular social and economic order deemed necessary by this small number of elites and external powers. On the ground, Western powers quickly moved from the initial aim of the mission to instil stability to creating government under the leadership of an unelected clientele. In reaction, Egypt, Ghana, and Guinea ordered their troops to disobey UN orders and to support the elected prime minister and head of government, Patrice Lumumba. The African states denounced Dag Hammarskjold, Secretary-General of the UN, and the Eisenhower Administration, for subverting UN procedures and mandates in an open attempt to subordinate the postcolonial desire for self-determination to Cold War contentions (Jackson 1982).

The manners in which the West instrumentalized UN procedures in the time before the intervention in the Congo are nearly identical to what transpired around Libya. Then, as now, once the West identified its allies and established control over the process, it placed humanity on the side of allies as 'the people'—in effect humans: those whose lives, ways of being, and property cannot be altered without defacing 'our' collective humanity. The opponents of these allies, almost always identical to the West's own, cease therefore to have an identity other than supporters of the regime whose transgression against humans and humanity has been certified by the West. Those elements of the population may be implied in general but they mostly remain non-nameable. Effectively, these populations cease to be citizens and fully human. They become merely an instrument of the anti-human. Their ways of being, lives, and property are thus compromised such that their physical elimination, displacement, and dispossession no longer matter as they would where the people were concerned.

As predicted by majorities of Africans at the time, the humanitarian concerns expressed for the populations of Benghazi—thereafter amalgamated with the insurgency as the People of Libya—were not extended for the populations residing in Western Libya, particularly Tripoli, Sirte, Bani Walid, and other places favourable to the regime. These populations lost their humanity by political fiat since they were depicted as supporters of the regime (when alive) or collateral damage (when eliminated). Likewise, whereas the intervention occurred in the first place to prevent attacks on Benghazi (of the people), the people of Bani Walid and Sirte could be sacrificed (for the people) by militias and their supporters formally christened as the people. With the permutation and replacement of the 'human' with the 'people' all political manoeuvres were allowed to destroy the very fabric of life and society for those who did not meet the requirements of the people. To the initiated in African politics, there are in today's Libya emergent scenarios of social disintegration, ethnic confrontation, regional disintegration, and maybe even a future civil war—as happened in the Congo.

Western discourses on Libya produced predictable political positions on the ground. As may be recalled, Libya National Transition Council would not negotiate, compromise, or reconcile. Why would they have when the largest armies in the world are committed to the destruction of the one obstacle to their own path to power? President Ahmadou Toumani Touré of Mali gave an indication of his own sentiment and those of his peers in an interview to Radio France Internationale (RFI). Asked by the reporter why he would not join the West (dubbed again by the interviewer as the International Community), Touré gave the following answer, which I paraphrase: 'We are asked to promote democracy in Libya against a man who holds power at the barrel of the gun and you want me to unseat him at the barrel of the gun and seat another group in his place. If Gaddafi's unwillingness to negotiate and compromise is the problem today why is the other side relying on forced removal?' (RFI 2011). Indeed, the current intransigence of the West and the TNC reveal a culture of intolerance that unsettles Africans of all political persuasions—and not just dictators who are destined to the dustbin of history as it were. It is still likely too that the outcome of the Libyan intervention would be the same as the anterior one in the Congo: that a group imposed by imperial powers and bolstered in its position as representative of the people by those powers would have no incentive to adopt a constitutional order and institutions that render it accountable to its populations, which extends beyond 'the people'.

Many wondered then why 'Africans' would object to the 'liberation' of Libya. Gaddafi came to power after worldwide contestations over the political, economic, and cultural inequities. The coup that brought him to power was bloodless and he financially supported and protected the King's family (the man he overthrew) for a number of years. Gaddafi helped to establish the Organization of Petroleum Exporting States (OPEC); supporting the Non-Aligned Movement, and African Unity, while engaging in activities that are undoubtedly reprehensible. Africans could not accept the notion that Gaddafi was a tyrannical man for over forty years. To be clear, the violence associated with Gaddafi's regime, which I earlier termed a national democratic deficit, was still an object of criticism for many Africans, but this criticism in no way legitimated violent intervention by the West; intervention with which Africans were all too familiar even in its most benign forms. Further, even on a continent accustomed to dictatorship and worse, the idea that considerable segments of the population could be excluded from the emerging political compact was horrifying. Human rights activists, constitutionalists, and civil society groups accustomed to fighting for democratic inclusion were the first to advocate for negotiating an inclusive social compact in Libya even as the majority denounced Gaddafi's positions.

Case study: the Suez Canal Crisis

The Suez Canal Crisis illustrates the ambiguous legacy of decolonization and, as such, has implications for postcolonial alternatives to international morality and law. Principally, it demonstrates the desire to make permanent Western authority over others based on regimes of truth that legitimized the implied violence and a commandment that legalized the subordination of the native to Western power. This commandment, according to Achille Mbembe (2001), has four properties: (1) a regime of exception that allowed the West to place itself above the common law; (2) historical regimes of privileges and immunities for Western decision-makers and persons; (3) the conflation of international morality with Western injunction to others; and (4) the circularity of sovereignty whereby the sovereignty of others is constantly negated to give precedence to Western-enacted international regimes that maintain the sovereign pre-eminence of Western powers.

Second, the resolution of the Suez Crisis shows the manner in which the US sought to update the commandment to account for postcolonial sensibilities but without relinquishing it. At the time of the Suez Crisis, the US was confronted with its loyalties to its allies—Great Britain, France, and Israel—and the need to discredit the invasion of Hungary by its Cold War nemesis as antithetical to the postwar order. The solution came when Lester Pearson, the Canadian external affairs minister, suggested the creation of a United Nations Emergency Force in Suez to keep the peace between the opposing forces until a political settlement could be achieved. President Eisenhower emerged thus from the crisis on the side of anti-colonial forces in the Third World while maintaining his traditional alliances. It follows that, even as he was hailed as a hero in the Third World, Nasser's regime was unable to bring about the postcolonial alternative regime of governance, production, and distribution so desired by his supporters—a warning to anyone who amalgamates decolonization and anti-colonialism with postcolonial success.

Background to the Suez Crisis

As has been argued postcolonialism arises from a temporal rupture in European modernity, following the end of formal colonial rule. It is preceded by anticolonialism, or opposition to colonial occupation or administration, and other anti-imperialist movements, including resistance to the so-called colonial penetration. In short, postcolonialism signals the decline of the European colonial order and associated 'truths'. The political arrangements and actors that emerged as alternatives to Western power made sense of the postcolonial moment by re-examining the intellectual, political, and moral foundations of colonialism. In the political instance, postcolonialism insists on a new international order free of the legacies of colonialism or colonial institutions. As actualized today, postcolonialism has distinct goals which can be traced to the 1955 Bandung Conference, the 1961 Non-Aligned Movement, and Cuba's Tricontinentalism, among others. The Bandung Conference assembled leaders of Africa, Asia, and Latin America under the stewardship of Chou En Lai of China, Jawaharlal Nehru of India, and Sukarno of Indonesia. Its purpose was to decolonize international practices on questions of foreign policy and development. The Non-Aligned Movement complemented the spirit of Bandung by underscoring the need for a community of interest to advance the single objective of equality, free association, and mutually in international affairs. Finally, the idea of Tricontinentalism was to develop a new ethos of power and subjectivity for the three concerned continents through foreign policy.

These and antecedent agendas and demands were partly reflected in the United Nations Charter proclamation of self-determination as one of the cornerstones of the international order. They motivated decisions by Gamal Abdel Nasser and other so-called Third World leaders, including the decision to nationalize the Suez Canal in 1956. Still, most accounts of the Suez crisis tell a story of a superpower balance of power, uneasy Cold War alliances, and the supposed recklessness of Third World nationalism. They might even refer to the event as the Suez Canal war. This is because Nasser's ambition to nationalize the canal resulted in a war of aggression against Egypt by Britain, France, and

Israel. The prevailing Western narrative of events leading to the war is based upon simple axioms. To summarize a long story, the canal was realized under the direction of Ferdinand de Lesseps, between 1854 and 1856, on concessions from Said Pasha, the viceroy of Egypt. It became operational on 15 December 1858 and, under agreement, was to be managed by the Suez Canal Company (also Compagnie Universelle du Canal Maritime de Suez) for ninety-nine years. Under European and American agreement, the canal was to be open to ships of all nations under a plan drafted by Austrian engineer Alois Negrelli. Come 1956, Nasser, a left-leaning Arab Nationalist, if not Pan-Arabist, decided to annul the regime governing the Suez Canal. Nasser was then cast as an ally of the Soviet Union. Nasser was said to be recklessly ambitious with little regard for the subtleties of international law. This narrative takes it for granted that Britain and France were obligated to reply to Nasser's actions, if only to deter similar actions by other Third World revisionists. Thus, Britain and France took umbrage at Nasser's decision to nationalize the administration of the canal. Israel was worried about the 'right of passage' of ships bound for the port of Eilat.

This narrative also poses the reactions of the world's two major powers—then, the US and the Soviet Union—as logical and delicate balancing acts. Accordingly, the US was a NATO ally of France and Britain but, on the geopolitical schemes of the Cold War, the Hungarian Crisis was a more efficacious terrain to fight Soviet power. The US also faced a potential public relations embarrassment in the Third World if it criticized the Soviet Union's military intervention in Hungary while condoning military intervention by former colonial powers in one of their former provinces. The Soviet Union was allied with Egypt but had greater worries for the Hungarian crisis, which threatened the very idea of communism. To show consistency in projecting its powers in defence of its allies, the Soviets had also promised to defend Egypt. In the end, the Franco-British-Israeli operation to take the canal was highly successful from a military point of view. But from a geopolitical perspective, it proved a diplomatic and ideological disaster for Britain and France. So too was the Israel occupation of the Egyptian Sinai.

Questioning conventional accounts of the Suez Crisis

This widely circulated reading satisfies realists and others, but it is a bit removed from the primary issues underlying the takeover of the Suez Canal by Egypt. To postcolonialism, the letters of the Suez agreements are not unimpeachable, and the decision by Britain, France, and Israel to wage war on Egypt was illogical, absurd, and reckless in its own way. For explanation, imagine this writer in his introductory course in international law on the topic of international regimes of waterways. Guinea, his country of birth, had been independent from France for less than two decades. The professor, a Frenchman, wrote on the board the name of three canals: the Suez Canal; the Panama Canal; and the Kiel Canal (Kaiser-Wilhelm-Kanal). He then proclaimed confidently that, although entirely within Egyptian territory, Suez was an international passageway. The Panama Canal, which cuts across the state of Panama, was actually the American canal. The Kiel Canal, on the other hand, was German property because it was located in Germany. You could imagine that, if the professor intended to communicate respect for international law, he was mistaken. Where he perceived normative certainty, this student and his friends perceived colonial hubris and arrogance. We could not make sense of the argument that Germany claimed proprietorship of the Kiel Canal due to its location but Egypt could not claim the Suez on account of colonial understandings. We were particularly incensed when, through an indiscretion, the law professor mentioned that the excavation of the Suez Canal was due mostly to the forced labour of poor Egyptians. Every student in the class could recall that unequal treaties, forced or slave labour, and discriminatory international regimes had in fact been the hallmark of colonialism!

The internationalization of the Suez Canal under private European management appeared to us to be a throwback to European notions of imperial sovereignty. Thus, whereas we were supposed to be outraged by Nasser's adventure, we wished we had been there for the cheers. Nasser was in fact right that the letter and spirit of colonial agreements were inconsistent with the postwar notion of

(continued)

self-determination. In this postcolonial contest, Nasser was alone. Nor was it unique to this circumstance that former colonial powers attempted to preserve colonial privileges against Egyptian claims. Nasser was preceded by Mohammed Mossadegh in Iran (1953) who was removed from power by Mohammad Reza Pahlavi, the Shah of Iran, and pro-monarchy forces in a coup led by British and US intelligence agencies. His sin: the desire to renegotiate turn-of-century oil deals that gave control of Iranian oil to British firms. Mossadegh and Nasser were nonetheless followed by many more Third World leaders and movements from Africa to Asia and Latin America. However corrupt it may appear today, the OPEC was partly connected to postcolonial insurgency against such residual colonial forms as reflected in the international regimes on waterways.

You might wonder why a simple lecture would offend anyone. But you would be mistaken in thinking that the justifications of unequal treaties, forced or slave labour, and discriminatory international regimes were mere political acts undertaken as a matter of expediency. This is not the case. Such actions were steeped in specific ways of thinking and relating to the world that were common among European and Western elites. Philosophers and political theorists condoned such actions and their processes through proprietary articulations of society and law; labour and property; and reason and moral sentiments. From the seventeenth century, European thinkers, including French *philosophes* and British utilitarians, developed historical understandings of societies and their institutions as bases for merits and entitlements. These understandings are complex and at times contradictory, and outside of the aims of this introduction. But, to elaborate on an earlier theme, they were grounded in presumed relationships of peoples to territory and economy, leading to conclusions that 'natives' had no firm moral connections to land that may result in property. The central view was that 'natives' were less industrious and lacked reason to properly perceive the collective good. In contrast, Europeans were assumed to be endowed with reason to master industry, to aspire to property, and to be nobly motivated. They were thus to bring science and value to the less fortunate, including through coercion. One could, therefore, extract concessions from a subservient Viceroy, enlist forced labour to dig a canal, make money on it, and call it the common good. In this light, Nasser's action annulled in one stroke centuries-old European assumptions about the relationships of 'native' populations to nature (or their environment) by reclaiming Egyptian rights to the canal. These assumptions, eloquently framed by the likes of John Locke and Montesquieu, had been the bases for Europe's extra-regional claims to sovereignty and property.

These justifications have not disappeared from disciplinary narratives today. When it is convenient, the discipline of IR has embraced past imperial follies and their rationalizations as state practice. It is not uncommon to come across the axiom that great powers have the greatest influence in the world and, as such, should be willing to use their capabilities to nudge international existence in particular directions. This assertion is made without questions about how particular great powers use their influence and the means and ends to which they apply their capabilities. Fortunately, considerable minorities among the citizens of great powers are somewhat sceptical of the implied wisdom.[2] From a postcolonial perspective, such truisms reflexively evoke memories of prejudices, discriminations, and privations. In such instances, the discipline appears more like an instrument of empire than a science.

Conclusion

Postcolonialism has a critical constructionist dimension; that is, it does not merely seek out points of convergence on planes of understanding of already-existing norms. Postcolonialism aspires to produce new forms of politics based on contingent and empathetic understandings of the trajectories of human societies. In this sense, postcolonialism conveys a sense of ethical and political possibilities after colonialism. It favours an ethos of egalitarianism, social justice, and solidarity. It has faith in its own reasonableness and decency (Scott 1999).

Featured book

Couze Venn, *The Postcolonial Challenge: Towards Alternative Worlds* (London: Sage, 2006).

Although postcolonial texts are not commonly available in international relations, Professor Venn's *The Postcolonial Challenge: Towards Alternative Worlds* is an interesting and important point of reference for students of international politics. It is lucidly written and, provides a comprehensive treatment of postcolonialism in the area of political economy. Venn demonstrates that postcolonial analyses must move beyond the strictures of Western hegemony as well as beyond the past and contemporary spatial allocations of resources and values. Venn calls this approach 'transmodern', and it advances propositions for new politics that befit a transmodern world and political economy.

Venn's interests, unlike those of Marxist and liberal political economists, are not primarily around questions of modernization, development aid, and foreign direct investment. Like Marxists, however, Venn pays attention to the structures of capitalism and its trajectories within different cultural spaces. Venn's text also deals with questions that may seem far removed from the concerns of students today but which are necessary to understand the stakes in postcolonial analyses. These include epistemology and ontology; history and power; rationality, authority, and truth; the conditions of rationalism and its base calculations and technologies; the relationships between rationality, truth, and authority; the import of cultures of knowledge and the politics of power; the utility of hierarchies of values as condition of expropriation under capitalism; and, finally, the technologies and languages of government.

The purpose of the related discussions is not to obscure but, rather, to demonstrate the necessity for envisaging different methods of investigation and modes of explanations of social events today. Students will require careful engagement with Venn's critical hermeneutics but the reading will pay off in terms of expanding students' understanding of the practices and institutions associated with modernity and transmodernity.

It is of interest to the analysis of global politics that Venn recalls the most important geopolitical events from the perspectives of postcolonial entities. Students seldom come across the acronyms of UNCTAD (United Nations Conference on Trade and Development), NIEO (New International Economic Order), GATT (General Agreement on Tariffs and Trade), MIGA (Multilateral Investment Guarantee Agency), and WTO (World Trade Organization) or terms such as 'Law of the Sea', 'Bandung Conference', and 'Non-Aligned Movement' in their regular classes. Venn points out that scholars of IR have erred in neglecting to pay attention to the actual configurations of the stakes in postwar contentions over such actors, events, and processes and the way in which these actors, events, and processes figure in the experiences of postcolonial entities. Venn draws out the insistence in postcolonial analyses on agency and the institutions of power and how these operate. They are all essential to imagining a future.

Postcolonialism is also certain of its responsibility and duty toward other members of the international community. Postcolonialism, in fact, aspires to a different kind of universalism, one based on deliberation and contestation among diverse political entities, with the aim of reaching functional agreement on questions of global concern. This kind of universalism differs from one resulting from universal injunctions by self-assured subjects.

In these regards, postcolonialism maintains consistent positions on politics that do not distinguish between the domestic, national, and international spheres. In the international instance, postcolonialism is mindful of the failure of hegemonic powers to integrate post-colonial states into the decision-making processes of the international system. Yet, post-colonialism's ambivalence on these and other questions of international morality does not flow from outright rejection of systems of thought, whether rationalism, universalism, humanism, liberalism, and the like. Postcolonial antipathy is directed at the imperial desire for hegemony, or the aspiration to unilaterally set the terms and rules of politics and culture; to singly adjudicate international outcomes; and/or to manage knowledge and the memory of international relations. In the domestic instance, postcolonialism also denounces, with equal vigour, the failure of postcolonial elites to integrate co-citizens—and/or domestic social and cultural formations—into democratic structures of governance within the state. Postcolonialism, thus, is a broad commentary on present models of politics, economy, and ethics.

In both instances, postcolonialism must confront anxieties of survival that arise among subjects in any fluid and uncertain context. Again, rather than oppose them, postcolonialism embraces fluxes and the resulting opportunities, including the hybridity of culture and identity (Bhabha 1994). To do so, postcolonialism must rethink the boundaries between self and others (Anzaldúa 1987) as well as recognize transculturation as an inevitable historical process (Moreiras 2001). Thus, postcolonialism seeks to connect with progressive elements at home and in the former metropolises in order to productively engage the fields of culture and identity in manners that eliminate violence and/or escape the problematic legacies of class hegemony, gendered exclusion, colonial domination, and capitalist exploitation (Scott 1999). All these themes are present in postcolonialism as articles or declarations of faith. The postcolonial order envisaged by postcolonialism would be more inclusive and solicitous. This future world would be based on tolerance toward self-criticisms and criticisms of the self by others; reverence for contingency and historical flows; and more fluid understandings of values, ethics, and the common good. You would not object to such a world, would you? If not, then you must always open your mind to new (and just) possibilities!

 Questions

1. Why is 'postcolonialism' as a phenomenon difficult to define and pinpoint as a single theoretical tradition?

2. What is the author's definition of postcolonialism?

3. What are some of the goals and agendas of postcolonialism?

4. How does postcolonialism approach 'truth' and 'knowledge'?

5. Discuss the postcolonial critique of Immanuel Kant and subsequent theories based upon the work of this theorist.

6. What is the postcolonial objection to 'human rights' as a 'universal value'?

7. How does Said's book *Orientalism* illustrate and elucidate the relationship between Europe and the East?

8. Describe the relationship between Orientalism and the discourses on terrorism including 'the War on Terror'.

9. How does postcolonialism's response to the Non-Proliferation Treaty illustrate its opinion about Western ideas of international morality and law?

10. What is the significance of the internationalization of the Suez Canal for postcolonialism?

11. What is the postcolonial approach to the future?

12. Compare the approaches of liberal internationalism, constructivism, and postcolonialism.

Further reading

Darby, Phillip (2000), *At the Edge of International Relations: Postcolonialism, Gender and Dependency* (Cambridge: Continuum International Publishing Group).
This book is interested in how a postcolonial perspective contributes or challenges traditional conventions in international relations theory.

Spivak, Gayatri Chakavorty (1999), *A Critique of Postcolonial Reason: Toward a History of the Vanishing Present* (Cambridge: Harvard University Press).
Divided between Philosophy, Literature, History, and Culture, this work gives extensive insight in to the colonial and postcolonial paradoxes in the Western intellectual tradition.

Nevzat, Soguk (1999), *States and Strangers: Refugees and Displacements of Statecraft* (Minneapolis: Minnesota University Press).
An important work on the ways refugee and refugee law challenge traditional concepts in International Relations such as the state and the citizen.

Chowdry, G. and Nair, S (2002) (eds.), *Power, Postcolonialism and International Relations; Reading Race, Gender and Class* (London and New York: Routledge, Advances in International Relations & Global Politics).
This collection covers a wide range of contemporary topics in IR from questions of the secular to recent debates over the future of human rights.

Grovogui, Siba N. (2006), *Beyond Eurocentrism and Anarchy: Memories of International Order and Institutions* (New York: Palgrave Macmillan).
This book re-visits a postwar encounter between a group of French-African intellectuals and Western elites as evidence of the importance of a genuinely global and equivocal perspective on IR.

Krishna, Sankaran (1999), *Postcolonial Insecurities: India, Sri Lanka, and the Question of Nationhood* (Minneapolis: University of Minnesota, Borderlines series).
Addresses the question of nation and state formation as a political and ethical project.

Biswas, Shampa (2001), '"Nuclear apartheid" as political position: race as a postcolonial resource?', *Alternatives: Global, Local, Political*, 26/4 pp. 485(38).
This piece continues the discussions about the colonial legacy of the Nuclear Non-proliferation Treaty.

Lynn Doty, Roxanne (1996) *Imperial Encounters: The Politics of Representation in North-South Relations* (Minneapolis: Minnesota University Press, Borderlines Series).
This book engages how policy-making is informed and even preceded by cultural and racial representations. Doty takes the position that politics is fundamentally interpretative.

 Notes

1. I say a place called Europe because I do not believe that Europe has a fixed identity and fixed traditions. I also wish to underscore historical co-dependencies among regions of the world.

2. On modernity, subjectivity, and violence see, for instance, Richard Ashley (1987), David Campbell and Michael Dillon (1993), and Chris Brown (1988).

 Visit the Online Resource Centre that accompanies this book for lots of interesting additional material. **www.oxfordtextbooks.co.uk/orc/dunne3e/**

14

Green Theory

ROBYN ECKERSLEY

 Reader's Guide

This chapter explores the ways in which environmental concerns have influenced International Relations (IR) theory. It provides a brief introduction to the ecological crisis and the emergence of green theorizing in the social sciences and humanities in general, noting its increasing international orientation, and then tracks the status and impact of environmental issues and green thinking in IR theory. It shows how ortho-dox IR theories, such as neorealism and neoliberalism,[1] have constructed environmen-tal problems merely as a 'new issue area' that can be approached through pre-existing theoretical frameworks. These approaches are contrasted with green IR theory, which challenges the state-centric framework, rationalist analysis, and ecological blindness of orthodox IR theories and offers a range of new green interpretations of interna-tional justice, development, modernization, and security. In the case study, climate change is explored to highlight the diversity of theoretical approaches, including the distinctiveness of green approaches, in understanding global environmental change.

Introduction

Environmental problems have never been a central preoccupation in the discipline of International Relations (IR), which has traditionally focused on questions of 'high politics' such as security and inter-state conflict. However, the escalation in transboundary ecological problems from the 1970s onwards saw the emergence of a dedicated sub-field of IR concerned with international environmental cooperation, which focused primarily on the management of common pool resources such as major river systems, the oceans, and the atmosphere. This scholarship has since grown apace with increasing global economic and ecological interdependence and the emergence of uniquely global ecological problems, such as climate change, the thinning of the ozone layer, and the erosion of the Earth's biodiversity. The bulk of research has focused on the study of environmental regimes, primarily from the evolving theoretical framework of neoliberalism, which has approached the environment merely as a new 'issue area' or new political problem, rather than a new theoretical challenge.

By the closing decades of the twentieth century, however, a growing body of green IR theory had emerged that called into question some of the basic assumptions, units of study, frameworks of analysis, and implicit values of the discipline of IR. Just as feminist discourses emerging from outside IR have exposed the gender blindness of much IR theory (discussed in **Chapter 11**), green IR theory, drawing on more radical green discourses from outside the discipline of IR, has helped to expose what might be called the ecological blindness of IR theory. Emerging primarily out of a critique of mainstream rationalist approaches (primarily neo- or structural realism as set out in Chapter 4 and neoliberalism discussed in **Chapter 6**), green IR theory has simultaneously drawn upon, and critically revised and extended, neo-Marxist inspired **International Political Economy** (**IPE**) and normative international relations theories of a cosmopolitan orientation. This new wave of green scholarship has reinterpreted some of the central concepts and discourses in IR and global politics, and challenged traditional understandings of security, development, and international justice with new discourses of **ecological security**, **sustainable development** (and reflexive modernization), and **environmental justice**.

The complex problem of global warming provides an especially illuminating illustration of the diverse ways in which 'real-world' environmental problems are refracted through different theoretical lenses in the discipline of IR. As we shall see, realists typically dismiss environmental problems as peripheral to the main game of international politics unless the consequences of climate change can be shown to impinge directly on national security. Neoliberals, in contrast, are more likely to offer advice on how to adjust incentive structures in the climate change regime to induce inter-state cooperation. Critical theorists, however, tend to reject such piecemeal, 'problem-solving' approaches that fail to address social and economic structures of domination (as noted in **Chapters 8** and **9**). The green voices in the global climate change debate have extended this line of critical inquiry to include neglected areas of environmental domination and marginalization, such as the domination of non-human nature, the neglect of the needs of future generations, and the skewed distribution of ecological risks among different social classes, states, and regions. As we shall see, it is this overriding preoccupation with environmental justice that unites the IPE and normative wings of green IR theory.

After tracking the emergence of green theory in the social sciences and humanities in general, this chapter explores how green theory has itself become more transnational and global, while critical IR theory has become increasingly green. Green IR theory is shown to rest at the intersection of these two developments. The chapter will also point to the different ways in which environmental issues have influenced the evolution of traditional IR theory. The diversity of theoretical approaches, including the distinctiveness of green theories, will be further highlighted through the case study of global warming.

The emergence of green theory

Environmental degradation caused by human activity has a long and complex history. However, until the period of European global expansion and the industrial revolution, environmental degradation generally remained uneven and relatively localized. The 'modern ecological crisis'—marked by an exponential increase in the range, scale, and seriousness of environmental problems around the world—is generally understood to have emerged only in the latter half of the twentieth century. Likewise, the 1960s is typically taken to mark the birth of the 'modern' environment movement as a widespread and persistent social movement that has publicized and criticized the environmental 'side-effects' of the long economic boom following the Second World War. Rapid economic growth, the proliferation of new technologies, and rising population in this period generated increasing energy and resource consumption, new sources (and rising levels) of pollution and waste production, and the rapid erosion of the Earth's biodiversity. While some environmental indicators had improved in some countries by the closing decades of the twentieth century, the overall global environmental assessment for the twenty-first century remains bleak. The United Nations Environment Program's Millennium Ecosystem Assessment (UNEP MEA), completed in March 2005, found that approximately 60 per cent of the examined ecosystem services that support life on Earth are being degraded or used unsustainably (Millennium Ecosystem Assessment 2005: 1).

The 'ecological crisis' is clearly an apt characterization of these developments although the phrase 'ecological predicament' probably best captures the peculiar conundrum facing policy-makers at all levels of governance, namely that environmental problems remain persistent and ubiquitous even though nobody intended to create them. Unlike military threats, which are deliberate, discrete, specific, and require an immediate response, environmental problems are typically unintended, diffuse, transboundary, operate over long time-scales, implicate a wide range of actors, and require painstaking negotiation and cooperation among a wide range of stakeholders. Indeed, environmental problems are sometimes described by policy analysts as 'wicked problems' because of their complexity, variability, irreducibility, intractability, and incidental character. Most environmental risks have crept up, as it were, on a rapidly modernizing world as the unforeseen side-effects of otherwise acceptable practices. As Ulrich Beck has put it, 'they are "piggy-back products" which are inhaled or ingested with other things. They are *the stowaways of normal consumption*' (Beck 1992: 40).

However, it did not take long for radical voices within the environment movement, and critical voices in the social sciences and humanities, to question not just the side-effects of economic growth but also the phenomenon of economic growth itself and the broader processes of modernization. This debate became highly politicized with the 'limits-to-growth' debate of the early 1970s. Influential publications such as the Club of Rome's *The Limits to Growth* report (Meadows et al. 1972) and *The Ecologist* magazine's 'Blueprint for Survival' (*Ecologist* 1972), offered dire predictions of impending ecological catastrophe unless exponential economic growth was replaced with 'steady-state' economic development. These debates coincided with the first United Nations Stockholm Conference on the Human Environment (1972), which formalized the emergence of the environment as a 'global issue'.[2]

From environmental issues to green theories

Environmental concerns, like feminist concerns, have left their mark on most branches of the social sciences and humanities. However, it was not until the late 1980s that a distinctly 'green' social and political theory emerged to give voice to the interrelated concerns of the new social movements (environment, peace, anti-nuclear, women's) that have shaped green politics. These movements also spearheaded the formation of a wave of new green parties in the 1980s at the local, national, and regional level (most prominently in Europe), based on the 'four pillars' of green politics: ecological responsibility, social justice, non-violence, and grass-roots democracy. These pillars have provided a common platform for new green party formations around the world, including in Africa, Latin America, and Asia. Indeed, green politics is the only new global political discourse and practice to emerge in opposition to neoliberal globalization.

While the term 'green' is often used to refer simply to environmental concerns, by the early 1990s green political theory had gained recognition as a new political tradition of inquiry that has emerged as an ambitious challenger to the two political traditions that have had the most decisive influence on twentieth-century politics—liberalism and socialism.[3] Like liberalism and socialism, green political theory has a normative branch (concerned with questions of justice, rights, democracy, citizenship, the state, and the environment), and a political economy branch (concerned with understanding the relationship between the state, the economy, and the environment). As we shall see, the international normative and political economy dimensions of this new green tradition are now discernible but they are less sharply etched than their domestic counterpart, largely because they are still in a formative phase of development.

In broad outline, the first wave of green political theory mounted a critique of both Western capitalism and Soviet-style communism, both of which were regarded as essentially two different versions of the same overarching ideology of industrialism, despite their differences concerning the respective roles of the market and the state. The green critique of industrialism formed part of a broader re-examination of taken-for-granted ideas about the idea of progress and the virtues of modernization inherited from the Enlightenment. Both liberalism and orthodox Marxism were shown to have developed on the basis of the same cornucopian premises, which assumed that the Earth's natural resource base could support unbridled economic growth, and that increasing growth and technological advancement were both highly desirable and inevitable. Both political traditions were shown to share the same optimism about the benefits of science and technology, and either explicitly or implicitly accepted the idea that the human manipulation and domination of nature through the further refinement of instrumental reason were necessary for human advancement. Green political theorists have taken issue with these Enlightenment legacies and highlighted the ecological, social, and psychological costs of the modernization process. They have criticized humanity's increasingly instrumental relationship with non-human nature, along with the subjugation of indigenous peoples and many traditional forms of agriculture. Drawing on the kindred disciplines of environmental ethics and environmental philosophy, which emerged in the late 1970s and early 1980s, green political theorists have called into question anthropocentrism or human chauvinism—the idea that humans are the apex of evolution, the centre of value and meaning in the world, and the only beings that possess moral worth. Rejecting such a posture as arrogant, self-serving, and foolhardy, many green theorists have embraced a new ecology-centred or 'ecocentric' philosophy that seeks to respect all life-forms in terms of their own distinctive modes of being, for their own sake, and not merely for their instrumental value to humans. From an ecocentric perspective, environmental governance should be about protecting not only the health and well-being of existing human communities and future generations but also the larger web of life, made up of nested ecological communities at multiple levels of aggregation (such as gene pools, populations, species, ecosystems). This perspective also draws attention to the limits to humanity's knowledge of the natural world, arguing that nature is not only more complex than we know, but possibly more complex than we shall ever know. Major technological interventions in nature are seen as invariably producing major social and ecological costs. Green theorists therefore generally counsel in favour of a more cautious and critical approach to the assessment of new development proposals, new technologies, and practices of risk assessment in general.

Some of these green themes—particularly the critique of the ascendancy of instrumental reason—were central to the first generation of Frankfurt school critical theorists (discussed in **Chapter 9**), who were the first Western Marxists to problematize the domination of nature and explore its relationship to the domination of humans. Whereas the mature Marx had adopted a Promethean posture towards nature and welcomed scientific and technological progress, the exploration by Theodor Adorno and Max Horkheimer of the 'dialectic of Enlightenment' pointed to the multiple costs to human and non-human nature that accompanied the increasing penetration of instrumental reason into human society and nature (Adorno and Horkheimer 1972). This general theme has been further developed (albeit in less pessimistic terms) by the second generation of Frankfurt school critical theorists, led by Jürgen Habermas. One of Habermas's enduring concerns has been to protect the 'lifeworld' from the march of instrumental rationality by ensuring that such rationality remains subservient to the practice of critical deliberation. Habermas's ideal of communicative rationality has served as a major source of inspiration in the development of green democratic theory and critical green explorations of the relationship between risk, science, technology, and society. Whereas orthodox Marxist theory had confined its critical attention to the relations of production, green theory has expanded this critique to include the 'forces of production' (technology and management systems) and what Ulrich Beck has called 'the relations of definition' that define, assess, distribute, and manage the risks of modernization.

There remains disagreement among green political theorists as to whether green politics should be understood as anti-modern, postmodern, or simply seeking more 'reflexive modernization', although the latter appears to have emerged as the most favoured approach. Indeed, the second wave of green political theory of the mid-1990s and beyond has been less preoccupied with critical philosophical reflection on humanity's posture towards the non-human world and more concerned to explore the conditions that might improve the 'reflexive learning capacity' of citizens, societies, and states in a world of mounting yet unevenly distributed ecological risks. The green critique of industrialism and modernization has not eclipsed the politics of 'left vs. right', but it has certainly placed the traditional distributive struggles between labour and capital, and between rich world and poor world, in a broader and more challenging context. Indeed, improving distributive justice while simultaneously curbing ecologically destructive economic growth has emerged as the central political challenge of green theory and practice, both domestically and internationally.

The transnational turn in green theory

In exploring the relationship between environmental justice and environmental democracy, the second wave of green political theory has become more transnational and cosmopolitan in its orientation. The first wave of green political theory sought to highlight the ecological irrationality of core social institutions such as the market and the state and many green political theorists had extolled the virtues of grass-roots democracy and ecologically sustainable communities as alternatives. The second wave of green political theory has been more preoccupied with critically rethinking and, in some cases, 'transnationalizing' the scope of many core political concepts and institutions with environmental problems in mind. This scholarship has produced new, local, transnational, deterritorialized or global conceptualizations of environmental justice (e.g. Low and Gleeson 1998; Schlosberg 2007), environmental rights (e.g. Hayward 2005), environmental democracy (Doherty and de Geus 1996), environmental activism (Wapner 1998), environmental citizenship (Barry 1999; Dobson 2003), and green states (e.g. Eckersley 2004; Barry and Eckersley 2005). There has also been an increasing engagement by green political theorists with some of the core debates within normative IR theory, particularly those concerned with human rights, cosmopolitan democracy, transnational civil society, and transnational public spheres. This scholarship has also fed into, and helped to shape, a distinctly green branch of normative IR theory concerned with global environmental justice. According to green theory, environmental injustices arise when unaccountable social agents 'externalize' the environmental costs of their decisions and practices to innocent third parties – particularly vulnerable communities in the Global South—in circumstances where the affected parties (or their representatives) have no knowledge of, or input in, the ecological risk-generating decisions and practices. Rob Nixon has described this process as 'slow violence' because it so often slips under the radar of political attention—unlike sensational environmental disasters that produce immediate harm (Nixon 2011).

Environmental injustices also occur when privileged social classes and nations appropriate more than their 'fair share' of the environment, and leave behind oversized 'ecological foot-prints' (Wackernagel and Rees 1996). The basic quest of green theory is, therefore, a double one: to reduce ecological risks across the board, and to prevent their unfair externalization and displacement, through space and time, onto innocent third parties.

Ultimately, environment justice demands: (1) recognition of the expanded moral community that is affected by ecological risks (i.e. not just all citizens, but all peoples, future generations, and non-human species); (2) participation and critical deliberation by citizens and representatives of the larger community-at-risk in all environmental decision-making (including policy-making, legislating and treaty-making, administration, monitoring, enforcement, and adjudication); (3) a precautionary approach to ensure the minimization of risks in relation to the larger community; (4) a fair distribution of those risks that are reflectively acceptable via democratic processes that includes the standpoint of all affected parties and public interest advocacy groups; and (5) redress and compensation for those parties who suffer the effects of ecological problems.

Green scholarship on questions of political economy has likewise become more globally focused, although discourses of economy–environment integration have always had a global dimension—even before the emergence of a distinctly green theory that identified with the concerns of the new social movement and green parties. The early 'limits-to-growth' debate had generated calls for radical policy changes to bring about a curbing or even cessation of economic growth (and, in some cases, population growth) to put a break on rising global environmental degradation. However, these calls proved to be both controversial and politically unpalatable. By the late 1980s, the limits-to-growth debate was eclipsed by the more appealing discourse of sustainable development, which had been widely embraced following the publication of *Our Common Future* (the Brundtland Report) by the World Commission on Environment and Development (1987). The Brundtland Report challenged the idea that environmental protection and economic development stand in a simple zero-sum relationship and it pointed to the opportunities for 'decoupling' economic growth and environmental deterioration by pursuing an environmentally friendly or sustainable development path. Sustainable development, according to the Brundtland Committee's pithy and oft-quoted formulation, is understood as development that meets the needs of present generations without sacrificing the ability of future generations to meet their own needs. A broad strategy of sustainable development was officially endorsed at the United Nation's Conference on Environment and Development ('the Earth Summit') in Rio de Janiero in 1992 and it continues to serve as the dominant meta-discourse of national and international environmental law and policy, despite the fact that it remains deeply contested and only weakly implemented.

While the Brundtland Report's intra- and inter-generational approach to equity is welcome, from a green perspective it still rests on an instrumental orientation towards the non-human world and ignores the case for biodiversity preservation for its own sake. Even more problematically, the Report optimistically assumed that sustainable development could be achieved by increasing economic growth rates. In defending an alternative conception of *ecologically* sustainable development, green political economists have rejected the dominant framework of neoclassical economics in favour of the new theoretical framework of ecological economics. For ecological economists, market mechanisms may provide an efficient allocation of resources but they can neither ensure a fair distribution of wealth and income relative to present and future human needs, nor ensure that the scale of the economy operates within the ecological carrying capacity of ecosystems. These matters are beyond the capacity of markets and must be addressed politically, through environmental education, community cooperation, societal contestation and negotiation, state regulation, and international cooperation.

Nonetheless, the general argument that there are synergies between more efficient capitalist development and environmental protection has been reinforced by the more recent, and mostly European-led, discourse of **ecological modernization** (Hajer 1995). Proponents of ecological modernization argue that stricter environmental regulation, economic competition, and constant technological innovation produce economic growth that uses less energy and resources and produces less waste per unit of gross domestic product (GDP). Far from acting as a break on growth, proponents of ecological modernization maintain that stronger domestic environmental regulation can act as a spur to further environmental/technical innovation, which enhances national economic competitiveness and forces an upward ratcheting of environmental standards. This 'win–win' approach has been warmly embraced, if not systematically implemented, by many members of the Organization for Economic Cooperation and Development (OECD), particularly in Western Europe, and it coincides with a shift towards the increasing use of market-based instruments in environmental policy.

While limits-to-growth advocates underestimated the synergies between capitalist development and environmental protection, green critics maintain that the discourse of sustainable development, and especially the more technologically oriented discourse of ecological modernization, have overestimated them. Improving the environmental efficiency of production through technological innovation is to be welcomed but it does not reduce aggregate levels of resource consumption and waste production. Indeed, gains in environmental efficiency typically enable improvements in economic productivity, rising incomes and further consumption and production. Moreover, not all environmental protection measures—such as biodiversity protection—are necessarily conducive to economic growth. In some cases, difficult political trade-offs are necessary. Finally, green critics argue that a simple strategy of technologically driven ecological modernization provides no means of addressing the deeply skewed distribution of ecological risks among different social classes and nations. In contrast, the Brundtland Report was concerned to promote intra- and intergenerational equity, but it relied on the 'trickle-down' effect brought about by increasing growth (with faster growth recommended for the South to enable it to 'catch up' to the North). From a green perspective, these recommendations encapsulate the sustainable development paradox: that environmental protection is best achieved by pursuing more (albeit environmentally efficient) growth, which generates more *aggregate* environmental problems (albeit at a slower rate).

In grappling with this paradox (which also sheds light on why environmental problems are such 'wicked' problems), green political theorists and green political economists have drawn on the new field of environmental sociology, particularly the sub-branch dealing with modernization and the risk society, which provides a direct challenge to neoclassical economics and neoliberal political ideology. For sociologists of the risk society, such as Ulrich Beck (1992), ecological problems persist because they are generated by the very economic, scientific, and political institutions that are called upon to solve them. The paradox of sustainable development, therefore, cannot be solved simply by the pursuit of more environmentally efficient means to achieve given ends. Rather, it is necessary to pursue 'reflexive modernization', which entails reflecting critically and continuously on the means *and* the ends of modernization. Following Christoff (1996), many green theorists now draw a distinction between 'weak' and 'strong' versions of ecological modernization. The former represents the 'technical fix' interpretation favoured by many OECD governments, and the latter represents the more critical, green approach of reflexive modernization. It is here that green IPE and green normative theory join forces in advocating a more 'ecologically informed' democracy that provides extensive opportunities for citizens to represent long-range, generalizable interests and to challenge the settled practices of risk definition, generation, distribution, and management.

Nonetheless, there remain internal divisions within green circles over whether capitalist economies, states, or the state system are indeed capable of becoming ecologically reflexive to the degree required to avert significant and ongoing environmental degradation. However, all agree that the intensification of economic globalization and the ascendancy of neoliberal discourses at the national and international levels have made the general green case harder to pursue. Nor is the anarchic structure of the state system well suited to resolving transnational and global ecological problems, especially global warming, which is one of the most complex and challenging collective-action problems facing the international community. Of course, IR scholars working in the broad traditions of realism, liberalism, and Marxism have well-developed (and diverging) views about the prospects of international environmental cooperation. As we shall see, green IR theory has largely defined itself in opposition to mainstream rationalist approaches to IR (principally neorealism and neoliberalism), while also taking on board green theory's critique of many elements of the Marxist tradition.

The greening of IR theory

Green IR theory shares many of the characteristics of the new IR theories emerging out of the so-called 'third debate' (also sometimes referred to as the 'fourth debate', see **Chapter 1**): they are generally critical, problem-oriented, interdisciplinary, and above all unapologetic about their explicit normative orientation. In their quest to promote global environmental justice, green IR scholars seek to articulate the concerns of many voices traditionally at the margins of international relations, ranging from environmental non-government organizations, green consumers, ecological scientists, ecological economists, green political parties, indigenous peoples, and, broadly, all those seeking to transform patterns of global trade, aid, and debt to promote more sustainable patterns of development in the North and South.

Green IR theory may be usefully subdivided into an IPE wing, which offers an alternative analysis of global ecological problems to that of regime theory, and a normative or 'green cosmopolitan' wing that articulates new norms of environmental justice and green democracy at all levels of governance. Both of these sub-fields remain indebted to critical theory, particularly the neo-Gramscian-inspired critical political economy of Robert Cox, and the cosmopolitan discourse ethics of Jürgen Habermas, and therefore can be located clearly on the critical/constructivist side of the rationalism versus constructivism debate in IR theory (this debate is discussed in **Chapters 1** and **10**).

Rationalist accounts and green alternatives

The two dominant rationalist approaches in IR theory—neorealism and neoliberalism—have tended to approach environmental problems as a 'new issue area' to be absorbed within their pre-existing theoretical frameworks rather as something that presents a new analytical or normative challenge. Whereas neo- or structural realists have been mostly dismissive of the 'low politics' of the environment, neoliberals have conducted extensive empirical work on regimes dealing with transboundary and global environmental problems. This scholarship has produced a range of useful insights that help to predict whether or not states are likely to cooperate in, or defect from, environmental regimes, along with a range of reforms for improving the effectiveness of such regimes. In general, dominant rationalist approaches have not explicitly engaged in normative theorizing, although neoliberals have openly acknowledged their problem-solving and reformist, rather than critical, orientation (Haas et al. 1993: 7). Their primary research purpose has been to observe, explain, and predict the international behaviour of states, and to suggest practical reforms that would improve the effectiveness of environmental regimes.

Both the political economy and normative wings of green IR theory have challenged these dominant rationalist approaches on four levels. First, green critics have directed critical attention to the normative purposes that are served by rationalist approaches by exposing the problematic environmental assumptions and ethical values that are implicit in neorealist and neoliberal analyses. In this respect, green IR theorists take seriously Robert Cox's observation that 'theory is always for someone and for some purpose' (Cox 1981). Neorealism, in particular, is criticized for 'normalizing' rather than challenging the environmentally exploitative practices sponsored by states. From their Hobbesian universe, neorealists maintain that rivalrous state behaviour is inevitable owing to the anarchic structure of the state system, and that it would be foolhardy for states to pursue environmental cooperation that did not confer relative gains. Of course, neorealist theorists do not personally endorse environmental exploitation but they remain unreflective about the political purposes served by their theories and therefore provide an apology for environmental exploitation and international non-cooperation. As we shall see, green IR theorists have also challenged the restrictive understanding of national security that has dominated realist theories of all persuasions and argued instead for a more comprehensive framework for understanding security that takes human well-being and ecosystem integrity, rather than states, as the fundamental moral and analytical reference point.

In contrast, neoliberals, from their Lockean universe, seek to create international regimes that optimize the 'rational exploitation' of nature, both as a 'tap' (in providing energy and natural resources) and as a 'sink' (via the waste assimilation services of the Earth, oceans, and atmosphere) in ways that expand the menu of state development options. However, their rational choice framework implicitly sanctions an instrumental orientation towards the non-human world and leaves little room for understanding or promoting alternative 'green identities' of particular states or non-state actors. Whereas neoliberals implicitly accept capitalist markets and sovereign states as background 'givens' to international regime negotiations, green IR theorists are concerned to expose the ways in which these social structures serve to thwart the development of more effective environmental initiatives. They also seek to give voice to new forms of counter-hegemonic resistance to neoliberal economic globalization. Like all critical theorists, green IR theorists emphasize the role of agents in transforming social structures—in this case, to promote environmental justice and sustainability.

Second, green IR theorists have added their weight to the critique of rationalist approaches pioneered by critical theorists and constructivists, who have exposed the limitations in the analytical frameworks and explanatory power of **positivist** IR theories. For example, neorealists predict that inter-state environmental cooperation is highly unlikely unless it can be induced or coerced by a hegemonic state, and that such cooperation will always remain vulnerable to shifts in the distribution of power (understood as the distribution of material capability). For neorealists such as Kenneth Waltz the 'tragedy of the commons' is generated by the anarchic structure of the state system, which is essentially unchanging. The only changing variable in this system is the distribution of material capabilities among states. Non-state actors and normative discourses are considered peripheral. Green theorists point out that neorealism provides a crude and incomplete account of international environmental politics. Indeed, one of the biggest growth areas in international treaty-making is in the environmental field, yet realists are at a loss to explain why or how this has occurred.

Although neoliberals offer a more plausible account of the evolution of international environmental cooperation, their framework of analysis is unable to provide a satisfactory account of the normative dimension of environmental regimes. Instead, neoliberals typically reduce environmental regimes to the outcome of a set of interest-based bargaining positions held by states, usually unpacked in terms of relative environmental vulnerability, relative capacity to adjust to environmental change, and the relative costs of adjustments. By contrast, green theorists point out that environmental regimes embody moral norms that cannot be reduced to state interests or capacities. Understanding why regimes have emerged to protect endangered species (such as whales or elephants), the atmosphere, the oceans, or wilderness areas (such as Antarctica) requires an examination of not only state interests but also national cultures and values, the role of scientists and transnational environmental advocacy networks, and the persuasive practices of regime negotiators and other 'norm entrepreneurs'. The deficiencies in rationalist regime theory have prompted some green IR theorists to develop alternative constructivist theoretical foundations for the study of environmental regimes (e.g. Vogler 2003).

More generally, however, green political economy scholarship has defined itself in opposition to rationalist regime theory. Indeed, the state-centric focus of rationalist regime theory is seen to deflect attention away from what is seen to be the primary driver of global ecological degradation and environmental injustices, namely the competitive dynamics of globalizing capitalism rather than the rivalry of states per se. A single-minded focus on states or 'countries' is also seen to be misguided, because it disaggregates global production and consumption in arbitrary ways and, therefore, misidentifies where social power, social responsibility, and the capacity to adjust lie. Capitalism operates at a global level in ways that leave highly uneven impacts on different human communities and ecosystems, with some social classes and communities leaving much bigger 'ecological footprints' at the expense of others. Merely punishing those countries that are, say, heavy aggregate polluters ignores the fact that many consumers and financial interests located elsewhere benefit from the pollution without taking any responsibility for the costs. In this respect at least, states are not always the most meaningful units of consumption, and aggregate figures of wealth or pollution in particular states say nothing about the vast disparities of wealth, income, and risks within those states. Instead of allocating blame and responsibility to particular states, green IPE theorists suggest that we should be monitoring and allocating responsibility along transnational commodity chains, from investment, resource extraction, production through to marketing, advertising, retailing, consumption, and disposal (Conca 2000: 149).[4] Indeed, one of the innovations of green IPE is that it focuses as much on global consumption as global investment and production (e.g. Princen et al. 2002).

Third, green IR theorists have directed their critical attention to the social agents and social structures that have systematically blocked the negotiation of more ecologically enlightened regimes. These critical analyses have been applied not only to ineffective regimes (chief among which is the Tropical Timber Agreement that is dominated by the timber industry and those states involved in the import and export of timber) but also to the relationship between overlapping regimes and to global governance structures in general. One prominent concern of green IR theorists is that international economic regimes, such as the global trading regime, tend to overshadow and undermine many international environmental regimes. This has sparked an ongoing green debate about the desirability and/or possibility of greening the World Trade Organization (WTO) versus setting up counter-institutions, such as a World Environment Organization, to balance the disciplinary power of the WTO.

Finally, green IR theorists have explored the role of non-state forms of 'deterritorialized' governance, ranging from the transnational initiatives of environmental NGOs (such as the Forest Stewardship Council, which has produced an influential certification scheme for forest products produced from sustainably managed forests) to the private governance practices of industrial and financial corporations, including the insurance industry. This new scholarship has produced a more complex and layered picture of global environmental governance that is able to recognize new, hybrid, and/or network patterns of authority that

Featured book

Matthew Paterson, (2000), *Understanding Global Environmental Politics: Domination, Accumulation, Resistance* (London: Palgrave).

Understanding Global Environmental Politics provides an exemplary illustration of the central theoretical preoccupations of green IR theory. The book provides a fundamental challenge to the basic questions and units of analysis adopted by mainstream (neoliberal institutionalist) regime theorists in the study of global environmental politics. The core question of mainstream inquiry is: 'what affects the possibility of states collaborating successfully to resolve particular transnational environmental problems?' (p. 1). Matthew Paterson argues that this narrow framing of the problem depoliticizes global environmental politics, breaks it down into discrete environmental issues and trends, restricts attention to international environmental negotiations and closes off any investigation into the social institutions that systematically produce ecological problems. The origin of global environmental change is seen to lie in an interstate tragedy of the commons and the absence of global political authority, or simply a set of discrete trends that are treated as exogenous to the conceptual inquiry. The anarchic state system is taken for granted and the analysis is confined to the relative vs. absolute gains debate, the role of institutions, the behaviour of states, and the influence of non-state actors on interstate negotiations.

Paterson argues that green IR theory should start with three more fundamental questions: (1) why have ecological problems arisen or how are they produced?; (2) what are the impacts of ecological problems on different social groups?; and (3) what should be the response? In reply to the first of these questions, he offers an interlocking structural explanation. That is, the production of ecological problems is understood as internal to the logic of four main power structures of global politics: the state system, capitalism, scientific knowledge/managerialism, and patriarchy. Building on a neo-Gramscian understanding of power structures as producing social identities and practices, Paterson teases out the different ways in which these four power structures work together to produce ecological problems on a routine basis. In response to the second question, he also highlights the skewed distribution of ecological risks and the distance in space and time between those who benefit from the social practices that produce them, and those who ultimately suffer. In response to the third question, he argues that the appropriate response is to resist these interlocking power structures and build smaller communities and steady-state economies based on egalitarian social principles.

Paterson has also helped to pioneer the study of everyday practices of consumption and production and the social identities that are produced. He illustrates his structural theory through a detailed examination of three case studies that are 'local everywhere': the construction of sea defences, driving cars, and eating McDonald's hamburgers. He shows how each of these local practices simultaneously produce global environmental problems in a systematic fashion and help to reproduce state, economic, scientific–technological, and patriarchal power structures.

straddle state jurisdictional boundaries or, in some cases, bypass the traditional hierarchical forms of governance typical of nation states.

In sum, green IR theory has self-consciously sought to transcend the state-centric framework of traditional IR theory and offer new analytical and normative insights into global environmental change. The case study on climate change provides a useful means of illustrating this contribution, from the critique of mainstream IR approaches through to the recommendation of alternative policy prescriptions.

Case study: the challenge of climate change

The problem of human-induced climate change represents one of the most challenging environmental problems confronting humankind. Atmospheric concentrations of greenhouse gases resulting from human activity have increased substantially from around 1750 and exponentially since the end of the Second World War, with the ten years from 1995 emerging as the warmest in the instrumental record (Intergovernmental Panel on Climate Change (IPCC) 2007: 30). Scientists predict that if greenhouse gas emissions continue unchecked, the world will face mass extinctions; water, energy, and food scarcity; the loss of coral reefs through coral bleaching; rising sea levels, along with coastal, and infrastructural damage; and human death and suffering from a growing incidence of 'extreme weather'. While the incidence of climate risks is expected to vary geographically, lower-income populations in developing countries are expected to suffer the most (IPCC 2007: 19). Climate change will also exacerbate existing inequalities in access to basic necessities such as health care, adequate food, and clean water. The inhabitants of small islands and low-lying coastal areas are particularly at risk from sea-level rise and storm surges.

In response to the alarming predictions of the IPCC's First Assessment Report in 1990, states negotiated the United Nations Framework Convention on Climate Change (UNFCCC), which was signed at the Earth Summit in Rio de Janeiro in 1992. The basic objective of the agreement is to achieve a 'stabilization of greenhouse gas concentrations in the atmosphere at a level that would prevent dangerous anthropogenic interference with the climate system' (Article 2). The Framework Convention also established basic principles of equitable burden sharing in Article 3, the most significant of which are that the parties should protect the climate system 'on the basis of equity and in accordance with their common but differentiated responsibilities and respective capabilities' (hereafter CBDR); that developed countries should take the lead in combating climate change; and that full consideration should be given to the specific needs and special circumstances of developing countries, especially those that are particularly vulnerable to the impacts of climate change.

No binding targets or timetables were included in the Framework Convention, partly at the insistence of the USA. To address this problem the parties negotiated the Kyoto Protocol 1997, under which industrialized countries agreed to reduce their aggregate levels of greenhouse gas emissions by an average of 5.2 per cent by the end of the 2008–12 commitment period (from a 1990 baseline), although different countries negotiated different targets. The Clinton administration signed the Kyoto Protocol in 1997 and agreed to reduce the USA's emissions by 7 per cent after negotiating a range of 'flexibility instruments' such as carbon trading that would lower the cost of compliance. However, it never presented the treaty for ratification to the US Senate due to strong domestic opposition. In 2001, the Bush administration expressly repudiated the Kyoto Protocol on the grounds that the US's Kyoto target would harm the USA economy, and that the Protocol was flawed because it did not require major developing countries, such as China, to undertake emission reductions in the same commitment period. Despite the non-cooperation of the world's most powerful state, the Kyoto Protocol became legally binding in 2005 following Russia's ratification in late 2004.

It is widely accepted that the first round of commitments made by the parties to the Kyoto Protocol will have a negligible effect on reducing aggregate global emissions. The IPCC has warned that global aggregate emissions must peak by 2015 and then decline by 80–90 per cent by 2050, and that developed countries must reduce their emissions by 25–40 per cent by 2020 to prevent dangerous climate change. Against this background, the Kyoto Protocol may be likened to a warm-up match, with the negotiations for a post-Kyoto treaty for the commitment period 2013–20 serving as the crucial 'main game' that will determine the fate of the Earth's climate.

However, the parties have struggled to produce a post-Kyoto treaty. In an effort to draw the USA back into the climate regime and to increase the engagement of the major emitters in the developing world, such as China and India, in 2007 the parties launched a new negotiation track for a Treaty on Long-Term Cooperative Action (the LCA treaty) alongside negotiations for a second commitment period to the Kyoto Protocol. Both agreements were to be signed at Copenhagen in 2009. Under the LCA track, it was agreed that developed countries would negotiate further emissions reduction commitments, that developing countries would negotiate nonbinding 'nationally appropriate mitigation actions', and that the parties would negotiate rules for funding, technology transfer and other assistance to developing countries to address mitigation and adaptation. However, as the deadline approached, tensions grew between the USA and major developing countries, particularly China and India. The USA insisted that the LCA treaty would be ineffective without significant commitments from all the major emitters. In response, China (supported by the G77) insisted that developing countries were under no obligation to accept internationally binding commitments given their significant development needs and the failure of developed countries to fulfil their leadership obligations under the Convention given their greater historical responsibility, capacity, and per capita carbon footprint. Since Bali, China has overtaken the USA as the world's largest aggregate emitter, but the average per capita emissions of China are only around one third of the USA's.

Despite the election of President Obama, who declared a commitment to tackle climate change, and despite an offer by the European Union (EU) to increase its Copenhagen emissions reduction target from 20 to 30 percent if other major economies undertook comparable commitments, no treaty was signed at Copenhagen in 2009. Instead, the conference produced a nonbinding political accord, known as the Copenhagen Accord. This agreement, which was forged outside the formal negotiating process by the US and the newly formed BASIC group (Brazil, South Africa, India, and China), accepted the need to prevent global warming of more than 2 degrees, promised significant financial support to developing countries, but merely invited parties to make nonbinding pledges to reduce emissions. While the Accord was officially endorsed a year later at the Cancún meeting, the negotiations for a LCA treaty were superseded at the Durban meeting in 2011 where the parties agreed to embark on a fresh round of negotiation for a new legal treaty to include all major emitters. This new treaty was to be signed in 2015, and to come into effect in 2020.

Durban was seen as a major diplomatic breakthrough for the EU insofar as China and India agreed, for the first time, to commit to a future treaty in return for the EU agreeing to a second commitment period under the Kyoto Protocol—despite the US's repudiation of Kyoto and its failure to fulfil its leadership obligations under the Convention. However, the price of this deal was the further postponement of more ambitious and binding commitments at a time when scientists were warning of a shrinking window of opportunity for effective mitigation action and a significant gap between what had been pledged under the Copenhagen Accord and what is required to avert dangerous climate change.

The international climate negotiations have been accompanied by significant developments in climate policy at the regional, national, and sub-national levels alongside the growth of international carbon markets. However, these developments have been patchy and many national governments have faced significant domestic opposition—particularly from energy-intensive industries—in their efforts to enact emissions trading schemes or impose a carbon tax to achieve national emission reduction targets.

Given the enormity of the climate change challenge, and the complexity of the issues involved, it is hardly surprising that it has elicited a diversity of theoretical analyses and responses from the discipline of International Relations (IR). However, the contribution of green IR theory is distinctive in two respects. First, it has offered an alternative analysis and explanation of the political problem and of the international negotiating process to that of mainstream rationalist approaches. Second, green IR theories have promoted new normative discourses that have generated alternative policy proposals to those that have dominated the international negotiations thus far.

Alternative green explanations

While the theoretical parsimony of realism served it reasonably well in accounting for relations between the superpowers during the Cold War, it has struggled to make sense of international environmental regimes, including the climate change negotiations. The problem for neorealists, in particular, is that they

(continued)

allow no or little room for any diversity of state international responses to climate change, since they regard all states, to borrow Kenneth Waltz's phrase, as 'like-units' and are therefore expected to respond in the same way to systemic pressures. However, this understanding cannot explain the significant differences in negotiating positions and national policy developments in different states. Neorealists cannot explain why 191 countries plus the EU have ratified the Kyoto Protocol, despite the USA's defection and the absence of any binding commitments from developing countries. While neorealists can explain laggards (such as the USA), they cannot explain leaders. For example, they cannot explain why the EU has aspired to be a climate leader and why it agreed to a second commitment period under the Kyoto Protocol in the absence of support from major emitters such as the USA, Japan, Russia, and Canada.

Neoliberals are able to offer a more plausible account of the outcome to date based on their analyses of state interests and capacities. However, in focusing their attention on the hard bargaining among states over the distribution of benefits and burdens of adjustment, neoliberals assume all states have the same national interests and sideline the larger ideational, normative and communicative context that shapes the social construction of interests and drives the negotiations. This includes differences in risk cultures in different jurisdictions, the scientific findings of the IPCC and the regime's burden sharing principles that have framed the negotiations and served as a major point of normative contestation between the USA and China/G77. These principles recognize asymmetrical obligations based on differing capacities and levels of responsibility among states in the developed and developing world. They acknowledge that industrialized countries are primarily responsible for past emissions and that it is necessary that they 'cut some slack' for developing countries to pursue their legitimate aspirations to improve the quality of life of their citizens, many of whom live in abject poverty. This normative framework, and the communicative context of domestic and international politics, is essential to understanding both the achievements and blockages in the international negotiations and in domestic politics. For example, both the USA and Germany are home to significant research programmes in climate science, yet climate scepticism and denial is high in the USA (including in Congress), and virtually absent in Germany (including the Bundestag).

While China and India now appear to have accepted that a high minded insistence that developed countries fulfil their leadership obligations before developing countries take on binding commitments is a recipe for regime failure, there is still a broad agreement that these commitments will be differentiated, and that developed countries have an ongoing obligation to assist developing countries, particularly those that are the least culpable and the most vulnerable.

Alternative green arguments

While green IR theorists give prominence to the role of justice norms in their analysis, along with the importance of critical discourse in transforming the modernization process (and the self-understanding of social actors), they are by no means starry eyed about progress to date on the climate change negotiations. Like all critical theorists, they are particularly attentive to the relationship between **knowledge and power** and concerned to expose exclusionary discourses and practices (Okereke 2008). They are concerned to improve the communicative context of domestic and international climate policy-making to ensure that the science of climate change is clearly aired, and the most vulnerable parties and communities are given a fairer hearing relative to the fossil fuel interests and industry groupings that oppose action on climate change. To this end, green Habermasians welcome the proliferation of transnational public spheres as key mechanisms for consensual social learning in response to new problems. More generally, they welcome the growing array of non-state actors who attend, criticize, and/or influence the climate negotiations as providing new forms of democratic accountability that transcend the limitations of 'executive multilateralism'. Indeed, some green theorists have suggested that regimes themselves may be regarded as public spheres insofar as they promote critical deliberation (Payne and Samhat 2004).

In addition to exposing distortions in the communicative context of the climate change negotiations and domestic policy-making, green IR theorists have also offered alternative ways of framing the global warming challenge, along with alternative policy prescriptions that they consider will provide a fairer and more lasting solution to the problem of human-induced climate change. For green theorists, the skewed distribution of the impacts of climate change graphically illustrates the problem of environmental injustice in general. Poor communities (particularly in the South) produce relatively low per capita carbon emissions relative to the affluent, consuming classes in the North yet it is predicted that they will suffer the most from global warming and will be less able to adapt to, or insure against, climate-related damage. The green ideal of environmental justice is a cosmopolitan ideal that argues that all individuals, irrespective of nationality or social class, should have an equal right to the energy resources and waste absorption services provided by the natural environment, provided the total use of resources and services remains safely within the ecological carrying capacity of the biosphere. This ideal cannot be realized by market mechanisms alone and it certainly cannot be realized by the strategy of weak ecological modernization that relies on technological fixes since it fails to cap aggregate levels of carbon emissions and ignores the maldistribution of risks associated with climate change. Rather, environmental justice requires extensive environmental regulation along with a significant redistribution of 'emissions space' in the atmosphere from the rich to the poor to ensure the simultaneous satisfaction of basic needs and environmental quality for all. One popular model is 'contraction and convergence' developed by the London-based Global Commons Institute, which proposes a major contraction of emissions by the rich countries and an eventual per capita convergence by all countries at a level that the atmosphere can safely absorb. This model provides developing countries with some room to grow, while also facilitating a considerable transfer of resources from the high per capita emitters to the low per capita emitters under carbon-trading schemes. In contrast, the negotiation of the post-Kyoto treaty is likely to follow the approach of the Kyoto Protocol, which avoided a principled-approach to the allocation of targets based on responsibility and capacity, and the best-available science, and simply left it to individual developed countries to choose their own targets. Moreover, some green critics argue that the 'flexibility instruments' introduced into the Kyoto Protocol, such as carbon trading and offsetting, enable those industries which can afford to purchase credits or offsets to continue their carbon pollution and avoid or defer the necessary green investment that would reduce their emissions at source. Flexibility thus serves to hollow out the responsibility of rich countries and undermine the UNFCCC norm that developed countries should lead the way in combating climate change by pioneering new, low carbon technologies and practices. While it is accepted that the participation of all major carbon emitters (including the USA, the EU, Russia, Japan, China, and India) is essential to the success of a post-Kyoto treaty, the terms of that participation must be such that environmental injustices are ameliorated rather than exacerbated.

Conclusion

Green IPE initially formed the backbone of green IR theory. However, it has been increasingly complemented by green normative inquiry, particularly in the wake of the increasing transnationalization of green political theory, which has injected a distinctly green voice into the more general debates about international justice, cosmopolitan democracy, and the future of the state. At the same time, many well-known cosmopolitan theorists, such as David Held, Andrew Linklater, Henry Shue, and Thomas Pogge, have turned their attention to the ethical and institutional implications of transboundary environmental harm.

While green political economists and green normative theorists remain united by their condemnation of environmental injustices, green IR theory is not without its internal tensions. First, green political economists are prone to adopt a stronger anti-statist position than green normative theorists, who tend to be more preoccupied with exploring how states and the state system might become more responsive to ecological problems. Whereas green political economists single out the competitive dynamics of global capitalism as the key driver of environmental destruction, green normative theorists argue that states represent the pre-eminent institution with the requisite steering capacity and legitimacy to impose ecological constraints on capitalism (Barry and Eckersley 2005). Democratizing states and the state system is thus a necessary step towards reflexive modernization, which is expected to yield a more ecologically constrained global capitalism.

Second, although most green IR theorists share the cosmopolitan norm that all those affected by decisions or risks should have some sort of say in making them (irrespective of nationality or locality), there remains a significant body of green communitarian theory (which includes bioregionalism, ecoanarchism, and ecofeminism) that emphasizes the virtues of place-based identity and ecologically sustainable local communities. For these theorists, extending an individual's sense of belonging to particular social and ecological communities, and cultivating a place-based identity (which includes an attachment to local flora, fauna, and landscapes), provides a far more potent political motivation to protect non-human species and victims of environmental injustice than does the more abstract idea of global citizenship or cosmopolitan democracy.

A further area of disagreement concerns the wisdom of conceptualizing ecological problems as security problems. Advocates of ecological security maintain that environmental problems—pre-eminent among which is global warming—should be considered a growing source of insecurity. Some environmental security scholars (who do not necessarily identify as green IR scholars) also argue that growing natural resource scarcity (particularly water), environmental degradation, and increasing numbers of 'ecological refugees' are likely to generate increasing conflict and violence both with and between states, and that states should include an ecological dimension in their national security strategies.

However, more sceptical green IR theorists have argued that framing ecological problems as a security issue in order to raise their status to a matter of 'high politics' could backfire. Instead of leading to a broader and more enlightened security agenda that will also 'green' the military, they suggest that the new discourse of ecological security may end up merely playing on traditional security concerns and possibly facilitating militarized solutions to the sustainability challenge. According to the sceptics, led by Daniel Deudney (1990), environmental threats and military threats are of a different order, and they should therefore be addressed differently. Conceptualizing ecological problems as security problems also betrays the core green values of non-violence and anti-militarism and deflects attention away from the important task of promoting ecologically sustainable development. Sceptics have also pointed to the dangers of linking environmental deterioration and scarcity with conflict, arguing that it represents a crude form of environmental determinism (e.g. Barnett 2001). Other green IR theorists have emphasized the potential for shared ecological problems to present peace-making opportunities by providing a basis for conducting collaborative research, stimulating dialogue, building trust, and transcending differences by working towards common environmental goals and strategies (Conca and Dabelko 2003).

However, Deudney's critique is directed against those who argue for the development of national environmental security strategies. It does not address green arguments for a more comprehensive conceptualization of ecological security that seeks to widen the moral referent or unit of analysis of security as well as extend traditional understandings of the sources of insecurity, responses to insecurity, and the conditions for long-term security. Proponents of this more expansive understanding argue that it has the potential to undermine traditional ideas of state territorial defence (along with the logic of the zero-sum game presumed by realists) and promote international cooperation towards long-term sustainability. This broader conceptualization also directs attention to value-complexity in security policy-making, enables a more critical scrutiny of the role of the military as a source of insecurity, and seeks a diversion of military spending to sustainability spending.

The internal debate over environmental security is indicative of green IR theory's strong anti-militarist posture. This may partly explain why green IR theory has yet to develop a considered or clear ethical position on a range of security-related debates, such as the appropriate relationship between order and justice in world politics or the appropriate use of force for humanitarian intervention or environmental protection (cf. Eckersley 2007). Nonetheless, green IR theory has undergone significant development in the last decade to the point where it is recognized as a significant new stream of IR theory. The new green discourses of environmental justice, sustainable development, reflexive modernization, and ecological security have not only influenced national and international policy debates. Taken together, they have also recast the roles of states, economic actors, and citizens as environmental stewards rather than territorial overlords, with asymmetrical international obligations based on differing capacities and levels of environmental responsibility. This recasting has important implications for the evolution of state sovereignty. If it is accepted that sovereignty is a derivative concept, the practical meaning of which changes over time in response to changes in the constitutive discourses of sovereignty, then to the extent that some of these discourses (on development, justice, and security) take on a greener hue, it is possible to point to 'the greening of sovereignty'. Moreover, to the extent that states—and citizens within states—become increasingly accountable to communities and environments beyond their own borders, then they may be characterized as transnational states and citizens rather than merely nation states or national citizens. Of course, the society of states is a long way short of this ideal. However, green IR theorists have brought this ideal into view and made it thinkable.

 Questions

1. What are the core criticisms made by the first wave of green political theory against liberal and socialist theories? Is green political theory modernist or postmodernist?

2. What is the cause of the ecological blindness of traditional IR theories?

3. In what ways has the second wave of green political theory become more transnational?

4. Why are green IR theorists critical of dominant discourses of sustainable development and ecological modernization? What alternatives do they propose?

5. What normative and analytical criticisms have green IR theorists levelled against mainstream rationalist approaches (neorealism and neoliberalism)?

6. What does green IR theory have in common with critical theory and constructivism? How does it differ from them?

7. How would you describe the different preoccupations of green normative IR theory and green IPE? What unites these two strands of green IR theory?

8. In what ways does the green analysis of the climate change negotiations differ from mainstream approaches?

9. Why are green IR theorists internally divided over the wisdom of conceptualizing ecological problems in the language of security?

10. What do you consider to be the major contribution of green IR theory to IR theory in general?

11. Are environmental problems a security threat?

12. What consequences do green theory and ecological concerns have for the concept of sovereignty and the role of the state?

Further reading

Bryant, R. and Bailey, S. (1997), *Third World Political Ecology* **(London: Routledge).**
Provides a systematic examination of green political economy questions from a Third World perspective.

Clapp, J. and Dauvergne, P. (2011), *Paths to a Green World: The Political Economy of the Global Environment* **(Cambridge, MA: MIT Press).**
Provides an excellent theoretical and practical introduction to the relationship between globalization and environmental degradation.

Dauvergne, P. (2008), *The Shadows of Consumption: Consequences for the Global Environment* **(Cambridge, MA: MIT Press).**
Maps the hidden social and ecological costs of globalization and growing consumption.

Eckersley, R. (2004), *The Green State: Rethinking Democracy and Sovereignty* **(Cambridge, MA: MIT Press).**
Develops a theory of the green state (and state system) from a critical constructivist perspective.

Gale, F. P. and M'Gonigle, R. M. (2000) (eds.), *Nature, Production, Power: Towards an Ecological Political Economy* **(Cheltenham: Edward Elgar).**
An edited collection providing a good illustration of recent innovative research in green political economy.

Käkönen, J. (1994) (ed.), *Green Security or Militarised Environment* **(Aldershot: Dartmouth).**
An edited collection providing a good overview of the ecological security debate.

LaFerrière, E. and Stoett, P. J. (1999), *International Relations Theory and Ecological Thought: Towards a Synthesis* **(London: Routledge).**
The first book to explore the intersection of IR theory and green political thought.

LaFerrière, E. and Stoett, P. J. (2006), *International Ecopolitical Theory: Critical Approaches* **(Vancouver: UBC Press).**
Provides a collection of essays that showcase critical theoretical approaches to global environmental politics that challenge managerial and economistic approaches to sustainable development.

Nixon, R. (2011), *Slow Violence and the Environmentalism of the Poor* **(Cambridge, MA.: Harvard University Press).**
Highlights the lack of political attention given to the 'attritional lethality' or 'slow violence' inflicted on vulnerable communities and ecosystems in the Global South through the failure to curb environmental problems such as deforestation, climate change, oil spills, and toxic drift.

Okereke, C. (2008) *Global Justice and Neoliberal Environmental Governance* **(London: Routledge).**
Argues that, although moral norms shape environmental negotiations more than regime theorists have acknowledged, neoliberal understandings of justice (based on mutual advantage, or upholding property rights) have dominated international environmental agreements more than environmental alternatives.

O'Neil, K. (2009), *The Environment and International Relations* (Cambridge: Cambridge University Press).
Highlights the strengths and limitations of traditional IR in understanding global environmental governance.

Paehlke, R. C. (2003), *Democracy's Dilemma: Environment, Social Equity and the Global Economy* (Cambridge, MA: MIT Press).
Examines the democratic challenge of achieving sustainability while improving social equity.

Paterson, M. (2000), *Understanding Global Environmental Politics: Domination, Accumulation, Resistance* (London: Palgrave).
Provides an excellent illustration of a green neo-Gramscian approach to understanding global environmental change.

Princen, T., Maniates, M., and Conca, K. (2002) (eds.), *Confronting Consumption* (Cambridge, MA: MIT Press).
Provides a path-breaking examination of the problem of over-consumption.

Schlosberg, D. (2007), *Defining Environmental Justice: Theories, Movements, and Nature* (Oxford: Oxford University Press).
Provides a comprehensive analysis of the theory and practice of environmental justice that includes distributive justice, recognition, participation, and capabilities.

Timmons Roberts, J. and Parks, B. C. (2007), *A Climate of Injustice: Global Inequality, North–South Politics, and Climate Policy* (Cambridge, MA: MIT Press).
Highlights how disagreement between rich and poor countries over how to distribute the burden of climate mitigation hampers international cooperation; they also provide new measures of climate inequality.

Important websites

Institute for Environmental Security. An international non-profit non-governmental organization established in 2002 in The Hague to increase political attention to environmental security as a means to help safeguard essential conditions for peace and sustainable development. **www.envirosecurity.org**

Global Commons Institute. An independent London-based institute, directed by Aubrey Meyer, devoted to 'shrinking and sharing' future global greenhouse gas emissions. **www.gci.org.uk**

Third World Network. An independent non-profit international network of organizations and individuals involved in issues relating to development, the Third World, and North–South issues, with a comprehensive environment link. **www.twnside.org.sg**

Wuppertal Institute. An independent research institute that conducts research on the social and ecological effects of globalization and develops strategies for sustainable globalization. **http://www.wupperinst.org/globalisation/**

Notes

1. In common with other chapters in the book, I am using neoliberalism as a shorthand for neoliberal institutionalism, and using neorealism as being synonymous with what John Mearsheimer (in Chapter 4) calls structural realism.

2. This period also saw the formation of the world's first proto-green parties in Australasia and Europe in direct response to the publication of *A Blueprint for Survival* (1972).

3. While the description 'green political theory' is widely used in Europe and Australasia, in North America it is more typically referred to as 'environmental political theory'.

4. For example, Mathew Paterson (2000) has provided an innovative green neoGramscian study that tracks the power of, and ecological shadow cast by, the global automobile industry, which includes a critique of 'car culture'.

 Visit the Online Resource Centre that accompanies this book for lots of interesting additional material. **www.oxfordtextbooks.co.uk/orc/dunne3e/**

15

International Relations Theory and Globalization

COLIN HAY

 Reader's Guide

This chapter seeks to establish what is at stake in the globalization debate(s) for contemporary International Relations (IR) theory. There is no field (or sub-field) of social and political analysis that has more invested in adjudicating claims as to the extent to which we have witnessed, are in the process of witnessing, or have yet to witness an epochal transition to globalization. Quite simply, the very term international relations is anachronistic if some variants of the globalization thesis are accurate. This chapter reviews both the existing debate on the extent and nature of globalization itself—What is it? Is it occurring? What are its consequences? How evenly distributed are they? What are its drivers?—and the stakes for a range of core theoretical perspectives in IR. It shows how the literature on globalization has developed over time, revealing how the nature of the debate has changed, and it illustrates this both theoretically and empirically by developing a case study of the impact of globalization on the development of the welfare state.

Introduction

It is difficult to conceive of a topic more controversial or that has given rise to a greater proliferation of literature in recent years than the nature, extent, and consequences of globalization. Nor is it easy to think of a field of scholarly inquiry that has more invested in such controversies and that literature than International Relations (IR) theory. For, quite simply, whether the political landscape can meaningfully be said to comprise national units that one might credibly describe as engaged in inter-national relations (literally, 'relations *between* nations') is at issue. If globalization, as for many, characterizes the contemporary period and if, as again for many, the extent of globalization is the degree to which the national recedes in significance, then globalization may already have ushered in an age of *post-*international relations (Rosenau 1990; Youngs 1999).

That, of course, is an immensely controversial claim. It is, moreover, not one that I will defend in this chapter. And, as we shall see, it is one that is challenged both by those who question the degree to which the contemporary landscape of world politics has, indeed, been globalized and by those who argue that it has, but who see globalization and international relations as far less mutually exclusive. As this perhaps already serves to indicate, the stakes of 'the globalization debate', for IR theory in particular, could scarcely be higher. Yet, as it also serves to indicate, in entering this debate we embroil ourselves in both a semantic minefield—in which terms like globalization do not always mean quite what we might assume them to mean—and an area of considerable empirical dispute—in which it seems almost no evidential claim remains uncontested.

That provides some important context for what is to follow. My aim in this chapter is to guide the reader through this battle-ground of evidential claim and counter-claim, conceptualization and re-conceptualization, definition and redefinition. In so doing I hope to establish what is at stake for IR in the globalization debate and also to show how the debate itself has at times come to be distorted by the extraordinarily high stakes for the chosen theoretical perspectives of its principal protagonists. The chapter proceeds in four core sections. In the first of these I consider the extent to which globalization itself might be seen to pose a challenge to the defining assumptions of IR theory, calling into question the very identify of IR as a field of scholarly inquiry. In the second I seek to unpack the semantics of the globalization debate. I show how both the extent to which we can credibly describe contemporary trends in terms of globalization and the implications of so doing depend crucially on what globalization is taken to imply. Define globalization inclusively and whilst there is plenty of evidence of globalization, its identification is of no great consequence. Conversely, set the definitional threshold higher and the significance of identifying globalization trends or tendencies is all the greater, but the evidence to substantiate such a description is all the more difficult to find. Having dealt with the semantics of globalization in the second section, we turn to the empirics of globalization in the third. This section deals separately with the extent and character of the process of economic globalization on the one hand, and its implications on the other. Here I advance a sceptical position showing that, with respect to economic globalization at least, it is only if we adopt the least exacting of definitional standards that the term globalization is easily reconciled with the available empirical evidence. Indeed, the more we examine the empirical evidence, the more globalization appears a less self-evident empirical fact and the less it seems to constrain domestic policy-making autonomy. This latter point is illustrated in the final section in which a case study is developed on the future of the **welfare state** in the advanced liberal democracies in an era of globalization.

What's at stake in the globalization debate?

It may seem somewhat odd to seek to establish what is at stake for IR theory in the globalization debate before considering what the term globalization might be taken to imply. The reasons for this are, however, simply stated. They are principally two-fold. First, as we shall see, there is no commonly accepted conception, far less definition, of globalization in the existing literature. Indeed, as much as anything, the debate about globalization is a debate about what we understand by the term. As a consequence we cannot turn to the definition of globalization to provide a simple point of access to the debate, for the question of definition is a far from innocent one theoretically. As this perhaps already suggests, we need to understand the nature of the debate before we can see what is at stake in defining globalization. Second, the debate about globalization within IR theory is, in fact, merely the latest incarnation of a longer running dispute between **state-centric** and non-state-centric theorists. It is important, then, that we understand the character of that evolving debate before we consider the language of globalization within which it is conducted today.

Perhaps more so than for any other field (or sub-field) of social and political analysis, IR theory's globalization debate is a negative rather than a positive one. That this is so is not difficult to explain. For arguably it is realism and neo- or structural realism (see **Chapters 3** and **4**), for so long the dominant perspectives in IR theory and the perspectives around which contemporary IR theory has arguably been built, that has most invested in the globalization debate—and most to lose. It is perhaps unremarkable, given this, that it is realists and neorealists who have tended to be most persistently dismissive of globalization's extent, its qualitative novelty and its system redefining qualities—indeed, invariably all three. And it is not difficult to see why realists might have something of a natural disposition to scepticism when it comes to globalization. For, as was described in rather greater detail in **Chapter 4**, the neorealist worldview is one that sees international politics through the eyes of the self-interested, self-contained, and above all sovereign state-as-actor. Realism, in other words, is predicated on a state-centric ontology. It is this state, according to realists, that is the dominant and, in many accounts, the only significant actor on the international stage. Yet according to the globalization thesis the days of the nation state are over.

As this suggests, IR theory's globalization debate is, in effect, an ontological dispute—between state-centrism and non-state centrism. As a consequence much—arguably too much—of its content is about the continuing relevance or the contemporary irrelevance (depending on one's worldview) of realism and neorealism as theoretical perspectives. But this is not to suggest that other theoretical perspectives—notably feminism (**Chapter 11**), constructivism (**Chapter 10**), critical theory (**Chapter 9**), poststucturalism (**Chapter 12**), and green theory (**Chapter 14**)—do not have a stake in the globalization debate or, indeed, much to contribute to our understanding of globalization itself. The key point, however, is that none of these alternative perspectives is predicated on ontological assumptions about the centrality or non-centrality of the state in international relations. As such they have rather less invested in the globalization debate than neorealism, neoliberalism, and indeed, **cosmopolitanism**. Each offers an analytical/theoretical perspective which can be brought to bear on the world system independently of its degree of globalization; each has relevance and critical purchase in both a state-centric and a non-state-centric world alike; and each perspective contains, amongst its advocates, globalists and sceptics.

The stakes are, by contrast, significantly higher for neorealists, neoliberals, and cosmopolitans. For each the degree of globalization is an index of the degree of relevance/irrelevance of their theoretical perspective. For both neoliberals and cosmopolitans globalization challenges practically all of realism's most cherished analytical assumptions. Their critique of realism's continued relevance can be summarized in a series of core claims.

1. The **sovereignty** and policy-making capacity of the nation state, on which realism is predicated, are both compromised to a very significant extent by the proliferation of cross-border flows beyond the purview and control of the state.

2. Globalization is associated with (or arises out of) a proliferation of issues that are global in scope and scale (such as climate change and the threat of global pandemics); these, arguably, nation states never had the capacity to deal with.

3. In response to such challenges, and whether at the behest of nation states or not, a range of genuinely trans-national institutions of global governance have developed which have changed fundamentally the character of world politics—taking us, as it were, beyond the era of the nation state.

4. This new multi-layered and multi-level political landscape is populated by a rather more disparate range of potentially consequential actors and that whilst this may include some (though by no means all) nation states, the nation state is no longer the principal, far less the sole significant, actor in world politics.

5. The emergent trans-national arena of political deliberation associated with globalization has served to increase the relative salience of matters of 'low politics' whilst relegating those of 'high politics' with which realism was principally concerned.

6. The process of economic globalization, in increasing the mobility of capital and hence its capacity to flit from national jurisdiction to national jurisdiction, has enhanced the power of capital relative to the state, with the effect that whole areas of domestic policy-making have essentially been depoliticized.

7. Taken together, these globalization-engendered challenges to realist assumptions constitute not only a refutation of realism as a theoretical doctrine but the passing of the era of the nation state with which it was inextricably linked.

The above discussion pits realism and neorealism squarely against globalization and the proponents of theories of globalization. And, indeed, for the most part that is precisely how the debate has developed, with realists/neorealists and their critics exchanging blows from either side of a rather deep theoretical chasm over the extent and implications of globalization. Yet this is by no means unproblematic as we shall see, and it has led to a fair amount of confusion and conflation that has certainly not helped to sharpen our analytical purchase on either the empirical or the theoretical issues involved here.

Let me explain. The point is that there has been something of a tendency in IR theory to reduce the debate about globalization to a debate about the relevance of the realist/neoreal-ist worldview (or ontology). That is unfortunate, for it has given rise to a further tendency to conflate a series of empirical, analytical, and theoretical claims that might usefully be sepa-rated and assessed independently of one another. In effect a series of empirical issues about the extent of globalization and a series of analytical questions about the implications of glo-balization for the nature of the world system have been used to provide a theoretical test of realism's relevance and the validity of the ontological assumptions (about the nature of the state and its centrality) on which it is predicated. This has resulted in an at times confusing debate which does justice neither to the analytical strengths and weaknesses of realism/neo-realism nor to the complex empirical issues involved in adjudicating the extent of globaliza-tion and its implications for the character of world politics. Realists, it seems, feel almost duty bound to deny the significance of globalization, just as their critics feel obliged to embrace it, seizing upon theories of globalization as if they provided an empirical refutation of realism. In fact, as we shall see, neither reaction respects the complexity and indeterminacy of the world system today. Realism/neorealism, (neo)liberal intergovernmentalism, and cosmopolitanism are perhaps best seen as lenses through which contemporary trends might be interpreted. Each is selective in what it considers and what it excludes from view. But the point is that world politics today is sufficiently multi-layered and multi-faceted for each to bring interesting and important issues into focus. It is wrong, then, to think that the world system can deliver a knock-down blow to the analytical assumptions on which any of these contending theories is predicated. As Richard Ned Lebow points out in his introduction to **Chapter 3** on classical realism, 'neorealism is unfalsifiable, and its rise and fall has little to do with conceptual and empirical advances'. Nor, it might be added, has it much more to do with the changing character of the world system. Moreover, even were we to conclude that the empirical evidence of globalization's extent and impact was sufficient to invalidate the realist paradigm, we would be quite wrong to infer from this that realism was never valid theoretically, nor that any of its contemporary challengers are thereby vindicated. By the same token, were we to conclude that realist assumptions had by no means been rendered anachronistic by the process of globalization to date, we would be just as wrong to infer from this that realism is the most appropriate way to analyse such trends. Empirical evidence cannot adjudicate ontological differences and theoretical choices of this kind, though it is all too often assumed that it can (see also Hay 2002).

If much of IR theory's globalization debate has pitted realist/neorealist 'sceptics' against neoliberal/cosmopolitan 'globalists' in the manner described here, then it is important to note that there are exceptions. Particularly interesting in this respect is an extremely respectful and temperate exchange between Barry Buzan (defending a particular conception of neorealism) and David Held (the key proponent of cosmopolitanism) published in the *Review of International Studies* (Buzan, Held, and McGrew 1998). Buzan's position is especially interesting here and is summarized in Table 15.1.

What is particularly interesting about this is that Buzan accepts almost all of the points seen by globalists as posing fundamental challenges for realism. He concedes that trans-national flows compromise the ease with which one might speak of nation states as sovereign; he concedes the growing salience of trans-national processes of governance whilst emphasizing the role of states in the promotion of such developments; he concedes the importance—indeed, the growing importance—of non-state actors on the international stage; and he concedes the higher salience of low politics relative to high politics, especially in those more interdependent parts of the world system. Moreover, though more implicit than explicit, his remarks would also seem compatible with the idea that world politics today is characterized by a proliferation of issues with which the nation state never had the capacity to deal effectively and that the constraints imposed by economic globalization have greatly diminished the capacity for domestic policy-making autonomy. Yet, despite all this, he manages to defend an (albeit qualified) form of realism. This he does, not by challenging the globalization thesis itself, but effectively by departmentalizing it. In so doing he makes four core claims:

1. In essence, globalization is an economic phenomenon whose implications as such are largely confined to certain (low political) domains—domains that realism was never especially concerned with.

2. Although the salience of such domains has undoubtedly increased, a significant proportion of international politics retains its realist character.

Table 15.1 Buzan's qualified defence of realism in a context of globalization

In his response to David Held's development of a cosmopolitan view of globalization, Buzan defends the continued relevance of the realist worldview and analytical perspective in a context characterized by certain globalizing tendencies. In so doing he concedes a number of points to the globalists.

1. The position Buzan seeks to defend 'the state is . . . the key political unit in the international system' (387); 'as long as the international system is divided into states the relations between states will have the characteristic of being about power politics' (388).

2. The concessions to the globalists 'in relation to the emergence of a world economy, and to some extent the development of a world society, and even in terms of transportation and communication systems, it is clearly naïve now to think of a world made up of sovereign states which "contain" everything' (390); 'where states have become very open and interdependent, then some of the realist theorising about the balance of power (and all that) is clearly less relevant . . . thinking about states in terms of traditional power politics is unhelpful' (390); 'states . . . get together sometimes with other actors, sometimes just with other states, to discuss issues of joint concern and sometimes they can hammer out a set of policies, a set of rules of the game, which enable them to coordinate their behaviour' (392).

3. The qualification of the concessions 'there are plenty of parts of the world in which the realist rules of the game still apply . . . the world is really divided into two or three spheres in which the rules of the game are quite different because the level of globalisation is very differently distributed' (390); 'in most areas of world politics . . . states are still the principal authorities' (391); 'globalisation is primarily an economic phenomenon. It is also in part a logistical phenomenon to do with transportation and communication and the ability to move goods, peoples, ideas, etc. around the world much faster and much more easily than before' (394); 'it is not clear what the alternative political structure to the state is, or how indeed we would make the transition from the current order to another' (394).

Note: All references are from Buzan, Held, and McGrew (1998).

3. Often independently of the process of economic globalization, states have increasingly, but only under certain highly specific conditions, effectively pooled their sovereignty in developing mechanisms of trans-national governance (whether regional or global) that reflect their mutual self-interest.

4. Both economic globalization and the involvement of states in such mechanisms of trans-national governance are both extremely unevenly distributed, with the effect that the lion's share of the content of international politics remains essentially statist and hence realist in character in spite of globalization.

This is a neat and self-contained position which, whilst ceding certain terrain to cosmopolitans like Held (2002, 2003) and neoliberals like Joseph Nye and Robert O. Keohane (see, for instance, Keohane and Nye 1977; Nye and Donahue 2000), suggests the core contribution that realism can make to IR theory even in a context of presumed globalization. Moreover, it indicates the potentially highly fruitful character of the interparadigm debate that globalization is capable of generating within IR theory—at least, once the attempt to use globalization to adjudicate between paradigms is put to one side. Yet there is still one problem with the position Buzan seeks to defend. For, however credible it may seem, and however creditable his concessions to the globalists are, they rest on a series of assumptions about economic globalization in particular that are of an empirical kind—assumptions which are simply not tested empirically. Ironically, Buzan may go too far in his concessions to the globalists. For, as we shall see in the third section of this chapter, for many so-called 'sceptics' evidence of the kind of economic globalization he seems to presume here is rather less forthcoming than one might think. Yet before considering such evidence directly, and having established the high stakes for IR theory of the globalization debate, it is first important that we establish quite what we mean by the term globalization anyway. It is to this potential conceptual minefield that we now turn.

The semantics of globalization

Thus far we have assumed that all protagonists in the globalization debate know exactly what they are talking about when they refer to the term 'globalization'. Moreover, we have assumed that, basically, they are all talking about the same thing. As will become clear, this is dangerously presumptuous on both counts. To be fair to them, they may in fact know precisely what they are referring to when they refer to the term 'globalization', but if that is the case they are seemingly exceedingly reluctant to share that with the reader. As a consequence protagonists in the same globalization debate repeatedly talk past one another, simply because they are talking about different things. This is not helped by the great many things that have been referred to in terms of globalization. As David Held and his co-authors suggest, globalization is 'the cliché of our times: the big idea which encompasses everything from global financial markets to the Internet but which delivers little substantive insight into the contemporary human condition' (Held et al. 1999: 1). And, recall, Held is an unapologetic if sophisticated globalist who in fact goes on to provide a rather exacting and extremely useful definition of globalization to which we will return in due course.

The simple point is that globalization has come to mean a variety of rather different things to a range of different authors. Moreover, given the vast array of processes and practices to which it is often (legitimately) used to refer even by the same author, it is perhaps hardly surprising that it has come so often to prove a source of confusion rather than clarity.

This can be seen even in the relatively brief exchange between Barry Buzan and David Held discussed above. For in the space of a few pages a great variety of rather different things are referred to in terms of globalization. Amongst these might be identified those listed in Table 15.2.

There is, of course, nothing wrong with referring to any of these processes in terms of globalization. Yet it is actually very difficult to think of some common property of factor that they all share by virtue of which we might label them instances of the same thing (globalization). Moreover, with respect to each and every item in the list there are choices involved; choices which need to be defended if the term globalization is not to obscure more than it reveals.

Take the first, for instance. Globalization is commonly associated with a variety of cross-border flows—typically flows of goods, investment, and information, but also holiday-makers, migrant workers, asylum seekers, environmental pollutants, infectious agents, and so forth. But the existence of such flows, and in some cases even the magnitude of such flows, is by no means unprecedented historically. So what is it precisely about the magnitude or

Table 15.2 Potential indices of globalization

1. Cross-border flows of goods, investment and information.

2. Trans-national processes of political deliberation and decision-making.

3. Inter-dependence between states.

4. The development of a world system whose dynamic and developmental trajectory is not reducible to the simple product of the units (states) which comprise it.

5. The proliferation of problems to which global solutions are required.

6. The development of institutions charged with responsibility for fashioning genuinely global public policy.

scope of such flows that might lead us to identify the contemporary period as one character-ized by globalization where that which preceded it was not? Oddly, this is a question which is very rarely posed. Each of these flows may be more or less global in character—and, pre-sumably, we would want to know that such flows were really quite global in character before we would be happy referring to them as instances of globalization. But quite how global do they have to be? And what does global mean here anyway?

Consider the flow of infectious agents. These are, of course, not exactly diligent observ-ers of national borders and so the cross-border transmission of infection is clearly as old as the existence of nominal borders that infectious agents might cross. Yet at what point might we legitimately start talking about the possibility of their globalization? When a farmer in Alsace sneezes and their neighbour in Germany catches a cold, is this globaliza-tion? When the Crusaders took their Western European viruses and bacteria to the Holy Lands was this an early form of globalization? When the crew of Christopher Columbus passed their pathogens to the people of North America, was this globalization? Or is glo-balization a term we should reserve to describe the (contemporary) era of mass public transportation across continents and the prospect of the proliferation of global pandemics that this threatens?

There are, of course, no 'correct' answers to questions like these; but there are choices which can be defended—and which *should* be defended if the concept of globalization is to increase our analytical purchase on such matters. In particular we need to ask ourselves whether all cross-border flows, for instance, are by definition instances of globalization, or whether such flows need to be trans-regional, trans-continental, or, indeed, genuinely glo-bal before they count as evidence of globalization. Similarly, we need to ask ourselves whether the question of globalization merely relates to the geographical character (the 'extensivity' in Held et al.'s (1999) useful terms) of such flows, or whether it also relates to their prevalence (or 'intensivity'). In other words, should the identification of processes of globalization just be about identifying *some* flows that are global in their geographical character or should it also be about identifying an increasing propensity for flows to be of that kind?

The point is that whether globalization is happening or not depends on what globaliza-tion is taken to imply—and there are fairly substantial differences amongst IR theorists on this point. Unremarkably, sceptics tend to adopt more exacting definitional standards than their globalist counterparts, taking some delight in pointing to the disparity between the real evidence (such as it is) and the rigours of such an exacting definitional standard. Globalists by contrast set for themselves a rather less discriminating definitional hurdle, with the effect that they interpret the very same evidence that often leads sceptics to challenge the globalization thesis as seemingly unambiguous evidence *for* the thesis. What makes this all the more confusing is something that I have already referred to—the seeming reluctance of authors on either side of the exchange to define clearly and concisely their terminology.

Yet though frustrating, this is hardly surprising. For, as in Table 15.2, a great variety of rather different things are referred to, often by the same author, in terms of globalization—and, as already noted, it is often extremely difficult to put one's finger on a single factor in respect of which each might be labelled an instance of globalization. As this suggests, we might well excuse the absence of a simple definition of globalization on the grounds that the phenomena to which it refers are multi-faceted and complex. Yet our generosity cannot extend to absolving IR theorists of their responsibility to be clear about how and why they are using the term. If globalization is multi-dimensional, then authors who deploy the term need to be able to specify the dimensions of globalization to which they are referring.

Pointing to potential *dimensions* of globalization may help us out here. No less helpful is one further factor—that like so many contested terms in the social sciences, globalization is perhaps better understood in negative rather than positive terms. In other words, we can learn quite a lot about what globalization *is*, by considering what it is not. In fact a review of the literature on globalization rapidly reveals a number of globalization's 'others'—terms presented alongside globalization but starkly counterposed to it. Amongst such oppositional pairings the following are perhaps the most obvious:

1. National vs. global. Referring to the level at which the centre of gravity of the world system might be seen to lie and the primary character of the cultures, economies, and polities within that system.
2. International vs. global. Referring to the character of supra-national decision-making processes and, specifically, to the extent to which these might be seen as trans- rather than merely inter-national in form.
3. Regionalization vs. globalization. Referring to the precise geographical scope and character of any particular process of integration.
4. Protectionism/isolationism vs. globalization/internationalism. Referring to the internal or external orientation of domestic level policy-making.

This is immediately instructive, revealing a range of rather different senses of globalization or, better perhaps, a range of *dimensions* of the term. Each is worthy of a brief commentary.

In the first of these conceptual pairings, globalization is counterposed and contrasted to the nation and the state (indeed, to the nation state). This distinction and contrast clearly lies at the heart of IR theory's globalization debate. Sceptics, typically realists and neorealists, continue to privilege the national level, conceptualizing world politics in terms of the interaction of distinct and nationally embedded political cultures. Globalists, by contrast, point to the transcendence of the national and its dissolution in a proliferation of cross-border flows. This, they suggest, generates a new global arena of political struggle and contestation that is literally, *supra*-national—above the level of the national.

The second conceptual opposition follows almost logically from the first. Yet the emphasis here is subtly different, the focus falling less on the constituent units of the world system than on the character of supra-national decision-making that follows. Here the global is counterposed to the international, globalization to internationalization. This opposition is equally central to the globalization debate in contemporary IR theory. Realist and neorealist sceptics continue to view world politics in state-centric and inter-national terms, denying in so doing the existence of a distinct realm of trans-national political deliberation that is not a simple aggregation of state-level preferences. By contrast, globalists, typically neoliberals and cosmopolitans, point to the increasing salience of trans-national institutions of govern-ance and to the existence of a distinct political process and dynamic at this level that is not reducible to the preferences of states.

The third conceptual opposition is rather different and takes us into issues that we have yet to discuss in any detail. It refers less to the character of the politics of the world system itself, than to how we might most accurately describe those cross-border flows we witness. In short, it takes us from largely conceptual/ontological issues to largely empirical matters. Here, as we shall see in more detail in the next section, trade economists and a range of criti-cal international political economists challenge the extent to which the term globalization captures well contemporary trends in economic integration. They suggest that it is important that we differentiate very clearly between regionalization and globalization and that, if we do so, we see rather clearer evidence of the former than the latter. This dispute is more empirical than theoretical and it is one to which we return in the next section.

Finally, globalization is also counterposed to protectionism and isolationism in the rather more specialist literature characterizing the orientations of domestic policy-makers and the choices they make. Policy-makers may embrace globalization by, for instance, promoting a global regime of free trade and free capital mobility both domestically and on an interna-tional stage; or they may resist globalization, shoring up their national defences against trade penetration and other trans-border economic flows through a series of protective tariffs and other restrictions.

As this discussion hopefully serves to indicate, globalization is indeed a multi-dimensional concept in that there are a variety of rather different senses of the term to which authors appeal, often in the same breath. Yet whilst this might seem to lessen the importance somewhat of specifying precisely a definition of globalization, it does not diminish the significance of the question 'How global does it have to be to count as evidence of globali-zation?'—indeed, it merely projects this question into a number of different dimensions. But sadly this is a question that is very rarely posed and on which it is difficult to find any consensus. Yet, if it is obviously asking too much of the existing literature to expect it to provide an answer to this question, we can at least be clear about how the term globaliza-tion will be employed in what follows. The definition I prefer is a relatively specific and exacting one; it is one that can be operationalized empirically (as we shall see) and it is one that differentiates very clearly between processes of regionalization and processes of globalization. All of these requirements are satisfied by the definition advanced by David Held and his colleagues. For them, 'globalization is a process (or set of processes) that embodies a transformation in the spatial organisation of social relations and transactions, generating trans-continental or inter-regional flows and networks of activity, interaction and power' (1999: 16).

The empirics of globalization: its extent and consequences

What counts as evidence of globalization is, as I have suggested, a semantic issue. Yet whether or not globalization is occurring and what, if any, consequences it has remain, in essence, empirical matters. It is appropriate, then, that having discussed the semantics of globalization in the previous section we now turn, albeit more briefly, to the empirics of globalization.

There is a vast and at times quite technical literature here which we cannot hope to survey in any depth in the space of a few pages (for far more detailed reviews see Hay 2005, 2009). And, what is more, it is a literature in which almost every claim is a contested one—at least in the sense that almost every empirical claim made is either a refutation or an attempted refutation of a claim made somewhere else in the literature. There is, nonetheless, a distinct pattern to the empirical evidence and to the debate that it has generated. In particular, as the debate has become more and more empirical in character—as, in effect, we have acquired greater and greater knowledge of the extent and consequences of globalization—so the balance of opinion has become more and more sceptical of the often hyperbolic character of the early globalist literature. Globalization, it seems, is less self-evidently a fact, rather more unevenly developed and potentially rather less consequential for domestic policy-making autonomy than was once assumed. This is certainly not to suggest that the world has not changed; but it is to suggest that the period of restructuring of the international system since the 1960s that we invariably label globalization is rather less unprecedented historically, rather less well described in terms of globalization, and rather less corrosive of state autonomy than many had tended to assume.

What follows, then, is an unmistakably sceptical view of globalization—yet one which is, as I hope to show, well substantiated empirically. I suggest that there is a significant and, indeed, a growing disparity between the simple presumption of globalization in much of the existing literature and the nature and trajectory of developments in the world system. The literature on which I draw in seeking to defend that claim is primarily economic in focus and the contents of this section reflect that focus. The reasons for this privileging of the economic in the existing literature and in this section are relatively simple. They are principally four-fold. First, it is far more difficult to gauge empirically the extent of political globalization than the extent of economic globalization. Economic flows, unlike their political equivalents, are recorded and quantified and their significance relatively easy to gauge. Political flows, by contrast, can really only be assessed qualitatively. Second, if we are interested in the extent to which the policy-making autonomy and capacity of the state has been eroded then it is vital that we consider the extent and consequences of economic globalization—since this is invariably seen as the most significant constraint on such autonomy. Third, many accounts depict globalization as, if not a purely economic phenomenon, then at least a principally economic phenomenon. It is, then, more plausible to extrapolate from the economic sphere than it is to extrapolate from any other. Fourth, and relatedly, if it can be shown that claims about economic globalization are exaggerated considerable damage is done to the globalization thesis since it is the economic sphere which is invariably presented as the most globalized of all social realms.

The empirical evidence assembled in the recent literature deals really with two different, if closely related issues—the extent and geographical character of the process of economic globalization (if we can call it that) on the one hand, and the consequences of economic

Table 15.3 The empirical case against the globalization thesis

The extent of globalization	The consequences of globalization
1. The integration of the world economy since the 1960s has yet to reach unprecedented levels, returning the international system to levels of economic integration last seen in the period between 1870 and 1914.	1. In contrast to the expectations of globalists, the relationship between public spending and globalization (economic openness) continues to be positive rather than negative; that positive correlation has, if anything, strengthened since the 1960s and 1970s.
2. Globalization is a poor description of the current phase of international economic integration, which is more accurately characterized as one of regionalization and so-called 'triadization'.	2. In contrast to the expectations of globalists, there is no inverse relationship between levels of inward foreign investment and a variety of indices of public spending, taxation, and labour-market, environmental, and other standards.
3. The current phase of financial integration has yet to produce either the convergence in interest rates across the globe or the divergence in rates of domestic savings and domestic investment anticipated in a fully integrated global capital market.	3. Whilst the liberalization of financial markets has increased the potential impact of speculative attacks on currencies, capital market participants are far less prone to penalize high levels of public spending and market-regulating interventions by the state than is conventionally assumed.

globalization (or, as much of this literature would prefer, 'complex economic interdependence') for the policy-making autonomy of the state domestically on the other. The findings of this literature are summarized in Table 15.3.

The extent of globalization

As indicated in Table 15.3, the empirical case against the standard depiction of the process of economic globalization comes in three parts. Perhaps the best known aspect of the sceptics' case is their observation that current levels of global economic integration, though far greater than at any point during the postwar period, are by no means unprecedented historically. In fact, as they show, both for levels of trade and capital flows, the world economy today is more closely integrated than at any point since the Second World War, but it is in fact no more integrated in aggregate terms than it was in the latter part of the nineteenth century and the early years of the twentieth century (Bairoch 1996; Hirst and Thompson 1999; Lewis 1981).

Though this is perhaps the most widely discussed aspect of the sceptics' case, it is probably also the least significant—and it is also the most misunderstood. In the end this is little more than the statement of an empirical fact—or, insofar as it is contentious, an empirical claim. The sceptics are often misunderstood as suggesting that the world economy has simply not changed. That is, in fact, a considerable distortion of the argument they present. What they are suggesting is that the current and ongoing re-integration of the world economy still has some way to go before it is, in quantitative terms, unprecedented historically. This is certainly an important finding, but it is by no means a definitive refutation of the globalization thesis in itself. It suggests, in particular, that we should be somewhat cautious of those accounts which infer historically unprecedented degrees of constraint on domestic policy-making autonomy from the quantitative force of globalization alone. Yet, we cannot conclude from this that globalization is not an unprecedented constraint on policy-making autonomy. For, as authors like Hirst and Thompson (1999: 27ff.) freely concede, in qualitative if not quantitative terms, there are very significant differences between the contemporary period and the last time the world economy was so closely integrated.

The second pillar of the case against the globalization thesis is rather more significant, though as yet rather less widely acknowledged. Trade economists have, for decades, mapped in detail trends in the global distribution of trade, differentiating in so doing between processes of trade integration that are intra-regional and those that are inter-regional in character. In recent years the techniques used in this literature have been taken up by a number of international political economists to map trends in the geographical distribution of trade and foreign direct investment (Frankel 1997, 1998; Hay 2006; Hirst and Thompson 1999; Petrella 1996). What this literature shows is that the term globalization is both a poor description and an *increasingly* poor description of the current trajectory of patterns of international economic integration. Their findings can be summarized as follows:

1. In almost all regions within the world economy, the pace of intra-regional integration currently exceeds that of inter-regional integration and has done so for some time; this is true for both trade and foreign direct investment.

2. As a consequence, the most powerful dynamic in the world economy today is regionalization not globalization.

3. In addition to such regionalizing tendencies, there is evidence of some regions within the world economy becoming ever more closely integrated.

4. Such inter-regionalization processes are, however, very unevenly distributed.

5. Accordingly, for the world economy as a whole the most accurate description of such trends is not globalization, but **triadization**, where the triad comprises the North American, South-East Asian, and European regional economies.

Taken together, these are extremely important findings, suggesting that the contemporary characterization of the international economy in terms of globalization is not only inaccurate but increasingly so. When it is considered that a significant proportion of contemporary policy-making, at both the national and trans-national levels, is predicated on the assumption that economies must increasingly demonstrate themselves globally competitive, the potential policy relevance of such findings is revealed.

The final pillar in the case against the standard globalization thesis is the most technical. Again, however, it has a potentially significant bearing on policy-makers' responses to the world of globalization they invariably presume they inhabit. The stylized algebraic models of the world economy which now guide economic policy-making in almost all national capitals invariably assume the existence of a fully integrated world financial market. Indeed, in essence, their contribution to economic policy-making is to derive from such assumptions an optimal set of policy settings appropriate for an era of globalization.

Yet such models also make a series of predictions about the world economy that are, in principal, testable empirically (see, for instance, Bayoumi 1990, 1997; Feldstein and Horioka 1980; Watson 2001). The problem is that such predictions are not borne out by the available empirical evidence.

The technical details need not concern us here (though see Hay 2005 and Watson 2001 for a more detailed review). Suffice it to note that two predictions, in particular, have troubled economists. These are:

1. That in an ever more globally integrated financial market, interest rates should converge and that, in a perfectly integrated world, financial market interest rate differentials should be eliminated—the persistence of interest rate differentials providing a simple index of the lack of global financial market integration.

2. That in an ever more globally integrated financial market the correlation between domestic savings and investment should fall and that, in a perfectly integrated capital market, it should fall to zero—the persistence of savings–investment correlations being an equivalent index of the lack of financial market integration.

The problem is that there is evidence of neither, with interest rate differentials and domestic savings–investment correlations proving rather more resilient than economists anticipated they should. The most obvious conclusion to draw from these results is that financial markets are not as well integrated globally as we tend to assume. That is an important point in its own right. More important still, however, is the point that financial markets are not as well integrated globally as policy-makers using (now) standard economic models assume them to be.

Case study: from the welfare state to the competition state?

The section on the empirics of globalization suggests, very strongly, that the era of the nation state as an effective policy-making instrument is far from over. Indeed, it is almost certainly the case that the state today consumes a greater share of global GDP than at any previous point in its history. Yet it would be wrong to infer from evidence like that reviewed in that section that the nation state is entirely unconstrained by globalization and that globalization has played no part in its contemporary transformation. Here IR theorists have also had much to say. In particular, Philip G. Cerny, in a series of important interventions (1995, 1997, 2000), has pointed to the role of globalization in the transition that he identifies from the era of the welfare state to that of the competition state in the advanced liberal democracies. His argument is summarized in the Featured Article text box and is considered here in more detail by way of a case study.

The debate over the prospects of the welfare state in the era of globalization is crucial for IR theory for three principal reasons. First, as we have seen, IR theory's globalization debate pits realists and neorealists against globalists. And, as we have also seen, the former stress the continued sovereignty and policy-making autonomy of the nation state, whilst the latter see these as having both been profoundly compromised by globalization. The point is that there is no more direct test of the extent of the state's sovereignty and policy-making capacity than its ability to provide for the welfare of its citizens. As such, the question of the future of the welfare state and, in particular, the assessment of the thesis that the state's role as a guarantor of its citizens' welfare has been subordinated to that of promoting competitiveness, is a core concern for IR theory.

Second, this is not just a question of the state's sovereignty or of its capacity to provide for its citizens. It is also, crucially to IR theory, a question of the relative power and influence of state actors and non-state actors—most obviously, trans-national corporations. For, if Cerny is right to identify the emergence of a competition state which subordinates all other policy imperatives to that of promoting the competitiveness of the national economy in a global environment, then the state today has become little more than a relay for the interests of capital. And, to the extent that this is accepted, it is surely with those interests and not with those of the state that IR theorists should now be principally concerned. Again, the consequences for state-centred IR theory are potentially considerable, the stakes of the debate considerable indeed.

Finally, and as already noted, IR theorists, like Ian Clark (1999) and Philip G. Cerny, have contributed much to our understanding of the development of the state. Cerny's argument on the rise of the competition state in the context of globalization is particularly interesting. What follows is a summary What follows is a summary of Cerny's argument (in the Featured Article box) and a discussion of its implications in today's global context.

 Featured article

Philip G. Cerny, (1997), 'Paradoxes of the Competition State: The Dynamics of Political Globalisation', *Government and Opposition*, 49/4: 595–625

Cerny's seminal contribution starts, like many before it, from the premise that in an era of heightened economic integration (or globalization), competitiveness becomes ever more central to economic performance. As trade and investment flows increase, so national economies are increasingly pitted against one another in an ever more intense competitive struggle. Those economies which are either innately uncompetitive or whose states impose upon them burdensome regulatory restrictions and unnecessary levels of direct and indirect taxation will lose ground—unless, that is, they reform their practices imposing on each and every form of state intervention an exacting competitive audit. Any such audit, Cerny suggests, reveals the welfare state to be an indulgent luxury of a bygone era—normatively desirable in its own terms, certainly, but an unsustainable burden on competitiveness in an era of globalization that can now no longer be afforded.

The argument here is simple and, in all likelihood familiar. Faced with a choice between national jurisdictions, mobile investors seeking to maximize profits will choose lightly regulated environments characterized by low levels of corporate and personal taxation over densely regulated environments with high levels of corporate and personal taxation. All things being equal, they will relocate their productive activities from economies with burdensome welfare states to those more committed to the free play of market mechanisms. In so doing they will serve to summon the passing of the era of the welfare state in the advanced liberal democracies. In its place, Cerny suggests, a new form of the state—the 'competition state'—is developing. Where the welfare state's principal priority was the promotion of the welfare of its citizens through the insulation of 'key elements of economic life from market forces', the competition state's principal strategy is one of 'marketisation in order to make economic activities located within the national territory . . . more competitive in international and trans-national terms' (1997: 258, 259). The competition state, he goes on, is a minimal or residual state when compared to its welfare state predecessor. It promotes the flexibility and dynamism of the economy through a series of fine-grained (microeconomic) interventions (typically on the supply-side, typically designed to incentivize competitive practices). In so doing it resists the (Keynesian) tendency to manage demand within the economy as a whole. It places competitiveness above all other priorities of government, subordinating social and labour-market policies to the promotion of a flexible economy capable of adapting rapidly to the changing pressures imposed upon it by the global market-place. Finally, it promotes welfare only to the extent to which this contributes unambiguously to the flexibility, productivity, and, above all, competitiveness of the economy as a whole.

(continued)

Cerny's paradigmatic account of the competition state under the conditions of globalization is compelling and it certainly seems to describe extremely well the reform trajectory on which many advanced liberal democracies are currently embarked. Yet it is not easily reconciled with the evidence considered in the section on empiric globalization and, even if it describes well the development of the competition state, can it credibly explain its emergence? A number of points might here usefully be made.

First, Cerny in fact relies upon a rather simple conception of the determinants of competitiveness in an open or integrated world economy. It is, moreover, one that is arguably at increasing odds with the available empirical evidence. Cerny assumes that competitiveness is to be gauged solely (or certainly primarily) in terms of the cost for which a business or economy can supply a good to market. As a consequence, all forms of taxation and all regulatory restrictions are burdens on competitiveness since they increase the costs of production (or, at least, the costs incurred by the business in the process of production). Couched in such terms it is not at all difficult to see how and why the welfare state might be seen as a burden on competitiveness. But cost is not the sole, or arguably even the principal, determinant of consumer choice in a complex market place. The quality, performance and pedigree of the goods on offer are just as important, arguably more so. Moreover, by and large, economies characterized by the highest levels of social welfare expenditure tend to compete in markets which are less price-sensitive than quality-sensitive. As the Swedes would have it, consumers do not buy Volvos because they are cheap. The point is that if we concede that there is more to competitiveness in international markets than cost minimization, then the competitive audit of the welfare state becomes far more complex than Cerny assumes it to be. High levels of societal welfare, though expensive in terms of high non-wage labour costs, may well be associated with a healthy and dedicated workforce, with cooperative rather than adversarial industrial relations, with high levels of human capital and product innovation, and with high domestic levels of consumer demand—all of which might be seen to correlate positively with economic performance.

Second, it is presumably for this reason that foreign direct investment continues to be attracted in disproportionate levels to the highest aggregate welfare spenders in the world economy and why levels of trade integration are positively and not negatively correlated with state and welfare expenditure. In short, there is little evidence to substantiate the thesis that the welfare state is, indeed, a drain on competitiveness.

These are crucial points. For they suggest that the trade-off that Cerny simply assumes between welfare expenditure/the welfare of one's citizens, on the one hand, and economic performance in an era of economic interdependence, on the other, is more imagined than real. As a consequence, the state's capacity to care for the welfare of its citizens may be less eroded by globalization than we, or indeed it, have tended to assume. Moreover, in so far as this is the case, it is the perceived interest of political actors in developing competition state-like entities, rather than the needs of capital per se, that is driving the development of the state today.

Third, as the discussion already begins to indicate, Cerny's rather dualistic distinction between the competitive-corrosive welfare state, on the one hand, and the competitive-enhancing competition state, on the other, is crude and overly simplistic. It is certainly the case that the welfare state can—and to some extent is being—reformed so as to increase its potential contribution to international competitiveness, but it is important not to lose sight of the considerable contribution to competitiveness that it has arguably always made. Indeed, the archetypal high public-spending Nordic welfare states were, throughout the postwar period, amongst the most open economies in the world. The welfare state has always gone hand in hand with economic openness; there is no evidence of that symbiotic relationship being eroded today. This, too, is an important point. For it reminds us of the need for IR theorists to consider the historically variant but always important relationship between political and economic interests in understanding the development of the world system. Though it has often failed to attract much attention from IR theorists, the state has always played a crucial role in determining domestic economic prospects. Arguably in this respect the era of globalization is no different.

Fourth, Cerny's account of the development of the competition state both assumes and, indeed, attributes causality to, a fully integrated world economy. As the previous section serves to indicate, that assumption is in fact increasingly problematic. The European economies which both pioneered the development of the welfare state and in which the majority of advanced welfare states are still located are ever more tightly integrated regionally. But by virtue of this fact they are arguably less exposed to the pressures of seeking competitive advantage in the global economy. The determinants of competitiveness for them are increasingly regional in character and, indeed, less global in character than at any point in the postwar period.

Finally, however accurate descriptively Cerny's account of the development of the competition state may be, it provides no credible explanation for this development—attributing causality rather vaguely to a fairly amorphous conception of globalization. The closest we get to a mechanism is the appeal to a neo-Darwinian process of natural selection in which the competitive advantage conferred by the development of the competition state ensures that it is emulated. Yet the problem with this is that there is no real evidence to suggest that competition states are more globally competitive than the welfare states they purportedly replaced. And whilst this remains the case, the argument that we have witnessed a decisive sea change in the relative balance of power between the state and capital, is unconvincing. Altogether more likely is that, in the absence of compelling evidence one way or the other, a series of largely neoliberal reforms have successfully been presented and promoted as determinants of economic prosperity—and implemented as such. In this respect the proliferation of competition state-like entities is less a confirmation of Cerny's thesis than it is an indication of the influence of many of the assumptions on which his thesis is predicated.

If that is indeed the case, much of the policy-making autonomy of the state and its capacity to care for the needs of its citizens remains intact—though whether it is perceived to remain intact is perhaps another matter.

Conclusion

This chapter has covered a fair amount of ground. Yet its conclusions can be relatively simply stated. As we have seen, globalization is often presented as a profound challenge to the very field of IR itself, calling into question the appropriateness and contemporary relevance of a continued focus on the relations between nations. Yet, as any sanguine assessment of the empirical evidence of globalization reveals, the current level of interdependence within the world system, though considerable, is not easily reconciled with the stronger variants of the globalization thesis. Nor is the term globalization necessarily a very accurate description of current realities and contemporary trends. Accordingly, whilst there is certainly much to be gained from a focus on processes of trans-national interdependence and global governance, there are still profound insights to be had from a more traditional focus on the state as a key if not the only actor on both the domestic and international stage. In the end neither focus is mutually exclusive. And whilst that remains the case, talk of post-international relations is somewhat premature.

Questions

1. What is globalization?

2. Is globalization good for us?

3. To what extent, if any, does globalization invalidate realism and neorealism?

4. Are globalization and IR anathema?

5. How intensive and how extensive do processes have to be before we can happily refer to them as globalized?

6. What is meant by 'triadization' and is it occurring?

7. Are globalization and regionalization antagonistic or mutually reinforcing trends?

8. Assess the sceptics' case against the globalization thesis.

9. Does the welfare state have a future in an era of globalization?

10. What is a competition state and how might it confer a competitive advantage upon a national economy in an era of globalization?

11. Is globalization compatible with democratic deliberation?

12. Is the state a victim or an agent of globalization—or both?

 ## Further reading

Buzan, B., Held, D., and McGrew, A. (1998), 'Realism versus Cosmopolitanism', *Review of International Studies*, 24: 387–98.
A fascinating exchange about the consequences of globalization for IR theory between a defender of a (qualified) realism and the key proponent of cosmopolitanism.

Cerny, P. G. (1997), 'Paradoxes of the Competition State: The Dynamics of Political Globalisation', *Government and Opposition*, 32/1: 251–74.
A clear and accessible statement of Cerny's influential 'competition state' thesis.

Clark, I. (1999), *Globalisation and International Relations Theory* (Oxford: Oxford University Press).
An excellent, careful, and judicious assessment of the implications of globalization for IR theory.

Held, D. (2003), 'Cosmopolitanism: Globalisation Tamed?', *Review of International Studies*, 29/4: 465–80.
A clear and accessible statement of the cosmopolitan position by its principal advocate.

Youngs, G. (1999), *International Relations in a Global Age: A Conceptual Challenge* (Cambridge: Polity).
A cogent if perhaps somewhat overstated critique of the limitations of state-centred IR theory in an age of globalization.

Important websites

Globalization guide. A globalization resource for students. **www.globalisationguide.org**

The Globalization Website. A resource for students and researchers compiling debates about th...
consequences of globalization. **www.sociology.emory.edu/globalization**

 Visit the Online Resource Centre that accompanies this book for lots of interesting additional material. **www.oxfordtextbooks.co.uk/orc/dunne3e/**

16

Still a Discipline After All These Debates?

OLE WÆVER

 Reader's Guide

This concluding chapter reflects on the aggregate picture produced by the preceding chapters. What kind of a discipline do these theories sum up to? The previous chapters spoke from the perspective of each theory observing itself and the world; now the discussion will be located at the level of the discipline as such. This chapter will examine the intellectual as well as social patterns of IR and discuss the discipline as a social system, its relations of power, privilege, and careers. For this it draws on theories from the sociology of science. It argues among other things that the discipline of International Relations (IR) is likely to continue whether or not 'international relations' remains a distinct or delineable object and that the central social mechanism of organization and control in the discipline lies in the control by theorists of the leading journals. The chapter also argues that the core of the intellectual structure in the discipline is recurring 'great debates'. Yet, both contextual factors and observable patterns in debate among the theories point to a loosening of the grip of great debates. This does not mean more agreement but less—we do not even agree on what to discuss any more. Nevertheless, the ultimate evaluation of the state and outlook of IR is positive about its ability to stay committed to the world and theory simultaneously, and therefore be of some occasional benefit.

Introduction

After visiting thirteen different theories, it would be nice to know how this all sums up. Is the whole more or less than the parts—do the theories challenge or support each other—and where is the study of International Relations (IR) heading? The authors of the chapters in this book have been tasked to look at the world through their own theory, and not surprisingly it all looks very promising for each of them. But, most likely, some theories are going to fare better than others, some will change and adapt, and given this, we would like to know what debates are likely to become pivotal in the future.

It would be a (common) illusion to discuss these questions as if they were either decided by 'reality' or by 'debate' about pure ideas. Most stock- taking exercises approach this task in one of two ways. Many point to international relations reality, to important questions or challenges, and predict that the discipline will change in relay fashion (terrorism and therefore theories of non-state actors, terrorism and therefore realism, terrorism and therefore liberal theories of cooperation, etc.). Correspondingly, histories of the disciplines are written in retrospect viewing the events through the theories that won the debate: it therefore looks as if the events caused the theories (Wæver 1998: 691–2). They did not. The second approach is to assume that the best argument wins, and therefore by checking in the debate who is right and wrong one knows how it will go (Katzenstein et al. 1998). However, I do not feel in a position to judge the contributions of all the wise colleagues in the chapters of this book. In any case, there is no reason to assume that the discipline will suddenly—and for the first time—develop according to the power of the better arguments, because like any social system it is a structured field permeated by relations of power. A theory from the USA is more likely to gain influence than one made in Nigeria, and if it comes from an Ivy League university that again increases its chances of success, and then there is gender and meta-theoretical bias to take account of, and so forth.

What we know about international relations is always contingent on the theory used—one cannot subtract the theory afterwards and get 'clean' knowledge of reality. Therefore, one only knows international relations when one knows IR. And one only knows the separate theories of IR, when one understands what they are doing to each other. Thus, the portrait of the discipline is not an aim in itself, but it is necessary to understand the past, present, and future of the theories which in turn is necessary to understand the world we study.

This exercise helps to answer another puzzle from the volume: in what sense are these different theories *IR theories*? Some of them come from other fields—from economics (game theory and neoliberal institutionalism), cultural studies (postcolonialism), philosophy (poststructuralism), political economy (Marxism), or from diverse sources (feminism)—and some of the theories even resist the concept of IR. Are they IR theories, nevertheless? The answer is yes, and this becomes clear when we understand the discipline as an institution, as is suggested in this chapter.

The aforementioned question provokes a follow-up. Why does the volume present *this* set of theories? Are there any limits to the number of theories one could choose? A selection can be justified because the theories are not living alone in the world; they play a relational game of **recognition** and mutual interest. When looking at the whole they form, it becomes possible to see what theories make up the discipline.

There is a further and even more basic follow-up. Does 'IR' exist? In what sense can we talk any more about a discipline of IR when most of the chapters here argue that the world is in significant respects post-international, globalized, or characterized by 'world politics' rather than international relations? When, furthermore, a number of the main theories refuse the label of IR theory themselves, and increasingly argue in favour of interdisciplinarity, what then becomes of the discipline of IR?

Therefore, the first question has to be whether IR is (still?) a discipline, and whether it is likely to remain one (or whether you wasted your time reading those preceding chapters about the theories of a disappearing discipline).

The discipline question

Conceptions of the discipline of IR

It is often discussed whether IR is a discipline or has been overtaken by fragmentation, multi-disciplinarity, hybridity, or—as argued most forcefully by rational choice theorists—by method-based (re-)integration with at least all of political science and potentially all social sciences (or more). Most ubiquitous are probably arguments pointing to the obsolescence of the domestic–international distinction, interestingly advanced by both rationalists and many critical theorists and poststructuralists (Milner 1998; Katznelson and Milner 2002; George 1994). Others emphasize more—and typically lament—the proliferation of theories, approaches, and sub-fields that make it harder and harder for a research community to recognize itself and its members (a question covered by Steve Smith in the **Introduction** to this volume). Much of the anxiety (and hope) about disciplinary demise rests on a false premise, that it is possible and necessary to have agreement over objects or definitions in a discipline.

Such debates assume that, to exist, a discipline demands (1) a clear and distinct object, or (2) agreement on a definition. The most widespread view is probably (1), in other words, disciplines exist because and to the extent that their *object exists*. There are living organisms, therefore biology; an economy and therefore economics; and people have psychological disorders and therefore psychology exists. From at least 1969 onwards, it should have been difficult to view things this way. Michel Foucault showed convincingly in the *Archeology of Knowledge* how disciplines do not mirror given objects—they constitute them or are formed together with the formation of their objects. The notions of 'economy' or 'psyche' as distinct objects form only at specific points in time and replace other ways to delineate and differentiate the world (Foucault 1972 [1969]).

What about position (2)? If the basis of a discipline does not lie in the object of study as such, because objects can be constituted and delineated in different ways, the basis must be in the *constant reproduction of a consensus* according to which the object exists. It would seem that the ability to continue to generate agreement in a community of researchers is the key to being and surviving as a discipline.[1] However, this is empirically as unfounded as (1): the history of science is full of disciplines that did not agree at all on their self-definition, subject matter, or methodology, and continued nevertheless. A recent example is organization studies (Knudsen 2003), to which one could add psychology and sociology which have been in this situation for most of their existence.

Strangely missing from the normal 'to be or not to be' discussions of the discipline is a third approach: (3) a conception of the discipline as focused on *power and institutions*. The omission of position (3) is strange because one would expect to find an interest in an analysis of power and institutions in a discipline dominated by realists and institutionalists. (This approach can even be recast as political economy for the critically minded.)

In light of position (3), we can see the discipline as real and reproducing—even in the absence of a clear and given object (international relations) and a shared agreement (IR). This becomes visible through a more external, sociological glance at our activity as IR scholars.[2] The usual discussion commits the fallacy of fairness, of assuming that the existence of disciplines or theories has to be deserved or earned. The result is a naivety we usually do not exhibit in relation to other things we study, only when we talk about the academic world. It goes generally for reflections on the discipline—the many stock-taking exercises about 'the state of the discipline'—that they are in the prescriptive key. For instance, it is common to lament the widespread practice of describing IR in terms of 'great debates' as if this is just some kind of 'bad habit', which 'we' can stop doing if we so decide (Lake 2011). But, as I will demonstrate in the next section, it is actually a part of the *structure* of the discipline; it serves purposes and removing it would have far-reaching effects. So change would affect relations of power and privilege, and therefore just to point out that 'we' should do things differently is slightly naive. It is idealistic in the good old moralistic sense of the word (Carr 1946). Prescription is fine, but when talking about 'the world out there' we usually assume that reform will turn out better if we first try to understand the patterns, structures, interests, and dynamics of a field. However, when discussing the discipline, because it is about 'doing our job', we tend to assume that one can talk directly about 'what we want to do'. Disciplines reproduce for reasons better explained by sociology of science than because of the state of the world or the practices of disciplinary cultivation.

Sociological explanation for the reproduction of disciplines

Thinking in terms of disciplines emerged gradually as the medieval university gave way to the modern research university, but what explains the staying power of disciplines is the relationship between them and the practical and social organization of the universities, a system that emerged at the turn of the twentieth century in the USA. Disciplines became more than categories in the organization of *knowledge*, and also crucial in the organization of *scholars* and *universities* (Abbott 2001; Clark and Youn 1976; Clark 1983; Geiger 2005: 55f.). Since at least the 1920s, the narrowness, over-specialization, and confinement of disciplines has been criticized, and new patterns predicted.[3] Waves of interdisciplinarity and large multidisciplinary projects came—and went (Campbell 1969; Abbott 2001: 122, 131–6). The disciplinary system proved surprisingly resilient. The main explanation for this is the departmental structure invented in the USA: 'academic disciplines in the American sense—groups of professors with exchangeable credentials collected in strong associations—did not really appear outside the United States until well into the postwar period' (Abbott 2001: 123, 2002: 207; for a comparative description of the situation in Germany, France, and the UK, see Abbott 2001: 123–5, 2002: 207–8). The system with 'departments of equals' and a PhD 'in something' was part of the solution to an administrative problem of a lack of internal structure in a rapidly expanding university system. It proved highly durable. The duality of internal organization and a system for structured career mobility externally—backed up by national disciplinary societies such as the American Political Science Association (APSA)—became self-reinforcing because it is self-penalizing to challenge the discipline (Abbott 2001: 126; cf. Hammond 2004). It becomes hard for single universities to challenge the disciplinary system, because their PhD graduates would lose their career options: they would no longer qualify as PhDs 'in xx'. Abbott further underpins this argument by pointing to mechanisms related to undergraduate education and the idea of 'the college major', which we do not need to go into here. The main point is that the system of disciplines as invented in the USA proved highly self-reinforcing. With the postwar dominance of US universities, the model spread. American universities often were the pinnacle of career prospects for foreigners too, so global disciplines became replicas of US ones, in turn leading to local accommodation in most countries to this format.

Disciplines, therefore, generally do not die, merge, or split just because their subject appears in a new light. Occasionally, splits happen, typically if a field receives generous funding for a long period (biology), and mergers can happen if an area is gradually losing influence (classics). But disappearance of a field is unlikely, and even more unlikely is a general reorganization of, say, all of the social sciences according to a new and better format, be that to get away from the nineteenth-century assumptions about society, state, and international built into the current disciplines (Wallerstein 2001 [1991]), or to implement a universal reorganization of social sciences according to the different branches of rational choice theory.

Waves of change have swept through the various disciplines, major **paradigms** have come and gone and the dominant format of research has changed in many disciplines, and yet the general map has been surprisingly constant. Why is it important that disciplines are more unshakeable than widely assumed? Because it refocuses our attention on the internal structure of the discipline, rather than assuming that its survival is all the time at stake. For instance, boundary drawing is usually less about actually ensuring the continuation of IR than it is part of power struggles within the discipline about who are to be included/excluded and who are more central than others (cf. Gunnell 1991; Guzzini 1998). Rather than mirroring the self-presentation of precarious disciplinary existence, it is more interesting to take IR as a continuing condition—for better and worse—and study its internal organization.

IR and political science

So disciplines reproduce as social structures. But an obvious objection could be that IR is a *sub*-discipline within political science. It is true that political science is a discipline, and it reproduces for the reasons given by Abbott and others. IR is not in an immediate sense a discipline of this kind—it is, in the vast majority of universities, political science that plays this dual institutionalization role of being a unit in each university and a (trans-)national scene for careers. However, a conception of political science as made up of a few sub-fields is endemic. In the USA it is typically the quartet of American politics, comparative politics, political theory, and IR; and in some European systems, comparative politics, political theory, public administration, and IR. This structure is neither necessary, natural, nor very old (Kaufman-Osborn 2006), but when the current four-fold structure finally emerged in the late 1950s (after a number of very different structures in the first half of the twentieth century), it quickly became stable and self-reproducing. Abbott's explanation can be extended down to the sub-disciplinary level. To prepare for careers in a discipline organized around these four sub-fields, one needs to have credentials in these terms.[4] Therefore, the four became self-reproducing and IR has staying power as a sub-discipline.

Among the four, it seems that IR has the strongest sense of independent disciplinarity (cf. the common use of the term discipline for both IR and political science in places like this volume). Part of the reason for this is that IR emerged with separate chairs and institutes partly independently of political science (especially in the UK and the European continent, see Goodwin 1951; Manning 1954), and leading professional organizations such as the International Studies Association (ISA) and its British counterpart (BISA) officially see themselves as interdisciplinary, despite the reality of overwhelming political science dominance. IR has its own journals and independent organizations and conferences, and therefore many tend to think of themselves as 'international relationists' rather than 'political scientists'. IR is a discipline within a discipline.

Many relevant challenges and dynamic factors influencing the discipline are noticed in its ongoing discussions, but often the factors are linked to the wrong questions due to the constant underestimation of the staying power of disciplines. Globalization in its many senses does upset the standard categories of domestic/international, medialization challenges the conception of politics, and so forth. But this is not likely to lead (all of) us beyond the discipline to new fields defined to mirror 'new realities'—rather these are important challenges that the discipline and its theories will try to make sense of in different ways. Similarly, increased fragmentation in the discipline is not likely to make it disappear, nor should it be a reason for romantic lamentation and calls for 'unity'; we should look systematically at the changes in the structure of the discipline and what this means for the kinds of knowledge it can produce.

Finally, the reluctance to celebrate the durability of disciplines is probably strengthened by the connotations of 'discipline' where poststructuralists and especially postmodernists (terms used as defined by Campbell, **Chapter 12**) play on the social control sense of 'discipline' (compare the discussion of 'disciplinarity' in Messer Davidow et al. 1993). This mock-etymology—fun as it is—should probably give way to the real origins of 'discipline'; in Latin *discere*, to learn. Since 'there are far more research problems than there are disciplines . . . a university organized around problems of investigation would be hopelessly balkanized' (Abbott 2001: 135; cf. Campbell 1969), and, due to a lack of abstraction, knowledge defined by a specific problem will constantly date before 'problem portable knowledge'. Therefore, 'disciplinary boundaries are, after all, necessary for the growth of knowledge' (Fuller 2002 [1988]: 197).

It is not that everybody should be doing IR theory, or that disciplinary knowledge is somehow privileged or finer than interdisciplinary, multi-disciplinary, or post-disciplinary work; only that there will *also* be IR theory. There are often good reasons to focus on a given issue, problem, or question and develop theory specifically for the purpose and at the interface between different disciplines. However, one of these disciplines will be one called IR, and a set of theories known as IR theories will go together with this field. Notably, there will be a certain premium on being recognized as a theory of a discipline, because these constitute the largest and most stable market for candidates and journals. New theories typically emerge not at the core of a discipline but at the interstices between disciplines, but they then face strategic choices about whether to cultivate an identity as co-founder of a new field (start founding journals and associations for it, as done by development research, feminism, communication studies, and many other fields in the early stages) or celebrate their radical homelessness, or stake a claim to being an IR theory (and typically make similar claims in other disciplines; compare, for example, feminism and poststructuralism). Even new and radical theories of IR fall back on the same institutional infrastructure—using the same techniques of persuasion at the conferences, writing for the top journals, gaining major research council grants, etc. So, while they may claim to be 'post-IR', to others this looks like a contestation *within* IR.

For instance, it is increasingly often observed that the discipline's Western (and especially American) perspective and categories often make it rather useless for Third World concerns (Tickner 2003). However, when attempting to develop 'post-Western IR' that takes into account more adequately the concepts and issues that matter in other parts of the world, a new dilemma immediately emerges: this kind of scholarship will be stronger if recognized by the discipline as being IR (Tickner and Wæver 2004, 2009).

There is and most likely will remain a discipline of IR and theories of IR too. That was step number one. The remaining questions are as follows. What kind of discipline is it? What is it doing? How is it changing? More specifically, I will, in the section on what kind of discipline IR is, look at the *social structure* of the discipline in order to describe in general how it is organized, and whether this organization is changing. It is not possible to understand the development in theories without understanding how the discipline is constituted and how it is changing. The aforementioned section looks at the *intellectual structure* of the discipline. This includes a discussion of the pattern within and among the specific theories: which ones are around and, especially, what pattern do they form in combination? What are the main axes of debate and are they changing? The conclusion addresses questions about relevance, cumulation, and progress.

What kind of discipline is International Relations? Changes in social structure

Social and intellectual structure

Academic disciplines have both social and intellectual structures. The *social* structures include institutions from the large and formal organization of disciplines grouped in faculties within universities, to smaller and often more informal ones such as procedures of refereeing in key journals. The discussion here will focus on the central question of how researchers within a given field relate to each other—how dependent they are on each other and through this how they are coordinated and 'ruled'. This is central because it is in the nature of science to be a relationship among colleagues: 'scientific fields are a particular work organisation which structure and control the production of intellectual novelty through competition for reputations from national and international audience for contributions to collective goals' (Whitley 1984: 81). 'They reward intellectual innovation—only new knowledge is publishable—and yet contributions have to conform to collective standards and priorities if they are to be regarded as competent and scientific' (Whitley 1986: 187). The publication system has become the central institution, and competition for influencing and directing other researchers through publications a central mechanism. In contrast to professions where you get certified once and for all, individual autonomy of scientists is very low, because one continues to depend 'on colleagues for approval and recognition throughout one's research career' (Whitley 1984: 25). Recognition is the central medium, but recognition from some colleagues counts more than from others—authority is concentrated with those who achieve power over knowledge goals and procedures.

Intellectual structures include how knowledge in the field hangs together—to what degree over arching theories or paradigms encompass the different contributions or unify them through clear methods or techniques, and thus the degree to which it is predictable to practitioners whether their work will count as novel and meaningful. (Social and intellectual structures are closely connected, but I will present them in this chapter separately for purposes of clarity.)

The variations among the sciences do not—as is often assumed—derive from the subject matter of the different disciplines as in the standard contrast between natural and social/humanistic sciences. It is not a sufficient explanation that the social world is more complex, or natural phenomena in their nature more mechanical and thus predictable. A good illustration of this is the difference between mid-twentieth-century physics and chemistry. In physics, you needed expensive equipment, whereas, in chemistry, most apparatus was available in university departments. Chemistry then showed much less concern with theoretical unification and much less coordination, and its sub-fields were not ordered into a single hierarchy of importance (Whitley 1984: 108—see also 89–90 and 256–7). Physics needed to be able to decide on an allocation of resources and developed not only a tighter social structure, but also an intellectual structure where sub-fields were subordinated to general theory. This example shows that it is not a question of 'natural scienceness'—much more a question of specific conditions that shape the organization of a field which in turn influences the kind of research output. Similarly, social sciences such as sociology, political science, and economics differ in their internal structure, not necessarily reflecting their subject matter but as a historically evolved arrangement.

Disciplinary structures change over time. Christian Knudsen (2003) tells the story of organization studies as going through quite different formations, from a single paradigm situation in the late 1950s to the mid-1970s, to two different kinds of more diverse formations in later decades. The shift was largely explained by the rapid growth of the field, which undermined the previous hegemony of one dominant research programme. Whitley (1984) often uses the example of the bio medical field, where dramatic increases in funding meant a fragmentation, because scholars were no longer dependent on a few gate keepers but could get funding from many different sources more easily.

So what is the social structure of IR?

First, the global structure: IR is 'an American social science' (Hoffmann 1977). Modern IR theory was born in the USA after the Second World War when IR first became a widely adopted discipline. The Cold War meant generous funding, and the US research community became by far the largest and, therefore, most attractive in which to succeed. American journals were seen as leading 'international journals', despite often publishing less than 10 per cent from scholars not at US universities (Wæver 1998; Breuning et al. 2005). In this situation, US scholars could afford to ignore work done outside the USA, and it was up to others to bring their work to the attention of US based universities, journals, and publishers—dominance through neglect. Recent years have witnessed increased attention to this pattern and to the marginalized voices—from the most articulate ones like the English school (**Chapter 7**) to the almost silenced Third World scholars. There has been discussion about whether this is 'only' a social injustice where non-US and especially non-Western scholars are underprivileged or whether there is a qualitative difference and IR would look different if written from elsewhere. One should recognize both the significant differences between IR in say Germany, the UK, the USA, and Japan (Wæver 1998; Kinnvall 2005; Inoguchi and Bacon 2001), and simultaneously the omnipresence of US style IR all over the world. The IR world is best viewed as a mix of a US/global system and national/regional ones with varying degrees of independence (Wæver 2003). The US scene is both national and the central global one (consider the status of the ISA as both a North American organization and de facto global IR convention) but, although others relate to this scene, they simultaneously operate on different conditions dependent on whether their home is in India, Germany, or Brazil. I cannot go into detail about the other ones here. In line with the book, I focus on the US/global discipline and only occasionally note the limits and problems of this model, but will not cover the variations as such (see Tickner and Wæver 2009).

The second layer of social structural analysis is then to understand the US centred one. What are its institutions, degree of coherence, and forms of power? A key category here is 'mutual dependence' (Whitley 1984, 1986, 2000).[5] Mutual dependence 'refers to scientists' dependence upon particular groups of colleagues to make competent contributions to collective intellectual goals and acquire prestigious reputations which lead to material rewards' (1984: 87). Increased mutual dependence generally leads to increased competition, increased cooperation/coordination, and stronger organizational boundaries and identity.

IR has some clear 'symptoms' of strategic dependence. Why? Why should IR scholars be dependent on colleagues? '[T]he more limited access to the necessary means of intellectual production and distribution, the more dependent do scientists become upon the controllers of such channels and the more connected and competitive are their research strategies likely to be'(Whitley 1984: 84f.). In some disciplines, this is a question directly about resources such as equipment. This is usually not the case in IR, although it matters who controls (or advises) the various (private) foundations and (public) research councils. To most researchers in the discipline, dependence is more a question of access to publications which, in turn, influences resource allocation.

Researchers are dependent upon those 'colleagues who dominate reputational organizations and set standards of competence and significance' (Whitley 1984: 86). In fields where you can contribute to a number of distinct problem areas and seek reputations from different audiences by publishing results in different journals, this dependence is much lower than in disciplines such as particle physics where journals form a clear hierarchy and audiences are clearly defined.

IR has a hierarchy of journals. In the USA there is a big market for academic posts and scholars are highly mobile. Universities form a hierarchy, and the way to climb up the ladder is via publications, meaning that the lead journals are the most important hurdle. And it is a high one, because the leading journals in the social sciences have acceptance rates as low as 11–18 per cent (compared to 65–83 per cent in the natural sciences) (Hargens 1988: 150); leading IR journals are now below 10 per cent. Conversely, access to scarce expensive equipment is limited in the natural sciences. This makes evaluation by foundations and hiring at leading and wealthy institutions relatively more central compared to evaluation on the basis of journal publications that take absolute priority in most social sciences. In most human sciences and some social sciences it is relatively easy to get an article published in *some* journal given the proliferation of journals, but there is a relatively clear intersubjective understanding of the value of different journals and publishing houses (Jordan et al. 2009; Goodson et al. 1999). Lead journals become absolutely central. Thus, the key to IR's relatively high strategic dependence is concentration of control over the means of intellectual distribution.

Articles about theory as such do not rank higher than empirical, application ones. On the contrary, there is a fatigue with more new theories or meta-theories and a premium (not least for *International Organization* which is often thought of as the pre eminent journal in IR) on theory testing. However, the journals are mainly defined, structured, and to a certain extent controlled by theorists. You become a star only by doing theory. The highest citation index scores all belong to theorists. Thus, the battle among theories/theorists defines the structure of the field, but the practice it stimulates is one where all sub-fields compete for making it into the lead journals. This is in contrast to the situation in economics, where there is a closed system dominated by pure theory (and the different specializations have their own journals, and an article of an applied nature usually cannot make it into the leading journals at all).

In IR, the result is a two tiered discipline. To get into the lower tier, you have to become accepted as competent in a sub-field. Most sub-fields are relatively tolerant, welcome new members, and are not terribly competitive. They are hierarchical, but the hierarchy is not settled internally, so there is not much to fight over. Top positions are gained by making it into the upper tier, that is, by publishing in the leading all round journals; this means convincing those at the centre about relevance and quality (you still have to prove technical competence to your fellow specialists because some of them will most likely be reviewers).

This specific structure explains the most often noticed peculiarity of IR: its fondness of 'great debates'. Debates ensure that theorists remain central but empirical studies are important (in contrast to economics).[6] Without recurrent debates, empirical work would break off and just apply the accepted theory. Debates are possible—and necessary—in the USA because of the one big national 'market'. The decisive resources for careers have moved out of local control and up to the national, disciplinary level. In the USA it is possible to compete for definition of the whole field; in Europe and elsewhere it is easier to maintain local peculiarities.

It is important to note that IR has historically been relatively coherent compared to, for example, sociology, which has tended to diversify into numerous kinds of sociology, has had less agreement on the hierarchy of journals, and has had less correspondence between what is discussed in one sub field and another. Many of the leaders typically did not establish themselves through theories of direct transferability, but through exemplary empirical works (books) that only implicitly presented a paradigm for the discipline at large. So for IR the infamous great debates actually constitute a form of coherence.

Change in social structure

If we turn from statics to dynamics, what does this kind of interpretation tell us about changes? What are the factors that could upset the structure? This is of course a large subject in itself, but to list a few strong candidates:

- The social boundary is important not because of a likely dissolution of the discipline as an institution but because changes in boundary drawing transform the internal set up of the discipline. Does authority over IR rest only with IR (and over political science only with political science)? Recent years have shown two rather different challenges. One is the surge of rational choice. Since this is a supra disciplinary movement it means that scholars across the sub-fields and across disciplines have views on who should be hired in, say, an IR position in a department.

- The second challenge to the social boundary is 'audience plurality and diversity' (Whitley 1984: 111). In many human sciences lay audiences have strong opinions, and positions within the field can therefore be built through success with these audiences. This has not usually been the case for IR—you could become a star in the media, but that does not necessarily count academically. However, increasingly, hiring criteria are starting to include not only research but teaching and public performances in the media. This too weakens the hold of the disciplinary elite who control the leading journals. Notably, status in the policy world does not correlate or follow from intra-academic debates (in which case this new factor would not shift much; the ultimate source of authority would be the same). Often theories can be highly successful academically and without policy influence, and increasingly policy research in think tanks happens without anchorage in IR theory (see Kahler 1993, 1997; Peterson et al. 2005; Wæver and Buzan 2007; Jordan et al. 2009). The arena for public expertise increasingly becomes a separate source of authority in the discipline.

- In the same direction pulls a general change in the nature and status of science related to the 'knowledge society'. One might at first think that the 'knowledge society' means increased status to academics. Not so. Science has become too important to be left to scientists (Gibbons et al. 1994; Fuller 2000). Politics is scientificized, but science becomes politicized. The effects of much natural science in particular are too momentous (genetic manipulation for instance) to be left to intra-scientific decisions. Due to risks (Beck 1992) as well as value for society, science can be only one voice in science-related decisions—economic and political voices count inside academe too.

The main factors influencing the social structure are, in the case of IR, pointing towards a loosening of central control and less forceful coordination through the combined mechanism of leading journals and theorists in mutual debate.

This kind of structural–institutional approach to the discipline does not imply that one should accept everything as unchangeable (or a given change as inevitable). There are lots of reasons to argue about how we would like to change our academic world (for example, the Perestroika movement, 2000; see Monroe 2005),[7] and the most useful arguments are probably those that focus on process or culture, that is, on what kind of attitude and forms of interaction we should cultivate in order to generate a more productive and searching discipline (Lapid 2002, 2003), rather than direct description of better end states. However, all such 'reformism'—and even revolutionary approaches—usually fare better when its protagonists have analysed the setting first, to understand the kind of social system they are trying to change, including its structures and relations of power.

Changes in intellectual structure? The end of great debatism?

Task uncertainty

A key technical term from the sociology of science is 'task uncertainty' (Collins 1975; Whitley 1984). The basic paradoxical combination in science of novelty and conformity creates a high level of uncertainty about what will count and succeed. Research cannot aim at repetitious and predictable results. Novelty is constituted in relation to background expectations and assumptions; and the more systematic, general, and precise these are, the clearer the task will be. There is less uncertainty where work techniques are well understood and produce reliable results and/or clarity about the most significant topics. If you have followed the rules in most natural sciences and done something not done before, this is almost by definition a contribution to knowledge especially if it has taken place in an important area. If criteria are more diffuse, you might get your submission back with evaluations like 'nothing new', 'too idiosyncratic and not comprehensible', 'not IR', or 'the question is not interesting and important enough'. IR neither has agreement on very strict techniques nor clear priorities:[8] great debates have served to organize the discipline instead.

The set up in IR with periodic great debates has been part of the structure of our discipline. It corresponds to a situation with a relatively high degree of integration but far from a complete, hierarchical integrated structure where every piece has its place in the larger architecture of collective knowledge. The debates serve to focus the discipline and to define both a hierarchy of forms of work—the leading journals concentrating on presenting and not least elaborating and testing the main theories—and to give a meaningful role to larger parts of what goes on.

Stop the great debates?

Great debates are decried these days and most commentators hope we are getting away from them. This is problematic for three reasons:

1. Critics of the great debates implicitly assume that the alternative is a more coherent discipline. By contrast, the field more likely will be less integrated if the routine of great debates were lost.

2. The debatism is part of the structure, so we must take it seriously to understand how our discipline works, and change will involve questions of power and privileges.

3. These debates help us in important ways to understand the theories themselves.[9]

Studying (and teaching) the great debates helps not only to understand the pattern or to track *what theories* are in the field, but also to understand what is *in those theories*, that is to say how they are structured. Understanding *why* they look the way they do makes it also easier to penetrate their inner logic and thereby to work with them, not least for a student.

Theories are shaped by their immediate social setting, that is, the academic scene (and only to a much lower degree by external factors relating to political developments). Theories are not developed in an ideal process of 'learning' and adjusting to the anomalies or weaknesses (Kuhn and Lakatos; see **Chapter 1**)—the academic scene is much more combative, and there are always a number of theories competing. Therefore, the landscape or 'fronts' explain to a very large extent what a given theory is 'up to', that is, why particular challenges are seen as decisive for this theory. To prove A or redefine B is important because of what this will mean in the current main fights. Therefore, a contemporary student of a given theory can best get to the nerve of this theory by understanding what it was designed to do originally—and, therefore, the student needs to have a good, graphic depiction of the scene as it was. Or as Peter Berger notes—in a phrase attributed to a 'somewhat cynical colleague—"the goal of every scholarly enterprise is to blow someone's theory out of the water'" (2002: 1).

To understand a theory implies knowing why it was created that way. In other words, to understand neorealism, it helps to have the IR scene of the 1970s as a setting, and see how Waltz intervened most cleverly into that by his strategic move of a structural re-launch of realism. Similarly, Keohane constructs his neoliberalism on the basis of rational egoists and as a theory that says a few important things. This is a strategic move given Waltz's triumph and the standards of evaluation that have transformed accordingly. Elements of poststructuralism gained a surprising conceptual centrality within the discipline in the 1980s because the former main battle line had lost intensity, and the constellation among IR theories allowed for a challenge to rationalism as such (Wæver 1996). Wendt's theory is state-centric, both for theory internal reasons (having to do with the structure–agency debate), but surely also for relational reasons—thereby it becomes a parallel to Waltz and Keohane, the third book on that top shelf. The result is the pattern of transformation of the discipline from the third to fourth debate—illustrated in Figure 16.1.

Out of the triangle of realism, liberalism, and radicalism (Marxism), emerges what I have labelled the 'neo neo synthesis' between neorealism and neoliberalism, which in turns stimulates the radicalization of an all out reflectivist critique. The long diagonal axis (upper left to lower right) became the main debate in the 1980s, while the remaining narrow intra-rationalist debate between neorealists and neoliberals (short arrow) became the other constitutive element of the fourth debate.

It is a general pattern in intellectual history that change rarely happens through a completely new set of positions taking over, but more often through gradual mergers and splits, whereby one constellation changes to another, and different differences get primacy. This pattern is underpinned by what Randall Collins has called 'the law of small numbers' (1998: 38, 81).

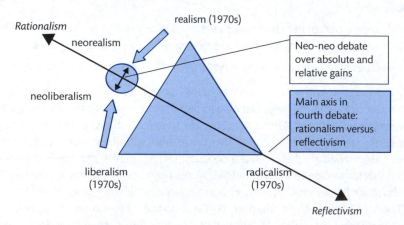

Figure 16.1 The 1980s: the fourth debate

Source: Adapted from Wæver (1996:165). Cambridge University Press.

Intellectual conflict is 'always limited by focus on certain topics, and by the search for allies' (Collins 1998: 1) and the number of positions that succeed in gaining general attention (and constitute active schools of thought which reproduce themselves for more than one or two generations) is typically *three to six*. There have to be rival positions, thus at least two, and then it is always easy to define a third in contrast to both. The upper limit is around six, because the need for allies and the scarcity of attention tend to make processes of multiplication beyond this self-defeating. IR has obeyed the intellectual law of small numbers, at least until recently.

Great debates—did they stop after all?

Great debates with shifting fronts and axes is the general long-term picture. But what about the current situation? Examining leading US journals, one finds little debate among general theories in the journals that are dominant in the IR discipline. In these—and *the* leading one, *International Organization (IO)*, in particular—distinct 'IR theory' has become marginalized and great debate references have almost disappeared. *International Security*, the leading journal on the security side of US IR, has had some limited discussion along the main axis of discussion in the fourth debate (rationalism vs. reflectivism) in the form of a discussion about moderate constructivism, while a debate over democratic peace largely followed the axis of the neo-neo debate (small arrow in Figure 16.1). The most vigorous debates have been intra-realist (offensive vs. defensive realism; cf. **Chapter 4**) and hardly count as 'great debates' for the discipline as a whole. *International Studies Quarterly* and *World Politics*, which share with *IO* the status as the top IR journals (Breuning et al. 2005), confirm the picture of very limited orientation in relation to any general map of IR.

A few years back, almost all articles in the USA fitted into a few main orientations and positioned themselves in relation to these, whereas the 'other' category, that is non-traditional theories, was much larger in several European and especially British journals (Wæver 1998). This underlines the general point that the discipline is organized with a US centre, and the great debates that focus the discipline therefore find their most complete representation in the leading US journals. The journals do not want to publish new theories all the time—the disciplinary rationality is that we should have a relatively limited set of theories (produced by the scholars at the top of the pyramid), and then others are supposed to use, test, and modify mildly. Therefore, many articles were either extensive applications of one theory or competitive tests of several. However, this kind of preferred article a decade ago is actually hard to find these days. Today, articles use lots of theory, and apply or test it—only it is not *IR* theory! The IR theory map lurks in the background as meta-references, but the operative theory in a typical *IO* article is a branch of sociological institutionalism, then a theory from economics, and then an ad hoc homemade model of norms or institution building. These are not derived directly from any general debates within IR. Similarly in more critical and/or European journals, only the theories imported from sociology, philosophy, and psychology are different ones.

Specific theories—what axes of debate?

The picture of no single great debate framing the entire field today is reinforced by the chapters of this volume. The picture of debates changes chapter by chapter. We seem to witness separate developments within each 'family'. Some (including me) have previously summed up the situation as a period where all theories turn inward and discussion runs among competing branches of each theory. However, this is too generalized and systematic a picture.

The theories are broad, parallel streams but their internal activity differs. How they are integrated, how participants interact and how much they refer to other streams varies. The brief survey here draws on the other chapters in this volume (and therefore gives no separate documentation or sources). I start with the theories that define the main debate among themselves. A little later I turn to the remaining theories/chapters.

- Structural realism is structured by competing theories within itself. The main debates are among offensive and defensive realism (and other developments of neorealism, like neo-classical and postclassical realism). The typical kind of study uses not quantitative methods or formal modelling but historical case studies to explore the very abstract general theoretical questions about causal relations between a few key variables (Walt 1999). Because structural realism is the core of US security studies, this format for presentation of research also characterizes attempts by other theories to break into mainstream security studies such as part of the democratic peace literature and soft 'constructivism' understood as 'ideational variables'.

- Neoliberalism has a quite different pattern. The typical *IO* article does not put the general theory in play (as the structural realist does), but draws on a specific theory or model from organization theory or economics. It is then tested or explored with one or more IR cases, as summarized in **Chapter 6** in this volume and in Moravcsik (2003). Optimistically, one could say the research programme adds more and more variables in a maturing construct. However, it is doubtful whether this really lives up to being a research programme in a Lakatosian sense, at least not a 'progressive' one, which would demand that the different theories are drawn from the same 'hard core' and are developing this (Lakatos 1970). Neoliberalism is not spreading out from a common core and filling out different niches, building a common construct. It is more a family of like minded attempts that are not easily compatible, additive, or cumulative. This broad family shares a general perspective on institutions and rational choice, but it is not a unified framework. Neoliberalists have no great debate internally like the one among structural realists, but they have a sense of working on middle-range theories with shared premises.

- Hard rational choice is absent from this book. It seems that it has lost some of its previous centrality—compared to, especially, the days of the relative/absolute gains debate—and it has found its place in various sub-settings (see Katznelson and Milner 2002). It has done so less as a unified research project than it was, probably because the core of theory development is outside the discipline—in economics—which makes it hard to keep together as an IR theory.

- Constructivism is marked first of all by debate between different 'degrees' of constructivism, some vis-à-vis the most approachable parts of the establishment (neoliberals) and some with poststructuralists. There is much less debate than in the late 1980s–early 1990s between the extremes, the 'rationalism vs. reflectivism' debate often characterized by a focus on neorealism as the quintessential rationalist theory. Also, much soft constructivist work has been published in leading journals where it has followed a pattern like the one outlined for neoliberalism above (cf. Sterling Folker 2000)—not developing one core theory (maybe because constructivism is not an IR theory but a meta-theory; Onuf 2002), but drawing on different middle range theories from, typically, sociology or organization theory to introduce specific mechanisms not found in constructivism per se.

- Poststructuralism shows a somewhat surprising tendency (despite Campbell's welcome plea for abstractions) to engage primarily with specific subjects (famine, migration, exceptionalism), and engage less with general theory debates both vis-à-vis the establishment and internally. This is especially the case for British poststructuralists who are hegemonic in this part of the discipline.

- Feminism, critical theory, and neo-Marxism tend to follow the pattern of poststructuralism and in this sense keep the category of 'reflectivism' somewhat valid. They position themselves against the 'establishment', but have less faith in the chance of getting anybody there to listen (Tickner 1997), so less is invested in any great debate. Still it is here that the fourth debate is most systematically invoked. As justification and explanation of the importance of radical work, the defects of mainstream scholarship continue to be Othered.

The overall pattern remains in line with my prediction from the last survey of the discipline (Wæver 1996, 1997; and Figures 16.1 and 16.2 in this chapter): the fourth debate is being transformed into a continuum, a series of debates along the same axis. Most strikingly, along the rationalism–reflectivism axis, we have several relatively similar debates at various points. For example, within constructivism it is evident that there are lively debates between mainstream and moderate constructivists (*International Organization* and *International Security*), conventional and consistent constructivists (**Chapter 10**), as well as ongoing debates over Wendt's contribution to constructivism.

Andrew Abbott (2001) has noticed how many debates in social science exhibit a fractal pattern, or 'self-similarity'. The debate over constructivism has taken on the same form and is repeated at any step along the axis. Any position can be attacked by a more radical constructivist or a more whole hearted materialist one. Or, to put it more fractally, within each position, the same debate reappears.

In line with the 1996–7 prediction, we do not have a new axis (the line has the same end points and the same location), and the pattern has shifted from debate to continuum—a dichotomy (reflectivism/rationalism) has changed to a range of possibilities, but defined in the same terms. The important article by Fearon and Wendt on 'rationalism vs. constructivism: a sceptical view' (2002) is in this respect both a symptom of this evolution and an instructive intervention showing how to proceed in this newly opened land. 'In short, we believe the most fruitful framing of "rationalism vs. constructivism" is a pragmatic one,

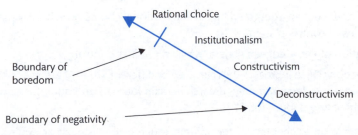

Figure 16.2 After the mid-1990s

Source: Wæver (1996: 169). Cambridge University Press.

treating them as analytical lenses for looking at social reality. . . . This prompts a concluding suggestion: that the rationalism–constructivism issue be seen not as a debate but as a conversation' (Fearon and Wendt 2002: 68).

Pinpointing our position in the genealogy of debates, we are still 'after the fourth debate'. Orientation still operates via the categories from the fourth debate as witnessed by most of the chapters in the present volume. There is not a lively and intense debate as in the late 1980s and early 1990s, but the categories are still around as the main signposts in the landscape. We are neither in a total interregnum, nor in a fifth debate. Neorealists and neoliberals each follow their own guiding pattern and spend little time explicitly on the fourth debate. They do not even debate much with each other. However, neoliberals and neorealists form internal debates simulating their classical first debate axis. The intra-realist debate follows the classical axis vis-à-vis liberals: defensive realism is closer to liberalism than offensive realism. Also the neoliberal debate is along the classical axis vis-à-vis realists: power vs. institutions (very clear in **Chapter 6**). Also this debate is 'self-similar' or 'fractal': you can at any step take a discussion between a more and a less tough Realpolitik interpretation.

The optimistic interpretation would be that each research programme in parallel tries to optimize itself through internal debate and we are preparing for the grand conclusion where all the theories are measured. This is not likely. This view overestimates both the parallelism of what happens within each, and assumes a non-existing agreement on the criteria for assessment. More likely, the meaning of this pattern is less coherence, less agreement.

A final alternative interpretation could be that diversity is temporary, because one theory is about to win. Each theory is to some extent internally relatively coherent. So, if one would come to control the whole, we would have coherence. The only serious candidate for this is rational choice. But there are three objections to the claim that it dominates the field. First, it is dominant only in the USA, not in Europe, or the rest of the world (Wæver 1998; Kinnvall 2005; Tickner and Wæver 2009); second, it faces quite stiff and possibly increasing resistance 'at home' in the USA (Walt 1999; Perestroika 2000; Monroe 2005); and third, it seems that— possibly driven by technology—recently large – N quantitative studies have become the preferred safe format for dissertations and also quantitatively gain ground in the mainstream journals, competing for the same method-based and scientific status in the discipline.

If we are then left with the diagnosis of less integration, why did this happen? Because of reality? Complexity? The end of the Cold War, the 'War on Terror', or globalization? Dissolution of disciplinary boundaries? Probably none of these. This is again the realist fallacy assuming the discipline reflects its object. A sociological explanation would return to the factors already discussed:

- The ironic effect of an attempted takeover by rational choice, which weakened the boundaries of control systems.
- Politicization of knowledge in general which diversifies control.
- Marketization which increases the relevance of different kinds of arena and thereby multiple career criteria: not only research in main journals and publishing houses but also teaching and public visibility.

If we look at the other chapters of the volume, much of the implicit or explicit disciplinary mapping takes the form of contrasting itself to all of modern IR theory, a kind of general dissatisfaction with all of Figure 16.1 (the fourth debate). The dissatisfied either emphasize the value of classical, more enduring approaches such as classical realism, classical liberalism, political theory, or Marxism; or they see a temporal move beyond this constellation into post-international theory as with postcolonialism, globalization theory, and green theory. Is the fifth debate to be found in this emerging pattern?

A final candidate for the future pattern could be a struggle over the role and character of theory. Although the chain of moves and countermoves, mapped here, were triggered by Ken Waltz, pushing in his seminal 1979 book for a much stronger role for theory as distinct from correlations and 'laws' (Wæver 2009), the mainstream has drifted back to a more empiricist, almost inductivist view of theory (more as advocated by King et al. 1994). When simultaneously theory debate weakens, as shown in this chapter, fewer new scholars enter the field as 'theorists', and the 'new normality' has become large N work. The launch in 2009 of a new journal defined and named as *International Theory*—across previous distinctions— could indicate a unifying theme/front: theoretical work vs. induction based correlation style learning. Predictably, some leading theorists within liberalism and especially realism have started to complain (privately?) about the decline of theory/theorists, and we might see the kind of re-alignment that is usually needed for new fronts to emerge, that is, a coalition between an embattled mainstream elite and critical scholars interested in theory for political reasons, unified in their resistance to number-crunchers testing senseless or uninteresting questions and devaluating the concept of 'theory'. An image of 'the end of theory' (accurate or not) might be the clarion call for a new move that reconfigures the disciplinary map (cf. Dunne et al. 2013)

Conclusion: What are we doing? How are we doing?

On the basis of the other chapters in this book, I have taken stock of where, what, and how IR is today, and in doing this use some theories from the sociology of science in order to obtain the necessary distance and do not aim to write one more article in defence of, and located in, a given IR theory.

This volume is introduced by an argument about the necessity of theory for the understanding of relevant political questions. Interestingly, this claim comes close to being a consensus in the discipline (although the degree of 'theoryness' is controversial as already argued). It agrees on both the following points:

- We should not do IR for IR's sake. IR should be relevant in some sense—not necessarily in the classical instrumental 'adviser to the Prince' sense of useful empirical knowledge which policy-makers draw on; it can also take the form of the poststructuralist political approach to discussing academic practices. Stephen Walt (1999) has as a neorealist attacked rational choice in security studies, primarily because it is not helpful.

- We should not give up theory for the sake of immediate relevance, because IR without theory (or method) is not really helpful in the long run. There are intense discussions between problem-driven and method-driven approaches but this is not about being theoretical or not; more it is a question of different sequences of theory, method, and issue according to different meta-theories. We see occasional appeals for the discipline to be less esoteric and more directly useful (Lepgold and Nincic 2001; Jentleson 2002; cf. Büger and Gadinger 2006), but most often the discipline refuses this trade off (Peterson et al. 2005; Maliniak et al. 2007; Wæver and Buzan 2007; Jordan et al. 2009). Its avoidance is assisted through a division of labour where think tanks such as the American Enterprise Institute in Washington or the Royal Institute of International Affairs in London focus exclusively on immediate policy.

The ideal in the discipline is relevance through theory. This rules out the route taken by many disciplines (natural, humanistic, and social ones) of treating the discipline as an end in itself. Often disciplines started as linked to a practical function, but gradually developed as an answer to their own questions—think literary studies or particle physics (Fuller 2002 [1998]: 191). Not IR. There is a general sense that the subject matter is too important for that—that IR is ultimately justified by the severity of its issues.

Many student readers of this book will be exasperated by the amount of theory, but it is a red herring to construct a debate for and against theory. Perhaps there is a more significant question. Are we getting better at theory? This is often discussed as progress or 'cumulation'. 'A good indicator for a noncumulative field is that it has a debate on whether cumulation is possible or not' (Fuchs 1993: 947). This debate on progress in IR often gets trapped because it is unfavourably compared with the process of cumulation that takes place in the natural sciences. However, Stephan Fuchs, among others, has argued that different specialities with different structures change through different processes. Some of the indicators associated with 'progress'—a fiercely competitive 'research frontier' especially—are not indicative of progress per se, but of a specific *kind* associated with the natural sciences. And the social sciences are unlikely to become this kind of 'high consensus, rapid discovery science' (Collins 1994). Not because there will be no discoveries, or because of a lack of empiricism, or too much ideological controversy, but because modern science since Galileo became organized around 'the practice of adapting or inventing technologies for purposes of research' (Collins 1994). Since new equipment is not central to social sciences, they are unlikely to get the same pattern of development.

This does not spell 'no improvement' in a general sense. Only through misleading standards of natural science (and labelling all else as relativism and 'anything goes') does the discipline fear that no judgements can be passed and nothing deemed better than anything else (Kratochwil 2003, 2006). In practice, we evaluate and value all the time—in the classroom, at the exam table, reviewing for journals, hearing a lecture—all the choices aim at improving the situation from our perspective. Naturally we often produce progress according to the criteria relevant today. (It would not necessarily have been progress seen from the perspective of a colleague doing what he or she did fifty or seventy-five years ago.) It is *our* progress.

As a young discipline, the ever-growing layers of reflection on predecessors produce increasing depth and sophistication not least self-reflection. Self-reflection grows both meta-theoretically (Lapid 2002, 2003; **Chapter 1** in this volume), through sociology of science based self-examinations, and politically (Smith 2004). IR increasingly understands itself and this is of great help in understanding the world, because as the case studies in the chapters of this volume show:[10] all the theories can tell us a lot about the 'real world' of 'international relations'. In a diverse discipline like IR, the challenge is not to achieve knowledge, but how to understand the multiplicity of it, and this is only possible when we understand both the world and the processes through which our understanding of it came about. By knowing how we know, we know more about what we know.

Questions

1. Why does a discipline not die or change if its subject matter changes shape in the real world?

2. When more and more important questions do not fit within the boundaries of distinct disciplines, should we not reorganize ourselves in interdisciplinary units defined by the things we study? What would be the advantages and disadvantages of this?

3. What are the most important resources to control in order to have influence within the discipline of IR?

4. The chapter mentions three factors whose change influences the social structure of the discipline. Can you think of other actual or potential changes in either society at large or academe that would change the discipline, and in what directions?

5. What are the main advantages and disadvantages of seeing the discipline in terms of 'great debates'?

6. Why has the narrative of great debates been so influential in IR?

7. If there is to be a fifth debate in IR what do you think it would look like?

 Further reading

Carlsnaes, W., Risse, T., and Simmons, B. A. (2002) (eds.), *Handbook of International Relations* **(London: Sage).**
Comprehensive overview of the discipline with articles covering theories, issue areas, concepts, and meta-theory. It succeeds surprisingly well in covering both American and European debates. Looking up any specific field, the article is likely to be a treasure trove of references and ideas for further research, but often very compact.

Friedrichs, J. (2004), *European Approaches to International Relations Theory: A House with Many Mansions* **(London: Routledge).**
This ambitious, short book contains, among other things, a report on Italian, French, and Scandinavian IR, their interpretation in terms of centre–periphery relationship to the USA, and a discussion of lessons about strategies to adopt for a more unified European IR.

Jordan, R., Maliniak, D., Oakes, A., and Peterson, S. (2009), 'One Discipline or Many? 2008 TRIP Survey of International Relations Faculty in Ten Countries', Reves Center and Arts and Sciences, College of William and Mary, Williamsburg, VA, February.
Survey where 2,724 IR scholars have answered questions about their theories, fields of specialization, methodology, ranking of journals and scholars, and much else including views on some policy issues. This third instalment in a series covers 10 countries but is most thorough for the USA and Canada.

Katznelson, I. and Milner, H. V. (2002) (eds.), *Political Science: State of the Discipline* **(New York and London: Norton).**
The latest 'authoritative' handbook sponsored by the American Political Science Association. Gives the same kind of dense overview as the previous text (although for all of political science), but interestingly it attempts to avoid the sub field structure and defines fields cutting across e.g. an IR/comparative politics divide.

Puchala, D. J. (2002) (ed.), *Visions of International Relations: Assessing an Academic Field* **(Columbia: University of South Carolina Press).**
Eight prominent scholars from very different approaches assess the field and present their visions for the discipline.

Sterling Folker, J. (2006) (ed.), *Making Sense of International Relations Theory* (Boulder, CO: Lynne Rienner).
All the main IR theories make sense out of 'Kosovo' (the crisis and NATO intervention in 1998–9), and the book is an excellent occasion for students to see (and compare) the theories in action. A unique and very informative exercise.

Tickner, A. B. (2003), 'Seeing IR Differently: Notes from the Third World', *Millennium: Journal of International Studies*, 32/2: 295–324.
Seminal article re examining key categories, including war and conflict, the state, sovereignty/autonomy, and nationalism, showing the value of Third World perspectives.

Tickner, A. B. and Wæver, O. (2009) (eds), *International Relations Scholarship around the World*, Volume 1 of 'Worlding beyond the West' series (London: Routledge).
The state of IR in all parts of the world is surveyed and explained, which makes quite concrete what the tensions and difficulties are for articulating new IR insights from the periphery.

 ## Notes

1. Classical examples of diagnoses of the discipline (of political science or IR) which pronounce a condition of disintegration and lack of coherence are Holsti (1985); Almond (1990); Katznelson and Milner (2002); Laitin (2004). For reflections on the discipline, see Gunnell (2002); Grant (2005). Put in more critical terms: hegemonic actors in the discipline carry out constant practices of boundary-drawing and exclusion to ensure a hegemonic conception of the discipline. However, this critical observation should not lead one uncritically to believe in an actual risk to the survival of the discipline. This boundary maintaining practice is primarily power politics *within* it.

2. See also the concluding section of Chapter 1 which stresses the importance of the internal structure of disciplines, and the importance of the academic world as the immediate social setting for the actions of theorists. See also Collins (1975, 1998).

3. It is widely believed that we are currently in or heading towards a novel situation in which the traditional disciplines are out of synch with major issues and concerns, and so many claim there is more room for multi-disciplinary work. This, however, is far from a new perception. '[T]he emphasis on interdisciplinarity emerged contemporaneously with, not after, the disciplines. There was no long process of ossification; the one bred the other almost immediately' (Abbott 2001: 312).

4. A recent survey of the hiring criteria used by department chairs supports this interpretation: 'First and foremost, the survey results establish "fit" as the most important factor across school types. Whether a job candidate works in the sub-field of the available position is of greater importance than anything else' (Fuerstman and Lavertu 2005: 734).

5. Whitley distinguishes between two kinds of mutual dependence, 'functional dependence' and 'strategic dependence'; for explanation and a detailed application of these concepts to IR, see Wæver (1998, 2003).

6. This showed statistically (in Wæver 1998: fig. 3) that a high proportion of articles in American journals fitted into the dominant categories compared to, especially, the British journals.

7. 'Perestroika' was a revolt—probably led by graduate students—in political science. It started in 2000 with an anonymous email signed 'Mr. Perestroika', attacking especially the dominance and privileging of rational choice and quantitative approaches in the journals and governance structure of the American Political Science Association. Much of the debate can be followed in the journal *PS: Political Science and Politics* and Monroe (2005).

8. Whitley subdivides task uncertainty, too (cf. note 5 on two kinds of mutual dependence): technical task uncertainty and strategic task uncertainty. The former refers to agreement about methods, the latter to agreement about priorities.

9. There has been much criticism of the accuracy of the debates as history writing (Wæver 1997; Wilson 1998; Schmidt 1998)—plus some rebuttals (Vigneswaran and Quirk 2005). Irrespective of their historical accuracy as general portrait, these powerful images had real effects as they structured key moves, which decisively shaped the discipline.

10. See Sterling-Folker (2006) for a similar exercise in which the different theories speak to the *same* case—Kosovo. The book shows that all have something important to say.

 Visit the Online Resource Centre that accompanies this book for lots of interesting additional material. **www.oxfordtextbooks.co.uk/orc/dunne3e/**

Bibliography

Abbott, A. (2001), *Chaos of Disciplines* (Chicago: University of Chicago Press).

—— (2002), 'The Disciplines and the Future', in S. Brint (ed.), *The Future of the City of Intellect: The Changing American University* (Stanford, CA: Stanford University Press).

Acharya, A. and Johnston A. I. (eds.) (2007), *Crafting Cooperation: Regional International Institutions in Comparative Perspective* (Cambridge: Cambridge University Press).

Adler, E. (1997), 'Seizing the Middle Ground: Constructivism in World Politics', *European Journal of International Relations*, 3/3: 319–63.

Adler, E. and V. Pouliot (eds.) (2011), *International Practices*. (Cambridge: Cambridge University Press).

Adorno, T. and Horkheimer, M. (1972), *The Dialectic of Enlightenment* (New York: Herder).

Aggarwal, V. K. (1998), 'Reconciling Multiple Institutions: Bargaining, Linkages, and Nesting' in V. K. Aggarwal, *Institutional Designs for a Complex World: Bargaining, Linkages, and Nesting* (Ithaca, NY: Cornell University Press), 1–31.

Alderson, K. and Hurrell, A. (2000), *Hedley Bull on International Society* (Basingstoke: Macmillan).

de Almeida, J. M. (2003), 'Challenging Realism by Returning to History: The British Committee's Contribution to IR Forty Years On', *International Relations*, 17/3: 273–302.

Almond, G. (1990), *A Discipline Divided* (Newbury Park, CA: Sage).

Anievas, A. (2010), *Marxism and World Politics* (London: Routledge).

Annan, K. (2004), 'Rwanda genocide "must leave us always with a sense of bitter regret and abiding sorrow", says secretary-general to New York memorial conference', 26 March 2004, press release. Available at: http://www.un.org/News/Press/docs/2004/sgsm9223.doc.htm, accessed 21 August 2007.

Anzuldúa, G. (1999), *Borderlands/La Frontiera*, 2nd edn. (San Francisco: Aunt Lute Books).

Appadurai, A. and Breckenridge, C. (1990), *The Making of a Transnational Culture: Asians in America and the Nature of Ethnicity* (New York: Berg Publishers).

Arato, A. and Gebhardt, E. (1991), *The Frankfurt School Reader* (New York: Continuum Press).

Arendt, H. (1964), *Eichmann in Jerusalem: A Report on the Banality of Evil* (New York: Viking).

Aristotle (1984), *The Complete Works of Aristotle: The Revised Oxford Translation*, edited by J. Barnes (Princeton, NJ: Princeton University Press).

Armstrong, D. (1993), *Revolution and World Order* (Oxford: Clarendon Press).

—— (1999), 'Law, Justice and the Idea of World Society', *International Affairs*, 75/3: 547–61.

Asad, T. (1993), *Genealogies of Religion: Discipline and Reasons of Power in Christianity and Islam* (Baltimore, MD: Johns Hopkins University Press).

Ashcroft, B., Griffiths, G., and Tiffin, H. (1990), *The Empire Writes Back: Theory and Practice in Post-colonial Literatures* (New York: Routledge).

Ashley, R. (1981), 'Political Realism and Human Interests', *International Studies Quarterly*, 25/2: 204–36.

—— (1984), 'The Poverty of Neorealism', *International Organization*, 38/2: 225–86.

—— (1987), 'The Geopolitics of Geopolitical Space: Towards a Critical Social Theory of International Politics', *Alternatives*, 12/4: 403–34.

—— (1988), 'Untying the Sovereign State: A Double Reading of the Anarchy Problematique', *Millennium: Journal of International Studies*, 17/2: 227–62.

—— (1989), 'Living on Border Lines: Man, Poststructuralism and War', in J. Der Derian and M. Shapiro (eds.), *International/Intertextual Relations: Postmodern Readings of World Politics* (Lexington, KY: Lexington Books), 259–322.

Ashley, R. and Walker, R. B. J. (eds.) (1990), 'Conclusion: Reading Dissidence/Writing the Discipline: Crisis and the Question of Sovereignty in International Studies', *International Studies Quarterly*, 34/3: 367–416.

Axelrod, R. (1981), 'The Emergence of Cooperation Among Egoists', *American Political Science Review* 75 (June).

Bacevich, A. (2005a), *The New American Militarism*. (Oxford: Oxford University Press).

Bacevich, A. (2005b), 'The Real World War IV', *Wilson Quarterly*, 29/1.

Bacevich, A. (2008), *The Limits of Power*. (New York: Metropolitan Books).

Bacevich, A. (2010), *Washington Rules*. (New York: Metropolitan Books).

Bagwell, K. and Staiger, R. W. (2004), *The Economics of the World Trading System* (Cambridge, MA: MIT Press).

Bain, W. (2003), *Between Anarchy and Society: Trusteeship and the Obligations of Power* (Oxford: Oxford University Press).

Bairoch, P. (1996), 'Globalisation Myths and Realities: One Century of External Trade and Foreign Investment', in R. Boyer and D. Drache (eds.), *States Against Market: The Limits of Globalisation* (London: Routledge), 173–92.

Baldwin, D. (1985), *Economic Statecraft* (Princeton, NJ: Princeton University Press).

Banks, M. (1984), 'The Evolution of International Relations', in M. Banks (ed.), *Conflict in World Society: A New Perspective on International Relations* (Brighton: Harvester Press), 3–21.

Barkin, S. (2003), 'Realist Constructivism,' *International Studies Review* 5: 325–42.

Barnett, J. (2001), *The Meaning of Environmental Security: Ecological Politics and Policy in the New Security Era* (London: Zed Books).

Barnett, M. and Duvall, R. (2005), 'Power in International Relations,' *International Organization* 59: 39–75.

Barnett, M. and Finnemore, M. (2004), *Rules for the World: International Organizations in Global Politics* (Ithaca, NY: Cornell University Press).

Barry, B. (1973), *The Liberal Theory of Justice* (Oxford: Clarendon Press).

Barry, J. (1999), *Rethinking Green Politics* (London: Sage Publications).

Barry, J. and Eckersley, R. (2005), *The State and the Global Ecological Crisis* (Cambridge, MA: MIT Press).

Bartelson, J. (1995), *The Genealogy of Sovereignty* (Cambridge: Cambridge University Press).

Bayoumi, T. (1990), 'Savings–Investment Correlations', *IMF Staff Papers*, 37: 360–87.

—— (1997), *Financial Integration and Real Activity* (Manchester: Manchester University Press).

Beardsworth, R. (2011), Cosmopolitanism and International Relations Theory (Cambridge, Polity).

Benjamin, W. (1968), *Illuminations*, edited and with an introduction by Hannah Arendt (New York: Schocken Books).

Beck, U. (1992), *The Risk Society: Towards a New Modernity*, translated by M. Ritter (London: Sage Publications).

Beck, U. (1999), *World Risk Society* (Cambridge: Polity Press).

Beitz, C. R. (1979/1999), *Political Theory and International Relations*, 2nd edn. (Princeton, NJ: Princeton University Press).

Beitz, C. R., Cohen, M., Scanlon, T., and Simmons, A. J. (eds.) (1985), *International Ethics* (Princeton, NJ: Princeton University Press).

Bensmaïa, R. (2003), *Experimental Nations: Or, the Invention of the Maghreb* (Princeton, NJ: Princeton University Press).

Benthall, J. (1993), *Disasters, Relief and the Media* (London: I. B. Tauris).

Berger, P. L. (2002), 'Introduction: The Cultural Dynamics of Globalization', in P. L. Berger and S. P. Huntington (eds.), *Many Globalizations: Cultural Diversity in the Contemporary World* (Oxford: Oxford University Press), 1–16.

Bernstein, R. (1979), *The Restructuring of Social and Political Theory* (London: Methuen).

—— (1983), *Beyond Objectivism and Relativism* (Oxford: Blackwell).

Bernstein, S. (2002), *The Compromise of Liberal Environmentalism* (New York: Columbia University Press).

Bhabha, H. (1994), *The Location of Culture* (New York: Routledge).

Bhaskar, R. (1978), *A Realist Theory of Science* (Hassocks: Harvester Press).

—— (1979), *The Possibility of Naturalism: A Philosophical Critique of the Contemporary Human Sciences* (Atlantic Highlands, NJ: Humanities Press).

Bin Laden, O. (2001), 'Text: Bin Laden's Statement', Al Jazeera, 7 October.

Blair, T. (2001), 'Statement on Military Action in Afghanistan', 7 October, available at: http://www.number-10.gov.uk/output/page1615.asp, accessed 8 January 2008.

—— (2004), 'Prime Minister's Press Conference', 25 May, available at: http://www.number-10.gov.uk/output/Page5860.asp, accessed 16 April 2009.

Bleiker, R. (1997), 'Forget IR Theory', *Alternatives*, 22/1: 57–85.

—— (2001), 'The Aesthetic Turn in International Political Theory', *Millennium: Journal of International Studies*, 30/3: 509–33.

—— (2005), *Divided Korea: Toward a Culture of Reconciliation* (Minneapolis: University of Minnesota Press).

Bohr, N. (1957), *Atomfysik og menneskelig erkendelse* (Copenhagen: J. H. Schultz Forlag).

Booth, K. (1995), 'Dare Not Know: International Relations Theory versus the Future', in K. Booth and S. Smith (eds.), *International Relations Theory Today* (Cambridge: Polity).

—— (1997), 'Discussion: A Reply to Wallace', *Review of International Studies*, 23/2: 371–7.

—— (ed.) (2005), *Critical Security Studies and World Politics* (Boulder, CO: Lynne Rienner Publishers).Booth, K. and Dunne, T. (2012), *Terror in our Time* (London: Routledge).

Bown, C. and Hoekman. B. (2008), 'Developing Countries and Enforcement of Trade Agreements: Why Dispute Settlement is Not Enough,' *Journal of World Trade*, 42/1: 177–203.

Brams, S. J. and Marc Kilgour, D. (1991), *Game Theory and National Security* (New York: Wiley-Blackwell).

Branigin, W. (2003), 'A Gruesome Scene on Highway 9: 10 Dead After Vehicle Shelled at Checkpoint', *The Washington Post*, 1 April, A01, Available at: http://www.washingtonpost.com/ac2/wp-dyn/A61229-2003Mar31?language=printer, accessed 7 April 2009.

Breuning, M., Bredehoft, J., and Walton, E. (2005),'Promise and Performance: An Evaluation of Journals in International Relations', *International Studies Perspectives*, 6/4: 447–61.

Brewer, A. (1990), *Marxist Theories of Imperialism: A Critical Survey*, 2nd edn. (London: Routledge).

Bronner, S. E. (2002), *Of Critical Theory and its Theorists*, 2nd edn. (New York: Routledge).

Brown, C. (1988), 'The Modern Requirement? Reflections on Normative International Theory in a Post-Western World', *Millennium: Journal of International Studies*, 17/2: 339–48.

—— (1992), *International Relations Theory: New Normative Approaches* (London: Harvester Wheatsheaf).

—— (1994), '"Turtles All the Way Down": Antifoundationalism, Critical Theory and International Relations', *Millennium: Journal of International Studies*, 23/2: 213–38.

—— (1997), *Understanding International Relations* (Basingstoke: Macmillan).

—— (2002), *Sovereignty, Rights and Justice* (Cambridge: Polity).

Brown, G. (2006), UK Chancellor Gordon Brown, BBC News, 22 April 2006, available at: http://news.bbc.co.uk/1/hi/uk_politics/4932988.stm, accessed 29 August 2007.

Brown, S., Coté, O., Lynn-Jones, S., and Miller, S. (eds.) (2011), *Do Democracies Win Their Wars* (Cambridge, MA: M.I.T. Press).

Brunkhorst, H. (2002), 'Globalizing Democracy Without a State: Weak Public, Strong Public, Global Constitutionalism', *Millennium* 31/1: 675–90.

Bryant, R. and Bailey, S. (1997), *Third World Political Ecology* (London: Routledge).

Bueno de Mesquita, B., Smith, A., Siverson, R., and Morrow, J. (2003), *The Logic of Political Survival* (Cambridge, MA: MIT Press).

Büger, C. and Gadinger, F. (2006), 'Große Gräben, Brücken, Elfenbeintürme und Klöster? Die Wissensgemeinschaft Internationale Beziehungen und die Politik—Eine kulturtheoretische Neubeschreibung', in G. Hellmann (ed.), *Forschung und Beratung in der Wissensgesellschaft* (Baden-Baden: Nomos).

Bull, H. (1996), 'International Theory: The Case for the Classical Approach', *World Politics*, 18.3: 361–77.

Bull, H. (1977/1995), *The Anarchical Society: A Study, of Order in World Politics* (London: Macmillan).

—— (2000), 'International Relations as an Academic Pursuit', in K. Alderson and A. Hurrell (eds.), *Hedley Bull on International Society* (Basingstoke: Macmillan).

Bull, H. and Watson, A. (1984), *The Expansion of International Society* (Oxford: Clarendon Press).

Burchill, S. et al. (1997), *Theories of International Relations* (Palgrave: Basingstoke).

Busch, M. L. (2000), 'Democracy, Consultation, and the Paneling of Disputes Under GATT', *Journal of Conflict Resolution*, 44/4: 425–46.

Busch, M. L. and Reinhardt, E. (2006), 'Three's a Crowd: Third Parties and WTO Dispute Settlement' *World Politics*, 58(3): 446–77.

Bush, G. W. (2001a), 'Address to a Joint Session of Congress and the American People', White House, 20 September, available at: http://www.whitehouse.gov/news/releases/2001/09/20010920.html, accessed 4 May 2006.

—— (2001b), 'President Discusses War on Terrorism', White House, 8 November, available at: http://www.whitehouse/gov/news/releases/2001/09/20011108.html, accessed 2 May 2006.

—— (2002), 'President Bush Delivers Graduation Speech at West Point', 1 June 2002, available at: http://www.whitehouse.gov/news/releases/2002/06/20020601-3.html, accessed 8 January 2008.

—— (2003), 'President Bush Rallies Troops at MacDill USAF Base', 26 March 2003, available at: http://www.whitehouse.gov/news/releases/2003/03/20030326-4.html, accessed 21 January 2008.

Butler, J. (1993), *Bodies that Matter: On the Discursive Limits of 'Sex'* (New York: Routledge).

Butterfield, H. and Wight, M. (1966) (eds.), *Diplomatic Investigations: Essays in the Theory of International Relations* (London: Allen & Unwin).

Buzan, B. (2001), 'The English School: An Underexploited Resource in IR', *Review of International Studies*, 27(3) 471–88.

—— (2004), *From International to World Society* (Cambridge: Cambridge University Press).

Buzan, B. and Little, R. (2000), *International Systems in World History: Remaking the Study of International Relations* (Oxford: Oxford University Press).

Buzan, B., Held, D., and McGrew, A. (1998), 'Realism versus Cosmopolitanism' *Review of International Studies*, 24/3: 387–98.

Buzan, B., Jones, C. A., and Little, R. (1993), *The Logic of Anarchy: Neorealism to Structural Realism* (New York: Columbia University Press).

Buzan, B., Wæver, O., and de Wilde, J. (1998), *Security: A New Framework of Analysis* (Boulder, CO: Lynne Rienner).

Bybee, J. S. (2002), 'Memo 14—Re: Standards of Conduct for Interrogation', in K. J. Greenberg, J. L. Dratel, and A. Lewis (2005), *The Torture Papers: The Road to Abu Ghraib* (Cambridge: Cambridge University Press).

Cameron, D. R. (1978), 'The Expansion of the Public Economy: A Comparative Analysis', *American Political Science Review*, 72(4): 1243–61.

Campbell, D. (1992), *Writing Security: United States Foreign Policy and the Politics of Identity* (Manchester: Manchester University Press).

—— (1998a), *Writing Security: United States Foreign Policy and the Politics of Identity*, 2nd edn. (Minneapolis: University of Minnesota Press).

—— (1998b), *National Deconstruction: Violence, Identity and Justice in Bosnia* (Minneapolis: University of Minnesota Press).

—— (2005), 'The Biopolitics of Security: Oil, Empire and the Sports Utility Vehicle', *American Quarterly*, 57/3: 943–72.

Campbell, D. and Dillon, M. (1993), *The Political Subject of Violence* (Manchester: Manchester University Press).

Campbell, D. T. (1969), 'Ethnocentrism of Disciplines and the Fish-scale Model of Omniscience', in M. Sherif and C. W. Sherif (eds.), *Interdisciplinary Relationships in the Social Sciences* (Chicago: Aldine Publishing), 328–48.

Caney, S. (2005), *Justice Beyond Borders: A Global Political Theory* (Oxford: Oxford University Press).

Caprioli, M. and Boyer, M. (2001), 'Gender, Violence, and International Crisis', *Journal of Conflict Resolution*, 45/4: 503–18.

Carlsnaes, W., Risse, T., and Simmons, B. A. (2002) (eds.), *Handbook of International Relations* (London: Sage).

Carr, E. H. (1946), *The Twenty Years' Crisis 1919–1939: An Introduction to the Study of International Relations*, 2nd edn. (London: Macmillan).

—— (1987), *What Is History?*, 2nd edn. (London: Penguin).

Cerny, P. G. (1995), 'Globalisation and the Changing Logic of Collective Action', *International Organisation*, 49/4: 595–625.

—— (1997), 'Paradoxes of the Competition State: The Dynamics of Political Globalisation', *Government and Opposition*, 32/1: 251–74.

—— (2000), 'Political Globalisation and the Competition State', in R. Stubbs and G. R. D. Underhill (eds.), *Political Economy and the Changing Global Order* (Oxford: Oxford University Press).

Césaire, A. (2000), *Discourse on Colonialism*, translated by J. Pinkham (New York: Monthly Review Press).

Chakrabarty, D. (2000), *Provincializing Europe: Postcolonial Thought and Historical Difference* (Princeton, NJ: Princeton University Press).

Chatterjee, P. (1986), *Nationalist Thought and the Colonial World: The Derivative Discourse?* (Minneapolis: University of Minnesota Press).

Chayes, A. and Chayes, A. H. (1993), 'On Compliance', *International Organization*, 47/2: 175–205.

Checkel, J. T. (1997), 'International Norms and Domestic Politics: Bridging the Rationalist–Constructivist Divide', *European Journal of International Relations*, 3/4: 473–95.

—— (1998), 'The Constructivist Turn in International Relations Theory', *World Politics*, 50/2: 324–48.

Cheyfitz, E. (1997), *The Poetics of Imperialism: Translation and Colonization from the Tempest to Tarzan* (Philadelphia: University of Pennsylvania Press).

Chin, C. (1998), *In Service and Servitude: Foreign Female Domestic Workers and the Malaysian 'Modernity' Project* (New York: Columbia University Press).

Christoff, P. (1996), 'Ecological Modernisation, Ecological Modernities', *Environmental Politics*, 5/3: 476–500.

Clapp, J. and Dauvergne, P. (2011), *Paths to a Green World: The Political Economy of the Global Environment* (Cambridge, MA: MIT Press).

Clark, B. R. (1983), *The Higher Education System: Academic Organization in Cross-national Perspective* (Berkeley: University of California Press).

Clark, B. R. and Youn, T. I. K. (1976), *Academic Power in the United States: Comparative Historic and Structural Perspectives* (Washington, DC: American Association for Higher Education).

Clark, I. (1999), *Globalisation and International Relations Theory* (Oxford: Oxford University Press).

—— (2005), *Legitimacy in International Society* (Oxford: Oxford University Press).

—— (2007), *International Legitimacy and World Society* (Oxford: Oxford University Press).

Cochran, M. (1999), *Normative Theory in International Relations: A Pragmatic Approach* (Cambridge: Cambridge University Press).

Cohn B. S. (1996), *Colonialism and its Forms of Knowledge: The British in India* (Princeton, NJ: Princeton University Press).

Cohn, T. H. (2005), *Global Political Economy: Theory and Practice*, 3rd edn (New York: Pearson Longman).

Colas, A. and Saull, R. (eds.) (2006), *The War on Terrorism and the American 'Empire' after the Cold War* (London: Routledge).

Coll, S. (2004), *Ghost Wars* (New York: Penguin).

Collins, R. (1975), *Conflict Sociology: Towards an Explanatory Science* (New York: Academic).

——(1994), 'Why the Social Sciences Won't Become High-consensus, Rapid-discovery Science', *Sociological Forum*, 9/2, 155–77.

——(1998), *The Sociology of Philosophies: A Global Theory of Intellectual Change* (Cambridge, MA: Belknap).

Conca, K. (2000), 'Beyond the Statist Frame: Environmental Politics in a Global Economy', in F. P. Gale and R. M. M'Gonigle, *Nature, Production, Power: Towards an Ecological Political Economy* (Cheltenham: Edward Elgar), 141–55.

Conca, K. and Dabelko, G. (2003), *Environmental Peacemaking* (Washington, DC: Woodrow Wilson Center Press).

Connolly, W. (1991), *Identity/Difference: Democratic Negotiations of Political Paradox* (Ithaca, NY: Cornell University Press).

——(2004), 'Method, Problem, Faith', in I. Shapiro, R. M. Smith, and T. E. Masoud (eds.), *Problems and Methods in the Study of Politics* (Cambridge: Cambridge University Press).

Constantinou, C. M. (1995), 'NATO's Caps: European Security and the Future of the North Atlantic Alliance', *Alternatives*, 20/2: 147–64.

——(1996), *On the Way to Diplomacy* (Minneapolis: University of Minnesota Press).

Cook, R. (2004), 'Bush Will Now Celebrate by Putting Fallujah to the Torch', *The Guardian*, 5 November.

Cooke, W. N. and Noble, D. S. (1998), 'Industrial Relations Systems and US Foreign Direct Investment Abroad', *British Journal of Industrial Relations*, 36/4: 581–609.

Copeland, D. C. (2000), *The Origins of Major War* (Ithaca, NY: Cornell University Press).

Coward, M. (2002), 'Community as Heterogeneous Ensemble: Mostar and Multiculturalism', *Alternatives*, 27/1: 29–66.

Cox, R. (1981), 'Social Forces, States and World Orders: Beyond International Relations Theory', *Millennium: Journal of International Studies*, 10/2: 126–55.

——(1983), 'Gramsci, Hegemony, and International Relations: An Essay in Method', *Millennium*, 12: 162–75.

——(1986), 'Social Forces, States and World Orders: Beyond International Relations Theories', in R. Keohane (ed.), *Neorealism and its Critics* (New York: Columbia University Press), 204–54.

Crawford, N. C. and Klotz, A. (1999), *How Sanctions Work: Lessons from South Africa* (New York: Palgrave Macmillan).

Crawford, N. (2001), *Argument and Change in World Politics: Ethics, Decolonization and Humanitarian Intervention* (Cambridge: Cambridge University Press).

Culler, J. (1982), *On Deconstruction: Theory and Criticism after Structuralism* (Ithaca, NY: Cornell University Press).

Daalder, I. H. and Lindsay, J. M. (2005), *America Unbound: The Bush Revolution in Foreign Policy*, revised edn. (Hoboken, NJ: John Wiley & Sons Inc.).

Dauvergne. P. (2008), *The Shadows of Consumption: Consequences for the Global Environment* (Cambridge, MA: MIT Press).

Davis, C. (2003), *Food Fights over Free Trade: How International Institutions Promote Agricultural Trade Liberalization* (Princeton, NJ: Princeton University Press).

Davis, N. A. (1991), 'Contemporary Deontology', in P. Singer (ed.), *A Companion to Ethics* (Oxford: Basil Blackwell).

Debrix, F. (1999), *Re-envisioning Peacekeeping: The UN and the Mobilization of Ideology* (Minneapolis: University of Minnesota Press).

de Goede, M. (2003), 'Beyond Economism in International Political Economy', *Review of International Studies*, 29/1: 79–97.

——(2005), *Virtue, Fortune and Faith: A Genealogy of Finance* (Minneapolis: University of Minnesota Press).

——(2006), *International Political Economy and Poststructural Politics* (Basingstoke: Palgrave).

Deitelhoff, N. (2009), 'The Discursive Profess of Legalization: Charting Islands of Persuasion in the ICC', *International Organization*, 63/1.

Deitelhoff, N. and H. Müller (2005), 'Theoretical Paradise-empirically lost? Arguing with Habermas', *Review of International Studies*, 31: 167–79.

Deleuze, G. (1988), *Foucault* (Minneapolis: University of Minnesota Press).

Der Derian, J. (1987), *On Diplomacy: A Genealogy of Western Estrangement* (Oxford: Blackwell).

—— (1992), *Antidiplomacy: Spies, Terror, Speed, and War* (Oxford: Blackwell).

—— (1994) (ed.), *Critical Investigations* (London: Macmillan).

—— (2001), *Virtuous War: Mapping the Military–Industrial–Media–Entertainment Network* (Boulder, CO: Westview).

—— (2003), 'Hedley Bull and the Case for a Post-Classical Approach', in H. Bauer and E. Brighi (eds.), *International Relations at LSE: A History of 75 Years* (London: Millennium Publishing Group).

Der Derian, J. and Shapiro, M. J. (1989) (eds.), *International/Intertextual Relations: Postmodern Readings of World Politics* (Lexington, KY: Lexington Books).

Descombes, V. (1981), *Modern French Philosophy*, translated by L. Scott-Fox and J. M. Harding (Cambridge: Cambridge University Press).

Deudney, D. (1990), 'The Case Against Linking Environmental Degradation to National Security', *Millennium: Journal of International Studies*, 19/3: 461–76.

Deutsch, K. W. (1957), *Political Community and the North Atlantic Area* (Princeton, NJ: Princeton University Press).

Devetak, R. 'Postmodernism', in S. Burchill, A. Linklater, et al. (eds.), *Theories of International Relations*, 2nd edn. (London: Palgrave), 181–208.

Devetak, R. (1995), 'The Project of Modernity and International Relations Theory,' *Millennium: Journal of International Studies*, 24/1: 27–51.

Diamond, L. (2004), 'What Went Wrong in Iraq?', *Foreign Affairs*, 83/September–October: 9–22.

Diels, H. and Kranz, W. (1956), *Die Fragmente der Vorsokratiker*, 7th edn. (Berlin: Weidmanische Verlansbuchhandlung).

Diez, M. and J. Steans (eds.) (2005), 'A useful dialogue? Habermas and International Relations,' *Review of International Studies*, 31/1.

Dillon, M. (1996), *The Politics of Security: Towards a Political Philosophy of Continental Thought* (London: Routledge).

—— (2000), 'Poststructuralism, Complexity and Poetics', *Theory, Culture and Society*, 17/5: 1–26.

—— (2003), 'Virtual Security: A Life Science of (Dis) Order', *Millennium: Journal of International Studies*, 32/3: 531–8.

Dillon, M. and Reid, J. (2001), 'Global Liberal Governance: Biopolitics, Security and War', *Millennium: Journal of International Studies*, 30/1: 41–66.

Dirks, N. B. (2001), *Castes of Mind: Colonialism and the Making of Modern India* (Princeton, NJ: Princeton University Press).

Dobson, A. (2003), *Citizenship and the Environment* (Oxford: Oxford University Press).

Doherty, B. and de Geus, M. (1996) (eds.), *Democracy and Green Political Thought: Sustainability, Rights and Citizenship* (London: Routledge).

Doty, R. L. (1993), 'Foreign Policy as Social Construction: A Post-positivist Analysis of US Counterinsurgency Policy in the Philippines', *International Studies Quarterly*, 37/3: 297–320.

—— (1996), *Imperial Encounters: The Politics of Representation in North–South Relations* (Minneapolis: University of Minnesota Press).

Downs, G. W., Rocke, D. M., and Barsoom, P. N. (2001), 'Is the Good News About Compliance Good News About Cooperation?' In *International Institutions: An International Organization Reader*, L. Martin, and B. Simmons (eds.) (Boston, MA: MIT Press) 279–306.

Doyle, M. (1997), *Ways of War and Peace: Realism, Liberalism, and Socialism* (New York and London: Norton).

Dreyfuss, R. (2003), 'The Thirty-year Itch', *Mother Jones* (March–April): 41–5.

Du Bois, W. E. B. (1999), *The Souls of Black Folk* (New York: Norton).

Dunne, T. (1998), *Inventing International Society: A History of the English School* (Houndmills: Macmillan).

—— (2005), 'System, State and Society: How Does It All Hang Together', *Millennium: Journal of International Studies*, 34/1, 157–70.

Dunne, T., Kurki, M., and Smith, S. (2013) (eds.), *International Relations Theories: Discipline and Diversity*, 3rd end. (Oxford: Oxford University Press).

Dunne, T. and Wheeler, N. J. (1999), *Human Rights in Global Politics* (Cambridge: Cambridge University Press).

Dunning, J. H. (1988), 'The Eclectic Paradigm of International Production: An Update and Some Possible Extensions', *Journal of International Business Studies*, 19/1: 1–32.

Eckersley, R. (2004), *The Green State: Rethinking Democracy and Sovereignty* (Cambridge MA: MIT Press).

—— (2007), 'Ecological Intervention: Prospects and Limits', *Ethics and International Affairs* 21/3: 275–396.

The Ecologist, reprinted as Goldsmith, E. (1972), *A Blueprint for Survival* (Harmondsworth: Penguin).

Edkins, J. (1999), *Poststructuralism and International Relations: Bringing the Political Back In* (Boulder, CO: Lynne Reinner).

—— (2000), *Whose Hunger? Concepts of Famine, Practices of Aid* (Minneapolis: University of Minnesota Press).

—— (2003), *Trauma and the Memory of Politics* (Cambridge: Cambridge University Press).

Edkins, J., Pin-Fat, V., and Shapiro, M. J. (2004) (eds.), *Sovereign Lives: Power in Global Politics* (New York: Routledge).

Edkins, J. (2011), *Missing: Persons and Politics* (Cornell: Cornell University Press).

Elsig, M. (2011), 'Principal-Agent Theory and the World Trade Organization: Complex Agency and 'missing delegation," *European Journal of International Relations*, 17/3: 495–517.

Elshtain, J. (1992), *Women and War* (Chicago: University of Chicago Press).

Enloe, C. (1990), *Bananas, Beaches and Bases: Making Feminist Sense of International Politics* (New York: Routledge).

——(2000), *Maneuvers: The International Politics of Militarizing Women's Lives* (Berkeley: University of California Press).

——(2010), *Nimo's War, Emma's War: Making Feminist Sense of the War in Iraq* (Berkeley: University of California Press).

Epp, R. (1998), 'The English School on the Frontiers of International Society: A Hermeneutic Recollection', *Review of International Studies*, Special Issue, 24: 47–63.

Erskine, T. (2003a) (ed.), *Can Institutions Have Responsibilities? Collective Moral Agency and International Relations* (New York and Basingstoke: Palgrave Macmillan).

Erskine, T. (2003b), 'Making Sense of 'Responsibility in International Relations – Key Questions and Concepts', in T. Erskine (ed.) *Can Institutions Have Responsibilities? Collective Moral Agency and International Relations* (New York and Basingstoke: Palgrave Macmillan), 1–16.

Erskine, T. (2008a), *Embedded Cosmopolitanism: Duties to Strangers and Enemies in a World of 'Dislocated Communities'* (Oxford: Oxford University Press).

Erskine, T. (2008b), 'Locating Responsibility: The Problem of Moral Agency in International Relations', in C. Reus-Smit and D. Snidal (eds.), *The Oxford Handbook of International Relations* (Oxford: Oxford University Press), 699–707.

Erskine, T. and Lebow, R. N. (2010) (eds.), *Tragedy and International Relations* (Basingstoke: Palgrave Macmillan).

Everest, L. (2004), *Oil, Power, and Empire* (Monroe, ME: Common Courage Press).

Fanon, F. (1968), *Wretched of the Earth*, translated by C. Farrington (New York: Grove Press).

Fattah, K. and Fierke, K. (2009), 'A Clash of Emotions: The Politics of Humiliation and Political Violence in the Middle East', *European Journal of International Relations*, 15/1: 67–93.

Fearon, J. and Wendt, A. (2002), 'Rationalism v. Constructivism: A Skeptical View', in W. Carlsnaes, T. Risse, and B. A. Simmons (eds.), *Handbook of International Relations* (London: Sage), 52–72.

Feldstein, M. and Horioka, C. (1980), 'Domestic Savings and International Capital Flows', *Economic Journal*, 90/358: 314–29.

Ferguson, K. and Turnbull, P. (1998), *Oh, Say, Can You See? The Semiotics of the Military in Hawaii* (Minneapolis: University of Minnesota Press).

Fetter, B. (1979), *Colonial Rule in Africa: Readings from Primary Sources* (Madison: University of Wisconsin Press).

Fierke, K. M. (2007), *Critical Approaches to International Security* (London: Polity).

Fierke, K. M. and Jorgensen, K. E. (2001), *Constructing International Relations: The Next Generation* (Armonk, NY: M. E. Sharpe).

Finnemore, M. (1996), *National Interests and International Society* (Ithaca, NY: Cornell University Press).

Finnemore, M. and Sikkink, K. (1998), 'International Norm Dynamics and Political Change', *International Organization*, 52: 887–918.

Foot, R. (2000), *Rights beyond Borders: The Global Community and the Struggle over Human Rights in China* (Oxford: Oxford University Press).

Foucault, M. (1972 [1969]), *The Archeology of Knowledge*, translated by A. M. Sheridan Smith (London: Tavistock Publishers).

——(1977), 'Nietzsche, Genealogy, History', in D. F. Bouchard (ed.), *Language, Counter-memory, Practice: Selected Essays and Interviews* (Ithaca, NY: Cornell University Press).

——(1979), *Discipline and Punish: The Birth of the Prison*, translated by A. Sheridan (New York: Vintage Books).

——(1982), 'Afterword: The Subject and Power', in H. L. Dreyfus and P. Rabinow, *Michel Foucault: Beyond Structuralism and Hermeneutics* (Brighton: Harvester Press), 208–26.

——(1984), 'What is Enlightenment?' in P. Rabinow (ed.), *The Foucault Reader* (New York: Pantheon Books), 32–50.

——(1988), *Politics, Philosophy and Culture: Interviews and Other Writings 1977–1984*, edited and with an introduction by L. D. Krittman, translated by A. Sheridan et al. (New York and London: Routledge).

Frankel, J. A. (1997), *Regional Trading Blocs: In the World Economic System* (Washington DC: Institute for International Economics).

——(1998) (ed.), *The Regionalisation of the World Economy* (Cambridge MA: National Bureau of Economic Research).

Fraser, N. (1997), *Justice Interruptus: Critical Reflections on the Postsocialist Condition* (New York and London: Routledge).

Friedrichs, J. (2004), *European Approaches to International Relations Theory: A House with Many Mansions* (London: Routledge).

Frost, M. (1986), *Towards a Normative Theory of International Relations* (Cambridge: Cambridge University Press).

—— (1996), *Ethics in International Relations* (Cambridge: Cambridge University Press).

Fuchs, S. (1993), 'A Sociological Theory of Scientific Change', *Social Forces*, 71/4: 933–53.

Fuerstman, D. and Lavertu, S. (2005), 'The Academic Hiring Process: A Survey of Departmental Chairs', *PS: Political Science and Politics*, 38/4: 731–6.

Fuller, S. (2000), *The Governance of Science: Ideology and the Future of the Open Society* (Buckingham: Open University Press).

—— (2002 [1988]), *Social Epistemology*, 2nd edn. (Bloomington: Indiana University Press).

Gale, F. P. and M'Gonigle, R. M. (2000), *Nature, Production, Power: Towards an Ecological Political Economy* (Cheltenham: Edward Elgar).

Galeano, E. (1985), *Genesis*, Memory of Fire Trilogy, Part 1 (New York: Norton).

Gallarotti, G. M. (1991), 'The Limits of International Organization: Systematic Failure in the Management of International Relations', *International Organization*, 45/2: 183–220.

Gates, S. and. Humes, B. D. (1997), *Games, Information, and Politics: Applying Game Theoretic Models to Political Science* (Ann Arbor: University of Michigan Press).

Gause III, F. G. (2011) 'Why the Middle East Studies Missed the Arab Spring', *Foreign Affairs* 90/4 (July/ August): 81–90.

Geiger, R. L. (2005), 'The Ten Generations of American Higher Education', in P. G. Altbach, R. O. Berdahl, and P. J. Gumport (eds.), *American Higher Education in the Twenty-first Century: Social, Political and Economic Challenges*, 2nd edn. (Baltimore, MD: Johns Hopkins University Press), 58–70.

Geiss, A., Brock, L., and Muller, H. (2006) (eds.), *Democratic Wars: The Dark Side of the Democratic Peace* (Houndmills: Palgrave Macmillan).

George, J. (1994), *Discourses of Global Politics: A Critical (Re)Introduction to International Relations* (Boulder, CO: Lynne Reinner).

Germain, R. D. and Kenny, M. (eds.) (1998), 'Engaging Gramsci: International Relations theory and the New Gramscians', *Review of International Studies*, 24: 3–21.

Gibbons, M., Limoges, C., Nowotny, H., Schwartzman, S., Scott, P., and Trow, M. (1994), *The New Production of Knowledge: The Dynamics of Science and Research in Contemporary Societies* (London: Sage).

Giddens, A. (1984), *The Constitution of Society: Outline of the Theory of Structuration* (Berkeley, CA: University of California Press and Cambridge: Polity).

Gilroy, P. (1993), *The Black Atlantic: Modernity and Double- consciousness* (Cambridge, MA: Harvard University Press).

Gilroy, P. (2005), *The Black Atlantic: Modernity and Double-consciousness* (Cambridge, MA: Harvard University Press).

Glaser, C. L. (1997), 'The Security Dilemma Revisited', *World Politics*, 50/1: 171–201.

Gleditsch, K. (2002), *All International Politics is Local: The Diffusion of Conflict, Integration, and Democratization* (Ann Arbor: University of Michigan Press).

Goldstein, J. and Keohane, R. O. (1993) (eds.), *Ideas and Foreign Policy: Beliefs, Institutions, and Political Change* (Ithaca, NY: Cornell University Press).

Goldstein, J., Kahler, M., Keohane, R. O., and Slaughter, A. (2000), 'Introduction: Legalization and World Politics', *International Organization*, 54/3: 385–99.

Goldstein, J. (2011), *Winning the War on War* (New York: Dutton).

Gong, G. W. (1984), *The Standard of 'Civilization' in International Society* (Oxford: Clarendon Press).

Gonzalez-Pelaez, A. (2005), *Human Rights and World Trade: Hunger in International Society* (London: Routledge).

Goodson, L. P., Dillman, B., and Hira, A. (1999), 'Ranking the Presses: Political Scientists' Evaluations of Publisher Quality', *PS: Political Science and Politics*, 32/2: 257–62.

Goodwin, G. L. (1951) (ed.), *The University Teaching of International Relations* (Oxford: Blackwell; Paris: Presses Universitaires de France).

Gordon, J. (1999), 'Economic Sanctions, Just War Doctrine, and the "Fearful Spectacle of the Civilian Dead"', *Cross Currents*, 49/3, available at: http://www.crosscurrents.org, accessed 3 August 2012.

Gramsci, A. (1971), *Selections from the Prison Notebooks*, edited by Q. Hoare and G. N. Smith (New York: International Publishers).

Grant, J. T. (2005), 'What Divides Us? The Image and Organization of Political Science', *PS: Political Science and Politics*, 38/3: 379–86.

Gregory, D. (1995), 'Between the Book and the Lamp: Imaginative Geographies of Egypt, 1849–50', *Transactions of the Institute of British Geographers*, 20/1: 29–57.

Grieco, J. M. (1990), *Cooperation Among Nations: Europe, America, and Non-Tariff Barriers to Trade* (Ithaca, NY: Cornell University Press).

—— (1993), 'Understanding the Problem of International Cooperation: The Limits of Neoliberal Institutionalism and the Future of Realist Theory', in D. A. Baldwin (ed.) *Neorealism and Neoliberalism: The Contemporary Debate* (New York: Columbia University Press).

Grovogui, S. N. Z. (1996), *Sovereigns, Quasi Sovereigns, and Africans: Race and Self-determination in International Law* (Minneapolis: University of Minnesota Press).

—— (2006), *Beyond Eurocentrism and Anarchy: Memories of International Order and Institutions* (New York: Palgrave Macmillan).

Guha, R. (1988a), 'The Prose of Counter-Insurgency', in R. Guha, G. Chakravorty Spivak, and E. Said (eds.), *Selected Subaltern Studies* (Oxford: Oxford University Press).

Guha, R. (1988b), 'On Some Aspects of the Historiography of Colonial India', in R. Guha, G. Chakravorty Spivak, and E. Said (eds.), *Selected Subaltern Studies* (Oxford: Oxford University Press).

Gunnell, J. G. (1991), 'In Search of the State: Political Science as an Emerging Discipline in the U.S.', in P. Wagner, B. Wittrock, and R. Whitley (eds.), *Discourses on Society: The Shaping of the Social Science Disciplines*, Sociology of the Sciences Yearbook (Reidel: Kluwer), 123–62.

—— (2002), 'Handbooks and History: Is it Still the American Science of Politics?', *International Political Science Review*, 23/4: 339–54.

Guzzini, S. (1998), *Realism in International Relations and International Political Economy: The Continuing Story of a Death Foretold* (London: Routledge).

Guzzini, S. (2005a) 'The Concept of Power: A Constructivist Analysis,' *Millennium*, 33: 495–521.

Guzzini, S. and A. Leander, eds. (2005b) *Constructivism and International Relations: Alexander Wendt and his Critics* (London: Routledge).

Haacke, J. (2005), 'The Frankfurt School and International Relations: on the centrality of recognition,' *Review of International Studies* 31(1): 181–94.

Haas, P. M., Keohane, R. O., and Levy, M. A. (1993) (eds.), *Institutions for the Earth: Sources of Effective International Environmental Protection* (Cambridge, MA: MIT Press).

Habermas, J. (1996), *Between Facts and Norms* (Cambridge, MA: MIT Press).

—— (1984), *The Theory of Communicative Action*. Volume 1. (Boston: Beacon Press).

—— (2006), *The Divided West*. (London: Polity Press).

Haggard, S. and Simmons, B. A. (1987), 'Theories of International Regimes', *International Organization*, 41/3: 491–517.

Hajer, M. (1995), *The Politics of Environmental Discourse: Ecological Modernization and the Policy Process* (Oxford: Clarendon Press).

Halliday, F. (1996), 'The Future of International Relations: Fears and Hopes', in S. Smith, K. Booth, and M. Zalewski (eds.), *International Theory: Positivism and Beyond* (Cambridge: Cambridge University Press), 318–27.

Hammond, T. H. (2004), 'Herding Cats in University Hierarchies: Formal Structure and Policy Choice in American Research Universities', in R. G. Ehrenberg (ed.), *Governing Academia: Who Is in Charge of the Modern University?* (Ithaca, NY: Cornell University Press).

Hansen, L. (2006), *Security as Practice: Discourse Analysis and the Bosnian War* (New York: Routledge).

Harbour, F. V. (1999), *Thinking About International Ethics: Moral Theory and Cases from American Foreign Policy* (Boulder, CO: Westview Press).

Harding, S. (1986), *The Science Question in Feminism* (Ithaca, NY: Cornell University Press).

Hargens, L. (1988), 'Scholarly Consensus and Journal Rejection Rates', *American Sociological Review*, 53/1: 139–51.

Harley, J. B. (1988), 'Maps, Knowledge, and Power', in D. Cosgrove and S. Daniels (eds.), *The Iconography of Landscape: Essays on the Symbolic Representation, Design and Use of Past Environments* (Cambridge: Cambridge University Press), 277–312.

Harvey, D. (1989), *The Condition of Postmodernity: An Enquiry into the Origins of Cultural Change* (Oxford: Blackwell).

Hawkins, D. G., Lake, D. A., Nielson, D. L., and Tierney, M. J. (2006), *Delegation and Agency in International Organizations* (Cambridge: Cambridge University Press).

Hay, C. (2002), *Political Analysis* (Basingstoke: Palgrave).

—— (2005), 'Globalisation's Impact on States', in J. Ravenhill (ed.), *Global Political Economy* (Oxford: Oxford University Press).

—— (2006), 'What's Globalisation Got to Do With It? Economic Interdependence and the Future of European Welfare States', *Government and Opposition*, 41/1: 1–22.

—— (2009), 'Towards a Global Political Economy?', in D. Lee, J. Steans, C. Hay, D. Hudson, and M. Watson, *International Political Economy* (Oxford: Oxford University Press).

Hayward, T. (2005), *Constitutional Environmental Rights* (Oxford: Oxford University Press).

Headrick, D. (1981), *The Tools of Empire: Technology and European Imperialism in the Nineteenth Century* (Oxford: Oxford University Press).

Hegel, G. F., (1977), *The Phenomenology of Spirit*, translated by A.V. Miller. (Oxford: Oxford University Press).

Heinze E. and Steele, B. (eds.) (2009) *Ethics, Authority, and War: Non-State Actors and the Just War Tradition* (New York: Palgrave Macmillan).

Held, D. (2002), 'Cosmopolitanism: Ideas, Realities, Deficits', in D. Held and A. McGrew (eds.), *Governing Globalisation* (Cambridge: Polity).

—— (2003), 'Cosmopolitanism: Globalisation Tamed?', *Review of International Studies*, 29/4: 465–80.

Held, D., McGrew, A., Goldblatt, D., and Perraton, J. (1999), *Global Transformations: Politics, Economics, Culture* (Cambridge: Polity; Stanford: Stanford University Press).

Herodotus (1998), *The Histories*, translated by R. Waterfield (Oxford: Oxford University Press).

Hersh, S. M. (2004), *Chain of Command: The Road from 9/11 to Abu Ghraib* (New York: Harper).

Herz, J. (1950), 'Idealist Internationalism and the Security Dilemma', *World Politics*, 2/2: 157–80.

Hesse, M. (1980), *Revolutions and Reconstructions in the Philosophy of Science* (Brighton, Sussex: Harvester Press).

Hirst, P. and Thompson, G. (1999), *Globalisation in Question*, 2nd edn. (Cambridge: Polity).

Hoffmann, S. (1977), 'An American Social Science: International Relations', *Dædalus*, 106/3: 41–60.

—— (1981), *Duties Beyond Borders: On the Limits and Possibilities of Ethical International Politics* (Syracuse, NY: Syracuse University Press).

Hoffman, M. (1987), 'Critical Theory and the Inter-Paradigm Debate,' *Millennium: Journal of International Studies* 23/1: 109–18.

Hollis, M. (1996), 'The Last Post?', in S. Smith, K. Booth, and M. Zalewski (eds.), *International Theory: Positivism and Beyond* (Cambridge: Cambridge University Press), 301–8.

Hollis, M. and Smith, S. (1990), *Explaining and Understanding International Relations* (Oxford: Clarendon Press).

Holsti, K. J. (1985), *The Dividing Discipline* (Boston, MA: Allen & Unwin).

—— (2002), 'Interview with Kal Holsti', A. Jones, *Review of International Studies*, 28/3: 619–33.

Honneth, A. (1995), *The Struggle for Recognition* (Albany, NY: SUNY Press).

Hooper, C. (2001), *Manly States: Masculinities, International Relations, and Gender Politics* (New York: Columbia University Press).

Hopf, T. (1998), 'The Promise of Constructivism in International Relations Theory', *International Security*, 23/1: 171–200.

Hopkins, A. G. (1997), *The Future of the Imperial Past*, Inaugural lecture, delivered 12 March (Cambridge: Cambridge University Press).

Horkheimer, M. (1992), *Critical Theory: Selected Essays* (New York: Continuum Press).

Horkheimer, M. and T. Adorno (1994), *Dialectic of Enlightenment.* (New York: Continuum Press).

Hourani, A. (1991), *A History of the Arab Peoples* (Cambridge, MA: The Belknap Press of Harvard University Press).

Howard, P. (2004), 'Why Not Invade Korea? Threats, Language Games and US Foreign Policy', *International Studies Quarterly*, 48/4: 805–28.

Howorth, J. (2007), *Security and Defence Policy in the European Union* (London: Palgrave).

Hoy, D. C. (2004), *Critical Resistance: From Poststructuralism to Post-critique* (Cambridge, MA: MIT Press).

Hughes, R. (1991), *The Shock of the New*, revised edn. (New York: Knopf).

Hulme, P. (1992), *Colonial Encounters: Europe and the Native Caribbean, 1492–1797* (New York: Routledge).

Human Security Research Project (2008), *Human Security Brief 2007* (Vancouver: Simon Fraser University). http://www.humansecuritybrief.info.

Huntington, S. (1996), *The Clash of Civilizations and the Remaking of World Order* (New York: Simon and Schuster).

Hurrell, A. (2002), 'Norms and Ethics in International Relations', in W. Carlsnaes, T. Risse, and B. A. Simmons (eds.), *Handbook of International Relations* (London: Sage), 137–54.

—— (2007), *On Global Order: Power, Values and the Constitution of International Society* (Oxford, Oxford University Press).

Hutchings, K. (1999), *International Political Theory: Rethinking Ethics in a Global Era* (London: Sage).

Huth, P. and Allee, T. (2002), *The Democratic Peace and Territorial Conflict in the Twentieth Century* (Cambridge: Cambridge University Press).

Iida, K. (2004) 'Is WTO Dispute Settlement Effective?' *Global Governance*, 10/2: 207–25.

Inoguchi, T. and Bacon, P. (2001), 'The Study of International Relations in Japan: Towards a More International Discipline', *International Relations of the Asia–Pacific*, 1/1: 1–20.

Intergovernmental Panel on Climate Change (IPPC) (2007), *Climate Change 2007—Synthesis Report: Summary for Policymakers*, http://www.ipcc.ch/pdf/assessment-report/ar4/syr/ar4_syr.pdf.

Jackson, J. H. (1998), *The World Trade Organization: Constitution and Jurisprudence* (London: Royal Institute for International Affairs).

Jackson, P. T. (2011), *The Conduct of Inquiry in International Relations: Philosophy of Science and Its Implications for the Study of World Politics* (London: Routledge).

Jackson, P.T., ed. (2004) 'Bridging the Gap: Toward a Realist-Constructivist Dialogue,' *International Studies Review*, : 337-352.

Jackson, R. H. (1990), *Quasi-states: Sovereignty, International Relations, and the Third World*, Cambridge Studies in International Relations 12 (Cambridge and New York: Cambridge University Press).

—— (2000), *The Global Covenant: Human Conduct in a World of States* (Oxford: Oxford University Press).

Jackson, R. and Sørensen, G. (1999), *Introduction to International Relations* (Oxford, Oxford University Press).

—— (2007), *Introduction to International Relations: Theories and Approaches*, 3rd edn (Oxford, Oxford, University Press).

James, C. L. R. (1989), *The Black Jacobins: Toussaint L'Ouverture and the San Domingo Revolution* (New York: Vintage).

Jameson, F. (1991), *Postmodernism, or, the Cultural Logic of Late Capitalism* (New York: Verso).

Jay, M. (1971), *The Dialectical Imagination* (Berkeley, CA: University of California Press).

Jentleson, B. W. (2002), 'The Need for Praxis: Bringing Policy Relevance Back In', *International Security*, 26/4: 169-83.

Jervis, R. (1999), 'Realism, Neoliberalism and Cooperation. Understanding the Debate', *International Security*, 24 (Summer): 42-63.

Joachim, J., Reinalda, B., and Verbeek, B. (2008), *International Organizations and Implementation: Enforcers, Managers, Authorities?* (London: Routledge).

Johnson, J. T. (1984) *Can Modern War Be Just?* (New Haven: Yale University Press).

—— (1991), 'Historical Roots and Sources of the Just War Tradition in Western Cultures', in J. Kelsey and J. T. Johnson (eds.), *Just War and Jihad: Historical and Theoretical Perspectives on War and Peace in Western and Islamic Traditions* (New York: Greenwood Press).

Johnston, A. I. (2001), 'Treating International Institutions as Social Environments', *International Studies Quarterly*, 45/4: 487-515.

Jones, R. J. B. and Willetts, P. (1984) (eds.), *Interdependence on Trial: Studies in the Theory and Reality of Contemporary Interdependence* (New York: St. Martin's Press).

Jordan, R., Maliniak, D., Oakes, A., and Peterson, S. (2009), 'One Discipline or Many? 2008 TRIP Survey of International Relations Faculty in Ten Countries', Reves Center and Arts and Sciences, College of William and Mary, Williamsburg, VA, February 2009.

Jørgensen, K. E. and Knudsen, T. B. (2006) (eds.), *International Relations in Europe* (London: Routledge).

Kahler, M. (1993), 'International Relations: Still an American Social Science?', in L. B. Miller and M. J. Smith (eds.), *Ideas and Ideals* (Boulder, CO: Westview Press).

—— (1997), 'Inventing International Relations: Still an American Social Science?', in L. B. Miller and M. J. Smith (eds.), *Ideas and Ideals* (Boulder, CO: Westview Press).

Käkönen, J. (1994) (ed.), *Green Security or Militarised Environment* (Aldershot: Dartmouth).

Kant, I. ([1795] 1970), *Perpetual Peace: A Philosophical Sketch* in H. Reiss (ed.), *Kant's Political Writings* (Cambridge: Cambridge University Press).

Kant, I. (1989), *Kant's Political Writings*. Edited by Hans Reiss (Cambridge: Cambridge University Press).

Katzenstein, P. (1996) (ed.), *The Culture of National Security: Norms and Identity in World Politics* (New York: Columbia University Press).

Katzenstein, P., Keohane, R. O., and Krasner, S. D. (1998), 'International Organization and the Study of World Politics', *International Organization*, 52/4: 645-85.

Katznelson, I. and Milner, H. V. (2002) (eds.), *Political Science: State of the Discipline* (New York and London: Norton).

Kaufman-Osborn, T. V. (2006), 'Dividing the Domain of Political Science: On the Fetishism of Subfields', *Polity*, 38/1: 41-71.

Kaye, D. (2011), 'Who's Afraid of the International Criminal Court?' *Foreign Affairs*, 90(3)(May/June): 118-30.

Keene, E. (2002), *Beyond the Anarchical Society: Grotius, Colonialism and Order in World Politics* (Cambridge, Cambridge University Press).

Kellner, D. (1989), *Critical Theory, Marxism and Modernity* (Baltimore, MD: Johns Hopkins University Press).

Keohane, R. O. (1984), *After Hegemony: Cooperation and Discord in the World Political Economy* (Princeton, NJ: Princeton University Press).

—— (1986) (ed.), *Neorealism and its Critics* (New York: Columbia University Press).

—— (1988), 'International Institutions: Two Approaches', *International Studies Quarterly*, 32/4: 379-96.

—— (1989), *International Institutions and State Power* (Boulder, CO, Westview).

—— (1993), 'Institutional Theory and the Realist Challenge After the Cold War', in D. A. Baldwin (ed.), *Neorealism and Neoliberalism: The Contemporary Debate* (New York: Columbia University Press).

Keohane, R. and Nye, J. (1971) (eds.), *Transnational Relations and World Politics* (Cambridge, MA: Harvard University Press).

—— (1977), *Power and Interdependence: World Politics in Transition* (Boston, MA: Little, Brown; Boulder, CO: Westview).

Kern, S. (1983), *The Culture of Time and Space, 1880–1914* (Cambridge, MA: Harvard University Press).

King, G., Keohane, R. O., and Verba, S. (1994), *Designing Social Inquiry: Scientific Inference in Qualitative Research* (Princeton, NJ: Princeton University Press).

Kinnvall, C. (2005), 'Not Here, Not Now! The Absence of a European Perestroika Movement', in K. R. Monroe (ed.), *Perestroika! The Raucous Rebellion in Political Science* (New Haven, CT: Yale University Press), 21–44.

Kinzer, S. (2003), *All the Shah's Men* (New York: Wiley).

Kinzer, S. (2006) *Overthrow: America's century of regime change from Hawaii to Iraq* (New York: Times Books).

Klare, M. (2004), 'Bush–Cheney Energy Strategy: Procuring the Rest of the World's Oil', *Foreign Policy in Focus Special Report*, January, http://www.fpif.org/papers/ 03petropol/politics_body.html, accessed 30 November 2005.

Klein, B. (1994), *Strategic Studies and World Order* (Cambridge: Cambridge University Press).

Knorr, K. E. and Rosenau, J. N. (1969) (eds.), *Contending Approaches to International Politics* (Princeton, NJ: Princeton University Press).

Knudsen, C. (2003), 'Pluralism, Scientific Progress and the Structure of Organization Studies', in H. Tsoukas and C. Knudsen (eds.), *The Oxford Handbook of Organization Theory* (Oxford: Oxford University Press), 262–86.

Kolakowski, L. (1969), *The Alienation of Reason: A History of Positivist Thought*, translated by N. Guterman (New York: Anchor Books).

Koremenos, B. (2001), 'Loosening the Ties that Bind: A Learning Model of Agreement Flexibility', *International Organization*, 55/2: 289–325.

Koremenos, B., Lipson, C., and Snidal, D. (eds.) (2003), *The Rational Design of International Institutions* (Cambridge: Cambridge University Press).

Korman, S. (1996), *The Right of Conquest: The Acquisition of Territory by Force in International Law and Practice* (Oxford: Clarendon).

Krasner, S. D. (1983) (ed.), *International Regimes* (Ithaca. NY: Cornell University Press).

—— (1991), 'Global Communications and National Power: Life on the Pareto Frontier', *World Politics*, 43/3: 336–56.

—— (1996), 'The Accomplishments of International Political Economy', in S. Smith, K. Booth, and M. Zalewski (eds.), *International Theory: Positivism and Beyond* (Cambridge: Cambridge University Press), 108–27.

—— (1999), *Sovereignty: Organized Hypocrisy* (Princeton. NJ: Princeton University Press).

Kratochwil, F. (1989), *Rules, Norms and Decisions: On the Conditions of Practical and Legal Reasoning in International Relations and Domestic Affairs* (Cambridge: Cambridge University Press).

—— (2000), 'Constructing a New Orthodoxy? Wendt's "Social Theory of International Politics" and the Constructivist Challenge', *Millennium: Journal of International Studies*, 29/1: 73–101.

—— (2003), 'The Monologue of Science', *International Studies Review*, 5/1: 128–31.

—— (2006), 'History, Action and Identity: Revisiting the 'Second' Great Debate and Assessing its Importance for Social Theory', *European Journal of International Relations*, 12/1: 5–29.

Kratochwil, F. and Ruggie, J. R. (1986), 'International Organization: A State of the Art or an Art of the State', *International Organization*, 40/4: 753–75.

Krause, K. (1998), 'Critical theory and Security' The Research Programme of Critical Security Studies, *Cooperation and Conflict*, 33(3): 298–333.

Kriesler, H. (2002) 'Through a Realist Lens', *Conversations with John Mearsheimer*, Institute for International Studies, University of California Berkeley, 8 April, available at: http://globetrotter.berkeley.edu/people2/Mearsheimer/mearsheimer - con5.html, accessed 6 May 2008.

Kuehls, T. C. (1996), *Beyond Sovereign Territory: The Space of Ecopolitics* (Minneapolis: University of Minnesota Press).

Kuhn, T. (1962), *The Structure of Scientific Revolutions* (Chicago: University of Chicago Press).

Kurki, M. (2011), 'The Limitations of the Critical Edge: Reflections on Critical Theory and Philosophical IR Scholarship Today', *Millennium*, 40/1: 126–46.

Lacher, H. (2006), *Beyond Globalization: Capitalism, Territoriality and the International Relations of Modernity* (London: Routledge).

Laclau, E. and Mouffe, C. (1985), *Hegemony and Socialist Strategy: Towards a Radical Democratic Politics* (London: Verso).

—— (1995), *Hegemony and Socialist Strategy* (London: Verso).

LaFerrière, E. and Stoett, P. J. (1999), *International Relations Theory and Ecological Thought: Towards a Synthesis* (London: Routledge).

LaFerrière, E. and Stoett, P. J. (2006), *International Ecopolitical Theory: Critical Approaches* (Vancouver: UBC Press).

Laffey, M. (2000), 'Locating Identity: Performativity, Foreign Policy and State Action', *Review of International Studies*, 26/3: 429–44.

Laitin, D. D. (2004), 'The Political Science Discipline', in E. D. Mansfield and R. Sisson (eds.), *The Evolution of Political Knowledge: Theory and Inquiry in American Politics* (Columbus: Ohio State University Press).

Lakatos, I. (1970), 'Falsification and the Methodology of Scientific Research Programmes', in I. Lakatos and A. Musgrave (eds.), *Criticism and the Growth of Knowledge* (London: Cambridge University Press).

Lake, D. A. (2011), 'Why "Isms" Are Evil: Theory, Epistemology, and Academic Sects as Impediments to Understanding and Progress', *International Studies Quarterly*, 55(2), 465–480.

Lake, D. A. (1993), 'Leadership, Hegemony, and the International Economy: Naked Emperor or Tattered Monarch with Potential?', *International Studies Quarterly* 37: 459–89.

Lang Jr, A. (2008), *Punishment, Justice and International Relations: Ethics and Order after the Cold War* (New York: Routledge)

Lapid, Y. (1989), 'The Third Debate: On the Prospects of International Theory in a "Post-positivist" Era', *International Studies Quarterly*, 33/4: 235–54.

——(2002),'Sculpting the Academic Identity: Disciplinary Reflections at the Dawn of a New Millennium', in D. J. Puchala (ed.), *Visions of International Relations: Assessing an Academic Field* (Columbia: University of South Carolina Press), 1–15.

——(2003),'Through Dialogue to Engaged Pluralism: The Unfinished Business of the Third Debate', *International Studies Review*, 5: 128–31.

Lebow, R. N. (2003), *The Tragic Vision of Politics: Ethics, Interests and Orders* (Cambridge: Cambridge University Press).

Lebow, Richard Ned (2008), *A Cultural Theory of International Relations* (Cambridge: Cambridge University Press).

Lepgold, J. and Nincic, M. (2001), *Beyond the Ivory Tower: International Relations Theory and the Issue of Policy Relevance* (New York: Columbia University Press).

Leysens, A. (2008), *The Critical Theory of Robert W. Cox: Fugitive or Guru?* (New York: Palgrave Macmillan).

Lewis, W. A. (1981), 'The Rate of Growth of World Trade, 1830–1973', in S. Grassman and E. Lundberg (eds.), *The World Economic Order: Past and Prospects* (Basingstoke: Macmillan).

Liberman, P. (1996), *Does Conquest Pay: The Exploitation of the Occupied Industrial Societies* (Princeton, NJ: Princeton University Press).

Ling, L. and Agathangelou, A. (2008), *Empire and Insecurity in World Politics: Seductions of Neoliberalism* (New York: Routledge).

Linklater, A. (1990), *Men and Citizens in the Theory of International Relations*, 2nd edn. (London: Macmillan).

——(1992), 'The Question of the Next Stage in International Relations Theory: A Critical Theoretic Point of View', *Millennium*, 21/2/: 77–98.

——(1996), 'The Achievements of Critical Theory', in S. Smith, K. Booth, and M. Zalewski (eds.), *International Theory: Positivism and Beyond* (Cambridge: Cambridge University Press), 279–98.

——(1998), *The Transformation of Political Community: Ethical Foundations of the Post-Westphalian Era* (Cambridge: Polity Press).

——(2005), 'The English School', in S. Burchill, A. Linklater, et al. *Theories of International Relations* 3rd edn. (London: Macmillan), 93–118.

——(2008), *Critical Theory and World Politics* (London: Polity Press).

Linklater, A. and Suganami, H. (2006), *The English School of International Relations: A Contemporary Reassessment* (Cambridge: Cambridge University Press).

Lipson, C. (2003), *Reliable Partners: How Democracies Have Made a Separate Peace* (Princeton, NJ: Princeton University Press).

Lisle, D. and Pepper, A. (2005), 'The New Face of Global Hollywood: Black Hawk Down and the Politics of Meta-sovereignty', *Cultural Politics*, 1/2: 165–92.

Little, R. (1996), 'The Growing Relevance of Pluralism?' in S. Smith, K. Booth, and M. Zalewski (eds.), *International Theory: Positivism and Beyond* (Cambridge: Cambridge University Press).

Locher, B. and Prügl, E. (2001), 'Feminism and Constructivism: Worlds Apart or Sharing the Middle Ground?' *International Studies Quarterly*, 45: 111–29

Locke, J. (1980), *Second Treatise of Government* (New York: Hackett).

Low, N. and Gleeson, B. (1998), *Justice, Society and Nature: An Exploration of Political Ecology* (London: Routledge).

Lu, C. (2006), *Just and Unjust Interventions in World Politics: Public and Private* (Basingstoke: Palgrave Macmillan).

Lukács, G. (1971), *History and Class Consciousness* (Cambridge, MA: MIT Press).

MacIntyre, A. (1981/1985), *After Virtue: A Study in Moral Theory*, 2nd edn. (London: Duckworth).

MacMillan, J. (1998), *On Liberal Peace: Democracy, War and International Order* (London: Tauris).

Maliniak, D. et al. (2007), *The View from the Ivory Tower: TRIP Survey of IR Faculty in the U.S. and Canada*, Reves Center and Arts and Sciences, College of William and Mary, Williamsburg, VA, February 2007.

Mann, J. (2004), *Rise of the Vulcans: The History of Bush's War Cabinet* (New York: Penguin).

Manning, C. A. W. (1954), *The University Teaching of Social Sciences: International Relations*, a report prepared on behalf of the International Studies Conference, UNESCO.

—— (1962), *The Nature of International Society* (London: G. Bell & Sons).

Mansfield, E. D. and Pollins, B. M. (2003), *Economic Interdependence and International Conflict: New Perspectives on an Enduring Debate* (Ann Arbor: University of Michigan Press).

Mansfield, E. and Reinhardt, E. (2003), 'Multilateral Determinants of Regionalism: The Effects of GATT/WTO on the Formation of Regional Trading Arrangements', *International Organization*, 57/4: 829–62.

Mansfield, E. and Snyder, J. (2005), *Electing to Fight: Why Emerging Democracies Go to War* (Cambridge, MA: MIT Press).

March, J. G. and Olson, J. P. (1989), *Rediscovering Institutions* (New York: Free Press).

Marchand, M. H. and Runyan, A. S. (2010) (eds.), *Gender and Global Restructuring: Sightings, Sites, and Resistances.* 2nd edn. (London and New York: Routledge).

Marcuse, H. (1964), *One-Dimensional Man* (Boston: Beacon Press).

Martin, L. (1992), *Coercive Cooperation: Explaining Multilateral Economic Sanctions* (Princeton, NJ: Princeton University Press).

Martin, L. and Simmons, B. (1998), 'Theories and Empirical Studies of International Institutions', *International Organization*, 52/4: 729–57.

Martin, L. and Simmons, B. (2001) (eds.), *International Institutions: An International Organization Reader* (Boston, MA: MIT Press).

Marx, K. (1977), *Capital*, Volume 1 (New York: Vintage).

—— (2000), *Selected Writings*, edited by D. McLellan, 2nd edn. (Oxford: Oxford University Press).

May, E. (ed.) (1993), *American Cold War Strategy* (New York: St Martin's).

Mbembe, A. (2001), *Postcolony* (Berkeley: University of California Press).

McCubbins, M. D. and Schwartz, T. (1984), 'Congressional Oversight Overlooked: Police Patrols Versus Fire Alarms', *American Journal of Political Science*, 28/1: 165–79.

McGrew, A. (2005), 'Globalisation and Global Politics', in J. Baylis and S. Smith (eds.), *The Globalisation of World Politics: An Introduction to International Relations*, 3rd edn (Oxford: Oxford University Press).

Meadows, D. H., Meadows, D. L., Randers, J., and Behrens, W. W. (1972), *The Limits to Growth: A Report to the Club of Rome's Project on the Predicament of Mankind* (New York: Universe Books).

Mearsheimer, J. J. (1990), 'Back to the Future: Instability in Europe after the Cold War', *International Security*, 15/1: 5–56.

—— (1994–5), 'The False Promise of International Institutions', *International Security*, 19/3: 5–49.

—— (2001), *The Tragedy of Great Power Politics* (New York: Norton).

Megill, A. (1994) (ed.), *Rethinking Objectivity* (Durham, OH: Duke University Press).

Memmi, A. (1965), *The Colonizer and Colonized* (Boston, MA: Beacon Press).

Messer-Davidow, E., Shumway, D. S., and Sylvan, D. J. (1993) (eds.), *Knowledges: Historical and Critical Studies in Disciplinarity* (Charlottesville: University Press of Virginia).

Mignolo, W. (1995), *The Darker Side of the Renaissance: Literacy, Territoriality, and Colonization* (Ann Arbor: University of Michigan Press).

Mignolo, W. (2000), *Local Histories/Global Designs: Coloniality, Subaltern Knowledges, and Border Thinking* (Princeton, NJ: Princeton University Press).

Mill, J. S. (1998), *On Liberty and Other Essays* (Oxford: Oxford University Press).

Millennium Ecosystem Assessment (2005), *Ecosystems and Human Well-being: Synthesis* (Washington: Island Press), available at: http://www.millenniumassessment.org/documents/document.356.aspx.pdf, accessed 23 June 2009.

Millennium Forum (2005), 'Barry Buzan's *From International to World Society?*', 34/1: 156–99. Contributions by Emmanuel Adler, Tim Dunne, and Barry Buzan.

Milner, H. (1998), 'Rationalizing Politics: The Emerging Synthesis of International, American, and Comparative Politics', *International Organization*, 52/4: 759–86.

Mitchell, R. B. (1994), 'Regime Design Matters: Intentional Oil Pollution and Treaty Compliance', *International Organization*, 48/3: 425–58.

Mitchell R. B. and Keilbach, P. M. (2003), 'Situation Structure and institutional Design: Reciprocity, Coercion, and Exchange', in B. Koremenos, C. Lipson, and D. Snidal (eds.), *The Rational Design of International Institutions*, (Cambridge: Cambridge University Press), 131–58.

Mitchell, S. M. and Hensel, P. R. (2007), 'International Institutions and Compliance with Agreements', *American Journal of Political Science*, 51/4: 721–37.

Mitzen, J. (2005), 'Reading Habermas in Anarchy: Multilateral Diplomacy and Global Public Spheres', *American Political Science Review*, 99/3: 401–18.

Moeller, S. (1999), *Compassion Fatigue: How the Media Sell Disease, Famine, War and Death* (New York: Routledge).

Mohanty, C. T. (1988), 'Under Western Eyes: Feminist Scholarship and Colonial Discourse', *Feminist Review*, 30/3: 61–88.

Monmonier, M. (1996), *How to Lie with Maps*, 2nd edn. (Chicago: University of Chicago Press).

Monroe, K. R. (2005) (ed.), *Perestroika! The Raucous Rebellion in Political Science* (New Haven, CT: Yale University Press).

Monteiro, Nuno and Keven Ruby (2009) 'IR and the False Promise of Philosophical Foundations', *International Theory*, 1(1): 15–48.

Montesquieu, C. L. S. (1973), *The Persian Letters* (New York: Penguin).

Moon, K. H. S. (1997), *Sex Among Allies: Military Prostitution in U.S.-Korea Relations* (New York: Columbia University Press).

Moravscik, A. (1998), *The Choice for Europe: Social Purpose and State Power from Messina to Maastricht* (Ithaca, NY: Cornell University Press).

—— (2003), 'Theory Synthesis in International Relations: Real Not Metaphysical', *International Studies Review*, 5: 131–6.

Moreiras, A. (2001), *The Exhaustion of Difference: The Politics of Latin American Cultural Studies* (Durham, OH: Duke University Press).

Morgan, T. C. and Schwebach, V. L. (1997), 'Fools Suffer Gladly: The Use of Economic Sanctions in International Crises', *International Studies Quarterly*, 41/1: 27–50.

Morgenthau, H. J. (1947), *Scientific Man vs. Power Politics* (London: Latimer Press).

—— (1948a), *Politics among Nations: The Struggle for Power and Peace* (New York: Alfred A. Knopf).

—— (1948b), 'Letter to Michael Oakeshott, 22 May 1948' *Morgenthau Papers*, B-44.

—— (1958), *Decline of Domestic Politics* (Chicago, IL: University of Chicago Press).

—— (1960), *Politics among Nations*, 3rd edn (New York: Alfred A. Knopf).

—— (1966), 'The Purpose of Political Science', in J. C. Charlesworth (ed.), *A Design for Political Science: Scope, Objectives and Methods* (Philadelphia, PA: American Academy of Political and Social Science).

—— (1972), *Politics among Nations: The Struggle for Power and Peace*, 5th edn. (New York: Alfred A. Knopf).

—— (1978), *Politics among Nations: The Struggle for Power and Peace*, 5th edn., revised (New York: Alfred A. Knopf).

Morrison, T. (1993), *Playing in the Dark: Whiteness and the Literary Imagination* (New York: Vintage).

Morton, Adam, D. (2003) 'Historicizing Gramsci: situating ideas in and beyond their context', *Review of International Political Economy*, 10: 118–46.

Mueller, J. and Mueller, K. (1999), 'Sanctions of Mass Destruction', *Foreign Affairs*, 78/3: 43–53.

Müller, H. (2004), 'Arguing, Bargaining and all That: Communicative Action, Rationalist Theory and the Logic of Appropriateness in International Relations', *European Journal of International Relations*, 10(3): 395–435.

Murphy, J. (2011) 'UK's "Moral Responsibility to Libya": UK Shadow Defence Secretary Jim Murphy speaks to Andrew Marr', *The Andrew Marr Show*, 23 Oct. 2011, available at: http://www.bbc.co.uk/news/uk-politics-15420417; accessed 20 April 2012.

Nagel, T. (1972), 'War and Massacre', *Philosophy and Public Affairs*, 1/2: 123–44.

Narang, N. and Nelson, R. (2009), 'Who Are Those Belligerent Democratizers? Reassessing the Impact of Democratization on War', *International Organization*, 63/2: 357–79.

Nardin, T. (1983), *Law, Morality, and the Relations of States* (Princeton, NJ: Princeton University Press).

—— (1996) (ed.), *The Ethics of War and Peace: Religious and Secular Perspectives* (Princeton, NJ: Princeton University Press).

—— (2008), 'International Ethics', in C. Reus-Smit and D. Snidal (eds.), *The Oxford Handbook of International Relations* (Oxford: Oxford University Press), 594–611.

Nardin, T. and Mapel, D. (eds.) (1992), *Traditions of International Ethics* (Cambridge: Cambridge University Press).

Navari, C. (2009), *Theorising International Society: English School Methods* (Palgrave: Basingstoke).

Neufeld, M. (1993), *Reconstructing International Relations Theory* (Cambridge: Cambridge University Press).

Neumann, I. B. (1996), *Russia and the Idea of Europe: A Study in Identity and International Relations* (London: Routledge).

Neumann et al. (2012) 'Forum on Critical Realism', *Review of International Studies*, 38(2).

Nicholson, M. (1996), *Causes and Consequences in International Relations: A Conceptual Study* (London: Pinter).

Nielson, D. L. and Tierney, M. J. (2003), 'Delegation to International Organizations: Agency Theory and World Bank Environmental Reform', *International Organization*, 57/2: 241–76.

Nixon, R. (2011), *Slow Violence and the Environmentalism of the Poor* (Cambridge, MA: Harvard University Press).

Nussbaum, M. and Cohen, J. (eds.) (1996/2002), *For Love of Country?* (Boston, MA: Beacon Press).

Nye, J. S. and Donahue, J. D. (eds.) (2000), *Governance in a Globalising World* (Washington, DC: Brookings Institute Press).

Oatley, T. H. (2003), 'Multilaterizing Trade and Payments in Postwar Europe', in B. Koremenos, C. Lipson, and D. Snidal (eds.) *The Rational Design of International Institutions* (Cambridge: Cambridge University Press), 289–210.

Oatley, T. and Nabors, R. (1998), 'Redistributive Cooperation: Market Failure, Wealth Transfers, and the Basle Accord', *International Organization*, 52/1: 35–54.

Obama, Barack (2009a) 'Barack Obama's Inaugural Address,' *New York Times*, 20 January.

Obama, Barack (2009b) 'Barack Obama's Cairo Speech,' *The Guardian*, 4 June.

Obama, B. (2009), 'President Obama Speech in Prague' (5 April 2009), http://www.whitehouse.gov/blog/09/04/09/Europe-Revisited-A-New-Image-a-New-Role/, accessed 12 April 2009.

Okereke, C. (2008), *Global Justice and Neoliberal Environmental Governance* (London: Routledge).

O'Neill, B. (1994), 'Chapter 29: Game Theory Models of War and Peace,' in R. Aumann and S. Hart (eds.), *Handbook of Game Theory with Economic Applications*, Volume 2 (Amsterdam: Elsevier), 995–1053.

O'Neil, K. (2009), *The Environment and International Relations* (Cambridge: Cambridge University Press).

O'Neill, O. (1975), 'Lifeboat Earth', *Philosophy & Public Affairs*, 4/3: 273–92.

—— (1986), *Faces of Hunger: An Essay on Poverty, Justice and Development* (London: Allen & Unwin).

Onuf, N. (1989), *World of Our Making: Rules and Rule in Social Theory and International Relations* (Columbia, SC: University of South Carolina Press).

—— (2002), 'Worlds of Our Making: The Strange Career of Constructivism in International Relations', in D. J. Puchala (ed.), *Visions of International Relations: Assessing an Academic Field* (Columbia, SC: University of South Carolina Press), 119–41.

Orend, B. (2006), *The Morality of War* (Peterborough, Ontario: Broadview Press).

Osiander, A. (1994), *The State System of Europe 1640–1990: Peacemaking and the Conditions of International Stability* (Oxford: Clarendon Press).

Østerud, Ø. (1996), 'Antinomies of Postmodernism in International Studies', *Journal of Peace Research*, 33/4: 385–90.

Oye, K. (1986) (ed.), *Cooperation Under Anarchy* (Princeton, NJ: Princeton University Press).

Paehlke, R. C. (2003), *Democracy's Dilemma: Environment, Social Equity and the Global Economy* (Cambridge, MA: MIT Press).

Pahre, R. (2003), 'Most-Favored-Nation Clauses and Clustered Negotiations', in B. Koremenos, C. Lipson, and D. Snidal, (eds.), *The Rational Design of International Institutions* (Cambridge: Cambridge University Press), 99–130.

Palan, R. (2000), 'A World of Their Making: An Evaluation of the Constructivist Critique in International Relations', *Review of International Studies*, 26/4, 575–98.

Paterson, M. (2000), *Understanding Global Environmental Politics: Domination, Accumulation, Resistance* (London: Palgrave).

Patomäki, H. and Wight, C. (2000), 'After Post-Positivism? The Promises of Critical Realism', *International Studies Quarterly*, 44/2: 213–37.

Pattison, J. (2010) *Humanitarian Intervention and the Responsibility To Protect: Who Should Intervene?* (Oxford, Oxford University Press)

Payne, R. A. and Samhat, N. H. (2004), *Democratizing Global Politics: Discourse Norms, International Regimes, and Political Community* (Albany, NY: State University of New York Press).

Pensky, M. (ed.) (2005), *Globalizing Critical Theory* (Lanham, MD: Rowman & Littlefield).

Peoples, C. (2009), *Justifying Ballistic Missile Defence: Technology, Security and Culture* (Cambridge: Cambridge University Press).

Perestroika, Mr. (2000), 'To the Editor, PS and APSR, On Globalization of the APSA: A Political Science Manifesto', posted on the Perestroika list serve, 26 October; reprinted in K. R. Monroe (ed.), *Perestroika! The Raucous Rebellion in Political Science* (New Haven, CT: Yale University Press), 9–11.

Peterson, S., Tierney, M. J., and Maliniak, D. (2005), *Teaching and Research Practices, Views on the Discipline, and Policy Attitudes of International Relations Faculty at the US College and Universities* (Williamsburg, VA: College of William and Mary).

Peterson, V. S. and Runyan, A. S. (2009), *Global Gender Issues* 3rd edn. (Boulder, CO: Westview).

Petrella, R. (1996), 'Globalisation and Internationalisation: The Dynamics of the Emerging World Order', in R. Boyer and D. Drache (eds.), *States Against Market: The Limits of Globalisation* (London: Routledge).

Pevehouse, J. (2005), *Democracy from Above: Regional Organizations and Democratization* (Cambridge: Cambridge University Press).

Pevehouse, J., and Russett, B. (2006), 'Democratic Intergovernmental Organizations Promote Peace', *International Organization*, 60/4: 969–1000.

Phillips, D. L. (2005), *Losing Iraq: Inside the Postwar Reconstruction Fiasco* (Boulder, CO: Westview Press).

Philpott, S. (2001), *Rethinking Indonesia: Postcolonial Theory, Authoritarianism and Identity* (London: Palgrave Macmillan).

Pillay, S. (2004), 'Anti-colonialism, Post-colonialism, and the 'New Man'', *Politikon: South African Journal of Political Studies*, 31/1: 91–104.

Pinker, S. (2011), *The Better Angels of Our Nature: Why Violence Has Declined* (New York: Viking)

Pocock, J. G. A. (2003), *The Machiavellian Moment: Florentine Political Thought and the Atlantic Republican Tradition* (Princeton, NJ: Princeton University Press).

Pogge, T. (1989), *Realizing Rawls* (Ithaca, NY, and London: Cornell University Press).

Pollack, M. A. (1997), 'Delegation, Agency, and Agenda Setting in the EC', *International Organization*, 51/1: 99–134.

Pollard, R. (1985), *Economic Security and the Origins of the Cold War* (New York: Columbia University Press).

Poovey, M. (1998), *A History of the Modern Fact: Problems of Knowledge in the Sciences of Wealth and Society* (Chicago: University of Chicago Press).

Popper, K. R. (1959), *The Logic of Scientific Discovery* (London: Hutchinson).

Posen, B. R. (1984), *The Sources of Military Doctrine: France, Britain, and Germany between the World Wars* (Ithaca, NY: Cornell University Press).

Prakash, G. (1999), *Another Reason: Science and the Imagination of Modern India* (Princeton, NJ: Princeton University Press).

Price, R. (2008), 'The Ethics of Constructivism', in C. Reus-Smit and D. Snidal (eds.), *The Oxford Handbook of International Relations* (Oxford: Oxford University Press), 317–26.

Price, R. and Christian Reus-Smit (1998), 'Dangerous Liaisons? Critical International Theory and Constructivism', *European Journal of International Relations*, 4/3/: 259–94.

Priest, D. and W. Arkin, (2011) *Top Secret America* (New York: Little, Brown).

Princen, T., Maniates, M., and Conca, K. (2002) (eds.), *Confronting Consumption* (Cambridge, MA: MIT Press).

Prügl, E. (1999), *The Global Construction of Gender: Home-based Work in the Political Economy of the 20th Century* (New York: Columbia University Press).

Puchala, D. J. (ed.) (2002), *Visions of International Relations: Assessing an Academic Field* (Columbia: University of South Carolina Press).

Ramsey, P. (1968/2002), *The Just War: Force and Political Responsibility* (Oxford: Rowman & Littlefield).

Rawls, J. (1971), *A Theory of Justice* (Oxford: Oxford University Press).

—— (1975), 'Fairness to Goodness', *Philosophical Review*, 84: 536–54.

—— (2005), *Political Liberalism*, expanded edn., Columbia Classics in Philosophy (New York and Chichester: Columbia University Press).

Reinhardt, E. (2000), 'Adjudication Without Enforcement in GATT Disputes', *Journal of Conflict Resolution*, 45/2: 174–95.

Reiter, D. and Stam, A. (2002), *Democracies at War* (Princeton, NJ: Princeton University Press).

Rengger, N. and B. Thirkell-White (2007), 'Editors' Introduction', *Review of International Studies*, 33 (Special Issue): 3–24.

Reus-Smit, C. (1999), *The Moral Purpose of the State: Culture, Social Identity, and Institutional Rationality in International Relations* (Princeton, NJ: Princeton University Press).

Review of International Studies (2001), Forum on the English school 27/3: 465–513.

Rhode, D. (2012) 'The Obama Doctrine' *Foreign Policy*, 27 February, available at: http://www.foreignpolicy.com/articles/2012/02/27/the_obama_doctrine, accessed 13 March 2012.

Risse, T. (2000), '"Let's Argue!": Communicative Action in World Politics', *International Organization*, 54/1: 1–39.

Risse, T., Ropp, S. C., and Sikkink, K. (eds.) (1999), *The Power of Human Rights: International Norms and Domestic Change* (Cambridge: Cambridge University Press).

Roach, S. C. (2010), *Critical Theory of International Politics: Complementarity, Justice, and Governance.* (London: Routledge).

Roach, S. C. (ed.) (2008), *Critical Theory and International Relations: A Reader* (London: Routledge).

Roben, V. (2008), 'The Enforcement Authority of International Institutions', *German Law Journal*, 9/11: 1965–86.

Roberts, A. and Guelff, R. (eds.) (1989), *Documents on the Laws of War*, 2nd edn. (Oxford: Oxford University Press).

Robinson, F. (1999), *Globalising Care: Ethics, Feminist Theory and International Relations* (Oxford: Westview Press).

Robinson, W. I. (2004), *A Theory of Global Capitalism* (Baltimore, MD: Johns Hopkins University Press).

Rochester, J. M. (1986), 'The Rise and Fall of International Organization as a Field of Study', *International Organization*, 40 (Autumn): 777–813.

Rorty, R. (1967) (ed.), *The Linguistic Turn* (Chicago: University of Chicago Press).

Rose, G. (1998), 'Neoclassical Realism and Theories of Foreign Policy', *World Politics*, 51 (October): 144–72.

—— (2001), *Visual Methodologies* (London: Sage).

Rosenau, J. N. (1990), *Turbulence in World Politics: A Theory of Change and Continuity* (Princeton, NJ: Princeton University Press).

Rosenberg, J. (1994), *Empire of Civil Society* (London: Verso).

Rosendorff, P. and Milner, H. V. (2003), 'The Optimal Design of International Trade Institutions: Uncertainty and Escape', in B. Koremenos, C. Lipson, and D. Snidal (eds.), *The Rational Design of International Institutions*, (Cambridge: Cambridge University Press), 69–98.

Rousseau, D. (2005), *Democracy and War: Institutions, Norms, and the Evolution of International Conflict* (Stanford, CA: Stanford University Press).

Roy, A. (1998), 'The End of Imagination', *The Guardian* (UK), 1 August.

Ruggie, J. G. (1986), 'Continuity and Transformation in the World Polity: Toward a Neorealist Synthesis,' in Robert O. Keohane (ed.) *Neorealism and its Critics* (New York: Columbia University Press).

Ruggie, J. G. (1998),'What Makes the World Hang Together? Neo-utilitarianism and the Social Constructivist Challenge', *International Organization*, 52/4: 855–85.

Rupert, M. (1995), *Producing Hegemony* (Cambridge: Cambridge University Press).

Rupert, M. and Smith, H. (2002) (eds.), *Historical Materialism and Globalisation* (London: Routledge).

Rupert, M. and Solomon, S. (2006), *Globalisation and International Political Economy* (Lanham, MD: Rowman and Littlefield).

—— (1993), *Grasping the Democratic Peace* (Princeton, NJ: Princeton University Press).

Rupert, M. (2009), 'Antonio Gramsci', in J. Edkins and N. Vaughan-Williams (eds.) *Critical Theorists and International Relations* (London: Routledge), 176–86.

Russett, B. and O'Neal, J. R. (2001), *Triangulating Peace: Democracy, Interdependence, and International Organizations*, Norton Series in World Politics (New York: Norton).

Said, E. (1979), *Orientalism* (New York: Vintage).

Sands, Philippe (2008), 'Stress Hooding, Noise, Nudity, Dogs', *The Guardian Weekend*, 19 April, 18–27.

Sayer, D. (1991), *Capitalism and Modernity* (London: Routledge).

Scarry, E. (1995), *The Body in Pain: The Making and Unmaking of the World* (Oxford: Oxford University Press).

Scheuerman, William S. (2011), *The Realist Case of Global Reform* (New York: Polity).

Scheuerman, W. E. (2008), *Frankfurt School Perspectives on Globalization, Democracy, and the Law* (London: Routledge).

Showstack-Sassoon, A. (2005), 'Intimations of a Gramscian approach to global civil society', in R. Germain and M. Kenny (eds.) *The Idea of Global Civil Society: Politics and Ethics in a Globalizing Era* (London: Routledge), 35–46.

Schlosberg, D. (2007), *Defining Environmental Justice: Theories, Movements, and Nature* (Oxford: Oxford University Press).

Schmidt, B. (1998), *The Political Discourse of Anarchy: A Disciplinary History of International Relations* (Albany: State University of New York Press).

—— (2008), 'International Relations Theory: Hegemony or Pluralism?', *Millennium: Journal of International Studies*, 36/2: 295–304.

Schmitt, R. (1997), *Introduction to Marx and Engels: A Critical Reconstruction*, 2nd edn. (Boulder, CO: Westview).

Schoenbaum, T. J. (1997), 'International Trade and Protection of the Environment: The Continuing Search for Reconciliation', *The American Journal of International Law*, 91/2: 268–313.

Schultz, K. (2001), *Democracy and Coercive Diplomacy* (Stanford, CA: Stanford University Press).

Schwartz W. F. and Sykes, A. O. (2001), 'The Economic Structure of Renegotiation and Dispute Resolution in the World Trade Organization', *The Journal of Legal Studies*, 31: 181–3, 188–92.

Scott, D. (1999), *Refashioning Futures: Criticism after Postcoloniality* (Princeton, NJ: Princeton University Press).

Searle, J. R. (1995), *The Construction of Social Reality* (London: Allen Lane; New York: Free Press).

Sending, O. L. (2002), 'Constitution, Choice and Change: Problems with the "Logic of Appropriateness" and its Use in Constructivist Theory', *European Journal of International Relations*, 8/4: 443–70.

Sending, J. O. (2002), 'Constitution, Choice and Change: Problems with the 'Logic of Appropriateness' and its Use in Constructivist Theory,' *European Journal of International Relations*, 8/4: 443–70.

Shapcott, R. (2001), *Justice, Community and Dialogue in International Relations* (Cambridge: Cambridge University Press).

Shapcott, R. (2010), *International Ethics: A Critical Introduction* (Cambridge: Polity).

Shapiro, M. J. (1988), *The Politics of Representation: Writing Practices in Biography, Photography and Policy Analysis* (Madison: University of Wisconsin Press).

Shapiro, M. J. and Alker, H. R. (eds.) (1996), *Challenging Boundaries: Global Flows, Territorial Identities* (Minneapolis: University of Minnesota Press).

Shepherd, L. (2008), *Gender, Violence, and Security: Discourse as Practice* (London: Zed Books).

Shue, H. (1980), *Basic Rights: Subsistence, Affluence and United States Foreign Policy* (Princeton, NJ: Princeton University Press).

Sil, R., and Katzenstein, P. J. (2010), *Beyond Paradigms: Analytic Eclecticism in the Study of World Politics* (Basingstoke: Palgrave Macmillan)

Silberstein, S. (2002), *War of Words: Language, Politics and 9/11* (London: Routledge).

Simmons, B. A. (2002), 'Capacity, Commitment, and Compliance: International Institutions and Territorial Disputes', *Journal of Conflict Resolution*, 46/6: 829–56.

Singer, P. (1972), 'Famine, Affluence, and Morality', *Philosophy & Public Affairs*, 1/3: 229–43.

Sjoberg, L. (2006), *Gender, Justice and the Wars in Iraq* (New York: Lexington Books).

Skinner, Q. (2002), *Visions of Politics: Regarding Method* (Cambridge: Cambridge University Press).

Smith, A. (1993), *Wealth of Nations*, edited by K. Sutherland (Oxford: Oxford University Press).

Smith, S. (1987), 'Paradigm Dominance in International Relations: The Development of International Relations as a Social Science', *Millennium: Journal of International Studies*, 16/2: 189–206.

——(1992), 'The Forty Years' Detour: The Resurgence of Normative Theory in International Relations', *Millennium: Journal of International Studies*, 21/3: 489–506.

——(1997), 'Power and Truth: A Reply to William Wallace', *Review of International Studies*, 23/4: 507–16.

——(2004), 'Singing Our World into Existence: International Relations Theory and September 11 Presidential Address to the International Studies Association, February 27, 2003, Portland, OR', *International Studies Quarterly*, 48/3: 499–515.

——(2008), 'Debating Schmidt: Theoretical Pluralism in IR', *Millennium: Journal of International Studies*, 36/2: 305–10.

Smith, S., Booth, K., and Zalewski, M. (eds.) (1996), *International Theory: Positivism and Beyond* (Cambridge: Cambridge University Press).

Snidal, D. (1985), 'The Limits of Hegemonic Stability Theory', *International Organization*, 39/4: 579–614.

Snyder, J. L. (1991), *Myths of Empire: Domestic Politics and International Ambition* (Ithaca, NY: Cornell University Press).

Smith, J. M. (2001), 'The Politics of Dispute Settlement Design', in L. Martin, and B. Simmons (eds.) *International Institutions: An International Organization Reader* (Boston, Massachusetts: MIT Press) 210–44.

Soguk, N. (1999), *States and Strangers: Refugees and Displacements of Statecraft* (Minneapolis: University of Minnesota Press).

Spero, J. and Hart, J. A. (2003), *The Politics of International Economic Relations* 6th edn. (Belmont, CA: Thompson Wadsworth).

Spivak, G. C. (1987), *In Other Worlds; Essays in Cultural Politics* (New York: Routledge).

Sterling-Folker, J. (2000), 'Competing Paradigms or Birds of a Feather? Constructivism and Neoliberalism Institutionalism Compared', *International Studies Quarterly*, 44/1, 97–119.

——(2001), 'Evolutionary Tendencies in Realist and Liberal IR Theory', in W. R. Thompson (ed.) *Evolutional Interpretations of World Politics* (New York: Routledge).

——(2002) 'Realism and the Constructivist Challenge: Rejecting, Reconstructing or Rereading', *International Studies Review*, 4: 73–97.

——(2002), *Theories of International Cooperation and The Primacy of Anarchy: Explaining U.S. International Monetary Policy-Making after Bretton Woods* (Albany, NY: SUNY Press).

——(ed.) (2006), *Making Sense of International Relations Theory* (Boulder, CO: Lynne Rienner).

Strange, S. (1983), '*Cave! hic dragones*: A Critique of Regime Analysis', in S. D. Krasner (ed.), *International Regimes* (Ithaca, NY: Cornell University Press).

——(1987), 'The Persistent Myth of Lost Hegemony', *International Organization*, 41/4: 551–74.

Swank, D. (2002), *Global Capital, Political Institutions and Policy Change in Developed Welfare States* (Cambridge: Cambridge University Press).

Thomas, D. C. (1999), 'The Helsinki Accords and Political Change in Eastern Europe', in T. Risse, S. C. Ropp, and K. Sikkink (eds.), *The Power of Human Rights: International Norms and Domestic Change* (Cambridge: Cambridge University Press).

Thompson, E. P. (1978), *The Poverty of Theory and Other Essays* (London: Merlin Press).

Thucydides (1954), *History of the Peloponnesian War*, translated by R. Warner (New York: Penguin).

——(1996), *The Landmark Thucydides: A Comprehensive Guide to the Peloponnesian War*, edited by R. B. Strassler (New York: Free Press).

Tickner, A. B. (2003), 'Seeing IR Differently: Notes from the Third World', *Millennium: Journal of International Studies*, 32/2: 295–324.

Tickner, A. B. and Wæver, O. (2004), 'Geo-cultural Epistemologies and IR: Montreal follow-up memo', unpublished paper.

Tickner, A. B. and Wæver, O. (eds.) (2009), *International Relations Scholarship around the World*, Volume 1 of 'Worlding beyond the West' series (London: Routledge).

Tickner, J. A. (1997), 'You Just Don't Understand: Troubled Engagements between Feminists and IR Theorists', *International Studies Quarterly*, 41/4: 611–32.

—— (2001), *Gendering World Politics* (New York: Columbia University Press).

Timmons Roberts, J. and Parks, B. C. (2007), *A Climate of Injustice: Global Inequality, North-South Politics, and Climate Policy* (Cambridge, MA: MIT Press).

Todorov, T. (1993), *On Human Diversity: Nationalism, Racism, and Exoticism in French Thought*, translated by C. Porter (Cambridge, MA: Harvard University Press).

Tormey, S. (2004), *Anti-capitalism: A Beginner's Guide* (Oxford: Oneworld).

Toulmin, S. (1972), *Human Understanding* (Oxford: Clarendon Press).

Traxler, F. and Woitech, B. (2000), 'Transnational Investment and National Labour Market Regimes: A Case of "Regime Shopping"?', *European Journal of Industrial Relations*, 6/2: 141–59.

Trouillot, M.-R. (1997), *Silencing the Past* (Boston, MA: Beacon Press).

True, J. (2003), *Gender, Globalization, and Post-socialism: The Czech Republic after Communism* (New York: Columbia University Press).

—— (2008), 'The Ethics of Feminism', in C. Reus-Smit and D. Snidal (eds.), *The Oxford Handbook of International Relations* (Oxford: Oxford University Press), 408–21.

United Nations (1999), Committee on Economic, Social and Cultural Rights, General Comment No. 12 'On the Right to Adequate Food' (art. 11) 12/05/1999, available at: http://www.unhchr.ch/tbs/doc.nsf/0/3d02758c707031d58025677f003b73b9, accessed 20 April 2012

US Department of State (2003), 'US Military Investigators Evaluating Civilian Checkpoint Deaths (Central Command Report, April 1: Iraq Operational Update)', available at: http://usinfo.org/wf-archive/2003/030401/epf205.htm, accessed 7 April 2009.

van der Gaag, N. and Nash, C. (1987), *Images of Africa: The UK Report*, available at: http://www.imaging-famine.org/images_africa.htm, accessed 25 June 2009.

van der Pijl, K. (1984), *The Making of an Atlantic Ruling Class* (London: Verso).

van der Veer, P. (2001), *Imperial Encounters: Religion and Modernity in India* (Princeton, NJ: Princeton University Press).

Van Evera, S. (1999), *Causes of War: Power and the Roots of Conflict* (Ithaca, NY: Cornell University Press).

Vigneswaran, D. and Quirk, J. (2005), 'The Construction of an Edifice: The Story of a First Great Debate', *Review of International Studies*, 31/1: 59–74.

Vincent, R. J. (1986), *Human Rights in International Relations* (Cambridge: Cambridge University Press).

Vogler, J. (2003), 'Taking Institutions Seriously: How Regime Analysis Can Be Relevant to Multilevel Environmental Governance', *Global Environmental Politics*, 3/2: 25–39.

Wa Thiong'o, N. (1986), *Decolonizing the Mind: The Politics of Language in African Literature* (Portsmouth: Heinemann).

Wackernagel, M. and Rees, W. (1996), *Our Ecological Footprint: Reducing Human Impact on the Earth* (Gabriola Island, BC: New Society Publishers).

Wæver, O. (1995) 'Securitization and Desecuritization', in R. D. Lipschutz (ed.), *On Security* (New York: Columbia University Press).

—— (1996), 'The Rise and Fall of the Interparadigm Debate', in S. Smith, K. Booth, and M. Zalewski (eds.), *International Theory: Positivism and Beyond* (Cambridge: Cambridge University Press), 149–85.

—— (1997), 'Figures of International Thought: Introducing Persons Instead of Paradigms', in I. B Neumann and O. Wæver (eds.), *The Future of International Relations: Masters in the Making?* (London: Routledge).

—— (1998), 'The Sociology of a Not so International Discipline: American and European Developments in International Relations', *International Organization*, 52/4: 687–727.

—— (2003), 'The Structure of the IR Discipline: A Proto- comparative Analysis', ISA paper, Portland.

—— (2004), 'Aberystwyth, Paris, Copenhagen: New 'Schools' in Security Theory and their Origins between Core and Periphery', paper presented at the annual meeting of the International Studies Association, Montreal, 17–20 March.

—— (2009), 'Waltz's Theory of Theory, *International Relations*, 23/2: 201–22.

Wæver, O. and Buzan, B. (2007), 'After the Return to Theory: The Past, Present, and Future of Security Studies', in A. Collins (ed.), *Contemporary Security Studies* (Oxford: Oxford University Press), 383–402.

Walker, R. B. J. (1987), 'Realism, Change and International Political Theory', *International Studies Quarterly*, 31/1: 65–86.

—— (1993), *Inside/Outside: International Relations as Political Theory* (Cambridge: Cambridge University Press).

Walker, R.B.J. (2009), *After the Globe: Before the World* (New York: Routledge)

Wallace, W. (1996), 'Truth and Power, Monks and Technocrats: Theory and Practice in International Relations', *Review of International Studies*, 22/3: 301–21.

Wallerstein, I. (2001 [1991]), *Unthinking Social Science: The Limits of Nineteenth-century Paradigms*, 2nd edn. (Philadelphia, PA: Temple University Press).

—— (2004), *World-Systems Analysis* (Durham, OH: Duke University Press).

Walt, S. M. (1998), 'International Relations: One World, Many Theories', *Foreign Policy*, 110: 29–35.

—— (1999), 'Rigor or Rigor Mortis? Rational Choice and Security Studies', *International Security*, 23/4: 5–48.

Waltz, K. N. (1959), *Man, the State, and War: A Theoretical Analysis* (New York: Columbia University Press).

—— (1979), *Theory of International Politics* (London: McGraw-Hill; New York: Random House; Reading, MA: Addison-Wesley).

—— (1993), 'The Emerging Structure of International Politics', *International Security*, 18/1: 5–43.

—— (1998), 'Interview', *Review of International Studies*, 24/3: 371–86.

Welsh, J. M. (2012), 'A normative case for pluralism: reassessing Vincent's views on humanitarian intervention', *International Affairs*, 87.5: 1193–204.

Wiggershaus, R. (1994), *The Frankfurt School: Its History, Theories, and Political Significance*, translated by Michael Robertson (Cambridge, MA: MIT Press).

Williams, Michael C. (2005) *The Realist Tradition and the Limits of International Relations*. (Cambridge: Cambridge University Press)

Williams, Michael C. (2007) *Realism Reconsidered: The legacy of Hans Morgenthau in International Relations* (Oxford: Oxford University Press).

Walzer, M. (1977/2006) *Just and Unjust Wars: A Moral Argument with Historical Illustrations*, 4th edn. (New York: Basic Books).

Wapner, P. (1998), *Environmental Activism and World Civic Politics* (Albany: State University of New York Press).

Warrior, R. A. (1994), *Tribal Secrets: Recovering American Indian Intellectual Traditions* (Minneapolis: University of Minnesota Press).

Wasserstrom, R. A. (ed.) (1970), *War and Morality* (Belmont, CA: Wadsworth).

Watson, A. (1992), *The Evolution of International Society* (London: Routledge).

Watson, M. (2001),'International Capital Mobility in an Era of Globalisation: Adding a Political Dimension to the "Feldstein–Horioka Puzzle"', *Politics*, 21/2: 81–92.

Weber, C. (1994), *Simulating Sovereignty: Intervention, the State and Symbolic Exchange* (Cambridge: Cambridge University Press).

—— (1999), *Faking It: US Hegemony in a Post-phallic Era* (Minneapolis: University of Minnesota Press).

Weldes, J., Laffey, L. Gusterson, H., and Duvall, R. (eds.) (1999), *Cultures of Insecurity: States, Communities and the Production of Danger* (Minneapolis: University of Minnesota Press).

Welsh, J. M. (1995), *Edmund Burke and International Relations* (Basingstoke: Macmillan).

Wendt, A. (1987), 'The Agent–Structure Problem in International Relations', *International Organization*, 41/3: 335–70.

—— (1992), 'Anarchy Is What States Make of It: The Social Construction of Power Politics', *International Organization*, 46/2: 391–425.

—— (1998), 'Constitution and Causation in International Relations', *Review of International Studies*, 24/5: 101–17.

—— (1999), *Social Theory of International Politics* (Cambridge and New York: Cambridge University Press).

Wheeler, N. J. (2000), *Saving Strangers: Humanitarian Intervention in International Society* (Oxford: Oxford University Press).

White, S. (1991), *Political Theory and Postmodernism* (Cambridge: Cambridge University Press).

White House (2002), *National Security Strategy of the United States* (17 September), available at: http://www.whitehouse.gov/nsc/print/nssall.html, accessed 19 December 2002.

Whitley, R. (1984), *The Intellectual and Social Organization of the Sciences* (Oxford: Clarendon Press).

—— (1986), 'The Structure and Context of Economics as a Scientific Field', in W. J. Samuels (ed.), *Research in the History of Economic Thought and Methodology*, Volume 4 (Greenwich CT and London: JAI Press), 179–209.

—— (2000), 'Introduction [to the second edition]. Science Transformed? The Changing Nature of Knowledge Production at the End of the Twentieth Century', in R. Whitley, *The Intellectual and Social Organization of the Sciences*, 2nd edn. (Oxford: Oxford University Press), ix–xliv.

Whitworth, S. (1994), *Feminism and International Relations: Towards a Political Economy of Gender in Interstate and Non-governmental Institutions* (Basingstoke: Macmillan).

Wiener, A. (2003), 'Constructivism: The Limits of Bridging Gaps', *Journal of International Relations and Development*, 6/3: 252–75.

Wiener, A. (2008), *The Invisible Constitution of Politics: Contested Norms and International Encounters* (Cambridge: Cambridge University Press).

Wight, C. (1996),'Incommensurability and Cross Paradigm Communication in International Relations Theory: What's the Frequency Kenneth?', *Millennium: Journal of International Studies*, 25/2: 291–319.

Wight, M. (1966), 'Why Is There No International Theory?', in H. Butterfield and M. Wight (eds.), *Diplomatic Investigations* (London: Allen & Unwin).

——(1977), *Systems of States*, edited by H. Bull (Leicester: Leicester University Press).

——(1978), *Power Politics*, edited by H. Bull and C. Holbraad (Leicester: Leicester University Press).

——(1991), *International Theory: The Three Traditions* (Leicester: Leicester University Press for the Royal Institute of International Affairs).

Wilensky, H. L. (2002), *Rich Democracies: Political Economy, Public Policy and Performance* (Berkeley, CA: University of California Press).

Wilson, P. (1998), 'The Myth of the "First Great Debate"', *Review of International Studies*, 24(Special Issue): 1–15.

Wittgenstein, L. (1958), *Philosophical Investigations* (Oxford: Blackwell).

Wohlforth, W. C. (1994–5), 'Realism and the End of the Cold War', *International Security*, 19/1: 91–129.

——(1999), 'The Stability of a Unipolar World', *International Security*, 24/1: 5–41.

Wood, E. M. (2003), *Empire of Capital* (London: Verso).

Woodward, B. (2004), *Plan of Attack* (New York: Simon & Schuster).

Wyn Jones, R. (1999), *Security, Strategy, and Critical Theory* (Boulder, CO: Lynne-Rienner Publishers).

World Bank (2007), *Little Green Data Book*, available at: http://siteresources.worldbank.org/INTDATASTA/64199955-1178226923002/21322619/LGDB2007.pdf.

Young, O. R. (1991), 'Political Leadership and Regime Formation: On the Development of Institutions in International Society', *International Organization*, 45/3: 281–308.

Youngs, G. (1999), *International Relations in a Global Age: A Conceptual Challenge* (Cambridge: Polity).

Zagare, F. C. and Kilgour, D. M. (2000), *Perfect Deterrence* (Cambridge: Cambridge University Press).

Zehfuss, M. (2002), *Constructivism in International Relations: The Politics of Reality* (Cambridge: Cambridge University Press).

Zinner, E. and Williams, M. B. (1999), *When a Community Weeps: Case Studies in Group Survivorship* (London: Bruner/Mazel).

Glossary

Explanatory note This glossary has been compiled by the editors, although it draws upon the definitions of key concepts provided by the contributors. In a small number of cases, different theories contest the meaning of key terms: where significant interpretive differences exist, we have endeavoured to make this clear in the descriptions here.

agency the capacity for purposive action, or the exercise of power. The role of 'agents' in social life is traditionally contrasted to the role of 'structures', such as institutions or norms. The agency–structure debate refers to the debate over the priority to be accorded to agents (individuals or states) as opposed to structures in shaping social life.

balance of power a dominant idea within realist and English school traditions of thought. For most classical realists, the balance of power was something that was contrived (i.e. actors had to cooperate to maintain the balance) whereas for neorealists the balance of power is akin to a natural equilibrium. For neorealists, states within the international system will automatically balance against any dominant state power. In English school thought, the balance of power is an 'institution' which requires not only cooperation but a shared belief that a balance of power is crucial if international order is to be achieved.

balancing where a threatened state accepts the burden of deterring an adversary and commits substantial resources to achieving that goal. The threatened state can mobilize its own resources or join with other threatened states to form a balancing coalition.

bandwagoning when a weaker states joins a stronger or dominant alliance in the context of the balance of power in the international system.

bargaining a branch of game theory which deals with situations in which all parties have a common interest in bargaining for a solution which improves the outcome for at least some and worsens it for none.

behaviourism/behavioralism a school of thought that, drawing on empiricist theory of knowledge and positivist philosophy of science, seeks to study human behaviour in reference to observable and measurable behavioural patterns. In IR the term 'behaviouralism' is more commonly used.

bipolarity a system in which there are only two great powers.

buck-passing where threatened states try to get another state to check an aggressor while they remain on the sidelines.

capitalism an historically particular form of social life in which social means of production are privately owned, and labour is commodified. Entailing a constellation of political, economic, and cultural aspects, capitalism involves a relation of class power in which the owning class controls the process of labour and appropriates its product. Marx respected the historic achievements of capitalist society, especially its enhancement of human productive powers, but was scathingly critical of the ways in which capitalism disempowered and dominated human beings, preventing them from realizing the potential for freedom which its historic achievements made possible.

central wars conflicts that involve all or almost all the world's great powers. The French Revolutionary and Napoleonic Wars (1792–1815), the First World War (1914–18), and the Second World War (1939–45) were all central wars.

clash of civilizations thesis a phrase coined by US political scientist Samuel Huntington who argued that the end of the Cold War had created conditions for a new form of international conflict based on ethnic and religious allegiances; civilizations were, he argued, the highest level of shared identity. In particular Huntington focused on possible conflict between the West and Islam, a claim which was widely cited by journalists and political leaders after the 9/11 attacks on the USA.

classical approach an alternative to behaviourism advocated by Hedley Bull. The classical approach eschews positivist commitments to a fact/value distinction, and their expectation that hypotheses should be testable. In its place, the English school puts an interpretive mode of inquiry that tries to understand historical and normative change by engaging with 'texts' such as legal treaties, speeches, and diplomatic discourses. Other characteristics of a classical approach include the inescapability of ethical considerations and a realization that the study of world politics must engage with (and interpret) the dilemmas faced by practitioners.

communitarianism an ethical perspective that sees obligations and allegiances to be defined with reference to distinct and discrete political communities, rather than with reference to the universal category of humankind (as is the case with cosmopolitanism). Within normative IR theory, communitarianism is usually placed in opposition to 'cosmopolitanism'. Many realists have adopted (often implicitly) a communitarian position, defending the ethical primacy of the state as the definer of valid moral and political rules.

competition state used by Cerny and others to refer to those states which subordinate all other policy imperatives to that of promoting the competitiveness of the national economy in a global environment.

complex governance a theory of global order that focuses on the role played by new global regulators who effectively provide the governance that was once the responsibility of sovereign states.

compliance compliance involves the extent to which states can be induced or encouraged to abide by international agreements. Neoliberals, in particular believe that the 'compliance problem' is one of the central dilemmas of International Relations. They see institutions as playing a key role in monitoring and enforcing compliance.

consequentialism a class of moral decision-making according to which the right thing to do is understood in terms of its likely consequences. Utilitarianism is one prominent type of consequentialist position. The everyday phrase 'the road to hell is paved with good intentions' neatly captures the dangers of not thinking about politics in consequentialist terms. Consequential-ism is generally placed in opposition to deontology.

constructivist feminism a branch of feminism in IR that focuses on the way that ideas about gender shape and are shaped by global politics, studying how states and other international actors' perceptions of their own and others' gender identities shape their behaviour in global politics.

correspondence theory of truth defines truth as correspondence with facts. For an advocate of the correspondence theory of truth, the observer can capture truth in statements that are true if they correspond to the facts and false if they do not.

cosmopolitanism an ethical perspective from which all individuals have equal moral standing, and obligations and allegiances are defined with reference to the universal category of humankind. While cosmopolitans are united in their advancement of normative commitments that cross state boundaries, they disagree on the institutional arrangement which is best suited to promoting cosmopolitan values. Cosmopolitanism is usually placed in opposition to 'communitarianism' within normative IR theory.

critical feminism a branch of feminism in IR that addresses the ideational and material manifestations of gendered identities and gendered power in global politics, committed to understanding the world in order to try to change it.

defection in neorealist and neoliberal thinking the problem of defection is a consequence of the anarchic international system. States fear that allies may not live up to their promises because there are frequently no penalties for breaking such commitments. States may also be concerned that others can 'free-ride'; in other words gain the advantage of a cooperative agreement without paying for any of the costs. Neorealists and neoliberals have engaged in a lively debate about whether institutions can mitigate the incentives to defect.

defensive realists structural realists or neorealists who argue that systemic factors put significant limits on how much power states can gain, which works to dampen security competition.

democratic peace advocates of democratic peace explain war and peace in the international system with reference to domestic-level variables. Their basic claim is that regime types (defined by institutional features, e.g. elections, decision-making structures, and culture) shape foreign policy inclinations of national decision-makers and their interactions on the international level. Democratic peace theorists, following Kant, argue that democratic domestic institutions are conducive to producing peace on the international level, especially among democracies.

deontology a class of moral decision-making according to which some acts are wrong in themselves, regardless of their consequences. One of the most famous deontological arguments was out forward by Immanuel Kant.

deterrence persuading an opponent not to initiate a particular action because the perceived benefits are outweighed by the anticipated costs and risks.

dialectical understanding of history an understanding of social life central to Marxism and critical theory that examines humans as embedded in social relations, which are themselves in process. Humans are seen as historical beings, simultaneously the producers and the products of historical processes. Accordingly, politics is understood in a relatively expansive sense as struggles affecting the direction of these processes of social self-production, rather than narrowly distributive struggles over who gets what. In contrast to the liberal conception of freedom as individual choice, a dialectical view suggests that freedom involves a process of social self-determination.

discourse the language and representations through which we describe and understand the world, and through which meanings, identities, and social relations are produced. According to social theorists who believe that social reality is constituted by and through discourse, claims to pre-discursive reality are unwarranted. Borrowing from the French philosopher Michel Foucault, discourse theorists recognize that power is at work in defining the terms of debate (*see also* 'knowledge and power'). Discourse is a term closely associated with poststructuralism and also postcolonialism.

dyadic in democratic peace theory the term dyadic is used to signify the particular character of a relationship between a pair of actors, usually states. The presumption here is that if these actors share democratic values and institutions they will not be inclined to consider force as an instrument for resolving any conflicts of interest between them.

ecological modernization refers to a strategy of continuous innovation in environmental technological development and environmental management systems, encouraged or forced by governments and pursued by firms, to increase the efficiency of energy and resource use and reduce waste production and pollution. This strategy is defended as both good for business and good for the environment.

ecological security there are numerous conceptualizations of ecological security, ranging from conservative to radical. Conservatives maintain that ecological problems are a new source of insecurity and inter-state conflict that require the development of national ecological security strategies. Radicals seek to widen the traditional state-centric approach to security questions, arguing that ecological problems challenge the very idea of territorial defence and demand inter-state cooperation over common environmental problems.

economic determinism the idea that processes intrinsic to the economy (narrowly understood) are the primary determinants of social and political life. Economic determinism was a predominant tendency among Marxists well into the twentieth century. Western Marxism and critical theory reacted against this tendency, insisting that dialectical processes could not be understood without active human agents, and that the ideological and political conditions of human social agency were essential to an understanding of the limits and possibilities of particular social orders.

economic sanctions import or export barriers or restrictions imposed on one state or international actor by another state or group of states for the purpose of obtaining political or economic concessions.

empiricism a theory of knowledge (an epistemology) that holds that knowledge should be grounded in empirical experience. Empiricist epistemology has been influential in informing positivist philosophies of science and is often seen to underlie positivist theories in IR theory.

environmental justice environmental justice advocates seek to reduce ecological risks and also prevent their unfair externalization and displacement, through space and time, onto innocent third parties. Green theorists have approached this challenge by exploring new and more extensive forms of democratic accountability by risk generators and more extensive forms of representation and participation by classes and communities (including non-human species and ecosystems) affected by ecological risks, irrespective of their nationality, social class, or geographic location.

epistemic realism the view in the social sciences that there is an external world, the existence and meaning of which is independent of ideas, beliefs, and theories, or the actions of an observer. Although underpinned by an empiricist theory of knowledge and the positivist philosophy of science, it is not synonymous with either.

epistemology a branch of philosophy that seeks to theorize how we gain knowledge about the world. One of the most influential theories of knowledge in modern philosophy has been empiricism, which has emphasized the centrality of empirical observation in obtaining and justifying knowledge (*see* 'empiricism').

essentialism a term used to describe the result of simplifying or organizing people on the basis of 'natural' or 'general' characteristics. Constructivism, feminism, and critical theory emphasize that differences among people are not natural or timeless, but some of the most vehement critics of essentialism tend to be found among the poststructuralists and postcolonialists.

explaining and understanding a distinction introduced into IR theory by Hollis and Smith (1990). 'Explanatory' theories seek to emulate natural sciences and explain general causes, while 'understanding' approaches aim to account for agents' actions 'from within' through interpreting actors' meanings, beliefs, and reasons for action.

foundationalism a term used to describe theories that believe that our knowledge can have foundations, either in reason and rationality (rationalism), systematic empirical observation (empiricism), or independent existence of reality (realism). Foundationalist theories are criticized by the so-called anti-foundationalist theorists, typically associated with poststructuralist perspectives.

gender a set of socially constructed characteristics describing what men and women ought to be. Feminists, who have pioneered the study of gender, contrast differences ascribed by society (gender variations) with differences that are biologically 'given' (sexual differences). While individual men and women may not embody all the socially ascribed characteristics, expectations about gender roles serve to empower men and disempower women.

gendered lens the use of gender as a category of analysis through which to filter understandings of global politics. This is a term famously used by Cynthia Enloe (1990).

great debates a disciplinary narrative that describes the historical development of IR scholarship. The first debate is said to have taken place between idealists and realists, the second debate between traditionalists and modernizers. The interparadigm debate in the 1970s and 1980s pitted realist, liberal, and Marxist theoretical viewpoints against each other. Finally, the debate between meta-theoretical positions variously described as a contest between explaining and understanding, positivism and postpositivism, and rationalism and reflectivism, engaged theorists from the 1980s onwards. This debate has been referred to as the 'third debate' by some (Lapid 1989) and as the 'fourth debate' by others who see it as a debate beyond the interparadigm debate (Wæver 1996).

hegemonic stability in the late 1980s a number of prominent neorealists and neoliberals argued that international order can be provided by a single hegemonic power. For this to succeed, the hegemon needed to define its long-term interests in ways that were compatible with the interests of others in the system. A key part of this argument is the link between hegemonic power and the creation of regimes and institutions to maintain order.

hegemonic war a war between two dominant or 'leading' powers (hegemons) within the international system. Many realists argue that the historical record suggests hegemons do not rise and fall peacefully.

hegemon or hegemony in realist thought used to refer to an international system dominated by a hegemon that dominates the system through its military and economic might. In Gramscian and critical theory thought, hegemony refers to a situation in which socially dominant groups secure their power by getting subordinate social groups to subscribe to their ideological vision, thereby effectively consenting to their social power and making the widespread use of direct (and obviously oppressive) coercive power unnecessary.

'how possible' question knowledge claims are sometimes categorized as answering one of three kinds of question: the 'what', the 'why', or the 'how possible' questions. 'How possible' questions differ from the other two in that they do not ask for knowledge of the causes of an event (why) or about the constitution of an object (what) but rather about the 'conditions of possibility' under which certain things/events/meanings can exist.

imperialism as seen by the Marxists, imperialism involves the deployment of (primarily coercive) state power in the service of capital accumulation. Classical theories of imperialism, developed in the early twentieth century, tended to emphasize economic determinism as the motor of imperial expansion, but contemporary recastings of the concept have framed it in more dialectical terms, emphasizing the integral roles of agency, ideology, and politics in the construction of capitalist world orders.

incommensurability a term associated with Thomas Kuhn's (1962) work referring to the incomparability of theoretical positions. A term widely used, perhaps unjustifiably, in the interparadigm debate in IR to characterize the mutually exclusive nature of theoretical views of the world by realist, pluralist, and globalist approaches.

interdependence interdependence involves a relationship of mutual dependence in which actions and interests are entwined. This relationship may produce unintended, undesirable, and reciprocal consequences, but participating actors also obtain important interests and benefits through their interconnection

international institutions sets of norms and rules designed by states to structure and constrain their behaviour and to facilitate cooperation. International institutions have traditionally been the focus of analysis of the neoliberal school of thought that has challenged realists' scepticism of their significance. Increasingly constructivism has also analysed the role of institutions in international politics.

International Political Economy (IPE) a branch of political inquiry that studies the intersection of international relations and political economy. Rather than privileging states over markets, as traditional IR has tended to, IPE examines both states *and* markets.

international regimes defined famously by Stephen Krasner (1983) as 'sets of principles, norms, rules, and decision-making procedures around which actors' expectations converge'. The notion of regimes was useful in opening up the study of international institutions away from a focus on formal international organizations towards recognition of more informal regimes.

international society closely associated with the English school, international society describes an institutional arrangement for promoting order. It can be said to exist when there are criteria for membership, and when those belonging to international society have shared values and believe themselves to be bound by the agreed rules. The values that are shared could be minimal (toleration) or maximal (highly interventionist to promote universal values).

international system a term widely used to describe the totality of state actors in global politics. While realists believe that the anarchical character of the system leads to self-help behaviour, both liberals and English school theorists have pointed to the possibility of 'societal' characteristics among states (see 'international society'). In classical English school thinking the term 'international system' refers to patterns of contact between the units (states in the modern period) which may be structured but are not rule-governed.

justice in European international society of the seventeenth and eighteenth centuries, justice was defined by sovereignty norms: what was just was the recognition of other states and granting them independence and respecting their territorial integrity. Yet sovereign states have never been able to contain justice claims. Questions about minority rights, the rights of non-European peoples enslaved during the colonial period, the rights of prisoners of war, and, increasingly, the call for equality and democracy, all presuppose a realm of justice beyond the domain of the society of states. A feature of late modern international relations is the growing sensitivity of all international actors to transnational justice claims.

just war tradition Western body of thought going back to scholastics such as Thomas Aquinas and revived by modern-day intellectuals such as Michael Walzer. At the heart of Just War thinking are questions about what is morally right in terms of whether force can be justified (*jus ad bellum*) and how it can be used (*jus in bello*).

knowledge and power many positivist IR theorists believe in the possibility of objective and value-neutral knowledge. Many postpositivists have, however, emphasized the importance of reflection on the social context of knowledge generation, which is often embedded in power relations. The relations of power and knowledge are emphasized especially by poststructuralists and postcolonialists who, following the work of Michel Foucault, emphasize the inevitable and mutually constitutive nexus of knowledge and power. Indeed, the poststructuralists and postcolonialists go beyond many other postpositivists in emphasizing that all knowledge is embedded in discursive constructions and strategies of power. In so arguing, these theorists are following Foucault's concept of power, which emphasizes the dispersal of power and its location in the techniques and practices of power rather than in a power centre.

liberal feminism a branch of feminism in IR that addresses the various material manifestations of women's subordination in global politics, usually through empirical analysis.

logic of appropriateness a term associated with March and Olsen (1989), used to describe the logic-informing actions that are taken in reference to rules and norms that define what constitutes legitimate behaviour. This term is contrasted to the 'logic of consequences' (*see next entry*).

logic of communication the validation of normative claims to truth through effective communication and/ or dialogue, in which the voluntary exchange of words, ideas and arguments leads to consensus.

logic of consequences a term used to describe the logic through which rational actors come to make decisions. When acting through the logic of consequences, actors conduct themselves on the basis of a rational calculation of which action produces an outcome that maximizes their interests. *See* 'logic of appropriateness'.

meta-theory inquiry into the underlying philosophical assumptions that inform theoretical approaches. Meta-theoretical inquiry engages with philosophical questions of ontology, epistemology, and methodology. Often referred to as 'theory about theory'.

methodology methodological schools of thoughts debate how we best gain evidence about the nature of the natural and the social world. Different theoretical approaches in the social sciences have contrasting understandings of the validity and hierarchy of social science methods. Key methodological avenues in the social sciences include quantitative, qualitative, discursive, and historical methods.

monadic in democratic peace theory the term monadic refers to the unique character of republican states in terms of their aversion to war. Unlike the weaker claim by democratic peace theorists that liberal states have made a separate peace, advocates of the monadic version believe that republican states will always and everywhere be peace-prone.

moral agent those agents that we understand to have moral responsibilities. In other words, we can expect moral agents to discharge certain duties and we can reasonably hold them to account for failing to do so. Moral agents are generally characterized by their capacities for deliberating over possible courses of action and their consequences and acting on the basis of this deliberation. Whereas many IR approaches make assumptions of agency, normative IR theory focuses on questions of moral agency and responsibility.

moral standing entities that have moral standing are understood to matter morally in their own right. They are objects of moral concern, or bodies towards which moral consideration is directed. For example, cosmopolitan positions in normative IR theory understand all individual human beings to have *equal* moral standing. By contrast, communitarian positions are often criticized for failing to take seriously the moral standing of those outside particular communities.

multipolarity a world in which there are three or more great powers.

mutually constituted a phrase used to refer to the dialectical relationship of two concepts or forces that simultaneously co-determine each other. For example, in the agency–structure debate some argue that agents and structures 'mutually constitute' each other (Giddens 1984), and thus have to be understood in reference to each other, rather than in isolation from each other.

normative IR theory a field of study that draws on a combination of political theory, moral philosophy, and IR in order to address explicitly ethical question about international politics.

offence–defence balance indicates how easy or difficult it is to conquer territory or defeat a defender in battle. If the balance favours the defender, conquest is difficult and war is therefore unlikely. The reverse is the case if the balance favours the offence.

offensive realists structural realists who maintain that states should attempt to gain as much power as possible, which works to intensify security competition.

ontology a branch of philosophy that studies the nature of being and existence. In IR all theorists make assumptions about the kinds of objects they conceive to exist in and to shape international politics. While many realists tend to argue that states are the key ontological units in international politics (*see* 'state-centric'), constructivists, feminists, and Marxists, for example, emphasize 'social ontologies' where the emphasis is on examining the social interaction and social relations between states or other actors (such as genders or classes).

order a concept which both realists and English school theorists consider pivotal. For realists, order is generally considered to consist in the absence of war. While they accept that order can be achieved, for example, through balance of power or deterrence politics, given the anarchical nature of the international system, order in the eyes of realists is always precarious. For the English school, given the specific context of international anarchy, the achievement of order is the only purpose that culturally diverse, sovereign 'units' can agree upon. The institutions of international society — diplomacy, the balance of power, peace conferences, great power management, international law — were primarily designed to achieve the goal of order upon which the liberty of the units depends.

paradigm a term associated with Thomas Kuhn's (1962) work referring to theoretical schools, or sets of principles, concerning the nature of science, that are accepted as exemplary in any given historical period.

pluralist international society a term associated with the English school that describes an institutional arrangement designed to sustain international order. R. J. Vincent (1986) used an 'egg-box' metaphor to explain pluralism. International society is the box and the eggs are states: we can assume that the eggs are valuable but also fairly fragile. The task of the box is to separate and cushion the eggs. Pluralism is defended by those who attach a premium to cultural diversity, and who are suspicious of particular states that regard themselves as ethical states with a duty to impose their values on others.

positivism a contested term in the philosophy of science and in IR theory. Generally understood to refer to a philosophy of science that is founded on (1) the empiricist theory of knowledge (which argues that sensory experience provides the only legitimate source of knowledge); (2) an assumption of 'naturalism' (the belief in the unity of natural and social sciences); and (3) the belief in the possibility of making fact–value distinctions (separation of normative, political, and ethical beliefs from 'factual' statements).

postcolonial feminism a branch of feminism in IR that is interested in the intersection of gender and cultural subordination, addressing the way that dominant gender and political relations are entrenched both in global politics and between feminists, depending on their class, race, and geographic location.

post-empiricism refers to debates in the philosophy of science which challenge the empiricist theory of knowledge by identifying how the social constitution of meaning, the linguistic construction of reality, and the historicity of knowledge are important for an understanding of science.

postpositivism an umbrella term for a number of approaches that criticize positivist approaches to knowledge generation. Postpositivists can be seen to include a heterogeneous group of theorists critical of the positivist approach to studying world politics, such as interpretive/hermeneutic theorists, poststructuralists, feminists, critical theorists, scientific/critical realists, and some, although not all, constructivists.

poststructuralist feminism a branch of feminism in IR that is particularly concerned with the way dichotomized linguistic constructions, such as strong/weak, rational/emotional, and public/private, serve to empower the masculine over the feminine.

principal–agent theory an approach to studying institutional relationships that focuses on the delegation of authority from principals, who have the right to make decisions, to their agents. Authority is delegated within specified constraints, and principals can change the structure of delegation if it is not operating to their satisfaction. Neoliberal scholars apply principal–agent theory to understand the autonomy of international organizations (IOs), treating member states as the principals and the IO's management and staff as agents.

Prisoner's Dilemma a game in which two players try to get rewards by cooperating with or betraying the other player. In this game, one of the most influential examples in game theory, it is assumed that the only concern of each individual player ('prisoner') is to maximize their own advantage, with no concern for the well-being of the other player. Because of the structure of the game, no matter what the other player does, one will always get a greater pay-off by defecting. However, the rewards of mutual cooperation are greater than those of mutual defection. Since in any situation playing defect is more beneficial than cooperating, rational players will defect even though they would be better off cooperating, creating the dilemma.

rationalism/rationalist theory form of theorizing that utilizes rational choice explanation in its explanatory framework (*see also* 'rationality' and 'Prisoner's Dilemma'). Keohane (1988) used this term to highlight the similarities between the neorealist and neoliberal theorists, who shared with each other the assumption of rationality and, further, tended to apply the rules of the positivist model of science in their research. Keohane contrasted rationalism with 'reflectivism' (*see below*).

rationality a rational actor calculates the costs and benefits of different courses of action and chooses the course of action that provides the highest net pay-off. Rational actors also behave strategically, meaning that they take into account the likely reactions of others to their choices and how those reactions will influence their own pay-offs. The rationality of state behaviour is an important assumption in neorealist and neoliberal theories.

Realpolitik associated with the realist school of thought in IR. *Realpolitik* is a term arising from Bismarck's foreign policy and is used to describe policies that concern themselves solely with the singular pursuit of the national interest.

reason a justification given by an actor for an action. Many argue that there is a difference between reasons and causes such that investigation of the 'reasons' of an action makes social inquiry distinct from causal analysis in the natural sciences. This is because reasons, for these interpretive scholars, cannot be said to act in a (causal) 'when A, the B' manner but have to be understood in reference to the complex social meanings that they are embedded in.

recognition refers to the act of acknowledging others as actors and as particular kinds of actors. States, for example, mutually recognize each other as states, thus constituting each other and themselves as such. They can also recognize each other as different kinds of states, for example, as democratic or autocratic states. Recognition is treated as a socially constructed category and is deemed important by many social constructivists and English school theorists in the construction of identity of actors.

reflectivism a term used initially by Robert Keohane (1988) to refer to theorists that reject the rational choice methods and the positivist approach to knowledge generation of the 'rationalist theorists' in the study of world politics. Reflectivism is often interpreted to incorporate various 'postpositivist' schools such as feminism, critical theory, but especially poststructuralism.

regionalization trend towards increasing and intensifying interaction between actors within a given geographical region.

revisionist states states looking for opportunities to use military force to alter the balance of power.

rule a philosophical term associated with social constructivist literature referring to a (set of) meaning(s) that is transmitted through language in social interaction and in reference to which actors formulate their thoughts and actions.

scientific realism philosophy of science that aims to overcome the limitations of the positivist philosophy of science. The key assumption that informs scientific realism, and its close associate 'critical realism', is the belief in the independent existence of reality (however,

not in accordance with 'epistemic realism' of the positivists, *see above*). Scientific and critical realists advocate deep ontological inquiry through conceptualization and epistemological and methodological pluralism.

security dilemma the paradox that occurs when a state seeks to improve its own security resulting in the decreased security of other states. Providing assurances to the contrary is not effective, realists argue, given the lack of trust between actors in a self-help world. At the heart of the security dilemma is the idea that security is a relative concept: all actors cannot have more of it.

social construction the process of bringing to existence objects or subjects through the process of social interaction and transmission of social meanings. Social constructions do not exist in nature but have come about through acts of human creation (*see* 'social facts').

social facts facts that, unlike so-called brute facts (Searle 1995), require social institutions or norms for their existence. Social facts, such as money or states, exist by the virtue of their social construction by actors.

social totality a metaphysical term that refers to the whole of society as an assemblage of concrete social and class relations.

sociology of science a field of inquiry that seeks to understand scientific knowledge and scientific practices in relation to the historical, social, and political environment of the practice of science.

solidarist international society a term associated with the English school, referring to the collective enforcement of international rules. Collective security, for example, could be considered a solidarist security architecture. In his original formulation, Bull associated solidarism, not only with collective enforcement, but beyond it, the guardianship of human rights. This is primarily why a great deal of solidarist literature in the 1990s was liberal in orientation. However, there is no a priori reason why solidarism needs to be thought of in liberal terms. It is quite possible for key actors in international society to use multilateral institutions to spread conservative values (as the Concert of Europe did in the early nineteenth century).

sovereignty a key characteristic or a norm in the international system/society denoting the independent, territorially self-standing, and self-determining qualities of states. There are many conceptions of the nature and role of sovereignty in international political life. Realists tend to see sovereignty as an expression of the power and autonomy of states. Postpositivist theorists, such as constructivist and poststructuralist theorists, seek to demonstrate the socially constructed nature of the assumption of sovereign states. Many theorists have also pointed to the erosion of the sovereignty of states in the context of globalization.

speech act a category of language that does not only describe or convey information but can be thought of as an act. For example, actions such as 'to promise' or 'to threaten' function through language and, hence, can be seen as speech acts.

state-centric theories that take as their key ontological objects state actors. Mainstream IR theories such as realism, neorealism, and neoliberalism take the state-as-actor as their point of departure. In addition, variants of constructivism can also be conceived of as state-centric, especially Wendt (1999).

status quo states states satisfied enough with the balance of power that they have no interest in using military force to shift it in their favour. Status quo powers are sometimes referred to as security seekers.

structural violence the violence done to people when their basic needs are not met. This includes the effects of malnutrition, domestic violence, gender subordination, poor education, poor health care, and so on.

sustainable development according to the Brundtland Report published by the World Commission on Environment and Development in 1987, sustainable development is development that meets the needs of the present generation without sacrificing the needs of future generations. However, the term remains deeply contested on ethical, political, and economic grounds. Much of this disagreement can be ultimately traced to different assumptions about what should be sustained, for whom, and by what means.

system/society an important fault-line especially in International Political Theory and English school theory demarcating mere interaction in the case of the former, but the presence of social relations among sovereign states in the latter. *See the individual entries on* 'international system' and 'international society'.

theory a central but contested term in natural and social sciences and in IR. In IR explanatory theorists tend to see theory as sets of statements that explain particular events, either in reference to a series of prior events or in reference to one or more causal variable. Critical theorists point to the role of theory in not only explaining, but also in simultaneously critiquing social systems. Constitutive theory examines the way in which social structures are internally constituted or how ideas or discourses constitute social objects. Normative theory examines the plausibility of ethical arguments about what 'ought to be'. Theory can also be seen to refer, more generally, to the frameworks of thought or knowledge through which we engage and give meaning to the world.

triadization trend towards increasing and intensifying interactions between actors in a triad, where the triad comprises the North American, South-east Asian, and European regional economies.

understanding *see* 'explaining and understanding'.

unilateralism when a state conducts its actions and reaches its foreign-policy decisions without consulting or cooperating with other international actors.

unipolarity a world in which there is only one great power. Global hegemony is synonymous with unipolarity.

welfare state a state whose principal domestic priority is the promotion of the welfare of its citizens through the provision of social and medical services.

world society shared values and common interests among the society of human kind. Depending on the degree to which values and interests converge, there will be an institutional dimension to world society: in the late twentieth and early twenty-first centuries, these institutions are primarily international non-governmental organizations that are prone to cajole and embarrass states into upholding their transnational commitments. It is important to note that world society is not the exclusive domain of actors with liberal values — the content of the transnational values (and action) may be extremely illiberal.

Index